PEASANT SOCIETY ❧ A READER

PEASANT SOCIETY
A Reader

JACK M. POTTER
MAY N. DIAZ
GEORGE M. FOSTER
University of California, Berkeley

LITTLE, BROWN AND COMPANY
BOSTON

LIBRARY OF CONGRESS CATALOG CARD NO. 67-24912

SECOND PRINTING

Published simultaneously in Canada
by Little, Brown & Company (Canada) Limited

PRINTED IN THE UNITED STATES OF AMERICA

Preface

PEASANT SOCIETY: A READER is planned to present the student with a sampling of current ideas about peasant society and culture. Since most recent studies of peasant life have been written by social anthropologists, we have given the book an anthropological direction. But the authors include, in addition to anthropologists, sociologists, an economist, a philosopher, and a social psychologist. The accounts they give are based principally but not entirely on first-hand field observations, although some authors have drawn upon historical materials to elucidate their points. Because space is limited and because we are interested in peasant society as a generic, worldwide type, rather than as a socioeconomic phenomenon of European history, we have not utilized the voluminous writings of historians and economists who have studied European peasantry.

The formal study of peasants in a nonhistorical, noneconomic context is very recent, going back scarcely twenty years, and as yet no full agreement has been reached on the most important theoretical and factual points that should be included in a university course on this subject. We have therefore deemed it desirable to discuss at some length, in the editors' introductions, characteristics of peasant society that we feel will give readers a general view of the field at its present stage. These introductions are signed because we found that, with the individualism that often characterizes anthropologists, we did not always agree on emphasis and weighting. But, both the items reprinted and their assignment to the several sections of the volume represent our collective judgments. Only after these decisions were made did we divide the task of preparing the introductory statements, in which each of us has assumed considerable latitude of interpretation.

In preparing a reader, editors are faced with a major decision: to seek comprehensive coverage by selecting brief sections from many items, or to gain depth by concentrating on relatively few major sources and reprinting them in their entirety. We feel the second course is preferable, since it does greater justice both to authors and to readers. In writing articles and chapters, authors customarily develop a point or series of points, the significance of which may be obscured by abridgment. We find that students learn more when they can stick with one author long enough to find out what he has in mind, than they can by spreading their effort over daubs and patches of several sources.

Following this philosophy, most of the studies that follow have been reproduced in their entirety, including notes and citations. In a few instances, usually because of length, it has been necessary to shorten or otherwise modify the original text. These changes are indicated in the appropriate places.

We wish to thank our colleagues who have given us permission to reproduce their works. Readers may be interested to know that all royalties from the sale of this book will be paid to the American Anthropological Association, and not to us. We hope that our efforts will contribute in a direct and tangible manner to the furtherance of anthropological research.

Jack M. Potter
May N. Diaz
George M. Foster

Table of Contents

PART ONE Peasant Society

PART TWO Peasant Economics

PART ONE

PEASANT SOCIETY

Introduction: What Is a Peasant?

George M. Foster

"Peasants," said Kroeber, "constitute part-societies with part-cultures." They are "definitely rural — yet live in relation to market towns; they form a class segment of a larger population which usually contains also urban centers. . . . They lack the isolation, the political autonomy, and the self-sufficiency of tribal populations; but their local units retain much of their old identity, integration, and attachment to soil and cults" (1948:284). When he wrote these lines, Kroeber was thinking primarily of European peasantry, and he regarded the topic — which occupied a single paragraph in an 800-page book — as an almost incidental observation. Yet with these few lines Kroeber sparked a re-examination in anthropological thinking of the question of cultural typology, and drew attention to the problem which, today, probably is examined by more anthropologists than any other. And with his customary economy of expression, he singled out the elements which, even today, are seen as central in peasant analysis.

To the average reader the word "peasant" connotes a historical, social, and economic aspect of life in Europe in the Middle Ages, when agricultural serfs clustered around great manors, or marginal farmers in small villages lived in juxtaposition to towns and cities, to which they came to sell their produce and buy the items they could not themselves provide. This is the sense in which peasants are discussed in the *Encyclopedia of Social Sciences* (von Dietze 1934). Today scholars see peasants in wider perspective, as a major societal type only incidentally related to time and place. Just as primitive society, industrial society, and perhaps plantation society are generic forms whose definition is not tied to a geographic or historical anchor, so now we look upon peasants as peoples whose styles of life show certain structural, economic, social, and perhaps personality similarities (although of course not identities), in contrast to these other basic forms, without reference to country or century.

Firth suggested the wider utility of the "peasant" concept when he argued that Malay fishermen could be better understood if this conceptual framework were used. The word "peasant," he pointed out, has a somewhat different meaning when applied to Oriental peoples than when applied to European communities. He felt, however, that the similarities were sufficiently great to justify the extension of the term: "Like the European peasantry the Oriental peasantry are communities of producers on a small scale, with simple equipment and market organization, often relying on what they produce for their subsistence" (1946:22).

Even earlier, John Embree, in writing about a Japanese village, recognized that peasants are a distinctive societal type: "A peasant community possesses many of the characteristics of a preliterate society, e.g., an intimate local group, strong kinship ties, and periodic gatherings in honor of some deified aspect of the environment. On the other hand, it presents many important differences from the simpler societies; each little peasant group is part of a larger nation which controls its economic life, enforces a code of law from above, and, more recently, requires education in national schools. The economic basis of life is not conditioned entirely by the local requirements. . . . The farmer's crop is adjusted to the needs of the state. In religion and ritual there are many outside influences to complicate the simple correlation of rites and social value, festivals and agricultural seasons. While full of local variations, the rituals and festivals are not indigenous to the community nor is the community spiritually self-sufficient" (1939:xvi).

It is curious that the study of peasant life is so little advanced. As Geertz has written, "The peasant is an immemorial figure on the world social landscape, but anthropology noticed him only recently" (1962:1). How recently is indicated by the fact that, except in Kroeber's 1948 *Anthropology*, the word "peasant" is found in the index of no general social anthropology texts until Keesing's *Cultural Anthropology* (1958) and Titiev's *Introduction to Cultural Anthropology* (1959). Both men — as do subsequent textbook authors — confuse peasants with that well-worn and now largely neglected concept of "folk." So, except for Redfield's *Peasant Society and Culture* (1956) and Wolf's recent *Peasants* (1966), readers must turn to periodicals for the theoretical literature on peasants.

If formal recognition of a peasantry as a major societal type, with a growing corpus of sociological theory to explain it, has come late, the same cannot be said of the field study of peoples we now call peasants. James Rennel Rodd's *The Customs and Lore of Modern Greece* (1892) is still an excellent source of information on peasant behavior in that country, and Edith Durham's Albanian writings (e.g., 1910, 1928) describe peasant peoples in detail. Perhaps the richest source of information on European peasants is found in a remarkable series of memoirs published by the Spanish Real Academia de Ciencias Morales y Políticas, during the years 1900 to 1916. These monographs, ostensibly limited to *derecho consuetudinario*, customary law, are in fact detailed provincial ethnographies. *The Irish Countryman* by Conrad Arensberg (1937), though not cast in the conceptual framework of a peasantry, is also required reading for anyone interested in the subject.

Winifred Blackman's *The Fellāhīn of Upper Egypt* (1927) is still a rewarding source of information about North African peasants, and the same may be said, for India, about the Wisers' wonderful little book, *Behind Mud Walls* (1963. First published 1934). Arthur Smith's *Village Life in China* (1899), although not written by an anthropologist, tells us a great deal about life in a traditional Chinese village.

In America, *La Población del Valle de Teotihuacán* (1922), edited by the late Mexican anthropologist Manuel Gamio, includes a description of peasant villagers of the central Mexican highlands, preceding Redfield's epoch-making *Tepoztlán* (1930) by eight years.

All these studies, and others like them from the same periods, have one important fact in common: Unlike most of the voluminous accounts of European peasantry based mainly on historical documents, they were written by people who described what they had seen in the field. Hence they are anthropological studies in the best sense of the word, and they illuminate the lives of peoples anthropologists now classify as "peasant."

The reasons that caused anthropologists and other social scientists to be slow to recognize peasants as a societal type need not concern us in detail at this point. It is enough to note in passing that anthropologists, at least, were describing peasants and speculating about appropriate models to explain peasant social forms and behavior long before they used the word in an operational sense. The principal reason for this delayed recognition appears to us to be the confusion between the concept of "folk society," as written about at length by Redfield, and that of "peasant society." Redfield, who pioneered peasant studies in America, first called peasants "folk" (as, for example, in the subtitle of *Tepoztlán: A Study of Folk Life*), only subsequently recognizing the greater appropriateness of the "peasant" concept. Because of professional cultural lag, a long line of American anthropologists, including one of the editors of this volume (Foster 1953), continued to talk about "folk" culture when in fact they were talking about "peasants." Probably because of this delay, only now is a sophisticated body of theory about peasants beginning to emerge.

With these preliminary points in mind, let us attempt to answer in greater detail the question: "What is a peasant?" This task is necessary because the types of societies that will concern us here, and the theories pertinent to them, will depend on our definitions. Almost without exception, anthropologists subscribe to Kroeber's part-societies–part-cultures definition of peasants, but they differ as to details. Firth, for example, finds that "the term peasant has primarily an economic referent. . . . The primary means of livelihood of the peasant is cultivation of the soil." Although stressing agriculture and self-sufficiency, Firth, as we have seen, extends the word "peasant" to include other small-scale producers, such as fishermen and rural craftsmen, pointing out that "they are of the same social class as the agriculturalists, and often members of the same families. As occupational groups they may even be separable only in theory, since many a peasant farmer is also a fisherman or craftsman by turns, as his seasonal cycle or his cash-needs influence him" (1950:503).

The emphasis on agriculture and self-sufficiency is implicit or explicit in many writings about peasants, yet we believe that stressing occupation and cultural content obscures the really important diagnostic criteria. These may be found by exploring Kroeber's definition, by asking the question: "Of what larger society, with what more complex culture, are peasants a part?" Redfield, although he never quite extricated himself from the conceptual pitfalls of folk society and the folk-urban continuum, showed the way to the answers. The word "peasant," he wrote in 1953, "points to a human type. . . . It required the city to bring it into existence. There were no peasants before the first cities. And those surviving primitive peoples who do not live in terms of the city are not peasants" (1953:31). The larger society of which peasants are a part, then, is urban society, the civilization of an entire region that is carried by the religious, political, commercial, and intellectual elite groups. Although these elites are often large landowners, they usually make their homes in cities, where their primary contacts are with the members of other upper socio-economic groups.

The peasant, Redfield believed, was, like the primitive tribesman, "indigenous," but unlike the tribesman, he "is long used to the existence of the city, and its ways are, in altered form, part of his ways. The peasant is a rural native whose long established order of life takes important account of the city" (1953:31). Later he wrote: "We are looking at rural people in old civilizations, those rural people who control and cultivate their land for subsistence and as a part of a traditional way of life and who look to and are influenced by gentry or townspeople whose way of life is like theirs but in a more civilized form" (1956:31).

Most writers who analyze peasant societies emphasize a structural relationship between village and city, with social, economic, political, often religious, and certainly temporal characteristics. In 1953, one of the editors of this volume described peasant society (following common usage at that period, he called it "folk society") as a half-society, "a part of a larger social unit (usually a nation) which is vertically and horizontally structured. The peasant component of this larger unit bears a symbiotic spatial-temporal relationship to the more complex component, which is formed by the upper classes of the *pre-industrial urban center*" (Foster 1953:163. Emphasis added). Later he emphasized that in speaking of peasants he was "not discussing simple communities of small-scale subsistence producers, wherever they may be found, but communities that represent the rural expression of large, class-structured, economically complex, pre-industrial civilizations, in which trade and commerce and craft specialization are well developed, in which money is commonly used, and in which market disposition is the goal for a part of the producer's efforts. The city is the principal source of innovation, and the prestige motivation brings novelty to the country" (Foster 1960–1961:175).

In defining peasants, Wolf aptly reminds us that "definitions are tools of thought, and not eternal verities" (1955:453). With this caution he limits peasants to agricultural producers (specifically excluding fishermen, and, by implication, craftsmen) who control their land and who aim at subsistence, not at reinvestment. At the same time he sees that the word "indicates a structural relationship, not a particular cultural content," and that a peasant society can be understood only as it relates to some larger integral whole (1955:454). Recently, Wolf has suggested that although the city is a likely product of the increasing social complexities that include peasants, it is not inevitable. Rather, he argues cogently, "it is the crystallization of executive power which serves to distinguish the primitive from the civilized, rather than whether or not such power controls are located in one kind of place or another. *Not the city, but the state is the decisive criterion of civilization* and it is the appearance of the state which marks the threshold of transition between food cultivators in general and peasants. Thus, it is only when a cultivator is integrated into a society with a state — *that is, when the cultivator becomes subject to the demands and sanctions of power-holders* outside his social stratum — that we can appropriately speak of peasantry" (1966:11. Emphasis added). We believe Wolf's recognition of outside power-holders as the key variable is correct; normally, if not always, such power is associated with the city.

Like most anthropologists, we agree that peasants are primarily agriculturalists, but we also believe that the criteria of definition must be structural and relational rather than occupational. For in most peasant societies, significant numbers of people earn their livings from nonagricultural occupations. It is not *what* peasants produce that is significant; it is *how* and *to whom* they dispose of what they produce that counts. When settled rural peoples subject to the jural control of outsiders exchange a part of what they produce for items they cannot themselves make, in a market setting transcending local transactions, then they are peasants. We see peasants as a peripheral but essential part of civilizations, producing the food that makes urban life possible, supporting (and subject to) the specialized classes of political and religious rulers and the other members of the educated elite. This elite carries what Redfield called the "Great Tradition," which gives continuity and substance to the sequences of advanced culture, and which lies in contradistinction to the "Little Tradition" — which characterizes villagers themselves.

Although peasant societies usually are based on agriculture, it does not follow that all farmers are peasants. The long-settled, skillful farmers of the pueblos in the American Southwest do not qualify as peasants, since their communities are (or were) largely autonomous in political control and religious leadership, and since they lacked major market mechanisms and did not draw upon a Great Tradition. In contrast, many of the village farmers of Nuclear America prior to the Spanish Conquest are generally thought of as peasants, since often they formed parts of states with autochthonous Great Traditions, with political and religious rulers, elaborately developed market systems, and other characteristics of civilizations including incipient writing. The technically competent and culturally sophisticated agricultural peoples of indigenous Africa south of the Sahara, on the other hand, are thought of by many anthropologists as "semipeasants" rather than true peasants, in spite of elaborate political states and economic systems of exchange. The anomalous position of some of these societies is made clear in Professor Fallers' contribution to this book. American farmers, even prior to the introduction of elaborate machinery, were not peasants; although they grew a good deal of what they ate, they were oriented toward a market economy, fluctuating prices, and supply and demand. And it seems stretching the point a bit, too, to speak of a contemporary peasantry in the industrialized parts of Europe.

The first settled farmers of the Near East were not peasants, even though their social relationships and the outward appearance of their villages must have been essentially the same as those of the first peoples that can be called peasants. These early settled prepeasants were turned into peasants with the appearance of the first towns or incipient cities — about 3,500 B.C. in the Near East, to use Wolf's date (1966:11) — in which political and usually religious control began to be exercised over the hinterland. We agree with Redfield that there were no peasants before the first cities. We wish to emphasize, however, that peasants are not a function of any city, *but of a particular kind of city* which, using Sjoberg's terminology, has come to be called the *preindustrial city* — the type which from the time of its appearance was the only kind of city until the industrial revolution brought into being the contemporary city. As pointed out in Professor Sjoberg's article, the preindustrial city can take several forms, but all are distinct from the modern city. The modern city, with the demands it places on rural communities for a labor force and for a market outlet for mass-produced goods, with the communication networks it brings into being, and with the superstates that tend to follow in its wake, does not produce peasants. Peasants survive into the modern world because of the phenomenon of cultural lag, but they are being transformed into postpeasants as the ancient cities on which they depended gradually are transformed into modern cities, or as revolutionary movements as in contemporary China bring precipitous change to rural areas.

Redfield wrote that "today more peasants are made as Indian or Chinese civilization moves into the communities of tribal peoples. As European civilization spread to the New World, secondary peasantry, with roots of culture different from that of the invaders, came and still come to be made" (1956:137). We think that this rarely if ever happens. Today's tribal peoples are coming into contact with an industrial world, and the demands this world makes on them produce urban workers or a rural proletariat, but not peasants. Few if any of the contemporary rural peoples of the new Africans strike us as peasants. Time moves too fast. However a particular peasant society came into being, and whatever the nature of its transformation, it achieved a relatively steady state in which it settled down into an unquestioned, if uneasy, acceptance of dominance by superior powers. In the formation of peasant communities, time to simmer is an essential ingredient. History today does not permit this kind of simmering. Simply because change comes slowly in traditional societies, peasants will be with us for a long time to come. But the supply is not being replenished. History, in turning former peasants into postpeasants, is steadily reducing the numbers of peasant societies (as contrasted to absolute numbers of people), and eventually there will be no more.

If the primary criterion for defining peasant society is structural — the relationship between the village and the city (or the state) — it is clear that the major focuses of interest will be found in these ties. They have a number of aspects, including the social, economic, religious, jural, historical, and emotional. But in all, it seems to us that the critical common denominator is that peasants have very little control over the conditions that govern their lives. Occupying as they do a very low socio-economic level in the states of which they are a part, they find that the basic decisions that affect their lives are made from outside their communities, and have always been so made. Peasants are not only poor, as has often been pointed out, but they are relatively powerless. Or at least they look upon themselves as powerless, for only in rare peasant revolutions, when they break out of their customary behavior patterns, have they been a force in world history. And even then they quickly seem to revert to the apathetic and quiescent state that normally characterizes their outlook on life.

Peasants know that control over them is held in some mysterious fashion by superior powers, usually residing in cities, just as supernatural control over them is held by enormously powerful beings whose abode is also outside the village community. Peasant leadership is normally weak; it is truncated and ineffectual in meeting other than the most traditional and routine demands. In part this is because the more powerful extra-village leaders who hold vested interests in peasant communities cannot afford to let local leaders rise, since they would constitute a threat to their control. And in part it is because the assumption of political power by local men means stepping out of the role of "ideal villager," since it upsets the equilibrium that is equated with social health (cf. "Limited Good" pp. 300–323). Whatever the reasons, for lack of effective local leadership peasant communities pay a grievous price, particularly in a changing world where tradition is no longer a sufficient guide to life.

Lacking effective political control and knowing it, peasants seek structural devices which permit them to maximize — the word seems hardly suitable — their pathetically meager opportunities, and almost always on an individual, or at most a family basis. Two devices, for their frequency, seem especially important. Patron-client patterns, in which peasant villagers seek out more powerful people who may be city dwellers, wealthy hacienda owners, religious leaders, or other individuals with the power to aid, are a significant element in most peasant societies. Patrons, who act as cultural intermediaries have variously been called "hinges" (Redfield 1956:43–44), "gate keepers" (Kenny 1960:18), "brokers" (Wolf 1956:1075–1076), and the like. Whatever they may be called by anthropologists, their role is mediating between the peasant and his Little Tradition, and the more powerful elements in his society, who participate in the Great Tradition.

Fictive kinship is the second common (but by no means universal) structural device through which peasants may fortify their position in their communities and in their wider societies. Although the institution is sometimes used to establish patron-client ties, with greater frequency it allies peasants with fellow villagers, and with people of similar position and status in other peasant settlements. Fictive kinship institutions, of which the Spanish and Spanish-American *compadrazgo* is the most widespread variant, resemble true kinship patterns, in that kinship or semi-kinship terminologies and forms of address are used, and some of the behavior appropriate to the relationship resembles that characterizing real kin. But, since true kinship need not — and usually does not — underlie these behavior patterns, the kinship motif is, in fact, fictive or ceremonial. Sometimes, of course, relatives are chosen to serve as fictive kin. Patron-client patterns and fictive kinship are discussed in greater detail, and are illustrated in readings, in the section on peasant social structure.

In the economic sphere, it is noteworthy that the peasant is also subject to his larger social unit. Only rarely and in unusual circumstances does he set the prices at which he sells, and perhaps never does he set prices at which he buys (other than in the impersonal sense of supply and demand, as he collectively exerts pressure on the market). All too often — in the modern world, at least — prices are determined by international forces; and in the traditional world, by local city monopolists who artificially rig prevailing prices. It is noteworthy, too, that whatever the form of control held by the elite, they usually drain off most of the economic surplus a peasant creates, beyond that necessary for a bare subsistence living and for local religious expenditures.

In religion it is usually the rituals and beliefs that are developed as a part of the Great Tradition that are more weakly reflected in village activities. The pattern may be that of the Sanskrit tradition seeping down to peasant and tribal levels, or that of what might be called folk Catholicism in Latin America and southern Europe, in which religious leaders (who may of course be peasants in origin) have been trained away from their homes in schools which partake of the Great Tradition. Usually the patterns of religious activities and beliefs in peasant society are determined in large measure by extravillage forces.

The emotional dependence of the peasant on the city presents an especially poignant case. Peasants throughout history have admired the city, and have copied many of the elements they have observed there. The city, with its glitter and opportunity, holds a fascination, like a candle for a moth. But at the same time, and for good cause, peasants hate and fear cities and the city dwellers who exercise control over them. Since time immemorial city people have alternately ridiculed, ignored, or exploited their local country people, on whom they depend for food, for taxes, for military conscripts, for labor levies, and for market sales. Peasants know they need the city, as an outlet for their surplus production and as the source of many material and nonmaterial items they cannot themselves produce. Yet they recognize that the city is the source of their helplessness and humiliation, and in spite of patrons half trusted, the peasant knows he can never really count on a city man. The Wisers described it well when they voiced the feelings of Hindu villagers: "In the cities they devise ways of exploiting us . . . when we get our money and want to take home some cloth, the shopkeepers get out the pieces which they have been unable to dispose of, and persuade us to buy them at exorbitant prices. We know they are laughing at us. But we want cloth, and the next shopkeeper will cheat us as badly as the last. Wherever we go in the town, sharp eyes are watching to tempt our precious rupees from us. There is no one to advise us honestly or to help us escape from fraudulent men" (1963:124).

And again, "You cannot know unless you are a villager, how everyone threatens us and takes from us. When you [the Wisers] go anywhere, or when a sophisticated town man goes anywhere, he demands service and gets it. We stand dumb and show our fear, and they trample on us" (1963:127).

In a culture-historical sense, peasant society is also dependent on and essentially formed by the city, from which it takes far more than it gives. Many writers think of peasant society as a grass-roots creation, a viable organism from which spring the basic cultural forms we call "peasant." Redfield, writing about songs and literature, by implication seems to assume the creativity of the peasant: "The popular song has an author; the folk song easily loses its composer. The question of communal composition does not arise in the realm of popular literature as distinguished from folk literature" (1930:6). Yet to focus attention on the dubious creativity of peasants is to lose sight of the really significant historical factor in peasant-city relationships. For, if we examine the content of any peasant community, we are struck by how many of its elements represent simplified, village manifestations of ideas and artifacts which originated in the city at an earlier period: religious beliefs and practices, linguistic forms, costumes, house furnishings, forms of social organization, and the like. This process was described some years ago by one of the editors of this volume: "Peasant cultures continually incorporate into their fabrics significant parts of the sophisticated, intellectual components of their own tradition [i.e., what Redfield shortly thereafter called 'Great Tradition']. . . . If the cultures here denoted as 'peasant,' on an empirical basis, are critically examined, it will be found that many of the most significant elements have filtered down from the sophisticated world of their own tradition of several centuries earlier. Time to simmer is an essential part of this concept of peasant culture, time to integrate diffused traits and complexes into the peasant fabric, to rework them and to make them harmonious with the functional whole. The time element may be, in part, what distinguishes a peasant culture from a recently acculturated group" (Foster 1953:164. "Peasant" has been substituted for the original word "folk").

Redfield noted the same fact: "This relatively stable relationship between peasant and city is in part shaped by the cultural advances of the city and the incorporation into peasant life of institutions developed in the course of this advance" (1953:35). And again, "The culture of a peasant community . . . is not autonomous . . . we discover that to maintain itself peasant culture requires continual communication to the local community of thought originating outside of it. The intellectual and often the religious and moral life of the peasant village is perpetually incomplete; the student needs also to know something of what goes on in the minds of remote teachers, priests, or philosophers whose thinking affects and perhaps is affected by the peasantry" (1956:68). Redfield saw this relationship as one between the "great tradition of the reflective few" of civilization, and the "little tradition of the largely unreflective many" (1956:70).

Peasant society, then, is hardly a "grass-roots" creation, produced by rural cultural inventiveness and vigor. Peasant societies are what they are — and thus stand in contrast to truly primitive tribal societies, which are somewhat more nearly grass-roots products — precisely because, throughout history, they have replenished and augmented their cultural forms by imitating customs and behavior of other members of their wider society. But since peasants comprehend imperfectly what they see in cities, the urban-inspired elements they acquire are reworked, simplified, and trimmed down so they can be accommodated to the less complex village existence. And because this process is slow, by the time urban elements are successfully incorporated into village culture, urban life has changed and progressed; thus, peasants are always doomed to be old-fashioned. No matter how hard they have tried, what they have believed to be the last word has almost invariably reflected the city forms of earlier generations.

Although cultural elements seem to flow principally outward and downward from city to peasant village, this is not the *only* direction of transmission. In lesser degree — perhaps especially in music, dance, literature, and the other arts — there is a return flow. Creative members of the Great Tradition of a particular society often look to their rural peoples for inspiration, and studies of song and dance, writing and painting, often reveal the influence the country and the peasant have had on the city elite. But, though we recognize the circular flow of culture implicit in the symbiotic relationship that binds peasant to urban dweller, we think it obvious that this flow is anything but evenly balanced.

We wish to express our opinion on two other points about which we think there is often confusion. Peasant society is often described as "intermediate" (Redfield 1930:217, Casagrande 1959:2), with the implication of its being "transitional" between one form and another. In Redfield's words, "The peasant village is a half-way house, a stable structure, along the historic road mankind takes between our imagined polarities" (1953:225). The words "intermediate" or "transitional" emphasize, it seems to us, the idea of the folk-urban continuum, which we feel is not at all suited as a model for understanding peasant societies. Peasant societies do not exist because they have crept from a primitive form toward city influences. Settled agriculturalists automatically and spontaneously *became* peasants when the first cities (or states, to use Wolf's modification of the concept) came into being, and when they lost their political and economic autonomy. "Half-way house," even though qualified as "a stable structure," still implies a relatively temporary state. It seems to us that a societal type that has existed for from 6,000 to 7,000 years — i.e., from the beginning of civilization — deserves recognition in its own right, not as "intermediate" or "transitional" but as a genuine social and cultural form to which half or more of the people who have lived since time began have conformed! The fact that peasants — like primitives — are on their way out in no way invalidates their right to be studied as a unique form.

The second point to which we wish to address ourselves has to do with the rate at which peasant societies change. Peasant society is often described as "static," which means "unchanging." Peasant societies, of course, have changed relatively slowly in the past. For, because of the symbiotic ties between peasants and urban peoples, the rate of change of the former is in significant measure governed by that of the latter. Peasants seem always to be trying to catch up with their urban brethren, who nonetheless are always a good many steps ahead of them. It is the *relationship* between city and village — the cultural lag that we always find, which keeps peasants backward and old-fashioned — that is, static. Once this cultural lag disappears, as it increasingly does in an industrial world, peasants disappear.

The articles in Part I were selected to illustrate some of the points touched upon in this introduction. In a classic paper, Gideon Sjoberg describes the social and economic characteristics of the preindustrial city, which, as we have seen, is inseparable from the concept of a peasantry. In "The Social Organization of Tradition," Robert Redfield offers a model — the Great Tradition versus the Little Tradition — now widely accepted by anthropologists to conceptualize the relationship between the *cultures* (rather more than the economic and political forms) of peasants and city peoples. Lloyd Fallers, using African materials, directs himself to the question of whether skilled farmers who market a part of their produce in towns are automatically peasants. In answering the question: "Are African Cultivators to Be Called 'Peasants'?" he concludes that whereas the term is apt in an economic and a political sense, in a cultural sense the African cultivator is not a peasant since his society lacks a Great Tradition, i.e., does not have (an indigenous) system of writing and the attendant "literary religious traditions which formed the bases for European and Asian high cultures." Finally, Morris Opler makes the very important point that peasants are tied not only to cities but to other peasant villages as well. Through social, religious, and economic networks they maintain close contact with people in neighboring villages, so that every peasant community is in fact a part of a much wider rural unity.

REFERENCES CITED

Arensberg, Conrad
1937 *The Irish Countryman: An Anthropological Study*. New York: The Macmillan Co.

Blackman, Winifred S.
1927 *The Fellāhīn of Upper Egypt*. London: George G. Harrap and Co.

Casagrande, Joseph B.
1959 "Some Observations on the Study of Intermediate Societies." *Intermediate Societies, Social Mobility, and Communication* (Verne F. Ray, ed.). Proceedings of the 1959 Annual Spring Meeting of the American Ethnological Society. Seattle: University of Washington Press. pp. 1–10.

Durham, M. Edith
1909 *High Albania*. London: Edward Arnold.
1910 "High Albania and Its Customs." *Journal of the Royal Anthropological Institute* 40:453–472.
1928 *Some Tribal Origins, Laws and Customs of the Balkans*. London: G. Allen and Unwin.

Embree, John F.
1939 *Suye Mura: A Japanese Village*. Chicago: University of Chicago Press.

Firth, Raymond
1946 *Malay Fishermen: Their Peasant Economy*. London: Kegan Paul, Trench, Trubner and Co.
1950 "The Peasantry of South East Asia," *International Affairs* 26:503–512.

Foster, George M.
1953 "What Is Folk Culture?" *American Anthropologist* 55:159–173.
1960–1961 "Interpersonal Relations in Peasant Society." *Human Organization* 19:174–178.
Gamio, Manuel (ed.)
1922 *La Población del Valle de Teotihuacán*, Tomo II. Mexico, D.F.: Dirección de Talleres Gráficos.
Geertz, Clifford
1962 "Studies in Peasant Life: Community and Society." *Biennial Review of Anthropology 1961* (B. J. Siegel, ed.). Stanford: Stanford University Press. pp. 1–41.
Keesing, Felix M.
1958 *Cultural Anthropology: The Science of Custom*. New York: Rinehart and Co.
Kenny, Michael
1960 "Patterns of Patronage in Spain." *Modern Community Studies in the Circum-Mediterranean Area, Anthropological Quarterly* 33:14–23.
Kroeber, A. L.
1948 *Anthropology*. New York: Harcourt, Brace and Co.
Redfield, Robert
1930 *Tepoztlán: A Mexican Village. A Study of Folk Life*. Chicago: University of Chicago Press.
1953 *The Primitive World and Its Transformations*. Ithaca, N.Y.: Cornell University Press.
1956 *Peasant Society and Culture*. Chicago: University of Chicago Press.
Rennell Rodd, James
1892 *The Customs and Lore of Modern Greece*. London: David Stott.
Smith, Arthur H.
1899 *Village Life in China: A Study in Sociology*. New York, Chicago, Toronto: Fleming H. Revell Co.
Titiev, Misch
1959 *Introduction to Cultural Anthropology*. New York: Henry Holt and Co.
von Dietze, C.
1934 "Peasantry." *Encyclopedia of the Social Sciences* 12:48–53.
Wiser, William H. and Charlotte Viall Wiser
1963 *Behind Mud Walls 1930–1960*. Berkeley and Los Angeles: University of California Press.
Wolf, Eric R.
1955 "Types of Latin American Peasantry: A Preliminary Discussion." *American Anthropologist* 57:452–471.
1956 "Aspects of Group Relations in a Complex Society: Mexico," *American Anthropologist* 58:1065–1078.
1966 *Peasants*. Englewood Cliffs, N.J.: Prentice-Hall.

The Preindustrial City

Gideon Sjoberg

In the past few decades social scientists have been conducting field studies in a number of relatively non-Westernized cities. Their recently acquired knowledge of North Africa and various parts of Asia, combined with what was already learned, clearly indicates that these cities are not like typical cities of the United States and other highly industrialized areas but are much more like those of medieval Europe. Such communities are termed herein "preindustrial," for they have arisen without stimulus from that form of production which we associate with the European industrial revolution.

Recently Foster, in a most informative article, took cognizance of the preindustrial city.[1] His primary emphasis was upon the peasantry (which he calls "folk"); but he recognized this to be part of a broader social structure which includes the preindustrial city. He noted certain similarities between the peasantry and the city's lower class. Likewise the present author sought to analyze the total society of which the peasantry and the preindustrial city are integral parts.[2] For want of a better term this was called "feudal." Like Redfield's folk (or "primitive") society, the feudal order is highly stable and sacred; in contrast, however, it has a complex social organization. It is characterized by highly developed state and educational and/or religious institutions and by a rigid class structure.

Thus far no one has analyzed the preindustrial city per se, especially as it differs from the industrial-urban community, although Weber, Tönnies, and a few others perceived differences between the two. Yet such a survey is needed for the understanding of urban development in so-called underdeveloped countries and, for that matter, in parts of Europe. Such is the goal of this paper. The typological analysis should also serve as a guide to future research.

ECOLOGICAL ORGANIZATION

Preindustrial cities depend for their existence upon food and raw materials obtained from without; for this reason they are marketing

From "The Preindustrial City" in *The American Journal of Sociology,* Vol. LX, No. 5 (March 1955), pp. 438–445. Reprinted by permission of The University of Chicago Press.

[1] George M. Foster, "What Is Folk Culture?" *American Anthropologist,* LV (1953), 159–73.

[2] Gideon Sjoberg, "Folk and 'Feudal' Societies," *American Journal of Sociology,* LVIII (1952), 231–39.

centers. And they serve as centers for handicraft manufacturing. In addition, they fulfill important political, religious, and educational functions. Some cities have become specialized; for example, Benares in India and Karbala in Iraq are best known as religious communities, and Peiping in China as a locus for political and educational activities.

The proportion of urbanites relative to the peasant population is small, in some societies about 10 per cent, even though a few preindustrial cities have attained populations of 100,000 or more. Growth has been by slow accretion. These characteristics are due to the nonindustrial nature of the total social order. The amount of surplus food available to support an urban population has been limited by the unmechanized agriculture, transportation facilities utilizing primarily human or animal power, and inefficient methods of food preservation and storage.

The internal arrangement of the preindustrial city, in the nature of the case, is closely related to the city's economic and social structure.[3] Most streets are mere passageways for people and for animals used in transport. Buildings are low and crowded together. The congested conditions, combined with limited scientific knowledge, have fostered serious sanitation problems.

More significant is the rigid social segregation which typically has led to the formation of "quarters" or "wards." In some cities (e.g., Fez, Morocco, and Aleppo, Syria) these were sealed off from each other by walls, whose gates were locked at night. The quarters reflect the sharp local social divisions. Thus ethnic groups live in special sections. And the occupational groupings, some being at the same time ethnic in character, typically reside apart from one another. Often a special street or sector of the city is occupied almost exclusively by members of a particular trade; cities in such divergent cultures as medieval Europe and modern Afghanistan contain streets with names like "street of the goldsmiths." Lower-class and especially "outcaste" groups live on the city's periphery, at a distance from the primary centers of activity. Social segregation, the limited transportation facilities, the modicum of residential mobility, and the cramped living quarters have encouraged the development of well-defined neighborhoods which are almost primary groups.

Despite rigid segregation the evidence suggests no real specialization of land use such as is functionally necessary in industrial-urban communities.

[3] Sociologists have devoted almost no attention to the ecology of preindustrial centers. However, works of other social scientists do provide some valuable preliminary data. See, e.g., Marcel Clerget, *Le Caire: Étude de géographie urbaine et d'histoire économique* (2 vols.; Cairo: E. & R. Schindler, 1934); Robert E. Dickinson, *The West European City* (London: Routledge & Kegan Paul, 1951); Roger Le Tourneau, *Fès: Avant le protectorat* (Casablanca: Société Marocaine de Librairie et d'Édition, 1949); Edward W. Lane, *Cairo Fifty Years Ago* (London: John Murray, 1896); J. Sauvaget, *Alep* (Paris: Librairie Orientaliste Paul Geuthner, 1941); J. Weulersse, "Antioche: Essai de géographie urbaine," *Bulletin d'études orientales,* IV (1934), 27–79; Jean Kennedy, *Here Is India* (New York: Charles Scribner's Sons, 1945); and relevant articles in American geographical journals.

In medieval Europe and in other areas city dwellings often serve as workshops, and religious structures are used as schools or marketing centers.[4]

Finally, the "business district" does not hold the position of dominance that it enjoys in the industrial-urban community. Thus, in the Middle East the principal mosque, or in medieval Europe the cathedral, is usually the focal point of community life. The center of Peiping is the Forbidden City.

ECONOMIC ORGANIZATION

The economy of the preindustrial city diverges sharply from that of the modern industrial center. The prime difference is the absence in the former of industrialism which may be defined as that system of production in which *inanimate* sources of power are used to multiply human effort. Preindustrial cities depend for the production of goods and services upon *animate* (human or animal) sources of energy — applied either directly or indirectly through such mechanical devices as hammers, pulleys, and wheels. The industrial-urban community, on the other hand, employs inanimate generators of power such as electricity and steam which greatly enhance the productive capacity of urbanites. This basically new form of energy production, one which requires for its development and survival a special kind of institutional complex, effects striking changes in the ecological, economic, and social organization of cities in which it has become dominant.

Other facets of the economy of the preindustrial city are associated with its particular system of production. There is little fragmentation or specialization of work. The handicraftsman participates in nearly every phase of the manufacture of an article, often carrying out the work in his own home or in a small shop near by and, within the limits of certain guild and community regulations, maintaining direct control over conditions of work and methods of production.

In industrial cities, on the other hand, the complex division of labor requires a specialized managerial group, often extra-community in character, whose primary function is to direct and control others. And for the supervision and co-ordination of the activities of workers, a "factory system" has been developed, something typically lacking in preindustrial cities. (Occasionally centralized production is found in preindustrial cities — e.g., where the state organized slaves for large-scale construction projects.) Most commercial activities, also, are conducted in preindustrial cities by individuals without a highly formalized organization; for example, the craftsman has frequently been responsible for the marketing of his own products. With a few exceptions, the preindustrial community cannot support a large group of middlemen.

The various occupations are organized into what have been termed

[4] Dickinson, *op. cit.*, p. 27; O. H. K. Spate, *India and Pakistan* (London: Methuen & Co., 1954), p. 183.

"guilds."[5] These strive to encompass all, except the elite, who are gainfully employed in some economic activity. Guilds have existed for merchants and handicraft workers (e.g., goldsmiths and weavers) as well as for servants, entertainers, and even beggars and thieves. Typically the guilds operate only within the local community, and there are no large-scale economic organizations such as those in industrial cities which link their members to their fellows in other communities.

Guild membership and apprenticeship are prerequisites to the practice of almost any occupation, a circumstance obviously leading to monopolization. To a degree these organizations regulate the work of their members and the price of their products and services. And the guilds recruit workers into specific occupations, typically selecting them according to such particularistic criteria as kinship rather than universalistic standards.

The guilds are integrated with still other elements of the city's social structure. They perform certain religious functions; for example, in medieval European, Chinese, and Middle Eastern cities each guild had its "patron saint" and held periodic festivals in his honor. And, by assisting members in time of trouble, the guilds serve as social security agencies.

The economic structure of the preindustrial city functions with little rationality, judged by industrial-urban standards. This is shown in the general nonstandardization of manufacturing methods as well as in the products and is even more evident in marketing. In preindustrial cities throughout the world a fixed price is rare; buyer and seller settle their bargain by haggling. (Of course, there are limits above which customers will not buy and below which merchants will not sell.) Often business is conducted in a leisurely manner, money not being the only desired end.

Furthermore, the sorting of goods according to size, weight, and quality is not common. Typical is the adulteration and spoilage of produce. And weights and measures are not standardized: variations exist not only between one city and the next but also within communities, for often different guilds employ their own systems. Within a single city there may be different kinds of currency, which, with the poorly developed accounting and credit systems, signalize a modicum of rationality in the whole of economic action in preindustrial cities.[6]

[5] For a discussion of guilds and other facets of the preindustrial city's economy see, e.g., J. S. Burgess, *The Guilds of Peking* (New York: Columbia University Press, 1928); Edward T. Williams, *China, Yesterday and Today* (5th ed.; New York: Thomas Y. Crowell Co., 1932); T'ai-ch'u Liao, "The Apprentices in Chengtu during and after the War," *Yenching Journal of Social Studies*, IV (1948), 90–106; H. A. R. Gibb and Harold Bowen, *Islamic Society and the West* (London: Oxford University Press, 1950), Vol. I, Part I, chap. vi; Le Tourneau, *op. cit.*; Clerget, *op. cit.*; James W. Thompson and Edgar N. Johnson, *An Introduction to Medieval Europe* (New York: W. W. Norton Co., 1937), chap. xx; Sylvia L. Thrupp, "Medieval Gilds Reconsidered," *Journal of Economic History*, II (1942), 164–73.

[6] For an extreme example of unstandardized currency cf. Robert Coltman, Jr., *The Chinese* (Philadelphia: F. A. Davis, 1891), p. 52. In some traditional societies (e.g., China) the state has sought to standardize economic action in the city

SOCIAL ORGANIZATION

The economic system of the preindustrial city, based as it has been upon animate sources of power, articulates with a characteristic class structure and family, religious, educational, and governmental systems.

Of the class structure, the most striking component is a literate elite controlling and depending for its existence upon the mass of the populace, even in the traditional cities of India with their caste system. The elite is composed of individuals holding positions in the governmental, religious, and/or educational institutions of the larger society, although at times groups such as large absentee landlords have belonged to it. At the opposite pole are the masses, comprising such groups as handicraft workers whose goods and services are produced primarily for the elite's benefit.[7] Between the elite and the lower class is a rather sharp schism, but in both groups there are gradations in rank. The members of the elite belong to the "correct" families and enjoy power, property, and certain highly valued personal attributes. Their position, moreover, is legitimized by sacred writings.

Social mobility in this city is minimal; the only real threat to the elite comes from the outside — not from the city's lower classes. And a middle class — so typical of industrial-urban communities, where it can be considered the "dominant" class — is not known in the preindustrial city. The system of production in the larger society provides goods, including food, and services in sufficient amounts to support only a small group of leisured individuals; under these conditions an urban middle class, a semi-leisured group, cannot arise. Nor are a middle class and extensive social mobility essential to the maintenance of the economic system.

Significant is the role of the marginal or "outcaste" groups (e.g., the Eta of Japan), which are not an integral part of the dominant social system. Typically they rank lower than the urban lower class, performing tasks considered especially degrading, such as burying the dead. Slaves, beggars, and the like are outcastes in most preindustrial cities. Even such groups as professional entertainers and itinerant merchants are often viewed as outcastes, for their rovings expose them to "foreign" ideas from which the dominant social group seeks to isolate itself. Actually many out-

---

by setting up standard systems of currency and/or weights and measures; these efforts, however, generally proved ineffective. Inconsistent policies in taxation, too, hinder the development of a "rational" economy.

[7] The status of the true merchant in the preindustrial city, ideally, has been low; in medieval Europe and China many merchants were considered "outcastes." However, in some preindustrial cities a few wealthy merchants have acquired considerable power even though their role has not been highly valued. Even then most of their prestige has come through participation in religious, governmental, or educational activities, which have been highly valued (see, e.g., Ping-ti Ho, "The Salt Merchants of Yang-Chou: A Study of Commercial Capitalism in Eighteenth-Century China," *Harvard Journal of Asiatic Studies*, XVII [1954], 130–68).

caste groups, including some of those mentioned above, are ethnic groups, a fact which further intensifies their isolation. (A few, like the Jews in the predominantly Muslim cities of North Africa, have their own small literate religious elite which, however, enjoys no significant political power in the city as a whole.)

An assumption of many urban sociologists is that a small, unstable kinship group, notably the conjugal unit, is a necessary correlate of city life. But this premise does not hold for preindustrial cities.[8] At times sociologists and anthropologists, when generalizing about various traditional societies, have imputed to peasants typically urban kinship patterns. Actually, in these societies the ideal forms of kinship and family life are most closely approximated by members of the urban literate elite, who are best able to fulfill the exacting requirements of the sacred writings. Kinship and the ability to perpetuate one's lineage are accorded marked prestige in preindustrial cities. Children, especially sons, are highly valued, and polygamy or concubinage or adoption help to assure the attainment of large families. The pre-eminence of kinship is apparent even in those preindustrial cities where divorce is permitted. Thus, among the urban Muslims or urban Chinese divorce is not an index of disorganization; here, conjugal ties are loose and distinctly subordinate to the bonds of kinship, and each member of a dissolved conjugal unit typically is absorbed by his kin group. Marriage, a prerequisite to adult status in the preindustrial city, is entered upon at an early age and is arranged between families rather than romantically, by individuals.

The kinship and familial organization displays some rigid patterns of sex and age differentiation whose universality in preindustrial cities has generally been overlooked. A woman, especially of the upper class, ideally performs few significant functions outside the home. She is clearly subordinate to males, especially her father or husband. Recent evidence indicates that this is true even for such a city as Lhasa, Tibet, where women supposedly have had high status.[9] The isolation of women from public life has in some cases been extreme. In nineteenth-century Seoul, Korea, "respectable" women appeared on the streets only during certain hours of

[8] For materials on the kinship system and age and sex differentiation see, e.g., Le Tourneau, *op. cit.*; Edward W. Lane, *The Manners and Customs of the Modern Egyptians* (3rd ed.; New York: E. P. Dutton Co., 1923); C. Snouck Hurgronje, *Mekka in the Latter Part of the Nineteenth Century*, trans. J. H. Monahan (London: Luzac, 1931); Horace Miner, *The Primitive City of Timbuctoo* (Princeton: Princeton University Press, 1953); Alice M. Bacon, *Japanese Girls and Women* (rev. ed.; Boston: Houghton Mifflin Co., 1902); J. S. Burgess, "Community Organization in China," *Far Eastern Survey*, XIV (1945), 371–73; Morton H. Fried, *Fabric of Chinese Society* (New York: Frederick A. Praeger, 1953); Francis L. K. Hsu, *Under the Ancestors' Shadow* (New York: Columbia University Press, 1948); Cornelius Osgood, *The Koreans and Their Culture* (New York: Ronald Press, 1951), chap. viii; Jukichi Inouye, *Home Life in Tokyo* (2d ed.; Tokyo: Tokyo Printing Co., 1911).

[9] Tsung-Lien Shen and Shen-Chi Liu, *Tibet and the Tibetans* (Stanford: Stanford University Press, 1953), pp. 143–44.

the night when men were supposed to stay at home.[10] Those women in preindustrial cities who evade some of the stricter requirements are members of certain marginal groups (e.g., entertainers) or of the lower class. The role of the urban lower-class woman typically resembles that of the peasant rather than the urban upper-class woman. Industrialization, by creating demands and opportunities for their employment outside the home, is causing significant changes in the status of women as well as in the whole of the kinship system in urban areas.

A formalized system of age grading is an effective mechanism of social control in preindustrial cities. Among siblings the eldest son is privileged. And children and youth are subordinate to parents and other adults. This, combined with early marriage, inhibits the development of a "youth culture." On the other hand, older persons hold considerable power and prestige, a fact contributing to the slow pace of change.

As noted above, kinship is functionally integrated with social class. It also reinforces and is reinforced by the economic organization: the occupations, through the guilds, select their members primarily on the basis of kinship, and much of the work is carried on in the home or immediate vicinity. Such conditions are not functional to the requirements of a highly industrialized society.

The kinship system in the preindustrial city also articulates with a special kind of religious system, whose formal organization reaches fullest development among members of the literate elite.[11] The city is the seat of the key religious functionaries whose actions set standards for the rest of society. The urban lower class, like the peasantry, does not possess the education or the means to maintain all the exacting norms prescribed by the sacred writings. Yet the religious system influences the city's entire social structure. (Typically, within the preindustrial city one religion is dominant; however, certain minority groups adhere to their own beliefs.) Unlike the situation in industrial cities, religious activity is not separate from other social action but permeates family, economic, governmental, and other activities. Daily life is pervaded with religious significance. Especially important are periodic public festivals and ceremonies like Ramadan in Muslim cities. Even distinctly ethnic outcaste groups can through their own religious festivals maintain solidarity.

Magic, too, is interwoven with economic, familial, and other social activities. Divination is commonly employed for determining the "correct" action on critical occasions; for example, in traditional Japanese and Chi-

[10] Osgood, *op. cit.*, p. 146.

[11] For information on various aspects of religious behavior see, e.g., Le Tourneau, *op. cit.;* Miner, *op. cit.;* Lane, *Manners and Customs;* Hurgronje, *op. cit.;* André Chouraqui *Les Juifs d'Afrique du Nord* (Paris: Presses Universitaires de France, 1952); Justus Doolittle, *Social Life of the Chinese* (London: Sampson Low, 1868); John K. Shryock, *The Temples of Anking and Their Cults* (Paris: Privately printed, 1931); Derk Bodde (ed.), *Annual Customs and Festivals in Peking* (Peiping: Henri Vetch, 1936); Edwin Benson, *Life in a Medieval City* (New York: Macmillan Co., 1920); Hsu, *op. cit.*

nese cities, the selection of marriage partners. And nonscientific procedures are widely employed to treat illness among all elements of the population of the preindustrial city.

Formal education typically is restricted to the male elite, its purpose being to train individuals for positions in the governmental, educational, or religious hierarchies. The economy of preindustrial cities does not require mass literacy, nor, in fact, does the system of production provide the leisure so necessary for the acquisition of formal education. Considerable time is needed merely to learn the written language, which often is quite different from that spoken. The teacher occupies a position of honor, primarily because of the prestige of all learning and especially of knowledge of the sacred literature, and learning is traditional and characteristically based upon sacred writings.[12] Students are expected to memorize rather than evaluate and initiate, even in institutions of higher learning.

Since preindustrial cities have no agencies of mass communication, they are relatively isolated from one another. Moreover, the masses within a city are isolated from the elite. The former must rely upon verbal communication, which is formalized in special groups such as storytellers or their counterparts. Through verse and song these transmit upper-class tradition to nonliterate individuals.

The formal government of the preindustrial city is the province of the elite and is closely integrated with the educational and religious systems. It performs two principal functions: exacting tribute from the city's masses to support the activities of the elite and maintaining law and order through a "police force" (at times a branch of the army) and a court system. The police force exists primarily for the control of "outsiders," and the courts support custom and the rule of the sacred literature, a code of enacted legislation typically being absent.

In actual practice little reliance is placed upon formal machinery for regulating social life.[13] Much more significant are the informal controls exerted by the kinship, guild, and religious systems, and here, of course, personal standing is decisive. Status distinctions are visibly correlated with personal attributes, chiefly speech, dress, and personal mannerisms which proclaim ethnic group, occupation, age, sex, and social class. In nineteenth-century Seoul, not only did the upper-class mode of dress differ considerably from that of the masses, but speech varied according to social class, the verb forms and pronouns depending upon whether the speaker ranked higher or lower or was the equal of the person being addressed.[14] Obviously, then, escape from one's role is difficult, even in the street

[12] Le Tourneau, *op. cit.*, Part VI; Lane, *Manners and Customs*, chap. ii; Charles Bell, *The People of Tibet* (Oxford: Clarendon Press, 1928), chap. xix; O. Olufsen, *The Emir of Bokhara and His Country* (London: William Heinemann, 1911), chap. ix; Doolittle, *op. cit.*

[13] Carleton Coon, *Caravan: The Story of the Middle East* (New York: Henry Holt & Co., 1951), p. 259; George W. Gilmore, *Korea from Its Capital* (Philadelphia: Presbyterian Board of Publication, 1892), pp. 51–52.

[14] Osgood, *op. cit.*, chap. viii; Gilmore, *op. cit.*, chap. iv.

crowds. The individual is ever conscious of his specific rights and duties. All these things conserve the social order in the preindustrial city despite its heterogeneity.

CONCLUSIONS

Throughout this paper there is the assumption that certain structural elements are universal for all urban centers. This study's hypothesis is that their form in the preindustrial city is fundamentally distinct from that in the industrial-urban community. A considerable body of data not only from medieval Europe, which is somewhat atypical,[15] but from a variety of cultures supports this point of view. Emphasis has been upon the static features of preindustrial city life. But even those preindustrial cities which have undergone considerable change approach the ideal type. For one thing, social change is of such a nature that it is not usually perceived by the general populace.

Most cities of the preindustrial type have been located in Europe or Asia. Even though Athens and Rome and the large commercial centers of Europe prior to the industrial revolution displayed certain unique features, they fit the preindustrial type quite well.[16] And many traditional Latin American cities are quite like it, although deviations exist, for, excluding pre-Columbian cities, these were affected to some degree by the industrial revolution soon after their establishment.

It is postulated that industrialization is a key variable accounting for the distinctions between preindustrial and industrial cities. The type of social structure required to develop and maintain a form of production utilizing inanimate sources of power is quite unlike that in the preindustrial city.[17] At the very least, extensive industrialization requires a rational, centralized, extra-community economic organization in which recruitment is based more upon universalism than on particularism, a class system which stresses achievement rather than ascription, a small and flexible kinship system, a system of mass education which emphasizes universalistic rather than particularistic criteria, and mass communication. Modification in any one of these elements affects the others and induces changes in other systems such as those of religion and social control as

[15] Henri Pirenne, in *Medieval Cities* (Princeton: Princeton University Press, 1925), and others have noted that European cities grew up in opposition to and were separate from the greater society. But this thesis has been overstated for medieval Europe. Most preindustrial cities are integral parts of broader social structures.

[16] Some of these cities made extensive use of water power, which possibly fostered deviations from the type.

[17] For a discussion of the institutional prerequisites of industrialization see, e.g., Bert F. Hoselitz, "Social Structure and Economic Growth," *Economia internazionale*, VI (1953), 52–77, and Marion J. Levy, "Some Sources of the Vulnerability of the Structures of Relatively Non-industrialized Societies to Those of Highly Industrialized Societies," in Bert F. Hoselitz (ed.), *The Progress of Underdeveloped Areas* (Chicago: University of Chicago Press, 1952), pp. 114 ff.

well. Industrialization, moreover, not only requires a special kind of social structure within the urban community but provides the means necessary for its establishment.

Anthropologists and sociologists will in the future devote increased attention to the study of cities throughout the world. They must therefore recognize that the particular kind of social structure found in cities in the United States is not typical of all societies. Miner's recent study of Timbuctoo,[18] which contains much excellent data, points to the need for recognition of the preindustrial city. His emphasis upon the folk-urban continuum diverted him from an equally significant problem: How does Timbuctoo differ from modern industrial cities in its ecological, economic, and social structure? Society there seems even more sacred and organized than Miner admits.[19] For example, he used divorce as an index of disorganization, but in Muslim society divorce within certain rules is justified by the sacred literature. The studies of Hsu and Fried would have considerably more significance had the authors perceived the generality of their findings. And, once the general structure of the preindustrial city is understood, the specific cultural deviations become more meaningful.

Beals notes the importance of the city as a center of acculturation.[20] But an understanding of this process is impossible without some knowledge of the preindustrial city's social structure. Although industrialization is clearly advancing throughout most of the world, the social structure of preindustrial civilizations is conservative, often resisting the introduction of numerous industrial forms. Certainly many cities of Europe (e.g., in France or Spain) are not so fully industrialized as some presume; a number of preindustrial patterns remain. The persistence of preindustrial elements is also evident in cities of North Africa and many parts of Asia; for example, in India and Japan,[21] even though great social change is currently taking place. And the Latin-American city of Merida, which Redfield studied, had many preindustrial traits.[22] A conscious awareness of the ecological, economic, and social structure of the preindustrial city should do much to further the development of comparative urban community studies.

[18] *Op. cit.*

[19] This point seems to have been perceived also by Asael T. Hansen in his review of Horace Miner's *The Primitive City of Timbuctoo, American Journal of Sociology*, LIX (1954), 501–2.

[20] Ralph L. Beals, "Urbanism, Urbanization and Acculturation," *American Anthropologist*, LIII (1951), 1–10.

[21] See, e.g., D. R. Gadgil, *Poona: A Socio-economic Survey* (Poona: Gokhale Institute of Politics and Economics, 1952), Part II; N. V. Sovani, *Social Survey of Kolhapur City* (Poona: Gokhale Institute of Politics and Economics, 1951), Vol. II; Noel P. Gist, "Caste Differentials in South India," *American Sociological Review*, XIX (1954), 126–37; John Campbell Pelzel, "Social Stratification in Japanese Urban Economic Life" (unpublished Ph.D. dissertation, Harvard University, Department of Social Relations, 1950).

[22] Robert Redfield, *The Folk Culture of Yucatan* (Chicago: University of Chicago Press, 1941).

The Social Organization of Tradition

Robert Redfield

I

Out of that anthropology which rested on studies of isolated primitive or tribal peoples arose the concept, "a culture." The Andamanese had a culture, the Trobrianders, the Aranda of Australia, and the Zuni. Each culture came to be conceived as an independent and self-sufficient system. Recently words have been found to make clear this conception of an "autonomous cultural system." It is "one which is self-sustaining — that is, it does not need to be maintained by a complementary, reciprocal, subordinate, or other indispensable connection with a second system." Such units — such cultures as those of the Zuni or the Andamanese — are systems because they have their own mutually adjusted and interdependent parts, and they are autonomous because they do not require another system for their continued functioning.[1] The anthropologist may see in such a system evidences of past communications of elements of culture to that band or tribe from others, but, as it now is, he understands that it keeps going by itself; and in describing its parts and their workings he need not go outside the little group itself. The exceptions, where the band or tribe relies on some other band or tribe for a commodity or service, are small and do not seriously modify the fact that that culture is maintained by the communication of a heritage through the generations of just those people who make up the local community.

The culture of a peasant community, on the other hand, is not autonomous. It is an aspect or dimension of the civilization of which it is a part. As the peasant society is a half-society, so the peasant culture is a half-

From "The Social Organization of Tradition" in *The Far Eastern Quarterly*, Vol. XV, No. 1 (November 1955). Reprinted by permission of The Association for Asian Studies, Inc. This paper is based on and is partly an excerpt from one of the four lectures delivered at Swarthmore College, under the auspices of the Cooper Foundation, in March, 1955. It was (in part) read at a meeting of the Central Section of the American Anthropological Society at Bloomington, Indiana, in April, 1955.

[1] "Acculturation: An Exploratory Formulation," The Social Science Research Council Summer Seminar on Acculturation, 1953 (Members: H. G. Barnett, Leonard Broom, Bernard J. Siegel, Evon Z. Vogt, James B. Watson), *American Anthropologist*, 56.6 (December 1954), 974.

culture.[2] When we study such a culture we find two things to be true that are not true when we study an isolated primitive band or tribe. First, we discover that to maintain itself peasant culture requires continual communication to the local community of content of thought originating outside of it. It *does* require another culture for its continued functioning. The intellectual, and often the religious and moral life of the peasant village is perpetually incomplete; the student needs also to know something of what comes into the village from the minds of remote teachers, priests or philosophers whose thinking affects and perhaps is affected by the peasantry. Seen as a "synchronic" system, the peasant culture cannot be fully understood from what goes on in the minds of the villagers alone. Second, the peasant village invites us to attend to the long course of interaction between that community and centers of civilization. The peasant culture has an evident history; we are called upon to study that history; and the history is, again, not local: it is a history of the civilization of which the village culture is one local expression. Both points, in recognition of both generic aspects of the peasant culture, were clearly made by George Foster when he reviewed recently his experiences in Latin-American communities and wrote that there the local culture "is continually replenished by contact with products of intellectual and scientific social strata," [3] and said also that "One of the most obvious distinctions between truly primitive societies and folk [peasant] societies is that the latter, over hundreds of years, have had constant contact with the centers of intellectual thought and development. . . ." [4]

How, as anthropologists working in the small community of peasants, are we to conceive and how are we to study that larger system, that compound culture, of which only parts appear to us in the village?

I think we might begin with a recognition long present in discussions of civilizations of the difference between a Great Tradition and a Little Tradition. Writing of Chinese religion, Wing-tsit Chan says "that instead of dividing the religious life of the Chinese people into three compartments called Confucianism, Buddhism and Taoism, it is far more accurate to divide it into two levels, the level of the masses and the level of the enlightened." [5] Writing of Islam, G. von Grünebaum discusses the ways in which the Great Tradition of the orthodox and the scholar is adjusted to or is required to take account of the Little Traditions of the common people in the villages. He distinguishes such accommodations of

[2] A. L. Kroeber, *Anthropology* (New York: Harcourt, Brace, 1948), 284.

[3] George M. Foster, "What Is Folk Culture?" *American Anthropologist*, 55.2, Part 1 (April–June 1953), 169.

[4] Foster, 164. In quoting this passage I venture to substitute "peasant" for "folk" to make the terminology fit that chosen for these lectures. I think Foster's "folk societies" are much the same as those I here call "peasant societies."

[5] Wing-tsit Chan, *Religious Trends in Modern China* (New York: Columbia University Press, 1953), 141 ff. See also, W. Eberhard, "Neuere Forschungen zur Religion Chinas, 1920–1932" *Archiv für Religionswissenschaft*, 33.3 (1936), 304–344, a discussion of *Staatskult and Volksreligion* in China.

Great Tradition to Little Tradition, as when a Christian cross sent by Saladin to Baghdad was first despised but in the end reverenced by even the orthodox, from such re-interpretations of doctrine as are forced on the Great Tradition by the Little, as when the expounders of Islam come to justify the cults of local saints by referring to Koranic passages about "familiars of the Lord." [6] At this point von Grünebaum, historian and humanist, is studying from the top the same phenomena which Westermarck, anthropologist, studied in Morocco from the bottom — in the local communities.[7] From India Professor V. Raghavan [8] has sent us a series of papers about the many kinds of specialists who in India teach and have taught the sanskritic tradition to the village peasants. Centuries ago certain sanskritic scholars used popular compositions, notably the epics and the *Purānas*, expressly for the purpose of teaching vedic lore to the people. Parts of these compositions "were recited to vast congregations of people gathered at sacrificial sessions by certain special classes of reciters." Professor Raghavan traces an unbroken tradition to the present day of deliberate provision, by ruler and by teacher, of recitations in vernacular languages, of the ancient Hindu epics into the villages of southern India and across to Cambodia. There was and there is an organization of specialists devoted to mediating between Great Tradition and Little. So Professor Raghavan, historian and humanist, follows the structure of this organization, pursues the course of its influences through Indian history, until he comes into the present day villages of south India where, as he puts it, "some sweet-voiced, gifted expounder" sits in temple or in house-front and expounds "to hundreds and thousands the story of the *dharma* that *Rāma* upheld and the *adharma* by which *Rāvana* fell." [9]

And in the village he finds already there, having entered so to speak by the back door, the anthropologist, a fellow not very well prepared to conceive and to study this structure of tradition, this organization of functionaries and of content of thought, into which the life of the village enters and on which the life of the village in part depends.

II

Coming from cultures which *are* autonomous systems, anthropologists have experience either with societies in which there is no distinction between Great and Little Traditions, or with societies in which

[6] G. E. von Grünebaum, "The Problem: Unity in Diversity," in *Unity and Variety in Muslim Civilization*, ed. by G. E. von Grünebaum (Chicago: University of Chicago Press, 17–37.

[7] Edward Westermarck, *Ritual and Belief in Morocco* (London: Macmillan, 1926).

[8] V. Raghavan, "Adult Education in Ancient India," *Memoirs of the Madras Library Association* (1944), 57–65; "Methods of Popular Religious Instruction, South India," MS; "Variety and Integration in the Pattern of Indian Culture," MS.

[9] Raghavan, "Methods of Popular Religious Instruction, South India," *MS*.

the upholders of an incipient Great Tradition are themselves members of that same small community and on the whole share a common life with the other members of it. Either there is but a single tradition to study or the specialization of knowledge that has developed is carried on through the generations within the local community and we need not go outside of it to report and account for it.

In reading Radcliffe-Brown on the Andaman Islands we find nothing at all about any esoteric aspect of religion or thought. Apparently any older person will be as likely to know what there is to know as any other. This diffuse distribution throughout the population of knowledge and belief may be characteristic of very large primitive societies of much greater development of the arts of life than the Andamanese enjoyed. Thus, among the Tiv of Nigeria, a tribe including about a million agricultural people, "there is no technical vocabulary, because there are no professional classes, and little specialization beyond that which is the result of sex or age. Every aspect of tribal life is everybody's business." [10] This is a primitive society without a great tradition. Among the Maori, however, ". . . two different aspects of all the superior class of myths were taught. One of these was that taught in the *tapu* school of learning, a version never disclosed to the bulk of the people but retained by the higher grade of *tohunga* (experts or priests) and by a few others. The other was that imported to the people at large, and this, as a rule, was of an inferior nature, more puerile and grotesque than the esoteric version." [11] And in West Africa, where aborigines had developed complex states, a distinction between what we might call a littler and a greater tradition appears in the control of elements of worship, recognized by the people as recondite and esoteric, by certain priests. Initiates into these cults are secluded for seven months of instruction in secret. Also, there are differences as between layman and specialist in the understanding of the religion: the priests of the Skycult in Dahomey see clearly distinctions among deities and their characteristics about which laymen are very vague.[12] Among Sudanese peoples reported by Professor Griaule [13] there is, apparently, extraordinary development of highly reflective and systematic specialized thought among certain individuals.

This ordering of some instances suggests the separation of the two traditions in societies that do not represent the great world civilizations. The content of knowledge comes to be double, one content for the lay-

[10] *Akiga's Story*, tr. and annot. by Rupert East (London: Oxford University Press, 1930), 11.

[11] Elsdon Best, *Maori Religion and Mythology*, Bulletin No. 10, Dominion Museum, Wellington (N.Z.: W. A. G. Skinner, Government Printer, 1924), 31–32.

[12] Melville Herskovits, *Dahomey, An Ancient West African Kingdom* (New York: J. J. Augustin, 1938), Vol. II, Ch. 26.

[13] Marcel Griaule, *Dieu D'Eau* (Paris: Les Éditions du Chêne, 1948).

man, another for the hierarchy. The activities and places of residence of the carriers of the great tradition may remain close to those of the layman, or the priests and primitive philosophers may come to reside and to work apart from the common people.

Had we been present at Uaxactun or at Uxmal when Maya civilization was doing well we should have been in a position to study Great and Little Traditions in an indigenous civilization. There the specialists developing the Great Tradition had come to live lives notably separate from those of the villagers and to carry forward elements of an indigenous culture into a much higher level of intellectual and speculative thought. Professor Pedro Armillas,[14] writing about this, tells us to think of Maya civilization as formed of two cultural strata corresponding respectively to the dominant aristocracy of the ceremonial centers and the hamlet-dwelling farmers; he thinks the lives of these two became increasingly distinct and separate. Indeed, I say, what the Old World and New World civilizations had in common is most importantly just what it is that makes a civilization anywhere: the separation of culture into Great and Little Traditions, the appearance of an elite with secular and sacred power and including specialized cultivators of the intellectual life, and the conversion of tribal peoples into peasantry.

But it is in the villages of the old indigenous civilizations — in China, Indonesia, Europe and India — that we anthropologists in fact most closely engage the structure of compound tradition, Great and Little. In Latin America we engage it also, but there the civilization is secondary, imposed by an invader on a village people with a different tradition. In Maya villages of the present day we have to take account of a double structure of tradition, one broken off, the other continuing and changing.

In our village studies in Old World civilizations especially we shall find, I think, that our efforts to understand a village will more and more require us to include in our subject matter institutions and states of mind that are far away from the village in time or space or both. We shall find ourselves improving our working communications with the humanist-historian. His studies are textual: he studies not only written texts but art and architecture as part of his textual corpus.[15] Ours are contextual: we relate some element of the great tradition — sacred book, story-element, teacher, ceremony or supernatural being — to the life of the ordinary people, in the context of daily life as in the village we see it happen.[16]

[14] Pedro Armillas, "The Mesoamerican Experiment," in "The Ways of Civilizations," ed. by Robert J. Braidwood, *MS*. Professor Armillas might not think of the Maya hamlet-dwelling farmers as peasant. He regards the world views of the elite and of the farmers as "sharply different."

[15] Stella Kramrisch, *The Art of India Through the Ages* (London: Phaidon Press), 1954.

[16] For this way of contrasting the two kinds of studies, I am indebted to Milton Singer.

III

These remarks are, I am sure you see, not so much a report as a forecast. I think that in pursuing our studies in the peasant communities that lie within the great civilizations the contextual studies of anthropologists will go forward to meet the textual studies made by historians and humanists of the great traditions of that same civilization. In doing this we shall expand our own contexts and extend our concepts. We shall find ourselves studying aspects of small communities that were absent or unimportant in autonomous primitive communities. We shall study the peasant community in its heteronomous aspects. And we shall move outside of that community to study institutions and groups that connect Little and Great Traditions in single structures of several distinguishable kinds.

I think it likely that it will be especially in the course of their studies of village India that anthropologists will come to develop these new forms of thought and to recognize new kinds of natural systems to study. It is in India that Great and Little Tradition are in constant, various and conspicuous interaction with the life of the local communities. It is there that the Great Traditions are in fact several; there the preeminent older tradition, the sanskritic, is itself a skein of related but distinguishable threads of teaching and institution. It is there that the teachings of reflective and civilized minds appear plainly in the festivals and in the ideals of peasantry. It is in India that a man's ascribed status, in the form of caste, is closely associated with the claim of that caste to greater or lesser participation in the rituals and ideals of life as inculcated in sanskritic teaching. Professor Srinivas, anthropologist, has studied the way in which certain villagers, with ways of life somewhat apart from the great vedic tradition of India, have been taking on, in part quite consciously, elements of Hindu culture. In recent generations this people, the Coorgs, have come to think of themselves as *Kṣatriyas*, people of the warrior caste or *varṇa* and have come under the influence of philosophical Hinduism to the point that four Coorgs, people once largely outside the vedic tradition, have become *sa̱nnyāsis*, dedicated holy men observing teachings of the Indian high tradition. And as the Coorgs have become Hinduized their place in the Indian hierarchy of status has risen.[17]

Western anthropologists began their studies in India, in most cases, with the study of the tribal peoples there, but in very recent years many of them have studied the peasant villages that are parts of Hindu, Muslim or modern civilizations. Some of them have become interested in the way

[17] M. N. Srinivas, *Religion and Society Among the Coorgs of South India* (Oxford: Clarendon, 1952). See also Bernard S. Cohn, "The Changing Status of a Depressed Caste," in *Village India*, ed. by McKim Marriott, (*Comparative Studies in Cultures and Civilizations*, ed. by Robert Redfield and Milton Singer) (Chicago: University of Chicago Press, 1955).

in which sanskritic elements of culture enter village life. In a recent paper Bernard Cohn [18] has told us how in a certain village the leather-workers have improved their position by adopting customs authorized by the high sanskritic tradition. Another American anthropologist who has considered Indian village life with regard to its connections with the sanskritic tradition is McKim Marriott.[19] In Marriott's village, Kishan Garhi, the religion consists of elements of local culture and elements of the high sanskrit tradition in close adjustment and integration. He finds "evidence of accretion and of transmutation in form without apparent replacement and without rationalization of the accumulated and transformed elements." Fifteen of the nineteen festivals celebrated in Kishan Garhi are sanctioned in universal sanskrit texts. But some of the local festivals have no place in sanskrit teaching; those that do are but a small part of the entire corpus of festivals sanctioned by sanskrit literature; villagers confuse or choose between various classical meanings for their festivals; and even the most sanskritic of the local festivals have obviously taken on elements of ritual that arose, not out of the great tradition but out of the local peasant life.

This kind of syncretization is familiar to students of paganism and Christianity, or of Islam in its relations to local cults in North Africa. Marriott proposes that the two-way interaction between little and great traditions be studied as two complementary processes to which he gives names. For one thing, the little traditions of the folk exercise their influence on the authors of the Hindu great tradition who take up some element of belief or practice and, by incorporating it in their reflective statement of Hindu orthodoxy, universalize that element, for all who thereafter come under the influence of their teaching. Marriott cannot quite prove [20] that the following was indeed an instance of universalization, but he suggests that the goddess *Lakṣmī* of Hindu orthodoxy is derived from such deities as he saw represented in his village daubed on walls or fashioned in images of dung: the natures and meanings of the high goddess and the local godlings are similar and some villagers identify the latter with *Lakṣmī*.

The opposite process, which Marriott calls parochialization, is that by which some sanskritic element is learned about and then re-formed by the villagers to become a part of their local cult. For example: a divine sage of

[18] Bernard Cohn, "The Changing Status of a Depressed Caste," in *Village India*.

[19] McKim Marriott, "Little Communities in an Indigenous Civilization," in *Village India*.

[20] Mr. Marriott kindly tells me something of the strong evidence for the conclusion that Lakṣmī has entered the great tradition relatively late and from the folk cultures of India. He quotes Rhys Davids and Renou and Filliozat to this effect. It appears that this deity was absent from early vedic literature, that early statues to her were set in places reserved for popular deities, and that the Buddhist canon castigates Brahmans for performing nonsensical, non-vedic rituals such as those to *Śrī Devī* (*Lakṣmī*), etc. (Marriott, personal communication.)

the sanskritic tradition, associated by the Brahman elders with the planet Venus, is represented by erection of a stone in the village. Brides are now taken here to worship with their husbands. But then the origins of the stone are forgotten; it comes to be regarded as the abode of the ancestral spirits of the Brahmans who put it there.

Marriott was able to learn something about the interaction of great and little traditions in bringing about the translation or substitution of meanings and connections of rite and belief because he had read some of the sources of Hindu orthodoxy and because in the village he studied he found some people much more than others in communication with those sources themselves. The village includes the educated and the ignorant, and the villager himself is well aware of the difference. A more educated villager calls himself a *sanātanī*, a follower of the orthodox and traditional way; a Brahman domestic priest distinguishes "doers and knowers"; the ordinary villager says that a certain ritual is *Nārāyaṇ*, a deity, inseminating the mortar in which the family husks grain, but an educated man of the same village says that it is a symbol of the creation of the world.[21] Where there are such differences as between villagers, the connections the village has with the philosopher or theologian can be traced in part by the anthropologist in his community study. The analysis then moves outward and upward to meet such investigations of the downward movement of orthodoxy or philosophy as is studied by von Grünebaum for Islam and Raghavan for Hinduism.

Although I know nothing of India save at second hand, I think I see in what is already coming from that field of work indications of some of the kinds of things that anthropologists will be thinking and observing as they come to relate village life to the civilization of which it is a part. They will be concerned with the comparisons of religious and other belief in the village with the content of sanskritic orthodoxy and with the avenues of communication — the teachers, singers, reciters — between the two. They will study the "cultural media," the ceremonies, songs, dances, dramas, recitations and discourses in which much of this communication is expressed. And they will attend to the specialists, the kinds of teachers, reciters, genealogists and historians, who mediate between Little Tradition and Great. So the anthropologist will at times leave the village to study these institutions and groups. McKim Marriott and Surajit Sinha have suggested to me an anthropological study of a temple

[21] Marriott says that in Kishan Garhi the more learned villager takes, in short, quite distinguishable positions toward great and little traditions. The latter, which he sees manifest in the doings of the uneducated villagers, is a matter of practice, is ignorance or fragmentary knowledge, is confusion or vagueness, and is expressed in concrete physical or biological images. The great tradition, which he thinks of himself as in larger degree representing, is theory or pure knowledge, full and satisfying, is order and precision, and finds for its expression abstractions or symbolic representations.

connected with village life. An Indian historian, K. K. Pillay,[22] has already published a study, from his point of view, of such a temple in Travancore. Also, the anthropologist will study one of those castes whose special function is to preserve and cultivate the history and the genealogy of that other caste on which it depends, or one of those castes of those who sing to their patrons traditional stories from the *Rāmāyaṇa* or the *Mahābhārata*. Shamrao Hivale[23] has written a book on one such caste and a study of another is under way under direction of Professor Srinivas. Such castes are corporate groups relating little and great tradition to one another.

Looked at in this way, the interaction of great and little traditions can be regarded as a part of the social structure of the peasant community in its enlarged context. We are concerned with those persisting and important arrangements of roles and statuses appearing in such corporate groups as castes and sects, or in teachers, reciters, ritual-leaders of one kind or another, that are concerned with the cultivation and inculcation of the great tradition. The concept is an extension or specialization of the concept of social structure as used by anthropologists in the study of more nearly self-contained societies than are peasant villages. We turn now to consider, for the compound peasant society, a certain kind of the persisting social relations, a certain part of the social structure. The relations between Muslim teacher and pupil, between Brahman priest and layman, between Chinese scholar and Chinese peasant — all such that are of importance in bringing about the communication of great tradition to the peasant, or that, perhaps without anyone's intention, cause the peasant tradition to affect the doctrine of the learned — constitute the social structure of the culture, the structure of tradition. From this point of view a civilization is an organization of specialists, kinds of role-occupiers in characteristic relations to one another and to lay people and performing characteristic functions concerned with the transmission of tradition.

We might, as does Professor Raymond Firth, reserve the phrase "social organization"[24] in connection with concrete activity at particular times and places. Social organization is the way that people put together elements of action in such a way as to get done something they want done. Social structure is a persisting general character, a "pattern" of typical relationships; social organization is described when we account for the choices and resolutions of difficulties and conflicts that actually went on or characteristically go on. Accordingly we might withdraw the title of this paper from its wider use and reserve it for the way in which elements

[22] K. K. Pillay, *The Sucindram Temple* (Madras: Kalakshetra Publications, 1953).

[23] Shamrao Hivale, *The Pardhans of the Upper Narbada Valley* (London: Oxford University Press, 1946).

[24] Raymond Firth, *Elements of Social Organization* (London: Watts, 1951), Ch. 2, 35 ff.

of action are put together in any particular case of transmission of the tradition. We shall be studying the social organization of tradition, then, when we investigate the way in which the school day is arranged in the conservative Islamic school, or when we study the way — as Norvin Hein has already done [25] — in which the festival of *Rām Līlā* is brought about in an Indian community, the peasants and the literate *paṇḍit* cooperating to the end that the sacred stories are acted out to the accompaniment of readings from the sacred text of the higher tradition. If there are problems of adjustment between what the more learned man would like to see done and what the lay people of the village think proper, or entertaining, these cases of social organization of tradition will be the more interesting. I remember lost opportunities to study the social organization of tradition in my own field work, especially one occasion when the Catholic parish priest and the local shaman of the Maya tradition took part, successively, in a ceremony of purification in a Guatemalan village. There were then many pushings and pullings, many matters of doubt, conflict and compromise, which I failed to record. In that case there were, of course, two more esoteric traditions, in some degree of conflict with each other, and both requiring some adjustment to the expectations of the villagers.

So we come to develop forms of thought appropriate to the wider systems, the enlarged contexts, of our anthropological work. In studying a primitive society, in its characteristic self-containment, its societal and cultural autonomy, we hardly notice the social structure of tradition. It may there be present quite simply in a few shamans or priests, fellow members of the small community, very similar to others within it. And in a primitive and preliterate society we cannot know much of the history of its culture. The structure of tradition in early Zuni is seen as a division of function within the tribal community and is seen as something now going on, not as a history. But a civilization has both great regional scope and great historic depth. It is a great whole, in space and in time, by virtue of the complexity of the organization which maintains and cultivates its traditions and communicates them from the great tradition to the many and varied small local societies within it. The anthropologist who studies one of these small societies finds it far from autonomous, and comes to report and analyze it in its relations, societal and cultural, to state and to civilization.

[25] Norvin Hein, "The Rām Līlā," *The Illustrated Weekly of India* (October 22, 1950), 18–19 (provided by McKim Marriott).

Are African Cultivators to Be Called "Peasants"?

L. A. Fallers

The term "peasant" has often been used of African rural folk, particularly when distinguishing them from political and religious elites in the larger and more complex societies. The word for the ordinary peasant cultivator in the kingdom of Buganda — *mukopi* — is commonly translated as "peasant," for example, and the literature of French Africa is full of references to "*paysans*." But most writers, one suspects, have used the word rather loosely; if pressed, most of us would be inclined to say: "Well, perhaps they are not *quite* peasants." Africanists tend to feel, perhaps, that the common folk of the complex African polities fall between the categories commonly utilized by those who have studied "peasant societies" in Latin America, Europe and Asia, on the one hand, and, on the other, those employed by students of aboriginal North American "tribes." They strike us as being not quite peasant, but not quite tribal — something in between, a *tertium quid*. We may try to understand more clearly just what this *tertium quid* quality consists in by comparing some African societies with the notion of the "peasant society" developed during the past twenty years by students of Latin American, Asian and European peoples. The point of this is not, of course, merely to play with definitions but rather to explore some of the implications of the fact — of which we are all aware — that the concept "peasant society" refers to a bundle of features which do not always go together. In doing this we may hope to indicate somewhat more precisely how these complex African societies resemble or differ from the classical peasant societies — thus satisfying our anthropologist's urge to fit all the peoples of the world into a grand classificatory scheme — and to suggest, indirectly, something about the significance of those peasant-like features which Africans do not share.

We may appropriately begin with Kroeber's definition (or description), since it has seemed to Robert Redfield, George Foster, Eric Wolf, and other peasant specialists to best describe their field of interest: "Peasants are definitely rural — yet live in relation to market towns; they form a class segment of a larger population which usually contains urban centers,

From "Are African Cultivators to Be Called 'Peasants'?" in *Current Anthropology*, Vol. II (April 1961). Reprinted by permission of the author and The Wenner-Gren Foundation for Anthropological Research, Inc.

sometimes metropolitan capitals. They constitute part-societies with part-cultures" (Kroeber 1948: 284). This last phrase — "part-societies with part-cultures" — we may take to be the heart of the matter. It can, however, be made somewhat more precise. On the one hand, the phrase *does* quite satisfactorily differentiate peasant societies from the societies we usually describe as "tribal" — societies whose constituent units, or segments, to use Durkheim's phrase, are all much alike and internally more or less homogeneous, in both structure and culture. Peasant societies, as Kroeber's definition suggests, are more differentiated, both socially and culturally. Peasant villages may all be much alike, but they are bound together into a larger whole by structures of a quite different kind, and the persons who man these other structures commonly have a different culture — a "sophisticated" or "urban" or "elite" or "high" culture. On the other hand, Kroeber's definition does not satisfactorily distinguish peasant societies from modern industrial ones, for the constituent units of these latter are also "part-societies with part-cultures" — even more partial than are those of peasant societies, because modern societies are even more differentiated. We may suggest that the single most important difference between peasant and modern industrial societies lies in the nature of their constituent units. Whereas in peasant societies the household and the local community remain the primary units, in modern industrial societies occupational structures dissociated from households and cutting across local community units become important centers of cultural and structural differentiation. It is the vast increase in the differentiation and autonomy of occupational structures which industrialization makes possible above all. Local communities thus lose their semi-self-sufficiency, the semi-detached quality which they still retain in the peasant society and which led Redfield to emphasize — indeed to over-emphasize in his earlier work, as Foster has pointed out — the similarity between the peasant village and the tribal segment (Redfield 1947; Foster 1953). Unlike the latter, the peasant community is not completely isolable, completely capable of self-sufficiency; but neither is it so completely knitted into a larger fabric by crisscrossing occupational structures as is the modern community. The latter cannot possibly be imagined in isolation from the larger society. In contrast, the peasant community is relatively self-sufficient, leading many observers to comment upon its frequent indifference to changes in the political superstructure and hostility to members of the elite. Perhaps we may usefully alter Kroeber's characterization to read as follows: A peasant society is one whose primary constituent units are semi-autonomous local communities with semi-autonomous cultures. In this way we may differentiate the peasant society from both the tribal and the modern industrial varieties. It is perhaps necessary to add that we think of these as ideal, not concrete, types; actual societies will be in varying degrees "tribal," "peasant," and "modern industrial." The types are a means toward greater understanding, not a device for pigeon-holing whole societies.

Now this semi-autonomy of constituent local communities, which we may take to be the differentiating characteristic of the peasant society, may be decomposed into a number of aspects, of which we may here consider three: (1) the economic, (2) the political, and (3) what we may call, perhaps not very satisfactorily, the "cultural." We shall examine each of these briefly, attempting to see how far they find counterparts in the more complex African societies. It should perhaps be repeated that we consider here only trans-Saharan pagan Africa, excluding the Muslim areas and Ethiopia.

1. In economic terms, a peasant is presumably a man who produces — usually through cultivation — mainly for his own household's consumption, but who also produces something to exchange in a market for other goods and services. This is the economic aspect of the peasant community's semi-autonomy (Firth 1951:87). In this sense, peasants abound in Africa. The vast majority of Africans were cultivators in pre-contact times — in some cases intensive and devoted cultivators. They also traded; the great markets of West Africa are famous, but also in most other parts of the continent there was a good deal of craft specialization and trade aboriginally. Cowrie shells, gold dust, ivory, iron bars and hoes in different areas provided semi-generalized media of exchange. In the more centralized states there was tribute, and sometimes even regular taxation, to support and augment the authority of the non-agricultural superstructure. In short, in the economic aspect of the matter there appears to be no problem. Economically, most Africans were traditionally peasants and with the opening of the continent to overseas trade they quite easily and naturally took up the cultivation of export crops in exchange for imported goods.

2. Politically, too, the more powerful African states had much in common with the Asian, European and American societies which are commonly classed as "peasant." The political aspect of the peasant society has received relatively little attention from anthropologists, perhaps because so often the societies which the peasant specialists study have long since been "decapitated" politically (to use Kidder's expressive phrase), the indigenous political superstructure being replaced by those of modern colonial or nationalist post-colonial states (Redfield 1956:78). The political aspect is thus the one least accessible to study through the anthropologist's traditional techniques of direct observation. We can learn more about this aspect of the society made up of semi-autonomous peasant local communities from social historians like Marc Bloch, from legal scholars like Maine, Maitland, Seebohm, and Vinogradoff and from comparative sociologists like Max Weber. The legal scholars who unravelled the political structure of medieval Western Europe and its characteristic unit, the manor, divided into two schools, the "Romanists" and the "Germanists," over just this question of the nature of the semi-autonomy of communities which lies at the heart of the peasant type (Vinogradoff 1892:1–39). The Romanists emphasized the vertical relationship

of the manor with the political hierarchy, associating it historically with the Roman *latifundiae* established in the area during the time of the Empire. The Germanists, on the other hand, saw in the manor and its surrounding "vill" essentially a development out of the old solidary Germanic village community. If we understand this literature correctly — and it is easy for an anthropologist to go astray in the writings of legal historians — both were right, in the sense that both tendencies were present. They were debating, in an historical idiom, the relative importance of the two dimensions which always seem to be present in the peasant society and which constitute the political aspect of the semi-autonomy of its constituent local communities: On the one hand there is the local community, hostile to the outside, sharing certain common rights in land and governed by local, often informal, mechanisms of social control; and on the other hand there is the hierarchy of patrimonial or feudal relations of personal superiority and responsibility (*noblesse oblige*) and subordinate dependence, which link the local community with the wider polity. Peasant political systems vary with the relative strength of the local community as against that of the vertical structure, as Eric Wolf (1955) has pointed out; and also, as Max Weber (1947:346–58) has shown, with the degree to which the latter is made up of appointed personal retainers as contrasted with hereditary feudal (using the term loosely) vassals.

These political peasant-like features, like the economic ones, are common enough in African states. The village community is a common feature everywhere (though it may be physically dispersed in scattered homesteads) and political hierarchies, where they exist, vary according to the degree to which they consist of appointed officials or hereditary chiefs. Africa is, of course, preeminently the continent of unilineal descent groups and this gives to both village communities and political superstructures a character which is less common in other regions. The village community often contains a core of lineage-mates and its corporate nature may be expressed in the idiom of unilineal descent (Fortes 1953; Smith 1956). There is an interesting range of variation according to whether strangers in such communities are relegated to a kind of second-class citizenship or are fictionally adopted into the core group. These phenomena are not, of course, universal in Africa. In the Interlacustrine area, the lineage is limited to such "domestic" functions as the control of inheritance and exogamy, and the village itself is defined purely territorially (Fallers 1960). In the political superstructure of African states, unilineal descent groups often hold corporate rights to chieftainship; and thus the hierarchy, which in medieval Europe tended to consist of dynasties of individual hereditary lords and vassals, in an African state like Ashanti, or in one of the Southern Bantu states, consists essentially of representatives of corporate descent groups (Busia 1951; Schapera 1955). In some other states, like Dahomey and Buganda, the hierarchy is essentially one of patrimonial retainers, resembling in this respect the states of the Islamic world and Byzantium more than those of feudal Europe (Herskovits 1938; Fallers 1960). In general, allowing for peculiarities resulting from differences in patterns of descent, the politics of the traditional African states seem to fall well within the peasant range.

3. Thus, there would seem to be no reason why African villagers should not be called "peasants" politically and economically. Doubts arise, however, when we turn to the culture that is characteristic of peasant life — that is, to the tendency, to which Redfield (1956), Foster (1953), and Marriott (1955), have drawn attention, for the economic and political semi-autonomy of the peasant community to be matched by a cultural semi-autonomy. The culture of the peasant community of the classic conception is a "folk" version of a "high culture"; it is neither the same as the latter nor independent of it, but rather a reinterpretation and reintegration of many elements of the high culture with other elements peculiar to the peasant village. It is this cultural semi-autonomy of the village, it would seem, which above all determines the relations which obtain between social strata in the peasant society. The elite possess, and live by, the high culture to a greater extent than do the peasants. The peasant, accepting the standards of the high culture to some degree, to that degree also accepts its judgment of him as ignorant and uncouth. At the same time, he possesses his own folk culture, containing high culture elements, and this provides him with an independent basis for a sense of self-esteem, together with an ideology within which he may express his partial hostility toward the elite and its version of the common culture. Excellent examples are provided by Homans' account (1940:368–370) of how thirteenth century English villagers caricatured the behavior of the elite.

Now it would seem to be just the relative absence of this differentiation into high and folk cultures which principally distinguishes the African kingdoms from the societies which have commonly been called "peasant." There is, of course, a substantial degree of cultural differentiation in many African societies. There are craft specialists with highly developed skills, and there are ritual specialists with great bodies of esoteric knowledge. There are courtly manners and there are recognized degrees of sophistication, ranging from the courtier who is "in the know" politically to the country bumpkin. Nevertheless, there remains an important difference between trans-Saharan pagan Africa in these respects and the differentiation which was possible in medieval Europe, China, India and Islam. The word "peasant" denotes, among other things, a degree of rusticity in comparison with his betters which we do not feel justified in attributing to the African villager.

Lacking the more pronounced degrees of cultural differentiation, the African states characteristically exhibit a somewhat different pattern of stratification. African villagers do not seem to feel the same degree of ambivalence toward the political superstructure that European, Asian and

Latin American peasants do because, not standing to the same degree in contrast to the possessors of a differentiated high culture, they do not to the same extent feel judged from above by a set of standards which they cannot attain. Correspondingly, there is less development of a differentiated folk culture as a kind of "counter-culture." Africans very commonly perceive themselves as being differentiated in terms of wealth and power but they do not often, except in the few real composite conquest states, view their societies as consisting of "layers" of persons with differential possession of a high culture. As is well known, they much more characteristically divide in terms of genealogical and territorial segments, even in instances where there are marked "objective class differences" in the Marxian sense. Not even those West African societies in which cities provided a basis for rural-urban cultural differentiation exhibit the degree of folk-high distinction commonly found in what we may now call the real peasant societies. Dahomean and Yoruba villagers were not separated from their urban cousins by a cultural gap of the same magnitude as that which divided medieval European and Asian countrymen from city folk (Herskovits 1938; Bascom 1951; Lloyd 1955).

In large part this difference is due simply to the absence in traditional Africa of the literary religious traditions which formed the bases for the European and Asian high cultures. Written records make possible a vastly greater accumulation and elaboration of high culture. Furthermore, the mere presence of writing places between the literate and the illiterate member of the same society a barrier which cannot easily develop in its absence. The peasant's suspicious hostility toward the member of the urban elite is in large part a product of his realization that the latter, in his ability to read and write, holds a weapon against which the peasant cannot easily defend himself.

Thus the traditional African villager was, we might say, a peasant economically and politically, but was not a peasant culturally. Perhaps it would be better to call him a "proto-peasant" or an "incipient peasant," for wherever literary culture has entered Africa, it has quickly made him more fully a peasant. Thus the Muslim Swahili peoples of the east coast and the Hausa of the Western Sudan were traditionally more peasant-like than their non-literate, pagan neighbors; and the modern Baganda and Ashanti, with their imported Western Christian high culture, are more fully peasants than were their great-grandfathers. We may suggest that one of the reasons why Christianity, Islam and their accompanying high cultures have been so readily accepted in many parts of Africa is that many African societies were structurally "ready" to receive peasant cultures.

REFERENCES CITED

Bascom, W. R.

1951 "Social Status, Wealth and Individual Differences Among the Yoruba." *American Anthropologist* 53:491–505.

Busia, K.
1951 *The Position of the Chief in the Modern Political System of Ashanti*. London: Oxford University Press for the International African Institute.
Fallers, Margaret C.
1960 *The Eastern Lacustrine Bantu*. International African Institute Ethnographic Survey of Africa, East Central Africa, Part XI.
Firth, R.
1951 *Elements of Social Organization*. London: Watts and Co.
Fortes, M.
1953 "The Structure of Unilineal Descent Groups." *American Anthropologist* 55:17–41.
Foster, G. M.
1953 "What Is Folk Culture?" *American Anthropologist* 55:159–173.
Herskovits, M. J.
1938 *Dahomey*. New York: J. J. Augustin.
Homans, G.
1940 *English Villagers of the Thirteenth Century*. Cambridge: Harvard University Press.
Kroeber, A. L.
1948 *Anthropology*. New York: Harcourt, Brace and Co.
Lloyd, P. C.
1955 "The Yoruba Lineage." *Africa* 25:235–251.
Marriott, McKim
1955 "Little Communities in an Indigenous Civilization," in *Village India* (McKim Marriott, ed.); pp. 171–222. American Anthropological Association Memoir 83.
Redfield, R.
1947 "The Folk Society." *American Journal of Sociology* 52:293–308.
———.
1956 *Peasant Society and Culture*. Chicago: University of Chicago Press.
Schapera, I.
1956 *Government and Politics in Tribal Societies*. London: Watts.
Smith, M. G.
1956 "Segmentary Lineage Systems." *Journal of the Royal Anthropological Institute* 88, Part 2:39–80.
Vinogradoff, P.
1892 *The Villainage in England*. London: Oxford University Press.
Weber, Max
1947 *The Theory of Social and Economic Organization*. Translated by A. M. Henderson and Talcott Parsons. New York: Oxford University Press.
Wolf, Eric
1955 "Types of Latin American Peasantry: A Preliminary Discussion." *American Anthropologist* 57:452–471.

THE EXTENSIONS OF AN INDIAN VILLAGE

Morris E. Opler

A villager in India, besides being a member of a distinguishable local community and interacting with many of its other members, has important ties of a more extensive nature, and participates in practices and understandings characteristic of wider areas. In discussions of the independence, viability and future of the Indian village it may be useful to keep the nature of these ties to the outside in mind and to consider their past history and the present trends in respect to them. So that concrete material may serve as a basis for discussion, data from Senapur, a village of Northcentral India in the Jaunpur district of Uttar Pradesh will be utilized. Senapur, as do all individual communities, presents some unique features, but we know that it is much like other villages of the region and we know that in respect to principal institutions, social structure, and most of the attributes that will be reviewed here it shares much with other villages of North India which have been described in the literature.

In the first place Senapur does not stand alone. It is one of a cluster of villages covering a seventy square mile area which have traditions of a common origin and descent. According to this tradition the area was conquered fifteen generations ago by a Kshatriya (locally called Thakur) leader. He, his sons, and his grandsons founded these related villages and his descendants are the Thakur residents of these villages. Advisers, servants, and retainers are said to have accompanied him, and *their* descendants account in part for the residents of the villages who are of other castes. Segments of the conquered early inhabitants allegedly remained to do agricultural labor and menial tasks. Newcomers attached themselves to the service of those already there. The Thakurs became the owners of the land they had conquered. Until recently they rented a great deal of it to others or permitted the use of it by families of other castes whose members served them in one or another capacity. Thus the descendants of the founder, members of the same clan and tradition, remained the dominant influence in this cluster of villages and made common cause. For instance, they had an assembly which met at a central place to consider matters of general and intervillage importance.

From "The Extensions of an Indian Village" in *The Journal of Asian Studies*, Vol. XVI, No. 1 (November 1956). Reprinted by permission of The Association for Asian Studies, Inc.

The founder of Senapur, a grandson of the conqueror of the area, inherited one-eighth of the total property. This included land which became sites of other villages. Consequently the Thakurs of Senapur have owned land in other villages of the area and therefore have had good reason for special interest in these other communities and for continual contact with them.

It is through the women that another set of connections has been established with outside villages. Village exogamy is practiced; brides must come from outside the village and the lines of communication and contact opened through this means are quite enduring. The process begins when representatives of a marriageable girl's family start out on a journey to find a suitable husband for her. If the search is successful a betrothal ceremony is arranged which again brings representatives of the two families together. The marriage usually takes place at the bride's village and home, where the bride's family plays host to a good-sized party of the groom's relatives and friends. If the bride is not yet mature she may not accompany her husband back to his village. Later, her journey to her husband's village is the occasion for another ceremony and procession. It is customary for young married women to visit their parental home for rather prolonged periods. This necessitates negotiations and attendants. Relatives of the married women frequently visit her. On certain ceremonial occasions presents of special foods and other gifts are carried to the home of the married daughter. The married daughter is expected to return to her father's village when marriages are celebrated in her family of birth and for other ritual occasions. Often, when she visits for prolonged periods, she brings a child or two with her to her father's home. The warm regard of the maternal grandparents for their daughter's children and of the mother's brother for his nephews and nieces is proverbial. Senapur brides come from a radius of a hundred miles. Often a distant village becomes well known through these affiliations, for several women may come to Senapur as brides from the same community. According to a census recently completed, several hundred villages are linked with Senapur by these marriage bonds. It must be remembered that approximately half of the adult population was born in other villages. Nor are the connections only with villages where Thakurs predominate, for each caste of the village has its own rules of village exogamy and its own conventions for finding mates for its young people.

Still another institution which forces a person to look beyond his own village is caste. Indeed he may belong to a caste which has few representatives in the village in which he lives and in that case he may have to seek social contacts with caste-fellows who live in other villages. At any important occasion involving ritual and feasting a family is likely to invite prominent members of the caste from other villages to attend. Respected leaders or elders of the caste from other villages may be asked to serve as arbiters of serious disputes. Caste assemblies which cross-sect village lines take measures to punish offenders and issue regulations which seek to enhance caste status. Regional and central caste organizations sometimes support worthy causes and educational institutions, and even issue pamphlets, magazines, and books to explain or promote caste affairs. Much of this is aimed primarily at educated urban dwellers, but the details of such ventures also reach the villages and evoke pride and caste loyalties. Some persons who have not fared well in Senapur take heart from these accounts of the better fortune of their caste-fellows elsewhere.

Customary work obligations, sometimes associated with caste, also take people out of the village and bring workers in. Indian economy calls for an elaborate division of labor. Many tasks are traditionally associated with certain castes. When a village does not have any or a sufficient number of artisans or workers of a given caste to perform certain tasks or services the work is carried on by individuals of other villages with the proper skills and caste background. In like manner, workmen of Senapur often have regular customers in neighboring villages as well as in their home village. A rough count suggests that thirty-five to forty castes are involved in the full round of practical and ritual services sought by an individual or family at one time or another in a rural community. Very seldom does any single village contain that many resident castes. Representatives of twenty-four castes live in Senapur, and this is a large number for any village. A rural area containing a number of villages can therefore to some extent be considered a work pool, with some villages utilizing the surplus labor of others and special skills being traded back and forth. Then, besides those who come to the village rather regularly to work, there are those who come occasionally or irregularly, venders of various sorts, mendicants, tinkers, and entertainers. And, in addition to those villagers who find employment out of Senapur but in the vicinity, there are also quite a few who find employment far from the village. At any one time nearly 15 per cent of the adult male population is working out of the village, many in places as far away as Bombay, Calcutta, and Assam.

That the village is for many purposes a part of a much larger unity and is recognized and felt as such is obvious when a widespread religious or political movement gains momentum. Then speakers and representatives visit the village or the vicinity and try to stir up interest and enthusiasm for their cause in the community. Within the last fifty years the Arya Samaj, the Independence movement, and the Land Reform movement have been channels through which voices and impulses transcending the local scene have reached and markedly influenced the village. Far from being insulated from the larger scene, the village was very much affected by the outbreak of 1857 against British rule, became a center of Arya Samaj religious reform activities, was involved in the disorders attending the "quit India" agitation of 1942, and is now rocked and torn by the present government's land reform program.

Religion has been another important link with the outside. Senapur has its own protective godling and its local shrines. Many rituals are personal, family, or annually recurring events celebrated in the village. But Senapur residents know about the famous shrines and temples in distant parts of the country and aspire to see at least some of them before they die. Famous religious centers such as Banaras, Gaya, and Prayag are not too distant, and hundreds of villagers have been to one or another of them. Shrine priests or their representatives visit the Senapur area to awaken interest in these pilgrimages. The sacred Ganges is relatively close to the village and the main bathing and ritual occasions find many Senapur villagers at one or another of the temples which dot its banks. There are certain temples, fairly far from the village but still in the general region, where certain life cycle rites are often carried out. One such place, for instance, is a favorite site for the hair-cutting ceremony which is ordinarily performed when the child is about five years of age. Even for the exorcism of ghosts and the propitiation of angry godlings village boundaries are often crossed. The famous practitioners (or *ojhās*) of the area are well known to the Senapur people and are frequently visited by sufferers in search of aid. The ailing and troubled from other villages also seek out Senapur curers. Another religious event brings a large number of visitors from surrounding communities; each year a religious pageant depicting scenes from the life of Rama, the incarnation of God Vishnu, takes place in Senapur.

Connection with the market town, too, exerts a strong outward pull on Senapur residents. It happens that the principal market town for Senapur is also the subdivisional headquarters, with its courts, land records office, officials, and government seed and agricultural implement store. Consequently official business as well as the bazaar draws the Senapur villager to this center.

The quest for education has taken the Senapur children across village boundaries many times. Senapur has had a primary school for a long time. Most of the children who attend school go to the Senapur primary school, though some who live in a hamlet of Senapur go to the nearer primary school of an adjoining village. Very recently a junior high school covering grades six to eight was established in the village. But a high school or college education can only be acquired outside of the village. A surprising number of boys of high-caste families of the village have received college educations and several have earned M.A. degrees.

In reviewing material of this kind, a number of points stand out quite clearly. One is that in spite of a well-defined separate identity, and an individual quality for which it is quite well known in the vicinity, Senapur leans heavily upon and interacts constantly with neighboring villages and the outside world. It has been quite possible to demonstrate this without even raising the question of economic self-sufficiency, without pointing out that Senapur today draws upon the outside market for cloth, many tools, dyes, kitchen utensils, matches, and kerosene, among other things.

In fact the evidences of outside contact which have been emphasized are less those that have to do with economy and traits of material culture than with tradition and common outlook, social and political organization, and religion. It might well be argued that a village like Senapur was and still is more self-sufficient and isolable in an economic sense than in respect to social organization and non-material culture.

Another point that seems worth noting is that the basic articulations of Senapur and Senapur people with other communities and far-flung places which we have noted is not a recent development or a consequence of modern systems of communication and transportation. They rest on ancient practices and patterns. Common traditions of origin and descent, with bards to celebrate them, are a very old feature of Indian life. Village exogamy is certainly nothing new. The market town and the place of pilgrimage are magnets which have drawn villagers to them for a very long time. Even departure from the village for outside employment is nothing new in principle. We know that Thakurs of Senapur have served in the military forces of rulers and nobles for over two hundred years.

It is therefore obvious that the picture sometimes presented of the self-contained, isolated, static Indian community leaves much to be desired. Rather, there has been a traditionally controlled mobility working through marriage arrangements, leadership patterns, caste, and religious centers. It is this circulation of services, brides, arbiters, and caste edicts across village boundaries which probably accounts for regional cultural cohesiveness. Much more attention must be paid to the nature and extent of these linkages if cultural and subcultural areas are to be accurately defined.

Those who tend to see the Indian village of the past as a self-sufficient and isolated entity are prone to argue that this isolation must break down rapidly under modern conditions and that village cohesiveness and isolability must yield to outside and particularly to urban influences and values. But this "self-sufficiency" has been more of a myth than a fact, as we have seen. And, in addition, the trend is not at all this simple and one-directional. The amount of employment outside the village may give the impression that the village is disintegrating and losing its active and ambitious males to urban blandishments. But such an interpretation seems hasty and doubtful when it is realized that extremely few of these workers intend to or actually do remain out of the village permanently. In most cases they leave the village with family permission and even urging to earn money for family purposes. In many cases money earned outside of the village has helped families to purchase village land, build better homes, arrange advantageous marriages, and stabilize and improve their positions and prospects in the village.

It must be remembered, too, that the democratically elected managing committees and assemblies have strengthened the hand and resources of village officials and governing bodies. The legally established local courts, serving villages and village circles, are designed to encourage the villages to settle their own problems. If these experiments succeed, individual villages and small groups of closely associated villages will take much more responsibility for the enforcement of law and order, the settlement of disputes and litigation, and the maintenance of facilities for public benefit. The present Indian central and state governments have embarked on a policy of decentralization in which the aim is to maximize the functions and importance of village governing bodies. On the basis of examples of this kind it can be persuasively argued that many recent ties with the outside and recent legal and political developments actually safeguard the future and integrity of the village rather than threaten it.

Often it is the pattern of outside contact rather than the fact of outside contact which is altered. It is quite true that improved transporation facilities, increased participation by India in world trade, and a higher industrial index have brought a great many commodities to the market town and from there into the village. But these increasing ties with the outside market have come at the expense of other ties and contacts. Cloth sellers, sellers of dyes, sellers of spices, dealers in cattle, and colorful merchants of various kinds used to visit the village regularly, often from far places, such as the Punjab. Now they rarely appear. If something has been gained by the easier access to the market, something too, has been lost. *Paṇḍās* or shrine priests and their representatives come less often now to persuade villagers to visit the holy spots where they and their family members carry out rites and administer to pilgrims from the area. Because of trains, buses, and bridges that span wide streams, a pilgrimage is no longer the formidable and time-consuming journey it once was, and the personal effort and direct association are not as necessary to insure a goodly flow of worshippers to the shrine. Thus, the relations with the outside are retained but mechanisms which help maintain them change in character.

An attempt has been made in this paper to see an Indian village in terms of its extensions, and as a part of larger units organized on social organizational, political, caste, or religious grounds. The involvement of Senapur villagers with organizations, places, and events outside of the village is considerable and it seems that this has been the case for a very long time. Yet it has not interfered with the separate identity and cohesiveness of the community, which in some respects is more marked than before. Like any unit in a segmentary social system, the Indian village has to be examined to determine in what respects it stands alone and parallels for its members the advantages and purposes of similar units, and in what respects it combines in various ways with other units to serve wider purposes.

PART TWO

PEASANT ECONOMICS

Introduction: Economic Relations in Peasant Society

May N. Diaz

The peasant as Economic Man must direct his activities toward two spheres, each of which has its own rules, its rewards and values, its characteristic sanctions.

On the one hand, he supports his family primarily and directly from what he and they produce as agriculturalists or, less often, as artisans or fishermen or herders. His actions and choices must be very directly related to the natural resources of land, water, weather, and sun, for he is closely bound in an ecological system that gives him less control over the natural world than that enjoyed by farmers with a more sophisticated technology. It is in this sense that he is close to nature, for he is not the Child of Nature, in mystical contact with the earth and sky, portrayed by romantic writers. The store of folklore, calendar customs, weather omens, proverbs, and rituals which are part of peasant culture in all areas of the world attests to his awareness of participating in an ecology. One also is made conscious of his view when one encounters his often stubborn resistance to new agricultural and other productive techniques, for he fears that any change in procedure is likely to increase the risks of an already risky enterprise. As social scientists would say: small technological changes may bring with them unanticipated consequences, threatening the operation of his production system.

The alternatives available to him as producer are limited by natural resources and technology; the area in which he can decide how to run his economic enterprise and how to dispose of his income is limited by the expectations shared with his fellow villagers and by the regulations imposed by the larger society. He must choose his course of action — whether to eat or sell the wheat; whether to give away, slaughter, or fatten the pig; whether to save a money profit or spend it on fireworks and flowers — according to the values of his community. Characteristically, in the peasant community, where the nonconformity of one frequently is seen as a threat to the cohesion of the whole, the limits are very narrow. The individual, wishing to maintain viable face-to-face relations with his fellow villagers, finds that he must play the economic game according to local rules. He dares not risk ostracism by becoming a free agent, for he depends on those around him for extra hands for building a house and for harvest, for spouses for his children, and for assistance at birth, death, and famine.

On the other hand, the peasant's economic activities are related to the larger society of which he is a part. The grain, fruit, meat, wine, pottery, fish, cotton, or flax he produces go not only to feed and clothe his family, but also to maintain the priests, artisans, merchants, bureaucrats, kings, and soldiers who make up the urban population or who are the carriers of the Great Tradition of his society. He is tied into a system of distribution and taxation in which his goods and services become part of a regional and national network of economic exchanges. In many cases he participates in an impersonal market where prices respond to supply and demand, and like Economic Man in an industrial society he makes economizing decisions in order to make a maximum profit.

Within the local context the peasant's economic goal is to use his resources — land and its natural products, labor, water and sun, and his knowledge of technology — to maintain his family directly, rather than to use the products of his labor as an investment for a money return. From this kind of orientation there follow certain social and economic consequences.

First of all, he tries to pass on to his children a means of subsistence. His primary resource is land. Whether the land is regularly transferred as a single unit or whether it is split among a number of heirs in part decides the kinds of social groups that form the building blocks of the agricultural production system. In the latter case the peasant society becomes an intertwined network of nuclear families; in the former it is made of alliances based on marriage and fictive kinship between multigenerational groups, bound into common enterprise and common interest by blood ties.

In some peasant societies it is felt that economic survival is possible only if the farm is kept intact, for some agricultural systems are viable only if kept at a certain size. For example, if it takes a multiplicity of activities to eke out a living from marginal lands — if one must hunt, fish, sow grain in small valleys, cultivate garden crops along fertile river banks, and keep goats on rocky mountain slopes — a large farm worked by many hands may support more people with greater efficiency and generosity than many small ones. A peasant economy relying heavily on livestock production also operates well with units larger than a single family.

A variety of kinship and inheritance rules have developed in order to define membership in a land-holding unit or peasant "corporation." The following examples are intended to be illustrative rather than exhaustive. In a unilineal society the "corporation" can be defined clearly by kinship. Thus the patrilineal *zadruga* of Yugoslavia was at one time a land-owning unit operating a common agricultural enterprise wherein the males were descendants of a common paternal ancestor and the females were in-marrying spouses. Such a group has ready means for maintaining solidarity and for calling upon the members' work and loyalty. Who belongs and who does not is clearly demarcated; "we" and "they" are unmistakable. The sense of common identity and interest is bolstered by tale and myth and the rituals associated with birth, death, and marriage.

In many — perhaps most — peasant societies, however, kinship is reckoned bilaterally, and no unit can be clearly defined by kinship alone. Additional rules must be invoked — primogeniture, for example, where only the first son or the firstborn holds title to the land. Other heirs are more or less compensated by money or other movable wealth, or are forced to leave and find other means of support, for the patrimony can support only one nuclear family. At different periods in history, younger sons have taken up other occupations, moved to cities, cleared new land, gone to sea, or emigrated. In Scandinavia the heir to allodial land inherited the right to hold, manage, and profit from the land, while his siblings retained the right to prevent the sale or breaking up of the property as well as to share in the products as long as they were working residents on the farm.[1] Thus assigning differential rights to the heirs allowed for the formation of a kin-based bilateral corporate group.

More commonly, however, it is expected (or required by law) that the land be divided among the heirs. Each farm unit is expected to support a single nuclear family. Following such a rule over several generations can splinter once-viable peasant farms into smaller and smaller units. Only where the land is fertile, water abundant, and intensive cultivation feasible can such a practice be continued without leading to increasing misery. Consequently, whatever the formal rule or law, peasants have found devices by which they attempt to protect the unity of a viable farm. Sons may be pushed or urged into taking up wage labor, or the family nest egg may be used to buy a ticket to the current version of the Promised Land. Irish peasants (Arensberg and Kimball 1940) give their daughters a dowry in money, attempt to find alternative occupations for younger sons, and leave the original unit intact for the male heir and his nuclear family. Friedl discusses a more complex dowry situation in modern Greece.

Land rights in peasant societies are not always vested in kinship groups, large or small, and inherited according to genealogy. In some communities of northern Europe before enclosure, in parts of Mesoamerica and Central Java, ownership of the land — in the sense of rights to manage, distribute, and dispose of the property — rests in the village community as a unit. Individual members are assigned plots to which they are given use rights. Their claims and those of their descendants rest on their continued par-

[1] Allodial land is the absolute property of the owner: "real estate held in absolute independence, without being subject to any rent, service, or acknowledgment to a superior — opposed to *feud*." *Merriam Webster New International Dictionary*. 2nd Edition.

ticipation in a nonkinship-based association, a fact which emphasizes the need to keep up amicable relations with fellow villagers and to behave in accordance with village expectations. Eric Wolf, in the article "Closed Corporate Peasant Communities in Mesoamerica and Central Java," in Part Three of this book, analyzes this kind of community in detail.

Clearly, corporate villages call forth strong claims on individuals in order to maintain solidarity, but in "open" peasant villages people also act so as to reinforce social cohesion — often at the expense of apparent economic goals or the individual's needs and wishes. Such cohesion may be desirable according to abstract values, but it also often is essential for the survival of peasant economies. Peasant farming is "labor intensive" rather than "capital intensive," as Wolf puts it, and additional workers are necessary at certain times of the year or for tasks that need to be accomplished in a single operation. Nuclear families must assure themselves of help with the harvest, for example, and even larger three-generational domestic units often cannot mobilize enough manpower to cope with engineering projects of any size, such as roadbuilding, diking, and canal maintenance. Extrafamilial ties are necessary even for the routine jobs of a peasant farm. Work groups are often called up on the basis of kinship and neighborhood or through the dyadic contract (see Foster, "The Dyadic Contract," in Part Three). In a few peasant societies, voluntary associations are formed (see Smith, "The Japanese Rural Community," in Part Three). Labor exchanges of this kind are often validated and celebrated by ritual and ceremony, by drinking, feasting, and dancing, so that participants feel they have gained in enjoyment for what they have contributed in work. In the context of the whole village economic system, inefficient labor is sometimes obtained at rather high cost, so that the employment of wage labor would seem more efficient in terms of the economy. In fact, when peasant societies begin to break down in the modern world, the greater efficiency of wage labor usually drives out co-operative forms, as Charles Erasmus has pointed out (1956). But looked at in reference to the operation of village society, such exchange contributes to the continuance of village integration; it is an investment for a social as well as an economic end.

Social integration is also served by actions that are part of the distributive system of the peasant economy. The dyadic contract — fictive-kin, friend, and neighborhood ties — is established and reinforced with gift-giving and the exchange of favors and services, thus increasing the flow and magnitude of the local economy just as Christmas gift-giving spurs on distribution in the United States. Diversification is also served thereby, for many exchanges are complementary — a handful of plums for an egg, repairing a plow for a haircut — so that the total inventory of goods and services available to any family is increased. And finally, a system of reciprocal gift-giving allows individuals an area of discretion in using their economic resources; a man can manipulate his small capital and his labor within comparatively short time units, somewhat maximizing his own economic interests. Peasants use patron and fictive-kin relations for their own advantages. They give now, to draw later, in an elementary, low-risk savings system.

On the other hand, social commitments often limit the capital which they can acquire, what they can spend, and how they can invest. Thus in "closed" communities — and often in "open" ones as well — egalitarian styles of life are insisted on. Acquiring more wealth than one's fellows suggests that one has somehow robbed them and snatched more than one's fair share (see Foster, "Peasant Society and the Image of Limited Good," Part Four). Conspicuous consumption arouses envy, as it does in modern communities, but rather than awakening increased competition in order to surpass the Joneses, it calls up negative sanctions — distrust, gossip, ostracism, and witchcraft. There are characteristic institutions whereby such "excess wealth" is siphoned off so as to enhance rather than weaken social cohesion. By spending on ritual, on feasts, on elaborate religious festivities, the individual acquires prestige, for he has used his wealth for the benefit of the community in ways which are meaningful to its members. On the other hand, he may be left with no capital.

Thus the peasant as an actor at the local level in the economic system finds his choices circumscribed by the social values of his community, by the relative poverty of his economic resources, and by his limited control over production. In the regional and national economic system, as buyer and seller in a network stretching beyond his acquaintance and often his imagination as well, he participates in interactions of a different character.

The market gives the peasant one of his most important ways of taking part in a larger society (see Skinner, "Marketing and Social Structure in Rural China"). In China, for example, the market town is the primary factor that binds farm and city together. The market town forms a nucleus to which peasant villages are connected as spokes to the hub of a wheel, so that regions are sets of market towns surrounded by satellite villages.

Other market systems in peasant societies may be patterned in other ways. Much of Mesoamerica and parts of China, for instance, have cyclical rather than centralized marketing, so that a market system consists of a series of markets held on different days in different places, allowing sellers and buyers access to several (cf. Silverman 1959). Certain villages specialize in particular crafts or products, but middlemen also carry wares from one to another. What is offered is complementary, although each market in the chain also offers some identical staples. Thus the entire region must be seen as a market system.

In much of northern Europe until the nineteenth century, marketing was done at fairs, held only a few times a year and drawing sellers and buyers from larger areas than either market mentioned above. Although peasants were customers at fairs, and sometimes sellers as well, the goods they contributed to the national and regional economy flowed as taxes and duties, the grain they produced for owners of manors and estates. The peasant did not sell his primary products in a market. He participated as a buyer and seller of livestock, a customer of drinking and gambling booths, an admirer of clowns and acrobats. The major volume of trade was in goods brought in by long-distance traders — laces, fine woolens, and linens the peasant could not afford to buy.

All these situations in which a peasant deals with an outsider share some characteristics. Buyer and seller act within roles specific to the economic context; they are "anonymous as to persons." Prices respond to supply and demand and are established by haggling. Commercial specialists play a major role, for only in some cases does the original producer sell directly to the ultimate consumer. The economic chain that forms a national distribution system is considerably more complex than that.

Although these markets often function remarkably like the model of a free market, there are some differences. The peasant, out of his customary reliance on personal relations and his sense of insecurity in the world outside the village, may set up traditional patron-client relations with particular sellers, or he may incorporate a town merchant into his fictive-kinship system. Mintz's article, "Pratik: Haitian Personal Economic Relationships," takes up some of these matters and points out that often such personalization is beneficial to both peasant and trader. It must also be noted that in Western history a market with legal restrictions, price control, and varied administrative restrictions has existed for long periods and in many places.

In the market the peasant makes decisions with a money profit in mind, as contrasted to his orientation toward family and community on the local level. Although the two goals are congruent, they are not identical. Each orientation may lead to varying patterns of action, e.g., in a large, impersonal market the peasant need not act according to the pressures exerted by local standards. It is in the inn of the market town that he can allow himself to boast and play rich man, and on the open field where horses are sold that he can drive a hard bargain to the ultimate degree of self-interest.

In traditional India a great many goods and services flow between peasant and elite through the *jajmani* system, sets of exchanges between castes, or rather between client members of castes. Propriety and virtues in the performance of economic services is validated by the religious system, wherein castes have been accorded ranks in a hierarchic system and certain services to perform for each other. Consequently, whereas the market system provides an impersonal means of integrating various strata of society into the economy, the *jajmani* system achieves integration through complementary actions, enforced by both religious and power sanctions. Lewis and Barnouw discuss *jajmani* exchanges and caste, pointing out that one cannot look at the system's functioning as effortless symbiosis, for it sets up not only rules for cooperating, but also areas of tension and strain.

Peasants live in a social world in which they are economically and politically disadvantaged. They have neither sufficient capital nor power to make an impression on the urban society. But they have no illusions about their position. Indeed, often they have no notion at all of that imaginary world which offers social mobility, entrepreneurs free to use their talents and resources to create new enterprises, and the possibility of economic growth, rather than a stability fluctuating on the edge of disaster. The devices they use to chart a course are modest. They are acts taken by a man with small capital and little prestige. Thus he gets credit by asking a patron for a loan, by being a traditional client of a particular shop (see Ward, "Cash or Credit Crops?"), by appealing to a moneylender, by giving away the major part of the perishable meat of a slaughtered animal in order to receive fresh meat when his friends slaughter theirs. He attempts to spread his risks by entering into complex arrangements whereby six of his piglets are fattened by six people in return for a set share of the meat after the slaughter. He saves by giving gifts and working for others, or by putting a penny a week into an association fund, receiving the total collection the week his turn comes. The modesty of his credit and banking systems must be held up against the fact that probably such were the institutions of most of the world's population for at least the last thousand years.

REFERENCES CITED

Arensberg, C. M., and S. T. Kimball
1940 *Family and Community in Ireland.* Cambridge: Harvard University Press.

Erasmus, Charles J.
1956 "Culture Structure and Process: The Occurrence and Disappearance of Reciprocal Farm Labor." *Southwestern Journal of Anthropology* 12:444–469.

Silverman, Sydel F.
1959 "Some Cultural Correlates of the Cyclical Market." *Intermediate Societies, Social Mobility, and Communication* (Verne F. Ray, ed.). Proceedings of the 1959 Annual Spring Meeting of the American Ethnological Society. Seattle: American Ethnological Society.

Dowry and Inheritance in Modern Greece

Ernestine Friedl

The farmers in the village of Vasilika, Boeotia, raise cotton and tobacco for sale. They also grow enough wheat to supply bread for their own families and for the shepherds they employ, and enough grapes to keep their households supplied with wine. The land on which these crops are grown, the machinery used to cultivate them, the houses in which the villagers live, and the money saved from the sale of the cash crops constitute the main forms of property for each village family. The success with which this property is handled largely determines the honor and prestige accorded each family by the villagers, and it contributes to the degree of pride a husband and wife and their children have in themselves.

What is considered success? The essential family obligation is to maintain a ratio between property and children such as to enable each child, when the property is divided into substantially equal shares among all the children, to maintain in his turn and for his family a decent standard of living. In other words, the villagers think of the elementary family as a kin group that conserves, accumulates, and transmits property from one generation to the next. The transmission of wealth is an important part of this trio of obligations. Property owned by a husband and wife who have no children to inherit it gives little satisfaction even when it means that the couple can maintain a relatively high standard of living.

Clearly, neither the forms in which wealth is reckoned nor the goals of the family with respect to it are unusual; they are certainly familiar to European rural societies. The occasion for this paper is the fact that the particular mechanisms by which property is inherited in Vasilika, with the social and cultural context in which they occur, have ramifications that seem especially worthy of note.

The patrimony is transferred to sons by inheritance or by gifts *inter vivos*, and to daughters by dowry. However, there is a strongly felt moral obligation to give marriageable daughters first lien on the property. The result is that the process for providing dowries for daughters and the pat-

From "Dowry and Inheritance in Modern Greece" in *Transactions of the New York Academy of Sciences*, Series II, Vol. 22, No. 1 (November 1959), pp. 49–54. Reprinted by permission of the author and The New York Academy of Sciences.

terns for the ultimate disposition of dowry properties have wide economic and social ramifications, some of which will be discussed here.

By Greek law and village custom each child is entitled to an equal share of property. While his children are still young, a farmer calculates approximately what he must give his daughters for dowries and what will be left for his sons to share. Sometimes it is obvious that the father's holdings, when distributed after his death to his sons in equal shares, will not be sufficient to support each of them. In such cases, one or more of the sons will be educated or trained for a nonfarming occupation. A son so trained is deemed to be drawing on his share of the patrimony. A family not only conserves its fields by educating its extra sons, but also gains added prestige by having a son in a white-collar civil service position or in a profession. The prestige of town occupations is so great that sometimes even an only son who is a promising student may be sent to continue his education in the gymnasium. The nearest gymnasium to Vasilika is approximately fifteen miles away, and some of the village boys go even farther. The attendance of a son at one of these schools entails a cash outlay for room, board, and appropriate clothing. These expenses must be paid out of income from the land. In addition, although this has become less important with increasing mechanization, the absence of the son at school deprives the family of the value of his services either on the farm or as a hired laborer on other properties. Thus, the villagers seem to feel that a son educated away from home receives, in the course of the years, the equivalent of all or a major part of his prospective inheritance. The situation is considered the same even with less prestige-giving types of training or education, such as apprenticeship to a barber or a tailor.

In the meantime, the farmer has other calls on whatever monies he can save after providing for the ordinary subsistence needs of his family. There is first the desire to have as much cash as possible to supplement the land he will give for his daughters' dowries. The more gold sovereigns he has, the less land he must part with and, therefore, the more will be saved for his farming sons. Second, his daughters need money to supply part of the materials necessary for their trousseaus. The selling of cotton and tobacco, each season, is therefore an occasion for deciding whether some cash is to be spent on yet another article of the trousseau. The father and his sons are also always constantly aware of the ultimate need to relinquish some of the land and some of the laboriously collected savings when the girls marry.

The burdens of fathers with daughters are not relieved by procuring well-dowered wives for their sons, contrary to what those familiar with dowry systems in other parts of the world might expect. If it were possible to use the incoming dowry of a son to provide the property needed for the marriage of a daughter, the social and economic consequences of the Greek dowry system would be entirely different. Alternately, if the Greek villager could avoid an actual transfer of property by having his son and his daughter marry the daughter and son of another farmer, as sometimes occurs in India, again the consequences would be different. Neither of these two alternatives is possible in Greek society. The fact is that the dowry, in every case, is considered property held in trust for the children of the newly married couple. It is therefore part of the descending patrimony of the new family and not part of the ascending or collateral patrimony of the groom. The bride's dowry can be used neither by the groom's father, nor by the groom himself, for the benefit of the groom's sisters. Indeed, the marriage contract may permit all or part of the wife's dowry to remain the property of the wife herself. Even when the groom has control or supervision over the dowry properties — this is the customary arrangement of the villages, whatever the provisions of the formal contract — he thinks of this property as separate from that which he has already inherited or will inherit from his father. The former is *príka yinekós*, woman's dowry, the latter is *patrikó*, paternal inheritance. As you walk around Vasilika with a villager, he will describe one field as having been part of the dowry his mother brought his father, another as land that he purchased with money drawn from his wife's dowry. A third and fourth plot, no longer his, were given respectively by his father as part of his sister's dowry, and by himself as part of his eldest daughter's when she married. The villager's remaining fields, apart from any that he may have bought or obtained by exchange in an ordinary real estate transaction, he calls patrikó, paternal, for he reckons as patrikó any land that was part of his grandfather's holdings, regardless of its original source. Thus, it takes at least two generations for dower land to be incorporated into the patrimony of the male line into which it comes. The dowry is therefore a mechanism by which property is transmitted from a woman to her children with a period of intermediate administration by her husband. With the dowry, the inheritance system is a bilateral one; a man receives property through the ancestors of both his father and his mother.

Once the dowry agreement has been made and the marriage has taken place, the actual disposition of the types of property that comprise the dowry has further consequences in the Greek countryside. The ultimate disposition is, in turn, related to the social framework in which the dowry system operates. Vasilika may be defined in Murdock's terms as a *patrideme*, a community in which there is more than one separate and distinct kin group related through males; one in which men bring their wives from other communities and expect to send their daughters and sisters to be married elsewhere. Village exogamy is not a moral ideal, but is the most frequent arrangement, partly because a large proportion of the two hundred and twenty inhabitants of Vasilika are too closely related through the patrilineal line to avoid the incest prohibitions of the Greek Orthodox Church, and also because one is likely to be able to make more advantageous marriages in other communities.

Therefore, let us consider the disposition of the dowry of a Vasilika girl who marries a farmer's son in Elatia, several miles away. The girl, of course, goes to live in Elatia, where she and her husband are entitled to a room in his father's house. In this room, the couple and their subsequent children sleep. Her trousseau supplies bedding and the personal touch for the room. In addition, the young couple is entitled to support from the joint efforts of the husband and his parents and siblings on the farm. The bride's dowry lands remain in Vasilika. Farming them requires either that her husband travel from Elatia to Vasilika to work the land himself, or that he engage one of his affinal relatives to work the land on shares. As he grows older, our Elatia farmer may prefer to exchange his wife's príka lands in Vasilika for some nearer his own village. The exchange might be arranged with a Vasilika man who brought his wife from Elatia or its vicinity. If the transaction requires additional payment, the cash may be drawn from the money part of the dowry that our Elatia farmer received with his Vasilika bride. Finally, if no reasonable exchange is practicable, the inconvenience of scattered land holdings may lead the Elatia farmer to sell the Vasilika dowry lands in order to purchase other land in or near his home.

A farmer son-in-law may also use the cash from his wife's dowry for capital outlays calculated to enhance the value of his children's patrimony. Therefore, he may buy major farm equipment, or additional land, or beehives, none of which will be merged with the assets of his paternal household, although the income drawn from the dowry-derived properties may be.

Let us now turn to the distribution of dowry properties that occurs when a village girl marries a townsman instead of a farmer, either in one of the provincial centers or in Athens. Here custom calls for a dowry that may include some land but comprises, as its principal element, a house in the town that must be habitable, although not necessarily complete, before the marriage can actually take place. The completion of the house remains the obligation of the father of the bride and may ultimately require the sale of some of his land to provide the necessary cash. Where a village girl marries an artisan or small tradesman living in a town, all or part of her dowry lands may be sold to establish her husband in business or to enable him to expand his enterprise. In all these instances, whatever dower lands there are in the bride's village, although they may be temporarily worked by affinal relatives on shares, are for the most part ultimately sold out of the bride's family.

The combination of village exogamy, patrilocal residence, and land as part of the dowry has the effect, therefore, of stimulating land transfers in the Boeotian countryside. Since some portion of each man's inherited lands, if he has any daughters, will pass into the hands of a different bilateral kin group, that is, a different elementary family, there is no opportunity to develop kin-associated holdings that will have the same boundaries for more than one generation. A son cannot expect to be farming exactly the same plots his father farmed, and he is even likely to own some lands in a village in which his father was entirely unknown. Indeed, a farmer cannot even expect, in the course of his own lifetime, to continue to farm the same land that constituted his holdings when he began as the head of a new elementary family. This situation effectively prevents the strengthening of the patrilineal lineage as a significant kin group in spite of a pattern of patrilocal residence.

It is very likely that the Boeotian situation also precludes the development of strong sentiments with respect to particular plots of land and may therefore account for, or at least reinforce, the instrumental attitude toward property characteristic of the Boeotian villages. Land is neither loved nor revered, nor is it considered an extension of oneself. It has value as a source of income; cash is needed for savings and dowries as well as for subsistence; therefore, new agricultural techniques which obviously improve crop yields are welcomed and easily absorbed into the farming practices of the community. Furthermore, if land is merely a source of income, other means of earning a living can be in direct competition with it. As I have already indicated, the fact is that in Vasilika nonfarming occupations in the towns have more prestige than farming, and merchandising, skilled trades, or semiskilled work such as driving a taxi are acceptable alternatives.

The late Robert Redfield discussed the apparently contrasting attitudes toward land of northern and eastern European rural peoples as compared to those of Mediterranean peasantries. In the north and east, land has personal and mystical associations, and the industrious pursuit of agriculture has strong moral value in and of itself. On the other hand, Redfield suggests that the Mediterranean people tend toward the instrumental view of land and the preference for town occupations just described for modern Boeotia (Redfield 1956). Redfield seeks an explanation for this difference in the relative wealth of farmers in the two areas, and also in the ancient Greek tradition of city-dwelling ultimately diffused throughout the Mediterranean area.

If we take our Greek community as an example of the Mediterranean group, it may be useful to compare it with a northern farming tradition, that of the Irish. In the Irish countryside, money is the only form the marriage portion takes. It is given by the bride's father to the groom's father; thus, the dowering of a daughter does not diminish the land holdings that the father of the bride must pass on intact to one of his sons. The result is a strong identification of a patrilineal line with a particular plot of land (Arensberg and Kimball 1940). That this kin identification with a particular plot is of intense importance to the Irish farmer may perhaps be shown most clearly by what happens in an Irish country family that has no male heirs. Here, the incoming son-in-law is expected to pay a money-bride price substantially in excess of the value of his bride's estate. The purpose of this excess payment, according to Arensberg and

Kimball ". . . may be . . . to overcome the anomaly felt at the reversal of the usual roles of sons and daughters." Perhaps Arensberg and Kimball's point may gain greater significance if viewed somewhat differently. I suggest that it is not so much the reversal of male and female roles that calls for the extra payment as the fact that an incoming son-in-law will ultimately change the patrilineal identity of the estate.

By contrast, a Greek incoming son-in-law is almost always a poor man whose own inheritance would be too small to support a family. When we questioned the villagers on whether such a son-in-law brings with him the equivalent of a bride price, the villagers looked surprised and said that if he had anything to bring, he would not be moving into his wife's household. In other words, the Greek incoming son-in-law has low social prestige because he is felt to be entering his wife's household in the role of a needed agricultural laborer, and the fact that the sons of the marriage will have his name is a secondary consideration. In the Irish countryside, the incoming son-in-law takes over the role of the proprietor of an estate that ultimately will be associated with his and not his wife's father's line, in a situation in which the identification of patrilineal lines with a given plot of land lasts for generations and is presumably a source of prestige and pride.

This comparison, although limited in scope, suggests that there is a connection between dowry and inheritance systems and attitudes toward land and land tenure. It would appear that, as in Greece, the bestowal of dowries representing an equal share of the inheritance for women, given at least partly in the form of fields, may well contribute to a practical, utilitarian attitude toward land simply because it prevents the development of unilaterally owned permanent estates and, instead, fosters land sales and exchanges. The converse would seem to be the case with communities such as those of rural Ireland, where a dowry is bestowed in the form of money, leaving the patrilineal land intact. Further use of comparative material, with strict attention to the operational details of various systems of dowry and inheritance, might establish a definite correlation between these and the attitude toward land and land tenure among the rural peoples of Europe.

REFERENCES CITED

Arensberg, C. M., and S. T. Kimball
1940 *Family and Community in Ireland*. Cambridge: Harvard University Press. pp. 113–116.

Redfield, R.
1956 *Peasant Society and Culture*. Chicago: University of Chicago Press. pp. 105–117.

Marketing and Social Structure in Rural China (Part I)

G. William Skinner

I set forth in this paper a partial description and preliminary analysis of rural marketing in China. This neglected topic has significance which ranges far beyond the disciplinary concerns of economics. It interests anthropologists in particular because marketing structures of the kind described here for China appear to be characteristic of the whole class of civilizations known as "peasant" or "traditional agrarian" societies. In complex societies of this important type, marketing structures inevitably shape local social organization and provide one of the crucial modes for integrating myriad peasant communities into the single social system which is the total society. The Chinese case would appear to be strategic for the comparative study of peasant marketing in traditional agrarian societies because the integrative task accomplished there was uniquely large; because the exceptional longevity and stability of Chinese society have allowed the marketing system in many regions to reach full maturity prior to the beginnings of modernization; and because available documentation of Chinese marketing over several centuries provides rich resources for the study of systemic development — of change within tradition.

Change which constitutes departure from the traditional system — which signals the onset of the transformation of a traditional agrarian society into a modern industrial society — can also be profitably approached through the study of rural marketing. Basic alterations in the distribution of markets and the patterning of marketing behavior provide a sensitive index of progress in modernization. Rural marketing thus deserves serious attention during each of the periods into which modern Chinese history can be divided — not excepting the contemporary Communist era. The subject takes on added significance during the most re-

From "Marketing and Social Structure in Rural China, Part I" in *The Journal of Asian Studies*, Vol. XXIV, No. 1 (November 1964). Reprinted by permission of The Association for Asian Studies, Inc. A preliminary version was prepared for the Seminar on "Processes of Change in Chinese Society," Toronto, Nov. 1–2, 1963, organized by the Subcommittee for Research on Chinese Society of the Joint Committee on Contemporary China. A reworked and abridged version of the sections on marketing communities was given as a Public Lecture at the London School of Economics and Political Science, Feb. 10, 1964. I am grateful for both opportunities.

cent decade because of the correspondences which can be demonstrated between the units of collectivization and marketing systems. It is part of my purpose in this paper to suggest that an adequate interpretation of developments since 1949 in the Chinese countryside must rest on a prior analysis of premodern peasant marketing.

Although the scholarly literature on local marketing in China is relatively meagre,[1] the raw materials for analysis are in abundant supply.

[1] On the side of documentary research, pioneering work was done by Katō Shigeshi. He and three other Japanese scholars have begun a systematic exploitation of *fang-chih:*

Katō Shigeshi, "Shindai ni okeru sonchin no teiki ichi" ["Rural Periodic Markets of the Ch'ing Dynasty"], *Tōyō gakuhō*, XXIII, No. 2 (February 1936), 153–204.

Kuramochi Tokuichirō, "Shisen no jōshi ["The Local Markets of Szechwan"], *Nihon Daigaku Shigakkai kenkyū ihō*, I (Dec. 1957), 2–32.

Masui Tsuneo, "Kanton no kyoshi" ["The Local Markets of Kwangtung"], *Tōa ronsō*, IV (May 1941), 263–283.

Yamane Yukio, "Min Shin jidai kahoku ni okeru teiki ichi" ["Periodic Markets in North China during the Ming and Ch'ing Periods"], *Shiron* VIII, (1960), 493–504.

Chinese scholars have produced two slighter pieces on rural marketing in earlier dynasties, for which contemporary gazetteers are unavailable:

Ho Ko-en, "T'ang-tai Ling-nan ti hsü-shih" ["Periodic Markets in South China during the T'ang Dynasty"], *Shih-huo*, V, No. 2 (1937), 35–37.

Ch'üan Han-sheng, "Sung-tai Nan-fang ti hsü-shih" ["Periodic Markets in South China during the Sung Dynasty"], *Li-shih yü-yen yen-chiu-so chi-k'an* (*Academia Sinica*), IX (1947), 265–274.

Field work on rural marketing was pioneered by Chinese sociologists. Ch'iao Ch'i-ming and Yang Mou-ch'un (Martin Yang), both trained in rural sociology at Cornell University, were the first to recognize the social significance of marketing systems. C. K. Yang's field study, conducted in 1932–33, remains a classic.

Ch'iao Ch'i-ming, *Hsiang-ts'un she-hui-ch'ü hua ti fang-fa* [*Methods for Mapping the Rural Community*], Chin-ling ta-hsueh, Nung-lin ts'ung-k'an, no. 31 (Nanking, May 1926).

Ch'iao Ch'i-ming, *Chiang-ning hsien Shun-hua-chen hsiang-ts'un she-hui-ch'ü chih yen-chiu* [*A Study of the Rural Community of Shun-hua Township, Chiang-ning hsien*], Chin-ling ta-hsüeh, Nung-lin ts'ung k'an n.s. no. 23 (Nanking, November 1934).

Yang Ch'ing-k'un (C. K. Yang), *A North China Local Market Economy*, mimeo. (New York: Institute of Pacific Relations, 1944).

Yang Mou-ch'un (Martin Yang), *A Chinese Village: T'ai-t'ou, Shantung Province* (New York, 1945).

Yang Mou-ch'un, "Chung-kuo ti chi-chen-ch'ü yü hsiang-ts'un she-ch'ü" ["The Traditional Market-town Area as a Modern Rural Community in China"], *She-hui-hsüeh k'an, I* (December 1963), 23–39.

Japanese field work in northern China has also produced a relevant literature, of which the two most important are:

Chūgoku Nōson Kankō Chōsa Kankōkai, ed., *Chūgoku nōson kankō chōsa* [*Investigations into the Customs of Chinese Villages*] (Tokyo, 1952–1958), 6 vols.

Amano Motonosuke, "Nōson no kenshi shijō" ["Traditional Rural Markets"]; "Nōson shijō no kōeki" ["Rural Marketing"], *Chūgoku nōgyō no shomondai* [*Problems of Chinese Agriculture*] (Tokyo, 1953), II, 69–174.

It remains to mention two useful field studies of marketing in Szechwan:

Liao T'ai-ch'u, "The Rape Markets on the Chengtu Plain," *Journal of Farm Economics*, XXVIII, No. 4 (November 1946), 1016–24.

J. E. Spencer, "The Szechwan Village Fair," *Economic Geography*, XVI, No. 1 (January 1940), 48–58.

Thousands of *fang-chih*, the gazetteers prepared locally for *hsien* and other administrative units, provide information in remarkable detail about local markets and often about the marketing process itself. These and other traditional documentary sources were supplemented during the pre-Communist era of transition by the descriptions of foreign observers, information reported in local newspapers, raw data compiled through fact-finding surveys, and even bits of scholarly field work. The richest resource for the study of rural marketing in mainland China, both before and after 1949, is the large body of potential informants from the mainland now resident in Taiwan, Hong Kong, and overseas — individuals who participated over a period of years in the marketing systems to which their native places belonged. Data for the present study are drawn from my own field work in Szechwan, 1949–50; [2] intensive interviews with a handful of emigré informants in the United States, Hong Kong, and Singapore; a large number of fang-chih; and a variety of other published works.[3] I have, nevertheless, barely tapped the potential sources, and this essay falls correspondingly short of comprehensive treatment.

The paper appears in separate installments. In this, the first part, attention is focused on the structure of marketing systems, and the analysis is essentially synchronic. The various aspects of change are reserved for treatment in the second part, to be carried in the *Journal's* next issue [*Journal of Asian Studies*, Vol. XXIV, No. 2, February 1965].

Part I begins with a consideration of two preliminary matters: the various types of markets and the principles of market-day scheduling. In subsequent sections, marketing structures are treated first as spatial and economic systems and then as social and cultural systems.

MARKETS AND CENTRAL PLACES

Central places — the generic term for cities, towns, and other nucleated settlements with central service functions — may be classified in a variety of ways. The approach taken here follows the lead of Christaller and Lösch.[4] In the analytical tradition which stems from these scholars, a given central place may be typed according to its position in interlocking spatial systems, within which economic function is associated

[2] Field work was made possible by grants from the Social Science Research Council and the Viking Fund (now Wenner-Gren Foundation).

[3] Research assistance was ably provided by Stephen M. Olsen and William L. Parish, Jr., both of Cornell University. I am also indebted, for assistance of one kind or another, to Hsiao Chih and John Liu of the Union Research Institute, Hong Kong; to Joseph P. L. Jiang, University of Singapore; and to Yinmaw Kau, Ichikawa Kenjirō, John T. Ma, and William John McCoy, Jr., all of Cornell University.

[4] The two classical studies are: Walter Christaller, *Die zentralen Orte in Süddeutschland* (Jena, 1933). August Lösch, *Die räumliche Ordnung der Wirtschaft* (Jena, 1944); page references are to the English translation: *The Economics of Location* (New Haven, 1954).

with hierarchical level.[5] It may be suggested that regularity in central-place hierarchies and consistency in the alignment of function with systemic position are enhanced by, if they do not actually result from, a condition of perduring "entropy" — many forces acting on the system of central places in many ways over a period of many centuries.[6] Be that as it may, in the case of China at the end of her long and relatively stable imperial era, central places are readily analyzed on the assumption that the economic function of a settlement is consistently associated with its position in marketing systems which are themselves arranged in a regular hierarchy.

The Chinese countryside supports settlements of bewildering variety. In this attempt to sort them into meaningful categories, I begin with the standard market town — a type of central place which appears to have been common to all regions of premodern agrarian China.

By late traditional times, markets had so proliferated on the Chinese landscape and were so distributed that at least one was accessible to virtually every rural household. They were considered essential, both as a source of necessary goods and services unavailable in the village community and as an outlet for local production. I term "standard" that type of rural market which met all the normal trade needs of the peasant household: what the household produced but did not consume was normally sold there, and what it consumed but did not produce was normally bought there. The standard market provided for the exchange of goods produced within the market's dependent area, but more importantly it was the starting point for the upward flow of agricultural products and craft items into higher reaches of the marketing system, and also the termination of the downward flow of imported items destined for peasant consumption. A settlement which is the site of a standard market (but not also of a higher-level market) is here called a "standard market town."

Settlement patterns below the level of the standard market town vary from one region to another. Nucleated villages are common throughout most of rural China, and in many areas these constitute the only settlement type below the standard market town. In some areas, however, certain "villages" support a type of market which I will here term "minor."

[5] It is convenience of exposition alone which dictates the introduction into this paper of a central-place typology prior to the description of systems. In fact, system analysis is prior to the construction of an appropriate typology.

[6] This hypothesis is merely an extension of the theory put forward by Berry to account for the fact that in certain traditional societies, China included, the sizes of central places exhibit a rank-size distribution. (In a distribution of this kind, the number of cases in each ascending size class is a regular progression from small to large, with no deficiencies in the middle range.) The extension is hardly daring in view of the established "compatibility of Christaller-Lösch type hierarchies and rank-size distributions of city sizes." Brian J. L. Berry, "City Size Distribution and Economic Development," *Economic Development and Cultural Change,* IX (July 1961), footnote 4, p. 573 and p. 582. See also Martin J. Beckmann, "City Hierarchies and the Distribution of City Size," *Economic Development and Cultural Change,* VI (April 1958), p. 246.

The minor market, popularly known as a "green-vegetable market," specializes in the horizontal exchange of peasant-produced goods. Many necessities are not regularly available, and virtually no services or imports are offered. It is of negligible importance as an entry point for locally produced goods into the larger marketing system. The sporadic occurrence of the minor market in rural China, its limited functions, and its peripheral position with regard to larger marketing systems lead me to consider it apart from the regular hierarchy of central places — as a transitional type which in most cases can be interpreted as an incipient standard market. Since it leads to no confusion, I use the term "minor market" to refer both to the market and to the settlement in which it is located.

In still other parts of China, of which the Szechwan Basin is the outstanding example, neither nucleated villages nor minor markets obtain. Peasants live in dispersed farmhouses or farmhouse clusters, and the only nodes on the economic landscape below the level of the standard market town are the small clusters of shops known as *yao-tien* (literally "small shops"). The exceptional character of human ecology in the Szechwan Basin should not, however, be overemphasized. The dispersed residential units of the Szechwanese countryside form themselves into natural groupings, each focused on a single *t'u-ti miao* (earth-god shrine), which may be termed "dispersed villages." When viewed as social systems, both the dispersed village of Szechwan and the nucleated village more commonly found elsewhere in China may be considered "village communities." The yao-tien, which appears sporadically on the Szechwanese landscape, is in some instances simply the "general store" of the dispersed village, and thus an equivalent of the group of shops commonly found in the largest of nucleated villages elsewhere in China. Other yao-tien — especially those consisting of several shops and situated at crossroads equidistant from two or three market towns — are the functional equivalent of minor markets elsewhere in China. They may be seen as incipient standard markets, and indeed several examples of standard markets established *de novo* within the memory of my Szechwan informants grew out of yao-tien.

It will be noted that the terminology suggested here reserves the term "village" for nucleated settlements which do not support markets.[7] "Village community" is a more inclusive term for residential social systems, nucleated or dispersed, which do not involve a market of any type. No generic term is proposed for minor markets or yao-tien, which are intermediate and transitional between village communities and standard market towns. "Market town," in the terminology used here, is limited to three types of central places positioned at adjacent levels of the hierarchical system of economic centers; each of the three corresponds to a type

[7] The use of the word "village" to refer to towns which are the site of standard markets is, however, common enough in the general literature. Spencer, for instance, uses "village" for "market town" throughout his Szechwan study even though it requires a definition of "village" (p. 48) which he admits does not hold for other provinces.

of market. The standard market, at the lowest of these three levels, has already been characterized. In ascending order, the other two types are here termed the "intermediate market" and the "central market." To begin with the latter, the central market is normally situated at a strategic site in the transportation network and has important wholesaling functions. Its facilities are designed, on the one hand, to receive imported items and distribute them within its dependent area and, on the other, to collect local products and export them to other central markets or higher-level urban centers. It will suffice at this point to say of the intermediate market simply that it has an intermediate position in the vertical flow of goods and services both ways. In the terminology being introduced here, a settlement which is the site of an intermediate market (but not also of a higher-level market) is termed an "intermediate market town." The "central market town" is similarly defined.

In general, as one moves in this hierarchical typology from each type of central place to the next higher, the number of households increases [8] while the proportion of the labor force engaged in agriculture falls. In addition, as one progresses from village to central market town, each type is more likely than the last to be walled and to support the worship of *ch'eng-huang*, the urban deity par excellence. The typical intermediate market town is at least partially walled and supports a shrine to ch'eng-huang. Central market towns and cities in traditional times were usually completely walled and had a full-fledged ch'eng-huang temple; this was true even of those centers which had no formal administrative status. Thus, position in the hierarchical typology of central places generally correlates with urbanism, whether defined in terms of variables familiar to the urban sociologist or in the common-sense terms of the Chinese layman.

PERIODICITY AND MARKET SCHEDULES

In Ch'ing China, as in most traditional agrarian societies, rural markets were normally periodic rather than continuous: they convened only every few days. This feature of traditional rural markets may be understood from several points of view.

On the side of the producer or trader, the periodicity of markets is

[8] It would appear that *within the same systems* there is seldom any overlap in the size of central places at different levels. That is, the local city normally will have more households than any of the central market towns dependent on it; each central market town has more households than any of the intermediate market towns dependent on it, etc. For instance, Chung-hsing *chen*, a central market town in Hua-yang hsien, Szechwan, contained approximately 2650 households in 1934. The intermediate market towns dependent on it were all markedly smaller, ranging in size from 360 to 900 households. In turn, each of the intermediate market towns had more households than did any of its dependent standard market towns. The intermediate market town of Chung-ho-ch'ang, to cite just one example at this level, had 900 households in 1934, while the size of its dependent standard markets ranged from 50 to 279. *Hua-yang hsien chih*, Min-kuo 23 (1934), ch. 1.

related to the mobility of individual "firms." The itinerant peddler, toting his wares from one market to the next with the aid of a carrying pole, is the archetype of the mobile firm in China. But equally characteristic of the traditional rural market are the wandering artisans and repairmen who carry their "workshop" about with them, and other itinerants purveying services of all kinds from letter-writing to fortune-telling. Why are these facilities mobile? In essence, because the total amount of demand encompassed by the marketing area of any single rural market is insufficient to provide a profit level which enables the entrepreneur to survive. By repositioning himself at periodic intervals, the entrepreneur can tap the demand of several marketing areas and thereby attain the survival threshold.[9] From the point of view of the itinerant entrepreneur, periodicity in marketing has the virtue of concentrating the demand for his product at restricted localities on certain specific days. When a group of related markets operates on coordinated periodic (as opposed to daily) schedules, he can arrange to be in each town in the circuit on its market day.

The diffuseness of economic roles in traditional China is also relevant in this regard, for a firm which is at once producer and trader finds periodicity advantageous even when only one market is exploited. Again, by concentrating demand on certain specific days, marketing periodicity enables such entrepreneurs to combine sales with production in an optimally efficient manner. This advantage accrues not only to the artisan in market-town shops, but also to the peasant engaged in cottage industry, and for that matter to the housewife who occasionally has eggs to sell. Each of these producers is his own salesman.

From the point of view of the consumer, the periodicity of markets amounts to a device for reducing the distance he must travel to obtain the required goods and services. We begin here with the restricted nature of those requirements on the part of the average peasant household. General poverty, value emphases on frugality, and traditional consumption norms all contributed to a minimal definition of subsistence needs in the peasant household. Furthermore, these needs were in considerable part supplied without recourse to marketing, for the peasant household produced (or received through wages in kind) much of what it consumed; self-sufficiency was a virtue. Under these circumstances, (1) no household needed to market every day, and (2) the number of households required to support a daily market was very large. In most parts of agricultural China, especially prior to the eighteenth century when the rural population was distributed relatively sparsely on the land, the number of households required to support a daily market would have meant marketing areas so large that villagers at the rim could not manage the trip to and from market in a single day. A market meeting only once in three or once

[9] For a sophisticated treatment of this aspect of periodic marketing see James H. Stine, "Temporal Aspects of Tertiary Production Elements in Korea," *Urban Systems and Economic Behavior*, ed. Forrest R. Pitts (Eugene, Ore., 1962), pp. 68–78.

in five days, however, could achieve a viable level of demand if only one-third or one-fifth as many villages fell within its dependent area. Thus, when markets are periodic rather than daily, market towns may be distributed far more densely on the landscape so that the most disadvantaged villagers can manage the trip to market in a reasonable period of time.[10] Even when the number of households within a marketing area increases to the point where sufficient demand is present for the market to convert to a daily schedule, from the point of view of the peasant consumer such a change offers little advantage if the household's needs are such that marketing only once every five or six days is the most efficient way to meet them.

It will be noted that the level of transport is a crucial variable no matter how one accounts for the periodicity of traditional markets. It is the "friction of distance" which limits both the demand area of the firm and the dependent area of a market. Thus the periodicity of markets in traditional agrarian societies is, in the last analysis, a function of the relatively primitive state of transport.

The pulsations of economic activity which occur as both mobile firms and mobile consumers converge on rural markets define one of the basic life rhythms in most traditional agrarian societies. A variety of marketing "weeks" obtain in China, the most widespread of which are based on the lunar decade or *hsün*. The three hsün begin respectively on the 1st, 11th, and 21st of the lunar month; in the case of 29-day months, the third hsün lacks one day. Marketing schedules based on the hsün are designated by citing the dates of markets in only the first of the three hsün in the lunar month. A "3-8 market" thus meets on the 3rd, 8th, 13th, 18th, 23rd, and 28th of the lunar month. The scheduling system which typically obtains in the more densely populated regions of South China may be cited here as an example. It provides three market days per hsün and consists of the following schedules:

1-4-7
2-5-8
3-6-9
4-7-10
1-5-8
2-6-9
3-7-10
1-4-8
2-5-9
3-6-10
[1-4-7]

It can be shown that the first three schedules plus either 4-7-10 or 3-6-10 provide not only the maximum regularity in the spacing of market days

[10] Stine (p. 70) puts the matter succinctly: "The consumer, by submitting to the discipline of time, is able to free himself from the discipline of space."

but also the most efficient distribution of market schedules on the landscape. These, in fact, were the most common schedules in the heart of the Szechwan basin, where my own field work was conducted.

MARKETING STRUCTURES AS SPATIAL AND ECONOMIC SYSTEMS

Any attempt to comprehend the social or economic dimensions of marketing structures inevitably makes certain assumptions about their spatial characteristics. One reason for analyzing these structures as spatial systems, then, is to make explicit the assumptions which underlie such remarks as I will be able to make about the economics and the sociology of marketing. Another reason is to facilitate the study of change, for as it happens the nature of systemic change — whether traditional or modern — becomes fully apparent only when the relevant data are spatially ordered.

In order to set forth meaningful propositions about marketing structures as spatial systems it will be necessary to have recourse to simple models. The most radical of the assumptions made in constructing them is that the landscape in question is an isotropic plain on which resources of all kinds are uniformly distributed. Theoretical considerations based on impeccable geometry and tolerably sound economics tell us that when such an assumption is made, market towns should be distributed on the landscape according to an isometric grid, as if at the apexes of space-filling equilateral triangles. In theory, too, the service area of each market should approach a regular hexagon.[11] These expectations apply anywhere in the world — neither the geometry nor the economics is peculiarly Chinese — and it is therefore of no particular moment to report that in six areas of China where I have been able to test the proposition, a majority of market towns have precisely six immediately neighboring market towns and hence a marketing area of hexagonal shape, albeit distorted by topographical features.[12]

[11] Proof of the proposition that the regular hexagon is the most advantageous shape for marketing areas is given in Lösch, Ch. X. In common-sense terms, it may be noted that the appropriate model has two requirements: Markets should be so distributed that (1) the most disadvantaged villager in any given marketing area is no more and no less disadvantaged than the most disadvantaged villager in any other area, and (2) the distance from the market of the most disadvantaged villager in each marketing area is minimal. The first requirement means that all marketing areas in the model must be of uniform shape and size. Since all parts of the landscape must be in some marketing area, the only possibilities are the three regular polygons which are "space-filling," namely, equilateral triangles, squares, and regular hexagons. The second requirement specifies that the more sides a polygon has the more efficient it is in this regard. To put it another way, as you move from the least advantageous position to the most advantageous position around the rim of the marketing area, the differential is maximal for triangular areas, intermediate for square areas, and minimal for hexagonal areas.

[12] The point is worth noting, however, because the only study of rural marketing in China which refers to the shape of marketing areas insists that they ". . . approach circular or square form." C. K. Yang, p. 39.

But are the hexagonal standard marketing areas discrete? That is, do the areas typically overlap? Or, if they fit together in the manner of hexagonal ceramic tiles, do certain of the villages lie *on* the boundary between two hexagons, oriented toward more than one standard market? Martin Yang, the first social scientist to map and describe a Chinese standard marketing system, has this to say: "On the whole, although there is no clear-cut line of demarcation, each market town has a definite and recognizable area, and looks upon the people of certain villages as its primary customers; in turn, it is regarded by the villagers as their town." [13] My research in Szechwan leads me to concur wholeheartedly: I had little trouble in ascertaining the limits of the standard marketing area which I was studying; the peasants within this area did the great bulk of their marketing in Kao-tien-tzu, the standard market town in question; and they considered it *their* market.[14] There are theoretical reasons, as I shall note in Part II [of this article; see p. 65 for reference], for expecting a standard marketing area in which new villages are being established to pass through a phase in which a small number of newly established villages are situated equidistant from two or three markets, but in a stable situation there is no theoretical reason for objecting to the assumption of essential discreteness which is supported by empirical evidence.[15]

If one assumes that standard marketing areas are in the ideal case discrete, hexagonal in shape, and dotted at regular intervals with villages, then geometric principles require an integral number of complete rings of villages around the town: either one ring (of 6 villages) or two rings (one of 6 and one of 12) or three rings (one of 6, one of 12, and one of 18), or still more. Which of these models best fits the Chinese case?

Empirical evidence clearly points to the two-ring model with its total of 18 villages. It is not that every known case of a standard marketing area has a close approximation of 18 villages. My assertion is based rather on (1) the finding that the ratio between villages and standard or higher-level markets on any sizable segment of the Chinese landscape *averages* very close to 18, and (2) the fact that variation in the ratios can be accounted for satisfactorily by a developmental model which moves from one 18-village-per-market equilibrium to another — but not by models which posit a stable equilibrium of 6 or 36 villages per market. (Data relevant to the second point must await Part II; here I can appropriately do no more than cite selected averages.) In the 1870's, the average

[13] Martin Yang, 1945, p. 190.

[14] C. K. Yang, p. 39, refers to the marketing areas of Tsou-p'ing hsien as ". . . economic cells, each . . . having its own boundary of operation . . ."

[15] Field workers have occasionally been misled in this regard by a failure to distinguish between standard and intermediate markets. Evidence that villagers attend two different markets — one standard and one intermediate — may be misinterpreted as an indication of their membership in two *standard* marketing systems.

number of villages per rural market was 17.9 in Hsiang-shan hsien and 19.2 in Ch'ü-chiang hsien, both in Kwangtung.[16] The classic field study of Chinese rural marketing — that of C. K. Yang in the 1930's in Tsou-p'ing hsien, Shantung — shows 21.4 villages per standard and higher-level market.[17] The *yin hsien t'ung-chih*,[18] compiled in 1937, one of the truly outstanding examples of Chinese gazetteer scholarship, presents detailed data which yield an average of 20.1 villages for each of its 82 periodic markets. I have been able to find records of contemporary date for the number of markets *and* villages over a really large area only in the case of Kwangtung in the 1890's; [19] the ratio of villages to rural markets for the province as a whole at that time was 19.6.

Our model, then, which is diagrammed as the basic pattern of Fig. 1, shows a hexagonal marketing area with the market town at the center, surrounded by an inner ring of six and an outer ring of twelve villages. As is empirically typical, the model calls for six major paths radiating out from the town.

These paths are at once the arteries and the veins of an economic system whose heart is the market in the town at its center. Along these paths, in the early morning hours of every market day, typically pass at least one out of every five adults living in the whole array of dependent villages. In T'ai-t'ou, the Shantung village described by Martin Yang, "some member from almost every household in the village is in the town on market day," [20] while in Luts'un, the Yunnan village studied by Fei and Chang, ". . . at least one went from each household each market day." [21]

During the few hours of market before the inward flow of villagers is reversed, the meagre facilities of the typical standard market town are sorely taxed. Most such towns have only one real street and lack a defined single marketplace altogether. Instead there is a multitude of petty marketplaces, one for each product. The grain market may be held in the temple courtyard, the pig market at the edge of the town, while each of the various items of perishable products and minor crafts produced locally has its customary marketing section along the main street. Even though most

[16] *Hsiang-shan hsien chih*, T'ung-chih 12 (1873), *ch.* 5; *Ch'ü-chiang hsien chih*, Kuang-hsü 6 (1800); data reproduced in Katō, p. 34.

[17] Data for this computation are given on pp. 5–6.

[18] *Yü-ti chih, ts'e* 3 for villages, *ts'e* 7 for markets.

[19] Fang chün-i Chang Jen-chün, comp. *Kuang-tung yü-ti ch'üan-t'u* [*Comprehensive Atlas of Kwang-tung*] Canton, Kuang-hsü 23 (1897), 2 vols.

[20] Martin Yang, 1945, p. 191.

[21] Fei Hsiao-t'ung and Chang Chih-i, *Earthbound China* (Chicago, 1945), p. 172. Households marketed much less often in Yits'un, another of the villages studied by Fei and Chang, but this village falls in an area which is marginal to agricultural China and in which marketing areas are immense. Of this, more in the following section.

For the Szechwan Basin, Spencer (p. 55) estimates that on any given market day throughout the year, on the average every other family is represented at market — a proportion which, from my own experience, seems low. It must also be noted that many households are represented by two or more members.

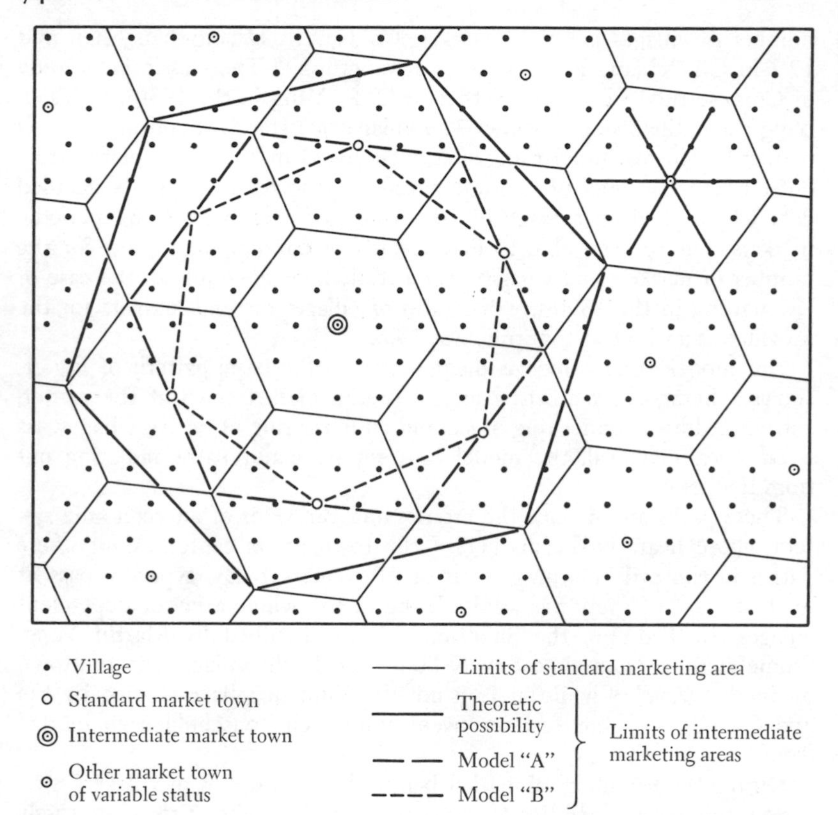

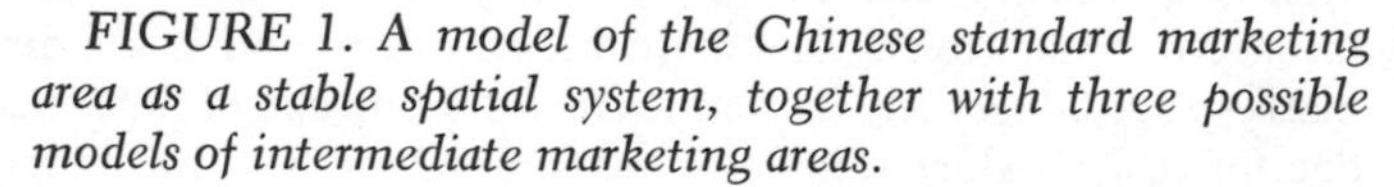

FIGURE 1. A model of the Chinese standard marketing area as a stable spatial system, together with three possible models of intermediate marketing areas.

sellers at any standard market are likely to be itinerants, the standard market town normally has a certain minimum of permanent facilities. These typically include — in addition to the socially important tea houses, wineshops, and eating places — one or more oil shops (selling fuel for wick lamps), incense and candle shops (selling the essentials of religious worship), and at least a few others offering such items as looms, needles and thread, brooms, soap, tobacco, and matches. Standard market towns normally support a number of craftsmen as well, including most typically blacksmiths, coffinmakers, carpenters, and makers of paper effigies for religious burning. A few crude workshops to process local products may also be located in a standard market town.

The standard market functions in the first instance to exchange what the peasant produces for what he needs. The peasant needs not only goods of the kind already suggested, but also the services of tool sharpeners and livestock castrators, medical practitioners and "tooth artists," religious specialists and fortune tellers, barbers, myriad entertainers, and even, on occasion, scribes. While many of these services are not available every market day, itinerants purveying all of them occasionally visit every standard market.

The standard marketing system also has a modest financial dimension. Shops in the town extend credit to regular customers. Certain shopkeepers and landowners lend money to peasants in transactions which may take place in the town on market day. The rotating credit societies of the peasant are also usually organized in the teahouses on market day and are thereby restricted to villagers from within the system.[22] In addition, certain landlords maintain an office in the town which collects rent from tenants.[23]

With regard to transport, village communities normally include a few landless peasants, as they are usually termed, who are regularly for hire as transport coolies. (Not only the local élite but also the stratum of the peasantry which is fully "respectable" eschew such public manual labor as carrying or carting bulky produce.) These men normally cart goods along the village paths serving a single marketing area and thus constitute another element in the standard marketing structure as a spatial-economic system.

While the activity which gives definition to the standard marketing system pulsates in accordance with the marketing week, it should not be imagined that its structure has no manifestation between market days. It is during what are in Szechwan colloquially called the "cold days" that many obligations incurred during the "hot" market day are met, and these, too, reinforce and express the total system. Grain sold to a buyer at market may be transported the next day. *Hsiao fan-tzu* ("petty commission agents") learn on market day which peasants have peanuts to sell and on the "cold days" visit their farms to make bids. Barbers travel along the village roads to give haircuts in those households which commissioned them at market. Carpenters, blacksmiths, and other artisans may also be hired at market to work in village households. These transactions all occur within the system defined in the first instance as the trading area of the standard market.

It is apparent from what has been described already that the standard marketing system, when viewed in spatial and economic terms, is but a subsystem of a larger structure. In particular, there is a regular movement

[22] Ch'iao Ch'i-ming, 1934, p. 15. In this study of a marketing community near Nanking, the intervillage membership of rotating credit societies is singled out for special notice.

[23] "The landlord has an office in the market-town and keeps in touch with his tenants on market-days." Li Mei-yun, *An Analysis of Social, Economic and Political Conditions in Peng-shan Hsien, Szechwan, China, Looking toward Improvement of Educational Programs,* unpublished dissertation in education, Cornell University, 1945, p. 223.

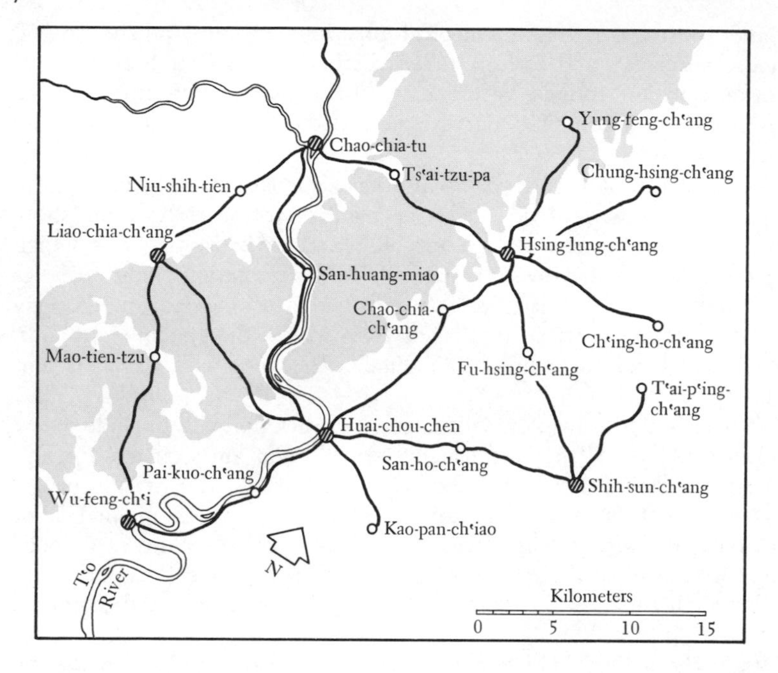
Chao-chia-tu
Yung-feng-ch'ang
Ts'ai-tzu-pa
Chung-hsing-ch'ang
Niu-shih-tien
Liao-chia-ch'ang
Hsing-lung-ch'ang
San-huang-miao
Chao-chia-ch'ang
Ch'ing-ho-ch'ang
Mao-tien-tzu
Fu-hsing-ch'ang
T'ai-p'ing-ch'ang
Huai-chou-chen
San-ho-ch'ang
Pai-kuo-ch'ang
Shih-sun-ch'ang
Wu-feng-ch'i
Kao-pan-ch'iao
N
T'o River
Kilometers
0 5 10 15

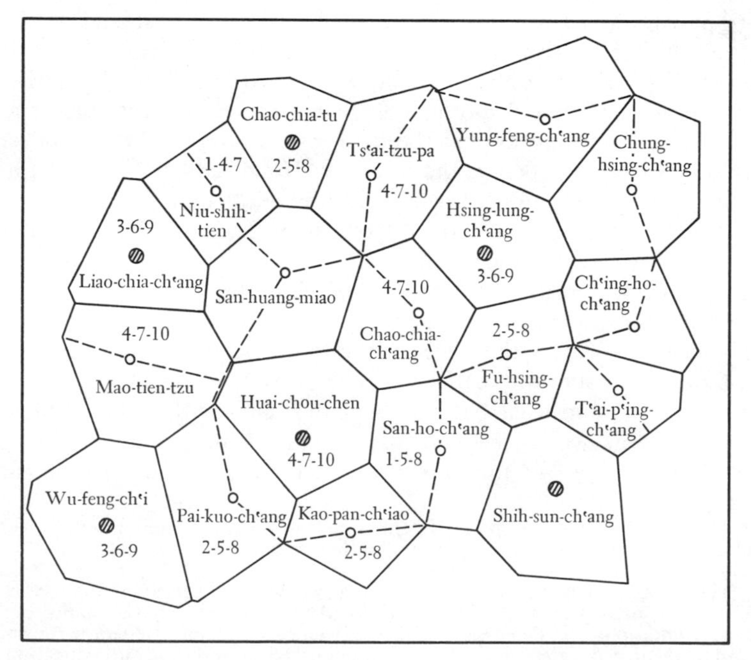
Chao-chia-tu 2-5-8
1-4-7
Ts'ai-tzu-pa 4-7-10
Yung-feng-ch'ang
Chung-hsing-ch'ang
Niu-shih-tien
Hsing-lung-ch'ang 3-6-9
Liao-chia-ch'ang 3-6-9
San-huang-miao
Chao-chia-ch'ang 4-7-10
Ch'ing-ho-ch'ang
Mao-tien-tzu 4-7-10
Fu-hsing-ch'ang 2-5-8
Huai-chou-chen 4-7-10
T'ai-p'ing-ch'ang
San-ho-ch'ang 1-5-8
Wu-feng-ch'i 3-6-9
Pai-kuo-ch'ang 2-5-8
Kao-pan-ch'iao 2-5-8
Shih-sun-ch'ang

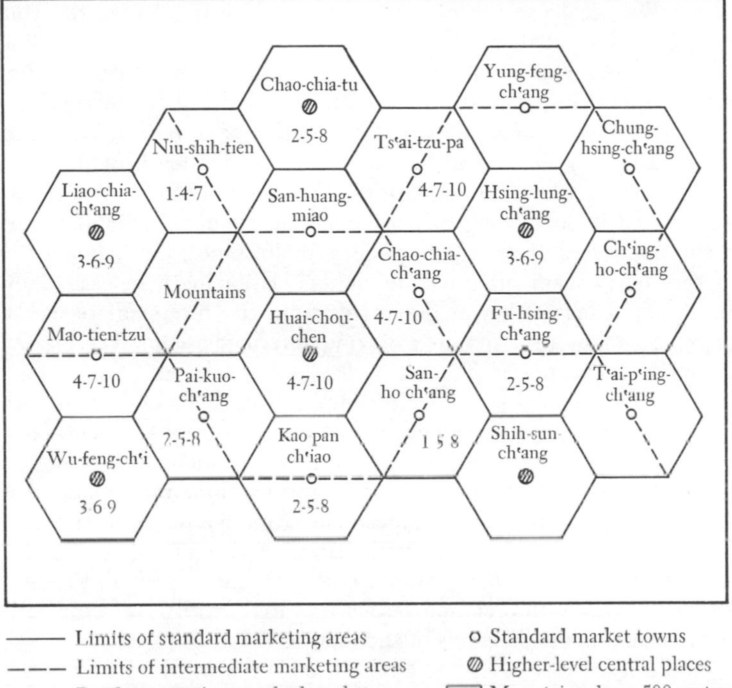

FIGURE 2. A portion of the economic landscape in Szechwan approximating Model A in the distribution of market towns.

2.1: The 19 market towns depicted lie between 35 and 90 km. northeast of Chengtu. Five markets (Yung-feng-ch'ang, Chung-hsing-ch'ang, Ch'ing-ho-ch'ang, T'ai-p'ing-ch'ang, and Shih-sun-ch'ang) are in Chung-chiang hsien, the other 14 in Chin-t'ang hsien. The mountains shown are part of the Lung-ch'üan range. The only roads mapped are those which connect standard to higher-level market towns.

2.2: First abstraction of the same landscape showing theoretic standard and intermediate marketing areas.

2.3: The same reduced to diagrammatic form. Compare with Model A as diagrammed in Figure 1.

both of goods and of mobile firms between the standard market town and the intermediate or still higher-level market towns to which it is immediately tied. I use the plural because in the usual case the standard market is dependent on two or three higher-level market towns rather than just one. The possibilities in this regard are presented in diagrammatic form in Fig. 1. The most inclusive of the three hexagonal intermediate marketing areas shown — the only model in which the standard market town is dependent on only one higher-level market town — appears to be relevant to the Chinese scene only where marketing systems are situated in something of a topographic cul-de-sac. Standard markets at the upper end of mountain valleys, for instance, are dependent solely on the downstream intermediate market. Even in these cases, however, the standard market towns downriver from the intermediate market are likely also to be oriented to a second intermediate market located still further downstream.

In China the great majority of empirical cases fit one or the other of the two less inclusive models labeled A and B in Fig. 1, or else fall in between them. Each standard market town is dependent on two higher-level market towns in the case of Model A, and on three in the case of Model B. An actual example of a Chinese landscape whose markets are distributed essentially in accordance with Model A is depicted in Fig. 2; and a comparable example fitting Model B is shown in Fig. 3. Both figures are designed to show the relation between spatial "reality" as conventionally mapped and model diagrams of the kind used in this paper.

In the usual case, then, a standard market is involved in two or three intermediate marketing systems rather than a single one. This fact points up a crucial distinction between the standard marketing system, on the one hand, and intermediate and higher-level marketing systems, on the other. Whereas the former is essentially discrete with regard to the inclusion or exclusion of component settlements, the latter are not. Whereas the stable equilibrium model of the standard marketing area shows *no* villages at the boundaries (and transitional models show only a small proportion of all villages at the boundary), the regular model of the intermediate marketing area shows *all* dependent standard market towns at the boundaries, equidistant from two or three higher-level market towns. In practice, while the territorial overlap of intermediate marketing systems is not great, it is crucial in the sense that, apart from the nucleus itself, all the primary nodes within the system are normally not exclusive to it.

A notable feature of the intermediate marketing system concerns the distribution of market schedules within it. In the literature on periodic marketing in China, it is usually imagined that schedules are simply distributed among markets in such a way that each shares the same schedule with as few of its neighbors as possible. The purpose of such dovetailing, as noted for instance by Spencer,[24] would be to make it possible for villagers to have an open market within reach almost every day and to

[24] Pp. 49 (Fig. 1 caption) and 51–52.

reduce competition among neighboring markets. However, not only have peasants little need or occasion to market more often than provided for by the schedule of their nearest standard market, but, in addition, it can be shown that schedules are not distributed in the simple manner affirmed or suggested in the literature. Rather, their distribution is designed to minimize conflict between the schedule of a given standard market and the schedules of the higher-level markets toward which it is oriented; the schedules of neighboring standard markets are essentially irrelevant. Stated another way, as new standard markets are established, a schedule will be selected which minimizes conflict with neighboring intermediate markets regardless of the schedules of neighboring standard markets.

The point may be illustrated by reference to the case of Chuan-p'eng-ssu, a market established in the Kuang-hsü reign in Chin-t'ang hsien, Szechwan.[25] At the time when it was established, there were four immediately neighboring markets with these schedules: 1-4-7 to the west, 2-5-8 to the northwest, 3-6-9 to the east, and 1-5-8 to the south. According to the principle of minimal conflict with all neighbors, the new market would have adopted a 3-6-10 or 4-7-10 schedule; at the very least it would have avoided any schedule including 5-8. In fact, the new market chose 2-5-8, for the simple reason that the towns to the west (1-4-7) and east (3-6-9) supported intermediate markets to which the new market would be oriented, whereas the towns with 2-5-8 and 1-5-8 schedules were standard market towns with which the newcomer would have minimal commercial ties.

As a consequence of this governing principle, neighboring standard markets often have the same schedule (note in Fig. 3.2 Lai-chia-tien, Kao-tien-tzu, and Hsin-tien-tzu, all with 3-6-9 schedules), whereas intermediate markets usually have no scheduling conflict with any of their dependent standard markets. This means that in areas of 3-per-hsün schedules, for instance, when the intermediate market has a 1-4-7 or 4-7-10 schedule, then all six of the dependent standard markets must share the only two harmonizing schedules which remain: 2-5-8 and 3-6-9. This situation is illustrated by the intermediate marketing system of which Chung-ho chen is the center (Fig. 3.2).[26]

It will be noted from Fig. 1 that, in addition to portions of the standard marketing areas of all dependent standard market towns, intermediate marketing areas include one complete standard marketing area at the center. This points up the important fact that an intermediate market

[25] *Chin-t'ang hsien chih*, Min-kuo 10 (1921), *ch*. 1. One of the market towns involved lies in Hua-yang hsien; the schedule of its market is given in *Hua-yang hsien chih*, Min-kuo 23 (1934), *ch*. 1.

[26] An equivalent example in a hsien where the 4-per-duodenum scheduling system is standard is provided by the intermediate marketing system centered on Pai-hsü (Shang-lin hsien, Kweichow), which has a *yin-shen-ssu-hai* schedule; its five dependent standard markets necessarily eschew Pai-hsü's schedule and share among them the two other possibilities. For market schedules see *Shang-lin hsien chih*, Kuang-hsü 2 (1876); data reproduced in Katō, pp. 26–27.

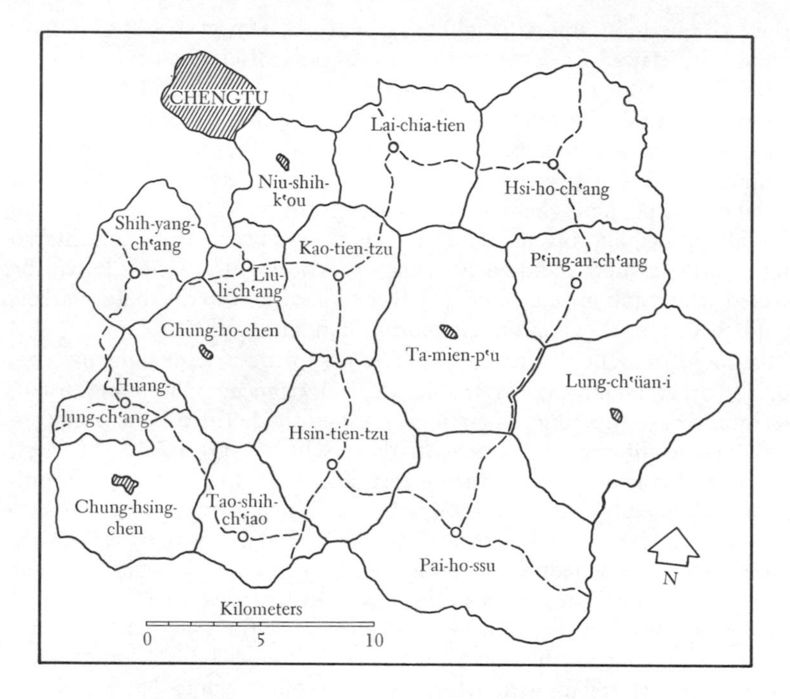
CHENGTU
Lai-chia-tien
Niu-shih-
k'ou
Hsi-ho-ch'ang
Shih-yang-
ch'ang
Kao-tien-tzu
Liu-
li-ch'ang
P'ing-an-ch'ang
Chung-ho-chen
Ta-mien-p'u
Huang-
lung-ch'ang
Lung-ch'üan-i
Hsin-tien-tzu
Chung-hsing-
chen
Tao-shih-
ch'iao
Pai-ho-ssu
N
Kilometers
0
5
10

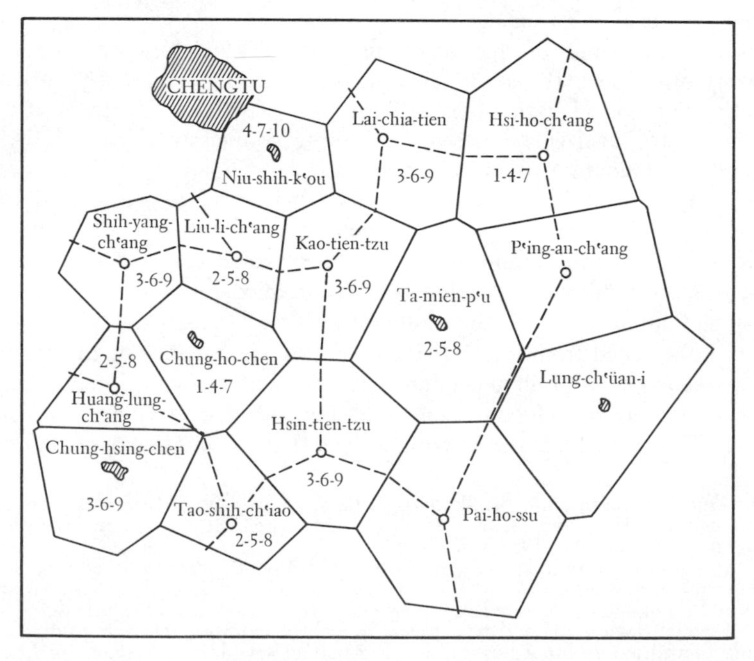
CHENGTU
4-7-10
Niu-shih-k'ou
Lai-chia-tien
3-6-9
Hsi-ho-ch'ang
1-4-7
Shih-yang-
ch'ang
3-6-9
Liu-li-ch'ang
2-5-8
Kao-tien-tzu
3-6-9
P'ing-an-ch'ang
Ta-mien-p'u
2-5-8
2-5-8
Huang-lung-
ch'ang
Chung-ho-chen
1-4-7
Lung-ch'üan-i
Hsin-tien-tzu
3-6-9
Chung-hsing-chen
3-6-9
Tao-shih-ch'iao
2-5-8
Pai-ho-ssu

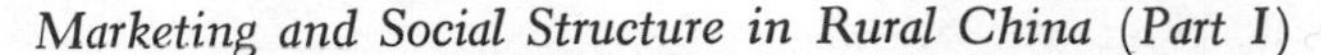

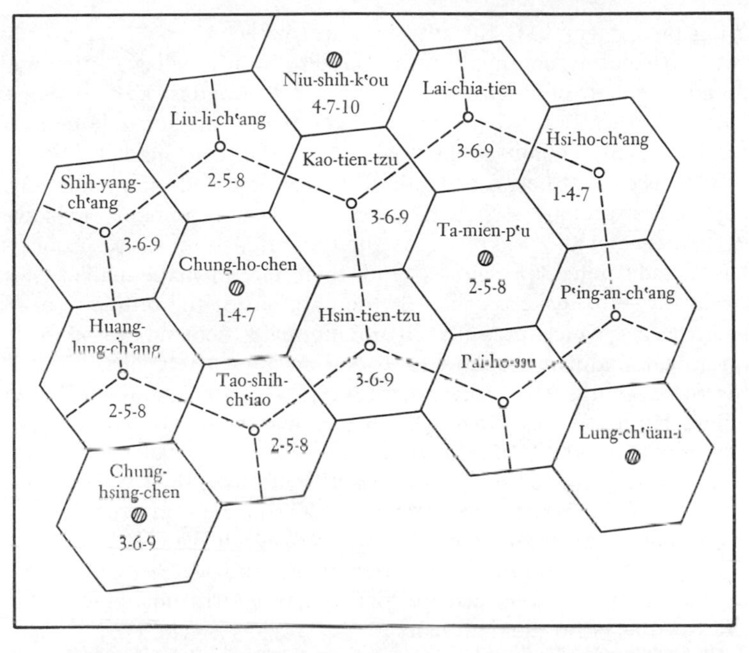

FIGURE 3. A portion of the economic landscape in Szechwan approximating Model B in the distribution of market towns.

3.1: The 15 market towns depicted lie to the southeast of Chengtu within a radius of 25 km. Three markets (P'ing-an-ch'ang, Lung-ch'üan-i, and Pai-ho-ssu) are in Chien-yang hsien, the other 12 in Hua-yang hsien. The terrain varies from flat to hilly; Lung-ch'üan-i is situated at the western foothills of the Lung-ch'üan mountain range. Marketing-area boundaries are only approximate.

3.2: First abstraction of the same landscape showing theoretic standard and intermediate marketing areas.

3.3: The same reduced to diagrammatic form. Compare with Model B as diagrammed in Figure 1.

town functions as the nucleus not only of the larger intermediate marketing system but also of a smaller standard marketing system.[27] As C. K.

[27] Everything which a peasant can do in his standard market can also be accomplished in his intermediate market. For those villages whose closest market is situated in an intermediate market town, the intermediate market is also the standard market.

Yang puts it (p. 14), the intermediate market town ". . . usually has two service areas, a primary area including nearby villages attending the market regularly or at least frequently, and a secondary area encompassing villages farther away where people come to the market only occasionally for items hard to obtain in their own . . . [standard] markets." [28]

Why is conflict between standard market days and intermediate market days so consistently eschewed? Clearly it is not primarily to serve the convenience of the peasantry. As the quotation from C. K. Yang's study has already noted, peasants attend their intermediate market only occasionally — to make purchases which are out of the ordinary, to obtain some service which peasants do not normally demand, to secure credit on an extraordinary scale, or to attend an annual religious festival. During three months when I lived with a typical peasant family in Szechwan, whose farmstead was three *li* from one market town, Kao-tien-tzu, and five li from another, Niu-shih-k'ou, the household head and his wife between them marketed forty-six times at the former, their standard market, and only three times at the latter, their intermediate market. In any case, the peasant's intermediate marketing needs would have been given ample scope by any scheduling distribution which provided out of every hsün or duodenum one intermediate market day which did not conflict with the schedule of his standard market.

The situation was rather different in the case of the local élite. Everything which set them apart from the peasantry encouraged their attendance at the intermediate market. They were literate, and in the intermediate as opposed to the standard market they could buy books and stationery supplies. Their style of life was if not exalted at least gentlemanly, and from time to time they needed to purchase foodstuffs, decorative items, or cloth of a quality which for a peasant would be sheer indulgence and hence unavailable in standard markets. They were men of comparative wealth, and the intermediate market town offered a range of opportunities for money lending and investment unmatched in their standard market towns. They were also men of leisure, and it was only in intermediate or higher-level markets that tea- and wine-houses especially equipped to fill the idle hours of leisured gentlemen were available. In short, while the regular needs of the peasants were met by the standard market, those of the local élite were met only by the intermediate market.

If the carefully attuned schedules as between an intermediate market

[28] The place of the intermediate market in the distribution system gives it certain economic advantages vis-à-vis neighboring standard markets in the competition for peasant (i.e. standard-market) trade. Prices paid for local produce tend to be slightly higher, and prices charged for imported items tend to be slightly lower in the intermediate markets than in standard markets. One therefore expects standard marketing areas centered on intermediate market towns to be somewhat larger than neighboring standard marketing areas centered on standard market towns.

and its dependent standard markets were for local élite a very real convenience, for many of the local traders they were an absolute necessity. A sizable proportion of the "mobile firms" in rural China followed a circuit limited to a single intermediate marketing system; their home base was in the intermediate market town, and they needed to return there periodically to dispose of what they were buying, to restock what they were selling, and simply to rest with their families.

A reference to Fig. 3.3 can illustrate how the intermediate market's exclusive schedule served the purposes of itinerant entrepreneurs. Take the case of the system centering on Chung-ho chen. A typical circuit would have the itinerant in the intermediate market for its market day on the 1st of the lunar month, in Huang-lung-ch'ang on the 2nd, Shih-yang-ch'ang on the 3rd, and back to Chung-ho chen for its market day on the 4th; on to Liu-li ch'ang on the 5th, Kao-tien-tzu on the 6th, and back to the central town for its market day on the 7th; then to Tao-shih-ch'iao on the 8th, Hsin-tien-tzu on the 9th, and back to Chung-ho chen on the 10th for a day of rest prior to entering the town's market on the 11th. Thus in each lunar *hsün* the itinerant completes a full circuit during which he has three market days at the intermediate market and one market day each at the six dependent standard markets. Those making circuits of this kind include purveyors of services with limited demand among the peasantry (the tooth artist, say, or the letter writer), artisans in crafts not usually represented among shops in the standard market town, hawkers of products imported from central markets or produced in the intermediate market town, and purchasing agents, of which more below.

Let us now look over the total complex of nested marketing systems and survey, first of all, the downward flow of merchandise. Exotic goods shipped to the central market town, and other goods produced in it, are distributed in part through the central market itself, in part by itinerants who circuit both intermediate and standard markets throughout the central marketing system, and in part to firms in the six intermediate market towns. Merchandise received by firms in each intermediate market town, together with other goods produced there, are similarly distributed: in part through the intermediate market itself, in part by itinerants who circuit standard markets within the intermediate marketing system, and in part to firms in the six standard market towns. The firms receiving goods in this downward flow consist, in the case of standard market towns, chiefly of small shops; in the case of intermediate market towns they include distributors who supply itinerants as well as dual wholesale-retail establishments; [29] and in the case of central market towns they include

[29] Cf. C. K. Yang, pp. 32–33: "Only four stores in Sunchiachen and seven stores in the County Seat [both intermediate market towns] do a very limited wholesale business along . . . with retailing which holds their main attention."

most prominently wholesalers equipped with warehouses. Merchandise which is consumed by the peasantry or required by petty craftsmen flows down through the system to every market; consumer goods for the local élite and supplies for artisans move no further down than the intermediate market; while consumer goods of interest chiefly to the bureaucratic élite, together with industrial supplies, normally go no further than the central market town itself.

The flow of goods upward through the marketing system begins when the peasant sells his product in the standard market, either to local consumers, to dealers based in the standard market who process and/or bulk the product, or directly to buyers who are visiting the standard market from higher-level market towns. Purchasing agents and buyers visit standard markets from central as well as intermediate market towns; they visit intermediate markets from local cities as well as central market towns. Whether the collecting firms are commercial houses or industries which process or consume the local products, these products are drawn up through the marketing system to ever higher-level centers.

In considering its significance for the interpretation of Chinese society as a total system, one must distinguish marketing from administration. To be sure, both were hierarchical systems in which the relevant territorial unit was larger at each ascending level. And in both, limited bureaucratic resources were concentrated at the higher levels: marketing systems below that of the central market, like administrative systems below the hsien, were subject to bureaucratic controls in only very attenuated form.

A fundamental difference is apparent, however, in the *manner* in which each of the two structures was articulated. Administrative units are, virtually by definition, discrete at all levels; every lower-level unit belongs to only one unit at each ascending level of the structure. Marketing systems, by contrast, are discrete *only* at the basic level, and each lower-level system is typically oriented to two or three systems at each ascending level. As a result, marketing structures, unlike administrative structures, take the form of interlocking networks. It is the joint participation of standard markets in two or three intermediate marketing systems, of intermediate markets in two or three central marketing systems, and so on, which articulates and unites the little local economies centered on each market town into, first, regional economic structures and eventually into a single society-wide economy. Thus, marketing had a significance for societal integration in traditional China which at once paralleled and surpassed — which both reinforced and complemented — that of administration.

The complexity of the whole, however, should not be taken to imply that the marketing system was either monolithic or tightly structured. Not only was there no one economic apex paralleling the administrative capital, but the flow of goods, which defined the structure, was seldom very heavy by modern standards. Moreover, as we shall see in the next section, each of the component standard marketing subsystems persisted in an economic subculture all its own.

MARKETING STRUCTURES AS SOCIAL SYSTEMS

Chinese marketing systems have important social as well as economic dimensions. The standard marketing system in particular is a unit whose social significance for the peasantry and for peasant relations with other groups deserves major attention. In order to suggest an emphasis suited to my purpose in this section, I shall call it henceforward the standard marketing *community*. There is good reason, I believe, for attempting to analyze this type of community not only as an intermediate social structure but also as a culture-bearing unit — the locus in the Chinese case of Redfield's "little tradition." [30]

Anthropological work on Chinese society, by focusing attention almost exclusively on the village, has with few exceptions distorted the reality of rural social structure. Insofar as the Chinese peasant can be said to live in a self-contained world, that world is not the village but the standard marketing community. The effective social field of the peasant, I will argue, is delimited not by the narrow horizons of his village but rather by the boundaries of his standard marketing area.

We may begin by asking how big this area normally is and how many people the community typically includes. So as to avoid the protraction of citing numerous examples, I present a set of estimates which incorporates and reconciles data from all relevant empirical cases available to me. Table 1, based on a simple graphic model, points up the obvious but nonetheless extremely important fact that the size of standard marketing areas varies inversely with density of population. In regions where the population is sparsely distributed on the land, marketing areas must be large in order to encompass enough demand to support the market; in densely settled regions they are small. The table also reveals a relationship which common sense does not necessarily foretell — namely, that the average population of marketing communities increases along with population density *only up to a point*. As densities rise above 325 persons per square kilometer — and as standard marketing areas fall below 27 square kilometers in size — the average population of marketing systems begins to decline. A full understanding of why marketing areas come

[30] Robert Redfield, *Peasant Society and Culture* (Chicago, 1956), p. 70 ff. It may, in the case of China, be only a minor distortion to conceive of the "great tradition" as unitary and homogeneous, but the variety and heterogeneity of its counterpart among the peasantry preclude any such conception. Instead of one "little tradition" there were many, and I allude here to the tendency for each to be associated with a standard marketing community.

to be as small as they are in very densely settled areas must await the analysis of change in Part II [of this article; see p. 65 for reference], but there is nothing mysterious about the kind of relationship which Table 1 shows between the population and the area of marketing systems. Given a steady decline in the size of marketing areas as one moves from densely to very densely populated regions, it is apparent that the point must eventually be reached wherever smaller areas cannot sustain ever larger agrarian populations. In agricultural China[31] at the end of the republican period, that point fell in the 300–350 density range.

Very large marketing areas of 150 or more square kilometers (at the top of the Table) occur only in mountainous regions and on the arid peripheries of agricultural China, where population is very sparsely distributed over a generally forbidding landscape. Only in such regions does one normally find marketing communities with as few as 3,000 people. At the other extreme, the very small marketing areas of 15 square kilometers or less (at the bottom of the Table) occur only on plains of exceptional fertility, situated in the typical case near major urban centers. The distribution by size of standard marketing areas in agricultural China may be summarized as follows:

Proportion of all standard marketing communities	*Range in average areas (sq. km.)*	*Range in densities: Persons per sq. km.*
5%	158-	- 19
15%	97-157	20- 59
60%	30- 96	60-299
15%	16- 29	300-499
5%	15	500-

The majority of standard marketing areas, then, are of a size which puts the most disadvantaged villager within easy walking distance of the town

[31] As used in this paper, "agricultural China" refers to a specifically defined contiguous area inclusive for the most part of what used to be called China Proper. The line separating agricultural from non-agricultural China was drawn along hsien boundaries (as of 1958) so as to include in the former practically all hsien with population densities of at least 10 per square kilometer. In lieu of a map defining this line, its course may be briefly described (in terms of 1958 provinces) as excluding approximately the northern third of Heilungkiang; including all of Kirin, Liaoning, Hopei, Shansi and Shensi; including a small portion of Inner Mongolia A. R., approximately two-fifths of Ningsia A. R., most of Kansu, and a few hsien in easternmost Tsinghai; and excluding the mountainous tracts in the west of Szechwan and Yunnan. Agricultural China (inclusive of Hainan but not Taiwan) incorporates 4,180,000 sq. km., as compared with 4,159,400 sq. km. in non-agricultural China (exclusive of Tibet and Chamdo). In 1958 there were 1,791 hsien-level units in the former, and 260 in the latter.

In general, land productivity is so low and population so thinly settled in what is here defined as non-agricultural China that marketing systems cannot exist in the form described in this paper.

— 3.4 to 6.1 kilometers.[32] In the modal case (see bottom of Table 1) marketing areas are just over 50 square kilometers in size, market towns are less than eight kilometers apart, and maximum walking distance to the town is approximately 4.5 km. The average (mean) population of the standard marketing community is somewhat over 7,000.

It is clear, then, that even in the case of the typical community — 1,500 households in eighteen or so villages distributed over fifty square kilometers — we are not dealing with a cozy primary group structured through bonds of great intimacy or intensity. On the other hand, unused as most students of China are to thinking of marketing systems as communities and given the burden of the relevant literature, we are likely to be led far astray in this regard. Let me illustrate with the community centered on Kao-tien-tzu, the standard market town which I studied in Szechwan. With some 2,500 households in 1949–50, it was an atypically large system.[33] Did the average peasant even recognize much less *know* the members of so many households?

If Mr. Lin, the 45-year-old peasant with whom I lived, may be considered at all typical, then the answer is yes. For Mr. Lin had a nodding acquaintance with almost every adult in all parts of the marketing system.[34] He could, moreover, identify and describe the community's leading élite families, in no matter which of the dispersed villages they lived. He knew details about peasant families on the other side of the market

[32] I see no merit in the notion that "walking distance" is in any sense a *determinant* of the size of marketing areas. Cf. C. K. Yang, pp. 14–15. If the spacing of market towns were somehow set simply to enable the most disadvantaged villager to walk to his market, carry out his business and return home during the daylight hours, then the size of standard marketing areas would vary within a narrow range. In fact, most of China's standard marketing areas are far smaller than any consideration of walking distance requires, and in areas on the periphery of agricultural China, they become so large that the one-way trip to market from disadvantageously situated villages takes more than one day. This would appear to be the case with a number of villages in the vicinity of Yits'un, Yunnan, if one may judge from the details supplied by Fei Hsiao-t'ung and Chang Chih-i, pp. 170–172.

[33] Standard marketing systems in northwestern Szechwan were atypically large in the late republican period because the area was relatively uncommercialized. See Part II [of this article; see p. 65 for reference].

[34] Exceptions were for the most part limited to the households of "outsiders" living on or near the highway at the northeastern rim of Kao-tien-tzu's marketing area. That part of the marketing area which lay nearest to Chengtu and through which the highway passed included in 1947 approximately 140 "downriver" Chinese, i.e., Chinese from provinces other than Szechwan, most of whom had come to the vicinity of Chengtu during World War II; and approximately 290 Szechwanese whose native place lay outside Hua-yang hsien. Few of these outsiders were peasants; some were shopkeepers in the *yao-tien* on the highway, others were rickshaw pullers or transport coolies who "worked" the intermediate marketing system centered on Niu-shih-k'ou, and still others were suburban residents with jobs in the city. Mr. Lin knew few of these individuals and cared little about them. "Outsiders" in the market town itself, however, were another matter. In 1947 there were 58 such individuals, including shopkeepers and schoolteachers; all were Szechwanese, and Mr. Lin knew most of them.

TABLE 1. AVERAGE AREA AND POPULATION OF STANDARD MARKETING COMMUNITIES, AS A FUNCTION OF POPULATION DENSITY; 1948 ESTIMATES FOR AGRICULTURAL CHINA*

	Density: persons per sq. km.	*Average population*	*Average area in sq. km.*	*Ave. distance traveled by most disadvantaged villager (km.)*	*Average distance (km.) between market towns*
	10	1850	185	8.44	14.6
	20	3160	158	7.80	13.5
	30	4080	136	7.24	12.5
	40	4800	120	6.80	11.8
	50	5300	106	6.39	11.1
	60	5790	96.5	6.09	10.6
	70	6160	88.0	5.72	9.91
	80	6500	81.3	5.59	9.69
	90	6750	75.0	5.37	9.31
	100	6980	69.8	5.18	8.98
	125	7460	59.7	4.79	8.31
	150	7870	52.5	4.50	7.79
	175	8050	46.0	4.11	7.12
	200	8240	41.2	3.98	6.90
	225	8350	37.1	3.78	6.55
	250	8570	34.3	3.63	6.30
	275	8720	31.7	3.49	6.05
	300	8850	29.5	3.37	5.84
	325	8870	27.3	3.24	5.62
	350	8790	25.1	3.11	5.39
	375	8660	23.1	2.98	5.17
	400	8640	21.6	2.88	5.00
	450	8100	18.0	2.63	4.56
	500	7850	15.7	2.46	4.26
	550	7320	13.3	2.26	3.92
	600	7140	11.9	2.14	3.71
	650	6760	10.4	2.00	3.47
	700	6370	9.1	1.87	3.24
Average for agric. China:	111	7140	64.4		
The modal case:	150	7870	52.5	4.50	7.79

* The curve which graphs the relationship between size of standard marketing area and population density is closer to the axes of ordinates and abscissas the more commercialized the agrarian economy. The specific curve from which the above figures for average areas were taken was designed to represent the situation in an agrarian economy commercialized to the extent that all of agricultural China was in 1948. Its contours derive from the data plotted for 76 hsien in south and southeastern Szechwan, but it was positioned somewhat closer to the axes in accordance with points on the graph provided by known cases of hsien more commercialized than any in Szechwan as of 1948. Justification for these procedures

town which most Americans would not know — and would not care to know — about their next-door neighbors. Mr. Lin's social knowledge of Kao-tien-tzu's marketing community was more impressive, perhaps, than that of the agricultural laborer who shared his compound or the transport coolie who carted his tangerines to market, but it paled by comparison with the informed social wisdom of any leisured gentleman among the community's local élite. The long-robed landlord might nod to only a favored few, but he recognized everyone he passed on the way to market and appeared to carry in his head a full dossier on each.

But is it after all so remarkable? The peasant in Kao-tien-tzu's marketing community had, by the age of fifty, attended his standard market more than three thousand times. He had, at least one thousand times on the average, been jammed into a small area along one street with the same male representative of every other household in that community.[35] He made purchases from peasant vendors whose homes lay in all directions from the town, and more to the point, he socialized in the teahouses with fellow peasants from village communities far removed from his own. Nor was the peasant alone in this, for in Kao-tien-tzu there was a teahouse for everyone, and few persons who went to market failed to spend at least an hour in one or two. Codes of hospitality and sociability operated to bring any community member who entered the door quickly to a table as somebody's guest. Inevitably an hour in the teahouse enlarged a man's circle of acquaintances and deepened his social knowledge of other parts of the community.

Let us pause at this point to note certain structural consequences of the fact that a peasant develops a fairly good social map of his standard

---

must await the treatment of commercialization and modernization in Part II [see p. 65 for reference].

The next-to-last column is computed from the average area according to the following formula for regular hexagons: $A = 2.598a^2$, where A is the area of the hexagon (i.e., of the standard marketing area) and a is the distance from its center to one of the six corners (i.e., the distance to be traveled from the most disadvantaged spot in the area). The last column is computed according to the formula $b = a\sqrt{3}$, where b is the distance between the center of two adjacent regular hexagons.

[35] This assertion takes into account the comparative stability in the membership of Kao-tien-tzu's marketing community from one generation to the next. The social knowledge gained during each market day is cumulative over a lifetime in direct proportion to the continuity of resident households and in inverse proportion to the amount of family migration into and out of the marketing community. Of the families in Kao-tien-tzu's community in the late 1940's, the great majority were a direct continuation of families already resident there at the turn of the century; of the new households, more had been formed through segmentation of local families than had been established by in-migrants. Even in the case of the small portion of the marketing area through which the highway passed (described in Footnote 34), no less than 80 per cent of the households included no one born outside the district in which they now lived. In the much larger portion of the marketing area away from the highway — including four-fifths of the community's population — over 95 per cent of all households consisted solely of locally born individuals. Cf. G. W. Skinner, "A Study in Miniature of Chinese Population," *Population Studies*, V (Nov. 1951), 91–103.

marketing area whereas the social terrain beyond it is largely unexplored. It means that the services he requires — whether of a midwife, a tailor, or a hired hand — will be sought for the most part from households within the system, thereby building up a modest network of patron-client relationships all contained within the standard marketing community. It means, as noted in the preceding section, that a man in need of funds is able to look far beyond the bounds of his own village in forming a rotating-credit society.

It means, too, that daughters-in-law tend to be taken from within the marketing community. Marriage brokers — who in Szechwan operated in certain teahouses of the market town — and mothers of marriageable sons are able with considerable assurance to scan the entire standard marketing community for potential daughters-in-law; seldom, however, do they know enough to find candidates from households outside the system. There is, in short, a distinct tendency for the standard marketing community to be endogamous for the peasantry. An interesting confirmation of this point comes from Jean Pratt Watts' study of a Hakka village community in the New Territories of Hong Kong: The most active and successful marriage broker in the village was a widow of means who indeed went with exceptional frequency to her market town, Tai Po, which has a daily schedule — where she kept tabs on marriageable girls in the larger community.[36] In consequence, the arrangements whereby one lineage traditionally gives its young girls as brides to another tend to be concentrated within standard marketing communities, as are also the more nearly *ad hoc* alliances which may have no immediate precedent. The affinal bonds of the peasant thus constitute another network which spreads through the standard marketing community and gives structure to the whole.

On the agnatic side of kinship, I suspect that the standard marketing community plays a role in lineage organization which may resolve a vexing analytical problem. New villages have traditionally been founded in China either by a single family or by a small group of patrilineally related families. The households in such a new settlement constitute in effect an offshoot of the lineage localized in their village of origin, often not far away. Through segmentation of this kind over a period of centuries, certain portions of the Chinese rural landscape have come to support a number of localized lineages of the same surname, all historically related by virtue of descent from a common ancestor, but each situated in a different village or market town.[37] Why is it that in some cases neighbor-

[36] Personal communication of 8 February 1964. Also see Jean A. Pratt, "Immigration and Unilineal Descent Groups: A Study of Marriage in a Hakka Village in the New Territories, Hong Kong," *Eastern Anthropologist*, XIII (1960), 147–158.

[37] Several examples from Chin-chiang hsien, Fukien, are cited by Father Amyot in his description of the home territory of the Philippine Chinese. Jacques Amyot, S.J., *The Chinese Community of Manila: A Study of Adaptation of Chinese*

ing localized lineages perpetuate or achieve organizational unity, whereas others, agnatically related through equally recent bonds, function as independent systems? My suggestion here is that, since peasant families have much social intercourse within their standard marketing community but little outside it, interlineage ties contained within a single marketing system are likely to be perpetuated whereas bonds between localized lineages sited in different standard marketing areas tend to erode with time. In the region of Szechwan where I did my research, Hakka families surnamed Lin were heavily concentrated in the three standard marketing areas centered on Kao-tien-tzu, Lai-chia-tien, and Ta-mien-p'u. The Lin households within each, however, seemed to be separately organized, with headquarters in teahouses of their respective market towns. Mizuno notes that in north China it is market towns rather than villages which normally support ancestral halls.[38] It may well be, therefore, that we should look to the standard marketing community as the usual locus of the "composite lineage."

I have another suggestive case to mention in this regard. In the standard marketing community of Kang-wei, Hai-ch'eng hsien, Fukien, an easy majority of the entire population belongs to a single composite lineage. The market itself was in 1948 controlled by the *ta-fang* (literally "great branch"), one of the component lineages localized in a village to the north of the market town. In the Kang-wei market the three grain measurers, the livestock agent and pig weigher, the chief of the palanquin bearers, and even the head of the beggars were all drawn from the ta-fang, and buyers from the ta-fang had special privileges at market. In this case, the ascendant social position of the ta-fang within the composite lineage is clearly expressed within the economic system of the marketing community. It would appear that just as the dominant branch in a localized lineage is, in appropriate circumstances, able to assert supreme power in the village community,[39] so the dominant localized lineage within a composite lineage may arrogate preponderant control in the marketing community.[40]

The case of Kang-wei also points up the fact that the power structure of a standard marketing community is, under the circumstances, unlikely

---

Familism to the Philippine Environment (Chicago, 1960), pp. 44–52. After noting that the villages in which lineages of the same surname are localized tend to be concentrated in a particular *hsiang*, Amyot states (p. 40): "In the usage of this area, the term *hsiang* may designate either a complex of villages and hamlets forming some kind of unity, or again, the largest village of the complex from which the latter derives its name. It is usually a market town."

[38] Mizuno Kaoru, *Hokushi no nōson* [*North China's Villages*] (Peking, 1941), p. 171.

[39] Cf. Maurice Freedman, *Lineage Organization in Southeastern China* (London, 1958), Chs. 8–9.

[40] Fang-chih themselves occasionally provide a glimpse of the controlling power which a dominant lineage holds in a particular market. See, e.g., Kuramochi, p. 25.

to be divorced from control of the market itself. In Szechwan during the republican period, the secret societies collectively known as the *Ko-lao hui* wielded supreme power at all levels of rural society — and the standard marketing community was no exception. It was, in fact, a most crucial unit, for lodges of the society were organized by, and limited in almost every case to, a single standard marketing community. There were two lodges organized within the standard marketing community centered on Kao-tien-tzu, one "clear" and one "muddy"; both had their headquarters and held their meetings in teahouses in the town. A majority of male adults belonged to one or the other, and on almost every market day members were able to conduct business with the officers of the lodge, who could be found in a particular teahouse. In Kao-tien-tzu, as in many other market towns of the Szechwan Basin, the market itself was controlled by one of the secret-society lodges. The positions of grain measurers, pig weighers, livestock middlemen, and certain other commission agents were reserved for society members, and a portion of each agent's fees was claimed for the coffers of the lodge.

Elsewhere in China, control of the market may be more widely dispersed among the several founding villages. A common arrangement in Shantung rotates responsibility for market management among the participating villages; during each hsün of the lunar month, a given village or several villages jointly undertake to provide and subsidize public measurers to render service as honest brokers free of charge. The examples cited by C. K. Yang, however, indicate that dispersed control of this kind is limited to minor markets and less important standard markets; in the case of intermediate markets (and apparently some of the larger standard markets), authority tends to be concentrated, both because communal control by the large number of villages involved is infeasible and because the commission fees at a large and prosperous market constitute too lucrative a prize to be ignored by groups with the power to claim it.[41]

The market itself, then, constitutes one focus of social structure within the marketing community. Another, of scarcely less importance, is often provided by the major temple of the town. To begin with, the committee which runs the temple is normally composed not only of devout townspeople but also of leading citizens with religious leanings who live in village communities throughout the marketing area. The annual fair, normally held in connection with the feast day of the temple's principal deity, is, however, too important an event to be left to the pious. In Kao-tien-tzu it was organized by a committee on which leading shopkeepers and the most powerful members of the landed élite both served. The local police unit which was formed every year at festival time to control the crowds and direct the procession, consisted in 1950 of some sixty volunteers including, again, individuals from all parts of the marketing

[41] C. K. Yang, pp. 18–20.

community. Moreover, the earthly domain of the temple deity himself was seen as corresponding to the standard marketing area. Each year the graven image of Tung-yüeh, a bureaucratic official of the underworld, was carried in procession through the area of his jurisdiction. The traditional route, which followed each of the main roads radiating from town, carried him in turn to Hung-men-p'u, Sha-ho-p'u, O-o-tien, and Ta-shih-tzu — each a yao-tien situated at one of the corners of the marketing area. In this manner, the religious festival provided an annual reaffirmation of the community's territorial extent and a symbolic reinforcement of its town-centered structure.

The discreteness of the standard marketing community is given religious expression in yet another way. Service groups of the devout participate in religious festivals by organizing joint offerings to the deity being celebrated and by participating as a group in the procession. Over thirty such groups took part in Kao-tien-tzu's annual fair in 1950, and with the exception of three from Chengtu, each group was limited in membership to a single standard marketing community, those from outside communities being identified by the name of the market town in question. It is likely that the *hsiang-hui* ("incense societies") and *shan-hui* ("mountain societies") which conducted pilgrimages to sacred shrines in traditional times were normally organized within the standard marketing community, if only because the bureaucracy discouraged organized religious activity on a larger scale.[42]

These examples indicate that a variety of voluntary associations and other formal organizations — the composite lineage, the secret-society lodge, the committee on arrangements for the annual fair, the religious service society — take the standard marketing community as the unit of organization.[43] Occupational groups, too, may be organized within the standard marketing community. One teahouse in Kao-tien-tzu was the meeting place of an association of animal breeders, another the headquarters of associations of carpenters and housebuilders. Still other voluntary associations, especially those related to agricultural production (crop-watching or irrigation societies, for instance), although not coterminous with the marketing community tended to be wholly contained within it.[44]

It remains to mention that the standard marketing community is the relevant context of organized recreation for the peasantry. Standard and higher-level markets constitute the arena of professional storytellers,

[42] Cf. Hsiao Kung-chuan, *Rural China: Imperial Control in the Nineteenth Century* (Seattle, 1960), pp. 313–14.

[43] An account of 1836 describes the establishment of an organization on Ho-nan island, near Canton, which can only be interpreted as a formalization of structure within a standard marketing community: "Twenty-four different villages have joined together to build a large house for purposes of general consultations; this stands at the market town. . ." *Chinese Repository*, IV (1836), p. 414. Cited in Hsiao, p. 309.

[44] Hsiao, pp. 288–289, 306–308.

theatrical troupes, blind singers, purveyors of games of chance, boxers, jugglers, performing medicine sellers, and magicians. Such professionals are notably absent not only from villages but in the usual case from minor markets as well. Just as market day brings relief from the tedium of rural life through the provision of recreational opportunities, so the temple fair affords the high point in the villagers' recreational year.

Insofar as this survey has demonstrated the structural reality of the standard marketing community, it will at the same time have provided a basis for assessing the extent to which such a community serves as a culture-bearing unit. There is in the literature a good deal of loose generalization concerning the cultural idiosyncrasy of Chinese villages. Each village, we are often told, has its own dialect, its own culinary specialities, its own version of the peasant hat, and so on. I strongly suspect, however, that when appreciable differences characterize the culture of adjacent villages, the villages in question will prove to belong to different standard marketing communities. It may well be true that in traditional times the typical peasant saw more of his fellow villagers than of all outsiders put together. But at the same time so much of his social interaction was with those from villages other than his own within the marketing community that it is difficult to imagine how cultural peculiarities of any magnitude could persist as between villages using the same standard market. By the same token, so little of the peasant's social intercourse brought him into contact with persons from outside his standard marketing community that the development of cultural distinctiveness as between marketing communities would appear inevitable. To the extent that the standard marketing community contained the peasant's life, it shaped the way he lived it. And if that community had long endured, it perforce carried on a little tradition of its own.

The most obvious case in point concerns the weights and measures associated with the marketing process itself. While they are standardized and in fact closely regulated within any one market,[45] considerable variation occurs from one standard market to another. In eleven markets investigated in 1932, C. K. Yang found ten different standards for the *tou*, the dry measure used to portion out grain. The *ta-ch'ih* ("big rule") used to measure homespun, and the *ta-ch'eng* ("big scale") for weighing bulky products likewise varied within a wide range from one market to the next.[46] In his study of crop marketing along the Peking-Hankow railroad, Ōhashi Ikuei found that purchasing agents working out of central market towns were forced to carry with them tables of equivalence for the weights and measures used in the various local markets of the system.[47] Data of this kind point up the relative independence and isolation of the standard marketing community *qua* economic system — and

[45] Documents specifying the weights and measures to be used in individual markets are cited by Kuramochi, p. 24, and by C. K. Yang, pp. 18–19.

[46] C. K. Yang, pp. 20–21. The situation in this regard was, as late as 1950, very similar in the Szechwan Basin.

[47] Cited in Amano, p. 156.

thereby point to the very circumstances which underlie the cultural idiosyncrasy of each. In the last analysis, it is traditional marketing patterns of long standing which account for the fact — to cite a typical example — that the cross-stitch designs with which every Szechwan girl painstakingly adorns the hangings for her bridal bed bear the characteristic stamp of her standard marketing community.

An equally obvious case in point concerns religious folklore, and in this regard many illustrations can be gleaned from Grootaers' geographical analysis of temples and folklore in northern China.[48] One of the maps shows, for instance, that the cult of Hei Lung, the Black Dragon, is concentrated in a single circumscribed section of Wan-ch'üan hsien, Chahar. Reference to large-scale maps of this region strongly suggests that this particular area, in which six temples to the deity in question are extant, is in fact the standard marketing area centered on the town of Chiu-p'u. In the marketing community of Kao-tien-tzu, the lore of Tung-yüeh and his hellish bureaucracy inevitably looms large in the peasant's conception of the other world, but in the religious culture of surrounding marketing communities, this deity and his court are of relative insignificance.

In the case of language, too, one expects minimal variation within a standard marketing community — in view of the massive amount of verbal interaction which takes place at market — but a degree of distinctiveness as between marketing communities. It occurred to me, when my informants in Szechwan used to discourse on the peculiarities of speech characteristic of the different markets, that the minimal unit of significance to the dialect geographer of China is precisely the standard marketing area.

I have little evidence concerning the social dimensions of higher-level marketing systems in China, but there are two points I should like to make in this connection. It seems clear that in many respects Chinese social structure at the lower-intermediate levels parallels the marketing structure described in the preceding section and, like it, takes the form of a hierarchical network. Let me illustrate once again with the case of Kao-tien-tzu. This standard market town is, in accordance with Model B, oriented toward three higher-level market towns, and hence a part of three different intermediate marketing systems (see Fig. 3.1). Each of these structural bonds is paralleled by hierarchical arrangements involving a number of different social organizations. I restrict myself to one example apiece: (1) Liao households in the Kao-tien-tzu marketing community are, like those surnamed Lin, organized into a composite lineage with headquarters in the market town, but the Liaos consider their organization to be merely a *branch* of the far more inclusive composite lineage which maintains an ancestral hall in Ta-mien-p'u, the intermediate market town to the southeast. (2) The Chih-chung *ju-yüan* ("Confucian

[48] Willem A. Grootaers, "Temples and History of Wan-ch'üan (Chahar), the Geographical Method Applied to Folklore," *Monumenta Serica*, XIII (1948), 209–216.

hall" — a benevolent society) of Kao-tien-tzu maintains close relations with a superior hall known as Chung-ho ju-yüan and situated in Chung-ho chen, the intermediate market town to the southwest. Finally (3), let me refer once again to the secret-society lodges which, while essentially independent, are nonetheless united into rather extensive federations. Kao-tien-tzu's lodge in one of these federations is tied in the first instance to its counterpart in Niu-shih-k'ou, the intermediate market town to the northwest.

It should be explicitly noted that these organizations are officered or controlled not by peasants but by leisured gentlemen, and that in general the links between organizations at the two levels are effected, if not by members of the local élite, then by the merchants who have business interests in both standard and intermediate market towns. In Kao-tien-tzu, to note a datum of similar import, peasant members of the secret society belong only to one or the other of the two lodges in their standard market town, whereas merchants and members of the local élite not infrequently find it advantageous to belong to a lodge in their intermediate market town as well.

This observation leads to my second point: marketing systems at each level in the hierarchy have a distinctive significance for interclass relations. From this point of view, the standard marketing community can be seen as the locus of such intercourse as petty traders have with the peasantry on the one hand and with the local élite (primarily through the mechanism of market control) on the other. But its primary significance pertains to the relations between peasantry and "gentry." Whereas many individual villages could boast of no families which were at once landed, leisured, and literate, every standard marketing community included in traditional times a number of so-called "gentry" families. And it was in the market town that these élitist families exerted "social control," to use the usual imprecise term. Every gentleman who aspired to even informal leadership normally held court in a particular teahouse at his standard market, and disputes among peasants in different village communities were usually mediated by such leaders in the teahouses on market days.[49] It was in the market town, too, that landlords or their agents dealt with tenants, and upper-class officials of the secret-society lodge made the policy decisions which affected peasant welfare throughout the community.

The concept of the local élite as an intermediary and a buffer between the peasantry and the bureaucratic élite is — though the terminology may seem peculiar — a familiar one. And so is the view of the petty trader as a middleman between the peasantry and the merchants in higher-level central places. Both functioned as "brokers" [50] who at once shielded the

[49] Li Mei-yun, p. 212.

[50] Eric Wolf refers to the Janus-faced qualities of the individuals who serve as "brokers" between community-oriented and nation-oriented groups. "Aspects of Group Relations in a Complex Society: Mexico," *American Anthropologist*, LVIII (1956), p. 1076.

peasant from an outside world which he distrusted and selectively filtered and transmitted to him its products — a few necessities of exotic origin, imperial edicts as "adjusted" to local conditions, bits of the great tradition as distorted by story tellers or of élite ideology as adapted by *hsiang-yüeh* lecturers.[51] My point here is simply that these Janus-faced "brokers" — whether cultural, political or economic — operated at the level of the standard market town, not the village. It was the standard marketing community which they linked to or — depending on one's perspective — isolated from the institutions of the larger society.

The social sphere of the *intermediate* market town [52] is essentially a world which the intermediaries of rural society have to themselves. Insofar as the intermediate marketing system is a social community, it is one which normally excludes both the peasantry and the bureaucratic élite. In the teahouses, winehouses, and restaurants of the intermediate market town, representatives of the local élite from the whole ring of surrounding standard marketing communities direct the affairs of the wider area served by the intermediate marketing system. The situation is comparable in the case of merchants, traders, and artisans whose business world is primarily confined within a given intermediate marketing system, for their intraclass affairs are also conducted in the intermediate market town. But perhaps the most interesting of the social relations peculiar to the intermediate marketing system are the interclass dealings between the gentlemanly élite and the merchants of the market town itself. For the crucial negotiations whereby, on the one hand, "gentry" capital is invested in the pawnbroking, moneylending, artisan manufacture, and commercial enterprise of the intermediate marketing system and, on the other, the capital of the artisan and tradesman is invested in agricultural land and translated into the coin of social respectibility — these dealings, too, are carried on in the teahouses and townhouses of market towns at this level.

The interclass significance of the *central* market town is distinguished by the addition to the field of the bureaucratic élite. It may be assumed that towns at this level are the locus not only of the various intergroup relations already noted for lower-level markets, but also of the critical

[51] Hsiao Kung-chuan's monograph is rich in detail concerning the interrelations between peasant villagers, members of the local élite, and bureaucratic officials. Many of these data are profitably analyzed in terms of local-élite brokerage between the peasantry and bureaucratic officialdom. For the hsiang-yüeh lecture system, see pp. 184–206.

[52] As noted in the preceding section the intermediate market town served as the center not only of an intermediate marketing system but also of a smaller standard marketing system, and the town had a dual function. Each intermediate market town was, for instance, the locus, on the one hand, of interclass relations between peasants and the local élite of its *standard* marketing area and, on the other, of interclass relations between traders and the local élite of its *intermediate* marketing system. It is nonetheless useful to keep the two functional levels analytically distinct. Certain teahouses and several of the winehouses of the intermediate market town were socially off-limits for the peasantry. These, together with the headquarters of many associations, must be seen as institutions relevant solely to the town's role as hub of an intermediate marketing community.

consultations which bureaucratic officials hold both with "gentry" leaders within their administrative jurisdiction and with leading merchants of the town. Morton Fried, describing the situation in Ch'u hsien, Anhwei, a small district seat and a central market town, notes that

> . . . successful landlords, merchants, artisans, and officials tend to associate socially on a basis of approximate equality. Wealthy landlords associate with wealthy merchants rather than with poor landlords; successful artisans prefer the company of wealthy merchants to that of indigent co-specialists. . . . The leadership of the various guilds is often vested in a gentleman of the town, the leadership of the combined guilds is always so vested.[53]

Ho Ping-ti's discussion of the relations between merchants and bureaucratic officials in the Ch'ing period [54] suggests that the picture painted by Fried as of 1948 can hardly be dismissed as a modern deviation produced by the new forces which came into play during the republican period.

Any view of traditional Chinese social structure which emphasizes parallels with the articulated marketing system must, increasingly at each higher level, take cognizance of the administrative system. My purpose in elaborating a somewhat unorthodox view is not to controvert earlier analyses which, following the bias of Chinese scholar-officials, assume the primacy of the administrative system. It is rather to urge balance — a recognition in future research that social structure in the middle range of traditional Chinese society is at once derivative of and enmeshed in two quite distinctive hierarchical systems — that of administration to be sure, but that of marketing as well.

[53] Morton H. Fried, *Fabric of Chinese Society* (New York, 1953), pp. 17–18.
[54] Ho Ping-ti, *The Ladder of Success in Imperial China* (New York, 1962), Ch. 2.

PRATIK: HAITIAN PERSONAL ECONOMIC RELATIONSHIPS

Sidney W. Mintz

The most visible features of Haiti's internal exchange economy are its market places. In 1954 there were 294 officially recognized and controlled market places in the Republic (Moral 1959:74). These are the intersection points in the trade network by which the bulk of Haiti's marketed agricultural product and its imports reach their consumers. Retail

From "Pratik: Haitian Personal Economic Relationships" in *Proceedings of the 1961 Annual Spring Meeting of the American Ethnological Society*, pp. 54–63. Reprinted by permission of the University of Washington Press. The writer is grateful to the Guggenheim Foundation and to the Social Science Research Council for grants which made the research for this paper possible.

stores are much less important than the market places, even in the large towns; in the countryside such stores are of little significance in economic life. In the capital, Port-au-Prince, and in large provincial centers such as Cap Haïtien and Les Cayes, storage depots and import houses are tied in with market place trade; but retail stores have limited importance outside the capital.

Trade is carried on by thousands of intermediaries, most of them women. In a population believed to total 3,400,000, Moral's estimates (1959: 84) suggest somewhat more than 50,000 female and 15,000 male traders. These figures are very probably too low; omitted are the large numbers of children under fourteen years engaged in petty trade, and the numerous part-time unlicensed intermediaries who slip in and out of trade.

Through the market places, producers and consumers are united in exchange, but few transactions involve only producer and consumer, since intermediaries successfully interpose themselves. Such intermediaries render many different services, including bulking, transport, minor processing and packing, storage, breaking bulk, moneylending, and the provision of short-term credit. They hold their places in the distributive process by offering these services at prices their customers are willing to pay; were they redundant, their customers would circumvent them.[1]

The competition for the privilege of serving as an intermediary is stern, since the Haitian economy has a large supply of labor in all sectors. Accordingly, each market woman seeks to protect her stake within the arena of exchange by various means. A paramount feature of the struggle to secure and to profit from the right to render service is the institutionalized personal economic relationship referred to in Haiti as *pratik*.[2] It is toward an examination of this relationship that the present paper is directed.

Moral writes:

L'attrait de l'argent est si fort dans les campagnes et la circulation monétaire si réduite que le "capitaliste" influent du bourg rural mène la spéculation pratiquement à sa guise grâce à une "clientèle" étendue dont la fidélité est maintenue soit par le jeu compliqué des avances, des engagements et des dettes, soit par le respect qu'impose la réussite, soit encore par la tradition de la "pratique." [3]

And he continues:

C'est le mot-clé du petit commerce rural. Il désigne à la fois le vendeur et

[1] Bauer (1954) has made the point eloquently for West Africa. Whether the intermediary's rate of profit is "unreasonable" does not appear to be a moral question but an economic one.

[2] Créole words are transcribed in the Laubach orthography, on which see Hall (1953). Créole words are italicized, and distinguished from French words by their orthography. The acute accent over "e" is as in French. Over "o," the grave accent forms the equivalent of the French open "o." The "ou" is as in French, the "ch" as in English "sh," and the "j" as in French "z." The circumflex indicates nasalization.

[3] "In the countryside the attraction of money is so great and currency circulation so limited that the influential 'capitalist' in the rural market town can speculate practically at will, thanks to a broad 'clientele,' whose good faith is preserved by the complex game of advances, pledges, and debts, by the respect due to success, or, again, by the tradition of 'pratik.' " [Editors' translation.]

l'acheteur. Il traduit surtout la confiance réciproque et la force de l'engagement oral dans une société où le document écrit est une rareté (1959:70).[4]

That *pratik* means both buyer and seller emphasizes the reciprocal nature of the relationships. Métraux (1951:121) points out that in Haiti "The women who buy and sell are on friendly terms, calling each other *bèl mè* (stepmother), *ma komè* (gossip) [i.e., "godsib" or ritual coparent] and *matelòt* (concubine of the same man)." In the *pratik* relationship, the participants are equals for purposes of trade.

A comparable terminology occurs in Jamaica, according to Katzin:

> The term "customer" is used by Jamaicans as a generic term applied to anyone with whom one has regular business dealings. Higglers call both those who sell to them and those who buy from them "my customers." One town higgler said: "The house buyers who buy from us are our customers, but country people call us customer and we call them customer. We are really the customer because we do the buying, but I don't know what we would call them, so we still call them 'customer' " (1959:19).

In Haiti, one "has *pratik*" (*gê pratik*) and "makes *pratik*" (*fè pratik*). The degree of intimacy and mutual benefit varies, but since the relationships are intended to stabilize and maintain one's role in distributive activity, they are always built up over time and have economic value for the participants. As such, pratik ties add to the regularity and patterning of internal marketing activity.

In an economy typified by unscientific agriculture and poor agricultural technology, inadequate processing and preservation media, primitive transport and communications facilities, feeble and dispersed demand, and very numerous small-scale producers and intermediaries, each with limited means, distribution is likely to have a markedly irregular character. This unevenness is magnified when seasonal variation in the supply of various goods, and in income, is often sharp. All of these conditions are characteristic of the Haitian economy. There is further some movement of individuals in and out of the distributive system with changes in season, status, and fortune. Under such circumstances, pratik relationships stabilize sequences of dyadic economic transactions. Taken together, they afford greater order to the distributive system as a whole.

The personal element in economic activity is of course not limited to economies of the Haitian sort. But certain features of such economies affect the ways that the relationships are worked out. Haiti is famous for its relatively plentiful supply of labor, its relatively scarce supply of capital, its agrarian and nonindustrial character, and its low productivity. On all of these counts it is the least developed economy in the Caribbean area, with the lowest per capita income, and probably the lowest standard of living for the whole of Latin America.

[4] "That is the key word in petty rural commerce. It refers to both the seller and the buyer. It expresses most of all the mutual trust and the strength of oral commitments within a society in which written instruments are rare."

Haiti is rural as well as agrarian. Moral demonstrates that the calculation that 12.6 per cent of the Haitian population is urban is arbitrary in the extreme; at most only approximately 8 per cent of the people live under even remotely "urban" conditions (1959:29–30). Country towns are above all political administrative centers. To some extent they also serve as regional entrepôts for agricultural produce moving out of the surrounding region, and for finished goods moving into it (Mintz 1960). Contact between the regional administrative centers and their countrysides, and between the various regions and the capital, rests to a considerable degree upon the distributive mechanisms of the internal market system. The sorts of information carried by market women and truckers in the course of their work include marketing intelligence, affecting the rate at which produce flows toward demand areas and helping to stabilize prices to some extent. The communication of a remote unsatisfied demand may even affect tendencies in production. In this sense intermediaries help to bring distant areas into firmer contact with the cities and with other regions by their activities. The distances covered in search of profit are staggering; to walk thirty miles in a day to acquire or dispose of stock is not unusual, and some women walk nearly twice that to attend particular market places. Such trips open regions and increase the likelihood that roads, trucks, and development activity will follow.

The nature of rural production in Haiti is such that relatively little agricultural land is held in large properties. Instead there are long-standing patterns of divided and subdivided small plots, worked by their owners, sharecropped, mortgaged, leased, rented, and held by customary tenure or by squatting. Agricultural production rests on a heterogeneous tenure situation, and is pursued on holdings which are prevailingly small. Farming itself is marked by crop diversification even on very small plots, by intercropping, and by successive harvests, up to four in a single year for some crops.

The rationale for maintaining highly diversified farms need not be considered here, but its relation to the distributive pattern is of interest. Rapid and efficient bulking of agricultural products for resale in cities or in other regions occurs readily only where production is quite specialized, or where many individual cultivators in a single subregion have very similar farm situations. Grapefruit from the north plain, onions from St. Raphaël, millet from Fond-des-Nègres, and rice from the Artibonite illustrate this sort of bulking to some extent. But even in these instances, the intermediaries may buy in relatively small quantities, limited by their available capital and media of transport, and their calculations of demand. Normally, the acquisition of stock by intermediaries for resale is a long, time-consuming procedure, involving personal dealings with a large number of individual producers or with other intermediaries.

Consumption both of finished goods and of agricultural produce exhibits certain parallels to production. The peasants customarily sell much of what they produce, and buy much of what they consume, but both sales and purchases are on a small scale. Whether it be millet, rice, cornmeal, root crops, greens, salt, spices, cloth, kerosene, cooking oils, soap, matches, or anything else, small sums are expended for small quantities. Such buying habits are analogous with the practice of selling off produce irregularly and in small quantities. These transactional habits are a function of the seasonal nature of the agriculture, its diversified character, the chronic shortages of cash, and the lack of adequate means of storage. They may also be conditioned by a cultural preference for small-scale and irregular expenditure of cash assets for consumption. Expectably, the distributive mechanisms which tie production and consumption together reflect their character.

Intermediaries are the living links between these two aspects of the economy. On the one hand they bulk produce when buying it up, on the other, they break bulk in resale. They render additional and incidental services, as noted, at the same time. The presence of an oversupply of individuals always ready to provide such services sharpens the competition between intermediaries, and keeps the costs of these services to the economy as a whole at a minimum. The constant search by large numbers of distributors both for supplies to be bought up for resale, and for loci of demand, helps to keep supply and demand in a more balanced relationship — as reflected in price changes — than would be the case were the number of distributors artificially reduced (Bauer 1954; Mintz 1957). It also serves to enhance the importance of the pratik relationships which are the major concern here.

A pratik may be either one who sells to a distributive intermediary or one who buys from a distributive intermediary. Since some products pass through the hands of more than a single intermediary, pratik relationships may tie together producer and middleman, or middleman and middleman, or middleman and consumer. For products which are bulked by an intermediary near the source of supply, and broken in bulk for resale by a retailer, the bulking intermediary may have pratik relationships with numerous small-scale producers on the one hand, and with several retailers on the other. Moreover, just as the producers may have pratik relationships with more than one bulking intermediary, so the retailers may have pratik relationships with numbers of consumers. Hence these ties form webs or networks of economic association.

The rationale behind the establishment of pratik is clearly economic in nature. This is confirmed by the results of scores of interviews with Haitian professional market women. Every such woman interviewed stated that she had pratik; and all of them made clear that the purpose of forming pratik ties is to secure and solidify the channels of trade. In general, the means for creating and maintaining pratik is by the granting of economic concessions. But obviously such concessions cannot be granted unilaterally, or they serve no economic purpose for one of the participants. Concessions (in the form of price, quantity, credit, or otherwise) are made by intermediaries both to producers and to consumers, and to yet other intermediaries. The reciprocal reward for these concessions takes the form of more assured pathways to supply and demand. In effect, the intermediary will be seen to be trading some portion of her potential profit in a theoretically random market situation, in return for some measure of assurance that she will be able both to acquire stock and then to dispose of it.

This point deserves some stress if only to clarify the wholly rational economic motives which lie behind pratik relationships. These ties are by no means uneconomic, noneconomic, or economically irrational; quite the contrary, in fact, since their existence demonstrates the Haitian market woman's clear recognition of the general character of the economy. Except in the instances of granting credit and lending money, and often even then, the guarantees that a pratik relationship will persist and continue to be mutually beneficial are personal and customary, not legal and contractual. But dishonesty on the part of a pratik will end the tie, and women who behave unethically in such relationships soon threaten their own stakes in the distributive process.

No market woman interviewed denied having pratik relationships with those who "buy from her hand"; some, however, fail to have these ties with those from whom they buy, if those others are producers. Intermediaries who buy from producers do not uniformly make pratik of them. Retailers — intermediaries who sell to consumers — are like intermediaries between intermediaries, having bilateral relationships. But on the consumer side, the nature of the pratik arrangement will differ.

Commonly the pratik is defined as a "good customer." [5] When an intermediary has pratik among producers from whom she buys, she may theoretically buy at a higher price, accept a smaller quantity for the same price, or advance a loan against a future crop. No one indicated that she bought less of a given product for the same price. The intermediary as buyer is acquiring stock, and wishes to do so to the limit of her capital. She may pay a little more in order to improve her access to more stock in the future. But she will not buy less from a single seller than her capital makes possible at one time, if this means having to seek out another seller of the same produce.

At the other end of the chain, the retailer who has pratik with her consumer customers is readier to make small concessions in price — giving a little more for the same amount of money — rather than giving the same amount of stock for less money. Where perishable goods are concerned, the retailer when bargaining will increase quantity rather than lower price as a matter of practice, even when not dealing with pratik who buy from her.

[5] From French "pratique." A typical definition of *pratik* is the following. "It means that you are selling. I come to buy from you each day. I need credit; you sell to me [on credit]; the money is 'content' that you sell to me. I always buy from your hand; I pay you well. That means 'pratik.' "

Perishability and like considerations (such as fragility, short harvests, and high unit costs) enter into the shaping of pratik relationships in other ways. The intermediary buying from her producer pratik is unlikely to offer to buy at higher than the going price if the product rots easily, as in the case of onions or tomatoes. The producer-seller is going to sell off to the first buyer who comes along and offers the going price. He cannot hold stock of this sort, even for short periods, given his lack of storage and refrigeration facilities. Correspondingly, the buying intermediary wins no future assurance of supply by offering more than the going price precisely because the producer-seller is unable to hold stock for her.

But in the case of relatively more durable stock — unhusked millet or dried corn for instance — the producer-seller may be in a position to retain his supply in anticipation of a price rise. With substantially imperishable stock, particularly rice, this is even more the case. In such instances, and where the buyer-intermediary regularly acquires stock from the producer, she may be willing to pay slightly more per unit of purchase when she buys. Her concessions increase her chances of acquiring stock when goods are scarce and resale profits potentially high.

Generally speaking, relationships with producers based on price concessions develop when such producers have relatively large stocks of imperishable goods. Peasants in this situation are able to "hold back" on two counts: better storage facilities, and more capital available for necessities. Less well-fixed producers, even of imperishable stocks, are more likely to have to sell off to any buyers, much as if their produce were subject to rapid spoilage.

In the case of items which spoil readily, the most common basis for pratik with the producer is by loans against a future crop. Such loans are made either to large-scale or small-scale producers of imperishables (with large-scale producers also winning concessions in price); but loans, to the exclusion of price concessions, predominate in transactions with producers of perishables.

Loans to producers are made in several ways. In the St. Raphaël region of the north, loans are made to producers of onions, which are subject to rather rapid spoilage, and to producers of rice and tobacco, both relatively durable. These loans are paid off in kind rather than in cash. Creditors are entitled to claim their stock at the very start of the harvest, at which time market prices are high. It appears to be the usual practice to estimate the price-to-be of the product and to lend money on these terms. Though some intermediaries claim that they have lost money on crop loans, the opening market prices for rice in the fall and onions in the spring make this unlikely. In the case of tobacco, however, marketing difficulties and the complaints some informants made indicate that they did lose money — some said they would advance no more money for tobacco crops, and this will probably affect the next year's tobacco crop.

Loans are usually advanced on the basis of acreage, or rather, on the estimated yield of a given acreage. The intermediary advances cash against the expected number of barrels of rice, or bags of onions, or bundles of tobacco to be harvested. She will either have some knowledge of the subject herself or depend on her husband or some trusted male friend in making such judgments. These estimates, though, are only a means for putting a reasonable ceiling on the loan, and do not affect the terms. Often the intermediary "buys" the total crop by making a flat cash payment before harvest, and claiming the entire harvest as it ripens.

Since it is likely that the producer who borrows from an intermediary will be turning over his product at harvest at a selling price below what he could get in the open market, it is relevant why peasants make such arrangements. The need for cash in the planting season is sometimes severe, while cash loans or credit are difficult to secure by other means. Loans made by intermediaries, though generally sealed by an informal contract, are generally small. The peasant does not normally put up his land or other real property as collateral, which he would be expected to do if he borrowed from a townsman or from a wealthy farmer. The intermediary who lends him money is probably resident in his community, and though she may handle more cash than he, their class position is not likely to be different. The pratik relationship itself is the basis for the loan even though the loan is contractual, and it is a relationship requiring some mutual trust and regard. When the budgets I collected are analyzed, it should be possible to specify the average earnings intermediaries in one community can make by investing their cash in this way. The lending intermediary in these cases takes two risks: one, of crop failure, and the other, of a market glut. Surely she does her best to protect herself in lending her capital to producers.

At the other end of the chain of intermediaries — that is, as between retailer and consumer — the character of pratik is different, both in kind and in scale. The retailer of vegetable produce in Port-au-Prince, for instance, whether itinerant house-to-house seller or stallkeeper in the large city markets, tries to acquire a group of steady customers. These customers are made and held by price and quantity concessions, but particularly by concessions in quantity. The "extra" — *dègi* or *tiyô* in Créole — is part of many transactions. All grains and legumes, for instance, are sold in units of tin cans of various sizes (Mintz 1961) normally heaped to spilling; the "extra" given in these instances is in excess of the heaped tin. In food measured by the lot or pile, the giving of an extra portion is sometimes more subtle. The Haitian squash (Créole: *militô*), the avocado, sweet potatoes, and many other perishable foods and some other items are sold in small piles. One will see a few such piles spread at the feet of a seller, and the differences between these piles are slight indeed, and difficult to measure. If the item in question varies much in size or quality, each pile will contain an assortment, and the piles are carefully prepared so that this will be so. "Extra" to pratik is then given by selecting the better items to make a pile, or by adding one or two additional units for the same price.[6]

On a given day at a particular time in any market, the going price for unit stock of this sort rapidly comes to be relatively uniform. The same is true for dried legumes such as rice, millet, corn and cornmeal, red and black beans, pigeon peas, and so on. Unless there is considerable variation in quality or condition, this uniformity of price will prevail. Prices for particular items take shape in a fashion surprisingly reminiscent of the textbook examples. The seller knows at what price a particular item sold on the previous market day; she also knows at what price she has risked buying. She sets her opening price in line with her expectations. If demand is steady and uncomplaining, she will raise her price but she rarely has to do this, since the asking price usually adjusts downward by small concessions until it becomes stabilized. If demand is slack (and customers voluble in their disdain), and other sellers are doing business at a lower price, she will reluctantly but quickly come down. What is worth remarking is the speed with which these adjustments are made, not over time or uniformly in different market settings, but for a given and particular situation. If there are a dozen sellers of cornmeal or red beans in a given market at ten o'clock in the morning — by which time the market has been in progress and prices have been finding their levels for several hours – it will be difficult to find a single seller whose price varies as much as a penny a unit for the stock in question. Exceptions occur, however, if the stock is very scanty and the demand high; if there are big variations in quality; or if sellers with very small stocks have the need to sell off very rapidly.

The implications of price uniformity for the pratik phenomenon are interesting. Each of the retailers of a certain product in the market may be expected to have pratik; they make these pratik and hold them essentially by giving more for less. But they remain in constant competition with other sellers of the same product, in terms of their asking price. Market women do not advertise their pratik. The pratik buyer comes to his or her pratik seller and inquires after the price of a certain good. The price quoted does not vary from that quoted to any other prospective buyer. But when the sale is consummated, the pratik buyer gets the product at a lower price — or else, and more typically, gets a greater quantity for the same price. Since this occurs only with pratik, it should not be thought that the intermediary is lowering the going price of her stock on the open market. The going price rises and falls in relation to supply and demand (Mintz 1959:24); price concessions of the sort described here are additional to general supply-demand based changes, or they may be thought of as occurring within the field of these wider changes.

The upshot of this is that two sorts of competition, very different from

[6] The same procedure is reported from Jamaica. Katzin writes (1959:87): "Some sellers favor their regular customers in other ways. To give 'brawta' or 'make-up' is the practice, all along the line from rural producer to retail buyer. This is identical with the British and American practice of giving something additional in a transaction."

each other, are occurring in the same setting. The first sort, and more important, is the competition of the open market, revealed by the emerging uniformity of the asking price at any one time for a given product in a single market. The second sort is the competition for pratik, proceeding behind the screen of apparent price uniformity. Not all buying pratik are granted the same measure of concession, nor even necessarily the same kind of concession. Intermediaries admit both to having buying pratik and to concealing the details of their pratik relationships from their competitors; these relationships are pervasive at the same time that they are partly hidden.

It remains to discuss pratik relationships between intermediaries. These are various in nature, but only one category will be treated, namely, relationships between wholesalers and retailers of agricultural products. Many agricultural items, such as dried grains, legumes, and fresh fruits and vegetables, are bulked by intermediaries who buy from numerous small producers and wholesale to retailers who break bulk in selling to consumers. Such a series includes a minimum of four participants: producer, bulker, retailer, and consumer. It is to the center of this series that attention is now directed.

Credit extension and concessions in quantity are the major means of tying retailer pratik to the wholesaler. Price reductions are also employed. Retailer pratik are to be found mainly in the capital, in and around the big markets, and in the provincial cities. Since the bulking intermediaries carry relatively large stocks, they will make pratik with numbers of retailers. Though the quantities of any one item carried by a bulking intermediary and those purchased by any single retailer vary enormously, the relative scale can be suggested. An onion bulker from the north will usually carry from about seven to about twenty sacks of onions to the capital to wholesale. These sacks hold approximately fifteen to sixteen No. 10 canfuls of onions when filled to bursting. A Port-au-Prince retailer may purchase one sack, or two, or even six, for resale by the pound or canful. The bulking intermediary will buy onions from the producer at, say, U.S. $7.00 the sack, and resell at U.S. $9.00, if the market is very brisk. For her trade at large, she will reduce the quantity of onions in each sack by one or two canfuls, and thus put together enough onions for an extra sack. When reselling her onions at the U.S. $9.00 rate, she may provide her pratik with one of two kinds of advantage: reduce the price per sack, or refill the sacks to their original overflowing. She may also be willing to sell to some of her established pratik on credit, giving them a week or ten days to sell off and repay her in the form of cash. Sometimes these credit arrangements include a carrying charge or interest. A bulking intermediary with many retailer pratik may be able to dispose of half or more of her stock through her pratik. Since onions are speculative, yielding good profits sometimes but glutting the markets at certain periods, pratik with retailers is decidedly advantageous to the bulking intermediary.

Pratik relationships seem to have a characteristic way of taking shape.

A bulking intermediary will call over a would-be buyer unfamiliar to her and invite her to buy. After some talk, if the seller likes the buyer's manner, she will make a very reasonable selling offer. As the sale is consummated, she will ask the buyer if she buys regularly on that day and at that place. If the answer is a friendly affirmative, she will say meaningfully: "Wait for me. I always come on this day. I come from such-and-such a town. I come here with the truck called so-and-so. I keep my stock here, at the depot of Madame X." With more talk, an understanding begins to emerge. Each woman will carefully watch the other's behavior on subsequent occasions, until there is genuine mutual trust. When vaunting the solidarity of a pratik, an intermediary will say: "When I go to Port-au-Prince, my pratik never lets me sleep in the depot — I sleep in her house." Or: "When X promises to buy eggs for me, she hides them from the other women, and will not consider their offers." [7] A buying pratik who knows her selling pratik is coming will wait at the proper place and time, refusing to buy stock from others that she is sure her pratik is carrying.

To the extent that her stock is committed in such arrangements, a selling pratik will refuse to sell to others until she has met her pratik buyer. One may be led to believe that the selling behavior of intermediaries is random or whimsical, and that they may refuse to make certain sales because of some irrational streak. It should be clear, however, that personalized economic relationships, while they modify somewhat the nature of the distributive process, arise precisely because intermediaries understand the basic character of the Haitian economy so well.[8]

A final point may be considered here. In the brief discussion of Haitian agriculture undertaken earlier, nothing was said of the economic and social arrangements by which work is done. Considerable emphasis is put on cooperative work groups by those writing on Haitian rural economy (Métraux 1951). But I think that in the Haitian countryside there is great economic individualism in agriculture, and in fact relatively little institutionalized cooperation. If this is true in agriculture, it appears to be even truer of marketing. Combines of intermediaries do not exist, and intermediaries do not at present form such combinations in order to bulk

[7] In this instance as in several described by Katzin for Jamaica, the economic rationality of such behavior is clearly demonstrated. Such examples make clear that the old woman on her way to market who refuses to sell her stock to a passing stranger at a very favorable price is not in fact behaving irrationally; quite the contrary. Nor does her unwillingness to sell demonstrate that her real purpose in going to market is merely to gossip with her neighbors, a charge which even local city people are fond of leveling at every opportunity. Careful examination of the Haitian situation throws light on James' claim (1942:771) that "The markets which are held throughout rural Haiti, many of them in the open country, are attended primarily for social pleasure, not for buying and selling."

[8] This understanding is often misunderstood to be a lack of commercial sophistication. James writes (1942:771): "The average rural Haitian is not a person of great ambition, nor one who takes naturally to the complexities of commercial life."

produce on a larger scale, reduce overhead, purchase trucks, fix prices, or otherwise act collectively in their own group interest. Intermediary activity has a highly fragmented individualistic character. But the pratik custom plays an integrating role. It is built up out of series or chains of dyadic relationships which persist through time, and are founded on mutual trust for mutual advantage. It may be that some observers of Haitian rural society have not noticed the variety of integrating social forms serving various ends. Ties of the pratik kind may be most common in those societies in which more extended formal social devices have never existed or have fallen into disuse. The kôbit and kòvé work societies of old have nearly disappeared from Haitian agriculture, to be replaced by day labor in most cases. But overmuch notice is still taken of these disappearing work groups since they have somehow caught the imagination of observers and visiting planners. Pratik relationships, partly because they occur mainly within the distributive system rather than wholly within production, partly because they seem socially narrow, fragile, and trivial alongside the work societies, have received little or no attention. It is at least worth considering whether cooperative economic activity in a country such as Haiti might not be realized more directly by careful prior analysis of dyadic relationships, than by the marshaling of nostalgic suppositions about an institution now nearly vanished from the scene.

REFERENCES CITED

Bauer, Peter T.
1954 *West African Trade*. Cambridge, Eng.: Cambridge University Press.

Hall, Robert A., Jr.
1953 "Haitian Creole." *American Anthropological Association Memoir* No. 74, April–June, 1953. Menasha, Wis.

Herskovits, Melville J.
1937 *Life in a Haitian Valley*. New York: Alfred A. Knopf.

James, Preston E.
1942 *Latin America*. New York: Odyssey Press.

Katzin, Margaret F.
1959 "Higglers of Jamaica." Ph.D. thesis, Northwestern University.

Métraux, Alfred, *et al.*
1951 "Making a Living in the Marbial Valley" (Haiti). *Occasional Papers in Education*, No. 10. Paris: UNESCO Educational Clearing House.

Mintz, Sidney W.
1957 "Aspects of the Internal Distribution System in a Caribbean Peasant Economy." *Human Organization*, XV (2): 18–23.
1959 "Internal Market Systems as Mechanisms of Social Articulation," in *Proceedings of the American Ethnological Society* (Verne F. Ray, ed.). Seattle: University of Washington Press.
1960 "A Tentative Typology of Eight Haitian Market Places." *Revista de Ciencias Sociales*, IV (2): 15–57.

1961 "Standards of Value and Units of Measure in the Fond-des-Nègres Market Place, Haiti." *Journal of the Royal Anthropological Institute,* 91:23–38.

Moral, Paul
1959 *L'Économie Haitienne.* Port-au-Prince, Haiti: Imprimerie de l'État.

CASTE AND THE JAJMANI SYSTEM IN A NORTH INDIAN VILLAGE

Oscar Lewis and Victor Barnouw

Although there is a great deal of literature about the caste system of India, very little attention has been paid to its economic aspects.[1] Most books and articles on caste have concerned themselves with the problems of its historical origin and development, with the rules and sanctions governing endogamy, food taboos, ritual purity, caste ranking, and the more dramatic injustices of untouchability. It is common in works about caste for the author to list the castes of a particular region with some account of the traditional occupation of each; but it is a curious fact that the author generally avoids what might logically seem to be a next step, an analysis of how these groups interact with one another in the production and exchange of goods and services. William H. Wiser, in his book *The Hindu Jajmani System,* was the first to describe in detail how such goods and services are exchanged in a rural Indian village. It is greatly to Wiser's credit that he was able to characterize *jajmani* relations *as a system.* Some knowledge of this system is crucial for an understanding of the economic aspects of caste in rural India.[2]

From "Caste and the Jajmani System in a North Indian Village" in *Scientific Monthly,* Vol. 83, No. 2 (August 1956), pp. 66–81. Reprinted by permission of the American Association for the Advancement of Science. The field work was done by Lewis with the aid of a number of Indian research assistants. Thanks are due especially to Kamal Prakash for his field assistance in connection with this paper. Thanks are also due to the Graduate Research Board of the University of Illinois for a grant that made possible Barnouw's collaboration in the library research and the writing of this paper.

[1] A caste is an endogamous social unit, membership in which is determined by birth; it is often associated with a particular occupation and with restrictions about the acceptance of food and water from other caste groups. Castes tend to be ranked, with the Brahmans being traditionally assigned the highest status and "untouchable" castes such as the Bhangi (sweepers) the lowest.

[2] W. H. Wiser, *The Hindu Jajmani System* (Lucknow 1936). There have been a few other works dealing with the relationship between caste and economics, notably S. S. Nehru's *Caste and Credit in the Rural Area* (Calcutta: Longmans Green, 1932). Kumar Goshal has emphasized the economic basis for the caste system in the following words: "Hindu reformers failed to make any headway against the caste system because it was rooted in the economy of India,

Under this system each caste group within a village is expected to give certain standardized services to the families of other castes. A Khati (carpenter) repairs tools, for example; a Nai (barber) cuts hair; but they do not necessarily perform these services for everyone. Each man works for a particular family or group of families with which he has hereditary ties. His father worked for the same families before him, and his son will continue to work for them, the occupation or service being determined by caste. The family or family-head served by an individual is known as his *jajman*,[3] while the man who performs service is known as the *jajman's kamin* or *kam karne-wala* (literally, worker). These are the terms used in northwestern India; in other parts of India where the system prevails other terms may be used.

It is a characteristic of this system to operate without much exchange of money. For it is not an open-market economy, and the ties between jajman and kamin are not like those of employer and employee in a capitalistic system. The jajman compensates his kamins for their work through periodic payments in cash or grain, made throughout the year on a daily, monthly, or bi-yearly basis. Kamins may also receive benefits such as free food, clothing, and residence site, the use of certain tools and raw materials, and so forth. To Wiser these concessions represent the strength of the system and are more important than the monetary payments.[4] Despite the increased use of money in recent years, the peasants nowadays tend

---

and only a change in that economy could bring about a change in the social structure. The economic system was stabilized at a low level, based upon more or less self-sufficient village communities which combined agriculture and handicrafts. Production was on a small scale, and for consumption rather than exchange. Everything moved in narrow, well-worn grooves fixed by custom. It was a precapitalist economic system, whose static quality could have been altered only by an expanding dynamic market for exchange of commodities. As long as this was lacking, the social relationships of the people could not possibly be altered." [Kumar Goshal, *The People of India* (New York: Sheridan House, 1944, p. 59)]. O. C. Cox was also aware of the importance of economic factors, as the following quotation shows: "The caste structure is fundamentally a labor structure, a system of interrelated services originating in specialized groups and traditionalized in a religious matrix." Cox quotes Pramathanath Bannerjea as follows: "The chief economic significance of the system is that it fixes absolutely the supply of any kind of labor. The scope given for the play of competition thus becomes limited, and consequently the law of demand and supply is rendered inoperative or oppressive in its operation. When any change takes place in the economic world, labor is unable to adjust itself. . . . Wages and prices have very often to be regulated by custom or some artificial means." [O. C. Cox, *Caste, Class, and Race* (New York: Doubleday, 1948), pp. 62, 67]. An awareness of the relationship between caste and economy, however, seems to be missing in even such a standard book as J. H. Hutton's *Caste in India* (Oxford University Press), in the revised edition of which (1951) there is no reference to the jajmani system or to Wiser's work.

[3] Webster's *Dictionary* (1950) defines *jajman* as "a person by whom a Brahman is hired to perform religious services; hence, a patron; client." The word derives from the Sanskrit *yajamana*, the present participle of *yaj*, to sacrifice. The term ultimately came to be used for anyone standing in the relationship of employer.

[4] W. H. Wiser, *The Hindu Jajmani System* (Lucknow, 1936), pp. 6–11.

to prefer grain payments to cash, since grain prices have risen so enormously in the past decade.[5]

When Wiser wrote his book, he did not know how general or widespread this system might be, although he referred to some passages in the works of other writers which suggested that it had a wide range of diffusion. This conclusion is supported by more recent studies, which give evidence for much the same kind of system in eastern Uttar Pradesh,[6] parts of Malabar and Cochin,[7] Mysore District,[8] Tanjore,[9] Hyderabad,[10] Gujarat,[11] and the Punjab.[12] Regional differences, of course, appear.

A major function of the jajmani system is to assure a stable labor supply for the dominant agricultural caste in a particular region by limiting the mobility of the lower castes, especially those who assist in agricultural work. If a kamin leaves the village, he must get someone to take his place, usually a member of the same joint family. This does not usually involve sale, and the jajman is not likely to object, as long as the position is filled. But such transfers are rare.[13] The kamins have valued rights and advantages which make them hesitate to move. We get a picture of this from the autobiography of a sweeper: ". . . my father's family have been serving a certain number of houses for the last few hundred years, from generation to generation. It was an unwritten law that if my family wanted to move out of the town to go somewhere else, they would have to find someone else in their place. In this matter the high castes have no choice as to who would work for them. If my people wanted to sell the work of the street in which they were working they could do so to another family of our own caste. The sale was only effected on condition that in that particular area no others of our community had any claim, and also that the people who bought it were satisfied that our family had been working there for at least two generations; the price would be fixed according to the income of the area. . . . But sales of this nature very rarely take place, as it means losing one's birthright and the family reputation. Also,

[5] See E. Eames, "Some Aspects of Urban Migration from a Village in North Central India," *Eastern Anthropol.* 8, 19 (1954).

[6] M. Opler and R. D. Singh, "The Division of Labor in an Indian Village," in *A Reader in General Anthropology*, C. S. Coon, ed. (New York: Holt, 1948), pp. 464–496. *See also* N. S. Reddy, "Functional Relations of Lohars in a North Indian Village," *Eastern Anthropol.* 8, 129 (1955).

[7] E. J. Miller, "Village Structure in North Kerala," *Economic Weekly*, Bombay, 9 Feb. 1952, pp. 159–164.

[8] M. N. Srinavas, "The Social System of a Mysore Village," in *Village India*, M. Marriott, ed. American Anthropological Association, 1955, Memoir 83, pp. 1–35; A. R. Beals, "Interplay among Factors of Change in a Mysore Village," *ibid.*, pp. 78–101.

[9] E. K. Gough, "The Social Structure of a Tanjore Village," *ibid.*, pp. 36–52.

[10] S. C. Dube, *Indian Village* (Ithaca: Cornell University Press, 1955).

[11] G. Steed, lecture notes, hectographed.

[12] M. L. Darling, *Wisdom and Waste in the Punjab Village* (London: Oxford University Press, 1934).

[13] According to M. Singh [*The Depressed Classes* (Bombay: Hind Kitabs, 1947), p. 98] Bhangis (sweepers) can sell their *jajmani* rights for as much as 200 rupees. *See also* Eames, p. 21; Reddy, p. 135.

this is the only means of livelihood open to us, and the richer the landlord we serve, the more prestige and honor we have . . ." [14]

Moreover, the community may put pressure on an individual to make him stay. Nehru cites the case of a village that instituted legal proceedings in a criminal court, seeking to insure that the village Lohar (blacksmith) should not migrate to another community, as he had threatened to do,[15] and Wiser describes the efforts of the people of Karimpur to keep a restless Dhobi (washerman) within the village.[16] Even if a jajman should be dissatisfied with his kamin's work, he would find it hard to replace him. "It is not easy for an agriculturist to remove a family attached to his household and secure the services of another. For example, A, a barber, is attached to the family of B, an agriculturist. If for any reason B is greatly dissatisfied with the services of A and wants those of another, he cannot abruptly dismiss A. His difficulty will not be in dismissing him, but in finding a substitute. Each of these castes has its own inter village council. Occupational castes have a developed trade unionism. . . . No one else would be willing to act as a substitute, for fear of being penalized by the caste *panchayat*. It may even be difficult for a number of families to join together and import a family belonging to that occupational caste from a different village. First, under these conditions of tension, an outside family would not come for fear of social pressure and ultimate ostracism for such an action. And if they do come, the caste fellows already in the village would make things very difficult, even unbearable, for them." [17]

Not every village has a full complement of specialists. In a survey of 54 villages in the mid-Gangetic valley, Nehru found that no single caste occurred in all the villages surveyed. Camars (leather workers) were found in only 64 per cent of the villages; Ahirs (herders) in 60 per cent; Brahmans, Nais, Lohars, and Telis in 40 per cent; Dhobis and Kurmis in 36 per cent; Kumhars in 30 per cent; and Baniyas in 16 per cent.[18] Nehru gives various reasons for the unexpectedly low figures of these caste groups. The Nai (barber), for instance, is a journeyman who goes from door to door and village to village. "No client needs him more than once a week and less than once a month. Also, the various festivals and ceremonies when his services are in urgent demand do not figure all too frequently in the village calendar. Hence alone or through a relation, one Nai can minister to the needs of more than one village; if the figures are an index, more than two villages." [19] The Dhobi (washerman), on the other hand, has a small representation because he serves primarily upper-

[14] Hazari, *An Indian Outcaste* (London: Bannisdale Press, 1951), pp. 12–13.

[15] S. S. Nehru, *Caste and Credit in the Rural Area* (Calcutta: Longmans Green, 1932), p. 27.

[16] Wiser, *The Hindu Jajmani System*, p. 123.

[17] Dube, *Indian Village*, p. 60.

[18] Nehru, *Caste and Credit in the Rural Area*, pp. 23–29.

[19] *Ibid.*, pp. 24–25.

caste or upper-class patrons. The womenfolk of most lower class families do the family wash. According to Singh, one seldom finds more than three Dhobi families in a village, and often only one catering to a group of villages.[20] Singh also says that the Bhangis (sweepers) are as sparsely scattered as the Dhobis, with their largest concentration in the towns.[21] Nehru explains that a single Baniya (merchant) can finance operations in villages within a radius of 10 to 20 miles or more; hence one need not expect to find Baniyas in every village.[22] The supply and demand factor suggests that there must be some mobility, despite the localizing function of the jajmani system.

Jajmani rights, however, which link one to certain families, may be regarded as a form of property passing from father to son. Like land property, it is equally apportioned among brothers when they separate.[23] Certain problems eventuate from this: "When a Lohar family multiplies and divides the work, each share comes to compass the work of fewer agriculturists unless they also multiply at the same rate. Of course when the latter multiply faster, the Lohars become responsible to a greater number of agricultural families, even though the extent of work may remain the same." [24] The apportionment of jajmani rights may prove to be very unequal, as Reddy has shown. From a table giving the number of jajmans served by ten Lohar families in Senapur, it appears that one Lohar family serves only seven jajman families, while another serves 37.[25] The rewards in grain and other benefits are of course proportionate. The jajmani system, then, provides some security in assuring one a position in society, but also gives rise to economic insecurity for some of the kamins.

In his pioneer work, Wiser summed up what seemed to him to be the advantages and disadvantages of the jajmani system in relation to the nation, the village community, the caste group, and the individual. On the whole, he emphasized the integrating and security-giving aspects of the system and described how it provided "peace and contentment" for the villagers.[26] Yet at other times, as we shall see, Wiser emphasized its attendant injustices. How the jajmani system affects the villagers who live by it, and what the future of the system may be in a developing money economy, are subjects that will be discussed in the latter part of this paper. First we will describe how the jajmani system functions at the present time in a particular village, Rampur, about 15 miles west of Delhi.[27]

[20] Singh, *The Depressed Classes,* p. 93.
[21] *Ibid.,* p. 95.
[22] Nehru, *Caste and Credit in the Rural Area,* pp. 26–27.
[23] Reddy, "Functional Relations of Lohars in a North Indian Village," p. 133.
[24] *Ibid.,* p. 130.
[25] *Ibid.,* p. 133.
[26] Wiser, *The Hindu Jajmani System,* p. 187.
[27] Rampur is 27 miles off the main Delhi-Fazilka road with which it is connected by a cart track. The village can also be reached from the Delhi-Ferozpur railway line. Gheora and Nanglio, the two nearest railway stations, are at a distance of a few miles from the village.

JAJMANI SYSTEM IN RAMPUR

There are 150 households at Rampur, with a total population of about 1,100. Twelve castes are represented in the village with the following distribution: 78 Jat families, 15 Brahman, 20 Camar (leather worker), 10 Bhangi (sweeper), 7 Kumhar (potter), 5 Jhinvar (water carrier), 4 Dhobi (washerman), 4 Khati (carpenter), 3 Nai (barber), 2 Chipi (calico printer or tailor), 1 Lohar (blacksmith), and 1 Baniya (merchant). Some caste groups often found in north Indian villages are not represented – for example, Ahirs, Telis, and Kurmis — but the list is quite representative and characteristic of the region.

The Jats are by tradition agriculturists and own all the land of the village, including the house sites, the land upon which the houses of the other castes are built. They are the principal *jajmans* for the other groups. According to the traditional mode of ranking, the Brahmans are superior to the Jats. The Brahmans do have the dominant position in Wiser's village of Karimpur, where they are the landowners and number 41 families in a population of 754.[28] But in Rampur the Brahmans are occupancy tenants of the Jats and are subservient to them.

The caste groups of Rampur have traditionally been related to one another through the mutual obligations of the jajmani system, the rules of which have been codified. Table 1 is an extract from the *wajib-ul-arz*, the customary law of Rampur, which specifies the kinds of work to be done by the different caste groups and the rates of compensation. The provisions of the wajib-ul-arz have legal effect, for British legislation continued to support these customary rules under civil law.[29]

It may be noted in Table 1 that various rights and duties are specified in connection with weddings. Marriages are the high points in the social life of a village and represent a great expenditure of wealth by the families concerned. All the castes, or most of them, are brought into some connection with a wedding, in which the importance of the family and the village are demonstrated, and in which a jajman's ties with his kamins may be strengthened. The same is true, to a lesser extent, of funerals and other *rites de passage*, as well as the village festivals. The service ties of the various caste groups are indicated in Table 2.[30]

Thirty or forty years ago a Khati at Rampur worked for his jajman all the year round. His work consisted of making plows and repairing them in the fields, and making plow yokes, three-legged stools, legs for string cots, and various farming implements. The wood was supplied by his jajman.[31]

[28] Wiser, *The Hindu Jajmani System*, p. 19.
[29] *Ibid.*, pp. 14–15.
[30] *Ibid.*, p. 70 ff.: and Hazari, *An Indian Outcaste*, pp. 13–15. S. Misra gives a list of payments at marriage and sacred-thread ceremonies to different "village servants" in a village in U.P.: "Earnings of Village Servants in U.P.," *Eastern Anthropol.* 5, 98 (1952).
[31] For a fuller list of items made by village carpenters, see Wiser, pp. 35–36.

The traditional payments for this work are specified in Table 1, but informants gave a somewhat different itemization as follows: (1) 45 *sirs* of grain from the wheat crop (in the dry season); (2) as much wheat fodder as one person can carry (in the dry season); (3) as much *jowar* (millet) fodder as one person can carry (in the rainy season) or (4) ½ *maund* (a unit of weight containing 40 *sirs; sir:* a weight of about 2 pounds) of green fodder (gram or peas).

A common form of payment, as specified in items (2) and (3) above and in the barber's list of rights in Table 1, is the provision that a man may take home from the crop as much grain as he can carry by himself. This is, of course, an elastic amount. A generation ago the village Lohar carried such a heavy load that he vomited blood on reaching home and died instantly.

In addition to the grain payments received from each jajman, a Khati also gets payments in cash or kind for noncustomary services such as the making of wheels, planks, handles of milling stones, and so forth. Daily meals are provided while the Khati is working at wedding preparations for a jajman's family, cutting the wood for fuel, and so forth, and he is feasted at the wedding itself and given 1 rupee[32] thereafter. Interservice relationships exist between the Khati and Nai, Dhobi, and Kumhar families. Each of the Khati families acts as jajman toward one Camar and one Bhangi family, which provide services for them and work at their weddings, when both families are feasted and given 1 rupee each.

While jajmani services are still exchanged, cash payment for carpentry is increasing, and jajmani ties have weakened. The Khatis have fewer jajmans than formerly. They seldom repair plows in the fields nowadays, and they are slow in completing jobs required by their jajmani obligations. The jajmans find that if they want to get work done on time, it is better to pay something in cash as well.

The famine of 1944–45 damaged the jajmani relationships between the Khatis and the Jats. Since grain was scarce, the Jats decided to reduce the customary dues. The village panchayat accordingly announced that the grain payments would be half the traditional amount that year. The Rampur Khatis and Lohars did not agree to these conditions and said that they would not work for their jajmans if they insisted on such terms. Six Jat families then broke off jajmani relationships with the Khatis and now do their own work, or else get it done by cash payments. Three of the Jat families have taken up carpentry. One of these families is dependent on carpentry as a full-time profession, while the other two are on a near-professional basis. The full-time Jat carpenter learned his trade while he was employed at the Civil Ordnance depot at the Delhi cantonment. The others learned the trade by themselves.

Only two of the four Khati families at Rampur now carry on the traditional trade. Two Khatis are teachers; one of these supplements his

[32] A rupee is worth about 21 cents.

TABLE I. RULES OF SERVICE, RAMPUR

Caste	*Type of service*	*Rights earned through service*
Khati (carpenter)	To repair agricultural tools.	1 maund of grain per year along with *ori* rights (2½ sirs of grain twice a year at each sowing season) (70).
Lohar (blacksmith)	To repair agricultural tools.	1 maund of grain per year along with ori rights.
Kumhar (potter)	To supply earthenware vessels and to render services of light nature at weddings.	Grains to the value of the vessels. Additional grain at the son's or daughter's marriage, according to status and capacity.
Hajjam (or Nai, barber)	To shave and cut hair; to attend to guests on their arrival and to render other services of light nature at weddings.	At each harvest as much grain as the man can lift by himself. Additional grain at the son's or daughter's marriage, according to status and capacity.
Khakrul (or Bhangi, sweeper)	To prepare cow-dung cakes; to gather sweepings, to remove dead mules and donkeys; to collect cots for extraordinary needs, and to render services at weddings.	Meals and *rabri* (a preparation made from churned curd and flour) twice a day; at each harvest as much grain as the man can lift by himself and also at the son's or daughter's marriage, according to status and capacity.
Camar (leather worker)	To assist in agriculture and give all kinds of light services.	One-twentieth of the produce.
	To do *begar* (compulsory labor), render ordinary service, and remove dead cattle.	One-fourth of the produce and the skins of dead cattle.

income by prescribing medicines. The trade of carpentry has seen some reverses in recent years. Bullock carts formerly had wooden wheels, which used to last for a year or two, and thus provided the Khati with a dependable source of income. But now iron wheels have taken their place. Out of 33 bullock carts at Rampur, 31 have iron wheels. Plank-making has also declined. People from Rampur now prefer to have their wood cut in Delhi by a buzz-saw. The two Khati carpenters at Rampur are in debt. One of them has two employed sons who help to ease his burden. The other Khati has some part-time work as a mason and also sells milk, but he is still in debt. The decline of the carpenter's importance in this village may be seen from the fact that whereas Rampur's 1100 inhabit-

TABLE 2. JAJMANI RELATIONSHIPS AMONG DIFFERENT CASTES IN RAMPUR

Number	*Caste*	*Serves*	*Is served by*
1	Brahman	2, 3, 4, 5, 6, 7, 8, 9, 10	3, 4, 6, 7, 8, 10, 11, 12
2	Jat		1, 3, 4, 6, 7, 8, 10, 11, 12
3	Baniya	1, 2, 3, 4, 5, 6, 7, 8, 9, 10, 11, 12	1, 4, 8, 10, 11, 12
4	Nai	1, 2, 3, 5, 6, 7, 8, 9, 10	1, 3, 8, 10, 11, 12
5	Chipi	1, 4, 10	1, 3, 4, 8, 10, 11, 12
6	Khati	1, 2, 3, 4	1, 3, 4, 8, 10, 11, 12
7	Lohar	1, 2, 3, 4	1, 3, 4, 8, 10, 11, 12
8	Kumhar	all	1, 4, 10, 11, 12
9	Jhinvar	(cash relationships)	(cash relationships)
10	Dhobi	all	1, 3, 4, 8, 11, 12
11	Camar	1, 2, 3, 4, 5, 6, 7, 8, 9, 10	8, 12
12	Bhangi	1, 2, 3, 4, 5, 6, 7, 8, 9, 10, 11	8, 10

ants are served by two or three underemployed carpenters, Wiser's village of Karimpur, with 754 inhabitants, had eight carpenter families whom Wiser described as being "constantly occupied." [33]

The single Lohar (blacksmith) in Rampur is also in debt. He formerly made and repaired his jajman's agricultural implements (axes, knives, and chopping tools) and during the harvest sharpened their sickles daily. In return, his jajmans paid him according to the schedule given in Table 1. The sale of tools was a supplementary source of income.[34]

Technological change is not responsible for the Rampur Lohar's poverty. He does not have the money to buy tools and equipment. His difficulties seem to stem largely from having too large a family; he married twice and had three children (all daughters) by his first wife and seven

[33] Wiser, *The Hindu Jajmani System*, p. 40.

[34] Reddy gives some details about the Lohar's work and payments in eastern Uttar Pradesh (p. 136). The work includes carpentry, which in Rampur would be done by the carpenter. "The carpentry that is needed in the construction of houses, major repairs of mechanical chaff-cutter and sugar-cane press and making of carts are outside the Jajmani system. Small repairs in the house or minor adjustments of the chaff-cutter and sugar-cane press are generally done by one's own Lohar *Parjan*. If the work takes less than an hour, the Lohar does not get any payment. If such work, however, extends over a few hours, he gets a nominal payment in grain that is sufficient for one meal. If the work outside the Jajmani system takes a whole day or more, he gets fixed wages."

children (four sons, three daughters) by the second. The marriages of his daughters put him in debt. The efforts of this man to support himself and his family show the difficulties of making ends meet in a village like Rampur. In order to pay off his debts, the Lohar decided to make some extra money by plying a horse *tonga* between Mundka and Rampur. So he borrowed 300 rupees at 15 per cent interest and bought a tonga. But then the Lohar fell sick and had to sell the tonga again for 150 rupees in order to pay for his treatment. Harrassed by his creditors, the Lohar left the village after handing over the charge of his jajmans to a Lohar from a neighboring village. A year later, when he returned to Rampur, the Lohar found it hard to get his jajmans back. His debts are still mounting, for the Lohar has to support his wife, four sons, two daughters, and two daughters-in-law. His eldest son, who is 16 years old, helps him in his work, but there are no other earning members in the family.

The "mixed" nature of the jajmani system at Rampur is illustrated in the cases of the Chipi and Dhobi. Two generations ago there were no tailors in Rampur, but a Chipi from Gheora came from time to time to stitch clothes. Then the villagers urged him to move in and stay. He did so, and his descendants (two families) still carry on the trade. The Chipis charge fixed rates in cash or kind for their work when dealing with Jat, Baniya, Khati, Lohar, or Jhinvar families However, in the case of the Nais and Dhobis they stitch clothes free of charge in return for the latter's services. For services at weddings, the Chipis receive from 15 to 30 rupees. They are supplied with earthenware by a Kumhar, who receives so much grain per vessel; a Dhobi washes their clothes without charge; and a Bhangi does all their sweeping in exchange for one *chappatti* [35] a day with leftover food and the occasional present of old clothes. These families are feasted and given money at Chipi weddings — 5 rupees for the Kumhar and 1 each for the Dhobi and Bhangi. A Camar is given 1 rupee at the weddings at which he assists, but there have never been interservice relationships between the Chipis and Camars.

There are four Dhobi families in the village, but two of the family heads have turned to other occupations — agricultural labor in one case and work in an ordnance plant in the other. The two remaining Dhobi families have 21 jajmans in Rampur between them and from 10 to 15 in a neighboring village. They receive from 10 to 20 sirs of grain from each jajman. They also have interservice relationships with Nai, Chipi, and Kumhar families, while some Bhangis do their sweeping at the chappatti-per-day rate. Formerly the Dhobis depended completely upon their local jajmans for a living, but nowadays they have customers in Delhi as well.[36]

[35] *Chappatti:* a wheat cake made of unleavened flour.

[36] For a good account of a Dhobi's work in a south Indian village, written at the end of the 19th century, see T. B. Pandian, *Indian Village Folk* (London, 1898), p. 23 ff.

Both social and technological changes have affected the position of the Nais, or barbers, in Rampur. The Nais used to cut the hair, toenails, and fingernails of their jajmans, while their wives shampooed the women's hair.[37] On harvest days the Nai at Rampur shaved his jajmans in the fields and received one sheaf from each one. After the harvest, the Nai was invited to take a load of as many sheaves as he could carry, or else he was given from 20 sirs to 1 maund of grain.

The Nai also served as marriage go-between. A barber was often commissioned by a girl's parents to find a suitable match for the daughter. When the barber had found a boy with the right qualifications, he was sent to the youth's home along with a Brahman to offer *tika*, the ceremonial placing of a forehead mark. The Nai received *neg jog* from the boy's parents, a gift consisting of 15 rupees in cash and a double cotton sheet; the Brahman received 9 rupees and a single sheet. It was the Nai who arranged the match; the Brahman's role was secondary. The Nai was thus a man of importance in the village. According to Wiser, the Nai and his wife were among the few people at Karimpur who devoted all their time to their jajmans. They had no time for farming.[38]

In recent years the Nai's position at Rampur has changed for the worse. About 25 years ago, a Jat panchayat at Bawana ruled that a Nai would thenceforth receive only 6 rupees as neg jog. The Bawana Nais refused to accept this ruling. The Jats then decided to dispense with Nais as go-betweens and to arrange their daughters' marriages themselves. In protest, the Nais stopped shaving and cutting their jajmans' hair, hoping that this would lead the Jats to resume the old system. Instead, it led some of the Jats to buy razors and to shave themselves, so that when the barbers took up their trade again, they found that they had lost some of their jajmans.

Meanwhile, changes in women's hair styles have adversely affected the Nain, or barber's wife. Formerly, hair was set above the head, and the barber's wife, who was expert in setting it after a shampoo, received 1 sir of grain for dressing it. The present hair style is simpler; any woman can now arrange her own hair. Thus she is apt to shampoo and dress it herself and seldom calls in a Nain.

One of the three Nais from Rampur is now working as a barber in Delhi, the second is a teacher, and the third is a truck driver in Delhi. But they all come back to Rampur on Sundays and give shaves and haircuts to their remaining jajmans.

Another group affected by recent panchayat rulings is the Kumhars

[37] "Shaving under the arms weekly, finger-nail cutting weekly, and toe-nail cutting fortnightly, are added to the tonsorial duties of the barber. Ordinarily hair is cut monthly except when his clients have their heads shaved for religious purposes or through choice. . . . At the time of a wedding he not only shaves the men in his own jajman's household, but he also shaves the guests from other villages — relatives of his jajmans." Wiser, pp. 38–39.

[38] Wiser, *The Hindu Jajmani System*, p. 40.

(potters), of whom there are seven families at Rampur. Except for one family whose head man is working in Delhi, each of the Kumhar families has a fixed number of jajmans to whom they supply clay vessels in exchange for specified amounts of grain.[39] The jajman must take earthenware from his own Kumhar and from none other. No other Kumhar would supply such vessels in any case, unless the jajman's own Kumhar lacked them. The Kumhars keep donkeys, which are needed for hauling clay from the riverbanks. These donkeys are lent out to jajmans when needed. This adds to the grain supplied by the latter — from 20 sirs to 1 maund of grain plus one bundle of dry fodder. A bundle of green fodder is also given from the *kharif* crop.[40] Still more grain may be obtained from weaving, a supplementary trade engaged in by Kumhars. There are also, of course, opportunities at weddings, when jajmans require many clay vessels for their guests, and when the Kumhars are feasted. On these occasions they receive about 2½ rupees and about 5¼ sirs of grain.

A commodity much needed by the Kumhars — and by all the other villagers as well — is cow dung. Since there are only 36 trees in the whole village (each privately owned and having a fixed monetary value), wood cannot be used for burning, and cow dung is the only available fuel. Everyone needs it for that purpose, but the Kumhars need more than others, for they must have plenty of fuel to fire their pottery. Firing takes place about seven times a year, and enough cow dung must be acquired each time. The competitive scramble for cow dung among the villagers has deprived the fields of manure for fertilizer. Faced with this problem, the village panchayat passed a ruling three years ago, prohibiting its collection and imposing a fine of 5 rupees on anyone who violated the rule. Much clandestine collecting no doubt takes place, but the Kumhars have now been compelled to buy much of their fuel. For each firing, about 9 rupees' worth of cow-dung cakes must be obtained. All the Kumhars are now heavily in debt and can hardly afford the extra costs. One Kumhar owes more than 500 rupees.

The handling of cow dung is traditionally the Bhangi's job. There are ten Bhangi (sweeper) families in Rampur, about half of which have found employment in Delhi or elsewhere. The remaining families still work for their jajmans. Bhangis used to receive a chappatti a day from the latter and 20 sirs to 1 maund of grain at harvest time. They were feasted at weddings and received 1 rupee in cash, together with the left-overs of the meal. For playing drums on the occasion of the birth of a

[39] "The Kumhar makes for village use, large round-bellied water jars, various types of jars used for milking, boiling, churning, etc., lids for water and milk jars, funnel-shaped tobacco pipe bowls, saucers which are used for the mustard oil lights, saucers for serving liquid foods at weddings, cups without handles, jars for storing grain, smaller jars for preserving spices and chutneys, feeding jars for cattle, and various other types of clay vessels." Wiser, pp. 45–46.

[40] *Kharif:* the rainy season and the crops planted during it.

son to a jajman, the Bhangis were given some *gur*[41] and wheat; while at a Bhangi wedding the jajman of the family presented 1 rupee and from 2½ to 5 sirs of grain. These obligations are no longer adhered to with regularity. Only a few jajmans give grain annually nowadays. Some do so if the Bhangi helps with the harvest, but the payment is small. One Bhangi who had 16 Jat families as jajmans helped nine of the families at harvest time. Three families gave him only 5 sirs of grain; the other six gave from 15 to 20 sirs. The women in most of the Jat and Brahman families at Rampur now handle cow dung and make cow-dung cakes themselves. However, the Bhangis are still indispensable as sweepers and removers of refuse from the home. So the jajmani relationship persists, although at a low rate of return for the Bhangis.

All the Bhangis at Rampur are heavily in debt and owe money to the Jats. In the past, they used to borrow money from their jajmans, either interest-free or at very low rates, but now they must pay from 12 to 18 per cent a year. Moreover, it is not easy to get loans. If a Bhangi approaches one of the Jats for this purpose, he may be told sarcastically to seek help from the Congress Party or from one of the politicians the Bhangi voted for on election day.

It is not surprising that the Bhangis have become hostile toward the Jats, as have the Camars, who will be discussed in a subsequent paragraph. This hostility has been fanned by some restrictive measures that have cut down the Bhangis' sources of income. The Bhangis formerly kept poultry. But the Jats were annoyed when the chickens made tracks over their freshly made cow-dung cakes, and they expressed their displeasure by manhandling some the Bhangis. No chickens are kept nowadays. The Bhangis also used to keep pigs. But the pigs, like the chickens, were apt to stray and spoil somebody's crops. The Jats told the Bhangis that the pigs would not be allowed to drink water at the village pond. Fines were imposed if pigs were found drinking there. The Bhangis therefore had to sell their pigs or else take them away to relatives in other villages. The loss of chickens and pigs meant a loss of supplementary income — not a small matter to people so deeply in debt.[42]

The greatest break with the jajmani system at Rampur has come from the Camars, traditionally the leather workers of India. They formerly removed their jajman's dead cattle, repaired their shoes and other leather objects, and helped them in agricultural work. George Briggs, writing as long ago as 1920, affirmed that the special role of the Camar in India's rural villages was doomed: "With the rise of the large-scale tanning industry in certain large centres, the village tanner's enterprise is being reduced to smaller dimensions. There is little likelihood that the rural

[41] *Gur:* a crude brown sugar which includes molasses.

[42] According to Mukerjee, however, some low caste groups have deliberately abandoned the raising of pigs and poultry in order to raise their status. See R. Mukerjee *et al.*, "Intercaste Tensions" (University of Lucknow, mimeographed, 1951), p. 14.

industry will survive. In this connection it is interesting to note that during the decade ending in 1911 there was a very marked decrease (36.9 per cent) in the number engaged in tanning, currying, dressing, and dyeing leather. At the same time the Camar population increased. Furthermore one of the results of the war has been a very great advance in large-scale tanning. The demand for village tanned leather is gradually being reduced to that of water-buckets and thongs. The former will be supplied more and more from chrome tanned leather, which is not a rural product at all, and finally, cheaper fabrics made from vegetable fibres will supplant leather for irrigation purposes. Slowly factory tanned leather will supplant village tanned leather in the village shoemaking industry." [43]

However, leather-working is only one of the Camars' traditional tasks. Ibbetson has described some of their duties in the Karnal tract, not far from Rampur: "The *Chamárs* are the coolies of the tract. They cut grass, carry wood, put up tents, carry bundles, act as watchmen and the like for officials; and this work is shared by *all* the *Chamárs* in the village. They also plaster the houses with mud when needed. They take the skins of all animals which die in the village except those which die on Saturday or Sunday, or the first which dies of cattle plague. They generally give one pair of boots per ox and two pairs per buffalo skin so taken to the owner." [44]

Table 3 gives some of the traditional obligations and payments for the Camars at Rampur.

Camars were formerly required to perform begar, including compulsory service for government officials who visited the village. In general, their position has always been a very low one, but recently they have been making efforts to raise their status and have discontinued some of their traditional jajmani obligations and services. They have developed mutual feelings of hostility with the Jats in consequence. During the past 20 years or so, the Camars seem to have been losing some of the sense of inferiority associated with their low caste status and untouchability. This has partly been due to the efforts of organizations such as the Arya Samaj, the Congress Party, and some of the other political parties in India. The Arya Samaj, a Hindu religious reform movement, has long campaigned against caste restrictions in this area, apparently with some effect. They held a conference in Rampur in 1910 at which some non-Brahman groups, principally the Jats, were persuaded to wear the sacred thread that was formerly reserved for the use of Brahmans. The Jats were urged not to feast Brahmans at cere-

[43] G. Briggs, *The Chamars* (London: Oxford University Press, 1920), p. 227. The increasing use of Persian wells has cut down on the demand for leather buckets.

[44] D. C. J. Ibbetson, *Report on the Revision of Settlement of the Panipat Tahsil and Karnal Parganah of the Karnal District*, 1872–1880 (Allahabad: Pioneer Press, 1883), pp. 116–117.

monial occasions, for this custom merely developed greediness in the latter caste. Besides, the speakers pointed out, village Brahmans are mostly illiterate, Brahmans only by birth, who have no real knowledge of the Vedas. In 1933, a second Arya Samaj conference was held at Rampur, this time directed against untouchability. The speakers told the Camars in the audience that unpaid begar service had no legal basis and that they should refuse to perform it. The speakers promised the Camars assistance if they got into trouble for refusing begar service. As a result, the Camars stopped rendering begar.

The Camars who carried away the dead animals of their jajmans used to eat the flesh of these animals. When previous attempts had been made to remove untouchability, the Jats had objected on the grounds that the Camars ate carrion. At the 1933 conference, the Arya Samaj speakers exhorted the Camars to give up eating the flesh of dead animals and to keep themselves and their homes clean so that untouchability could be removed. The Camars took a vow to do so. Most of the Jats at the conference then drank water at the hands of the Camars. These Jats were subsequently boycotted by the Brahmans for this violation of caste rules.

Despite this gesture on the part of some of the Jats, tensions developed between the Jats and the Camars. These had been manifest before the 1933 conference. In 1926 the Camars refused to pay the traditional house tax (*kudhi-tarif*) of 2 rupees per year to the Jats. The Camars of the few surrounding villages raised 450 rupees, a tremendous sum at that time, and took the case to the court. However, the other non-Jats of the village, still dependent upon the Jats as their kamins, did not support the Camars. All the Jat factions united in opposing the Camars. The case dragged on for two years, and the Jats finally won. However, the Camars still refused to pay the tax, and a court decree was obtained by the Jats for the auction of the Camars' property. Both of the *lambardars* (headmen) of the village along with other Jats led by the court-appointed officer, went to the house of the leader of the Camars and forcibly confiscated some brass vessels, *ghi*, and cotton, all of which were taken to a Jat's house, where they were held until the tax was paid.

A few years later the Camars and Jats fought another court case. This time the Camars brought criminal proceedings against some Jats who had beaten them for carrying meat in their pots. Then, in 1938, the house tax question came up again. During the preceding ten years, the Jats had failed to collect the house tax, which they now demanded in lump sum. When the Camars pleaded inability to pay, the taxes during this ten-year period were forgiven. But the Camars went on to pay taxes from 1938 to 1947. There were three other court cases between the Camars and Jats from 1930 to 1947. In one case, the Jats asked the Camars to assign a man each day to keep a day watch to guard Jat harvests against animals and thieves. When the Camars refused, the

TABLE 3. SERVICES RENDERED AND PAYMENTS RECEIVED BY CAMARS, RAMPUR

Occasion	*Services rendered*	*Payment received*
Boy's marriage	1. Felling trees, cutting wood for fuel. 2. Providing a watch at the house after the wedding party has left. 3. Accompanying the wedding party; attending to the bullocks at the bride's home.	1. Meals when cutting wood. 2. 1 rupee at departure of the wedding party. 3. 1 rupee at departure of the wedding party from the bride's home. 4. 1 rupee and some grain (usually 5 to 10 sirs of wheat).
Girl's marriage	1. Cutting wood for fuel. 2. Assistance in reception of wedding party. 3. Feeding their bullocks. 4. Keeping watch where party camps. 5. Making repairs in the house.	1. Meals for the whole family four times during the three-day stay. 2. 1 rupee at wedding party's departure. 3. 1 rupee, wheat (usually 5 to 10 sirs), and clothes after the wedding.
Ordinary service	1. Work without payment for officials (begar). 2. Repairs of jajman's shoes. 3. Work in extraordinary situations (illness or death, and so forth). 4. Help in harvesting. 5. Removal of dead cattle.	1. Meals on days of work for jajman. 2. 1 sir of grain at harvest time. 3. Grain left over on the threshing floor. 4. One-fortieth of the grain produce (minimum 2 to 5 maunds). 5. Animal carcases taken.
Extraordinary service	1. Full time work in harvesting *rabi* crop. 2. Full time work in harvesting kharif crop.	1. One-twentieth of the produce. 2. One-tenth of the produce if 100 maunds or over; more if the kharif crop is is less. 3. Meals given on work days.

Jats took the case to court. A compromise was reached in which the Camars agreed to a night watch rather than a day watch. The Camars interpreted this as a victory, and they became more aggressive, severing all their occupational and ceremonial relations with the Jats, including the burial of dead animals. After about six months, however, they resumed the removal of dead animals and maintained this service until the time of Indian independence. During World War II, many Camars from Rampur were employed in a nearby ordnance depot and in other military jobs, which gave them an opportunity to take an independent stand.

With the coming of independence, the position of the Camars was strengthened both legally and ideologically. Now the Jats could no longer enforce the provisions of the wajib-ul-arz, which specified the traditional village duties. The Camars stopped the payment of the house tax and the handling of dead animals. However, with the more limited opportunities for employment after the war, the Camars once again became dependent on the Jats. This put them in a difficult position vis-à-vis the Jats because they had openly opposed the latter in the panchayat and had supported the Congress Party candidate, who was opposed by most of the Jats.[45]

Giving up the practice of removing dead animals was a gradual process. For a while, the Camars removed only those animals that had died a lingering death from badly smelling wounds. The Jats disposed of other carcasses by burial. This violated provisions laid down in the wajib-ul-arz. Previously, when a Jat had buried a bullock, the Camars had reported the matter to the police, who then had the carcasses dug up and turned over to them. If the skin were decomposed, the Jat was made to pay the cost of the skin to his Camar.

The burial of animals by the Jats, however, was not without precedent. A mass burial of animals used to take place at *aikta* ceremonies, when there was a cattle epidemic. On these occasions, a curer was brought to the village, and all the livestock was brought together in one place. The curer performed some ritual actions and burned incense near the animals, all of which were then driven beneath a sacred stick. Ganges water was sprinkled about in all the houses. No outsiders were admitted into the village on this day, nor could any of the villagers leave. Various taboos prevailed; no iron utensils were used, flour was not milled, chappattis were not cooked, and houses remained unswept. The ceremony began on a Saturday and lasted until Sunday evening. At these times the Jats used to seek the Camars' permission to kill and bury the cattle, but this permission was readily granted, for the Camars also wanted the epidemic to end. Gradually, however, the Jats began to perpetuate the practice of burying dead cattle.

In 1934–35 the Camars temporarily gave up removing dead animals, partly because of objections raised by a doctor, who claimed that they were skinned too near the villagers' homes. Two years later, when a different place was set aside for the skinning, the removal of dead ani-

[45] For a similar dilemma, see "The Changing Status of a Depressed Caste," based on reports by Bernard S. Cohn, in *Village India*, M. Marriott, ed. American Anthropological Association, 1955, Memoir 83.

mals was resumed rather half-heartedly by the Camars. In 1947, on the eve of Indian independence, the Camars at Rampur gave up the practice altogether and have not resumed it since.

After the 1933 Arya Samaj conference, when the Camars gave up rendering begar service, the Jats began to cut down on the amounts of grain given them, claiming that the stipulations in the wajib-ul-arz had been violated by the Camars. Some of the latter say that this was a mere excuse on the part of the Jats. The main factor, according to them, was the increased price of grain.

Another factor must have been the increasing fragmentation of land. When the size of land holdings was large, and when they could not be managed without outside help, the traditional assistance of the Camars was sought and welcomed by the Jats; but as land holdings became smaller and families larger, and as pressure on the land brought about further fragmentation, the assistance of the Camars became less crucial. This was, of course, a gradual process; it did not happen overnight.[46]

Technologic changes have also had their effect. A mechanical iron cane crusher has now supplanted the old wooden type of crusher and obviated the large work crew that managed the old machine. Chaff cutting machines have supplanted the old tools used for that purpose. The Jat land-owners are now less dependent on Camars in these areas.

Meanwhile, the Camars have been trying to raise their socioreligious status by following higher-caste practices and giving up the consumption of dead animal flesh. Their ties to their *jajmans* have weakened. Gradually they have given up repairing the latter's shoes, another of their traditional jajmani obligations.

The opportunity to enter schools is now a new channel to higher status. None of the older Camars at Rampur can read or write, but 85 per cent of their boys aged 6 to 15 are attending school. In Kanjhawla High School, the untouchables and higher-caste boys eat together, while in the local school young Camars and Jats sit side by side. Since 1949 a Camar has been elected to the newly constituted intervillage council of four villages.

During World War II new kinds of employment were made available to the Camars, and some went to Delhi to work. Although there has been a postwar contraction of employment, four of the 21 Camar families at Rampur have found employment outside the village. Two work as agricultural laborers for one or two months a year at daily wages. Some work as occasional day laborers. Three Camar families do weaving, four

[46] Some aspects of the conflict between the Jats and Camars at Rampur have been dealt with in O. Lewis, "Group Dynamics in a North-Indian Village: A study in Factions," *Economic Weekly*, Bombay 6, pp. 423–425, 445–451, 477–482, 501–506 (1954). A discussion of land tenure, population pressures, and related economic problems appears in O. Lewis, "Aspects of Land Tenure and Economics in a North-Indian Village," in *Economic Development and Cultural Change* 4, No. 3, 279–302 (1956).

have taken up a guava garden on a contract basis, and four have started vegetable growing. Some raise cattle to supplement their income. Only two Camars in the village are shoemakers.

One of the Camars was asked why the other Camars did not also make shoes to supplement their income. He answered that capital is needed to buy cured hides, which cost from 50 to 60 rupees. Even if they somehow managed to buy a hide, they would have to sell shoes on credit and in most cases get only grain in return. The problem of getting funds for another hide would remain as before. The informant was questioned as follows:

"How did you manage it before?"

"We used to remove the dead cattle and tan the hides ourselves."

"Couldn't that system be revived?"

"Most of us don't want to skin leather any more."

"But couldn't you find just one man who would agree to do it for the others?"

"Well — that's a good idea. But all the other villagers would have to agree."

As it is, under the present system, all the hides at Rampur are going to waste, buried in the earth year by year. If cured hides cost from 50 to 60 rupees, this represents an enormous loss to the villagers.

It is not only low-caste groups that have abandoned their jajmani obligations at Rampur. The Brahmans have also done so. They formerly used to officiate at marriages and other ceremonies at the homes of their jajmans, at which times they received from 20 sirs to 2 maunds of grain and fodder. Every day during the cane-crushing season, a farmer would set aside from 1½ to 2 sirs of gur for his Brahman. Brahmans had traditional roles to play at festivals such as Kanagat and Makar Sankrant, at which they were feasted, and also in the event of a Kaj, a celebration in honor of the dead. The Arya Samaj, as has been noted, has expressed opposition to the feasting of Brahmans, and the Jats have been influenced by this point of view. Partly for this reason — perhaps also for the sake of economy — they have stopped feasting Brahmans. A Kaj has not been given for several years, and at festival times the Brahmans are seldom fed. (Cows or young girls are sometimes fed instead.) The Rampur Brahmans, for their part, claim that they regard the acceptance of food and charity as demeaning and that they prefer not to accept it. The Brahmans no longer settle marriage agreements, cook food at weddings, or carry on priestly functions. Four of the Rampur Brahmans are now cultivators, although only two make this their sole means of support. One of the Brahmans is a tailor, another sells milk.

There is one Baniya (merchant) family in the village which owns a shop. According to Wiser, the Vaisyas, who are absent in Karimpur, do not form an essential part of the Hindu jajmani system. This grouping would include the Baniya. Wiser quotes Sir Henry Maine to the effect that "the grain dealer (Vaisya) is never a hereditary trader incorporated with the village group." [47] The villagers at Rampur, however, speak of the Baniya as if he took part in the jajmani system. He has jajmani-type relationships, at least, with the Brahman families in Rampur and is served by Nais, Dhobis, Kumhars, Camars, and Bhangis. Besides selling grain and other commodities, the Baniya enters certain records in an account book for the benefit of some Rampur families. The gift of money (*neota*) presented at a wedding is recorded in this book, for the same sum must be paid back when there is a marriage in the donor's household. The Baniya receives 2 rupees for this service. He also keeps records, without charge, of loans made by one man to another. The Baniya was formerly paid for weighing grain, but most people weigh the grain themselves nowadays, and the Baniya has lost this source of income. According to Ibbetson, the Baniyas in the Karnal tract give a ball of gur on the day after Holi and some parched rice or sweets on Divali to the proprietors "in recognition of the subordinate position which they occupy in the village." [48]

The following sums up the present situation of the jajmani system: The system is still functioning in Rampur, a village close to Delhi, the nation's capital. Despite modern improvements, technological changes, India's five-year plans, the influence of reformist movements, and political ideologies, the system is not yet dead. However, changes are taking place. The Camars have stopped fulfilling some of their jajmani obligations toward the Jats, who have reciprocated in turn. There are also indications of tension between the Jats and the Bhangis, although the latter continue to serve their jajmans. The Brahmans have lost their priestly functions. The Dhobis, who formerly depended completely upon their local jajmans, now have customers in Delhi as well. The Khatis and the Lohar are abandoning their traditional trades. The Nais have lost their roles as marriage go-betweens as well as some of their opportunities as barbers.

Most of the lower caste villagers — and many of the Jats — are in debt. Some have been led to change their occupations and have gone to Delhi to look for work. Technological changes and the increasing land fragmentation have reduced the need for help in agriculture among the Jat families. Meanwhile, the Arya Samaj and some of the political parties have preached, with some effect, against caste restrictions. All these factors have led to a loosening of jajmani ties and obligations.

DISCUSSION

In a chapter in which he weighed the advantages and disadvantages of the jajmani system, Wiser drew an essentially benevolent picture of how it provided "peace and contentment" for the villagers.[49] The account by Opler and Singh has a similar emphasis: "Not only does

[47] Wiser, *The Hindu Jajmani System,* p. 143.
[48] Ibbetson, p. 118.
[49] Wiser, *The Hindu Jajmani System,* p. 187.

everyone have some place within the Hindu system, but it is significant that every group, from the Brahman to the Camar caste, has been somehow integrated into the social and ceremonial round of the community and has been given some opportunity to feel indispensable and proud." [50]

Our picture of Rampur, however, leads to a quite different assessment, for it seems evident that the relationship between jajman and kamin lends itself to the exploitation of the latter. Land ownership is the basis of power in Rampur. All the village land, including the house sites, is owned by the Jats; the other castes are thus living there more or less at the sufferance of the Jats. It was this crucial relationship to the land, with the attendant power of eviction, that made it possible for the Jats to exact begar service from the Camars in the past and still enables them to dominate the other caste groups. Moreover, some of the latter, such as the Bhangis, are deeply in debt to their jajmans. This gives the Jats an additional hold over their kamins.

Although Wiser's definition of the jajmani system and his theoretical discussion of it stress the element of reciprocity, most of his own data point to the asymmetrical nature of the power relationship. The same exploitative situation can be shown to exist in other areas where the jajmani system is found. Writing of a village near Lucknow, Majumdar and his colleagues write that the higher caste people always try to humiliate the lower castes. "The Thakurs dictate the most ruthless terms to the Chamars who take their fields as share croppers." [51] Reddy notes that a Lohar receives much less for his work from his Thakur jajmans than he gets from other castes.[52] Reddy also mentions that Lohars get beaten by their jajmans for delinquencies in their obligations.[53] Even Wiser, despite his favorable assessment, showed awareness of the harsh realities

[50] Opler and Singh, p. 496. The institution of caste has, of course, been lauded and attacked by various writers both in India and the West. H. Maine described it as "the most disastrous and blighting of all institutions," and R. Tagore called it "a gigantic system of cold-blooded repression." But Abbé Dubois, who was often critical of Indian customs, referred to caste as "the happiest effort of Hindu legislation." Gandhi expressed both points of view at different times. "Historically speaking," he once averred, "caste may be regarded as man's experiment or social adjustment in the laboratory of Indian society. If we can prove it to be a success, it can be offered to the world as a leaven and as the best remedy against heartless competition and social disintegration born of avarice and greed." But Gandhi also wrote, "Caste has nothing to do with religion. It is harmful both to spiritual and national growth." These quotations from Gandhi come from N. K. Bose, Ed., *Selections from Gandhi* (Navajivan, Ahmedabad), pp. 232, 234. That of Dubois is from J. A. Dubois, *Hindu Manners, Customs, and Ceremonies,* translated by H. K. Beauchamp (Clarendon Press, Oxford, 1947), p. 28. The quotations from Maine and Tagore are drawn from L. S. S. O'Malley, *Indian Caste Customs* (Cambridge University Press, Cambridge, 1932) p. vii.

[51] D. N. Majumdar *et al.*, "Intercaste Relations in Gohanakallan, a Village near Lucknow," *Eastern Anthropol.* 8, 211 (1955).

[52] Reddy, p. 137.

[53] *Ibid.*, pp. 139–140.

of the power relationship in *The Hindu Jajmani System.* But this awareness was given a much sharper expression in the book *Behind Mud Walls,* which was written in collaboration with his wife Charlotte Viall Wiser: "The leaders of our village are so sure of their power that they make no effort to display it. The casual visitor finds little to distinguish them from other farmers. . . . And yet when one of them appears among men of serving caste, the latter express respect and fear in every guarded word and gesture. The serving ones have learned that as long as their subservience is unquestioned, the hand which directs them rests lightly. But let there be any move toward independence or even indifference among them, and the paternal touch becomes a strangle-hold . . . in every detail of life have the leaders bound the villagers to themselves. Their favour may bring about a man's prosperity and their disfavour may cause him to fail, or may make life so unbearable for him that he will leave the village." [54] It is also evident from Wiser's data that the upper castes receive much more than the lower castes in goods and services.[55]

That the ownership of land, including house sites, is the crucial factor, appears in other areas as well. "In the good old days," writes Darling of the Punjab, "village servants were in complete subjection to their 'masters,' and this is still largely the case in the feudal north and west. There the fear of ejection from the village is a yoke which keeps the head bowed, and only those who own their own house and courtyard dare assert themselves." [56] An informant told Gittel Steed: "You have seen the whole Bakrana, every house probably. Have you seen any house that can be called a good house? This is because everyone is frightened of being driven out at any time. No one wants to build a good house here." [57] "That the *zemindar* is all-powerful in such places need hardly be stressed," writes Mohinder Singh. "The threat of demolishing a man's dwelling or ejecting him therefrom are powerful weapons in his hand for extorting begar. Till recently the cultivators did not have any rights in their house sites." [58]

While the landowners are generally of higher caste in Indian villages, it is their position as landowners, rather than caste membership per se, that gives them status and power. In Karimpur, where the Brahmans are the landowners, the traditional caste hierarchy obtains. But in Rampur the Jats own the land, and the Brahmans are subservient to them. Majumdar and his colleagues present a similar picture in their description of the village near Lucknow: "The respect which the Brahmins enjoy is merely conventional; in daily life, however, the Brahmins

[54] C. V. Wiser and W. H. Wiser, *Behind Mud Walls* (New York: Agricultural Missions, 1951), pp. 18–19; see also Cohn, p. 61.

[55] Wiser, *The Hindu Jajmani System,* pp. 70–71; Misra, "Earnings of Village Servants in U.P.," p. 98.

[56] Darling, p. 272.

[57] G. Steed, lecture notes, hectographed.

[58] M. Singh, *The Depressed Classes* (Bombay: Hind Kitabs, 1947), p. 193.

are treated on an equal footing with the other castes. . . . The Thakurs are the most influential group of people in the village because they are economically better off. They own most of the agricultural land in the village. They are the landlords who give employment to the other caste-people. The various other castes serve the Thakurs as their dependents." [59] Opler and Singh also report that in Madhopur the Brahmans, "in spite of their top position in the orthodox social scale, are not influential. The reason is that they are economically dependent on others." [60] In Madhopur it is the Thakurs who own the land, more than 82 per cent of it, and it is they who form the dominant caste, as in the study just cited. In another village described by Opler and Singh, a lower caste Ahir is headman of the village and leader of the village panchayat. He owns 50 acres — "the only villager who has actual ownership of any substantial portion of village land." [61] In an early work by Russell and Hira Lal, an area is discussed where Kunbis have higher-than-usual status. "The only reasonable explanation of this rise in status appears to be that the Kunbi has taken possession of the land and has obtained the rank which from time immemorial belongs to the hereditary cultivator as a member and citizen of the village community." [62]

Since the passing of *zamindari* abolition bills, the key power of landowners may have been curtailed in certain areas. Majumdar and his colleagues, for example, report that in the village they studied near Lucknow, where zamindari abolition has taken place, Camars now refuse to perform begar, while the barbers refuse to draw water for the Thakurs and will not wash their utensils or remove their leaf-plates any more.[63] However, the occurrence of begar since Indian independence has been noted in some areas — by Gittel Steed,[64] for example, and by Shridhar Misra.[65]

A qualification may be suggested, that while a landowner may have both tenants and kamins, the two groups need not be identical. He may have kamins who are not his tenants. This point is made by Opler and Singh, who also note that when there are disputes between Thakurs, the tenants align themselves with their landlords.[66] Perhaps a more crucial

[59] Majumdar *et al.*, p. 193.

[60] M. E. Opler and R. D. Singh, "Two Villages of Eastern Uttar Pradesh," *Am. Anthropol.* 54, 180 (1952), p. 180.

[61] Opler and Singh, "Two Villages of Eastern Uttar Pradesh," p. 187.

[62] R. V. Russell and R. B. Hira Lal, *The Tribes and Castes of the Central Provinces of India* (London, 1916), vol. 4, p. 22.

[63] Majumdar *et al.*, pp. 191–192.

[64] G. Steed, lecture notes, hectographed.

[65] S. Misra, "Caste Survey in Two Modal Villages with Stereotyped Discriminations," in "*Intercaste Tensions*" (28, p. 58). In a rural survey conducted by Misra, 11 out of 40 persons examined on the subject of *begar* admitted that they had to do *begar* at the instance of *zamindars*. Such *begar* usually takes the form of ploughing without payment once a year. For some striking descriptions of *begar* during the period of British rule, see G. Emerson, *Voiceless India* (New York: John Day, 1944), pp. 28, 173.

[66] Opler and Singh, "The Division of Labor in an Indian Village," p. 495.

consideration, however, is that the Thakurs in Senapur, like the Jats in Rampur, form a caste group that may (despite factional cleavages and differences in wealth) join ranks in solidarity vis-à-vis the lower castes in crucial issues. All the Jat factions in Rampur, for example, united in opposing the Camars over the house-tax matter.

The lower castes, theoretically at least, have a potential retaliatory weapon in the boycott, or withdrawal of their services. Thus, when the Nais of Rampur were informed of a decision by the Jats to reduce the neg jog paid at weddings, they stopped shaving and cutting their jajmans' hair in protest. But the sequel is instructive: The Jats retaliated by buying razors and shaving themselves. This shows that such protests may prove to be self-defeating. It also indicates that the jajmani system may be disrupted by action of either the jajmans or the kamins, or by the cumulative effect of both.

As the jajmani system declines, a great deal of tension is bound to develop between the landed and the landless, between the upper and lower castes, particularly since the system's decline is concomitant with a great increase in population and a decrease in the size of landholdings. Although the dominant position of the Jats is not yet in jeopardy in Rampur, their influence over the lower castes has been much reduced, and the demands of the lower castes have increased. It would therefore seem that the jajmani system contains some explosive potentialities and that, as the system continues to weaken, we may expect to see a heightening of the conflict between the dominant and subordinate castes in villages such as Rampur.

Meanwhile, despite the weakening of the jajmani system and the inroads of a money economy in Rampur, the social aspects of the caste system have changed very little. The rules of endogamy are not questioned.[67] Despite the influence of the Arya Samaj, the traditional caste rules governing interdining and the taking of water still prevail. The Jats will not share their hookahs with Camars or Bhangis or sit on the same string-cots with them.[68] When community project speakers address the people of Rampur in would-be democratic assemblages, the Camars remain on the outskirts of the crowd. Patterns of hierarchy and social distance persist, and the psychology of caste still permeates interpersonal relationships.

In some ways caste identifications have even strengthened in Rampur. Among the Jats the emphasis on caste loyalty may represent a defensive reaction to the weakening of the jajmani system, while among the Camars it signifies a united stand vis-à-vis the higher caste landowners.

[67] Caste endogamy is still the rule even in large cities, as was shown in a study by N. P. Gist, "Caste Differentials in South India," *Am. Sociol. Rev.* 19, 138 (1954). "Out of some two thousand married Hindu household heads who supplied information," writes Gist, "only nine stated that they and their wives belong to different castes." These surveys were made in Mysore and Bangalore.

[68] *See also* Cohn in *Village India*, p. 61.

A similar point, on a broader scale, has been made by Srinavas, who discusses the ways in which the modern political system, including universal adult franchise, has strengthened caste.

"The principle of caste," writes Srinavas, "is so firmly entrenched in our political and social life that everyone including the leaders have accepted tacitly the principle that, in the provincial cabinets at any rate, each major caste should have a minister (And this principle has travelled from our provincial capitals back to our village panchayats — nowadays the latter give representation on the panchayat to each caste including Harijans). In the first popular cabinet in Mysore State, headed by Shri K. C. Reddy, not only were the ministers chosen on a caste basis, but each had a secretary from his own sub-sub-sub caste. And today in Mysore this principle is followed not only in every appointment, but also in the allotment of seats in schools and colleges. . . . voting is on a caste basis, and voters do not understand that it is immoral to demand that the elected minister help his caste-folk and village folk. . . . no explanation of provincial politics in any part of India is possible without reference to caste. . . . In general, it may be said that the last hundred years have seen a great increase in caste solidarity and the concomitant decrease of a sense of interdependence between the different castes living in a region." [69]

While this may perhaps be overstating the case, it is a necessary corrective to the more widely held assumption that caste is crumbling rapidly. The decline of the jajmani system, then, will not necessarily be followed by an automatic or speedy disintegration of the caste system. Instead, caste may continue to take on new functions and manifestations.

[69] M. N. Srinavas, "Castes: Can They Exist in India of Tomorrow?" *Economic Weekly*, Bombay, 15 Oct. 1955, pp. 1231–1232. For some other discussions of the new functions of castes, see D. R. Gadgil, *Poona, A Socio-Economic Survey* (Poona: Gokhale Institute, 1952), part 2, p. 187; B. Ryan, *Caste in Modern Ceylon* (New Brunswick, N.J.: Rutgers University Press, 1953), p. 321; K. Davis, *The Population of India and Pakistan* (Princeton, N.J.: Princeton University Press), p. 175.

Cash or Credit Crops? An Examination of Some Implications of Peasant Commercial Production with Special Reference to the Multiplicity of Traders and Middlemen

Barbara E. Ward

> When I first knew Sarawak practically every Chinese Bazaar was an exact copy of every other except in size. The days of plate glass windows, show cases and English speaking assistants had not arrived. The same goods were stocked in the same way — rather higgledy-piggledy to our lights — but according to a system of their own. Boxes of rice, carefully graded according to quality. Tubs of various pastes, all rather smelly but undoubtedly good — pickled eggs of some antiquity, strings of vermicelli, exotic looking Chinese dried fruits, layers and layers of salt fish, salt, sugar, bits of shark, birds-nests; all these foods which the people love. Behind were bales of calico, that unbleached cloth known as "blachu," dark blue cotton, bright red cotton. Bundles of cheap flowered cloths, imitation "batik" sarongs, and butter muslin. Straw hats, sock suspenders, purse belts, singlets, made-up bow ties, and hair ribbons. Tiger balm, camphor oil, Dr. Williams' Pink Pills, and Vaseline. Tin plates, kettles, clogs, and pocket knives — what a collection! — but all desirable to the people. Candidly, I don't know how all these shops carried it all. Then of course the ways of Chinese commerce are a mystery to us. *In a small town you might get twenty or thirty of these shops, all the same and all receiving custom.*[1]

Many writers have remarked the multiplicity of apparently identical small shops and petty traders in many parts of the non-Western world. Many have taken the line that this reduplication is necessarily uneconomic, only to be explained by the "irrationality" of the local people or, as here, the "mysteries" of the Orient. In certain parts of the British

From "Cash or Credit Crops? An Examination of Some Implications of Peasant Commercial Production with Special Reference to the Multiplicity of Traders and Middlemen" in *Economic Development and Cultural Change*, Vol. VIII, No. 2 (January 1960), pp. 148–163. Reprinted by permission of The University of Chicago Press.

[1] J. B. Archer, *Autobiography*, unpublished ms. quoted in T'ien Ju-K'ang, *The Chinese of Sarawak*, London School of Economics Monographs on Social Anthropology No. 12, London, 1953, p. 37.

Colonial Empire, notably Uganda, attempts were early made to limit the numbers of retail traders by insisting upon a system of licences which would, it was believed, protect the "genuine" traders from such "uneconomic" competition. The multiplicity of middlemen to be found in the export trade of many of the colonial territories was (and is) often under a similar fire of criticism both from the local administrations and from Whitehall.

Recently there has been a reversal of attitudes, if not on the part of governments, at least on the part of some economists and economic historians. P. T. Bauer [2] in particular has emphasized that there are certain essential economic services concerned with both the distribution of consumer goods and the collection of primary produce which can best be supplied for a largely peasant producing population by a great multiplicity of middlemen. In the following pages attention is drawn to the significance in this respect of one other essential service: namely, the provision of credit.

THE FIELD

The material on which the following observations are based has been drawn mainly from the British Crown Colony of Sarawak, with supporting evidence from Hong Kong, the Federation of Malaya, Uganda, and Ghana.

With the exception of Malaya and Hong Kong, the territories under consideration in this paper are overwhelmingly composed of peasant producers.[3] Even in Malaya at least 40 per cent of the total production of rubber comes from small-holdings,[4] and in Hong Kong I am confining my attention solely to the 25,000 or so people who draw their livelihood from the family-based production of the inshore fishing grounds.

SMALL-SCALE COMMERCIAL PRIMARY PRODUCTION REQUIRES MIDDLEMEN

The common characteristic of those sections of these several societies which are concerned with commercial primary production by peasants is not the crop, nor the rhythms and methods of production — for these are all different — but the need to put the primary product on the market in order to obtain any reward at all. It is here in the marketing and especially the first level (produce-buying) marketing of the primary products that comparable features are to be looked for.

Rubber, sago, fish, coffee, cotton, cocoa differ fundamentally in production, but share one negative property in that none in itself provides

[2] P. T. Bauer, *West African Trade*, Cambridge, 1954, ch. 2.

[3] R. W. Firth, *Malay Fishermen: Their Peasant Economy*, London, 1946, pp. 22–27 and *passim*.

[4] Figures refer to 1953 production. Federation of Malaya, *Annual Report for 1954*, London, 1955.

subsistence for its producer: all have to be marketed. Most, also, have to be processed in some way, or ways, essential to their final acceptance on the world markets, to which they must in addition be "communicated" through the often complex systems of overseas export. Both processing and communication may be difficult, even impossible, for the peasant producer himself to perform. Sarawak's sago must be refined, bagged, and shipped to Singapore; Uganda's cotton must be ginned and exported to America, Britain, or India; much of Hong Kong's fish must be dried and salted or made into pungent red sauce, and although most of it is eaten in the colony itself, no fisherman has the time or skill to see to his own retailing. Thus, as has often been remarked, because peasant producers themselves do not usually have the requisite time or skill to do more than start their produce on the first rung of the market ladder, societies in which their type of commercial production predominates necessarily require middlemen to take over the primary products and handle them on their way to the wider markets.

There is an obverse to this situation: commercial primary producers require not only to sell but to buy. A society of this kind therefore necessarily also demands middlemen in the distributive trades, from the big importers in the ports down to the small shopkeepers, street hawkers, and so forth who go to the most minute villages and settlements up-country.

It is thus with the relatively small-scale trade with which peasant producers are involved that this paper is primarily concerned. Estate workers (wage laborers) have a place in this trade, but only as buyers of consumer goods (including foodstuffs), not as sellers of primary produce. Peasant producers, whether small landholders or fishermen, are involved in both buying and selling.

Despite the lack of exact enumeration, there is no doubt that except where they have been deliberately restricted by administrative action, the numbers of small-scale middlemen in the societies under consideration are large. So are those of retailers. How is this to be accounted for?

Obviously, one explanation lies in the difficulties of transport and communication in underdeveloped territories. Cocoa farmers in the depths of the Ghana rain forest, sago gardens up the Oya River in Sarawak cannot all be visited easily by one or two large-scale produce buyers, and cannot all be served easily by one or two large central stores. Though it carries force, however, this argument does not explain why — to let just one example stand for many — one small Hong Kong fishing village, with a total population (including women and small children) of just over 400, had (in 1953) room for two almost identical general shops and made use of the services of up to 13 fish buyers.[5]

[5] All data for Hong Kong are drawn from my own field notes. I am deeply indebted to the Committee for Foreign Languages and Cultures set up by H. M. Treasury (the Scarborough Committee) for enabling me to spend the years 1950–1953 in Hong Kong.

My suggestion is that such a state of affairs is at least partly to be accounted for by the fact that in many of the small-scale kinds of situation we are considering here, a large proportion of the everyday commercial transactions — produce-buying, retailing, paying for services of all kinds, including those of a predominantly "social" nature such as funerals, weddings, etc. — is carried on by means of some form of credit arrangement. In the vast majority of cases the creditor parties to such arrangements themselves have very little capital, and the number of debtors they can serve is therefore closely restricted. Furthermore, these are nearly always arrangements of personal trust made between individuals who are well acquainted with each other, and there is a limit to the number of individuals any one creditor can know well enough to trust in this way, even if he has (as he usually has not) a relatively large stock of capital.

The rest of this paper is devoted to amplifying and defending this point of view.

THE DEPENDENCE UPON CREDIT

In a book entitled *The Chinese of Sarawak, A Study of Social Structure,* T'ien Ju-K'ang [6] describes in detail the relationship which exists between Chinese primary producers and Chinese middlemen in that country. This is based upon an elaborate system of credit.

In Sarawak the Chinese village shopkeepers are at the same time the lowest level middlemen in the rubber trade. This congruence of middlemen and retailer roles in one individual is not particularly common; it simplifies but does not essentially alter the general picture. T'ien claims that "in effect these Chinese village shopkeepers in Sarawak who own some capital act as loan making capitalists and bankers, while the planters, who have none, constitute a labour force in their employ." [7]

What happens in fact is that, although a Chinese rubber planter in Sarawak does his shopping in the street markets for cash, and also pays for larger items — such as furniture, a bicycle, a radio, a watch, school-fees, or a wedding for his son — with cash (very often borrowed), he gets most of his everyday supplies of rice, other groceries, kerosene, hardware, etc., from the village shop of his choice on credit. The middleman-retailer (i.e., the shopkeeper) keeps a small notebook for each planter family. In it he writes down a credit and debit account of rubber (or other produce) against "groceries." (The account is always kept in money values; there is no question of barter.)

Rubber planters who have a long-standing connexion with the shop simply send their rubber sheets in, almost every afternoon, often by the children, trusting the shopkeeper to write down the correct current price. Others may spend a longer time each day ascertaining the current price and making sure that it is

[6] *Op. cit., passim.*
[7] *Ibid.,* p. 37.

correctly entered. In either case the next daily step is to order the daily grocery supplies — from the same shop. If all goes well, the value of the rubber brought in may be just enough to cover the cost of necessities, if not each day, then at least over a reasonably short period. . . . Through a long process of accumulation it has now become established that by paying off only a portion of his outstanding debt a regular client can always get further provisions on credit. As the average rubber holding is small and the price of rubber low, a client can almost never pay off the whole debt. . . . [8]

Moreover, be it noted, neither he nor his creditor expects him to do so.

The uglier word for "credit," of course, is "debt." The Chinese planters in Sarawak are continuously in debt to their local Chinese middlemen-*cum*-retailers. It is a situation which may well give scope for unscrupulous exploitation. But to stress only this potential (albeit sometimes real) evil, without appreciating the indispensability of both the middleman's function and the provision of credit and without even noticing the safeguards which in fact exist, is to be unrealistic.

We earlier discussed the essential nature of the middleman's function in societies which depend largely upon peasant primary production. We have now shifted our interest to the apparently equally indispensable requirement for some system of credit. The small planters alone would not be able to get their produce out to the markets, nor would they be willing to produce at all without consumer goods to buy. At the same time they are extremely short of cash. In these circumstances the credit system acts as a kind of lubricant which keeps the machinery of production going. Thus the export of primary produce depends as much upon the rural retailers and middlemen as it does upon the peasant small holders.[9]

The sago-producing areas of another part of Sarawak further demonstrate the essential, lubricating nature of credit.[10] Northeast of Kuching, in the Third Division of Sarawak, an indigenous people — the Melanau — are engaged almost exclusively in the small-scale peasant production of sago flour. This they produce by rather arduous methods and then sell to the local middlemen in the sago trade for further processing and resale. These middlemen are all Chinese. Like their counterparts in the rubber trade, they are also local retailers and manage their businesses in the same way. It is quite clear, from the published description, that they fully appreciate the economic significance of the credit system, for they deliberately use their position to compel the sago farmers to keep up a steady supply of flour.

The Melanau do not share the Chinese passion for work: rather than

[8] *Ibid.*, p. 43.

[9] Moreover, as T'ien points out, "it is not only the primary producers who are in difficulties. The rural middlemen-*cum*-retailers, too, are faced by an apparently insoluble dilemma. They cannot afford to go on lending in this way, but they can do nothing else either, for only by allowing credit in return for part payment can they hope to get any return at all" (*ibid.*, p. 44).

[10] H. S. Morris, *A Melanau Sago Producing Community*, London, 1954.

time being money to them, they take the line that money is time — money being valued only insofar as it can buy prestige and time for leisure and conversation. Thus a Melanau family which has produced a certain amount of sago flour will hope to sit back for a while. Knowing this, the Chinese middleman-retailers do their best to keep the Melanau in the red so that they can continually be reminded of their debts and urged to bring in more sago under threat of having their supplies of credit cut off. In this way two purposes are served: on the one hand, the retailers' clientele is bound ever more closely to him, thus making poaching by other traders (or, incidentally, the entry of new traders, including of course non-Chinese) difficult; on the other hand, and from the point of view of the economy as a whole more importantly, the flow of sago to the exporters is maintained and at a fairly steady rate.

A very similar state of affairs obtains in the fishing villages of Hong Kong. A small fisherman is likely to be in debt to his fish dealer (middleman) because he has had to borrow cash from him at some time or another in order to buy new gear, or repair his boat, or marry his son — for example. In return, he gives no security other than a lien on future catches. Boats and gear are not "mortgaged," but in effect, future catches are. The middleman recoups his loan by installments (usually at Chinese New Year) and takes interest by deducting from the price of the fish which he can get in the official markets. It pays both producer and middleman that their relationship should be an everlasting one: the fisherman knows he can raise a loan without delay; the dealer has a steady source of income. Indeed, like their compatriots in Sarawak, these small-scale fish middlemen do not expect ever to call in all their loans, nor do the fishermen expect ever to pay up completely.

Unlike the Sarawak agriculturalists, however, the Hong Kong fishermen usually maintain at least two credit relationships, for the middlemen in the fish trade are not usually connected (at least not directly) with retail business. For his groceries and so forth a fisherman must go to separate local shops. He cannot usually pay fully in cash, not having enough, but if personally known to the shopkeeper can open a credit account on which to buy daily necessities. (Once again, as in Sarawak, large items are bought with cash — usually borrowed from the fish middlemen — and street marketing is also always done in cash.) When the Chinese New Year comes round the theory is that all debts should be paid. Sometimes they are. More often, the fisherman seeks out the shopkeeper, entertains him at some expense in the teahouse, and confers with him as to how much should be paid off. (He does exactly the same thing with his fish middleman.) An installment or a loan keeps credit open for the next year. Usually the prices entered in such credit accounts with the shops are not higher than those paid by cash buyers, but a percentage may be added to the total sum in the books (the actual rate often varying with the relationship of the debtor to the shopkeeper).

The successful continuance of Hong Kong's fishing industry, no less than that of Sarawak's cash crop economy, depends upon the existence of a working system of credit and/or of loans. For Malaya the works of Bauer [11] and Firth [12] tell a similar tale, and it seems that in the eastern parts at least of Uganda [13] and the cocoa areas of Ghana [14] something similar may be true: at least in all the peasant producing areas of these territories, locally organized systems of credit and/or loan-giving are well established. I am not trying to argue that all those who give cash loans or allow credit to peasant primary producers do so out of a sense of social obligation. Of course they do nothing of the sort, and of course they take whatever economic (or other) advantage of the position of relative power which the status of creditor implies that they can. On the other hand, they are performing an essential economic service, for which no other agency exists at present.[15] Moreover, as we shall have cause to mention again, most of them are small men, very frequently themselves indebted to others, and in the last resort, as dependent upon their own debtors as these latter are upon them. Finally, in the very multiplicity of creditors lies part, at least, of the debtors' safeguard.[16]

THE MULTIPLICITY OF CREDITORS

But it is this multiplicity with which we are here concerned. Others have argued the significance of credit, but rather less attention has been paid to the multiplicity of creditors.

Two essential features of the types of credit system under discussion are: (1) the creditors themselves are normally small men with very limited amounts of capital at their disposal; (2) credit is almost invariably given without security in the full sense, simply on the personal reputation of the debtor, or rather one should say on the personal knowledge of the creditor. These two facts between them account for the multiplicity of creditors and hence very largely for the multiplicity of small-scale middlemen and retailers.

Little appears to have been published about the amounts of liquid capital available for cash lending to primary producers. It is information which would, in any case, be not too easily obtained in the field. Nevertheless, some indications that it is often very small do exist. As regards the granting of credit by village shopkeepers, it is well-known that in these two territories at least, and in Malaya, a small village shopkeeper

[11] P. T. Bauer, *The Rubber Industry, a Study in Competition and Monopoly*, London, 1948.

[12] *Op. cit.*, ch. VI.

[13] Dr. J. la Fontaine, verbal communication.

[14] Polly Hill, *The Gold Coast Cocoa Farmer*, ch. V, VI, VII.

[15] P. T. Bauer has on several occasions pointed to the safeguards provided by the existence of large numbers of middlemen competing among themselves. See, for example, his *Rubber Industry in Malaya*, p. 361 ff., and *West African Trade*, ch. 18.

[16] I.e., credit sales amounting to this sum.

is often himself dependent for stock buying upon a credit account with another businessman (sometimes another retailer) higher up the scale. In Sarawak, indeed, there appears to be a regular "ladder" of credit accounts of this kind leading right up from the small rural bazaars to the importers in Kuching, who themselves may be in a somewhat similar relationship with bigger firms in Singapore.

As for the personalization of credit, that too is well authenticated. One small shopkeeper in a Hong Kong fishing village told me: "I give credit to anyone who anchors regularly in our own bay; but if it is someone I don't know well, then I think twice about it unless I can find out all about him." T'ien makes much the same point when he describes how small Chinese rubber planters in Sarawak tend always to patronize shopkeepers with the same surnames as themselves. The notion is that shared surname implies shared kinship, and kinsmen are by definition "known" and trustworthy. It is, indeed, fairly obvious that small-scale peasant producers are not likely to be able to get credit on any other than personal terms such as these. Much of the work of the cooperative movement in underdeveloped territories is based precisely — and successfully — upon just this argument. In other words, the successful working of a system of commercial primary production by peasants requires the existence of a credit system that is not only extensive but also highly personalized. But if credit is to be advanced only to personal acquaintances, then there is a limit — and a fairly low limit — to the number of clients any one creditor can have.

Figures collected by T'ien in Sarawak and by myself in Hong Kong give ample evidence in support of this common sense observation. Writing of the scale of the rural credit system in Sarawak, T'ien reports: "At one point along the Simanggang Road there are about 15 shops. Most of these are small, single-line establishments, but 7 are fairly large grocery-*cum*-rubber-dealer stores. Of these the 3 most recently opened have each about $2,000 out on loan, 4 others between $4,000 and $6,000, and one, the largest and oldest . . . claims an outstanding loan of about $7,000. In a certain bazaar in the Bau area there are a dozen grocer-dealers. Six of them claim to have advanced goods to the value of between $4,000 and $5,000, five $5,000, and one, the largest . . . as much as $10,000. In one coastal bazaar the majority of the 20 grocer-dealers stated in 1949 that they had advanced between $1,000 and $2,000 worth of goods, but 2 claimed $8,000 and the largest . . . stated himself that he was owed as much as $15,000." [17] T'ien points out that all these figures were collected by direct questioning of shopkeepers, and it is possible that an element of boasting may have led to exaggeration,

[17] The Straits dollar was at that time worth about 2/6d sterling. Thus the sums mentioned here range from about £125 to about £1,850. The term "grocer-dealers" refers to shopkeepers described elsewhere in my text as "middlemen-retailers."

in which case the actual value of goods advanced on credit would be even less. It seems, for example, that other shopkeepers did not share the last man's estimate of his own position, but suggested that the true sum was probably about one-third or even one-half smaller.

The amounts owed to the shops by individual debtors range in value from about $50 to about $2,000.[18] For example, the distribution of debts owed to one shopkeeper in the Bau area is listed by T'ien as follows: [19]

Amount owed	Number of debtors
$ 40– 50	9
51–100	15
101–200	21
201–300	24
301–400	9
401–500	2
501–600	1
601–800	2

Now these are not very large sums. Say a rural shopkeeper has outstanding credit accounts amounting to $2,000. This means that he has at the most 10 credit customers with a $200 debt each, or, if the average debt were as low as $50, which is unlikely, this still would give him only 50 credit customers. Yet nearly all custom is done on credit; it is no wonder that there is such an apparently disproportionate number of traders.

My own figures for the inshore fishermen of Hong Kong tell very much the same story. The two small centres of Tai Po and Sai Kung in 1951–52 were the main marketing bases for 327 and 322 fishing boats respectively. In Tai Po there were only three successful middlemen and a small, fluctuating, number of less successful ones. But Tai Po itself housed a wholesale fish market, and it was easily possible for very many Tai Po fishermen to market their own catches direct. In other words, most Tai Po fishermen do not require the handling services of a middleman. The successful Tai Po middlemen were those three who had enough capital to be able to provide the service the fishermen could not perform for themselves: they could all make loans. But between them they did not have more than about $H. K. 14,000,[20] at most, out on loan in 1952. At, say, $H. K. 100 a client — and most loans would be larger — this gives an average of about 46 or 47 clients apiece. In Sai Kung, where the nearest wholesale market is at Kowloon, fourteen miles away overland, there were 16 middlemen to the 322 fishing boats enumerated there in 1952. Some

[18] I.e., about £6. 5. 0d. to about £250.
[19] *Ibid.*
[20] I.e., about £850. The Hong Kong dollar is worth about one-half of the Straits dollar, and was at this time valued at about 1/3d or approximately 16 to the £ sterling.

Sai Kung area fishermen take their own fish direct by sea to the market; some even accompany it overland; but even assuming that all dealt exclusively through these middlemen, there would be 20–21 fishermen only to each one. Actually, of course, the Sai Kung middlemen were not all equally successful. Once again the successful ones were those who were able to make loans (usually from funds supplied to themselves on loan from further up the market ladder in Kowloon), but again, the number of clients was quite small — between about a dozen and about two score.

Now it is my suggestion that the small size of these various clienteles is not to be wondered at, because the creditors themselves have little capital to invest (and much of that little is itself in the form of credit) and because no creditor can be expected to know more than, say, perhaps one hundred people well enough to extend personal credit to them. Indeed, the maximum number of such relationships of personal trust may well be considerably less.

The hypothesis to which we are led may be stated as follows: if, in a population which depends upon a wide distribution of credit, no creditor can be expected to have more than a limited number of debtors, then necessarily that population must include (or have access to) a large number of creditors.

It follows that if, as in Sarawak and Hong Kong, the most usual sources of rural credit are the local middlemen and retailers, there must, irrespective of transport and other factors, be expected to be a large number of these people. As indeed there are.

TESTING THE HYPOTHESIS

The most obvious and satisfactory test for this hypothesis would be an examination of its corollary. That is, to discover what, in the kind of economic situation we are considering, creditors with more liquid capital available for investment actually do with it. Do such men advance personal credit to more individuals than whatever the expected maximum for their particular community may be? Or do they simply make bigger loans but keep the number of debtors reasonably small? Or do they break out of the personalized system altogether, and go in for "more businesslike" arrangements, demanding security and fixed terms, putting pressure upon defaulters, and so forth, and if so, at what point on the increasing scale of their activities does this change begin? Or is it more usual for increased capital to be used not for individual loans of this kind at all, but for other forms of investment — land, building, expanding business of various kinds?

These and similar problems lie outside the scope of this paper. They would appear to be crucial to understanding how societies largely dependent upon peasant commercial production may proceed to more differentiated forms of economy. All that I am in a position to do here, however, is to consider my hypothesis, which is already supported by data from Sarawak and Hong Kong, in the light of evidence from other underdeveloped territories in which certain of the conditions which obtain in these two territories do not apply. I shall refer very briefly to Malaya, Uganda, and Ghana.

But first it is necessary to take note of the significance of certain distinctions.

DIFFERENT TYPES OF PURCHASE

Examples of different types of purchase were quoted earlier. They fall into three simple categories, as follows: first, all extraordinary once-and-for-at-least-a-long-time types of expenditure (buying a bicycle, a boat, a sewing machine, clothing, paying for a son's wedding, or a funeral), as well, of course, as those for which official regulations demand payment in money (taxes, school or medical fees, etc.) are made in cash. The payments may be spread out a little, if agreement to do this can be made, but there is not usually a long delay in completion. Such payments which are usually fairly large are made either out of a man's own resources or from loans he has raised from a third party or parties. They are not made on credit accounts.

Second, all petty purchases in street markets or from hawkers, as well as payments for small services (such as bus or ferry fares, hair cuts, entertainment expenses, small religious offerings) are also usually paid in cash. Such small outgoings usually come from the purchaser's own pocket, or possibly an immediate loan of a purely friendly nature.

The third form of purchase is made on a credit account. Goods bought in this way are usually daily necessities (where these have to be obtained from retailers), for example: rice, sugar, tea, kerosene, perhaps cigarettes.

Thus the first type of expenditure (A) often leads to the creation or reinforcement of a loan relationship, the second (B) usually requires the use of ready money, and only the third (C) involves the steady use of a credit account. Some such threefold distinction seems to be widespread. The explanation appears simple. Few peasant (or wage-earning) primary producers are likely to have enough ready cash available to make one of the large-scale payments demanded by type A goods and services out of their own pockets. At the same time the sellers of type A goods and services are usually specialists and/or non-local residents in the bigger trading centers who, in a situation where only personal security is acceptable, cannot be expected to give credit. The purchaser therefore must resort to borrowing cash from someone who does trust him. Type B goods and services, requiring relatively very small if very frequent sums, are sold by individuals who are also not in a position to give credit, whether because they have far too little capital themselves, or because they are (often) itinerant or (often) temporary petty traders with inadequate personal knowledge of their customers. It is only type C purchases which, because they are necessarily recurrent and localized and consist of goods which can be successfully stocked only in a permanent building and by at least a relatively full-time and experienced trader, are truly suitable for the type of personal credit account which we have described.

It is therefore necessary to consider in what circumstances daily necessities, particularly staple foodstuffs, do have to be purchased in this way.

DIFFERENT TYPES OF DAILY NECESSITIES, PARTICULARLY FOODSTUFFS

In the modern world it is no longer possible to find any commercial primary producers who are at the same time completely self-sufficient in their own subsistence. Nevertheless there are many who are self-sufficient in at least certain respects. These differences in degree of self-sufficiency are particularly significant insofar as they concern the people's daily necessities.

All the primary producers discussed here make regular purchases of such items as tea, sugar, kerosene. In Sarawak, Hong Kong, and Malaya they also depend upon regular purchases of something more fundamental, namely, rice, and imported rice at that. By strong contrast the staple food of Uganda's cotton and coffee growers and Ghana's cocoa farmers is home grown or purchased (often in already cooked form) from local markets to which they have been taken from the hands of local growers.

THE SIGNIFICANCE OF THESE DIFFERENCES: CREDIT ACCOUNTS

A population completely dependent upon the purchase of imported supplies of its staple food, as are the landless fishermen of Hong Kong upon rice, is necessarily closely tied to the retailers of that commodity who, by its very nature, must be at least relatively substantial men — unless, indeed, they are government agencies, as has happened in the past in Hong Kong, and seems to be the rule in China at present. Such men are likely to be in a position to allow at least some credit buying. Hong Kong's inshore fishermen are, as we have seen, usually involved in credit relationships with their rice suppliers, who are very often their tea, sugar, and kerosene suppliers too. Similarly in Sarawak the rubber and sago producers do not grow their own rice, but buy it from the local stores at which they have the credit accounts already described. Professor Bauer [21] wrote of a similar thing in Malaya, and Dr. Benedict [22] has described it also for Mauritius.

[21] Personal communication. See also Burton Benedict, "Cash and Credit in Mauritius," *The South African Journal of Economics*, Vol. 26, No. 3, September 1958, pp. 213–221.

[22] Dr. J. la Fontaine personal communication. I am indebted to both Dr. la Fontaine and Dr. Benedict for their willingess to allow me to quote from their answers to my questions about their field material from Uganda and Mauritius.

But in Uganda and Ghana the basic condition for this situation does not exist to the same degree. Tea, sugar, kerosene, etc. may be purchased from shops, but they can also be acquired from petty traders, and the staple foodstuffs are either home grown or bought with cash in the street markets; they are not imported. There is therefore less need for a close dependence upon shopkeepers than in the rice-importing countries, and one would not then expect Uganda and Ghana to exhibit such a development of credit account purchasing or such a multiplicity of general stores in the rural areas. It seems likely that this expectation is in accordance with the facts.

Nevertheless, to say this is not to invalidate the hypothesis that where credit purchasing does exist each creditor shop necessarily has a restricted number of customers, and therefore a multiplicity of such shops is only to be expected. On the contrary, such evidence as I have appears to support this hypothesis on two counts. First, there is some evidence of credit purchasing in Uganda which we shall examine. Second, there is clear evidence that in Ghana the number of rural lenders of money is markedly high for the size of the rural population, a fact which gives *prima facie* support for the basic assumption on which this hypothesis rests.

Let us consider these two counts in turn.

CREDIT RETAILING: UGANDA

We may consider the case of the Bagishu coffee growers of eastern Uganda. All coffee has, by law, to be sold exclusively to local cooperative societies, whose agents make a first initial payment in cash and thereafter hand over paper receipts for each lot of coffee as it is brought in, until such time as the whole shall have been sold upon the world market, when the receipts are presented for money. Small general stores in this coffee area allow credit to their customers, taking the receipts for security. This practice, which is explicitly illegal, is beyond the means of the smallest stores, whose owners tend to buy retail and sell at slightly enhanced prices. The rather more substantial storekeepers, however, both give credit and make cash loans against the security of the coffee receipts, which are also used to secure loans made by other (i.e., non-shopkeeper) individuals and even actually as money. Dr. la Fontaine, who spent two years on field work among the Bagishu, describes how widely the network of debts is spread, especially just before the coffee harvest, "when everybody owes money to everybody else"; she also agrees that, even though coffee receipts are used to secure the debts, a shopkeeper (or anyone else) would be unlikely to extend credit facilities to complete strangers, whereas on occasion he does give them to a well-known customer on personal trust alone.

We may ask how big a credit clientele any one shopkeeper in the Bagishu area has. Dr. la Fontaine's estimate is that a "big" man may have as many as 20–25 credit customers. Yet "almost everybody" takes advantage of these credit facilities. The inference is plain that there must be a fair multiplicity of general stores in this part of Uganda.[23] It is unfortunate that the complete census of Uganda, taken in 1948, has not yet been published, which makes it impossible to provide a numerical test for this inference.

CREDIT RETAILING: GHANA

Bauer's study of West African trade includes a passage which makes it clear that all the often multiple stages of merchandise trade between the importing firms and the ultimate consumer make substantial use of credit. He gives no information about credit purchases by peasant consumers, however, and it seems likely that the extreme multiplicity of agents in the distributive trade in West Africa (which takes the form of an immense multiplication of petty traders rather than of identical general stores) is to be explained without reference to the number of credit customers any one retailer can be expected to have.[24] We have already suggested that there is likely to be less demand for credit purchasing on the part of Ghanaian cocoa farmers who eat local produce than of, say, Sarawak rubber planters who eat imported rice.

Nevertheless, many Ghanaian cocoa farmers do make intensive use of credit facilities of other kinds, and it is to these that we turn now for our second examination of evidence which has bearing on the main theme of this paper.

LOANS: GHANA COCOA FARMERS

Evidence of the demand for credit is provided by the history of the Agricultural Loans Board which was set up in Ghana (then known as the Gold Coast) in 1950. "In the space of less than two years 73,000 requests for or inquiries about loans were made to it. Nearly 30,000 [largely illiterate] farmers submitted formal applications on an eight-page form; they applied for a total of some £50 millions." The Board suspended operations in 1953, having made loans totalling £1,320. The Minister of Agriculture stated that the government was now considering whether it might not be better to decentralize the machinery, looking round for some other body who might be in closer touch with the farmer from day-to-day, and who accordingly would be in a better position to know the standing of a particular farmer.[25]

The existing suppliers of credit are certainly in close day-to-day touch

[23] The Bagishu apparently pay cash for small purchases and to hawkers, pedlars and petty traders. They also pay cash, saved or borrowed, for big (i.e., type A) purchases (e.g., bicycles). The credit arrangements described above are for such items as: tea, sugar, meat, kerosene.

[24] Bauer's description of credit trading extending even down to the petty retail stage refers only to market women selling on credit to clerks and other workers in government service or mercantile firms and gathering round the office doors to collect their debts on payday. See *West African Trade*, pp. 61–62.

[25] Hill, *op. cit.*, p. 70.

with the cocoa farmers. We have seen that these farmers do not, as far as we know, make purchases on credit accounts. On the other hand, they can and do borrow cash — usually in the form of loans against the security ("pledge") of land, usually land under cocoa. The details of these arrangements differ considerably from any we have so far discussed, but the question which is basic to the present enquiry can still be posed: namely, are the creditors in these transactions numerous or few in relation to the primary producing population?

Miss Hill describes the practice of pledging cocoa farms as follows: "When a . . . cocoa farmer wants to borrow money for (say) six months or longer (usually longer) he often finds it convenient to do so by means of pledging his farm to a lender. The farm provides the lender with security for the debt, and the usufruct provides the borrower with a means to pay interest on the loan as well as, in many cases, with the means for repayment. Pledging . . . is a kind of indigenous mortgage system."[26] Although a good deal is known about the relationships between debtor and creditor under this system, it is naturally not possible to indicate the average numbers of debtors per creditor for the country as a whole. Creditors do not lend themselves to providing this kind of statistical information, and practices vary from place to place. But "in many areas the creditor who has had farms pledged to him by more than two or three debtors would seem to be very rare. The typical creditor perhaps has one or two farms pledged to him."[27]

Here too, then, is a society of peasant primary producers in which there is a high demand for credit (here in the form of cash loans) and in which it seems that the proportion of creditors to debtors is high. Certain other points are also clear. For example, very few Ghanaian creditors are professional moneylenders. They do not make lending their sole occupation but continue to pursue other work, and as a result they are not a class apart. Indeed, it appears that they are even less a class apart from the local primary producers than the Far Eastern middlemen-retailers we have considered above, for most of the Ghanaian cocoa pledgees are themselves cocoa farmers, living in the same area as their debtors, and many of them are closely related to or very friendly with their debtors. Certainly it seems that the necessary condition is that the creditor should be personally assured of his debtor's reliability. In this case he needs to know also his debtor's land and its productivity, but Miss Hill suggests that there is an even more important consideration! "I have never met a creditor who was willing to cope with more than a small number of farms: the supervision of the labourers is too much work."[28]

[26] *Ibid.*, p. 48.

[27] Personal communication.

[28] Personal communication. In an unpublished ms., Miss Hill remarks further upon the rarity in the cocoa areas of the large creditor. In her experience the largest clienteles contained only about twenty people. The average sums borrowed were small. I am greatly indebted to Miss Polly Hill for allowing me to quote from her unpublished work and also for her personal communications and criticism.

CONCLUSION

The evidence from Ghana, and possibly also that from Uganda — though administrative control probably accounts largely for the apparent absence of credit facilities (or at least their failure to be reported) there — shows that the earlier implication that credit account purchasing, as found in Sarawak, Malaya, Hong Kong, and Mauritius, might be universal for peasant commercial producers, was incorrect. Peasants who live on home grown (or locally produced) foodstuffs can subsist without recourse to credit purchase. Even they may use cash advances to tide them over the harvest period, however, and the Ghana evidence in general shows that when they reach a rather higher than subsistence level (which it is the whole trend — and aim — of commercial crop production to develop) they are likely to require loans of cash for expenditure of type A described above. Miss Hill has pointed out that it is the *poorest* Ghanaian cocoa farmers who do *not* pledge their farms. She adds, significantly: "*in their ability to borrow cocoa farmers are a favoured class compared with most other people,* favoured by the fact that they own something worth pledging and that there are those of their number who want to lend." [29] The cocoa farmers having farms to pledge are in much the same position as houseowners in, say, England who have property to mortgage: they are by no means the poorest members of the community, nor are they usually considered unfortunate or worthy of special governmental assistance to help wipe out their debts.

Indeed, it might be suggested that the similarities between some of the methods of entering into a credit relationship in peasant producing populations and in the West are closer than might be expected. If a private individual here in England wants to borrow money or open a credit account, he too has to establish his credentials, and in the last resort this means that he too depends on personal knowledge on the part of his creditor. This applies to loans from building societies and even from the banks, which do not have a multiplicity of branches stretching into quite small villages for nothing. It applies still more to the multitude of more or less "private" mortgages negotiated by solicitors on behalf of their clients. It could be argued that this function of the local solicitor in England (together with others that also require his personal acquaintance with his clients) largely explains the otherwise rather surprising multiplicity of small legal firms existing in every small town in

[29] Unpublished ms., my italics. Miss Hill notes the reasons which induce a cocoa farmer to borrow money. In many cases loans were raised for expenditures of type A, but in many others they were to meet the expenses of a sudden "calamity." As Miss Hill herself points out, however, calamities which can be recouped by monetary loans are more likely to happen to the relatively well off. A man may borrow to replace a damaged lorry or because he was unable to meet commitments (such as the payment of school fees) from which he was unwilling to withdraw, but a truly poverty stricken peasant does not own lorries or send his children to school at all.

the country. There is certainly a very large proportion of creditors to debtors in these "private" relationships.

Evidence from other primary producing areas is required, but in general it does seem that one concomitant of commercial production at this level and the rising standards of expenditure that go with it is a demand on the part of the primary producers themselves for credit and/or loan facilities. These may take various forms, according partly to the types of expenditure involved and partly to the availability of capital and its location. From our point of view here the significant question is: from whose hands is this credit or loan obtained? I am not concerned with the question of the ultimate source of the capital, but with the direct relationship between the primary producer borrower and his personal creditor. It seems that there are three main types of source: local middlemen (produce buyers), local retailers, and each other.[30] In all these cases, no matter what the type of credit arrangement, there is a limit to the number of debtors per creditor. This limit is usually set by two factors: first, the small amount of capital available to the creditor; and second, the necessity for the creditor, who in the circumstances we are discussing nearly always has to act on his own sole responsibility, to have personal knowledge of the character and circumstances of his debtor.

It follows that there must be a relatively large number of creditors, and in those territories in which they are also produce buyers and/or shopkeepers, a multiplicity of middlemen and shops.

[30] Some or all of these roles may overlap in one and the same individual. In Sarawak, middleman-retailer; in Ghana many a cocoa farmer is also a middleman in the cocoa trade and at the same time a creditor or debtor in the pledging system.

PART THREE

PEASANT SOCIAL ORGANIZATION

Introduction: The Social Life of Peasants

May N. Diaz and Jack M. Potter

Peasants must face the common problems of people everywhere. They must marry, establish families, and relate to kinsmen in a way that presupposes mutual obligations and expectations. They must get along with fellow villagers well enough to be able to call on them for economic, social, and ritual aid in time of need Because basic resources usually are scarce, they must find ways of minimizing or softening competition that would be disruptive in a social order as tightly knit as a peasant community.

Peasants must also maintain viable relations with people outside their community. Some of these people are their social and economic peers, and live in villages similar to their own. People from other villages may be sources of spouses, or they may provide the aid and protection villagers need when they travel away from home, in visiting religious shrines, or in the long-distance trading of local commodities that characterizes some peasant societies. Because they live in a hierarchically differentiated society, peasants also face the problem of relating to a social, economic, juridical, and cultural entity which vastly surpasses the limits of their local worlds. They must come to terms with classes and individuals who have or may have vast powers over them but who also, when properly manipulated, can aid the individual peasant in many life situations.

Peasant social institutions are thus Janus-faced — looking both toward the requirements imposed by the larger political and economic order and toward the customary expectations of the peasant community. They also have developed a variety of forms: a traditional Chinese community shows many differences from an Indian village, which in turn has organized itself in ways quite distinct from a Mediterranean or a Mexican settlement. But variety is not infinite, and once we look for similarities rather than differences, it is remarkable how often structural parallels appear. Sometimes these parallels result from historical influence, and spring in part from a common heritage: many Spanish American patterns for example, trace their beginnings to the Mediterranean world. At other times the parallels seem to be due to limited possibilities: fictive kinship forms, for instance The *compadrazgo* of Spanish America has no apparent historical connection with the Nepalese *mit* (Okada 1957), yet those institutions are similar and fulfill many of the same functions. Generic similarities among great diversity make peasant social organization a fertile field for comparative study.

At present, comparative studies are still in an embryonic stage. We are just beginning to recognize and explore crucial problems. The literature on peasants is rich in ethnographic detail, but comparative and theoretical studies are so few that a synthesis is still in the future. All we can do here is to point to some generic similarities found in peasant societies, note the range of variation, and point to what, in our judgment, are some of the major problem areas. In the brief introduction that follows, peasant social life is considered in four closely related categories: (1) family and marriage, (2) intravillage organization, (3) the peasant village as a social unit, and (4) peasants in relation to their wider society.

FAMILY AND MARRIAGE

Characteristically, in peasant societies the domestic unit is also the production unit: a group of kinsmen (sometimes with a few additional persons who are not relatives) bound together in such a fashion that their roles as family members also define their roles as producers and consumers. The cohesion of the domestic group is given further reinforcement by ceremony, religion, and the view in each culture of how things ought to be.

The domestic unit varies in form from one society to another. It is related to the needs of particular farming and other productive systems, and both helps to shape and is shaped by the norms and values of the culture. Although one might expect to find that peasant societies have certain characteristic residential units, in fact family types vary from three generation extended families — defined patrilineally (e.g., Yugoslavia, India, China), in a rare case or two matrilineally (e.g., Minangkabau of Central Sumatra), or bilaterally (as in parts of traditional Scandinavia) — to two-generation nuclear families composed of one married couple and their unmarried offspring.

Three factors, however, suggest that the variation is less far-reaching than it seems at first glance. First, inheritance patterns, as well as the requirements of particular ecological systems, strongly affect household composition (see Diaz, "Economic Relations in Peasant Society," above). Second, residence rules and ideal family types reflect people's views of what they can expect and what they should do if all other things are equal; since all other things seldom are, the statistical incidence of a given family type may depart sharply from what the society's members state to be the rule. In most peasant groups nuclear families are the most common domestic unit even though formal patterns of kinship reckoning, inheritance, rule of residence, and the members' own statements point toward extended families as typical. Third, as Wolf points out (1966:70–73), the conditions with which the peasant must contend as a consequence of the increasing industrialization in this century — extreme land pressure, increasing reliance on wage labor, and intensified cultivation for the market — force larger family units to break up into nuclear family households. Thus, for this moment in history at least, more peasants live in two-generation nuclear families than in any other kind of domestic unit.

Although peasants, like people everywhere, set certain limits within which marriages are forbidden, the precise definition of who cannot marry whom varies considerably. Where there are unilineal kin groups, one can expect that a rule of exogamy prevails: one must marry outside of one's patrilineage or clan; but where the family forms the only bounded kinship group and one's kin ties are based on a personal kindred, the limits are usually stated according to the number of links distant from ego. In each case, fictive kin are usually considered as if they were blood kin in determining an individual's eligibility.

Often, peasants define rules of exogamy and endogamy with reference to territory. Although it is difficult to make defensible generalizations about these prohibitions, where a peasant's social identity is primarily defined in reference to some group in addition to the family, such a group often is memorialized in marriage regulations, and the rules of endogamy or exogamy may support group cohesion. Thus, an entire village or the territorial sections of a village (e.g., neighborhoods or *barrios*) may be endogamous, so that already existing kin and neighborhood ties influence and are reinforced by marriage patterns. Such a structural principle followed to its logical conclusion would make intravillage and intervillage integration exceedingly difficult if no mediating devices established ties with other groups. Both economic bonds and ceremonial practices can increase social relations between groups, but marriage and affinity may affect these in a complex manner (see Diaz, "Opposition and Alliance in a Mexican Town," below). On the other hand, marriage rules may make it necessary to set up alliances with other groups by requiring marriage outside the village. Or, dual rules may apply, as in India, where caste endogamy and village exogamy tend to maintain rigid, hierarchically ranked and separate groups while also continuing and renewing intervillage ties. Economic considerations are important in most peasant marriages. Since one of a peasant's major economic resources is land, he calculates assiduously how much certain matches will affect his gaining or losing this precious resource, and marriages are often arranged to consolidate holdings.

INTRAVILLAGE ORGANIZATION

Although it may be that the peasant family is the most self-sufficient small unit found in any society, it cannot exist as a social isolate. Peasants must be able to call upon members of other families for mutual economic, social, and emotional support. Kinship is just one of the ways in which peasants structure interfamily ties within the village.

Some are formal, such as fictive kinship, caste, associations, and ties based upon common residence. Others are informal — friendship, neighborliness, and particularly the dyadic ties which are coming to be recognized as so important in many peasant communities — but no less effective in contributing to the functioning of village life. In some peasant societies, all these social patterns are utilized; in others only a few are stressed, to the neglect of others.

Kinship ties between peasant households are of three kinds: those based on "blood," affinity, and fictive kinship. For a discussion of the social bonds created through affinity see "Peasants and Their Wider Society," page 164 below.

Blood ties provide one of the calls on loyalty and support that members of one household group can expect of another. Whatever the rule of descent, the kinship system enables a peasant to form a work group for harvest or to designate individuals to whom he is bound by duties and obligations and from whom he can expect services and favors. It provides him with *one* universe of roles and norms, but, contrasted with the overriding importance of kinship in tribal societies, among peasants it provides only one means of social integration and order.

No characteristic of peasant social organization has attracted more interest than fictive kinship. Briefly, it is a tie between two or more people that is conceptually similar to real kinship, using kinship terminology or something similar formally brought into being by a ritual act, and, once established, usually lasting the lifetimes of the participants. Fictive kinship, like true kinship, usually involves an incest taboo. But there are important differences, and participants in such systems are well aware that the two systems are not one. Generally, fictive kinship is not a factor in inheritance rules, which is one of the major functions of true kinship systems. The *compadrazgo* system, first recognized in Latin American peasant communities, is the classic type of fictive kinship. Its enormous flexibility and its ability to function in widely varied social contexts, as pointed out by Mintz and Wolf, explains its vitality as well as its changing character as time passes. Historically, of course, it springs from Catholic ritual, and was brought from Europe to America. It is also important in Catholic and Greek Orthdox Europe, although in recent times the system has not proliferated there to anything like the extent we find in America.

A comparable institution is described for north India (Freed 1963), and is known in Nepal under the term *mit* (Okada 1957), in Tibet as *ganye* (Miller 1956), and in Japan as the *oyabun-kobun* (Ishino 1953). In the peasant societies where it is found, in addition to strengthening bonds between social and economic equals, it also provides an ideal way of tying together people of different social classes or religions. In the Balkans, it is a major device shaping the often less than harmonious relations between Moslems and Christians. In periods of rapid social change, fictive kinship also shows greater flexibility than true kinship systems and, where present, it often can be adapted to new conditions, as in Japan, where some industrial organizations are organized according to the oyabun-kobun.

Kinship — real and fictive — contributes to the social integration of a peasant community at a moment in history, binding together the living, but it also provides a thread of continuity, a way of tying persons to both the past and future. For peasants the tie connecting generations is particularly important in the consolidation and inheritance of land (again see Diaz, "Economic Relations in Peasant Society," above). Each kind of kinship reckoning defines kinsmen, a grid of persons relevant to those areas of life in which kinship is important, and each kind has predictable social consequences in the groupings it creates.

Anthropological theories about social structure are, in large measure, based on societies organized on segmental, unilateral principles. The fact that a majority of peasant societies (e.g., most Latin American and European peasant societies, and parts of Asia, such as Thailand) reckon kinship on a bilateral basis is therefore particularly important. A society based on the bilateral principle, with its correlate, the kindred, affords (as contrasted to unilineal systems) a flexibility in individual relationships which many peasant communities find to be advantageous. It seems to permit, in effect, an option in selecting those people with whom one maintains his most intense economic, friendship, and emotional ties, normally not found in societies organized on a unilateral kinship basis. Major theoretical insights into how social relationships may be arranged have already been derived by analyzing bilaterally organized peasant communities, and further theoretical progress will undoubtedly stem from the analysis of this most common of familial forms.

Notwithstanding the apparent predominance of this type of kinship, in many peasant societies kinship is reckoned patrilineally (e.g., Yugoslavia and Albania, the Arab world, and parts of south and east Asia). Often patrilineages, by far the most prevalent kin group found among peasants, are formed on this base. It is quite proper, in fact, to recognize the peasant societies organized around patrilineages as one basic type of peasant social structure.

In southeastern China prior to the Communist revolution entire villages were composed of one corporate patrilineage, and social relations within these "lineage villages" were organized mainly around lineage ties (Freedman 1958). In its extreme form, the Chinese lineage village was comprised of men descended from a common agnatic ancestor, the entire village forming a corporate kin group that owned and managed ancestral halls and the ancestral estates attached to them. Some village leaders were recruited on the basis of their kinship seniority within the lineage, and these councils of elders formed a body which made decisions for the group as a whole and attempted to resolve disputes and conflicts. Almost all of village life revolved around the lineage.

Lineage villages of a somewhat different type, called *dōzoku*, which include both real and fictive kin organized in hierarchic fashion, are described for northern Japan (Beardsley, Hall, and Ward 1959:34, 269–272, 274).

In other peasant societies villages are often comprised of two or more lineages. These multilineage villages are the characteristic form of village organization in most parts of China, and are also found in Korea, Japan, India, the Near East, and in traditional Zadruga-based communities of southeastern Europe.

The caste principle is another important means of organizing peasant social life, and, of course, is particularly common in India: in no other peasant society is it as effective in structuring relationships both within and between communities. Its very size and complexity, and the fact that those who know its workings best fail to agree on its nature, make us reluctant to attempt to discuss it here. Caste-like institutions are found, though, in several other peasant societies. Parts of traditional China (Potter 1964) had lower-caste groups who acted as servants to the dominant groups in rural villages. In Japan, in both urban and rural areas, the *eta* are an outcaste group similar to the untouchables of India. The eta stigma, in fact, has not yet been eradicated from modern Japan. And in Medieval Europe caste-like distinctions between serfs and nobility were crucial features of the manorial system.

The associational principle, like caste, is not found in all peasant societies, but where it is utilized, it may be enormously important, particularly in East Asia, traditional China, Korea, and Japan, where important affairs were carried out within the context of non-kin based associations. In traditional China, irrigation societies, money-lending clubs, burial associations, village-guard associations, and assorted religious associations all were significant in structuring village life. In the villages of central Japan similar associations were common, and almost all important communal tasks were performed by means of village-wide associations. In one sense it seems possible to say that the village itself was an association based upon common residence.

In other parts of the peasant world, associations are much less important. In Latin America, for example, the striking thing is the relative *absence* of a sense of association, which makes it extremely difficult for peasants in this area to organize to meet the challenges of the modern world. Those associations which do exist are primarily religious, their ends limited to maintaining the cult.

The intensity of the principle of association varies in Europe. Where peasants are fishermen, the spirit of association is usually strong. The occupational hazards are so great, particularly for open-sea fishermen, that in his own interest the fisherman usually sees the importance of submitting to a superior, democratically constituted authority within a *gremio* (in Spain) or similar organization in other maritime areas. Associations are sometimes found in other parts of Europe as well. In Old

Castile, adolescent and postadolescent boys formed "bachelor's clubs" to support each other in courting, and to provide social diversions. Burial societies are also common in Catholic European peasant communities. But nowhere else, it seems, are associations utilized as much as in East Asia. In India, for example, associations are virtually absent among the peasantry.

Territorial subdivisions based on common residence are often used by peasants to organize some aspects of social life within the village. In the Mediterranean and in Latin America, settlements almost always are divided into two or more units — called barrios in the Spanish and Spanish American world — which are socially and ritually important in community life. Where such divisions are found, each unit emphasizes its solidarity by allegiance to a common symbol such as a patron saint, a holy place, or a legend, which serves as a basis for the mutual identity and interest of the residents. Ceremonials and festivities may further accentuate the unity of each division of the town, and hostility toward outsiders — and sometimes open fighting — may punctuate group boundaries symbolically. Village subdivisions may also help regulate marriage, since exogamy or endogamy, or a tendency in either direction (the most usual pattern) characterizes some societies.

In China and other parts of Asia, territorial divisions are also important. Here, however, instead of forming independent foci of social solidarity they reinforce existing social divisions within the community, such as those based upon caste, lineage, or simply the temporal split that separates early settlers from late arrivals to the village. In China, for example, guardian deities often divide villages into two or more areas inhabited by different lineages or different branches of a large lineage.

Because of what has just been said, the very different picture of community definition in Bali described by Geertz is particularly important. Here, the reader will notice a model of intersecting planes of social organization based on temple association, residence, land ownership, kinship, and other factors is more effective in conveying an understanding of society.

Dyadic ties, a structural principle rather than a formal institution, have come to be recognized in recent years as an effective conceptual device whereby the social features of many peasant communities can be comprehended more effectively than within the framework of formal institutions. Foster describes this model as he sees it in a Mexican village, and Hollnsteiner, as she finds it in a Philippine barrio. Friedl has noted the model's utility in describing a Greek community (1962:74), and Phillips depicts it in Thailand (1965:22). Although the evidence is not yet sufficiently good to speak with confidence of correlations, it seems quite possible that the dyadic concept will prove especially valuable in enabling us to understand societies based on bilateral kinship systems, rather than unilateral systems, as well as those in which the spirit of voluntary association is weakly developed or lacking altogether.

THE VILLAGE AS A SOCIAL UNIT

Since Kroeber, scholars engaged in studying peasants have seen peasant villages as part societies and part cultures. They are not like isolated primitive communities because they exist within a wider society and polity that affects peasant culture and peasant social institutions. This veiwpoint, however, can be carried too far because, in a real sense, most peasant villages *are* little communities in which most important activities of life take place. As Redfield (1955:133) suggested, a fuller understanding of peasant communities can be obtained by adopting a dialectical point of view: on the one hand the village is seen as a society in itself; and on the other hand, its dependent ties with the wider society are emphasized (e.g., Opler's article in Part I of this volume).

At first glance, a peasant village appears to be a social isolate. It usually (but not always) consists of a residential area with its surrounding fields, bounded by and separated from neighboring communities. The separateness of the peasant village is almost universally symbolized in a ritual structure, whether it is the imposing ancestral hall of a village in southeastern China that extends the ancestral shadow over village houses, or the rustic village churches of Mexico and Spain. Religious symbols reflect a degree of social reality because the peasant village is not as dependent on the wider society of towns and cities as a rural community in a modern industrial state. The state apparatus could disappear overnight and an individual village could still manage to survive; with regional cooperation it could survive indefinitely, because its solidarity with the wider society (borrowing a phrase from Durkheim) is more mechanical than it is organic.

In analyzing the structure of peasant society, the first thing that strikes one is that usually (but by no means always) a peasant's primary point of identification is with a village, and not with a family, kin group, or caste. This feature stands in strong contrast to those societies (in anthropological literature perhaps best analyzed in Africa) in which the primary point of reference is the clan or lineage. When asked who or what they are, most peasants answer by claiming membership in a named community which usually (but again not invariably) is a bounded, clearly visible geographical entity. Just as an African tribesman is bound forever to his clan or lineage, in a traditional world a peasant tends to be bound forever to his natal village. Pitt-Rivers has pointed out how in southern Spain those born within a community remain "sons of the pueblo" until their dying day, regardless of where they may go to live (1954:7). The importance of this territorial and geographical principle, as contrasted to kinship, cannot be overestimated in trying to understand peasant society.

Within the limits allowed by the state, peasant villages from time immemorial have developed social institutions that complement national institutions and are capable of solving most important problems in maintaining an orderly community life.

To maintain social control within the village, peasants develop informal legal mechanisms that often contrast sharply with the more impersonal legal forms of the state. Almost universally, peasants are suspicious of the state, and as far as possible prefer to settle disputes within the village where all members are known as full human beings. The legal system of the village, based upon local custom, is much more informal and personalistic than the state legal apparatus. Moreover, the primary aim of most attempts at social control within the village is to resolve disputes in such a manner as to preserve harmony and repair tears in the fabric of interpersonal relations, whereas the state is more likely to seek repressive punishment.

A good example of the distinction between the Great and Little Traditions of law is traditional China. Over the centuries the state had developed extensive law codes to regulate criminal behavior, and had established regular courts in which magistrates dispensed formal justice. Chinese peasants, however, were loath to place themselves before the magistrate because they would be subject to torture, used to extract confessions, and because the bribes that court underlings demanded as a price for their support in a hearing often bankrupted a family. Most disputes were settled in the village context, where local gentry and lineage elders held informal hearings to solve disputes and enforce local customs. In disputes between villages, prominent local men were called in as mediators. Such village "courts" in rare cases invoked sentences of death or banishment upon incorrigible criminals or persons guilty of incest, but usually disputes were settled by assigning fines or by having the offending party give a banquet for those whose rights had been transgressed. Only in serious disputes, or when the parties refused to accept mediation, were cases taken before the magistrate. Smith describes similar informal procedures used by Japanese peasants to maintain social control; and further examples can easily be found in other peasant societies.

Like law, political behavior within peasant villages often strongly contrasts with the political system imposed by the state. Typically, there is both a formal and an informal political structure, even where local political functionaries are state appointees. Within the peasant village, wealthy and prestigious men often have more authority and power than state officials, and usually nothing important is decided without their approval. Political directives passed down through the state administration are by no means automatically carried out by local leaders; usually there is a lengthy process of compromise with lower-ranking state officials, and often state directives are evaded or simply ignored.

Making decisions on behalf of an entire village usually involves informal consultation among important members until a consensus is reached. Since the peasant community is usually an intimate, face-to-face social unit, ignoring any of the important men might lead to the formation of bitter factions and cliques that might seriously disrupt village life. If unanimous agreement among important villagers is not reached, the matter is usually dropped and not pursued further. Decisions are almost always arrived at by informal consultation behind the scenes; formal meetings, if held at all, do little more than rubber-stamp agreements previously made.

Life in most villages is certainly not a rustic communal paradise. Communities frequently are rent by bitter factional disputes, whether they are between political parties, different lineages, different castes, or merely different cliques grouped around strong men. In such situations it is almost impossible to obtain a consensus for joint action on the part of the village as a whole.

Peasant communities vary considerably in the extent to which they can regulate their own affairs, free from state interference; and they vary in the extent to which they form corporate groups, i.e., groups which have a legal personality independent of their members, have effective internal organization for making decisions on behalf of the entire village, and own common property. The extent to which villages form corporate groups depends on the attitudes of the villagers themselves, the kind of state superstructure within which they operate, and the possibility for social and geographical mobility in the wider society. In "Closed Corporate Peasant Communities in Mesoamerica and Java," Wolf discusses a type of community which, due to special historical circumstances, maintains a communal jurisdiction over land, restricts its membership, maintains a religious system of its own, enforces mechanisms which ensure the redistribution or destruction of surplus wealth, and upholds barriers against the entry of goods and ideas produced outside the community. It is in this type of community that Foster's "Image of Limited Good" ethos is particularly likely to be manifested.

At the other extreme are "open" communities in which land is freely alienable and there are few corporate holdings, membership in the village is fluid, communal control over surplus wealth is not so strong that class differences are eliminated, and access to sources of wealth, power, and prestige in the wider society is possible.

These bipolar types can in part be related to social change in the modern world: the closed community is probably more characteristic of classical peasant societies as they existed before modernization; whereas the open community characterizes societies which are in the process of modernizing and industrializing. This explanation is not complete, however, because even in traditional times peasant societies exhibited much variation in this respect. Villages in traditional China, and especially in those areas of China which had much commercial activity, were more open than closed, although they exhibited features of both types. In most Chinese villages land was alienable and it was possible for villagers to rise in status within the community by diligent farming, and outside the community by engaging in commerce or by passing the imperial civil service examinations and becoming a government official. There were, of course, few Horatio Algers in traditional China; but a herd boy who studied the Confucian classics while tending his water buffalo *could* become a high official of the empire, proving that traditional China allowed more social mobility to the peasantry than most other peasant societies around the world. Consequently, many Chinese villages were by no means homogeneous, and class distinctions were an accepted and important principle of village life. Other peasant societies probably fall somewhere between the closed communities described by Wolf and the more open communities of traditional China.

PEASANTS AND THEIR WIDER SOCIETY

All peasantries have developed ways of dealing with persons of superior wealth, power, and prestige, whether these persons are officials, wealthy landlords, merchants, or simply educated men who know the world outside the peasant village and are able to operate effectively in it. Peasants seek ties with such persons in order to gain increased economic security, to have political protection, and to have some powerful person on whom they can rely when dealing with persons and institutions in the wider society. In many peasant societies, such as those in Latin America and the Mediterranean area, these ties are formalized as patron-client relations which, as Foster points out, can be usefully conceptualized as vertical forms of the dyadic contract. In return for his services to peasants, the patron gains prestige and has his status validated in the eyes of society. By accumulating large numbers of clients dependent on him, he also gains in political power. As Silverman points out, such patron-client relations were extremely important in Italian society a few decades ago, although they have recently become less important. Hollnsteiner describes a similar relationship in Philippine society, in which patron-client ties are enforced through fictive kinship.

Patrons, together with persons of importance in rural society, such as the Chinese gentry, the local nobility of Medieval Europe, and the Indian Brahmans, form hinge groups which fulfill the necessary function of mediating between elites and peasantry — the two "halves" of peasant societies. Members of such hinge groups have been described as "cultural brokers" (Wolf 1956), who transmit elements of the cultural Great Tradition to the peasantry. In addition to their functions as cultural brokers, members of hinge groups often assume leadership among the peasants, exercising power and authority on the levels of society beneath the state administration. They also act as a buffer group, representing the peasantry's interests to officials, and protecting the peasantry as far as possible from the arbitrary exercise of state power. On the other hand, such groups also act as political brokers, transmitting and interpreting state policy to the peasantry and often taking the state's part or acting in accord with their own interests when dealing with peasants.

The classic example of hinge group functioning in a traditional peasant society is the Chinese gentry-scholar-official class, which for more than two thousand years played a leading role in Chinese society. This status group was comprised of men who had passed at least the lowest rung on the Chinese imperial examination system, an attainment which made them eligible for political office in the state bureaucracy and gave them high status and a privileged position in society. While playing their role as government officials, these men represented the interests of the state and their own class against the peasantry. Most of them never rose high enough in the examination system, however, to gain official position, and spent most of their lives in their native villages. Gentry members, with prestige derived from their Confucian education and power from official contacts, led most organizations on the local level of Chinese society. All villages wished to have such members of the elite on whom they could call to represent their interests in the world outside their village, especially since the gentry could deal with magistrates as social equals. Prestigious members of the gentry group acted as mediators in solving disputes within villages or between villages. Most local militias were led by gentry members; and in times of dynastic decline these men often became military leaders and could preserve or overthrow dynasties. In addition, the less successful members of the gentry became teachers in local village schools and were instrumental in transmitting the Confucian tradition to China's rural inhabitants. In all these ways, this group was perhaps the most important in traditional Chinese society. Since all were trained in the Confucian tradition and shared common values and a common status-ethic, they were important in serving to integrate Chinese society. The same might be said of the Brahmans of traditional India or the local nobility of Medieval Europe.

In addition to these vertical relationships that reach upward and outward from the peasant village, connecting peasants to persons of greater power and prestige, peasantries also establish horizontal ties that connect them to members of other villages and towns in the surrounding countryside. Redfield has aptly named these horizontal relationships "the countrywide network" (1956:50). The countrywide network has many dimensions: economic, religious, social, and political.

The peasant village is not economically self-sufficient, depending upon a wide network of persons to whom peasants sell their surplus handicrafts and produce, and from whom they purchase the goods that they themselves do not produce. In most peasant societies the economic network is spread intricately across the countryside, spaced with markets of varied sizes and organization, ranging from temporary local markets to permanent towns (see Skinner's article in Part Two). Here the peasant could meet economic specialists such as itinerant peddlers, merchants, repairmen, moneylenders, and pawnbrokers, with whom he had to relate. In peasant societies, usually, relations between peasants and merchants are carried out through go-betweens who, acting on the basis of personal acquaintance, negotiate the exchange of products.

It is probable, as Skinner has written (see his article in Part Two) that the market networks of each peasant society have a discernible structure, although little work has been done on this problem. Arrangements vary from society to society: in some areas, such as China, the market areas also formed units in which social relations other than economic exchange were extremely important. Whatever form the economic network takes, it is one means by which peasants are drawn outside their villages and are forced to deal with some of the other kinds of people who make up their society.

Economic networks are supplemented by religious networks in many peasant societies. In India the areas served by important temples form a kind of religious community, however diffuse. The pilgrimages common in Islamic areas of the Near East and the pilgrimages of Japanese peasants to major Shinto shrines also show the religious ties that draw the villagers out of their village world and force them to deal with priests and other villagers who share a common religious allegiance.

Economic and religious networks are supplemented by relations of kinship and marriage. In many peasant societies, as in China, village and lineage exogamy is the rule, forcing peasants to seek wives in other village communities, and in return give their daughters in marriage outside their native village. These marriage networks sometimes are bounded by the market town area, as in China (cf. Skinner), but often radiate outward in diminishing intensity from each individual village. It is evident that a village of some one thousand persons might have affinal ties with hundreds of other villages in the surrounding countryside, forming social bonds that the peasant can use to supplement the relationships that he enjoys in his native village.

In societies like that of China, where corporate patrilineages and patriclans are a basic feature of social structure, lineage ties between village branches often establish important social bonds across the countryside. In India, caste relations also extend across village boundaries and solidary groups are created which span myriads of villages, decreasing the social isolation of the individual village community.

The countrywide network in many peasant societies also includes associations for mutual protection, or for carrying out irrigation works. In rural Japan, irrigation societies often included many villages in large coastal valleys (Beardsley, Hall, and Ward 1959:276); and similar irrigation societies are found in some parts of China. In traditional China it was common in periods of unrest for villages to band together in leagues which organized village guards to protect themselves against the intrusion of bandits and hostile armies.

Finally, an extremely important part of the countrywide network in all peasant societies are the administrative units created by the state, which establish political relationships that cut across village boundaries. In Mexico and Spain, villages are combined into municipalities; in China, groups of villages were organized into rural townships which sometimes combined a score of villages into one administrative unit. Japan's *mura* is another example. Since state policy in almost all traditional societies varies from one historical period to the next, the administrative arrangements experienced by a single peasant village are diverse indeed. Sometimes these administrative divisions correspond to natural economic or social units; and sometimes, as in China (see Skinner's article in Part Two) these two kinds of ties diverge.

The peasant village is thus clearly not an isolated whole, it has both vertical and horizontal ties extending from the village to the larger society and civilization of which it forms but one small part. A point equally worth stressing, touched upon in our discussion of administrative arrangements, is that it is impossible to understand the social life of any peasant community without taking state policy and its history into account. Peasants are crucially affected by the actions and decisions of elite groups who man the state apparatus and who are the creators and carriers of civilization; peasantries can be fully understood only when seen in the context of their total civilization. Almost every facet of peasant social life here examined has been affected by decisions and policies that emanate from outside the world of the peasant village.

REFERENCES CITED

Beardsley, R., J. Hall, and R. Ward
1959 *Village Japan*. Chicago: University of Chicago Press.

Freed, Stanley A.
1963 "Fictive Kinship in a North Indian Village." *Ethnology* II:86–103.

Freedman, Maurice
1958 *Lineage Organization in Southeastern China*. London School of Economics Monographs on Social Anthropology, No. 18. University of London: The Athlone Press.

Friedl, Ernestine
1962 *Vasilika, a Village in Modern Greece*. New York: Holt, Rinehart & Winston.

Ishino, Iwao
1953 "The Oyabun-kobun: A Japanese Ritual Kinship Institution." *American Anthropologist* 55:695–707.

Miller, Beatrice
1956 "Ganye and Kidu: Two Formalized Systems of Mutual Aid among the Tibetans." *Southwestern Journal of Anthropology* 12:157–170.

Okada, Ferdinand E.
1957 "Ritual Brotherhood: A Cohesive Factor in Nepalese Society." *Southwestern Journal of Anthropology* 13:212–222.
Phillips, Herbert P.
1965 *Thai Peasant Personality: the Patterning of Interpersonal Behavior in the Village of Bang Chan*. Berkeley and Los Angeles: University of California Press.
Pitt-Rivers, J. A.
1954 *The People of the Sierra*. London: Weidenfeld and Nicolson.
Potter, J. M.
1964 "Ping Shan: the Changing Economy of a Chinese Village in Hong Kong." Unpublished Ph.D. dissertation. University of California, Berkeley.
Redfield, Robert
1955 *The Little Community: Viewpoints for the Study of a Human Whole*. Chicago: University of Chicago Press.
1956 *Peasant Society and Culture*. Chicago: University of Chicago Press.
Wolf, Eric
1956 "Aspects of Group Relations in a Complex Society: Mexico." *American Anthropologist* 58:1056–78.
1966 *Peasants*. Foundations of Modern Anthropology Series. Englewood Cliffs, N.J.: Prentice-Hall.

Opposition and Alliance in a Mexican Town

May N. Diaz

In anthropology, the term "alliance" has of late taken on, on the one hand, a narrow and highly specific meaning in terms of kinship and, on the other, a wide and generalized one in terms of the nature of the new contractual relationship formed between groups. We have, like poets, been playing on the double meaning of the term. In the common, nonanthropological usage a marriage alliance is usually seen as the union of two families, while a political alliance refers to a compact for specific purposes with defined limits entered into by two independent entities. We have meant both these things when we have talked about marriage regulations and the ties formed thereby between groups.

In this paper I intend to examine the question: In what way is a

From "Opposition and Alliance in a Mexican Town" in *Ethnology*, Vol. III, No. 2 (April 1964). Reprinted by permission of the publisher. The research on which this paper is based has been financed by a grant from the National Science Foundation and was done under the supervision of Professor George M. Foster of the University of California, Berkeley.

political alliance formed by a marriage? The problem is a complex one, but here I shall only deal with what one can learn from an examination of the customary ritual.

The data come from a west central Mexican town, a community made up of just under 6,000 persons, Spanish-speaking but considered Indian in culture by both their neighbors and themselves. It is located within commuting distance of the city of Guadalajara. About half of the households are supported by family pottery-making, while the rest are predominantly small farmers and unskilled workers in agriculture and industry. Kinship is reckoned bilaterally. Social integration within the community is maintained by a network of dyadic relationships (cf. Foster 1961), characterized by reciprocity and validated by the exchange of goods and services.

Integration is also maintained in part by the delicate balance of opposition in a system of four barrios or quarters and by ties which cross their boundaries. The town is divided into four equal territorial units (for some purposes these are arranged into a dual division). At one time the quarters were formal administrative units, and some townspeople still assume this to be the case, although in fact the barrio administrative offices no longer exist. Today the quarters function partly in terms of economic specialization and ritual, but they also provide a means of social identification for oneself and all others in the community, as well as a focus for the expression of hostility.

Until about ten years ago the constant undercurrent of hostility between barrios would erupt from time to time in the form of wars or of raids in which a gang of young males from one quarter would come riding on horseback into another part of town and capture a girl. Neither the wars nor the raids take place any longer, but *robo* or stealing is still a regular way of obtaining a girl and, in some cases, a wife.

Although in a few cases robo is a genuine capture of a girl who has caught the fancy of a young man, ordinarily the abduction occurs with the consent of the bride-to-be and after a period of courtship. A young man enlists the aid of a few of his friends; his *pandilla* or gang is usually composed of age-mates who were neighborhood playmates in his younger days. His brothers and other males with whom he has respect relations are not members. The girl is waylaid while she is on an errand and is carried off outside of town — nowadays usually in an automobile. She stays with the groom-to-be at least one night. On the couple's return, the girl is placed under the protection of the household of one of his relatives or godparents. Unless this step of placing the girl in a comparatively neutral household is taken, the formal proceedings to effect a marriage can go no further.

The groom selects someone to present his case to the bride's family. The delegate may be a relative, but no particular kinsman is preferred, although ordinarily neither his father nor his brothers are expected to perform this service. Again a certain amount of "neutrality" is expected of the peacemaker. He is accompanied by a few friends of the groom and, if possible, by a *compadre* (co-godparent) of the bride's father whose presence will assure the party of being received by the father. The groom does not go along, but he provides cigarettes and a bottle of tequila.

The visit follows a clear and highly formalized pattern. Its first stage consists of polite and general conversation on such topics as the weather, the planting season, or community affairs. I am indebted to Dr. Octavio Romano for the suggestion that such conversation helps to place the proceedings within the context of the community as a whole and thereby makes possible continued communication between the opposing parties. This stage is terminated by the peacemaker producing the bottle and the cigarettes. The passing of these items marks successful arrival at the place in the proceedings where the purpose of the visit can be openly acknowledged. As the meeting goes on, the bottle is passed at various intervals to mark points at which some degree of agreement has been reached.

The visitors try to emphasize whatever bonds of real or fictive kinship exist between themselves and the father of the bride. If he is the first cousin of a grandparent, he may be addressed as uncle; if he is a second cousin, he may be called *primo* (first cousin) rather than *pariente* (relative).

The formality of the behavior up to this point creates an atmosphere of respect between the participants in a situation in which there is likely to be a good deal of antagonistic emotion. Respectful behavior establishes distance between the actors in the scene. It allows the father of the bride to maintain his self-respect while he settles the future of a daughter whose loss of virginity has besmirched his honor. The forms of address used evoke mutual obligations of kinsmen and thus help to set up the lines through which communication can take place.

Once the purpose of the call has been stated openly, the tone of the proceedings changes. This is the stage at which the role-players attempt to establish the strength of their bargaining position. The father is hurt, unhappy, outraged. The groom's representatives try various strategies: the groom is a good but impetuous boy who has seen the error of his ways and is eager to make amends; the family is honorable and wishes to make things right; the couple have already undergone a civil ceremony and want their parents' blessing before the religious marriage is performed. With great reluctance the father gradually begins to consider the possibility of an agreement. He withdraws and consults with his wife. In a few cases he may refuse to give his approval, but usually he decides to make the best of a bad situation. The rest of the ritual in cases of robo is quite simple, consisting of a civil ceremony in the town hall and a brief religious rite occurring inconspicuously in the midst of the early morning Mass.

Obtaining a bride by stealing is an accepted way of embarking on a marriage. It is the preferred form when the groom feels that he is unlikely to be able to obtain the approval of his future father-in-law beforehand. Bride stealing most often occurs across barrio boundaries. It still carries with it the connotation of being a raid — even when the girl goes willingly. The girl's father reacts as if it were literally a robo, a capture, and the groom's relatives respond by going through formal peacemaking proceedings. Marriage by capture emphasizes some of the lines of antagonism inherent in the town structure, and, in addition, it dramatizes them in a series of symbolic acts, even in cases where the stealing is nominal.

In the first place, the forms emphasize the traditional roles of man and woman. The male is seen as an active force, as masculine power; the female as passive, as receptive, as not intruding her own will. Marriage is symbolized as the joining of two unlike units, of two people who occupy mutually exclusive roles. It is not dramatized as a relationship entered into by mutual consent. The event is celebrated by aggression on the one hand and by submission on the other.

Second, bride stealing reinforces the split between the two affinal groups. From the beginning of the marriage the groom's and the bride's relatives are assumed to be in opposition. The negotiations which take place so that the required rites can be performed are not viewed as the merging of two families but as diplomatic proceedings between two opposing groups, who compromise, and enter into a compact, while still maintaining their sovereignty.

This form of marriage re-enacts the separation of the territorial units of the town. The stealing of the bride from another quarter binds together the men of one group in opposition to another. It separates "us" from "them" — those of us who belong together and those whom we fight.

If the girl has not been captured, marriage rites begin with another kind of diplomatic deputation to her father. The composition of the visiting group is about the same, but the content of the negotiations varies somewhat. The girl's father has the customary right to make certain kinds of demands. He may set a *plazo*, or term, and postpone the marriage for a certain amount of time while giving his consent; or he may postpone the decision completely for several months. He also has the right to request an assortment of foodstuffs to be delivered at the time of the wedding. In some cases he may itemize details, demanding so many kilos of meat and maize and so many donkey-loads of firewood. If the groom's family fails to fulfill this part of the contract, the bride's father may refuse to allow her to be taken to the groom's house, even though both civil and religious ceremonies have been completed.

During the period of plazo, the betrothed girl is in a state of transition from the status of being unmarried to that of being married, from membership in one household to that in another. According to more conservative usages, the young man is expected to provide his fiancée with laundry soap and charcoal, so that she can learn to wash and to cook. If she becomes ill during this time, her fiancé is expected to pay for medicine because, as one informant put it, "she is not completely of the family of her father any more."

The traditional wedding involves three days of festivities, the first of these occurring on the day preceding the church ceremony. The animals necessary for the wedding feast are killed, and a gathering is held at the house of the groom. This is frequently a heartfelt farewell to bachelorhood, celebrated with drinking, music, and a supper prepared from the more perishable parts of the animals. Meanwhile the bride has gone to confession, having been escorted to church by the wedding *madrina* (godmother or sponsor). If the madrina does not appear to perform this duty, the bride cannot leave the house of her own accord, and the wedding rites cannot proceed. Similarly, on the wedding day the sponsors are expected to provide an automobile and music to escort her to church. If these items are not provided, the parents of the bride may refuse to *entregarla* ("deliver her").

After the standard Roman Catholic rite in the church the wedding party goes to the sponsors' home for breakfast and then moves on to the bride's home, where the "wedding reception" is held. Up until this point her parents (and particularly her mother) have taken little active part in the wedding; they may not even have attended the church ceremony. The bride now comes home, escorted by her girl friends, the groom, his relatives and friends, and the wedding sponsors. They carry large clay vessels filled with wedding food, provided by the groom's family. The food for the total series of festivities is contributed in part by members of the groom's kindred and by neighbors in his territorial unit. People outside the nuclear family thus ratify and support the contract and the alliance. They reinforce their own alliance with the groom's family and thereby provide support in the arrangements made with the bride's kinsmen.

The procession to the bride's home is brought to a climax and ends in a sham battle. At present this is only enacted during carnival periods, but in the past it was part of the regular proceedings, and in some other towns of the state of Jalisco which share a similar cultural base it continues to be practiced throughout the year (Ramírez Flores 1960). Those who consider themselves to be partisans of the bride's family meet the wedding party at the door of her father's home. Both contingents pelt each other with eggshells filled with water, ashes, and perfume. When the fun and horseplay have come to an end, the emissaries carry the food into the bride's father's house. In what is considered a solemn and emotional moment in the ceremonials, the wedding sponsors take the two sets of parents off privately and ask them to greet each other with a formal embrace. This is a difficult time for many people; it is reported to be a moment of strain, an occasion when both sets of participants must capitulate, a time when fathers weep openly.

Feasting continues all night in the houses of both the bride and the groom, but the bride must return to her godmother's home to spend the night there. Rights *in uxorem* are not given to the bridegroom until after the bride the following morning has performed a ceremonial service of washing the dishes in his parents' house and of serving *atole* (a traditional maize gruel) to the wedding guests there. Later during the day everyone goes to the bride's home for yet another feast — the *tornaboda* — which terminates the ceremonial.

Through all the comings and goings, the talks, the obligations, a series of general themes can be discerned: (1) the bride is "delivered" in a literal sense as if she were a symbol of the validation of an agreement; (2) the contingents and supporters of the bride and of the groom remain separate both symbolically and actually during most of the rites; (3) the full series of necessary steps can be taken only if there are mediators — peacemakers, sponsors, advisers; (4) the contract is not final until the day of the tornaboda, prior to which the treaty or compact can be abrogated at several points in the process.

At various places in the three days' activities it is obvious that the drama proceeds as if the bride were not acting of her own accord but were literally being "given" in marriage as part of a transaction with a larger sphere of reference. She cannot leave the house without her godmother as escort, and her father has the option of not allowing her to be taken out of the house if the conditions of the wedding contract have not been fulfilled — even in extreme cases when she has already been married by both church and state. The service which she performs on the last day for her husband's family symbolizes the final act of her passage from one family group to another.

The delivery of the bride is accomplished without the merging of the two families at any point in the proceedings except for the embrace, which, as it were, ratifies the compact between the two sets of parents. Although during most of the three days the groups do not even see each other, the contract can be formed and made binding because the traveling back and forth from one to another gives formal recognition to the importance of both units. Again, as in bride-stealing, the ceremonies resemble diplomatic proceedings between two sovereign and distinct units. Direct communication can take place only with the help of a mediator; often it could not take place at all without the tact and the manipulations of a practiced diplomat, for the affinal groups are expected to be not only distant but openly hostile as well.

The ceremonial of forming a marriage alliance thus shares with that of forming a political one a common narrative, a common set of specific events. It does not necessarily, however, create the same kind of bond. Whereas an alliance by marriage may give a passport into enemy territory and add new people to the category of those from whom one may hope to get (without being assured of getting) support and aid, the same alliance defines opponents without providing machinery for evoking solidarity. Although membership in a town quarter is exclusive — no one can be both a member and a nonmember, or be a member of more than one unit — no one speaks for the quarter. No one is its collective representative; no one has formed an alliance on its behalf. Consequently the bonds formed by a marriage alliance are, after the wedding, binding only on the husband and wife; for everyone else, their maintenance depends on repeated validations, on the choice to make active what is a latent contract. The diplomatic proceedings have produced a safe-conduct and a temporary armistice.

REFERENCES CITED

Foster, G. M.
1961 "The Dyadic Contract: A Model for the Social Structure of a Mexican Peasant Village." *American Anthropologist* 63:1173–1192.

Ramírez Flores, J.
1960 "Matrimonio: Indígenas de Zacoalco." *Jalisco en el Arte* (J. R. Alvarez, ed.) Guadalajara.

AN ANALYSIS OF RITUAL CO-PARENTHOOD (COMPADRAZGO)

Sidney W. Mintz and Eric R. Wolf

As anthropologists have been drawn into the study of Latin American cultures, they have gathered increasing amounts of material on the characteristic cultural mechanisms of *compadrazgo*. This term designates the particular complex of relationships set up between individuals primarily, though not always, through participation in the ritual of Catholic baptism.

This rite involves, among its various aspects, three individuals or groups of individuals. These are: first, an initiate, usually a child;

From "An Analysis of Ritual Co-Parenthood (Compadrazgo)" in *Southwestern Journal of Anthropology*, Vol. VI (Winter 1950). Reprinted by permission of the authors and the editors of the *Southwestern Journal of Anthropology*. All translations are by the authors unless otherwise indicated. The writers wish to thank the University of Puerto Rico and the Rockefeller Foundation for their sponsorship of the Puerto Rico Social Anthropology Project. Field data gathered by the authors and their colleagues on this Project have been used in the present article.

secondly, the parents of the initiate; third, the ceremonial sponsor or sponsors of the initiate. It thus involves three sets of relationships. The first links parents and child, and is set up within the confines of the immediate biological family. The second links the child and his ceremonial sponsor, a person outside the limits of his immediate biological family. This relation is familiar to most Americans as the relation between godfather or godmother and godchild. The third set of relationships links the parents of the child to the child's ceremonial sponsors. In Spanish, these call each other *compadres* (Latin *compater-commater*, Spanish *compadre-comadre*, Italian *compare-commare*, French *compere-commere*, German *Gevatter-Gevatterin*, Russian *kum-kuma*, etc.), literally co-parents of the same child. The old English form of this term, *godsib*, is so unfamiliar to most English-speaking people today that they even ignore its hidden survival in the noun "gossip" and in the verb "to gossip." In English, as in the Ecuadorian *compadrear*, the meaning of the term has narrowed to encompass just one, if perhaps a notable characteristic of *compadre* relations. Most other aspects of this relationship have, however, fallen by the wayside. In contrast, in Medieval Europe, the compadre mechanism was of considerable cultural importance, and in present-day Latin America, its cultural role is attested by its frequent extensions beyond the boundaries of baptismal sponsorship.

> The thing itself is curious, and quite novel to an Englishman of the present day [wrote Edward B. Tylor in 1861 [1]]. The godfathers and godmothers of a child become, by their participation in the ceremony, relations to one another and to the priest who baptizes the child, and call one another ever afterwards *compadre* and *comadre*. . . . In Mexico, this connexion obliges the *compadres* and *comadres* to hospitality and honesty and all sorts of good offices towards one another; and it is wonderful how conscientiously this obligation is kept to, even by people who have no conscience at all for the rest of the world. A man who will cheat his own father or his own son will keep faith with his *compadre*. To such an extent does this influence become mixed up with all sorts of affairs, and so important is it, that it is necessary to count it among the things that tend to alter the course of justice in the country.

In this article, the writers hope to present some material dealing with the historical antecedents of the compadre mechanism, and to discuss some of its present-day functional correlates.

Emphasis in studies of compadrazgo to date has largely centered on attempts to identify a European or Indian background for its various component traits.[2] Other studies have dealt with the diffusion of the complex in certain parts of Latin America, and the diversity of functions which it has assumed.[3] A recent trend has been to consider the compadre system as a significant feature of a putative Criollo culture.[4]

[1] Tylor, 1861, pp. 250–251.

[2] Parsons, 1936, pp. 524–525; Redfield and Villa R., 1934, pp. 373–374; Foster, 1948, p. 264.

[3] Paul, 1942.

[4] Committee on Latin American Anthropology of the National Research Council, 1949, p. 152.

The present writers hope to deal with the compadre system rather in terms of possible functional relationships to other aspects of culture, such as the family, the status system, the system of land ownership, the legal system, the role of the individual in culture, and so forth. We shall especially emphasize its functions in furthering social solidarity. We shall employ the term "horizontal" to designate the direction which the compadre mechanism takes when linking together members of the same class. We shall use the term "vertical" to indicate the direction it takes when tying together members of different classes. Finally, we hope to discuss compadrazgo not only in terms of the ethnographic present, but also in terms of its past functions, that is, in terms of its historical context.

I. HISTORICAL ANTECEDENTS

This section will deal with the historical development of compadrazgo and its functional implications in the past.

We have seen that in Catholic practice, a sponsor aids in the initiation of a new member into the Church. He must be an established member of the religious community. His presence and ministrations in effect testify that the new candidate is willing and able to receive the prescribed initiatory rite. In Catholic theory, this initiatory rite is regarded as a form of spiritual rebirth, and an analogy is drawn between the role of the biological father in the process of conception on the one hand and the role of the sponsor as a spiritual father on the other. This notion of spiritual affinity has in turn given rise to notions of spiritual kinship, and laid the basis for the formation of ritual kin relationships through the mechanism of sponsorship at baptism.

Each of these three ideas has a separate history. Each is made up in turn of strands derived from different cultural backgrounds. The notion of sponsorship finds no warrant in the New Testament, and Canon Law refers to "custom" as the judicial basis upon which the precept rests.[5] It may derive in part from Jewish practice at circumcision where a witness is required to hold the child undergoing the ritual. This witness is called by a term derived from the Greek.[6] In this connection, it is perhaps significant that the Eleusynian Mysteries of the Greeks also made use of sponsors.[7] The term "sponsor" itself represents an adaptation of a term current in Roman legal terminology where *sponsio* signified a contract enforced by religious rather than by legal sanctions.[8] Finally, we know that the primitive Church used sponsors to guard against the admission of untrustworthy individuals, clearly an important function in the early days of persecution. Hence the term *fidei iussores*, those who testified to the good faith of the applicant, by which sponsors were also known.

[5] Kearney, 1925, p. 4.
[6] Bamberger, 1923, p. 326.
[7] Drews, 1907, p. 447.
[8] Kearney, *op. cit.*, pp. 33–34.

The second component, the notion of spiritual rebirth, may also represent the product of several divergent traditions. However, this aspect of the institution falls outside the province of the present article.

The aspect of ritual kinship derived from sponsorship at baptism underwent its own special development. During the period of St. Augustine (A.D. 354–430), parents usually acted as sponsors for their own children. This custom was so widespread that Bishop Boniface was of the opinion that no one but parents could act as sponsors for the child's baptism. In a letter to Bishop Boniface, St. Augustine discussed this point, and drew attention to cases in which the sponsors had not been the parents. Slave owners had acted as sponsors for children borne by their slaves; orphans had been baptized with the aid of unknown third persons who had consented to act as sponsors; and exposed children had been initiated under the sponsorship of religious women.[9]

Roughly a hundred years later, the Byzantine emperor Justinian, who ruled from A.D. 527–565, first issued an edict prohibiting marriages between spiritual relatives. The terms *compater* and *commater* first appeared in A.D. 585 and 595, within the confines of the Western Church. Thus we may note first that a separate set of sponsors tended to be a later development from a stage in which parents and sponsors were the same people; and secondly, that this separation must have been effected within both the Eastern and Western Empires roughly between the first quarter of the fifth century and the end of the sixth century A.D. Nevertheless, full acceptance of this separation and consequent exogamy took place only gradually. From the evidence noted by the Byzantine historian Procopius, we may judge that in the beginning of this period, godparents still actually adopted their godchildren.[10] In A.D. 753 St. Boniface could still write:

> The priests throughout Gaul and France maintain that for them a man who takes to wife a widow, to whose child he has acted as godfather, is guilty of a very serious crime. As to the nature of this sin, if it is a sin, I was entirely ignorant, nor have I ever seen it mentioned by the fathers, in the ancient canons, nor in the decree of the pope, nor by the apostles in their catalogue of sins.[11]

But the Council of Munich, held in A.D. 813, prohibited parents from acting as sponsors for their own children altogether, and in the books of the Council of Metz of the same year, parents and sponsors are clearly referred to by separate sets of terms.

The next two hundred years witnessed a wider and wider extension of the ties of ritual kinship, and a concomitant growth of the exogamous group. A Council of Metz held in A.D. 888 attempted to restrict the development, but without effect. The incest group, biological as well as ritual, was extended to cover seven degrees of relationship. There was an increase in the number of ceremonials at which sponsors officiated,

[9] Kearney, *op. cit.*, pp. 30–31.
[10] Laurin, 1866, p. 220.
[11] Boniface (English transl.), 1940, pp. 61–62.

accompanied by an increase in the number of people executing distinctive roles at any one ceremony who could be included in the circle of kin. Finally, the number of sponsors executing any given function grew as well.

Where baptism and confirmation had originally been one set of rites, they grew apart and became two separate ceremonies, within the area dominated by the Western Church. This separation is documented for the Frankish kingdom in the eighth century, and was accompanied by the development of two different sets of sponsors, for baptism and for confirmation.[12] Since confirmation was looked upon as a completion of the baptismal act, confirmation sponsors similarly became ritual kin. In the Eastern Church, however, baptism and confirmation remain d one rite, but different sets of sponsors and hence ritual relatives were added for a hair-cutting rite as well as for "wet" baptism.[13] The Western Church, in turn, added ritual kin relationships with a "catechismal" godfather, who was present at ceremonies and abjurations preceding the baptismal act. For a long time it was also believed that the sacrament of confession produced a bond of ritual kinship between the father confessor and the confessant, until Pope Boniface VII abrogated this relationship in A.D. 1298.

But as the number of ceremonies productive of ritual kin relations grew, so grew the number of people who were geared into kinship arrangements. First, the Western Church extended spiritual relationships to cover the officiating priest, the sponsors, the child, the child's parents, and their respective children. Thus we get spiritual fraternity as well as spiritual co-parenthood. In this context, we may recall that the final ban against priests' marriages and concubinage was not issued until the Council of Trent (A.D. 1545–63). Finally, the number of sponsors increased, until general custom admitted between one and thirty baptismal sponsors.[14] While Pope Boniface abrogated ritual kin relationships arising from the confessional, he decreed at the same time that all the sponsors who were present at any given ceremony entered into valid ritual kin relationships, and necessarily became part of the widening exogamic circles.

Despite the largely formal nature of the material that deals with the growth of ritual kin ties during this period, we may perhaps venture some guesses as to possible functional correlates of the mechanism, and attempt to delimit some of the factors in its formation.

Ecclesiastical legislation on the subject tends to center in two main periods: in the ninth century A.D. on the one hand, and in the period from about A.D. 1300 to the end of the sixteenth century on the other. The interim period witnessed highest development of the feudal order.

[12] Laurin, *op. cit.*, p. 220.
[13] Durham, 1928, p. 304.
[14] Tuschen, 1936, p. 61.

Its main cultural conditions may briefly be restated. Ownership of land was vested in the feudal lord. He also owned a share of the labor of the serfs who lived on his land. In return he granted the worker rights to use the land, ownership of certain tools, and the right to consume some of the agricultural and handicraft goods which he produced. The mutual obligations and services which made up this system were maintained by custom, and this complex of custom operated largely through face-to-face relationships between its carriers. We hope to indicate that the compadre mechanism and its ritual kin correlates were a functioning part of the class system implicit in this basic relationship.

Many writers have suggested that the compadre mechanism superseded earlier relationships of a tribal character based on actual or fictitious ties of blood. Thus Kummer feels that "it subordinated the community of blood to the community of faith." [15] Tomasic notes that the compadre mechanism maintained itself within Dinaric society while blood brotherhood declined.[16] He sees some relationship between this phenomenon and "the strengthening of the power of the state," and states that the compadre mechanism "was transferred from the tribal to the state level." With the growth of the state and its formal institutions, compadrazgo thus served to manipulate the increasingly impersonal structure in terms of person-to-person relationships.

In more specific fashion, Dopsch has related some forms of artificial relationships and "brotherhood arrangements" among feudal tenants to changes in the pattern of inheritance.[17] When the power of the large landowners was at its peak during the declining phase of the Roman Empire and during the initial period of feudal consolidation, tenants inherited rights of tenure from their neighbors in the absence of descendants in the direct line. With changes away from the predominance of large landowners, and towards increased political centralization, this right of neighbor inheritance gave way to inheritance on the part of other relatives of the deceased, notably on the part of siblings. Blood or ritual brothers then became an asset in the struggle "to lighten the economic and social duties with which the landowners burdened their tenants." [18] During this period, inheritance of tenure on the manor within the same household became more secure, the greater the number of potential heirs and workers. Horizontally phrased mechanisms like the Latin *adfratatio* and the Visigoth *hermandad* kept the land within the group of ritual and blood brothers, and prevented its reversion to the lord's demesne. The Church, anxious to establish itself as an independent landowner in its own right, capitalized on this change in the process of inheritance to press its own claims. It accomplished this through the enforcement of religious rulings regarding exogamy.

[15] Kummer, 1931, p. 789.
[16] Tomasic, 1948, p. 80.
[17] Dopsch, 1918–20, vol. 1, p. 378.
[18] *Ibid.*

The marriages within the kin group and within the group of affinal relatives heavily reinforced the weight of the old Germanic limitations on the right of the individual to dispose of property, and as a result put the Church in a disadvantageous position.[19]

These limitations were used against the Church by its main adversaries in the struggle over land, the lay aristocracy and feudal lords. When the Church prohibited marriage within seven degrees of relationship, it prohibited it among all persons who for any legal purpose could claim blood relationship with each other.[20] This struggle was won by the Church, which in the process acquired almost complete control over legislation covering the making and execution of testaments.

Thus we may trace the early increase in exogamy to three different, yet interdependent factors: the attempt of the serfs to maintain their economic status; the attempt of the people to manipulate the growing structure of the state and the growing number of formal institutions through the use of a mechanism with which they were familiar; and the attempt of the Church to establish itself as an independent owner of landed property. In the final analysis, all three factors are but facets of the growing centralization of the feudal structure. This process took place in the main at the expense of the lay aristocracy. In the struggle the Crown attempted to play off Church and serfs against the feudal barons; the Church supported Crown and serfs against its lay competitors; and the serfs looked to both Crown and Church in their effort to increase their rights on the estates of the lay aristocracy.

Just as the increase in ritual brotherhood and in the size of the exogamic group may relate to this early stage of development of feudal tenures, so the great increase in compadre relationships and ritual kin prohibitions connected with them appear to relate to later changes in the tenure of serfs in relationship to their feudal lords.

The outstanding characteristic of the compadre mechanism is its adaptiveness to different situations. As the structure of the situation changes, so we may expect to see the compadre mechanism serve different purposes. As tenure became increasingly fixed within individual households, these units were also drawn into individual vertical relationships to the manorial administration. These different relationships crystallized into different rules for different groups of people on the manor. Far from being homogeneous, manorial custom took clear note of this process of differentiation. Under feudal conditions, then, one of the main functions of the compadre relationship was to structure such individual or family relationships vertically between the members of different classes.

In medieval France, "parents attempted to win for the baptismal candidate material advantages through their choice of godparents."[21]

[19] Dopsch, 1918–20, vol. 2, p. 227.

[20] Maitland and Pollock, 1923, pp. 387–388.

[21] Henninger, 1891, p. 31.

In Germany, "poor people invited individuals of higher status to become godparents to their children. . . . The nobles reversed this custom and invited their subjects, or at least their subjects' representatives, as *compadres*." [22] Mercenaries asked nobles to serve as godparents; day laborers asked their employers or the service staff of the manor. Officials often asked the city council, and the city budgets of the time show that the outlays arising from these ceremonial duties were often charged to the city treasury.[23] A "luminous instance" of how the mechanism was manipulated in daily practice is furnished by Coulton.[24] Monks were not allowed to stand as godparents, for fear that increased material benefits thus derived might weaken the centralized structure of the Church. But in 1419, the abbot of a French monastery which had suffered grievously under the ravages of war petitioned the Holy See for a dispensation from this ruling. "Seeing that the favor of nobles and of other powerful folk is most necessary and opportune to the said monks for the preservation of their rights; seeing also that, in these parts, close friendships are contracted between those who stand as godparents and the parents of the children," he argued in favor of initiating compadre relationships with some forty nobles.

The second function of the mechanism was to solidify social relationships horizontally among members of the same rural neighborhood. It is expressed in linguistic terms in the widening of the meaning of the word "compadre" to include the term "neighbor." In Andalucia, for example, the term "compadre" is easily extended to cover any acquaintance and even strangers.[25] In the Tyrol, the word *Gevatterschaft* (compadre group) is used to draw a contrast to the *Freundschaft* (the group of relatives, from the old meaning of the word *Freund* = relative). Hence also the English word, "gossip," derived from *godsib*,[26] and the use which Robert Burns makes in his poetry of such Scottish terms as *cummer* and *kimmer* to designate any woman from the neighborhood, a gossip, or a witch.[27]

One of the outstanding functions of the neighborhood group during the period of the later Middle Ages was the struggle against prevailing forms of feudal tenure. The eleventh century saw the beginning of the fight to resist labor services on the lord's land "by a sort of passive resistance." [28] During the twelfth and the thirteenth centuries, tenants consolidated to their own advantage the various rights of tenure which they enjoyed. "Begun in the twelfth century, emancipation was mainly achieved . . . by individual or collective acts of enfranchisement . . . generally brought about through a revolt of the inhabitants of a seignorie." [29] This struggle was often carried on with the aid of Crown and

[22] Boesch, 1900, pp. 26–27.
[23] *Ibid.*
[24] Coulton, 1936, p. 264.
[25] Donadin y Puignan, p. 863
[26] Weekly, 1921, p. 654.
[27] Warrack, 1911, p. 117.
[28] Ganshof, 1941, p. 295.
[29] Ganshof; *op. cit.*, p. 319.

Church, which supported the claims of serfs and tenants in order to undermine the position of the lay aristocracy. Not the least of these claims was directed against the feudal regulations governing marriage.

One of the most direct consequences of the extension of the exogamic group through ritual kin ties was to put pressure on existing provisions for a stable labor supply. Marriage off the manor meant the loss of property to one of the feudal lords, and he exacted compensation. A serf was not permitted to marry off the manor without payment of an indemnity variously known as *formariage*, *foris*, or *merchet*. Extension of kinship ties through ceremonial sponsorship inevitably brought nearer the day when most of the inhabitants of a village would be ritually related, and yet unable to pay the fee required for marriages outside the estate. Conflicts might for a while be avoided through refusal to marry and baptize in church, through systematic choice of godparents from the group of blood relatives,[30] or through systematic choice of sponsors from one family.[31] The two last-named techniques are reported for modern Bulgar villages. Yet these devices proved temporary, especially in the smaller communities.[32] At first, lords tried to meet the situation of increasing migration and marriage off the manor by local agreements,[33] but in the thirteenth and fourteenth centuries, the payment of merchet fell into disuse altogether. Serfs acquired the right to marry off the manor when they took over their fathers' land, or bargained with their lords for the privilege of marrying without interference. When a bargain was struck, the serfs had the exemptions written down in the manorial rolls, to be certain of proof when the actual occasion arose.[34]

The special charters won by the peasantry during these times gave rise to a special kind of neighborhood solidarity, reflected, in terms of the present problem, in attempts to include all the members of the neighborhood within the compadre network. Thus we may note a Bosnian practice of including Muslim members of the community by making them sponsors on special occasions, until in 1676 the Holy Office issued a decree against "the admission of heretics as sponsors, even though the strongest reasons of friendship and familiarity prompted the choice of such a person." [35] Also, in some areas neighbors acquired special rights as witnesses in legal proceedings, surviving until recently in the right of the Serb compadre to defend his *kum* in court, and to act as witness for him.[36]

In passing we may mention that the pattern of sponsorship permitted of easy extension into other spheres of activity. Thus, the organizations of medieval journeymen used both the components of baptism and

[30] Boesch, *op. cit.*, p. 26.

[31] Sanders, 1949, p. 129.

[32] Laurin, *op. cit.*, p. 262. For parallels in modern Bulgaria, cf. Handjieff, 1931, pp. 36–37.

[33] Nabholz, 1941, p. 506.

[34] Bennett, 1938, pp. 241–242.

[35] Kearney, *op. cit.*, p. 58.

[36] Ploss, 1911, p. 325.

sponsorship in initiating apprentices to their ranks,[37] and knights who aided a candidate for initiation into knighthood went by godfather and compadre terms.[38]

Finally, we must mention the sanctions of the Church in the enforcement of exogamy. In setting new norms for its tenants, it acted in its own self-interest in competition with the lay aristocracy which jealously guarded and reinforced its position of immunity. In extending Canon Law, and at the same time stressing dispensations from it, the Church added a source of income. Canon Law is man-made law, and the Pope has the right, by virtue of his office, to change its stipulations at will. For sixteen groschen a commoner could marry his blood relatives of the fourth degree of relationship, not to speak of ritual kin relations,[39] and a price list for the years 1492–1513 specifically states that "in spiritual relationships paupers are not dispensed, and the composition is three hundred ducats; nevertheless, one hundred are commonly paid." [40] Coulton has pointed out that enforcement to the letter of Canon Law would have meant "papal dispensations . . . in almost every generation of almost every village in Europe," [41] and the law was often honored in the breach. But punishment struck hard, as in the case of one John Howthon of Tonbridge who was whipped three times around market and church for having married a girl to whom his first wife had been godmother.[42]

As the Middle Ages draw to a close, we find an increasing number of local attempts to restrict the extension of exogamy through ritual kin ties, on the part of both Church and state. A number of synods, held between the years 1310 and 1512, tried to set limits to the number of sponsors at baptismal ceremonies, but failed.[43] In 1521 the German Estates petitioned the Pope for redress of a series of wrongs. Their complaint against ritual kinship derived from baptismal sponsorship heads a list of some sixty-odd complaints.[44] The German Reformation directed its attack against the custom. "This is the work of fools," Luther said.[45] "Because in this way one Christian could not take another one, because they are brother and sister among themselves. These are the money snares of the Pope." Luther declared that "love needs no laws whatsoever," and that "no man has the right to create such laws." He spoke out sharply against "these stupid barriers due to spiritual fatherhood, motherhood, brotherhood, sisterhood, and childhood. Who but Superstition has created these spiritual relationships? . . . Behold, Christian freedom is suppressed due to the blindness of human superstition." [46] His collected proverbs stress the purely mundane and neigh-

[37] Erich, 1936, p. 275; Siemsen, 1942, pp. 61, 67.
[38] Corblet, 1882, vol. 1, p. 180.
[39] Flick, 1936, vol. 1, p. 122.
[40] Lunt, 1934, vol. 2, pp. 525–526.
[41] Coulton, 1926, p. 80.
[42] Howard, 1904, p. 365.
[43] Laurin, *op. cit.*, p. 263.
[44] Münch, 1830, vol. 1, p. 344.
[45] Luther, 1539, p. 301.
[46] Luther, 1520, pp. 477–478.

borly aspects of the compadre mechanism, and advocate that just as "good fences make good neighbors," so they also make for good relations among compadres.[47] As early as 1550, Saxony restricted the number of baptismal sponsors to between seven and nine for nobles, and to three for burghers. Under pressures from within and without, the Church also reformed its stand at the Council of Trent (1545–63). It restricted ritual kin relationships to the baptizing priest, the child, the child's parents and the child's sponsors. But it put an end to spiritual fraternity, spiritual relationships between the sponsors themselves, and spiritual relationships arising from catechismal sponsorship. It restricted to one or to a maximum of two the number of sponsors at baptism, and the number of sponsors at confirmation to one. Again, state authorities followed suit, and the rules governing baptism issued by the Duke of Altenburg for the year 1681 are typical for a whole series of German cities. These rulings restricted the number of sponsors according to one's estate. Nobles were permitted more sponsors than burghers and artisans, burghers and artisans more than peasants.[48] The Austrian Emperor Joseph II restricted to only two or three the number of sponsors at baptism, although a much larger number had been chosen in earlier times.[49]

The rationale for these restrictions emerges perhaps most clearly in rulings prohibiting peasants from seeking their compadres in the towns, and "since rich people were often selected as *compadres*," people were prevented from asking unknown persons for the service.[50] We may note that the bulk of the restrictions coincide with the period which witnessed the rise of Protestantism and the early beginnings of industrial civilization. The new ethic put a premium on the individual as an effective accumulator of capital and virtue, and was certain to discountenance the drain on individual resources and the restrictions on individual freedom implicit in the wide extension of ritual kin ties. As a result the compadre mechanism has disappeared almost completely from areas which witnessed the development of industrial capitalism, the rise of a strong middle class, and the disappearance of feudal or neo-feudal tenures. Within these areas compadrazgo has lost its function most completely within the classes in which the family no longer forms the primary unit of production. This would include the economically mobile upper and middle classes on the one hand, and the industrial wage-earning working class on the other. In both these segments, kinship mechanisms became increasingly non-functional, and tended to be replaced by more impersonal, institutionalized forms of organization. Within these same areas, however, kinship mechanisms have been retained most completely where peasants have not yet become farmers. This point of transition comes where production is still largely for immediate consumption rather than for accumulation, and where the familial unit still forms the active basis

[47] Luther, 1900, p. 348.
[48] Boesch, *op. cit.*, p. 32.
[49] Ploss, *op. cit.*, p. 330.
[50] Boesch, *op. cit.*, p. 32.

of economic life. In Europe, as a whole, it has been retained most completely in such areas as Spain, Italy, and the Balkan countries where the development of industrial capitalism, the rise of a middle class, and the disintegration of the feudal order has been less rapid. To this extent Robert Redfield is justified when he called compadrazgo a Southern European peasant custom.[51] It is from Southern Europe that the complex was transmitted to Latin America, along with the call to baptize the infidels and to bring them into the fold of the Christian community as an addition to the faith through baptism, and as an addition to the riches of the Spanish Empire through labor.

II. FUNCTIONAL ANALYSIS

The Catholic ceremonial complexes, when carried to the New World, were to develop under conditions very different from those of fifteenth-century Europe. Alienation of Indian lands through such devices as the *repartimiento* and the *encomienda* proceeded concurrently with the wholesale conversion of millions of native peoples to Catholicism. The functioning of such mechanisms as compadrazgo in Latin American communities is strongly colored by four hundred years of historical development within this new setting. Yet there is little material on the cultural significance and usages of the compadre mechanism during the Colonial period. Certainly considerable research needs to be carried out on the processes of acculturation following early contact. Analysis of the social functioning of compadrazgo in its American beginnings is but a minor aspect.

Historical sources attest that baptism of natives had proceeded from the time of first contact. Fray Toribio de Benavente writes that in the fifty-five year period between 1521 and 1576 more than four million souls were brought to the baptismal font.[52] The evidence is good that emphasis was not on prior instruction in the catechism, but rather on formal acceptance of the faith. Father Gante and an assistant, proselytizing in Mexico, claim to have baptized up to fourteen thousand Indians in a single day. In all, Gante and his companion stated that they baptized more than two hundred thousand souls in a single Mexican province.[53]

Baptism was a sacrament designed to remove the stigma of original sin. The acquisition of godparents purported to guarantee to the initiate religious guidance during the years following his baptism. Actually, Spaniards who were members of exploring parties frequently served as sponsors for Indian converts, and thus fulfilled but a formal ritual necessity.[54] We can assume that most of the social implications of the compadre mechanism developed but slowly at first, if for no other reason than this.

Yet the baptismal ceremony established an individual in the Catholic

[51] Redfield, 1930, p. 141.

[52] Quoted in Rojas Gonzalez, 1943, p. 193.

[53] Bancroft, 1883, p. 174.

[54] Espinosa, 1942, p. 70 *passim*.

universe, and perhaps by virtue of its symbolic simplicity, it was readily accepted by many native populations. Redfield, Parsons, Foster, and Paul, among others, have sought to differentiate between aboriginal and Catholic elements in the modern Latin American ritual.[55] Parsons, Redfield, and Paul have felt further that certain derivations of the modern godparental ritual have come from the adaptation of this ceremonial form to pre-Columbian ceremonies and social patterns. The Maya of Yucatan possessed a native baptism so like the Catholic ritual that, according to one authority,

> some of our Spaniards have taken occasion to persuade themselves and believe that in times past some of the apostles or successors to them passed over the West Indies and that ultimately those Indians were preached to.[56]

The Aztecs also had a kind of baptism, and in addition, godparents of sorts were chosen in an indigenous Aztec ear-piercing ceremonial, according to Sahagun.[57] Paul feels there may even have been an aboriginal basis for the compadre aspect of the complex in the existence of various kinds of formal friendship among native peoples.[58]

But it is impossible to generalize about the ease with which aboriginal ceremonial procedure could be accommodated to the new sacrament, as endorsed by the Church. The most important modern social result of the baptismal ceremony in practice — the creation of a security network of ritual kin folk through ceremonial sponsorship — seems rather to be due to the institution's inherent flexibility and utility, than to any preexisting pattern with which the new complex might be integrated. Present-day folklore concerning the fate of an unbaptized child [59] suggests that a strong emphasis on the moral necessity for baptism was made from the start. In modern practice, however, whether the people in a given culture will feel that baptism requires the official approval and participation of representatives of the Church varies considerably. The evidence is that once the secular utility of this sacred institution was established, and the native populations could count on the fulfillment of those reciprocal obligations which godparentage and compadrazgo entailed, the Church might not even be consulted. Makeshift ceremonies, consummated without orthodox clerical approval, became so widespread as to be illegalized by ecclesiastical ruling in 1947, except in cases where the child's death seemed imminent before official baptism.

As has been indicated, the mechanism of godparenthood took shape originally as a means for guaranteeing religious education and guidance to the Catholic child. This aim was achieved through the ritual kinship established between the newborn infant, its parents, and its godparents,

[55] Redfield and Villa R., *loc. cit.*; Parsons, *loc. cit.*; Foster, *loc. cit.*; Paul, *op. cit.*, p. 79 *passim*.

[56] Lopez Medel, quoted in Landa, 1941, p. 227.

[57] Sahagun, 1932, pp. 34–35.

[58] Paul, *op. cit.*, pp. 85–87.

[59] Redfield and Villa R., *op. cit.*, p. 169; Parsons, 1945, p. 44; Paul, *op. cit.*

at the baptismal ceremony. The relationship frequently was reinforced, or extended with new sponsors, at other life crisis ceremonies, including confirmation and marriage.

From the original Catholic life crisis ceremonial sponsorship, godparenthood has been elaborated in various Latin American communities into the ceremonial sponsorship of houses, crosses, altars, or carnivals,[60] circumcision,[61] the future crop,[62] commercial dealings,[63] and so on. Gillin lists fourteen forms of compadrazgo for a single community.[64] In certain cases, it cannot be said with any certainty whether the new adaptation was developed locally, or constitutes a carry-over of some kind from some older European elaboration.

In general, ritual ties between contemporaries seem to have become more important than those between godparents and godchildren. This point is elaborated by Gillin in his discussion of the Peruvian community, Moche. He writes:

> The essence of the system in Moche is an "artificial bond," resembling a kinship relationship, which is established between persons by means of a ceremony. The ceremony usually involves a sponsorship of a person or material object by one or more of the persons involved, and the ceremony itself may be rather informal. However in Moche it seems to be placing the wrong emphasis to label the whole system . . . "ceremonial sponsorship." . . . The emphasis in Moche is upon the relations between sponsors of an individual or thing, and between them and other persons — in other words, relations between adults rather than between adults and children or things.[65]

While the custom derives primarily from a conception of spiritual parenthood, modern Latin American emphasis seems to be rather on ritual co-parenthood; the compadre-compadre relationship outweighs the godparent-godchild relationship.

The ritual complex has been demonstrated to be of so flexible and adaptable a nature that a wide group of individuals can be bound together ceremonially. Paul makes the points that the mechanism of compadrazgo may be used either to enlarge numerically and spatially the number of ritually related kin on the one hand, or to reinforce already existing blood or ritual ties on the other. These contrasting motives he calls "extension" and "intensification." [66] The authors of the present article feel that whether the compadre mechanism will be used prevailingly to extend or to intensify a given set of relationships will be determined in a specific functional-historical context.

In modern Latin American communities, there is clear patterning of choice. Compadres may be chosen exclusively from within one's own family, or perhaps blood kin will be preferred to outsiders. In other com-

[60] Gillin, 1945, p. 105.
[61] Beals, 1946, p. 102.
[62] Parsons, 1936, p. 228, n. 96.
[63] Zingg, 1938, pp. 717–718.
[64] Gillin, *loc. cit.*
[65] Gillin, *op. cit.*, p. 104.
[66] Paul, *op. cit.*, p. 57.

munities, on the other hand, one pair of godparents may serve for all of one's children, or compadres chosen from outside one's own family may be rigidly preferred. The present writers are convinced that the rare usages of compadrazgo in inheritance indicate the lack of utility of this mechanism in dynamically affecting prevailing patterns of ownership. It is a mechanism that can be used to strengthen existing patterns, but not to change them. In the two cases in which compadrazgo plays any role in determining land inheritance, land is held by the village community, and all that is inherited is temporary right of use.[67] Marital impediment under Canon Law, a factor of continuing importance in much of the New World,[68] and the selection of compadres within the kin group or outside it, are also factors bound together functionally and historically. This problem lies beyond the scope of the present article.

Compadrazgo, once accepted by a social grouping, can be moulded into the community way of life by many means. It is a two-way social system which sets up reciprocal relations of variable complexity and solemnity. By imposing automatically, and with a varying degree of sanctity, statuses and obligations of a fixed nature, on the people who participate, it makes the immediate social environment more stable, the participants more interdependent and more secure. In fact, it might be said that the baptismal rite (or corresponding event) may be the original basis for the mechanism, but no longer its sole motivating force. Some brief examples will demonstrate the institution's flexibility.

In Chimaltenango,[69] two compadres

> will lend each other maize or money ("as much as six dollars"). . . . Two *comadres* should visit each other often and they may borrow small things readily from one another. When one is sick, or when one has just had another child, her *comadre* should come bringing tortillas for the family, and she should work in her *comadre's* house "like a sister."

In Peguche,[70] "white compadres are an asset for anyone who has business in Otovalo or Quito."

In Tzintzuntzan,[71]

> On the economic level, the *compadrazgo* system forms a kind of social insurance. Few are the families which can meet all emergencies without outside help. Often this means manual help at the time of a fiesta, or the responsibility of a *carguero*. Sometimes it means lending money, which near blood relatives do not like to do, because of the tendency never to repay a debt. But *compadres* feel obliged to lend, and no one would have respect for a man who refused to repay a *compadre*.

In San Pedro de Laguna,[72]

> The practical purpose motivating the selection of Ladinas as *comadres* is the belief that they can cure infant illnesses and have access to the necessary medi-

[67] Wisdom, 1940; Villa R., 1945.
[68] Herskovits, 1937, p. 98.
[69] Wagley, 1949, p. 19.
[70] Parsons, 1945, p. 45.
[71] Foster, *op. cit.*, p. 264.
[72] Paul, *op. cit.*, p. 92.

cines. The Indians store no medicine. But the Ladinas — by virtue of their cultural tradition and their greater income — customarily have on hand a number of drugstore preparations. The godparent bond imposes on the Ladina the responsibility of coming to the medical aid of her Indian godchild. The first year or two is correctly considered to be the most critical period of the infant's life. Hence the natives sacrifice long-run considerations in favor of providing a measure of medical protection during the infancy of the child . . .

Evidence from studies of two communities in Puerto Rico suggests that the compadre relation may be invoked to forestall sexual aggressions.[73] Cases are mentioned where a man concerned about the attentions of a family friend to his wife, sought to avoid trouble by making his friend his compadre. Thus a new and more sacred relationship was established.

Among the Huichol,[74] the compadre relationship

unquestionably strengthens Huichol social organization outside the family, which is not strong. Though *compadres* are not under economic bonds to each other, the injunction to be kind and friendly prevents drunken fights and brawls, which are the greatest source of weakness in Huichol society.

One form of compadrazgo is

specifically organized to avoid aggression between two *compadres: "el compadrazgo de voluntad."* People say that where there are two bullies in the same *barrio,* they will conclude a "non-aggression pact" and make themselves *compadres de voluntad,* which means that they can no longer fight each other.[75]

The persistence of compadrazgo in very secularized contexts, and its existence in such cases even without the sponsorship of a person, object, or event, is evidence of its frequently high social and secular plasticity.

The formal basis for selecting godparents for one's children — religious guidance, and if necessary, the adoption of orphaned children — is sometimes carried out. Gamio mentions this traditional usage in the Valley of Teotihuacan,[76] Redfield and Villa R. for Chan Kom,[77] Villa R. for Tusik,[78] Rojas Gonzales for the Mixe and Zoque,[79] and Wisdom for the Chorti.[80] Among the Chorti,

the godfather often acts in every way as the actual father in the event of the latter's death. He gives his ward advice, gets him out of difficulties, sometimes trains him in a man's work, and may act as his parent when he marries. The same is done by the godmother for her female godchild. If both parents die, and the godchild is young, the godparent may receive the portion of the property which the child inherited, and put it to his own use, in return for which he must bring up the child as one of his own family. As soon as the young man or

[73] Wolf, 1950, ms.; Manners, 1950, ms.

[74] Zingg, *op. cit.*, p. 57.

[75] Wolf, *op. cit.*

[76] Gamio, 1922, vol. 2, p. 243.

[77] Redfield and Villa R., *op. cit.*, p. 250.

[78] Villa R., *op. cit.*, p. 90.

[79] Rojas Gonzales, *op. cit.*, pp. 204–205.

[80] Wisdom, *op. cit.*, pp. 293–294.

woman becomes eighteen years of age, his inheritance is made up to him by his godfather. Where there is more than one minor child, each godfather receives his ward's share out of the total property, each child going to live in the home of its own godfather, leaving the adult children at home.

This usage is of particular interest because the compadre mechanism can be seen here as a link in the process of inheritance. Yet final property rights in this society are vested in the village, and not in the individual. A single case of the same kind of usage is mentioned by Villa R. for the Maya Indian community of Tusik.[81] Yet compadrazgo cannot override the emphasis on group land tenure in either of these societies. The mechanism is flexible and adaptable specifically because it usually carries with it no legal obligations — particularly regarding inheritance. Paul makes this point clearly when he writes that,

Unlike the involuntary ties of kinship those of ritual sponsorship are formed on the basis of choice. This enables godparenthood to serve as the social link connecting divergent income groups, disparate social strata, and separated localities. Affinity too may cut across class and locality through the practices of hypergamy and intermarriage. But the frequency with which such irregular forms of marriage occur throughout the world is sharply limited by strong social pressures operating to keep the unions within the class or community. This is understandable in view of the fact that marriage is the means by which the in-group perpetuates itself. Because no such considerations of social recruitment impede the formation of godparent bonds between persons of different social strata, godparenthood more readily serves as a mechanism for intergroup integration.[82]

It may be fruitful to examine cases of compadrazgo as examples of mechanisms crosscutting socio-cultural or class affiliations, or as taking place within the socio-cultural confines of a single class. The authors believe such patternings will prove to be determined, not haphazard in character, nor determined solely along continuums of homogeneity-to-heterogeneity, or greater-to-lesser isolation. Rather they will depend on the amount of socio-cultural and economic mobility, *real and apparent*, available to an individual in a given situation. There is of course no clear-cut device for the measurement of such real or apparent mobility. Yet the utility of compadrazgo might profitably be examined in this light. The aim would be to assess whether the individual is seeking to strengthen his position in a homogeneous socio-cultural community with high stability and low mobility, or to strengthen certain crosscutting ties by alignment with persons of a higher socio-cultural stratum, via reciprocal-exploitative relationships manipulated through compadrazgo. Some examples may illuminate the problem.

The Maya Indian people of Tusik,[83] a community in east central Quintana Roo, Yucatan, are homogeneous in a tribal sense, rather than having a mono-class structure. Says Villa:

[81] Villa R., *op. cit.* p. 90.
[82] Paul, *op. cit.*, pp. 72–73.
[83] Villa R., *op. cit.*

There are no classes here in the sense that different groups of people have different relations to the production and distribution of economic goods; in the sense that some people own land on which other people work, or that some people are engaged in producing goods while others are engaged in distributing them or in servicing the rest of the population. As we have already pointed out, everyone in the subtribe has the same relation to the land as everyone else; the land is commonly held by the subtribe, and a man's rights to a piece of land rests only on the right that he has put agricultural labor into the land and is entitled to the products of his labor. Every man makes *milpa* — even the sacred professionals earn their living as farmers — and since the secular division of labor is practically nonexistent, there are no merchants or artisans.

The economic life of the group centers about maize, and the people consume all that they produce. Labor for other men is rare, and when done, payment in kind prevails. The only cash commodity is chicle. Says Villa:

Apparently all the people of the subtribe enjoy the same economic circumstances. Nothing one observes in their ordinary, daily behavior suggests the existence of differences in accumulated wealth. . . . The acquisition of wealth is related directly to the personal ambition of the individual, for there are no differences in opportunity and no important differences in privilege. The principal source of wealth is the extraction of chicle, which is within the reach of all. . . . This equality of opportuntiy is a recent matter, for some years ago when the chiefs had greater authority, the lands of the bush were distributed by them and the best portion preserved for their own use. In some cases men were thus able to enrich themselves through special advantage.

Regarding compadrazgo, the grandparents of the child to be born, preferably the paternal ones, are chosen. If they are not alive, chiefs or *maestros cantores,* as persons of prestige and good character, are selected. It is noteworthy that no mention is made of any choice of travelling merchants as compadres, although

the travelling merchants are the natives' main source of contact with the outer world. It is they who bring into the region . . . the most important news from the city. . . . The arrival of the merchant is the occasion for the people to gather together and excitedly discuss the events he relates to them, and in this atmosphere the merchant's own friendly ties with the natives are strengthened.

Chicle is sold, and commodities bought through these travellers, but apparently ritual kinship is not used to bind them with the community.

In marked contrast to the isolated, subsistence crop, tribal culture of Tusik, we may examine two communities which exhibit cultural homogeneity under completely different conditions. They are fully integrated economically, and to a great degree welded culturally into national cultures. The first of these is Poyal.[84]

Barrio Poyal is a rural community on the south coast of Puerto Rico,

[84] Mintz, 1950, ms.

in an area of large-scale sugar cane production, with corporate ownership of land and mills. The lands are devoted exclusively to the production of the single cash crop. While the barrio working population forms what is practically a mono-class isolate, compadres could be selected among the foremen, administrators, public officials, store owners, and so forth. Instead, there is an overwhelming tendency to pick neighbors and fellow workers as compadres. A man who seeks a wealthy compadre in Poyal is held in some contempt by his fellows; a wealthy compadre would not visit him nor invite him to his house. People remember when the old hacienda owners were chosen as godparents to the workers' children, but this practice is totally outmoded now. A local land-owning group no longer exists in Poyal.

Compadre relationships generally are treated reverentially; compadres are addressed with the polite *Usted*, even if they are family members, and the compadre relationship is utilized daily in getting help, borrowing money, dividing up available work opportunities, and so forth. However, as more and more Poyal workers migrate to the United States, the utility of many compadre ties is weakened.

Another example of the same category is Pascua,[85] a community of essentially landless, wage-earning Yaqui Indian immigrants who, with their descendants, form a village on the outskirts of Tucson, Arizona. The economic basis of Pascua life bears certain striking resemblances to Barrio Poyal: the almost total lack of subsistence activities, the emphasis on seasonal variation, the emphasis on wage-earning as opposed to payment in kind, and so on. Says Spicer:

> Existence is wholly dependent on the establishment of relationships with individuals outside the village. If for any reason the economic relations of a Pascuan with outside persons are broken off for an extended period, it becomes necessary to depend upon other Pascuans who have maintained such relations.

While the economic linkages are exclusively with external sources of income and employment, the compadre structure is described

> as an all-pervasive network of relationships which takes into its web every person in the village. Certain parts of the network, here and there about the village, are composed of strong and well-knit fibers. Here the relationships between *compadres* are functioning constantly and effectively. Elsewhere there are weaker threads representing relationships which have never been strengthened by daily recognition of reciprocal obligations. These threads nevertheless exist and may from time to time be the channels of temporarily re-established *compadre* relationships.

Spicer notes that:

> sometimes in Pascua sponsors are sought outside the village in Libre or Marana, or even among the Mexican population of Tucson.

[85] Spicer, 1940.

But everything suggests that the ritual kinship system here functions predominantly within the wage-earning, landless mono-class grouping of the Yaqui themselves. Spicer's description of compadrazgo is probably the most complete in the literature today, and the Pascua system appears to be primarily between contemporaries in emphasis, and as in Barrio Poyal horizontal in character.

These three cases, Tusik, Barrio Poyal, and Pascua, illustrate the selective character of compadrazgo and some of its functionings, within small "homogeneous" groupings. The mechanism plainly has considerable importance and utility and is treated reverentially in all three places. Yet while Tusik is isolated and lacks a class character, Barrio Poyal and Pascua are both involved in wage-earning, cash crop, world market productive arrangements where the homogeneity is one of class membership only, and isolation is not characteristic.

In Tusik, compadrazgo is correlated with great internal stability, low economic mobility, ownership of land by the village, and the lack of a cash economy and class stratification. In Barrio Poyal and Pascua compadrazgo correlates with homogeneous class membership, landlessness, wage-earning, and an apparent growing identity of class interest.

An interesting contrast is provided by Gillin's study of Moche. This is a Peruvian coastal community which, according to the Foreword,

> is in the last stages of losing its identity as an Indian group and of being absorbed into Peruvian national life. . . . Surrounded by large, modern haciendas, Moche is "Indian" only in that its population is largely Indian in a racial sense, that it has retained much of its own lands, that it exists in a certain social isolation from surrounding peoples, retaining a community life organized on a modified kinship basis, mainly of Spanish derivation. . . . Its lands, however, are now owned individually, and they are being alienated through sale and litigation. It is on a cash rather than subsistence basis economically. . . . Many Mocheros even work outside the community for wages, and some are in professions. . . . Formal aspects of native social organization have disappeared, and contacts with the outside world are increasing.[86]

In Moche, the compadre system would expectably be subject to the same stresses as those suffered by any other local social institution. Yet

> the whole idea of this type of relationship has been carried to extremes in Moche. There are more types of *padrinazgo* [i.e. godfatherhood] in this community than in any other concerning which I have seen reports. This fact may be linked with the absence of spontaneous community organization and solidarity.

Gillin finds evidence for fourteen different kinds of compadre relations. As to the choice of compadres, Gillin says:

> Godparents may be blood relatives, but usually the attempt is made to secure persons who are not relatives of either of the parents. Not only Mocheros, but

[86] Gillin, *op. cit.*; Foreword by Julian H. Steward.

in these days, trusted *forasteros* [i.e. outsiders] are chosen. From the point of view of the parents it is desirable to choose godparents who are financially responsible, if not rich, and also persons who have "influence" and prestigeful social connections. The real function of godparents is to broaden, and, if possible, increase the social and economic resources of the child and his parents and by the same token to lower the anxieties of the parents on this score.

In a later section, however, Gillin states that he does not feel that socially defined classes as such exist in Moche.[87]

It is extremely noteworthy that the mechanism of compadrazgo has maintained itself here in the face of what appears to be progressively accelerating social change. We wonder whether the elaborations of the mechanism's forms may be part of the community's unconscious effort to answer new problems. It must increasingly face the insecurity of growing incorporation into the national structure and increasing local wage-based, cash crop competition. This may call forth an increased emphasis on techniques for maintaining and strengthening face-to-face relationships. Eggan's study of Cheyenne kinship terminology[88] suggests that the kinship structure is sensitive to rapid social change if the changing terminology reflects genuine structural modifications. Ritual kinship structures may react to the weakening of certain traditional obligations by spreading out to include new categories of contemporaries, and therefore potential competitors.

Other examples suggest that vertical phrasings of the compadre system may take place in situations where change has been slowed at some point, and relationships between two defined socio-cultural strata, or classes, are solidified. San Jose is a highland coffee and minor crop-producing community of Puerto Rico.[89] The frequency distribution of land shows a considerable scatter, with 55 per cent of the landowners holding 10 per cent of the land at one extreme, and 5 per cent holding 45 per cent of the land at the other. Thus, while Tusik people hold their land communally, Barrio Poyal and Pascua people are landless, and Moche people are largely small landowners with no farm over four acres, San Jose people are in large part landowners with great variability in the size of holdings. While a large part of the agricultural population is landless, agricultural laborers in San Jose may be paid partly in kind, and frequently will be given in addition a small plot of land for subsistence farming. Production for wages is largely of the main cash crop, coffee.

In the rural zones of this community, a prevailing number of the compadre relations tie agricultural workers to their landholding employers, or small land-holders to larger ones. Thus a large landowner may become compadre to twenty smaller landowners living around his farm. In isolated areas, where the "community" is defined entirely in familial terms, most compadre relationships take place within the family. Yet it must

[87] Gillin, *op. cit.*, pp. 107, 113.
[88] Eggan, 1937.
[89] Wolf, *op. cit.*

be recognized that members of the same family, and brothers of the same filial generation, may be variously landowners, sharecroppers (*medianeros*), and laborers.

Compadrazgo in San Jose may help in the stabilization of productive relations between large and small landholders, or between landholders and their sharecropping employees and laborers. Interesting in this connection is the fact that the economic basis in San Jose is much less exclusively cash than in Tusik, Barrio Poyal, or Pascua. The land tenure pattern in San Jose does not appear to be changing rapidly. Compadrazgo relations are phrased vertically, so as to crosscut class stratification, quite probably serving in this connection to solidify the relationships of people to the land. There is evidence of landowners getting free labor out of their laborer brothers who have been made compadres. Contrariwise, laborers bound by compadrazgo to their employers are accustomed to rely on this bond to secure them certain small privileges, such as the use of equipment, counsel and help, small loans, and so on.

The authors know of no fully documented study of compadrazgo in the context of an "old-style" plantation or hacienda. Siegel's material on the Guatemalan plantation community of San Juan Acatan indicates that the Indians there often invite Ladinos with whom they come in contact to sponsor the baptisms of their children. But Siegel adds that the relationship in this community is "virtually meaningless." [90] The authors of the present article would in general predict that plantation laborers, either bound or very dependent on the plantation, with daily face-to-face contacts with the owner or *hacendado* would seek to establish a reciprocal coparental relationship with the owner. Historical material from old informants in Barrio Poyal offer evidence of this tradition, now markedly altered in the pure wage, absentee ownership context.

The mechanism may be contrasted, then, in several distinct contexts. In the first context are Tusik, Barrio Poyal, and Pascua. These communities are alike in their "homogeneity," and the horizontal structuring of the compadre system; yet they are markedly different in other respects. Tusik is tribal and essentially isolated from the world market, while Barrio Poyal and Pascua are incorporated into capitalistic world economies, and are fully formed working class strata.

In the second context is San Jose, with its varied land ownership pattern, its mixed (cash and subsistence) crop production and its several classes. Through the vertical phrasing of its compadre system, San Jose demonstrates a relatively stable reciprocity, economic and social, between the landed, large and small, and the sharecroppers and laborers.

In the third context is Moche. Land is held predominantly in small plots; the crops, as in San Jose, are both cash and subsistence, and while Gillin doubts the existence of classes, certainly the compadre system is

[90] Siegel, quoted in Paul, *op. cit.*, p. 72.

described as a vertical structuring one. Here, too, the elaboration of face-to-face ceremonialism may help to slow the accelerated trend toward land concentration, a cash economy, and incorporation into the world market.

III. CONCLUSION

In the first section of this article, the writers traced the relationship between land tenure and the functioning of ritual kin ties under conditions of European feudalism. During this period, ritual kin ties gradually changed from bonds of blood brotherhood to those of compadre relationships. This accompanied a change from neighbor inheritance to the family inheritance of tenure. As these changes in the pattern of land tenure took place, the ritual ties were shifted correspondingly from a horizontal cementing of relationships to a vertical phrasing of artificial kinship at the height of feudalism.

With the breakdown of feudal land tenures and the increased assertion of peasant rights, such ritual ties were again rephrased horizontally to unite the peasant neighborhoods in their struggle against feudal dues.

Under conditions of advanced industrial development, mechanisms of social control based on biological or ritual kin affiliations tend to give way before more impersonal modes of organization. Compadrazgo survives most actively in present-day Europe within the areas of lesser industrial development. From one such area, Spain, compadrazgo was carried to the New World, and developed here in a new historical and functional context.

In the second section of this article, five modern communities with Latin American culture were analyzed to show the functional correlates of the compadre mechanism. In cases where the community is a self-contained class, or tribally homogeneous, compadrazgo is prevailingly horizontal (intra-class) in character. In cases where the community contains several interacting classes, compadrazgo will structure such relationships vertically (inter-class). Last, in a situation of rapid social change compadre mechanisms may multiply to meet the accelerated rate of change.

REFERENCES CITED

Bamberger, M. L.

1923 *Aus meiner Minhagimsammelmappe* (Jahrbuch für Jüdische Volkskunde, vol. 1, pp. 320–332).

Bancroft, H. H.

1883 *History of Mexico* (San Francisco).

Beals, R. L.

1946 *Cherán: A Sierra Tarascan Village* (Institute of Social Anthropology, Publication no. 2, Washington, D.C.: Smithsonian Institution).

Bennett, H. S.
1938 *Life on the English Manor* (New York).
Boesch, H.
1900 *Kinderleben in der Deutschen Vergangenheit* (Monographien zur Deutschen Kulturgeschichte, vol. 5, Leipzig).
Boniface
1940 *The Letters of Saint Boniface* (Engl. transl., New York).
Committee on Latin American Anthropology, National Research Council
1949 *Research Needs in the Field of Modern Latin American Culture* (American Anthropologist, vol. 51, pp. 149–154).
Corblet, J.
1882 *Histoire Dogmatique, Liturgique et Archéologique du Sacrement de Baptême* (vol. 1, Geneva).
Coulton, C. G.
1926 *The Medieval Village* (Cambridge).
1936 *Five Centuries of Religion* (vol. 3, Cambridge).
Donadin y Puignan, D. D.
no date *Diccionario de la lengua Castellana.* (vol. 1, Barcelona).
Dopsch, A.
1918-20 *Wirtschaftliche und Soziale Grundlagen der Europäischen Kulturentwicklung* (2 vols., Vienna).
Drews, P.
1907 "Taufe, Liturg, Vollzug" (in *Realenzyklopädie für Protestantische Theologie und Kirche,* vol. 19, Leipzig).
Durham, M. E.
1928 *Some Tribal Origins, Laws, and Customs of the Balkans* (London).
Eggan, F.
1937 "The Cheyenne and Arapaho Kinship System" (in *Social Anthropology of North American Tribes,* F. Eggan, ed., Chicago).
Erich, O.
1936 *Wörterbuch der Deutschen Volkskunde* (Leipzig).
Espinosa, J. M.
1942 *Crusaders of the Rio Grande* (Chicago).
Flick, A.
1936 *The Decline of the Medieval Church* (vol. 1, New York).
Foster, G. N.
1948 *Empire's Children: The People of Tzintzuntzan* (Institute of Social Anthropology, Publication no. 6, Washington, D.C.: Smithsonian Institution).
Gamio, M.
1922 *La Población del Valle de Teotihuacán* (3 vols., Mexico).
Ganshof, F. L.
1941 "Medieval Agrarian Society in its Prime: France, the Low Countries, and Western Germany" (in *Cambridge Economic History of Europe from the Decline of the Roman Empire,* vol. 1, Cambridge).
Gillin, J.
1945 *Moche: A Peruvian Coastal Community.* (Institute of Social Anthropology, Publication no. 3, Washington, D.C.: Smithsonian Institution).

Handjieff, W.
1931 *Zur Soziologie des Bulgarischen Dorfes* (thesis, Leipzig).
Henninger, E.
1891 *Sitten und Gebräuche bei der Taufe und Namengebung in der Altfranzösischen Dichtung* (thesis, Halle a. S.).
Herskovits, M. J.
1937 *Life in a Haitian Valley* (New York).
Howard, G. H.
1904 *A History of Matrimonial Institutions* (vol. 1, Chicago).
Kearney, R. J.
1925 *Sponsorship at Baptism According to the Code of Canon Law* (thesis, Catholic University of America).
Kummer, Bernhard
1931 "Gevatter" (in *Handwörterbuch des Deutschen Aberglaubens*, vol. 3, Berlin).
Landa, Diego de
1941 *Landa's Relación de las Cosas de Yucatan* (English transl., A. M. Tozzer, ed.: Papers, Peabody Museum of American Archaeology and Ethnology, Harvard University, vol. 18).
Laurin, F.
1866 *Die Geistliche Verwandtschaft in ihrer geschichtlichen Entwicklung* (Archiv für Katholisches Kirchenrecht, vol. 15, Mainz).
Lunt, W. E.
1934 *Papal Revenues in the Middle Ages* (vol. 2, New York).
Luther, M.
1520 "Von der babylonischen Gefangenschaft de Kirche: von de Ehe" (in *Reformatorische Schriften, Luthers' Werke*, vol. 2, 1924, Leipzig).
1539 "Tischreden: Anton Lauterbach's Tagebuch aufs Jahr 1539" (in *D. Martin Luthers' Werke*, Kritische Gesamtausgabe, vol. 4, 1916, Weimar).
1900 *Sprichwörtersammlung* (Thiele, ed., Weimar).
Maitland, F. W., and (Sir) F. Pollock
1923 *History of English Law* (vol. 2, Cambridge).
Manners, R. A.
1950 *A Tobacco and Minor Crop Community in Puerto Rico* (manucript).
Mintz, S. W.
1950 *A Sugar-Cane Community in Puerto Rico* (manuscript).
Münch, E.
1830 *Vollständige Sammlung aller älteren und neueren Konkordate* (vol. 1, Leipzig).
Nabholz, H.
1941 "Medieval Agrarian Society in Transition" (in *Cambridge Economic History of Europe from the Decline of the Roman Empire*, vol. 1, Cambridge).
Parsons, E. C.
1936 *Mitla: Town of the Souls* (Chicago).
1945 *Peguche: A Study of Andean Indians* (Chicago).

Paul, B. D.
1942 *Ritual Kinship: With Special Reference to Godparenthood in Middle America* (Ph.D. thesis, University of Chicago).
Ploss, H.
1911 *Das Kind in Brauch und Sitte der Völker* (3rd ed., vol. 1, Leipzig).
Redfield, R.
1930 *Tepoztlan: A Mexican Village* (Chicago).
——— and Alfonso Villa R.
1934 *Chan Kom: A Maya Village* (Publication no. 448, Washington, D.C.: Carnegie Institution of Washington).
Rojas Gonzales, F.
1943 *La Institucion del Compadrazgo entre los Indigenas de México* (Revista Méxicana de Sociologia, vol. 5, no. 1).
Sahagun, B. de
1932 *A History of Ancient Mexico* (Engl. transl., Nashville).
Sanders, I.
1949 *Balkan Village* (Lexington).
Siemsen, R.
1942 *Germanengut im Zunftbrauch* (Berlin-Dahlem).
Spicer, E.
1940 *Pascua: A Yaqui Village in Arizona* (Chicago).
Tomasic, D.
1948 *Personality and Culture in Eastern European Politics* (New York).
Tuschen, A.
1936 *Die Taufe in der Altfranzösischen Literatur* (thesis, Bonn).
Tylor, E. B.
1861 *Anahuac* (London).
Villa R., A.
1945 *The Maya of East Central Quintana Roo* (Publication no. 559, Washington, D.C.: Carnegie Institution of Washington).
Wagley, Ch.
1949 *The Social and Religious Life of a Guatemalan Village* (American Anthropological Association, Memoir no. 71).
Warrack, A.
1911 *A Scots Dialect Dictionary* (London).
Weekly, E.
1921 *An Etymological Dictionary of Modern English* (London).
Wisdom, Ch.
1940 *A Chorti Village in Guatemala* (Chicago).
Wolf, E. R.
1950 *A Coffee Growing Community in Puerto Rico* (manuscript).
Zingg, R.
1938 *Primitive Artists: The Huichols* (University of Denver Contributions to Ethnology, Denver).

SOCIAL STRUCTURE AND POWER IN A PHILIPPINE MUNICIPALITY

Mary R. Hollnsteiner

[*Editors' Note:* Important differences distinguish Hulo, Bulacan from many other peasant communities. Its population is about 15,000 — much larger than that of most peasant communities — and, lying only fifteen miles from Manila, it has been subject to strong urban influences in recent years. Moreover, fishing rather than agriculture is its basic economic activity. Yet Mrs. Hollnsteiner feels that "the real society I have chosen is basically peasant," and we agree with her. Hulo is divided into ten *barrios*, the basic village units in the Philippines. Eight of these stretch in a contiguous line along a road, and two are somewhat separated from this populated strip. Most of these nuclei fall within the 1,000–2,000 population range, which makes them directly comparable to peasant communities elsewhere in the Philippines, and in other parts of the world.]

No discussion of power in Hulo is possible without taking into account the community's social structure. The statuses and the accompanying roles fashion the meaningful relationships which characterize Hulo society. Where power is concerned a network of supporters is crucial to the person interested in gaining and maintaining power. These followers are provided through the alliance system, a network of reciprocal relationships whose members extend to one another and expect mutual assistance and loyalty.

One is expected to go all out for an ally. He may be a kinsman, a compadre, a neighbor, or a friend. These relationships in themselves do not guarantee membership in one's alliance. It is when a kinsman, compadre, neighbor, or friend is emotionally close, and therefore tagged as an ally, that he can really be counted on. His well-being becomes the well-being of the group, and the group's collective welfare becomes his welfare. Allies can shift, however, since one who does not prove his loyalty in time of need is cast aside, and since new close relationships are constantly being formed as circumstances activate potential alliance ties. Persons outside one's alliance group are not really one's concern since presumably they belong to another alliance group and find their security through the members of that group.[1]

From *The Dynamics of Power in a Philippine Municipality* by Mary R. Hollinsteiner. Reprinted by permission of the author and the Community Development Research Council (University of the Philippines).

[1] For the concept of the alliance system in lowland Philippine society I am grateful to Frank Lynch, S.J. See his *Social Class in Bikol Town* (Chicago: University of Chicago, 1959), pp. 49–55. Regarding closeness, Lynch adds, "To be close is to be on intimate terms, friendly, affectionate, attentive, sympathetic, and actively interested in each other. It is the quality of a good friend. Its opposite is to be distant, which suggests a coolness of feeling between the two, or unfriendliness, uneasiness, disinterest, and perhaps even complete estrangement, whether the persons be blood relatives or not." (p. 53).

I will here discuss four basic social relationships which are a result of or culminate in the structuring of an alliance network: kinship, *compadrazgo* or ritual kinship, reciprocity, and associational ties. The significance of the role expectations connected with these relationships will be explored in the light of their bearing on the functioning of the power system.

FOUR BASIC STRUCTURAL RELATIONSHIPS

There are three types of kinship operative in Hulo: consanguinity, affinity, and ritual kinship or compadrazgo. Consanguinity refers to blood kinship, which is generated by the sharing of a common ancestor. It links an individual to the family into which he is born and reared. In the Philippines, descent is reckoned bilaterally, which means that one is equally related to both his father's and mother's consanguine kin with no preference structurally for either side. A distinction is made, however, in the degree of closeness of the blood relationship, one's nuclear family assuming far more importance than the extended kin. Since the Filipino inherits a network of kin from each of his parents, he has a vast number of relatives.

This number is further augmented by the acquisition of affinal kin, or in-laws, upon his marriage. His spouse's relatives become his as well. While his relation to the latter is affinal, his children's relation to them will of course be consanguineal.

The third type of kinship grouping found among the Christian Filipinos is ritual kinship, or compadrazgo. Originally introduced into the Philippines as part of the Roman Catholic heritage, the compadre system was intended by Church authorities to ensure the child's education in the faith. The godparents acquired at baptism and confirmation were to be additional spiritual guardians in case the parents were unable to discharge their duty.[2] The Hulo child refers to his godparents as *ninong* and *ninang;* they in turn refer to him as their *inaanak* and to his parents as *kumpare* and *kumare*, adaptations of the Spanish *compadre* and *comadre*.

Compadrazgo has also been extended to marriage. The bride and groom refer to the witnesses as ninong and ninang and become the latters' *inaanak sa kasal* (godchildren through marriage sponsorship). Official Catholic practice does not provide any spiritual relationship between the bridal pair and the witnesses, or obligations for the latter other than

[2] Although only two official sponsors are necessary, the child often acquires several more godparents through the unofficial *katuwang* practice. While the official godparents carry the child during the ceremony, the *katuwang* or "co-sponsors" stand next to the child and merely touch it. Their relationship to the child is the same as that of the official sponsors in actual practice. They also become the compadres of the child's parents. For a more comprehensive discussion of compadrazgo, see Robert B. Fox and Frank Lynch, S.J., "Ritual Co-parenthood," *Area Handbook on the Philippines*, vol. 2 (Chicago: University of Chicago for the Human Relations Area Files, 1956), pp. 424–30.

that of testifying to the fact of marriage if asked to do so by competent authority.[3] Yet, in accordance with general Philippine practice, Hulo weddings make the witness-couple relationship that of godparent-godchildren. The couple's parents and the witnesses become compadres. As in baptism and confirmation, the godparents for a marriage usually belong to the peer group of the couple's parents, or are of higher status. Thus, although official practice emphasizes the vertical relationship between sponsors and sponsored, the socially important bonds are in reality between the co-parents, or compadres.

While consanguine, affinal, and ritual kinship provide important bonds on which close and enduring relationships can be established, the system of reciprocal obligations forges strong links, too.[4] As an operating principle in Philippine society, reciprocity helps define one's position in relation to others for it comes into play when a transfer of goods or services takes place between individuals. Except where the exchange is contractual or quasi-contractual in nature, the recipient is expected to develop *utang na loob* (literally, a debt inside oneself, or sense of gratitude) to the donor and repay his favor sometime in the future in a form acceptable to the donor. Thus, a spiral of reciprocal favors is built up, for when the favor done is a service which cannot be repaid in kind, or which cannot be measured quantitatively, one cannot really tell when one's debt has been discharged. Indeed, some services can never be repaid — the saving of a life, for example.

The system of reciprocal obligations is further complicated by the relative statuses of the dyad involved in the exchange. In the case of status equals, one tries to repay with interest, which means that the creditor position is held now by one, now by the other. Where a clearly superordinate-subordinate relationship of some permanence occurs, as in the case of the landlord and tenant, the subordinate party is not even expected to repay with interest. In fact, partial payments suffice because they indicate recognition of the indebtedness, and, therefore, the appropriate sense of gratitude on the utang na loob debtor's side.

An alliance system may be held together by the framework of kinship, compadrazgo, and reciprocal obligations, but self-interest also provides a motivation. Where people do not feel bound by the first three pressures to align with a certain segment, then they are free to choose that course of action which will be most advantageous for them. Alignment with a segment from which they can expect benefits in the not too distant future is thus a practical move. This type of pragmatism is especially apparent in the political sphere.

One might ask where simple friendship fits into the scheme outlined above since it has not been mentioned apart from the other relation-

[3] *Ibid.*, p. 425.

[4] For a more comprehensive discussion of reciprocity, see Mary R. Hollnsteiner, *Reciprocity in the Lowland Philippines* (Quezon City: Ateneo de Manila, Institute of Philippine Culture Papers No. 1, 1961). This article also appears in *Philippine Studies*, vol. 9, no. 3, (July 1961), pp. 387–413.

ships. Its exclusion does not mean non-existence; on the contrary, friendship and the feeling of closeness and confidence implied is one of the basic features of the alliance system. It is interwoven into the other relationships; indeed, it is the integrating feature which holds the system together. For example, in contrast to affectively distant kin, the favorite relative is actually incorporated into one's segment or alliance group, as evidenced by a high frequency of interaction not evident in relation to other, less favored consanguine kin, who are only potential members of one's segment. That these binding relationships overlap is exemplified in the friend who may be a prospective in-law, should one's sister look upon him favorably as a marriage partner. Failing an affinal relationship, a friend can always be made *like* a close relative by incorporation into one's compadre network. Furthermore, a friend would not be worthy of the term if he did not foster camaraderie in innumerable ways, all of which require reciprocal demonstrations of loyalty and support. Though his motives may in some instances appear primarily exploitative, the fact of his being counted an ally remains as long as he carries out the role of the good friend.

Friendship is thus generally subsumed into the other four relationships. The latter are by no means mutually exclusive. There are cases, for example, where consanguine kin are chosen as baptismal sponsors, or where one selects a compadre on the basis of self-interest. The measure of a compadre's merits is often how well he has responded to his utang na loob obligations. Thus, one principle of alliance formation may foster another. A more detailed discussion of each of these structural relationships is here appropriate if we are to analyze how they impinge on the individual.

The Filipino is taught from childhood that his primary loyalties belong to his nuclear family and, by extension, to his other kinfolk. Any celebration in his family requiring a feast always finds relatives there, from oldest to youngest. The child is rarely excluded from any family parties, regardless of the late hour to which they may last. From babyhood he finds security in the warmth of family ties and in the knowledge that he has a corps of persons whose particular duty it is to aid him when he needs it, and whom he in turn should help when the occasion demands.

He is taught to revere his elders and care for his aged relatives when they can no longer take care of themselves; a sister who might be only a year or two older than himself is given the honorific term, *ate*, and the older brother, *kuya*, in Tagalog. The individual must also look toward the other end of the scale and share the responsibility for taking care of his younger siblings. All these duties are so deeply inculcated that should he for some reason not conform to his expected role in relation to kinsmen who have been close to him, he feels guilty and suffers the social disapproval of his family. If the transgression is extremely serious, he may even find himself estranged from them.

However, a note of caution must be injected into any discussion of the Filipino family. So much has been said and written about the closeness of family ties, that is, the obligation a Filipino feels to support not only his nuclear family but also his extended kin (in contrast to the system in most Western societies) that the tendency until recently has been to presume that this responsibility toward relatives *always* overrides all other non-kin ties.

This is not so; relatives do *not* always take precedence. In a system of bilateral descent, the individual can trace a blood relationship to so many people that to care equally about all of them becomes impossible. He must draw a line somewhere and select consciously or unconsciously those among his relatives with whom he will associate closely. These become members of his alliance group. While other relatives have a potential claim on his support, he may actually favor a compadre or a non-relative in his segment over these more socially distant relatives.

Lynch [5] puts this idea in pithy form when he states, "Relatives are important but the importance is often relative." His Bikol data [6] support the argument that kinship is of secondary importance in a small endogamous community, where most people are related to one another. Personal considerations often supersede kin allegiance while the value system and the class system of the community support the economic system more than the kinship system. He concludes:

> Should the society in question be one like Canaman he may find the consequences of kinship considerably curtailed. Given a society with wealth in the hands of a few, and to be passed down to few; given a society largely in-married and dwelling in a small settlement; given also a bilateral generational kinship structure featuring widely extended bonds and the overlapping of personal kindreds, then competition among kinsmen for the favor of wealthy and powerful kin seems almost unavoidable. By the nature of the case, moreover, this competition will in most cases be on grounds other than genealogical claims. For putting aside skills, which are simple and widely shared, and education, which the public schools have largely equalized for him and his peers, the lower class person (and most Canaman townsmen *are* lower class) is left with the advantage he might get by physical proximity, affability, attentiveness, and services rendered. In a community where most men are kin, a man must live by the friends he makes.

With regard now to compadrazgo, Foster's statement [7] about that institution in Spanish-America might equally well apply to the Philippines. "The complexity of compadrazgo in the New World surpasses

[5] Frank Lynch, S.J., "A Philippine Village: Report From the Field," *Anthropology Tomorrow*, vol. 6, no. 2 (University of Chicago Department of Anthropology, 1958), p. 16.

[6] Frank Lynch, S.J., "Limitations of Kinship in a Small Community," Paper presented at the 35th Annual Meeting of the Central States Anthropological Society at Madison, Wisconsin, May 14–16, 1959, pp. 12–13.

[7] George M. Foster, "What Is Folk Culture?" *American Anthropologist*, vol. 55, no. 2, Part 1 (April–June 1953), p. 167.

that of Spain, and appears in very considerable measure to be the result of local elaboration to meet felt needs in the emergent social structure of Post-Conquest America."

The compadre system of the Philippines provides an institutionalized means of formalizing a friendship between status equals or of bringing closer together persons of high and low status. By ritually incorporating a non-relative into one's kin grouping, one is in effect dispensing with the need for extreme care in one's dealings with that individual, allowing a more relaxed attitude in his presence as one would have with a socially close relative. Furthermore, the compadre's brothers and sisters can also be called compadres; if they perform the roles expected of a compadre, then they too become members of one's alliance group. Fictive kinship is even extended to the children of the sets of compadres, who are *kinakapatid* (like siblings) to one another.

That selectivity enters in among consanguine kin is shown by the already mentioned fact that relatives are often asked to be baptismal sponsors. This seems to be true particularly among the upper class families of the town. In a study of compadrazgo in Bikol following up Lynch's findings, Arce established that marriage sponsors usually come from a class higher than that of the parents of the bridal pair, in contrast to baptismal sponsors, who may be of equal or superordinate status. In the case of marriage, the elite are therefore forced to seek suitable marriage compadres from outside the town.[8] Observations in Hulo tend to bear out Arce's conclusions.

Equal status compadrazgo usually involves asking a friend of long standing to sponsor one's child at baptism. Exploitation of the relationship does not lurk so prominently here as it does in cross-class compadrazgo. Special treatment is still expected from the other person but the potential reciprocal favors tend to be more or less of the same type. The feeling of honor and satisfaction on the part of the friend asked is perhaps greater than in the cross-class case since he knows that real friendship and a desire to cement further that mutual attraction has precipitated the request rather than any ulterior motives.

Many Manila born and bred people seem to be embarrassed at the obviously exploitative nature of cross-class compadrazgo and choose equal status compadres for baptism. One might speculate that since in Manila even the closest friends and relatives do not see one another so often as they might in the barrio, they feel a need to forge stronger links with those people whom they truly like. Even here, however, a significant exception would be the Manila politician, who puts compadrazgo to good use.

[8] Wilfredo F. Arce, "The Characteristics of Ritual Kinsmen in a Small Community" (Unpublished thesis for Master of Arts, Quezon City: Ateneo de Manila, 1961); and Frank Lynch, S.J., "A Philippine Village: Report from the Field," *Anthropology Tomorrow*, vol. 6, no. 2 (University of Chicago Department of Anthropology, 1958), p. 26.

Perhaps the more important aspect of compadrazgo is its class-bridging aspect. Its function here is to provide a means of ordering hierarchical relations (landlord-tenant, employer-employee, high-low status), a channel for upward mobility, and possibly a mechanism of out-migration from the rural to urban areas.[9]

That the system can be used to advantage is apparent when tenant asks landlord or employee asks employer to be a child's godparent. The employee hopes for more rapid promotion and other forms of special treatment in the office, while the tenant strengthens his claim to at least continued tenant status in that his landlord-compadre will not likely cast him off the land. The tenant may also expect special consideration in the repayment of his loans to the landlord.

At any rate proper observance of one's compadre duties is highly valued in Hulo. This usually entails granting, insofar as possible, any favors sought by a compadre. It is easy to see how valuable this system can be where the power structure is concerned. For it opens up important channels of communication between the elites and important persons outside the community, especially in Manila, between the high status elites and the lower status residents of the town, and within the classes comprising the town.

While the traditional political elite group of Hulo (Juan, Javier, de la Cruz, etc.) tend to restrict their marriage partners to those of at least equal status, they utilize compadrazgo to enhance relationships with their subordinates, so that they build up a network of ritual relationships which supplement the inadequacies of the consanguine and affinal systems. If a family belonging to this elite group seems particularly friendly with a lower status individual or family with whom they interact fairly frequently in a political party, community, or religious organization, the lower status family will almost inevitably ask this elite family to sponsor their next child in baptism, wedding, or confirmation rites (the last not being considered by the people as important as the first two.) Once asked to be a godparent, no Hulo resident, including the elites, can humiliate the asker by refusing; he must accept. The widespread belief that one courts bad luck by refusing to be a godparent puts additional pressure on the prospective sponsor.

There are community mechanisms which regulate this request, however, otherwise the traditional elite would find themselves constantly burdened with the expenses and responsibilities attendant to being a sponsor. Ideally a lower status family must be quite sure before putting the question that the person asked wants to be a compadre and will sincerely accept the asker into his alliance system. To attain this assurance, the asker (often an intermediary) sounds out the elite family beforehand

[9] Robert B. Fox and Frank Lynch, S.J., "Ritual Co-parenthood," *Area Handbook on the Philippines*, vol. 2 (Chicago: University of Chicago for the Human Relations Area Files, Inc., 1956), pp. 429–30.

in subtle, euphemistic language. He would not dream of asking the question point-blank, for this would bare the possibility of a humiliating evasive answer and worse, an obviously reluctant "yes" eventually. By expressing himself euphemistically, the asker can provide the asked with an escape in case of reluctance. The actual outcome is usually that the asked party takes the hints and proposes in a half-jesting manner that he really should be the godparent of the child. Or he shows interest in the child and makes a point of asking who its godparents will be. This gives the asker the necessary and awaited cue. If the asked party does not provide this cue in a reasonable length of time despite several opportunities, the matter can be dropped with neither side losing face (*hiya*). In any case, the matter is rarely discussed openly until the two are absolutely sure that they understand each other and agree tacitly to establish a compadre relationship.

In the majority of cases, despite misgivings about the expense involved, the elite accept such a request in the spirit in which it is made — as an honor. The non-politically minded traditional elite, however, are less interested in making close contacts with lower status individuals and thus do not interact in community-wide organizations as much as do the traditional, politically-minded elite and the new professional-entrepreneurial elite. The first group is not primarily interested in being known as power individuals on the local level, while the last two groups actively seek the satisfaction which only the possession of power in their town will bring them.

Since the compadre relationship institutionalizes close ties, both sets of compadres are happy with the arrangement. Although the reciprocal favors are of different types in the superordinate-subordinate case, the higher status family rendering material benefits and prestige and the lower status family giving loyalty and the prestige of yet another family added to the superordinate family's list of compadres, each party has gotten what he needs so badly from the other.

The advantage of having elite compadres is that they must fulfill their expected role by providing generously. This begins with the initial ceremony. In the case of a baptism, the parents can be sure that their child will have a fine quality baptismal dress, the most expensive first class baptism complete with the loud, prolonged ringing of the church bells, a private ceremony right in front of the altar, and a suitable gift. For weddings, the elite godparents can be counted upon to pay the church fees, to give a fitting gift, to provide a band for the procession to the church, and to invite a group of their important relatives and friends whose presence graces the reception and enhances the prestige of the parents.

Once the ceremony is over, the godparents (who usually number more than two despite the church policy of discouraging numerous sponsors for one baptism) retire to the elaborate feast prepared by the parents and their relatives. Here the new members of the kin group meet their newly acquired "family" and greet them with cries of "Kumpare" and "Kumare" in place of the impersonal first names used by the town residents, or instead of the more formal "Mang Pedro" or "Mr. Cruz" used formerly. After a dutiful peek at the child who is the immediate cause of the festivities, the visitors promptly rejoin the merry throng.

The newly baptized child seems to be the least important individual in the gathering called to celebrate his entrance into the Christian world. Only a handful of relatives go to the church to witness the actual ceremony. Should the child die later on, the compadre relationship does not lapse but continues just as strongly as before, provided the compadres work at it as usual.

The godchild's obligations to his godparents entail visiting them at least once a year at Christmas and receiving money or a gift. He must accompany his parents to any baptismal, wedding, funeral, and a more recent innovation, birthday gathering, connected with his godparents. His solicitude is not wasted, for when he is in need of a job years later his godparents may be expected to help him secure one if they are in a position to do so.

Compadrazgo, then, provides an important structural basis of action. The ritual kinsman vies in importance with the non-nuclear consanguine kinsman. The common saying in Hulo that blood is thicker than water is behaviorally defined as absolute for the nuclear family but relative for extended kin. If one must choose between extended kin and a stranger, then the kin ties normally take precedence. But where other considerations enter in, such as a compadre relationship, a debt of gratitude, or self-interest, then extended kin may well take second place if they are not emotionally close enough to belong to one's alliance group.

While relatives must work to maintain the sense of solidarity inherent at least potentially in their kinship relations, compadres must work harder. To keep up this closeness, the individual makes sure he invites his relatives and compadres to any festive gathering he may hold. Each visits the other as often as possible, the lower status family going more often to the higher status family's house than vice versa. If small excursions to recreation spots in the area or to a Manila movie are planned by a housewife, a few favored relatives and compadres are asked to accompany her. She takes some food with her to their houses in case of a baptism, wedding, or funeral, participates in the nine-day prayers for the dead, helps serve at the meals that go with all three crises, and contributes a present for the baby, money if related to the groom's family, and again money to the family of the deceased.

If one family has a car, jeep, or carretela, the members will lend it to a favored relative or compadre should he ask to borrow it. If they have close contacts with persons in Manila who are in a position to give jobs, they try to get their needy relatives or compadres and the latter's relatives and compadres placed there. When someone gets sick, they approach a doctor-relative or compadre for treatment either for free or for a lower rate. The person who has personal contacts in Manila hospitals, especially government institutions with large free wards, is invaluable to his associates. For he can manage to enter them as patients, often a formidable task with the large number of persons in the city seeking entry to government hospitals and charity wards of private hospitals.

These are only some of the deeds which develop closer relationships between relatives, compadres, and friends. For each favor done, utang na loob comes into play. Failure to keep up these close contacts by supporting the system of reciprocal obligations causes the drifting apart of compadres (or any kind of ally, for that matter) until their ritual relationship is dormant. This happens not infrequently since most persons have several compadres not all of whom continue to be highly favored and not all of whom consciously work at keeping the ties alive. Should a compadre or relative shirk a definite obligation despite his owing a large measure of utang na loob, he has not fulfilled his expected role and, if the case is severe enough, becomes estranged from his creditor. One can conveniently drop a compadre who has failed to live up to his role as a ritual member of the kin group. An erring relative can similarly be detached emotionally, although the likelihood of reconciliation will be greater because of the mediation which upset relatives will insist upon.

The concepts of utang na loob and hiya deserve special attention as they are moral forces in the regulation of behavior. Their proper maintenance is one of the major values of Philippine society. As indicated earlier utang na loob may be translated as "sense of gratitude" or "debt of gratitude." The term hiya embraces the feelings of shame, embarrassment, guilt, and shyness. The two concepts are closely related; together they keep the social system in good working order. Utang na loob defines any situation harboring it since each person has an approximate idea of where he stands in relation to the other. Hiya seems to stem either from the non-existence or non-observance of utang na loob. In the case of non-existence an undefined situation is created where each actor is not sure of what his responses ought to be, while in non-observance, hiya develops or should develop from a person's sense of not having lived up to the utang na loob expectations of another. Both are powerful elements of the value system and provide the strong moral compulsion which initiates action and maintains cultural expectations.

In a society where favoritism is the rule rather than the exception, any individual builds up a continuous series of utang na loob relationships. The spiral never really ends because with the repayment of one side's debt of gratitude for a past favor, a reciprocating obligation is built up on the other side. In keeping with the highly familistic orientation of Philippine society whereby an individual represents his family, utang na loob is not limited to an individual-to-individual relationship but is rather seen as operative from family to family. Naturally, the individual who did the most to help is the focus of this attention but the immediate family of the favor-doer can expect some deferential treatment, too, as an offshoot of the transaction.

When a person deliberately ignores a debt of gratitude in Hulo, this is cause for much bitterness on the part of the person ignored. Although the debt had no specific time limit, when an opportunity for repayment arises, and the creditor desires payment, then the debtor is morally obligated to do his part. Failure to do so is strongly censured by the community at large, unless mitigating circumstances are present.

THE ROLE OF THE INTERMEDIARY

The widespread use in Philippine society of intermediaries to approach a person on behalf of another person also hinges very greatly on the concepts of utang na loob and hiya. In Hulo, when a person (A) goes to visit another person (C) with the intention of asking a favor, he rarely goes alone unless he is closely related or on very familiar terms with the person being visited. Person (A) will hesitate to approach any person not in his alliance system unless he has with him someone (B) who is allied to that individual. Without B (the intermediary), A will be too hiya or embarrassed to talk to C as their relationship is not such as to provide a basis for the opening of delicate negotiations. Moreover, A realizes that C owes him nothing, that is, has no utang na loob to him and, therefore, will not feel compelled to help A. (If C did have utang na loob to A, then A could approach C directly.) But if A can find a relative, compadre, utang na loob creditor, or other ally of C's, then he creates a defined situation where the mere existence of an alliance puts the visitors at ease; they know they have the right through the intermediary's relationship to ask a favor of C.

Armed with a basket of mangoes, or crabs, or large fish, or any special food which is suitable as a gift, A picks up B and together they go to C's house. The gift is not intended as a bribe but as a means of putting A and B in a slightly higher bargaining position than they would otherwise be. The latter would be hiya if they came to the house emptyhanded like beggars, asking but giving nothing in return. The conversation touches on many subjects unrelated to the purpose of the visit, queries about a mutual friend or relative, and so on, the major parts of the conversation being carried on by B and C while A sits quietly by offering comments now and then. At last the time comes for the aim of the visit to be broached. C has known all along of course that the visit is not solely a social one but he must wait politely until his guests find an opening to broach the subject. If he is pressed for time, he can throw in cues here and there to hasten the process. If the visitors know on the other hand that he has an engagement, they will get to the point more quickly since the maintenance of his goodwill is highly important.

The intermediary (B) broaches the topic and A adds his explanations. Because C has a special relationship with B, he will listen to the request and decide accordingly. If his utang na loob to B is strong, then he will feel a strong moral compulsion to grant the favor if he can or at least talk to the right people to see that it gets done, using intermediaries himself if necessary. In any case, he usually promises that he will see what he can do and sincerely tries to do it, something which he would not feel so necessary if the requests had not come from someone to whom he feels utang na loob.

In granting the favor, C does so primarily because B asked him and only secondarily because A needs it. B is now the one who owes a debt of gratitude to C even though he may not directly reap the material benefits that go with the favor, as A will. But A in turn now has utang na loob to B for his intercession in the matter. A also has utang na loob to C although not as much as he does to B since C did the favor mostly for B rather than for A. B carries the burden of the debt owed to C. Of course, if B and A find out later that C has not tried his best to accomplish what he promised, then they will not feel they owe him any gratitude and may even take the opposite attitude, one of resentment that C did not try to discharge his utang na loob to B in the way and at the time that B requested it. This brings on the accusation of C as being *walang utang na loob* or "ingrate" in not being honorable enough to recognize his debt of gratitude. This may be followed by the charge of *walang hiya*, or "shameless," because of his shirking repayment of a debt of gratitude when it could have and should have been paid. These epithets are two of the greatest insults that can be levelled against any Filipino.

The number of intermediaries possible in any single request situation varies. Often C, in turn, is cast into the role of intermediary since someone above him who is close to him may have to decide on the granting of the favor. The chain can be extended even further but is of course weakened if carried too far since the responsibility is dispersed and the time factor enters in when too many individuals along the chain must communicate up and down the line.

SUMMARY

1. The local power system is in effect an interlocking arrangement of many ego-centered alliances.

2. These ego-centered alliances are made especially by selecting from among those already joined to ego by bonds of kinship, ritual kinship (compadrazgo), reciprocal obligations, or associational ties.

3. Since the average Filipino has a large number of kin on both his mother's and father's side, he must distinguish between those who are emotionally close and those who are not.

4. The nuclear family, however, is automatically within one's circle of intimates.

5. Compadrazgo provides a particularly effective means of incorporating persons outside the nuclear family into one's alliance system.

6. There are two kinds of compadre relationship:

   a. where the two sets of compadres know one another and are equal in status;

   b. where the two sets of compadres know one another and are not equal in status, one being subordinate to the other.

7. Once the alliance has been made, the expected role of each partner is that of the good friend, whose loyalty and support can be relied upon.

8. An alliance, once made, must be nurtured by frequent contact and by reciprocal services, which develop a binding sense of gratitude between the participants.

9. It is recognized that, outside one's nuclear family, failure to cultivate one's relationships properly may result in the dissolution of these alliances and the creation of new alignments with a new constellation of partners. Hence, there is a continuous shift in the personnel belonging to any one alliance.

10. A person in a conflict situation because his loyalty and support are demanded by opposing sets of allies usually aligns either with the side to which he owes the greatest debt of gratitude or with the one which he feels will give him greater benefit.

11. *Hiya* (shame) strongly encourages the observance of one's *utang na loob* (sense of gratitude) to another by acting as a negative sanction on the non-observer.

12. Given the personalized nature of alliance relationships and, conversely, the social distance of non-allies, frequent use is made of intermediaries for soliciting favors, reconciling feuding parties, and generally getting things done.

13. Although a chain of intermediaries may develop in the course of transmitting a request to the proper persons, the recipient of the favor feels the greatest utang na loob to the intermediary immediately above him in the chain. He also feels indebted of course to the other intermediaries and the ultimate benefactor.

The Dyadic Contract: A Model for the Social Structure of a Mexican Peasant Village

George M. Foster

Tzintzuntzan is a peasant village of 2,200 inhabitants (1965) on the shores of Lake Pátzcuaro, in Michoacán state, 230 miles west of Mexico City. For many years it has been largely Spanish-speaking and mestizo in culture, but formerly it was Tarascan Indian, and its nearest neighbor villages are still Tarascan. A majority of families earn their living from pottery making, but farming is also important, and there is some fishing and day laboring on highway maintenance and in the fields of the few farmers with more land than they can cultivate alone. Socially and economically the village is relatively homogeneous. Real social classes are absent, and there are no families with disproportionate power and influence. The importance of the Catholic Church, and the complete absence of minority religious groups, further emphasize the community's homogeneous quality. Tzintzuntzan is dependent economically on the local and national markets to sell pottery and fish and to purchase much food, clothing, and other staples. Its political and legal organizations and its religious system are directed from outside. In the classic sense of the word "peasantry," it is a part-society existing in a symbiotic relationship with the urban centers of the Mexican nation.

The inhabitants of Tzintzuntzan lie near the bottom of the Mexican socio-economic pyramid. Individually and collectively they have limited power, influence, and economic security. They see themselves facing a hostile and dangerous world, from birth until death, in which the good things in life are in short supply, and in which existence itself is constantly threatened by hunger, illness, death, abuse by neighbors, and spoliation by powerful people outside the community. Society and culture provide the Tzintzuntzeños with formal institutions and behavior patterns within the framework of which they struggle to "defend" themselves and their families in this essentially unequal battle. When asked how things are going, a man may reply, *Pues, me defiendo*, that is, "I am managing to defend myself." Or, in the face of a nearly hopeless situation, he may ask, often a bit belligerently, *Con qué me defiendo?* that is, "With what do you think I'm going to defend myself?"

To defend oneself means, in the narrow economic sense, to be able to make both ends meet, to have enough to house, clothe, and feed a wife and children. But in the wider sense the expression implies the ability to face up to all the natural and supernatural threats that fill the peasant villager's world, to have effective means to counterattack in the face of any specific emergency.

The ideal of successful defense is to be able to live *sin compromisos*, to be strong, masculine, independent, able to meet life's continuing challenges without help from others, to be able to avoid entangling alliances. Yet, paradoxically, the struggle to reach this goal can be made only by saddling oneself with a wide variety of obligations. Strength and independence in fact always depend on the number and quality of the ties one maintains. Hence the whole course of life consists of manipulating and exploiting the institutions and behavior forms one knows in order to achieve desirable obligations, to tap social resources so that life's dangers will be minimized and its opportunities maximized. On a formal and institutional level an individual is aided in his "defense" by family, godparenthood (*compadrazgo*), and friendship ties. These are legitimate forms of support in which obligations and expectations — whether or not honored in any specific instance — are clearly spelled out.

Yet most important of all in Tzintzuntzan's social structure is an informal, unnamed principle of reciprocity that underlies all formal ties, cross-cutting them at every point, serving as the glue that holds society together and the grease that smooths its running. This reciprocity principle, which I call the "dyadic contract," can be thought of as a sociological model which reconciles the institutional roles already described with the real behavior that can be observed. Its particular utility as a model lies in the fact that it explains the behavior of people in all the situations in which they find themselves: between those of the same socio-economic status, between people of different statuses, between fellow villagers, between villagers and outsiders, and between man and the beings of the supernatural world.

The dyadic contract model postulates an informal structure in which the really significant ties within all institutions are largely achieved (hence selective) rather than ascribed (hence nonselective). The formal social institutions of Tzintzuntzan present each individual with a nearly infinite number of people with whom he has culturally defined bonds implying mutual obligations and expectations. But no individual could possibly fulfill all the roles imposed upon him by the statuses he occupies in his village's institutions; he is forced to pick and choose, to concentrate on relatively few. In other words, the formal institutions of society provide everyone with a panel of candidates with whom to interact; the individual, by means of the dyadic contract mechanism, selects (and is selected by) relatively few with whom significant working relationships are developed.

In Tzintzuntzan everyone, from an early age, begins to organize his societal contacts outside the nuclear family, and even to some extent within it, by means of a special form of contractual relationship, and as he approaches and reaches adulthood, these relationships grow in importance until they dominate all other types of ties. These contracts are informal, or implicit, since they lack ritual or legal validation. They are based on no idea of law, and they are unenforceable through any authority, even one as diffuse as public opinion. They exist only at the pleasure of the participants. They are noncorporate, since social units such as extended families, barrios, or villages are never bound. Even nuclear families cannot truly be said to enter into contractual relationships of this type with other families.

These contracts are essentially dyadic: they bind *pairs* of contractants rather than groups. The importance of this distinction is clear when we remember that in Tzintzuntzan there are no vigorous voluntary associations or institutions in which an individual recognizes identical or comparable obligations to two or more people. Each person is the center of his private and unique network of contractual ties, a network whose overlap with other networks has little or no functional significance. That is, *A*'s tie to *B* in no way binds him to *B*'s partner, *C*. *A* may have a contractual relationship with *C* as well, but the fact that all three recognize comparable bonds gives rise to no feeling of group association. An individual conceptualizes his relationships with others as a focal point at which he stands, from which radiate a multiplicity of two-way streets; at the end of each is a single partner, completely separate from all the others.

The people (or beings) with whom a villager forms these ties include persons of comparable socio-economic position both within and without the community, people of superior power and influence, and supernatural beings such as Christ, the Virgin Mary, and the saints. Contracts develop between members of a family as close as siblings; they bind compadres beyond the formally defined limits of the institution; and they closely unite friends and neighbors.

Since no ritual or legal forms validate dyadic contracts, what evidence justifies the model? And how can a villager himself be sure he is in fact closely tied to someone else, who also recognizes their special relationship? An outsider in Tzintzuntzan quickly learns of an elaborate pattern of reciprocity, occurring almost entirely between pairs of individuals, in which goods and services are continually exchanged. Some of the exchanges are easily visible, as when plates of steaming food are carried by children from one house to another. Other manifestations of the exchange pattern are not so readily seen, as when a compadre or friend speaks for another in a ceremonial act. But in its totality the reciprocity system validates, maintains, and gives substance to the implicit contractual networks. The symbolic meaning of these exchanges (as contrasted to purely economic activities) is accepted without question by all villagers. They know that as long as a person continues to give to and receive from a partner, he may rest assured that that particular relationship is in good order. When an exchange relationship between two people terminates, it is overt evidence to both that the contract is dead, regardless of the formal institutional ties or the religious validation which may continue to bind the participants. During the life of a contract, each partner expects to receive something he wants or needs from the other, at times, in ways, and in forms that are clearly understood by both. Each partner, in turn, acknowledges his obligation to give something to the other, again at times, in ways, and in forms that are a function of the type of relationship involved.

Two basic types of contractual ties may be recognized, depending on the relative statuses of the partners. "Colleague" contracts — the expression is mine, and not the villagers' — tie people of equal or approximately equal socio-economic position, who exchange the same kinds of goods and services. These contracts are phrased horizontally, and they can be thought of as symmetrical, since each partner, in position and obligations, mirrors the other. Colleague contracts operate primarily within Tzintzuntzan, but they also tie villagers to individuals in adjacent peasant communities.

"Patron-client" contracts — again the expression is mine — tie people (or people to beings) of significantly different socio-economic statuses (or order of power), who exchange different kinds of goods and services. Patron-client contracts are thus phrased vertically, and they can be thought of as asymmetrical, since each patrner is quite different from the other in position and obligations. Patron-client contracts operate almost exclusively between villagers and nonvillagers (including supernatural beings), since socio-economic differences in Tzintzuntzan are seen as so slight as to preclude the role of patron.

In addition to these informal, implicit contracts, villagers of course also recognize formal and explicit contracts, represented by such acts as marriage, establishing compadrazgo ties, and buying and selling property. These contracts rest on governmental and religious law, are legally or ritually validated through specific acts, and are usually registered in writing; most are enforceable through the authority of the particular system that brings them into being. They often are dyadic, but they may also bind several people, as when the baptism of an infant brings two parents, two godparents, and a godchild together. These formal contracts may be but are not necessarily congruent with the informal dyadic contracts, since the latter cut across all formal institutional boundaries and permeate all aspects of society. For example, two compadres are bound by formal ties validated in a ritual ceremony. This tie may be reinforced and made more functional by an implicit dyadic contract, making the two relationships congruent. Or two people may sign a paper authorizing one to sharecrop a field of the other; this formal relationship may be underlain as well by the general exchange pattern that spells a dyadic contract between the two signers.

With these preliminary remarks we can examine in more detail how this contractual system functions, first considering ties between colleagues and second those between patrons and clients. Between colleagues, reciprocity is expressed in *continuing* exchanges of goods and services. The goods and services are tangibles; incorporeal values play little part in the system. For example, a partner whose special knowledge about a glazing process is a trade secret is not likely to instruct a dyadic partner just because they exchange many other things. Over the long term the reciprocity is complementary, because each partner owes the other the same kinds and quantities of things. Over the short term the exchanges are not necessarily complementary, because a material item or service offered to partner A by partner B does not require subsequent return of the same thing to cancel the obligation (it may in fact require something different, as pointed out in the following paragraph). Rather, it is a question of long-range equivalence of value, not formally calculated yet somehow weighed so that in the end both partners balance contributions and receipts. In the usual situation each member of the dyad simultaneously counts a number of credits and debits which are kept in approximate balance.

Within the long-term complementary pattern, there are short-term exchanges, often noncomplementary, in which a particular act elicits a particular return. For example, a friend fixes a bride's hair for the wedding; the friend must be invited to the wedding feast, or if for any reason she cannot come, food must be sent to her from the scene of the dining. One compadre organizes a saint's day *mañanitas* predawn serenade for another compadre, providing guitar players, a chorus, and a tray of fruit and flowers. The honored compadre reciprocates by inviting the serenaders in for drinks and food. But these specific, noncomplementary exchanges are merely minor oscillations within the long-term, major dyadic patterns which bind partners over years and decades. The noncomplementary saint's-day exchange probably will be made complementary later in the year, when the second compadre returns the favor.

A very important functional requirement of the system is that *an exactly even balance between two partners never be struck.* This would jeopardize the whole relationship since, if all credits and debits somehow could be balanced off at one time, the contract would cease to exist. At the very least a new contract would have to be gotten under way, and this would involve uncertainty and possibly distress if one partner seemed reluctant to continue. The dyadic contract is effective precisely because partners are never quite sure of their relative positions at a given moment. As long as they know that goods and services are flowing both ways in essentially equal amounts as time passes, they know their relationship is solidly based.

The forms of exchanges can be examined in terms of services and goods offered and reciprocated in ritual and nonritual settings. These lines are not hard and fast in the minds of Tzintzuntzeños, however, and a material return in a nonritual setting may help counterbalance a service previously offered in a ritual setting, and so on around the circle of logical possibilities.

Services lent in a ritual context usually are associated with life crises such as baptism, confirmation, marriage, and death. They include a compadre's go-between services to make peace after an elopement, making funeral arrangements for a godchild who dies a "little angel," help and comfort extended on the occasion of a death, such as sitting up all night at the wake with a bereaved husband or wife, and the like. Goods offered in a ritual context include the financial responsibilities of marriage godparents, the expenses incurred by a baptismal godfather when his godchild dies young, aid to a father with the costs of his son's marriage, and particularly the help given partners when they are faced with major fiesta expenses. When a man is a mayordomo (called *carguero* in Tzintzuntzan), he visits the homes of relatives, compadres, and friends with whom dyadic contracts are recognized, asking them to "accompany" him, that is, to contribute foodstuffs and money. Emphasizing the ritual character of this transaction is the fact that raw foodstuffs equal to about half that given are returned following the fiesta.

At ceremonial meals, such as a saint's day fiesta, a wedding, a baptism, or a funeral, guests bring pots in which they pour surplus food from the heaping dishes served them. This is taken home to be eaten the following day. At any festive meal some people invited are unable to come, and others not specifically invited must be remembered. After the guests have been served children are sent to the homes of those who have not come with plates of hot food, so they too can share in the festivities.

Services in a nonritual context take an unlimited number of forms. One helps nurse a sick friend or relative, gives a hypodermic injection without the usual small charge, purchases something on request in Pátzcuaro, loans a stud boar without asking the usual fee, sews a dress or makes a picture frame free of charge. Any one of a thousand helpful acts is considered, and remembered, as a service incurring some form of reciprocal obligation.

In a nonritual context goods are exchanged when neighbors drop in to borrow an egg, a few chiles, or some other food or household item immediately needed. When men went to the United States as braceros they always borrowed money from friends and relatives, returning the money upon completing their contracts and adding as well some item such as a pair of nylon stockings or a sport shirt which served to keep alive the exchange relationship. A person with heavy medical expenses expects to receive money as an outright gift and as a loan, thus simultaneously being repaid for earlier transactions and incurring new obligations.

The continuing informal exchange of food and drink is particularly important in maintaining the dyadic contract. Except on ceremonial occasions invitations to meals almost never occur. But when someone —

a relative, a neighbor, a compadre, or a friend — with whom the exchange pattern is fully developed drops in, he or she usually is not allowed to leave without being offered whatever food is available: a tortilla, perhaps with a fried egg or beans, a bit of candied sweet potato, a glass of milk, a cup of coffee, or fresh fruit. The nature of the food or drink is not important, but if they are offered they *must* be accepted. Failure to accept proffered food or drink seriously jeopardizes an exchange relationship, since it appears to represent a denial of mutual understanding and friendly feelings, which are basic to the dyadic contract.

The food and drink exchange, important in all institutions, seems especially so between friends and neighbors. Because the ties to these people are unstructured, in a formal sense, in contrast to those of the family and the compadrazgo, even greater attention to constant reaffirmation of the relationship is deemed desirable. The offering of food and drink is the quintessence of this reaffirmation, and if someone professes friendship but fails in this informal exchange, he is said to be a "friend with his lips on the outside," that is, not a genuine friend.

Food exchanges tell us something else about dyadic contracts: they are not all of equal intensity. The situation is similar to that of American friendship patterns in which we see, visit, and interact more with some friends than with others, but the friends we see less often are still qualitatively different from mere acquaintances or professional associates, since we do recognize social and other obligations toward them. High-intensity contracts can be distinguished from low-intensity contracts by the way in which food is handled. If we see some people almost always being offered food when they come to a house, we may be sure that a high-intensity dyadic contract is operating. If continuing exchanges of various types with other people are noted, but less thought is given to informal offerings of food, then we know the contract is of lesser intensity.

In colleague contracts, as has been pointed out, a functional imperative of the system is that an even balance in exchanges never be struck, since only when partners simultaneously recognize both obligations and expectations as being outstanding do they feel a relationship is in good order. Conceptually, a precise balancing of debits with credits is tantamount to terminating a contract. Consequently, behavior that suggests the striking of an even balance, or the desire to strike an even balance, is interpreted as unfriendly, and normally to be avoided — unless, of course, an individual does in fact wish to terminate a relationship. To put the matter in a slightly different way, behavior forms between partners that confirm or reaffirm recognition of a contract are highly valued, whereas behavior forms which do not reaffirm recognition of a contract, or which may suggest the speaker or actor feels the contract is no longer very important, are seen as threatening and hostile. Once the importance of this point is grasped, certain aspects of behavior in

Tzintzuntzan which at first seem puzzling and incomprehensible fall nicely into place.

When I first began to take presents to people in Tzintzuntzan I was much disturbed when they were accepted with what seemed to me a distressing lack of enthusiasm, bordering on ungraciousness. At most a perfunctory *gracias* would be mumbled, and often nothing at all would be said. I feared I was not pleasing, or that more had been expected of me. Then I realized that this was a standard behavior pattern between the villagers themselves. When a tray of uncooked food, covered by a cloth, would be sent as a contribution to a *carguero's* fiesta expenses, his wife would accept it unceremoniously at the door, carry it without looking under the cloth to the kitchen, unload the tray, and return it and the cloth to the donor with no more comment than normal passing of the time of day.

This "lack of courtesy" among a normally courteous and ceremonially minded people puzzled me until I realized that the objects offered were viewed not as gifts, but rather as one among many items forming the exchange system existing between partners, an item for which repayment would be made in another way at a later date. The Tzintzuntzeños recognize — realistically, I think — that in their society there can be such a thing as a "gift" given quite apart from an existing or a potential exchange pattern between people only in a very special sense. Any favor, whatever its form, is part of a quid pro quo negotiation, the terms of which are recognized and accepted by the participants.

Both linguistic and other behavior forms show why the word "gift" is inappropriate to describe the goods and services that are exchanged in Tzintzuntzan. In American society a gift is thought of as something transferred from one person to another without measurable compensation. That it may, in fact, be part of a continuing exchange pattern is beside the point. A gift is accepted with enthusiasm and with thanks, verbally expressed, which symbolize something more than the courtesy thanks that accompany commercial transactions, since the words are recognized, subconsciously at least, as striking a conceptual balance with the donor's thoughtfulness.

In Spanish thanks are expressed in two distinct linguistic forms: *gracias* (literally the plural form of "grace"), usually translated into English as "thank you," and *Diós se lo pague*, meaning "May God (re)pay you for it." The first form serves for casual, informal interchanges of no moment between persons of equal status, or equal status at least as far as the occasion that calls forth the word is concerned. But *Diós se lo pague* is used in an entirely different sense, in which the thanker acknowledges the great difference in position and the fact that the object or service can never be reciprocated. Beggars, for example, acknowledge alms with this expression. Only by asking God's favor for the donor can the beggar in any way repay the giver; neither expects any other balance. An item acknowledged with *Diós se lo pague*, then, can properly be considered a gift in the American sense. An item or act acknowledged by *gracias* is something else, for the form is a courtesy and nothing more.

In Tzintzuntzan both forms are used. I hear *Diós se lo pague* when I give something considered by the recipient to be far outside the normal patterns of friendship exchange, such as a substantial monetary contribution to help with unusual medical expenses. When I give lesser items, such as a cut of cloth for a skirt or dress — something within the normal range of exchanges — I may hear *gracias*, or perhaps nothing at all. The recipient and I know the item given will be reciprocated with pottery, a tule-reed figure, fish, or something else commanded by the recipient; the cut of cloth is not a gift, nor are the pottery, the figure, or the fish.

The usual absence of verbal thanks and visible enthusiasm accompanying exchanges does not mean, of course, that the transactions are cold, calculated, and emotionless. People enjoy these transactions enormously; it is gratifying to know one is living up to his obligations, and that one's partners continue to value the association. Some of the fundamental values of the culture are expressed in the exchange acts themselves, and people sense and appreciate this fact, even though they would have trouble verbalizing it.

Another form of linguistic behavior which at first thought seems contrary to reason can be explained by the feeling that behavior suggesting a desire to terminate a contract is threatening, while behavior reaffirming the desire to continue a contract is reassuring. In Tzintzuntzan an individual often greets an acquaintance, or acknowledges the presence of a stranger on a trail, with *Adiós*, the common Spanish form of "goodbye," and more literally, "(I commend you) to God." Conversely, he very rarely says *Adiós* when taking leave of a friend, preferring some such form as *Hasta luego*, *Ándale* ("Run along"), *Nos vemos* ("We'll be seeing each other"), or — perhaps most frequently — *No nos despedimos* ("We won't say goodbye"). I think it clear that for a partner to say *Adiós* is potentially dangerous, for it can be interpreted to mean that he does not expect to see his partner for a long time, that he is perhaps tired of him and does not really want to continue the relationship implied in the contract. Or it may imply that the speaker is unwilling or unable to honor his obligations. The expression *Adiós* is therefore conceptually equivalent to *Diós se lo pague* in giving thanks for a gift; it is perceived as balancing the equation of obligations and terminating the relationship. Partners thus prefer to take leave of each other with a verbal expression that emphasizes the continuity of their relationship by expressing the belief, and hope, that they will soon again be together.

But why *greet* a stranger or acquaintance by saying "Goodbye" to him? The use of *Adiós* in this context is consistent with the perception of interpersonal relationships described earlier. An individual cannot be a partner to all the world, and many of the people he sees, and with whom he has some contact, cannot be his partners, and should not be mistaken in assuming that, for a particular act, he wishes to initiate a contract. *Adiós*, then, is both an expression of social distance, and a device to maintain it, a way to recognize the absence of a contractual tie. It is courteous and respectful, but not at all intimate. It says, in effect, "I see you, I greet you, I wish God to go with you, I respect you — but I must remind you that we have no claims on each other."

With patron-client contracts, in contrast to colleague contracts, one of the two partners is always of significantly higher position, from which stems the power which permits him to be a "patron" to the other. The Spanish word *patrón* has several related meanings: an employer of workers, a ceremonial sponsor, a skipper of a small boat, the protecting saint of a village or parish, the protecting saint to all people who bear his (or her) name. All these definitions are correct for Tzintzuntzan. A patron, it is clear, is someone who combines status, power, influence, authority — attributes useful to anyone — in "defending" himself or in helping someone selse to defend himself. But a person, however powerful and influential, is a patron only in relation to someone of lesser position — a client who, under specific circumstances, he is willing to help. Tzintzuntzeños all look up to a number of patrons. Each recognizes the saint whose name he bears as *mi santo patrón*, and everyone knows San Francisco is patron of the village. All accept the Virgin of Guadalupe as patron of America and Mexico, and consequently as their patron as well. In addition, a few adults refer to people in Pátzcuaro, Morelia, and other towns as *mi patrón*, because of relationships in which they assume the position of subordinate partner. Tzintzuntzeños have no corresponding word for themselves as clients. Since they represent near-bottom in the Mexican socio-economic hierarchy, they do not look down upon others from the lofty position of patron, and they do not think of the relationship as one in which a person may be either patron or client, depending on relative position and power.

Analytically, two basic types of patrons may be distinguished in Tzintzuntzan: (1) human beings, and (2) supernatural beings. The former include politicians, government employees, town and city friends, godparents or compadres of superior status, influence, or special abilities, and church personnel, especially the local priests. The latter — the supernatural patrons — are God, Christ, the Virgin Mary, and the saints, the last three in any of their geographical or advocational manifestations. All human patrons, except the local priests, are from outside Tzintzuntzan, since the status differences that are essential for a patron-client relationship are lacking within the community. Supernatural patrons are those associated with the local churches or with family altars, as well as those found in more distant communities.

As is true of colleague contracts, the partners' recognition of mutual obligations underlies and validates the patron-client system. There are, however, two important differences in exchange patterns. First, the patron and client exchange different kinds of goods and services, and second, *whereas all colleague contracts are continuing, some kinds of patron-client exchanges are noncontinuing, or short-term.* That is, a particular good or service offered by a prospective client requires an immediate and specific return from the potential patron. If the offer is reciprocated, the patron-client contract is established, but the act of reciprocation either simultaneously terminates the contract or establishes conditions for termination in the near future. To be more specific, patron-client relationships involving human beings are like colleague contracts, in that goods and services are exchanged as time passes, with no attempt to strike a balance, since this would cancel the contract. In some instances in which the patron is supernatural, the relationship continues for a long period, with no attempt to strike an exact balance. But in many other instances, and particularly those in which a supplicant asks for help in time of sickness or other crisis, the obligation incurred by the granting of the request is canceled out, or balanced off, by the supplicant's compliance with his vow. Hence, no contract exists until the request is granted, and no contract exists after the supplicant complies. This type of patron-client contract is terminated by striking what is recognized as an even bargain between the contractants, the very act that is zealously avoided by colleague contractants so that their relationship *will not* be terminated.

Tzintzuntzeños, recognizing their humble position and lack of power and influence, are continually alert to the possibility of obligating a person of superior wealth, position, or influence, thereby initiating a patron-client relationship which, if matters go well, will buttress the villagers' security in a variety of life crises that are only too certain: illness, the sudden need for cash, help in legal disputes, protection against various forms of possible exploitation, and advice on the wisdom of contemplated moves.

Exploiting the compadrazgo system is one of the most obvious ways of gaining a patron, and wealthy city relatives, local ranchers (of whom there are only a few), and storekeepers in nearby Pátzcuaro with whom one may have commercial relations are common targets. When Pánfilo Castellano's son Lucio was married, his wife's nephew, who had become a successful Pátzcuaro doctor, agreed to be marriage godfather. A preexisting family tie was thereby strengthened, and the new godfather was under strong obligation to help with free medical attention, possible loans, and advice that the greater experience of a town dweller makes possible. Pánfilo and his wife, in return, expect to take presents from time to time to their nephew, to invite him to family fiestas and meals in Tzintzuntzan, and perhaps to drum up trade among ill villagers.

Patron-client compadrazgo relationships, although formally identical to those binding socio-economic equals, are in fact recognized as quite distinct by all participants. This is especially apparent in linguistic usage. Compadres of the same status usually are extremely formal with each other, in theory at least dropping the familiar second person singular personal pronoun *tú* in favor of the formal *usted*. Client compadres, of course, are extremely formal with their patron compadres, as with all other human patrons, but patron compadres, almost without exception, address their village compadres with the familiar tú, so that the relative status of the two partners is never in doubt.

Although the compadrazgo institution is an excellent way to establish a patron-client contract, less formal acts also work well. One day while I sat with Silverio Caro in his roadside pottery stand, a small car drove up with three people. Silverio greeted the driver, "*Buenos días, doctor*," in such a way that it was clear they had had previous contact. After buying several pieces of pottery the doctor and his friends left. Silverio then explained that this was a relatively new doctor in Pátzcuaro whom he had consulted professionally, and it became clear to me that he was carefully building a relationship with him. The regular price of the merchandise selected was $16.50, but Silverio had charged only $13.00. If, on future visits to Pátzcuaro, the doctor were to show a bit more consideration than usual, or go out of his way to show friendship in some other way, Silverio would take presents of pottery and feel that his relationship with the doctor was good health insurance.

Within Tzintzuntzan, although there are wealth differences, there are no social distinctions sufficiently great to justify using the patron-client concept to describe personal relationships, with the single exception of the priests. The three priests who have served in recent years have been reluctant to accept compadrazgo ties, although they have done so on rare occasions, thereby establishing patron-client bonds. But other less specific ties exist. The priests need helpers to maintain church ritual, to arrange flowers and candles on altars, to clean the buildings, and to supply them with some of their food. They, in turn, can confer extra spiritual blessings on their supporters, and they can, because of their education and knowledge of the world, give temporal advice as well. So, it seems to me, it is proper to think of the priests as participating in exchange relationships with the villagers, in which they are patrons and the villagers are clients.

In these patron-client relationships between human beings, one notes both similarities to and differences from the colleague contracts. As with the latter, the relationships are continuing, and neither patron nor client attempts to strike an immediate balance, which both recognize would terminate the contract. But unlike the colleague contracts, the partners are not equals, and make no real pretense to equality. It is, in fact, this asymmetry, and particularly the ability to offer one's partner something distinct from that which he offers, and to receive something one's fellows do not have at their disposal, that makes the system worthwhile. Within the village local colleague ties provide a man with all he needs, at peak periods of demand, of the kinds of goods and services to which he himself also has access. The patron's utility lies in the fact that he can provide things not normally available in the village, things that at times are badly needed.

At first glance the patron-client compadrazgo, which is formally as well as informally contractual, appears to contradict the dyadic principle: in its important forms it binds a minimum of five and a maximum of eight people (e.g., for baptism, the child, parents, and godparents; for marriage, the godparents, the couple, and the parents of both bride and groom). The contradiction, however, is more apparent than real, since the *meaningful exchange-based* ties which underlie the system's formalities seem normally to involve dyads only. Above all, the patron is always an individual.

Just as individuals cast about among human beings for patrons, so do they turn to the saints, and to the various manifestations of Christ and the Virgin, testing their willingness to enter contractual relationships with them (i.e., by helping, by responding to overtures). Some of the resulting dyadic contracts are, like all those previously described, continuing, in that an even balance is never struck. Other contracts are rather different, in that they are called into being for a specific crisis, in response to the supplications of a human being. If the contract is made, i.e., if the supernatural being grants the request of the supplicant, the latter is obligated, at his earliest convenience, to fulfill his part of the bargain, to strike the balance by complying with his offer. This terminates the contract. An individual may try to renew the contract at a later time for a new crisis, but, as will be seen, he often will attempt a contract with a different patron on each new occasion.

Continuing patron-client contracts with supernatural beings are best seen in the pattern of daily prayers and lighting of candles practiced by most villagers. Every home has one or more simple altars, usually a shelf with a few wilted or artificial flowers and guttered candles beneath several pictures of Christ, the Virgin, and an assortment of saints. This low-pitched daily homage is believed to gain the protection of the beings invoked, not for specific crises, but against the thousand and one unthought dangers that lie in wait for the unwary. In the room in which Laura Prieto sleeps and sews, the wall altar holds pictures of the Virgin of Guadalupe, as well as of several other virgins and saints. When she sits down to sew, or at other times when she "just feels like it," she lights a vigil light "to all of them." She is paying her respects, asking them to continue to watch over her in return for this attention. Her mother pays little attention to this altar, but she prays to the Virgin of Guadalupe before arising in the morning, and Divine Providence is the object of a credo before she goes to sleep. In return, the mother hopes to receive her "daily necessities." Laura's stepfather is addicted to Souls in Purgatory and Our Lady of Perpetual Help, to both of whom he prays daily. In other homes the pattern is similar.

A noteworthy point in this pattern is that altars are not really centers of family rites, even though several members may light candles. Each member of the family has his special responsibility toward the patrons he has selected, who he feels favor him. No one, except upon special request, is responsible for acts of deference and respect for other family members. If Laura is away for a day or two on a pilgrimage, her mother feels no compulsion to light candles to Laura's patrons, although she will certainly ask her own patrons to care for her daughter. In the continuing type of relationship with supernatural patrons, the dyadic pattern that characterizes other village relationships is the rule.

Apart from what may be called "obligatory" patrons — Christ and the Virgin, shared by all villagers — how does one select continuing patrons? There is no rule; one simply follows hunches or whim, as in the case of Laura, who decided to add San Martín de Porres to her altar after hearing about him in a radio soap opera. Manuel Herrera, with impeccable logic, says he supposes the Virgin is really the most powerful. After all, *Ella tiene más parentesco con el Mero Jefe*, "She's most closely related to the Big Boss."

Noncontinuing or short-term contracts with supernatural patrons are best seen in the practice of votive offerings. When an individual faces a crisis, such as illness, accident, or an unusual need for money, he (or she) makes a *manda* or *promesa*, a vow or solemn promise to a saint or to one or another of the many images or manifestations of Christ or the Virgin, to do some pious act known to be pleasing to the patron. In the simplest pious acts, for rather minor crises, the petitioner lights a candle and prays, or hangs a silver *milagro* at the altar of the patron invoked. The silver (sometimes base metal) votive offerings are small representations of parts of the body such as an arm, a leg, eyes, breasts, or even an entire body in kneeling posture, or of pigs, goats, sheep, horses, or cattle. The one selected depends, of course, on the nature of the supplication: a pig for a lost or sick sow, and an arm for a sore arm.

In more serious crises the client promises the patron to wear a *hábito*, a plain religious garment, for a number of months, and to refrain from all kinds of public entertainment and amusements if the request is granted. Women who suffer from headache or who are otherwise sickly, and who may believe their long hair is an excessive drain on their systems, occasionally cut off their braids and hang them at the altar of the Virgin, pleading for relief. Guadalupe Huipe recently offered her braids to the *Imaculada* image of the Virgin, and to comply with her promise painstakingly glued each hair to a skullcap to be worn by the Virgin. Ofelia Zamora did the same thing 20 years ago, but with the passage of the years the hairs fell out and the Virgin became a bit bald, so Guadalupe had the opportunity to do something she felt would be particularly welcome to the Virgin.

When a person finds himself in sudden, grave peril, he commends himself to one of the advocations of Christ or the Virgin, and if he is saved, he orders a *retablo,* in classic form a painted metal sheet which graphically portrays the danger, shows the patron floating in the sky, and at the bottom has a line or two describing the miracle. For other grave crises, or in the hope of very special favors, a supplicant promises the Santo Entierro advocation of Christ to assume the role of penitent during one or more Good Fridays, either hobbling about with leg shackles or carrying a wooden cross along a prescribed route through the village. In other cases — usually illness — one appeals to a "miraculous" saint or image of Christ or the Virgin in another town, promising to go on a religious pilgrimage to fulfill the vow if the request is granted.

Several examples will show how the system works.

Valentín Rivera on two occasions has taken silver votive oxen to the church of San Antonio in Morelia, for aid in finding lost animals. San Antonio is patron of animals, and he is also very skilled in helping people find things such as, for farmers, lost animals, and — for young maidens — husbands. Benigno Zúñiga has taken silver eyes and a silver leg to the altar of Nuestro Señor del Rescate, both times for personal illness. Few if any adults have not, at some time or other, made use of ex-votos.

Laura Prieto was afflicted with giant urticaria, which caused her great suffering. She visited a Pátzcuaro doctor, who prescribed medicine, and then she appealed to the Virgin of Health ("the most miraculous Virgin in Pátzcuaro"), promising to wear the Virgin's "habit" for six months if she were relieved. Within a week she was much improved, so Laura bought the costly, heavy, scratchy wool, made the dress, wore it six months, and faithfully abstained from all public recreation. The doctor received no credit.

Most painted retablos in Tzintzuntzan are dedicated to the "miraculous" Señor del Rescate, whose extraordinary powers were noted sixty years ago when he was credited with saving the village from decimation by smallpox. One, showing a painting of Christ on the cross, with a woman kneeling below, bears the legend, "I give thanks to the very miraculous Señor del Rescate for having saved my life in a dangerous operation April 10, 1950, from which I nearly died. I offer myself with all my heart to El Señor. Glafira Ceja who resides in Ciudad Júarez, Chihuahua." A second, large, framed, hand-lettered script without a picture says simply, "A miracle which the Señor del Rescate did for me. I give my most sincere thanks to our Señor del Rescate for having saved my life when I was a prisoner in the Pátzcuaro jail in 1919. Eligio Carrillo."

Of the nineteen retablos hanging in 1961, twelve were related to health, and seven dealt with personal problems such as finding a lost animal, delivery from prison or drunkenness, and avoidance of military service. All but one were placed by the individual who was in danger or great need; the exception was a man who gave thanks for his wife's restored health. Curiously, only one of the retablos was hung by a Tzintzuntzeño: a widow who thanks Our Lady of the Sacred Heart for the "miracle" of making it possible for her to have a house. Why this discrimination by local people? As far as El Señor del Rescate is concerned, Benigno Zúñiga probably speaks for the village when he says this Christ *es casi de la familia*, is almost a member of the family, and can be approached successfully in a number of simpler ways, such as vigil lights and silver votive offerings. It looks as if it is a case of distant fields looking greener. San Juan de las Colchas, and San Juan de los Lagos, says Micaela, are where Tzintzuntzeños like to hang retablos.

Illustrating the pilgrimage pattern, Manuel Herrera, while working as a bracero in California, fell ill, not gravely, but enough so he feared he would lose work time, a critical matter for a man on a short-term contract. He promised the Virgin of the Rosary in Coeneo, about fifty miles from Tzintzuntzan, that if she cured him quickly he would make a pilgrimage to her church to light a 5-peso candle in her honor. He recovered without lost time, and shortly after his return to Mexico he visited Coeneo as promised.

The way in which noncontinuing, short-term contracts with supernatural patrons differ from continuing contracts should be apparent from the examples given. Except for the offering of ex-votos and candles and prayers, *the vow or promise is conditional upon the patron granting the request*. The offering of the would-be client, the promise of a pious act, must be carried through only if the patron in fact fulfills his (or her) part of the bargain, which is the act that brings the contract into being. Laura would not have worn her habit if she had not greatly improved; the retablos would not have been hung if the favors requested had not been granted; and Manuel would not have gone to Coeneo if he had become seriously ill. "Thus we really lose nothing," says Laura's very practical mother, in explaining how the system works. Neither patron nor client is under long-term or continuing obligation to his partner as a consequence of a successful exchange. The relationship is a one-time, one-subject affair, and with an exact balance of obligation struck both partners are free to go their own ways, perhaps but not necessarily coming together at a future time.

Although Christ and the Virgin may be appealed to in a general sense, and in any specific manifestation, and any saint may be approached, some are recognized as especially powerful or "miraculous" (like the Virgin of Health in Pátzcuaro), while others are particularly efficacious for certain things. San Judas Tadeo, for example, helps people find lost objects. If he is appealed to, and fails to help, his picture is turned to the wall or placed face down on a chair as punishment, in spite of the fact that the priests inveigh against this impious act.

In general, though, an eclectic approach is utilized in seeking special aid. When Macaria Gómez feared a gall-bladder operation, her daughter Victoria promised to wear the habit of the Virgin of Health for three months if the operation were not necessary; her daughter Laura promised to make a pilgrimage the 400 miles to the famous Virgin of San Juan de los Lagos (two neighbors had told her this virgin was "especially miraculous"); one friend promised the Virgin of Counsel in Santa Clara del Cobre to bring Macaria with her on pilgrimage; another friend promised the Virgin of the Rosary in Coeneo to bring Macaria with her; whereas her stepdaughter simply vowed alms to El Señor del Rescate. Macaria avoided the operation, but is in some doubt as to who receives credit. Her husband Manuel, in addition to the Virgin of the Rosary in Coeneo, has at some time appealed to El Señor de la Misericordia in Capula, to Santiago, patron saint of Capula, to El Cristo in San Juan de los Conejos, near Uruapan, to El Señor de la Exaltación in Santa Fe, to the Holy Virgin in the abstract, and to most of the saints and pictures of Christ and the Virgin in the Tzintzuntzan churches.

To appreciate fully patron-client relationships, both between human beings alone, and with the supernatural, one must understand the concept of *palanca*, or "lever." Broadly speaking, the palanca is *a way of access to a patron*, a device to reach someone with "leverage." "For example," Micaela once said to me with disarming candor, "I want something from you, but I don't want to ask you directly, so I ask Mariquita (Mary Foster) to approach you. She is my palanca." And again, "When I ask a friend to help, I say *Que me hagas una palanca*, you be my lever." A palanca, it is clear, is a go-between, someone with whom ego feels on reasonably close terms, who can be helpful in getting to the real patron. A palanca is, perhaps, a semi-patron as well as a patron. He can help in himself, but his real value resides in his ability to influence favorably the ultimate source of power.

As previously mentioned, priests are reluctant to accept compadrazgo ties with villagers. Consequently their nieces or sisters who keep house for them are deluged with requests to be godmothers, and they often accept. These women are looked upon as palancas. The relationship with them is not particularly valued in itself, but it is assumed that via them the client can more easily gain the ear of the priest in time of need; they are the lever, the device to achieve the desired end. This rather cynical view of the approach to a priest is seen in the saying *Por el santo se besa la piaña*, which means that in order to reach the saint who may help one, the supplicant must be prepared to kiss the pedestal on which the saint's image stands.

Although the word "palanca" is used only for human beings, it is clear that this concept is equally applicable to the supernatural. In trying to work out the pattern, I commented to Micaela that the person who wants to get ahead looks for palancas, tries to get them in debt by offering a meal or doing some other favor, but one is merely trying, and until the potential palanca comes through, one doesn't know. Nevertheless, a person keeps searching for the best palancas. "*Es la misma cosa con los santos*," said Micaela with considerable feeling, "It's the same thing with the saints." One continually tries different saints, shopping around, hoping to find the most influential ones, or the ones that can be most helpful to the petitioner. When I suggested to other informants that saints were really palancas, most were shocked; but a few, not too upset to speculate, said in effect, "Yes, that's really the way it is."

The concept of the palanca also helps us in understanding the real nature of the patron-client relationship with saints. The saints, and the Virgin Mary as well, in one sense are patrons in that the contract is made with them, but ultimately they are only palancas, or go-betweens. "*Cuando Diós no quiere, los santos no pueden*," the saying goes. "When God doesn't wish it, the saints can't do it." The saints and the Virgin are, then, advocates, special pleaders, whom one can approach more readily than God. They will handle your case when presented with it, but only if God wishes it can they be successful, and must the fee be paid, in the form of the petitioner complying with his vow.

CLOSED CORPORATE PEASANT COMMUNITIES IN MESOAMERICA AND CENTRAL JAVA

Eric R. Wolf

One of the salient aims of modern anthropology, conceived as a science, is to define recurrent sequences of cause and effect, that is, to formulate cultural laws. This paper is concerned with recurrent features in the social, economic, and religious organization of peasant groups in two world areas, widely separated by past history and geographical space: Mesoamerica [1] and Central Java.[2] These have been selected for

From "Closed Corporate Peasant Communities in Mesoamerica and Central Java" in *Southwestern Journal of Anthropology*, Vol. 13, No. 1 (Spring 1957). Reprinted by permission of the author and the editors of the *Southwestern Journal of Anthropology*. This paper represents an effort to contribute to the aims and methods of the Project for Research on Cross-Cultural Regularities, directed by Julian Steward at the University of Illinois. The writer was Research Associate of the Project from 1954–55. He is grateful for comments and suggestions to Julian Steward, Robert Murphy, and Charles Erasmus, as well as to those friends of the Project who heard a reading of a first draft of this paper at the Symposium on Cross-Cultural Regularities, held at the University of Illinois on June 16th, 1955.

[1] For a definition of Mesoamerica in culture-area terms, see Kirchhoff, 1952, pp. 17–30. In this paper, the term is used as short-hand for Mexican and Guatemalan communities which conform to the configuration discussed. See Wolf, 1955, pp. 456–461.

[2] Central Java is a region of rice-growing nucleated villages with a tendency to

comparison, because I have some measure of acquaintance with Mesoamerica through field work, and a measure of familiarity with the literature dealing with the two areas.

The cultural configuration which I wish to discuss concerns the organization of peasant groups into closed, corporate communities. By peasant I mean an agricultural producer in effective control of land who carries on agriculture as a means of livelihood, not as a business for profit.[3] In Mesoamerica, as in Central Java, we find such agricultural producers organized into communities with similar characteristics. They are similar in that they maintain a body of rights to possessions, such as land. They are similar because both put pressures on members to redistribute surpluses at their command, preferably in the operation of a religious system, and induce them to content themselves with the rewards of "shared poverty." They are similar in that they strive to prevent outsiders from becoming members of the community, and in placing limits on the ability of members to communicate with the larger society. That is to say, in both areas they are corporate organizations, maintaining a perpetuity of rights and membership; and they are closed corporations, because they limit these privileges to insiders, and discourage close participation of members in the social relations of the larger society.

Outright communal tenure was once general in both areas. In Java, such tenure still survived in a third of all communities in 1927, while land in more than a sixth of all communities was still redistributed annually. Such land consisted of the community's most valuable land, the irrigated rice fields.[4] Yet even where communal tenure has lapsed, jurisdiction over land by the community remains important. Communities may deny or confirm the rights of heirs who have left the village to inherit village lands; [5] they may take back and issue land to someone else if a member leaves the community; [6] or they may take back land issued if a member commits a crime.[7] Aliens may settle in such a community as sharecroppers, but may not inherit or buy the land they work.[8] Community members have priority in the purchase of village lands.[9] And members do not have the right to pledge their land as security.[10]

Estimates concerning the survival of land-holding communities in Mesoamerica tend to vary greatly. McBride estimated that in Mexico, in 1854, there were some 5,000 "agrarian corporations" in possession of

communal land tenure. It was also the main center of commercial sugar and indigo production which promoted communal tenure and dense populations. Western Java is characterized by cattle-breeding rather than by agriculture; Eastern Java is occupied by small hamlets, scattered among individually held rice fields (Furnivall, 1939, p. 386). Central Java is used as short-hand for Javanese communities which conform to the configuration discussed.

[3] Wolf, 1955, pp. 453–454.

[4] Boeke, 1953, p. 65.

[5] S'Jacob, 1951, p. 144.

[6] Haar, 1948, p. 85; Oei, 1948, pp. 24–25.

[7] Haar, 1948, p. 85.

[8] Haar, 1948, p. 119; S'Jacob, 1951, p. 143.

[9] Boeke, 1953, p. 31; Haar, 1948, p. 97.

[10] Haar, 1948, p. 113.

11.6 million hectares, but that in 1923 land-holding communities survived only in "certain out-of-the-way parts of the country." [11] Tannenbaum, in turn, calculated that in 1910 about 16 per cent of all Mexican villages and 51 per cent of the rural Mexican population lived in "free villages," that is, villages not included in some large estate.[12] This computation has been criticized by Simpson who follows Luis Cabrera in holding that "by the end of the Díaz regime [in 1910] . . . 90 per cent of the villages and towns on the central plateau had no communal lands of any kind." [13] A recent estimate holds that in 1910, 41 per cent of land-holding communities still maintained communal tenure, though on an illegal basis.[14] Today, there is a general tendency to maintain communal tenure on hillsides and forests, but to grant private ownership over valley bottoms and garden plots.[15] Even in such cases, however, communities can and do prohibit the sale of land to outsiders and limit the right of members to pledge land as a security on loans.[16] In contrast to Central Java, periodic re-allotment of land to community members seems to be rather rare in Mesoamerica.[17]

Peasant communities in both areas show strong tendencies to restrict membership in the community to people born and raised within the boundaries of the community. The community is territorial, not kinship-based.[18] Rules of community endogamy further limit the immigration of new personnel. These rules are characteristic of Mesoamerica; they occur only occasionally in Central Java.[19]

Membership in the community is also demonstrated by participation in religious rituals maintained by the community. In Java, each community is charged with the maintenance of proper relations with its spirits and ancestors. The rituals which serve this function cannot be carried on by the individual.[20] Each year the land is ritually purified (*slametan bresih desa*), the community spirit is feasted (*sedekah bum*), and offerings are made to the souls of the dead (*njadran*).[21] The religious official — in the past usually the chief, but nowadays more often the land supervisor and diviner of the community [22] — is looked upon as "a personification of the spiritual relation of the people to their land." [23] In Mesoamerica, there is no evidence of ancestor worship or propitiation as

[11] McBride, 1923, pp. 133, 135.
[12] Tannenbaum, 1929, pp. 30–37.
[13] Simpson, 1937, p. 31.
[14] González Navarro, 1954, p. 129.
[15] Aguirre and Pozas, 1954, pp. 192–198; Carrasco, 1951, pp. 101–102; Tax, 1952, p. 61.
[16] Aguirre, 1952a, p. 149; Carrasco, 1951, p. 102; Carrasco, 1952, p. 17; Lewis, 1951, p. 124; Tax, 1953, pp. 68–69; Wagley, 1941, p. 65.
[17] Tax, 1952, p. 60.
[18] Haar, 1948, pp. 51, 71; Lekkerkerker, 1938, p. 568; Guiteras, 1952, pp. 99–100; Redfield and Tax, 1952, p. 33.
[19] Haar, 1948, p. 155; Redfield and Tax, 1952, p. 31.
[20] S'Jacob, 1951, p. 140.
[21] Haar, 1948, pp. 24, 28; Kattenburg, 1951, p. 16; Ploegsma, 1936, p. 4; Supatmo, 1943, p. 9.
[22] Haar, 1948, pp. 91–92.
[23] *Ibid.*

such.[24] Yet each community tends to support the cult of one or more saints. The functions associated with these cults are delegated to members of the community. A man gains social prestige by occupying a series of religious offices charged with these functions; these tend to be ranked in a prescribed ladder of achievement. Often, they carry with them a decisive voice in the political and social affairs of the community.[25] Apparently only members of the community are normally admitted to such religio-political participation.

In both areas, the community motivates its members to expend surpluses in the operation of a prestige economy. The prestige economy operates largely in support of the communal religious cult, and allied religious activities. In Central Java, where cattle are symbolic of landownership,[26] wealth is expended conspicuously in cattle sacrifices, as well as in a large number of ritual feasts (*slametans*) offered by private individuals to ward off evil or difficulties, to celebrate special events in the life cycle, to mark holidays, and to emphasize stages in the production of rice.[27] Similarly, pilgrimages to Mecca earn prestige at the cost of large stores of surplus wealth. In 1927, the cost of such a pilgrimage was estimated at 1,000 florin. In that year, 60,000 Indonesians made the voyage, spending 60 million florin in the process, "an enormous sum for so poor a country." [28] In Mesoamerica, adult members of the community generally undertake to finance part of the cult of one or more saints, when they assume religious office. Expenditures may prove economically ruinous, though they earn great social prestige for the spender.[29]

In both areas, we not only encounter a marked tendency to exclude the outsider as a person, but also to limit the flow of outside goods and ideas into the community. This tendency is often ascribed to "inherent peasant conservatism" or to adherence to "static needs," but may actually represent the complex interplay of many factors. Villagers are poor, and unable to buy many new goods. The goods purchased must be functional within peasant life. Peasant needs in both areas are met by marketing systems which serve only the peasantry, and which are organizationally and culturally distinct from other marketing systems within the larger societies to which they belong. Such markets also have similar characteristics. They tend to offer a very high percentage of objects manufactured

[24] I should like to express a guess that further field work might reverse this statement. It is possible, for instance, that the cemetery plays a much greater symbolic role in Mesoamerican life than is generally suspected. The Mazatec of the Papaloapan River valley, about to be resettled, took great care to transfer the bones of their dead from their old to their new villages (Pozas, personal communication). The annual feast of the dead may have more communal function than is generally assumed.

[25] Cámara, 1952; Redfield and Tax, 1952, pp. 36–38.

[26] Boeke, 1953, p. 46.

[27] Geertz, 1956, pp. 138–140; Landon, 1949, pp. 156–158; Supatmo, 1943, p. 9.

[28] Vandenbosch, 1942, p. 27.

[29] Aguirre, 1952a, pp. 234–242; Cámara, 1952, pp. 155–157.

by peasant labor within the peasant household. They show a high proportion of dealings between primary producers and ultimate consumers. They are characterized by small purchases due to the limited amount of consumer purchasing power. In both areas, moreover, we find regular market days in regional sequence which make for a wide exchange of an assortment of local products, probably much larger than any store-keeper could hope to keep in his store.[30] Such markets can only admit goods which are congruous with these characteristics. The goods sold must be cheap, easily transportable, adaptable to the limited capital of the seller. Only goods such as these will reach the peasant household.

In both areas, moreover, peasant communities maintain strong attitudes against accumulated wealth. In Mesoamerica, display of wealth is viewed with direct hostility. In turn, poverty is praised and resignation in the face of poverty accorded high value.[31] We have seen how much surplus wealth is destroyed or redistributed through participation in the communal religious cult. In Java, there are similar pressures to redistribute wealth:

> . . . every prosperous person has to share his wealth right and left; every windfall must be distributed without delay. The village community cannot easily tolerate economic differences but is apt to act as a leveller in this respect, regarding the individual as part of the community. . . .[32]

Surplus wealth thus tends to be siphoned off, rather than to be directed towards the purchase of new goods.[33]

It is further necessary to point out that closed corporate peasant communities in both areas are socially and culturally isolated from the larger society in which they exist. The nature of this isolation will be discussed below. This general isolation of the peasant community from the larger society is, however, reinforced by the parochial, localocentric attitudes of the community. In Mesoamerica, each community tends to maintain a relatively autonomous economic, social, linguistic, and politico-religious system, as well as a set of relatively exclusive customs and practices.[34] In Gillin's words, "the Indian universe is spatially limited and its horizon typically does not extend beyond the limits of the local community or region." [35] In Central Java, similarly, each community is a separate sociocultural universe.[36] Such localocentrism is a form of "ignorance [which] performs specifiable functions in social structure and action." [37] It serves

[30] Re Java, see Boeke, 1953, pp. 48, 75; Lekkerkerker, 1938, pp. 728–729; Ploegsma, 1936, p. 24. Re Mesoamerica, see Foster, 1948b, p. 154; Pozas, 1952, pp. 326–338; Whetten, 1948, pp. 357–360. Whetten's account is a summary of a manuscript by B. Malinowski and Julio de la Fuente, entitled "The Economics of a Mexican Market System," which unfortunately has never been published.

[31] See e.g. Carrasco, 1952, pp. 47, 48; Lewis, 1951, p. 54; Tumin, 1950, p. 198; Tumin, 1952, pp. 85–94.

[32] Boeke, 1953, p. 34. See also Geertz, 1956, p. 141.

[33] See Kroef, 1956, p. 124.

[34] Redfield and Tax, 1952, p. 31; Tax, 1941, p. 29.

[35] Gillin, 1952, p. 197.

[36] Ploegsma, 1936, p. 5.

[37] Moore and Tumin, 1949, p. 788.

to exclude cultural alternatives by limiting the "incentives on the part of individuals of the groups in social interaction to learn the ways of their neighbors, for learning is the psychological crux of acculturation." [38] In Mesoamerica, such exclusion of cultural alternatives [39] is strongest in the area of the *costumbres,* those religious and social features of the community which — in terms of this paper — help to maintain its closed and corporate character.[40] In Java, similarly, communities show a tendency to

> . . . preserve a balance by averting and fighting every deviation from the traditional pattern.
>
> . . . when the villager seeks economic contact with western society, he does not enjoy the support of his community. Quite the contrary. By so doing he steps outside the bounds of the community, isolates himself from it, loses its moral support and is thrown on his own resources.[41]

Peasant communities in both areas thus show certain similarities. Both maintain a measure of communal jurisdiction over land. Both restrict their membership, maintain a religious system, enforce mechanisms which ensure the redistribution or destruction of surplus wealth, and uphold barriers against the entry of goods and ideas produced outside the community.[42] These resemblances also mark their differences from other kinds of peasant communities. They form a contrast, for instance, with the "open" peasant communities of Latin America where communal jurisdiction over land is absent, membership is unrestricted, and wealth is not redistributed.[43] They also contrast with the peasant communities of a society like pre-British Uganda where access to scarce land was not an issue, and where local groups consisted of client families, united in temporary allegiance to a common chief by hopes of favors, bounty, and booty in war, yet able to change their residence and to better their life chances through changes in loyalties when these were not forthcoming.[44] Differences also appear when the corporate communities discussed in this paper are compared with the peasant communities of China. In China, free buying and selling of land has been present from early times. Communities are not endogamous and rarely closed to outsiders, even where a single stratified "clan" or *tsu* held sway. Constant

[38] Hallowell, 1955, p. 319.

[39] Linton, 1936, pp. 282–283; Moore and Tumin, 1949, p. 791.

[40] Beals, 1952, pp. 229–232. See also Beals, 1946, p. 211.

[41] Boeke, 1953, p. 29, p. 51.

[42] Communities in both areas are also characterized by a tendency to nuclear rather than extended family organization, and by a tendency to divide access to land equally among the filial generation (Haar, 1948, p. 71; Kattenburg, 1951, p. 10; Redfield and Tax, 1952, p. 33; Aguirre and Pozas, 1954, pp. 181–182). I have not discussed these similarities in this paper, because I feel that closed corporate community organization can coexist with various kinds of families and various systems of inheritance, as long as these do not imply loss of land to outsiders. This will be the case, for instance, even where we have extended families or lineages, as long as only sons inherit rights to land and residence after marriage remains patrilocal.

[43] Wolf, 1955, pp. 461–466.

[44] Roscoe, 1911, p. 13, p. 269.

circulation of local landowners into the imperial bureaucracy and of officials into local communities where they acquired land prevented the formation of closed communities. Moreover, state controls maintained through control of large-scale water works heavily curtailed the autonomy of the local group. In such a society, relations between individual villagers and individual government officials offered more security and promise than relations among the villagers themselves.[45] Peasants may thus be found organized into many kinds of communities; only some, however, live in closed corporate bodies of the kind described here.

These casual contrasts afford another insight. In each case, the kind of peasant community appears to respond to forces which lie within the larger society to which the community belongs rather than within the boundaries of the community itself. The "open" peasant communities of Latin America "arose in response to the rising demand for cash crops which accompanied the development of capitalism in Europe."[46] Pre-British Uganda was characterized by political instability at the top, considerable personal mobility, and frequent shifts in personal allegiances, all of which found expression in the character of its local groups. Similarly, efforts to understand the peasant community in China purely in its own terms would be foredoomed to failure. These considerations suggest that the causes for the development of closed corporate communities in Mesoamerica and Central Java may derive from the characteristics of the larger societies which gave rise to them.

Historically, the closed corporate peasant configuration in Mesoamerica is a creature of the Spanish Conquest. Authorities differ as to the characteristics of the pre-Hispanic community in the area,[47] but there is general recognition that thoroughgoing changes divide the post-Hispanic community from its pre-conquest predecessor.[48] In part, the new configuration was the result of serious social and cultural crises which destroyed more than three-quarters of the Indian population, and robbed it of its land and water supply.[49] Population losses and flight prompted colonial measures leading to large-scale resettlement and concentration of population.[50] The new Indian communities were given rights to land as local groups, not kinship-wise; [51] political authority was placed in the hands of new local office holders and made elective; [52] tribute and labor services were placed on a new basis; [53] and "the rapid growth of Indian *cofradias* (sodalities) after the late sixteenth century gave to parishioners a series of organized and stable associations with which personal and communal

45 See e.g. Fei, 1953; Fried, 1953; Fukutake, 1951; Hu, 1948, p. 91; Wittfogel, 1935; Wittfogel, 1938; Yang, 1945, pp. 132–142.

46 Wolf, 1955, p. 462.

47 For a recent statement of conflicting views, see Monzón, 1949.

48 For a masterly exposition of these changes, see Gibson, 1955.

49 E.g. Wolf and Palerm, 1955, pp. 277–278.

50 Zavala and Miranda, 1954, pp. 39–41.

51 *Idem*, pp. 70–74.

52 *Idem*, p. 80; Aguirre, 1952b; Gibson, 1955, pp. 588–591.

53 Zavala and Miranda, 1954, pp. 85–88; Miranda, 1952.

identification might readily be made." [54] In Java, similarly, corporate peasant communities did not take shape

> until after the coming of the Dutch, when for the first time the village as a territorial unit became a moral organism with its own government and its own land at the disposal of its inhabitants.[55]

At the time of the Dutch conquest, there was still "an abundance of waste" in Java; [56] slash-and-burn farming was carried on quite generally; population densities averaged only 33.9 persons per km^2.[57] The closed corporate peasant community in Central Java thus represents an attempt to concentrate both population and tenure rights.

> Over the greater part of Java it was only on the introduction of land revenue from 1813 onwards that villages were reduced to uniformity and their lands bound up into a closed unit, and during this process there were numerous references to the splitting and amalgamation of villages, and to the promotion of hamlets to the status of independent villages.[58]

In the two areas, then, the closed corporate peasant community is a child of conquest; but this need not always be so The corporate community of pre-1861 Russia, the *mir*, was the product of internal colonization, rather than of foreign domination imposed by force of arms.[59] The corporate peasant community is not an offspring of conquest as such, but rather of the dualization of society into a dominant entrepreneurial sector and a dominated sector of native peasants. This dualization may take place in peaceful as well as in warlike circumstances, and in metropolitan as well as in colonial countries.[60]

Both in Mesoamerica and Central Java, the conquerors occupied the land and proceeded to organize labor to produce crops and goods for sale in newly established markets. The native peasantry did not command the requisite culturally developed skills and resources to participate in the development of large-scale enterprises for profit. In both areas, therefore, the peasantry was forced to supply labor to the new enterprises, but barred from direct participation in the resultant returns. In both areas, moreover, the conquerors also seized control of large-scale trade, and deprived the native population of direct access to sources of wealth acquired through trade, such as they had commanded in the pre-conquest past.[61]

Yet in both areas, the peasantry — forced to work on colonist enter-

[54] Gibson, 1955, p. 600.
[55] Furnivall, 1939, p. 13.
[56] *Idem*, p. 12.
[57] Klaveren, 1953, p. 152.
[58] Furnivall, 1939, p. 11.
[59] See e.g. Simkhovitsch, 1898, pp. 46–81.
[60] The concept of a "dual" structure of colonial societies has been advanced by Boeke, 1953. It is not necessary to subscribe to all parts of the author's theory, nor to his predictions regarding the future, to appreciate the utility of his concept in the analysis of social and cultural systems.
[61] For Java, see Furnivall, 1939, pp. 43–44; Kolff, 1929, p. 111; Leur, 1955, p. 92; Schrieke, 1955, pp. 3–79; for Mesoamerica, see Gibson, 1955, pp. 586–587.

prises — did not become converted into a permanent labor force. The part-time laborer continued to draw the larger share of his subsistence from his own efforts on the land. From the point of view of the entrepreneurial sector, the peasant sector remained primarily a labor reserve where labor could maintain itself at no cost to the enterprises. This served to maintain the importance of land in peasant life. At the same time, and in both areas, land in the hands of the peasantry had to be limited in amount, or the peasantry would not have possessed sufficient incentive to offer its labor to the entrepreneurial sector. It is significant in this regard that the relation between peasant and entrepreneur was not "feudal." No economic, political, or legal tie bound a particular peasant to a particular colonist. In the absence of such personal, face-to-face bonds, only changes in the general conditions underlying the entire peasant economy could assure the entrepreneurs of a sufficient seasonal supplement to their small number of resident laborers. This was accomplished in Mesoamerica in the course of the enforced settlement of the Indian population in nucleated communities during the last decades of the 16th century and the first decade of the 17th. By restricting the amount of land in the hands of each Indian community to six and one-half square miles, the Crown obtained land for the settlement of Spanish colonists.[62] A similar process of limiting the land frontier of the native population was introduced in Java. If access to land thus remained important to the peasantry, land itself became a scarce resource and subject to intense competition, especially when the peasant population began to grow in numbers.

With possibilities for accumulation limited to money-wages obtained in part-time employment and to occasional sales of agricultural produce or products of home crafts at low prices, peasant agriculture remained dependent on the expenditure of labor, a labor furnished by growing numbers of people living off a limited or decreasing amount of land. The technology of the peasantry thus remained labor-intensive, when compared with the capital-intensive and equipment-intensive colonist enterprises. Peasant technology is often described as "backward" or "tradition-bound," in disregard of many items such as second-hand Singer sewing machines, steel needles, iron pots, nails, tin-cans, factory-woven goods, aniline dyes and paints, etc. which may be found in the peasant inventory. It is backward only because the peasant is a captive of the labor-intensive technology with which he must operate. He must always weigh the adoption of a new good against the balance of his resources. This balance includes not only financial or technical resources, but also "resources in people" to whom he must maintain access by maintaining proper cultural behavior. These human relations he could only disregard at the price of sharply increasing life risks. The labor-intensive tech-

[62] Zavala and Miranda, 1954, p. 73.

nology in turn limits the amounts and kinds of technological change and capitalization which he can afford, as well as his consumption and his needs.

The social and economic dualization of post-conquest Mesoamerica and Java was also accompanied in both areas by dualization in the administrative sphere. By placing the native communities under the direct jurisdiction of a special corps of officials responsible to the home government rather than to officials set up by the colonists, the home government attempted to maintain control over the native population and to deny this control to the colonists. By granting relative autonomy to the native communities, the home government could at one and the same time ensure the maintenance of cultural barriers against colonist encroachment, while avoiding the huge cost of direct administration. Thus, in Mesoamerica, the Crown insisted on the spatial separation of native peasants and colonists,[63] and furthered the organization of the native population into nucleated communities with their own relatively autonomous government. It charged these native authorities with the right and duty to collect tribute, organize corvée labor and to exercise formal and informal sanctions in the maintenance of peace and order.[64] In Java, the government relied from the beginning on the coöperation of the autonomous communities, by making use of the traditional channels of intermediate chieftainship. Administrative "contact with village society was limited to a minimum." [65] After a period characterized by emphasis on individualism and distrust of native communalism during the second half of the 19th century, the Dutch administration reverted to reliance on the closed corporate peasant community at the beginning of the 20th century.[66]

Once the dualized system of administration began to operate, however, the colonists themselves found that they could often use it to their own advantage. In Central Java the sugar industry has preferred to rent land in block from native villages, and to draw on the total supply of labor in the village, rather than to make deals with individual villagers. Since sugar can be rotated with rice, such rental agreements have usually specified that sugar cultivation by the colonist enterprise could be followed by food production on the same land by native peasants in an orderly rotational cycle. Thus

> the sugar cultivation of the estates and the rice and other cultivations of the population are, as it were, co-ordinated in one large-scale agricultural enterprise, the management of which is practically in the hands of the sugar factory.[67]

[63] Zavala and Miranda, 1954, pp. 38–39.
[64] Aguirre, 1952b, p. 291; Chávez Orozco, 1943, p. 8; Gibson, 1955, p. 590; Zavala and Miranda, 1954, p. 82.
[65] Kroef, 1953, p. 201. See also Furnivall, 1939, pp. 118, 126, 217.
[66] Furnivall, 1939, pp. 182–187, 294–295.
[67] Kolff, 1929, p. 111. See also Haar, 1948, p. 85; Kolff, 1929, pp. 122–124; Pieters, 1951, p. 130; S'Jacob, 1951, pp. 144–145.

In the last years before World War II, the total area of land rented from native corporate communities did not exceed 100,000 hectares or 3 per cent of irrigated rice land. In boom years it might have been 6 per cent. But sugar production was concentrated in Central Java, and there covered a large part of the arable area.[68] I have argued elsewhere that a somewhat similar symbiotic relation between corporate peasant community and colonist enterprise can be discovered in Mesoamerica. There even the voracious haciendas reached a point in their growth where absorption of corporate peasant communities into the estates put too great a strain on the control mechanisms at their disposal, and where they found systematic relations with such communities on their borders beneficial and useful.[69]

Within the native sector, administrative charges in both areas were thus placed largely on the community as a whole, and only secondarily on the individual. This was especially true of tribute payments and labor services. In Central Java the demands on land-holders became so great

> that land-holding was no longer a privilege but a burden which occupants tried to share with others. . . . Again, in many parts of Java, the liability to service on public works was confined by custom to land-holders; and, as officials wished to increase the number of hands available for public works, and the people themselves wished to distribute and reduce the burden of service on such works, it was to the interest of both officials and land-holders that the occupation of land should be widely shared. This encouraged communal possession and obliterated hereditary social distinctions.[70]

In Mesoamerica also, tribute and labor charges were imposed on the whole community during the 16th and 17th centuries. Only around the beginning of the 18th century were they charged to individuals.[71] The constant decrease of the Indian population until the mid-17th century, the flight of Indians into remote refuge-areas, the exodus of Indians to the northern periphery of Mesoamerica and to permanent settlements on colonist enterprises all left the fixed tribute-payments and corvée charges in the hands of the remnant population. It is reasonable to suppose that these economic pressures accelerated tendencies towards greater egalitarianism and levelling, in Mesoamerica as in Java. It is possible that the disappearance of status distinctions between nobles and commoners and the rise of religious sodalities as dispensers of wealth in religious ceremonial were in part consequences of this levelling tendency.

It is my contention that the closed corporate peasant community in both areas represents a response to these several characteristics of the larger society. Relegation of the peasantry to the status of part-time laborers, providing for their own subsistence on scarce land, together with the imposition of charges levied and enforced by semi-autonomous local

[68] Pieters, 1951, p. 131.
[69] Wolf, 1956.
[70] Furnivall, 1939, pp. 140–141.
[71] Zavala and Miranda, 1954, p. 85.

authorities, tends to define the common life situation which confronts the peasantry of both societies. The closed corporate peasant community is an attempt to come to grips with this situation. Its internal function, as opposed to its external function in the social, economic, and political web of the dualized society, is to equalize the life chances and life risks of its members.

The life risks of a peasantry are raised by any threat to its basic source of livelihood, the land, and to the produce which is raised on that land. These threats come both from within and without the community. Natural population increase within the community would serve to decrease the amount of land available to members of the community, as would unrestricted purchase and hoarding of land by individual community members. Thus, as long as possible, closed corporate peasant communities will tend to push off surplus population into newly-formed daughter villages. More importantly, however, they will strive to force co-members to redistribute or to destroy any pool of accumulated wealth which could potentially be used to alter the land tenure balance in favor of a few individual families or individuals. Purchase of goods produced outside the peasant sector of society and their ostentatious display also rank as major social threats, since they are prima facie evidence of an unwillingness to continue to redistribute and destroy such accumulated surplus. They are indications of an unwillingness to share the life risks of fellow villagers according to traditional cultural patterns. Among most peasant groups, as indeed among most social groups anywhere, social relations represent a sort of long-term life insurance. The extension of goods and services at any given moment is expected to yield results in the future, in the form of help in case of threat. Departure from the customary distribution of risks, here signalled by a departure from the accepted disposal of surpluses, is a cause for immediate concern for the corporately organized peasantry, and for its immediate opposition. Similarly, unrestricted immigration and unrestricted purchase of land by outsiders would both serve to decrease the amount of land available to community members, as it would endanger the pattern of distribution of risks developed by community members over time. Hence the maintenance of strong defenses against the threatening outsider. It must be emphasized that these defenses are required, because the closed corporate community is situated within a dualized capitalist society. They are neither simple "survivals," nor the results of "culture lag," nor due to some putative tendency to conservatism said to be characteristic of all culture. They do not illustrate the "contemporaneousness of the non-contemporaneous." They exist, because their functions *are* contemporaneous.

This is not to say that their defensive functions are ultimately adequate to the challenge. The disappearance of closed corporate peasant communities where they have existed in the past, and the lessening number of surviving communities of this type, testify to the proposition that in the long run they are incapable of preventing change. Internal population surpluses can be pushed off into daughter villages only as long as new land is available. Retained within the boundaries of the community, they exercise ever-increasing pressure on its capacity to serve the interests of its members. The corporate community may then be caught in a curious dilemma: it can maintain its integrity only if it can sponsor the emigration and urbanization or proletarianization of its sons. If the entrepreneurial sector is unable to accept these newcomers, these truly "marginal" men will come to represent a double threat: a threat to their home community into which they introduce new ways and needs; and a threat to the peace of the non-peasant sector which they may undermine with demands for social and economic justice, often defended with the desperation of men who have but little to lose.

Secondly, while the closed corporate peasant community operates to diminish inequalities of risks, it can never eliminate them completely. Individual member families may suffer losses of crops, livestock, or other assets through accident or mismanagement. Some member families may be exceedingly fertile and have many mouths to feed, while others are infertile and able to get along with little. Individuals whose life risks are suddenly increased due to the play of some such factor must seek the aid of others who can help them. Some of these risks can be met through the culturally standardized social relations of mutual aid and support; some, however, will strain these relations beyond their capacity. Individuals may then in desperation seek aid from members of their community or from outsiders whose aid is tinged with self-interest. It would seem that even the most efficient prestige economy cannot be counted on to dispose of all surplus wealth in the community. Pools of such wealth tend to survive in the hands of local figures, such as political leaders, or nobles, or usurers, or store-keepers. Such individuals are often exempt from the everyday controls of the local community, because they occupy a privileged position within the economic or political apparatus of the larger society; or they are people who are willing to pay the price of social ostracism for the rewards of a pursuit of profit and power. Such individuals offer the needy peasant a chance to reduce his risks momentarily through loans or favors. In turn, the peasant in becoming their client, strengthens the degree of relative autonomy and immunity which they enjoy in the community. Such internal alliances must weaken communal defenses to a point where the corporate organization comes to represent but a hollow shell, or is swept aside entirely.[72]

REFERENCES CITED

Aguirre Beltrán, Gonzalo

1952a *Problemas de la Población Indígena de la Cuenca del Tepalcatepec* (Memorias del Instituto Nacional Indigenista, no. 3).

[72] Wolf, 1956.

1952b *El Gobierno Indígena en México y el Proceso de Aculturación* (America Indígena, vol. 12, pp. 271–297).

Aguirre Beltrán, Gonzalo, and Ricardo Pozas Arciniegas

1954 "Instituciones Indígenas en el México Actual" (in Caso et al., *Métodos y Resultados de la Política Indigenista en México*, pp. 171–272, Memorias del Instituto Nacional Indigenista, no. 6).

Beals, Ralph

1946 *Cherán: A Sierra Tarascan Village* (Smithsonian Institute of Social Anthropology, Publication no. 2).

1952 "Notes on Acculturation" (in Tax, ed., *Heritage of Conquest*, pp. 225–231, Glencoe: Free Press).

Boeke, J. H.

1953 *Economics and Economic Policy of Dual Societies: As Exemplified by Indonesia* (New York: Institute of Pacific Relations).

Cámara Barbachano, Fernando

1952 "Religious and Political Organization" (in Tax, ed., *Heritage of Conquest*, pp. 142–164, Glencoe: Free Press).

Carrasco, Pedro

1951 *Las Culturas Indígenas de Oaxaca, México* (America Indígena, vol. 11, pp. 99–114).

1952 *Tarascan Folk Religion: An Analysis of Economic, Social and Religious Interactions* (Middle American Research Institute, Publication no. 17).

Chávez Orozco, Luis

1943 *Las Instituciones Democráticas de los Indígenas Mexicanos en la Época Colonial* (México, D.F.: Ediciones del Instituto Indigenista Interamericano).

Fei, Hsiao-Tung

1953 *China's Gentry* (Chicago: University of Chicago Press).

Foster, George M.

1948 *The Folk Economy of Rural Mexico with Special Reference to Marketing* (Journal of Marketing, vol. 12, pp. 153–162).

Fried, Morton H.

1953 *Fabric of Chinese Society* (New York: Praeger).

Fukutake, Tadashi

1951 *Chūgoku Nōson Shakai no Kōzō* [Structure of Chinese Rural Society] (Tokyo: Yūhikaku Publishing Co.).

Furnivall, J. S.

1939 *Netherlands India: A Study of Plural Economy* (Cambridge: Cambridge University Press).

Geertz, Clifford

1956 *Religious Belief and Economic Behavior in a Central Javanese Town* (Economic Development and Cultural Change, vol. 4, pp. 134–158).

Gibson, Charles

1955 *The Transformation of the Indian Community in New Spain 1500–1810* (Journal of World History, vol. 2, pp. 581–607).

Gillin, John

1952 "Ethos and Cultural Aspects of Personality" (in Tax, ed., *Heritage of Conquest*, pp. 193–212, Glencoe: Free Press).

González Navarro, Moisés
1954 "Instituciones Indígenas en México Independiente" (in Caso et al., *Métodos y Resultados de la Política Indigenista en México*, pp. 113–169, Memorias del Instituto Nacional Indigenista, no. 6).

Guiteras Holmes, Calixta
1952 "Social Organization" (in Tax, ed., *Heritage of Conquest*, pp. 97–108, Glencoe: Free Press).

Haar, B. ter
1948 *Adatlaw in Indonesia* (New York: Institute of Pacific Relations).

Hallowell, A. Irving
1955 *Culture and Experience* (Philadelphia: University of Pennsylvania Press).

Hu, Hsien Chin
1948 *The Common Descent Group in China and its Functions* (Viking Fund Publications in Anthropology, no. 10).

Kattenburg, Paul
1951 *A Central Javanese Village in 1950* (Cornell University Department of Far Eastern Studies, Data Paper no. 2).

Kirchhoff, Paul
1952 "Mesoamerica" (in Tax, ed., *Heritage of Conquest*, pp. 17–30, Glencoe: Free Press).

Klaveren, J. J. van
1953 *The Dutch Colonial System in the East Indies* (Rotterdam: Drukkerij Benedictus).

Kolff, G. H. Van der
1929 "European Influence on Native Agriculture" (in Schrieke, ed., *The Effect of Western Influence on Native Civilizations in the Malay Archipelago*, pp. 103–125, Batavia: Kolff).

Kroef, Justus M. van der
1953 *Collectivism in Indonesian Society* (Social Research, vol. 20, pp. 193–209).
1956 *Economic Development in Indonesia: Some Social and Cultural Implications* (Economic Development and Cultural Change, vol. 4, pp. 116–133).

Landon, Kenneth Perry
1949 *Southeast Asia: Crossroad of Religions* (Chicago: University of Chicago Press).

Lekkerkerker, Cornelis
1938 *Land en Volk Van Java* (Groningen-Batavia: Wolters).

Leur, Jacob Cornelis Van der
1955 *Indonesian Trade and Society: Essay in Asian Social and Economic History* (The Hague-Bandung: W. Van Hoeve Ltd.).

Lewis, Oscar
1951 *Life in a Mexican Village: Tepoztlán Revisited* (Urbana: University of Illinois Press).

Linton, Ralph
1936 *The Study of Man* (New York: Appleton-Century).

McBride, George McCutchen
1923 *The Land Systems of Mexico* (New York: American Geographical Society).

Miranda, José
1952 *El Tributo Indígena en la Nueva España durante el Siglo XVI* (México, D.F.: El Colegio de México).
Monzón, Arturo
1949 *El Calpulli en la Organización Social de los Tenochca* (México, D.F.: Instituto de Historia).
Moore, Wilbert E., and Melvin M. Tumin
1949 *Some Social Functions of Ignorance* (American Sociological Review, vol. 14, pp. 787–795).
Oei, Tjong Bo
1948 *Niederländisch-Indien: eine Wirtschaftsstudie* (Zürich: Institut Orell Füssli A.G.).
Pieters, J. M.
1951 "Land Policy in the Netherlands East Indies before the Second World War" (in Afrika Instituut Leiden, org., *Land Tenure Symposium Amsterdam 1950*, pp. 116–139, Leiden: Universitaure Pers Leiden).
Ploegsma, Nicolas Dirk
1936 *Oorspronkelijkheid en Economisch Aspect van het Dorp op Java en Madoera* (Leiden: Antiquariaat J. Ginsberg).
Pozas Arciniegas, Ricardo
1952 *La Situation Économique et Financière de l'Indien Américain* (Civilization, vol. 2, pp. 309–329).
Redfield, Robert, and Sol Tax
1952 "General Characteristics of Present-Day Mesoamerican Indian Society" (in Tax, ed., *Heritage of Conquest*, pp. 31–39, Glencoe: Free Press).
Roscoe, John
1911 *The Baganda* (London: Macmillan).
Schrieke, Bertram J. O.
1955 *Indonesian Sociological Studies* (The Hague: W. Van Hoeve).
Simkhovitsch, Wladimir Gr.
1898 *Die Feldgemeinschaft in Russland* (Jena: Fischer).
Simpson, Eyler N.
1937 *The Ejido: Mexico's Way Out* (Chapel Hill: University of North Carolina Press).
S'Jacob, E. H.
1951 "Observations on the Development of Landrights in Indonesia" (in Afrika Instituut Leiden, org., *Land Tenure Symposium Amsterdam 1950*, pp. 140–146, Leiden: Universitaure Pers Leiden).
Supatmo, Raden
1943 *Animistic and Religious Practices of the Javanese* (New York: East Indies Institute of America, mimeo.).
Tannenbaum, Frank
1929 *The Mexican Agrarian Revolution* (Washington: Brookings Institution).
Tax, Sol
1941 *World View and Social Relations in Guatemala* (American Anthropologist, vol. 43, pp. 27–42).
1952 "Economy and Technology" (in Tax, ed., *Heritage of Conquest*, pp. 43–65, Glencoe: Free Press).

1953 *Penny Capitalism: A Guatemalan Indian Economy* (Smithsonian Institution Institute of Social Anthropology, Publication no. 16).

Tumin, Melvin M.

1950 *The Hero and the Scapegoat in a Peasant Community* (Journal of Personality, vol. 19, pp. 197–211).

1952 *Caste in a Peasant Society* (Princeton: Princeton University Press).

Vandenbosch, A.

1942 *The Dutch East Indies* (Berkeley: University of California Press).

Wagley, Charles

1941 *Economics of a Guatemalan Village* (Memoirs, American Anthropological Association, no. 58).

Whetten, Nathan L.

1948 *Rural Mexico* (Chicago: University of Chicago Press).

Wittfogel, Karl A.

1935 *Foundations and Stages of Chinese Economic History* (Zeitschrift für Sozialforschung, vol. 4, pp. 26–60).

1938 *Die Theorie der Orientalischen Gesellschaft* (Zeitschrift für Sozialforschung, vol. 7, pp. 90–122).

Wolf, Eric R.

1955 *Types of Latin American Peasantry* (American Anthropologist, vol. 57, pp. 452–471).

1956 *Aspects of Group Relations in a Complex Society: Mexico* (American Anthropologist, vol. 58, pp. 1065–1078).

———, and Angel Palerm

1955 *Irrigation in the Old Acolhua Domain, Mexico* (Southwestern Journal of Anthropology, vol. 11, pp. 265–281).

Yang, Martin

1945 *A Chinese Village: Taitou, Shantung Province* (New York: Columbia University Press).

Zavala, Silvio, and José Miranda

1954 "Instituciones Indígenas en la Colonia" (in Caso et al., *Métodos y Resultados de la Política Indigenista en México*, pp. 29–169, Memorias del Instituto Nacional Indigenista, no. 6).

The Japanese Rural Community: Norms, Sanctions, and Ostracism

Robert J. Smith

The persistence of the hamlet (*buraku*) in modern Japan is one of the most interesting evidences of continuity and stability in the

From "The Japanese Rural Community: Norms, Sanctions, and Ostracism" in *American Anthropologist*, Vol. 63, No. 2 (June 1961). Reprinted by permission of the author and the American Anthropological Association. The writer would like to acknowledge the support of the Social Science Research Center, Cornell University, for this and related research.

process of industrialization of that country. This important and still viable unit of society has been the object of study by a number of anthropologists in recent years and was dealt with at length in the classic study of Suye-mura (Beardsley, Hall, and Ward 1959; Norbeck 1954; Smith and Cornell 1956; Embree 1939).

The hamlet as a social unit shows marked solidarity even in the postwar period of increasing modernization of the countryside. Varying greatly in size, it is nevertheless a community in which face-to-face relations are far and away the most important, where every member household joins in cooperative endeavor in the maintenace of the irrigation system, roads, paths, and ditches, and where every hamlet wedding and funeral is attended by a representative of every household. Cooperative effort is, in some hamlets, extended to house construction and barn-raising, and many hamlets illegally hold common lands. A man wishing to convert one of his upland fields to paddy must, in many areas, secure the approval of the hamlet association. Buraku tend to vote as a unit in local elections, each casting its ballots for a candidate previously agreed upon as the one most likely to concern himself with the interests of the hamlet in village politics (Smith and Cornell 1956:17).

As a sub-unit of the village (*mura*) or town (*chō*) administrative unit, the buraku has no legal identity (Ward 1951:1025–1040), but it commands far more loyalty and support than any unit other than the household (*ie*). It has a head and its functions as an association are many. Although the predominant tone is one of cooperative effort, it would be an error to imagine that no tensions exist in such a community, but to a remarkable degree the individual is ready to set aside personal interest in favor of the community. Households within a buraku may feud and a man always has his enemies, but it is customary to subordinate such considerations to the requirements of community interest in what are defined as important matters.

It is precisely in the definition of what is important that the buraku reveals most clearly its essential character, for norms are clearly stated and closely sanctioned.

> When in any group or social system there is a high consensus on the *standards* of conduct, ordinary social interaction continually reinforces conformity by precept, example, approval (respect, affection, etc.), and a great variety of complex and often unconscious mechanisms. Behavior is incessantly and subtly corrected by the responses of others; firmly interdependent expectations are integrated into mutually supporting self-other patterns. Incipient nonconformity is subject to immediate and unanimous attempts at control, and overt nonconformity occasions reaffirmation of the threatened norms through disapproval and the imposition of sanctions (Williams 1960:376).

Among the various norms of a given society, those that are *institutional* for any particular person are felt as "moral imperatives" closely identified with the individual's sense of self-respect, violations of them being followed by guilt, shame, horror, self-deprecation, etc. For a whole group *or* society, probably the best index to institutional norms is the occurrence of severe penalties for violations. Such penalties are truly institutional, however, only if supported by an effective consensus of the society (Williams 1960:30).

The Japanese hamlet provides us with an excellent case in which the penalties are institutional in Williams' sense and in which the community still retains vestiges of its earlier power to enforce them through consensus. Above all, emphasis is placed on internal harmony and the presenting of a solid front to the outside world. This surface unity is specifically maintained by the imposition upon buraku members of the stricture to avoid any act which would cause the hamlet to "lose face." In fact, the hamlet will often pool its resources to prevent just such a loss of face, as in the community in which the author worked from 1951 to 1952 (Smith and Cornell 1956:17). During this period the central government was requisitioning rice on the basis of annual quotas assigned by the village office to individual households. In theory, the grain was to be turned in to the collection station by each household, but in practice each hamlet collected the quotas of all its members and submitted the total amount as a group. There was some competition among the hamlets of the village to be the first to fill its quota and it had been the practice to post the names of early-reporting hamlets on the village notice-board on the main road.

In the hamlet there were two widows who lacked any help at all on their farms and since it was clearly a severe hardship for them to submit any grain, all the other member households joined to make up the amount officially required of these two women. In the official report the fiction is maintained that the women did submit their rice. Now this action accomplished several things. First, it permitted the buraku to submit its quota early, thus gaining for it some prestige in the village. Second, it spared both the widows and the community the loss of face which would have followed their failure to meet their quotas, for the government would otherwise have forced a sale of grain. Third, it demonstrated to all the residents of the hamlet, to the two women concerned, and to any outsider who cared to take note that the community takes pride in its group spirit and is still able to care for its own.

The hamlet is, then, a unit in which the individual has a considerable psychological investment. He will subordinate much of his individuality to its requirements and pressures on the analogy of his subordination of personal interests to those of his household. All residents of a hamlet are more or less actively concerned for its reputation and say slightingly of communities which seem less concerned with such matters that they "know no shame."

How does the hamlet ensure the participation of its members in cooperative activities? As in most small communities, gossip is a powerful sanction, being one of the ways in which subtle correction of inappropriate behavior is attempted. As Williams has pointed out in the quotation above, incipient nonconformity is subject to immediate attempts at control. Should a household fail to provide an adequate feast for those attending a wedding of one of its members, tongues will wag. If the daughter of a household is thought too free with her affections, word will get back to her family very quickly. Were a man to build what others consider an overly pretentious house, people will comment on his lack of judgment and label him a fool. Should a man prove always contentious in meetings of the hamlet association, there are many indirect ways to let him know that he is going too far. There are, then, many norms which a household or an individual may violate that are not particularly firmly promoted by the community and for violation of which the penalties are rather mild. The residents of a hamlet can, by these means, usually insure a degree of conformity on the part of potentially disturbing elements. As Cornell has pointed out:

> There is a high correlation between public disfavor of an individual and the degree to which he has violated approved patterns of behavior. Theft and adultery produce the most serious social disturbances, but profligacy, indolence, extreme self-interest, and idle gossip also contribute a goodly share (Smith and Cornell 1956:230).

Norbeck reports that:

> The nonconformist has greater difficulty than the physically abnormal in adapting himself to the community. Social sanctions for the nonconformist begin with ridicule and may extend to avoidance and dislike (Norbeck 1954:117–118).

There are, inevitably, some people against whom these relatively mild sanctions are imposed in vain. Twenty years ago Embree (1939:174) reported that the common solution for the "individualist" misfit was to emigrate and, although the colonies no longer exist to drain off such people, migration to the cities is still a possibility. This is a course of action more easily taken by an individual than by a family or household, however, which means that there may be resident in a hamlet an individual who cannot or will not move, or a household generally disliked by the rest of the community. Such people are described as unneighborly or difficult and are a constant irritant, refusing to adhere to the customary usages of the hamlet, being niggardly with money and produce, and failing to give their wholehearted support to community projects.

Faced with such a problem, the buraku will try by all means at its disposal to make allowances for the troublemaker while attempting to force him back into line. Trouble in any form is disliked and a buraku will go to great lengths to avoid internal dissension for fear that it may lead to a permanent scar on the placid face of community relations.

> Hamlet solidarity implies . . . an explicit acceptance of the value of harmony in the hamlet. Factional rivalries, which often exist, are kept below the surface, and when they break out into open conflict, as they sometimes do with a bitterness intensified by long repression, there is general distress and any one in a position to do so lends a hand in mediation and pacification (Dore 1959:361).

Open breaches do occur within hamlets, then, and it is worthy of note that these almost always follow violation of a universally held obligatory norm. There are limits to the deviance tolerated by a hamlet and when these limits are passed, the buraku may move to impose the ultimate sanction at its disposal, the ostracism of a member household. This practice is known as *mura-hachibu,* meaning literally "village eight-parts" and refers to the virtually complete severing of community ties with an offending household. The etymology of this word is in doubt, but at least one authority (Takeuchi 1938) holds that it derives from the word *hajiku* (to repel, to reject, to snap). There are, however, other folk-etymologies, one of which is worth noting here. It is often said that there are "ten parts" to relationships within a hamlet. These are occasions upon which some kind of aid or joint ceremonial participation among member households occur and are (1) rites of passage linked with the life-cycle, (2) marriage and wedding ceremonies, (3) death and funeral observances, (4) construction of buildings, (5) fires, (6) sickness, (7) floods or water damage, (8) leaving on a journey, (9) birth and related ceremonies, and (10) memorial observances for the ancestors.[1]

The contention is that an ostracized household can expect help on only two of these ten occasions; thus, eight parts of the relationship with other member households are abrogated. In one prefecture, for example, it is reported that only in the event of death in a household or a natural disaster will other members of the hamlet rally round. In another area, the "two parts" remaining are extension of aid after a fire and attendance at weddings in the ostracized household.

Ostracism does not now mean that the household is actually forced to remove from the settlement, although two or three generations ago this was sometimes done.[2] In former days there were at least three categories of offense against hamlet norms which merited this punishment.

[1] These are respectively, *kan, kon, sō, kenchiku, kaji, byōki, suigai, ryokō, shussan* and *nenki.*

[2] Arai (1959:176) maintains that in feudal Japan exile was considered a far more serious sanction than ostracism, since the latter permitted the offender to continue to reside in the community. An exile (*mura-kando*) was ejected from the community physically and was free to go anywhere, but he could not re-enter the village. Arai points out that this was a satisfactory solution from the village point of view but that it made a great deal of trouble for society at large by throwing into it a small, irresponsible population of drifters. The central government of Tokugawa (1615–1868) actually urged villagers to keep the offender in the community as a pariah and legislation repeatedly recommended that such a family be forced to live in a small hut on the edge of the community. It is clear from this evidence that the formalization of village sanctions owed much to external pressures by feudal authorities rather than representing a simple evolution within buraku society itself.

They were: (1) starting a fire through carelessness, (2) setting a fire deliberately, and (3) murder. It is the more usual practice for a mura-hachibu to be permitted to remain in the settlement subject to virtually complete cutting of ties with other households. This is a severe hardship in an agricultural buraku, for it deprives a household of all aid which they might otherwise expect to receive. Neighbors who formerly helped with making rice seed beds, transplanting, harvesting, and threshing will not aid the mura-hachibu. No one will visit him or greet him on the road. The ostracized household may not attend hamlet association meetings where important decisions are made, nor may it employ such community facilities as exist. Marriage of its sons becomes difficult, since few would risk sending their daughters to an ostracized household, and the stigma of being a member of such a houschold would be a formidable obstacle to a girl's chance for marriage. Where the offense is considered particularly heinous, even small children of the household will be shunned by adults and schoolmates alike, but often avoidance is directed chiefly at the adult members of the household (Kida 1957:86).

Before proceeding to a discussion of some representative cases, it would be well to point out that the practice of mura-hachibu has, in a number of court decisions, been found illegal and in recent years has been specifically labeled "a violation of human rights." Consequently, the practice of mura-hachibu is an extreme example of the imposition of extra-legal sanctions by a community in an effort to preserve internal harmony.

The accounts of how ostracism actually comes about are agreed in their essentials, although there are regional variations not only in the name for the practice but in procedural matters. One hamlet household brings a complaint against another; the hamlet association reaches a unanimous decision (majority decisions ordinarily are not recognized in rural Japanese deliberations) for ostracism; a formal document is drawn up notifying the offending household of its exclusion from the social life of the community, often beginning with the charge that "they disturbed the harmony of the otherwise peaceful community" (Steiner 1956:198). Dore (1959:490–491), translating a Japanese source, offers a remarkable series of documents. The offense was the theft of some heads of millet from a field, the culprit having been caught in the act. The documents comprise (1) a letter from the hamlet association announcing the expulsion of the offender's household for one year, (2) a letter of commendation from the hamlet association to the man who had apprehended the thief and reported the theft, and (3) a letter, countersigned by a guarantor, from the head of the ostracized household to the hamlet association, apologizing for the misdeed and accepting the punishment.

The family appears to have been an old, well-established one which had gradually been losing its former power in village affairs. There is reason to believe that the punishment, which was largely vindictive, was engineered by a new power group of families which formerly had little influence in the community. Only one other family, also on the wane as a power in the village, had been punished according to the same set of rules.

Although some features of this case are unusual, as we shall see, an important fact stands out as characteristic of Japanese society. That is, of course, that the household is held accountable for the acts of all its members. Since the hamlet association is made up of member households, not of individuals, it follows that sanctions for deviant behavior are imposed upon an entire household. What is less ordinary about this particular case is first the fact that the period of ostracism is specified. While it happens that a mura-hachibu is often readmitted to the community, this usually occurs only after some time has elapsed and a variety of negotiations entered into. The second unusual feature is that ordinarily a single theft would not be sufficient to bring about ostracism. Even petty thievery, especially when it is defined as kleptomania, will move most people only to keep things out of reach or to watch the pilferer to see that he has no opportunity to steal (Smith and Cornell 1956:204; Norbeck 1954:117). It is, in fact, not so much from a desire to protect the household of a thief, but rather to preserve the hamlet's good name that theft is covered up. Should pilfering really get out of hand, however, the hamlet may mobilize itself to meet the mounting threat to community harmony.

The two offenses against the community which are most likely to lead to ostracism are exposing the community to a public loss of face and disturbing the peace and harmony of the hamlet. At least five other kinds of action are thought to have one or both of these undesirable effects:

1. Reporting any community decision or action with which one disagrees to the police or other formal authority, or making it public in any way not ordinarily approved by the hamlet.
2. Failing to maintain an established obligation with other hamlet households, including failure to participate in hamlet sacred and secular group observances such as shrine festivals, association meetings, and meetings of the mutual credit association where these exist.
3. Failing to acquiesce in a decision of the hamlet association.
4. Petty thievery, although this is by no means as universally sanctioned by eventual ostracism as are the first three.
5. Exhibiting a tendency to hostility and to making deliberately critical and undiplomatic statements in public, thus shaming and disturbing others.

It is not surprising, then, that the people most liable to ostracism by their fellow hamlet members are:

1. Those who have an established reputation for being unneighborly, who are said to be sharp dealers and chronic objectors to hamlet decisions.
2. Households which are more affluent than others in the hamlet and

thus need not fear the loss of cooperative aid, or against whom vengeful action is at last being taken by long resentful hamlet members.

3. Households not primarily engaged in agriculture nor dependent upon it for a livelihood who might, if shopkeepers, lose the trade of their own hamlet but not that of the village generally.

4. Those who commit a single outrageous offense so intolerable as to mobilize the hamlet to swift action, but who may have no other history of deviance or hostility.

All of these types are people who are willing to flaunt buraku regulations in some way, who take obvious and frequent advantage of what Williams calls "a 'permissive' zone of variation around even the most specific and strongly supported norms" (Williams 1960:373). But even such people, who might easily ignore pressures to conformity, usually will not do so. This is not so much because economic sanctions are any longer particularly threatening, but because a household ordinarily simply does not want to be socially isolated.

> In a strict sense, to suppress individual wants for the sake of . . . solidarity is voluntary, not compulsory: but the penalties and risks of a contrary course are considerable (Beardsley, Hall, and Ward 1959:258).

There is one remaining point to be made. Given the kind of community which the Japanese buraku is, and given the style of life found in most such communities, it comes as no surprise to discover that the maintenance of this formal sanction places a strain upon the hamlet. Not the least of the parties inconvenienced is the village office, which must deal with the mura-hachibu entirely apart from his former hamlet, sending out two copies of all notices and requests where one was sent before. The presence in the midst of a hamlet of one ostracized household is at best an inconvenience. First, with the loss of a household, many gaps appear in hamlet groupings — the youth clubs, the women's clubs, shrine groups, work gangs, and mutual labor groupings. Second, the presence of a mura-hachibu is a clear notice to the rest of the world that the hamlet was, in the final analysis, unable to secure conformity and "right behavior" from one of its members. Third, it should not be forgotten that a mura-hachibu household usually has some friends and probably some relatives in the hamlet and, although ostracism was unanimously agreed upon, this does not preclude the existence of some sentiment for eventual readmission of the household. While it may be far from their thoughts at the time of expelling the offenders, the hamlet households, as well as the mura-hachibu themselves, eventually begin to consider ways of healing the rupture in community relations.

Restoration of equal status would be to the advantage of all concerned, for the inconvenience is in many ways mutual, but it is usually required that the mura-hachibu submit a written admission of wrong-doing and an apology, together with a formal request for readmission to the hamlet. The obvious implication is that the wrong is entirely with the offenders and that only complete confession of error will serve to reconfirm the rightness of the hamlet's reaction to deviation from its norms. It is true, nevertheless, that these formal apologies are usually secured only after elaborate and more or less secret negotiations between the hamlet association and the mura-hachibu, through the services of a go-between. This go-between is most often a relative or friend of the ostracized household who does not reside in the same hamlet, or he may be a powerful man in the village who has been asked by the offender or the association to exert his influence in restoring relations between the two parties. As in so many other contexts in Japanese society, the use of a go-between insures both parties against loss of face in the event that the discussions are broken off. If the talks are successful, however, the go-between agrees to serve as guarantor for the mura-hachibu and at a meeting of the hamlet association it is he who makes the actual presentation of the letter of contrition while the head of the offending household sits in the lowest seat of the gathering. The go-between also presents on behalf of the mura-hachibu a nominal sum of money and some *sake* to the group. The association, acknowledging the aid of the intermediary, publicly announces the readmission of the household and its restoration to its former status.

It is restored at least in theory. People do not forget, of course, that a certain household was at one time ostracized and the fact may be mentioned to the inquisitive outsider. Such a family must take a bit more than ordinary care to see that it does nothing to indicate bad faith with the hamlet. But by and large, status is restored, and, in the village studied by the author, the head of the household which had been ostracized thirty years before while he was still a small boy was head of the hamlet association, a position which in its normal rotation about the twenty-odd houses of the buraku had again come to his.

In terms of the institutionalization of norms and sanctions, the buraku of Japan affords an example of a social grouping based on residence in which the status of violators of obligatory norms may ultimately be determined by consensus of the community. However much the power of the buraku may have waned in recent years, it can still, in many parts of Japan and for a variety of offenses, invoke the threat of ostracism as a powerful deterrent to the deviant.

REFERENCES CITED

Arai, Kōjirō
1959 "Seisai" (Sanctions). *Nihon Minzokugaku Taikei* (Outline of Japanese Ethnology) 4:173–188. Tokyo: Heibonsha.

Beardsley, Richard K., John W. Hall, and Robert E. Ward
1959 *Village Japan*. Chicago: University of Chicago Press.

Dore, Ronald P.
1959 *Land Reform in Japan*. London: Oxford University Press.

Embree, John F.
1939 *Suye Mura, a Japanese Village*. Chicago: University of Chicago Press.
Fukutake Tadashi, ed.
1954 *Nihon nōson shakai-no kōzō bunseki* (Structural Analysis of Japanese Agricultural Village Society). Tokyo: Tokyo Daigaku Shuppan Kai.
Kida, Minoru
1957 "The Laws of the *Buraku*." *Japan Quarterly* 4:(1)77–88.
Norbeck, Edward
1954 *Takashima, a Japanese Fishing Community*. Salt Lake City: University of Utah Press.
Smith, Robert J., and John B. Cornell
1956 *Two Japanese Villages*. Ann Arbor: University of Michigan Press.
Steiner, Kurt
1956 "The Japanese Village and Its Government." *Far Eastern Quarterly* 15:(2)185–200.
Takeuchi, Toshimi
1930 "Mura no seisai" (Village Sanctions). *Shakai Keizai Shigaku* (Social and Economic History Society) 8:(6)1–31.
Ward, Robert E.
1951 "The Socio-political Role of the *Buraku* (hamlet) in Japan." *American Political Science Review* 45:(4)1025–1040.
Williams, Robin M., Jr.
1960 *American Society*. New York: A. A. Knopf, 2nd edition.

Form and Variation in Balinese Village Structure

Clifford Geertz

As all things Balinese, Balinese villages are peculiar, complicated, and extraordinarily diverse. There is no simple uniformity of social structure to be found over the whole of the small, crowded countryside, no straightforward form of village organization easily pictured in terms of single typological construction, no "average" village, a description of which may well stand for the whole. Rather, there is a set of marvelously complex social systems, no one of which is quite like any other, no one of which fails to show some marked peculiarity of form. Even contiguous villages may be quite differently organized; formal elements — such as

From "Form and Variation in Balinese Village Structure" in *American Anthropologist*, Vol. 61, No. 6 (December 1959). Reprinted by permission of the author and the American Anthropological Association. The field work upon which this study is based was carried out from August 1957 to July 1958, with a three month break from January to March 1958, under a grant from the social sciences section of the Rockefeller Foundation, administered by the Center for International Studies, Massachusetts Institute of Technology. I am indebted to

caste or kinship — of central importance in one village may be of marginal significance in another; and each of the twenty-five or so villages sampled in the Tabanan and Klungkung regions of south Bali in 1957 — a total area of only some 450 square miles — showed important structural features in some sense idiosyncratic with respect to the others. Neither simplicity nor uniformity are Balinese virtues.

Yet all these small-scale social systems are clearly of a family. They represent variations, however intricate, on a common set of organizational themes, so that what is constant in Balinese village structure is the set of components out of which it is constructed, not the structure itself. These components are in themselves discrete, more or less independent of one another: the Balinese village is in no sense a corporate territorial unit coordinating all aspects of life in terms of residence and land ownership, as peasant villages have commonly been described, but it is rather a compound of social structures, each based on a different principle of social affiliation and adjusted to one another only insofar as seems essential. It is this multiple, composite nature of Balinese village structure which makes possible its high degree of variation while maintaining a general formal type, for the play between the several discrete structural forms is great enough to allow a wide range of choice as to the mode of their integration with one another in any particular instance. Like so many organic compounds composed of the same molecules arranged in different configurations, Balinese villages display a wide variation in structure on the basis of a set of invariant fundamental ingredients.

Perhaps the best systematic formulation of this type of village structure is to conceptualize it in terms of the intersection of theoretically separable planes of social organization. Each such plane consists of a set of social institutions based on a wholly different principle of affiliation, a different manner of grouping individuals or keeping them apart. In any particular village all important planes will be present, but the way in which they are adjusted to one another, the way in which they intersect, will differ, for there is no clear principle in terms of which this intersection must be formed. The analysis of village structure therefore consists in first discriminating the organizational planes of significance and then describing the manner in which, in actual fact, they intersect.

In Bali, seven such planes are of major significance, based on: (1) shared obligation to worship at a given temple, (2) common residence, (3) ownership of rice land lying within a single watershed, (4) commonality of ascribed social status or caste, (5) consanguineal and affinal kinship ties, (6) common membership in one or another "voluntary"

---

my research assistant E. Rukasah of the Fakultas Pertanian in Bogor, Indonesia, and to my wife Hildred Geertz for significant contributions to this study. This paper was written during a fellowship at the Center for Advanced Study in the Behavioral Sciences, and I am indebted to many of my colleagues at the Center for their criticism and comments on earlier drafts. For general views of Balinese culture, see Bateson and Mead (1942), Covarrubias (1936) and Korn (1936).

organization, and (7) common legal subordination to a single government administrative official. In the following paper, I will first analyze each of these planes of organization, then describe three villages as examples of differing modes of intersection of these planes, and finally offer a discussion of some of the theoretical implications of this type of village organization.

PLANES OF SOCIAL ORGANIZATION

1. Shared Obligation to Worship at a Given Temple. Bali is a land of temples. One sees them everywhere — under the village banyan tree, in the midst of rice fields, by waterfalls, in the centers of large towns, by a graveyard, at the sea edge, on a lake island, in every houseyard, at the mountain top — everywhere; of all sizes and in all conditions of repair; all or most showing the traditional form: the high brick walls, the intricately carved split gate, the tall pagodalike altars with their storeyed thatched roofs.[1] And there are no ruins in Bali: to each of these thousands of temples there is attached both an hereditary priest and a definite congregation of worshipers obligated to perform detailed ritual activities within its walls at fixed intervals, most commonly every six months. Such a congregation is said to *njungsung* the temple — literally to carry it on its head, as women carry nearly everything in Bali, including the elaborate offerings they bring to the temples on festival days.[2] Every family in Bali, unless it be Christian or Moslem, carries at least a half dozen temples — called *pura* — on its head.

Of the great variety of pura, by far the most important to the Balinese are the *Kahyangan-Tiga*. *Kahyangan* is an honorific word for temple (meaning literally "place of the gods"), indicating a pura of unusual importance, and *tiga* means three — thus, "the three great temples." There are probably over a thousand sets of such temples in Bali, with membership ranging from fifty up to several thousand families; the three temples concerned in any particular locality are the *Pura Puseh*, or origin temple, theoretically the temple built at the time of the first settlement of the area; the *Pura Dalam*, or graveyard temple for the spirits of the local dead; and the *Pura Balai Agung*, or "great council temple" (of the gods), dedicated primarily to maintaining the fertility of the surrounding rice fields. At the first two of these temples festivals are held once in every 210-day Balinese year, at the third once in a lunar year, the specific days depending upon the tradition of the individual temples. At such festival times the gods are conceived to descend from heaven, remain for three days, and then return to their home, and the congregation is obligated to entertain them during the time of their stay by means of complex offerings, elaborate rituals, and skillful artistic performances under

[1] For a more detailed description of Balinese temple forms, see Covarrubias (1936).

[2] A Balinese temple festival is described in detail in Belo (1953).

the general direction of the temple priest and the secular head of the temple. The cost of the festivals, the rather large amounts of labor involved, and the general upkeep of the temples falls on each member of the congregation equally, and this group is typically organized in some fairly complicated manner to achieve these ends.

As mentioned, Kahyangan-Tiga membership is defined territorially, each Balinese belonging to just one of the sets. Nevertheless, one cannot say, as have most scholars, that he belongs to the temple of his "village," and thus that Kahyangan-Tiga can be translated "the three village temples," because only in the limiting case are the boundaries of the basic territorial political unit, here called the hamlet, and of the Kahyangan-Tiga congregation coterminous; in most instances, the religious and political units are not coordinate but cross-cut one another. Whatever the Balinese village may or may not be, it is not simply definable as all people worshiping at one set of Kahyangan-Tiga, because people so obligated to worship commonly form a group for no other social function — political, economic, familiar, or whatever. The congregation of the Kahyangan-Tiga is, in essence, a specifically religious body; in most cases it comes together only at the obligatory temple festivals.[3] Thus, the oft-repeated and much-loved rites at these temples serve to form one crucial bond among rural Balinese of a generally territorial sort, but this bond balances off against other bonds formed in terms of more concretely social activities rather than, as is typical of religious ties, directly reinforcing them.

Besides the Kahyangan-Tiga there are dozens of other types of temples, with different bases in terms of which their congregations are formed: there are ricefield temples, at which worship the men who own land within a particular irrigation society; there are kinship temples, supported by members of a single patriline; there are caste temples where only people with a given rank worship; there are associational temples formed on a voluntary companionate basis, their obligations being inherited by their descendents; there are state temples attended by people subject to a single lord, and so on. Again, some of these correspond to concrete social groups with other, nonreligious purposes, some do not; some are almost inevitably found, some but rarely; some are obligatory for all men, some are voluntary. Thus, by plotting temple types in a locality, one plots the general shape of the local social structure but not its specific outlines. The temple system of the Balinese countryside forms a relatively fixed stone and wood mold in terms of which rural social organization expresses itself, and the semi-annual festivals in each temple dramatize

[3] It is also a legal community in that all the people in a single Kahyangan-Tiga congregation follow the same general rules regarding hamlet membership, marriage, inheritance, cooperative work, etc., rules which differ in detail from Kahyangan-Tiga group to Kahyangan-Tiga group. Sometimes this law community is headed by a Bendesa Adat, or customary law chief, who gives advice and direction on problems of custom. But, again, it is only in the odd case that this customary law community happens to coincide with a concrete political community.

the sorts of ties out of which Balinese peasants build their collective life. But it does not stamp that life into any simple or unvarying form, for within the general mold the possibilities for variations in stress, combination, and adjustment of social elements seem almost limitless.

2. *Common Residence*. As most Indonesians, Balinese live in a clustered settlement pattern, their walled-in house-compounds jammed against each other in an almost urban fashion so as to conserve rice land in the face of tremendously dense and growing population.[4] Within such clusters the basic territorial political unit is the hamlet, or *bandjar*. Bandjar, which may or may not be spatially isolated, depending upon the size of the settlement, contain anywhere from a dozen to several hundred nuclear families, averaging perhaps about eighty or ninety. In most parts of Bali, the bandjar may be rather simply defined as all those people subject to the decisions taken in one hamlet meeting house, or *balé bandjar*. Bandjar meetings of all male household heads are usually held in this balé once in a 35-day Balinese month, at which time all important policy decisions for the hamlet as a corporate unit are made, mainly by means of a "sense of the meeting" universal agreement process. As the temple is the focus of the religious community, so the meeting house — a wall-less, peaked-roof, Polynesian-looking structure usually located in the center of the hamlet — is the focus of the political community.[5]

To the bandjar are allocated the sort of general governmental and legal functions common to peasant communities in most parts of the world. It is responsible for local security, for the legitimation of marriage and divorce and the settlement of inheritance disputes, and for the maintenance of public works such as rural roads, the meeting house, and the local market sheds and cockpit. Commonly it will own a gamelan orchestra and perhaps dancing costumes and masks as well. As in many, but not all, parts of Bali, house-land is corporately owned by the bandjar as a whole, the hamlet also may regulate the distribution of dwelling places, and so control immigration. For serious crimes it may even expel members, confiscating their house-land and denying them all local political rights — for the Balinese the severest of social sanctions.

The hamlet also has significant tax powers. It may fine people for infractions of local custom, can demand contributions for public entertainments, repairs to civic structures, or social welfare activities more or less at will, and can exercise the right to harvest all rice land owned by bandjar members — the members as a whole acting as the harvesters — for a customary share of the product. Consequently, most bandjar have sizeable treasuries and may even own rice land, purchased out of income,

[4] Total Balinese population for 1954 is estimated at 1,500,000, with a mean density around 700 per square mile. In the thickly settled areas of South Bali densities reach up over 1,500 per square mile (Raka 1955).

[5] In the Tabanan area balé are lacking in most hamlets, meetings being held in the open air beneath a banyan tree or in a temple courtyard.

the proceeds of which are also directed to public purposes. Nowadays, a few bandjar even own trucks or buses, others help finance local schools, yet others erect cooperative coffee shops.

Finally, the bandjar also acts as a communal work group for certain ritual purposes, especially for cremations, which, along with temple festivals, are still the most important ceremonies in Bali, although their size and frequency have been reduced somewhat in the years since the war.[6] When an individual family decides to cremate, all members of the bandjar are obligated to make customary contributions in kind and to work preparing the offerings, food, and paraphernalia demanded for as long as a month in advance. Similar cooperation, but of lesser degree, is often enjoined for other rites of passage, such as tooth filing, marriage, and death. The bandjar is thus at once a legal, fiscal, and ceremonial unit, providing perhaps the most intensely valued framework for peasant solidarity.

The heads of the hamlet are called *klian*, literally "elder." In some bandjar there is but one, most often two or three. Sometimes there are as many as four or five, usually reflecting either a large bandjar or one sharply segmented into strong kin or other subgroups, in which all important cross-cutting minorities must be given a role in bandjar leadership. Nowadays klian are usually elected for five years and then replaced by a new set, often chosen by the outgoing group with the approval of the bandjar meeting, so as to avoid electioneering. Klian are assisted by various lesser officials, whose jobs are usually rotated monthly among the members of the bandjar. Though the klian lead the discussion at the bandjar meeting, hold the public treasury, direct communal work, and commonly are men of some weight in the local community they are not possessed of much formal authority. In line with the general Balinese tendency to disperse power very thinly, to dislike and distrust people who project themselves above the group as a whole, and to be very jealous of the rights of the public as a corporate group, the klian are in a very literal sense more servants of the bandjar than its masters, and most of them are extraordinarily cautious about taking any action not previously approved in the hamlet meeting. Klian, who are unpaid and have no special perquisites, feel that their position mainly earns them the right to work harder for the public and be more abused by it; wearily, they compare their job to that of a man caring for male ducks: like the drake, the bandjar produces lots of squawks but no eggs.

3. *Ownership of Rice Land Lying within a Single Watershed.* Unlike peasant societies in most parts of the world, there is in Bali almost no connection between the ownership and management of cultivable land on the one hand and local political (i.e., hamlet) organization on the other. The irrigation society, or *subak*, regulates all matters having to do with the cultivation of wet rice and it is a wholly separate organiza-

[6] For descriptions of these ceremonies, see Covarrubias (1936).

tion from the bandjar. "We have two sorts of custom," say the Balinese, "dry customs for the hamlet, wet ones for the irrigation society."

Subak are organized according to the water system: all individuals owning land which is irrigated from a single water source — a single dam and canal running from dam to fields — belong to a single subak. Subak whose direct water sources are branches of a common larger dam and canal form larger and less tightly knit units, and finally the entire watershed of one river system forms an overall, but even looser, integrative unit. As Balinese land ownership is quite fragmented, a man's holding typically consisting of two or three quarter- or half-acre plots scattered about the countryside, often at some distance from his home, the members of one subak almost never hail from a single hamlet, but from ten or fifteen different ones; while from the point of view of the hamlet, members of a single bandjar will commonly own land in a large number of subak. Thus as the spatial distribution of temples sets the boundaries on Balinese religious organization, and the nucleated settlement pattern forms the physical framework for political organization, so the concrete outline of the Balinese irrigation system of simple stone and clay dams, mud lined canals and tunnels, and bamboo water dividers provides the context within which Balinese agricultural activities are organized.

Though organizational details and terminology differ widely from region to region, there are elected chiefs — usually called *klian subak*, as opposed to *klian bandjar* — over the subak, while the higher levels of watershed and river system organization are coordinated by appointed officials of the central government as the heirs of the traditional irrigation and tax officials of the old Balinese kingdoms. But, again, it is primarily the subak as a whole which determines, in the light of its inherited traditions, its own policies.

The subak is responsible for the maintenance of its irrigation system, a task involving almost continual labor, for the apportionment of water among members of the subak, and for the scheduling of planting. It levies fines for infractions of rules (stealing water, ignoring planting directives, shirking work, and so on), maintains the subak temples and carries out a whole sequence of ritual activities connected with the agricultural cycle, controls fishing, fodder gathering, duck herding and other secondary activities in the subak, and so on and so forth. In most of the larger subak today the actual irrigation work — the constant repair of dams and canals and the perpetual opening and closing of water gates involved in water distribution — is carried out by only a part of the subak membership, called the "water group," which then receives a money payment from those not so working, the amount again being determined by the subak as a whole. Complex patterns of share tenancy, involved systems of controlled crop rotation, varying modes of internal subak organization, and the increasing efforts by the government water officials to improve inter-subak coordination complicate the whole picture. But everywhere the status of the subak as an independent, self-regulating, corporate group with its own rules and its own purposes remains as unchallenged today as it was in the times of the Balinese kings.

4. Commonality of Ascribed Social Status. The Balinese, like the Indians from whom they have borrowed (and reformulated) so much, have commonly been described as having a caste system. They do, in the sense that social status is patrilineally inherited, that marriage is fairly strictly regulated in terms of status, and that, save for a few unusual exceptions, mobility between levels within the prestige system is in theory impossible and in practice difficult. But they do not in the sense of possessing a ranked hierarchy of well-defined corporate groups, each with specific and exclusive occupational, social, and religious functions all supported by elaborate patterns of ceremonial avoidance and commensality and by a complex belief system justifying radical status inequality. Were the term "caste" not so deeply ingrained in the literature on Bali, it might be less confusing to speak of the Balinese as having a "title system," for it is in terms of a set of explicit titles, passing from father to child and attached to the individual's name as a term both of address and reference, that prestige is distributed.

Following Indian usage, the Balinese divide themselves into four main groups: Brahmana, Satria, Vesia, and Sudra. Since in such a classification more than 90 per cent of the population falls into the fourth category, a more common division for everyday use is made between *Triwangsa* ("the three peoples"), the first three groups taken as a unit, and the *Sudra,* which in a broad and not altogether consistent way corresponds to the gentry-peasantry distinction common to nonindustrial civilizations generally. Each group is then subdivided further in terms of the title system, the actual basis of the individual's rank in the society. Given a sample list of titles — *Ida Bagus, Tjokorda, Dewa, Ngakan, Bagus, I Gusti, Gusti, Gusi, Djero, Gde* — any but the most uninformed Balinese could tell you they were placed in a generally descending order of status, but only a small minority of theorists could tell you that the first was a Brahmana title, the next four Satria, the next three Vesia, and the last two Sudra.[7] In making status distinctions a man thinks and talks in terms of titles, not in terms of caste.

In general, a man may marry anyone of the same title or lower, a woman anyone of the same title or higher — thus hypergamy. In pre-Dutch times (i.e., before 1906, for South Bali only came under direct Dutch control at the beginning of this century) miscaste marriages were punished by exile or — particularly in the case of a Triwangsa girl and a Sudra man — death. Even today a girl marrying down is commonly "thrown away" by her family, in the sense that she is no longer recog-

[7] Only a minority of Sudra, considered to have higher prestige than the mass because of former affinal or political ties to higher status groups, have true address and reference titles. Most Sudra have no address title at all.

nized as kin and all social intercourse between her and her parents ceases. Under modern conditions such breaches often heal after some years have passed, particularly if the mismatch is not too great; but miscaste marriages are in any case very rare even today.

As the number of Triwangsa is so much less than the number of Sudra, status regulation of marriage means that the patterns of affinal connection tend to work out rather differently for the two groups, in that most Triwangsa marriages are hamlet exogamous, i.e., interlocal, while most Sudra marriages are hamlet endogamous, i.e., intralocal. This contrast lifts the horizontally linked Triwangsa up as a supra-hamlet all Bali group over the highly localized Sudra; a pattern congruent, of course, with the fact that the Triwangsa almost completely monopolized the interlocal, superordinate political and religious roles of the traditional Balinese state structure, as they do today of the Balinese branch of the Indonesian civil service.

The caste (or title) composition of any given hamlet (or temple group, or irrigation society) varies very widely. In one locality one may find representatives of a wide range of titles in a smooth gradient from the highest to the lowest, in another only very high and very low ones, in a third only middle range or only very high ones, in a fourth nothing but Sudra, and so on. And, as caste is a crucial factor in both political and kinship organization, such differences entail important differences in social structure. Prestige stratification in Bali is a powerful integrative force both on the local and on the island-wide levels.

5. *Consanguineal and Affinal Kinship Ties.* Descent and inheritance are patrilineal in Bali, residence is virilocal, but kinship terminology is classic Hawaiian — i.e., wholly bilateral and generational. The major exception to patri-descent and residence is that a man who has no sons may marry a daughter uxorilocally and designate her as his heir; her husband abandons his rights in his own patriline, as a woman does at marriage in the normal case, and moves to his wife's home to live. As this almost always occurs in cases where male heirs are lacking, Balinese genealogies show a noticeable ambilineal element, in that a certain percentage of the ties are traced through women rather than men.

The basic residential unit is the *pekarangan* or walled house compound, which in kinship terms may house groups which range from a simple nuclear family up to a three or more generation extended patrifamily. Typically two or three nuclear families, often with various unattached or aged patri-relatives, occupy a single pekarangan, but occasionally compounds with as many as ten or fifteen families, related through a common paternal grandfather, may be found, particularly among the upper caste groups. In addition to being a residential unit, the compound is a very important religious unit, for each compound group supports a small temple in the northeast corner of the yard dedicated to its direct ancestors at which twice yearly ceremonials must be given. Finally, the compound is usually divided into kitchens, called *kuren,* typically one nuclear family to a kitchen, but sometimes two or three, and it is this kitchen group which is the basic kin unit from the point of view of all superordinate social institutions: it is the kuren which is taxed for the Kahyangan-Tiga temples, which is allotted a seat in the meeting house, which must send a worker to repair the dam or participate in the harvest, which is the rice-field owning unit, and so on.

Above the compound and the kitchen one commonly finds, within any given hamlet, from one to ten or so (largely but not entirely) endogamous corporate kin groups called *dadia.*[8] Such dadia are basically ritual units, but they may also act as collective work groups for various social and economic tasks, may provide the main framework for informal social intercourse outside the immediate family for its members, may serve as an undivided unit in the local stratification hierarchy, and may form a well-integrated faction within the general hamlet political system. The degree to which it takes on these general social functions differs rather widely from village to village. In some villages dadia organization is the central focus of social life, the axis around which it revolves; in others it is of relatively secondary importance; and in a few villages, especially semi-urbanized ones, dadia may not exist at all.

Rarely is the whole hamlet population organized into dadia, and sometimes only a definite minority will be. This is so because of the manner in which dadia are formed. When a family line begins to grow in size, wealth, and local political power, it begins to feel, as a consequence of what is probably the central Balinese social value, status pride, a necessity for a more intensified public expression of what it takes to be its increased importance within the hamlet. At this point the various households which compose the line will join together under a chief elected from among them to build themselves a larger ancestral temple. This temple will usually be built on public, hamlet-owned land, rather than within the confines of one of the houseyards, thus symbolizing the fact that the line has come to be of consequence in the jural-political domain as well as in the domestic. The semi-annual ancestor worship ceremonies the group carries out now become more elaborate, stimulated, as is the building and (as the group continues to grow in power, size, and wealth) periodic renovation of the temple itself, by status rivalry with other local dadia.

Often within the large dadia, subgroups have differentiated and become corporate groups in their own right. These sub-dadia (the Balinese refer to them by a variety of terms) are composed of members of the dadia who know or feel themselves rather more closely related to one another than to the other members of the dadia. Even when there are sub-dadia, not all members of the dadia will necessarily belong to one of

[8] In most Balinese villages, marriage is preferentially within the dadia and, if possible, with the father's brother's daughter.

them. Sometimes a majority will remain free-floating dadia members and will have no sub-dadia ties at all. In one large dadia, for example, there were five sub-dadia accounting for sixty of the eighty or so kitchens in the dadia, the other twenty having no sub-dadia membership. It is the dadia, not the sub-dadia, which is the fundamental group, though the latter also often takes on important social functions.

As noted, the particular functions allocated to kin groups vary from place to place and the integration of these groups with each other and with the other social institutions becomes complex. Also, the number and relative size of kin groups in a given hamlet make a notable difference in how both the kin groups themselves and the hamlet function. A hamlet with, say, one large dadia and four small ones, will differ in both organization and operation from one with three medium large ones plus one or two small ones, or with five or six of roughly equal size. Such issues cannot be pursued here; but it should be clear that kinship, rather than shrinking to a concern with primarily "familial" matters as tends to occur in many peasant societies, remains in Bali an important organizing force in the society generally, albeit but one among many such forces.

6. *Common Membership in One or Another Voluntary Organization.* The Balinese term for any organized group is *seka;* literally, "to be as one." Thus the group of hamlet people is called the *seka bandjar*, the irrigation group is called the *seka subak*, and there are *seka dadia, seka pura,* and so on. But beyond these formal, more or less obligatory groups, there are thousands of completely voluntary organizations dedicated to one or another specific purpose, which are just called seka. These cross-cut all other structural categories and are based wholly on the specific functional ends to which they are directed.

There are seka for housebuilding, for various kinds of agricultural work, for transporting goods to market, for music, dance, and drama performances, for weaving mats, moulding pottery, or making bricks, for singing and interpreting Balinese poetry, for erecting and maintaining a temple at a given waterfall or a particular sacred grove, for buying and selling food, textiles or cigarettes, and for literally dozens of other tasks. Many bandjars have seka for such highly specific purposes as hunting coconut squirrels or building simple ferris wheels for holiday celebrations. Such voluntary seka may have a half dozen or a hundred members, they may last for several weeks or for years, the sons inheriting the fathers' memberships. Some of them build up quite sizeable treasuries and profits to divide among the members, some have yearly feasts of celebration, others even lend their earnings at interest.

As seka loyalty is a major value in Balinese culture, these voluntary groups are not just peripheral organizations but a basic part of Balinese social life. Almost every Balinese belongs to three or four private seka of this sort, and the alliances formed in them balance off those formed in the more formally organized sectors of Balinese social structure in the complex cross-cutting social integration characteristic of the island. From one point of view, all of Balinese social organization can be seen as a set of formal and voluntary seka intersecting with one another in diverse ways.

7. *Common Legal Subordination to a Single Government Administrative Official.* In addition to hamlet, irrigation society, and Kahyangan-Tiga temple organization, there is another sort of territorial unit at the rural level which stems from the organization of the Indonesian governmental bureaucracy as it reaches down into the Balinese countryside. This is the *perbekelan,* so called because it is headed by an official called a *Perbekel.* Before the Revolution the Perbekel was appointed by his Colonial superiors; since it, he is elected by his constituency. He still serves until either he retires or a movement to unseat him develops. He is always a local man, in most cases set apart from his neighbors only in having somewhat more education (although in line with the traditions of Balinese statecraft, higher titled people tend to be preferred for the role). He has under him anywhere from two to a half dozen *Pengliman,* also local men, also elected, each with his own bailiwick within the perbekelan. Both Perbekel and Pengliman are paid, but not very well, by the Government according to the number of kitchens in their domain. As it is through them that the policy directives, propaganda exhortations, and social welfare activities of the Djakarta political elite filter down to the mass of the peasantry and from them that reports on local conditions start back up, they form a kind of rural civil service, a miniature administrative bureaucracy constructed out of local elements.

As might be expected, the arbitrarily drawn boundaries of perbekelan do not, save in the odd case, coincide with any other unit in Balinese society, past or present; rather, they group from four to ten hamlets into what seemed to logical, efficient Dutch administrators to be logical, efficient administrative units. The result is that the hamlets involved not only may have no traditional ties with one another but may even be traditionally antagonistic, while other hamlets of long and continuing association may be separated by perbekelan boundaries. The Perbekel is thus placed in a rather anomalous position for, although his superiors tend to regard him as a "village chief" and expect him to have important traditionally based executive powers, his constituents tend to regard him as a government clerk and consequently not directly concerned with local political processes at all, the direction of which they conceive to lie in the interlocked hands of the temple, hamlet, irrigation society, kin group, and voluntary organization chiefs. The Perbekel is not governing an organic unit, but one which in most cases feels rather little internal solidarity at all and, though he may have some traditional status in the particular hamlet within the perbekelan of which he himself happens to be a member, he is unlikely to have much in the others.

As the Indonesian state increases its activities in an attempt to bring the country into the modern world, the Perbekel both becomes more and more important and feels more and more keenly the uncertain nature of his position. The degree to which he is able to assert his role, to secure his dominance over traditional leadership in matters concerning the national state, and to make a true political unit of the perbekelan varies with several factors: whether or not he is energetic and intelligent, whether or not he is the descendent of a traditional local ruling family, whether or not his perbekelan happens to include hamlets having long-term bonds with one another, whether or not there are a number of young, educated men who will support and encourage his "modernization" efforts, and so on. As with the other planes described, the role of the perbekelan unit in rural Balinese social structure is not describable in terms of any static typological construct, but can only be seen as ranging over a certain set of organizational possibilities.

THREE BALINESE VILLAGES

Thus far in the analysis of Balinese rural social structure the concept "village" has been studiously avoided, mainly because it is used by the Balinese in several mutually contradictory ways. Sometimes "village" (*desa*, a Sanskrit loan word) is used as a synonym for bandjar (the basic rural political unit); sometimes to refer to the Kahyangan-Tiga (temple congregation); sometimes, especially by urbanites and government officials, to the region under a single Perbekel; and, perhaps most commonly, for a vaguely demarcated region in which the planes of organization intersect in such a way that the people living within the region have rather more ties with one another than they do with people in adjacent regions. In this last and rather fuzzy sense, "village" refers to the integrative as opposed to the analytic aspects of rural social structure, and it is in this sense that the term will be used here. A village is not a hamlet, a temple group, or a perbekelan, but a concrete example of the intersection of the various planes of social organization in a given, only broadly delimited locality.

1. *Njalian.* In pre-Dutch times the seat of a minor lord and a secondary market center, Njalian lies at the western edge of the former kingdom and present regency of Klungkung, and is one of the more complexly organized villages of Bali. In Njalian virtually nothing is coordinate with anything else and the crisscrossing of loyalties reaches an almost unbelievable degree of intricacy. The perbekelan of Njalian — the present Perbekel is the head of the traditional ruling house, a *Tjokorda* by title — contains the rather large number of about 3,000 kitchens distributed among eight hamlets, six contiguous within one large settlement cluster and two spatially isolated some two or three kilometers away. There are four sets of Kahyangan-Tiga temples. To one set belong the members of four of the contiguous hamlets, to a second

set belong those of one hamlet in the main cluster and one of the segregated ones, to a third set belong only the members of the other isolated hamlet, and to the fourth only those of the other hamlet in the major cluster:

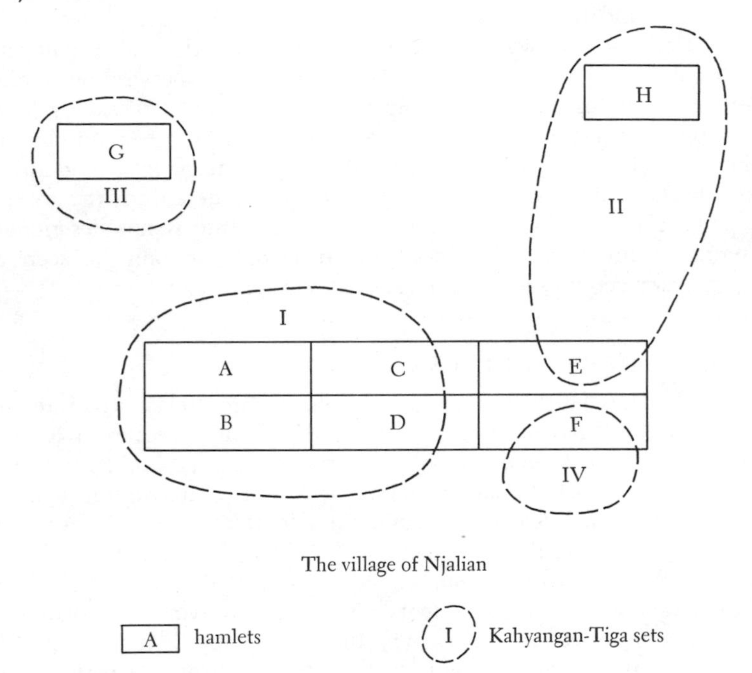

The village of Njalian

Even this rather involved diagram greatly oversimplifies the situation. In the first place, many people living in the territory of one hamlet are legally members of another. Further, the coordination of the temple sets with the hamlet boundaries is very recent, being instituted over strong opposition by the present Perbekel in 1950, and still very imperfect. Before the change, a man belonging to hamlet A would often belong to temple set IV, or a man in E to set I, and so on, and to some extent this still occurs, for traditional allegiances are difficult to reorganize by administrative fiat. Still further, the four bandjar in temple set I — A, B, C, and D — are not really territorial at all; though the meeting houses involved are distributed as shown, members of the hamlets attached to them are randomly interspersed through the whole A-B-C-D area. This sort of nonterritorial hamlet organization is actually frequent in Bali and was ignored above for purposes of descriptive simplicity. Finally, in Njalian the unit cooperating at a cremation — called a *patus* — is not coincident with the hamlet as it is in most other places. Instead, hamlet A is divided into two such collective work groups for cremations, B forms but one patus, C two, and so on. Thus a man may well have his hamlet alliance in one place (not even necessarily where he lives), his temple ties in a second, and his cremation obligations in yet a third, though of course in a majority of cases some of these affiliations may be merged.

Since Njalian contains representatives of a wide range of caste titles, the interaction of the status hierarchy with the hamlet and temple systems adds yet another dimension of complexity. Hamlet A consists entirely of Brahmana and higher Satria people, including the ruling family, but some lesser Triwangsa belong to B, C, D, and E, mixed in among the Sudra. Hamlets F, G, and H are wholly Sudra, with F consisting of but a single dadia kin group, a rather uncommon occurrence. Caste affects temple organization too. In temple set I the death temple was until two years ago divided by a low wall; the Sudra organized their festival separately and held it on one side of the wall, the Triwangsa held theirs on the other. But this has been changed for reasons of economy and democracy, and now all worship together. Voluntary organizations, of which there are literally dozens, irrigation societies, two main ones being involved in this area, and some thirty or forty kin groups also complicate social relationships, though kinship is evidently less important here as an organizing force than in many other villages.

In such an admittedly extreme case of cross-cutting social groupings, the problem of integration, of mutual adjustments among the groups, is a very pressing one. At times open fights have broken out between leaders of various groups over the question of who had prior rights on the services of members common to them. Heavy concurrent demands often mean that work is only hastily done; when the slit gong is beaten to call together members of a given group, many people fail to appear because they either were too far away to hear the gong or thought that it was being sounded for another group to which they were not obligated. To rationalize this situation the Perbekel has instituted a monthly meeting of all important group leaders — fifty people or so — in which he tries valiantly to get them to coordinate their several efforts. He has also attempted to territorialize the system more by making hamlet and temple membership dependent on residence but, though he has had a little success in this direction, most of his efforts have been resisted by the villagers who, he claims, prefer things to be complicated. Despite the fact that he is the traditional ruler of the area, that he has been Perbekel for thirty years, and that he now has the whole Indonesian State behind him, he says that there is really very little he can do in reforming village institutions. People bow and act subservient, but they do just as they wish.

2. *Tihingan.* Although it lies only six miles or so east of Njalian, in the heart of the former kingdom of Klungkung, Tihingan differs from Njalian in most of its important features. Unlike Njalian, Tihingan has never been the seat of a lord, has relatively few Triwangsa

and the Perbekel is a Sudra. Unlike Njalian, social affiliations, though complexly organized, are quite systematically integrated rather than randomly crosscutting. And unlike Njalian, there are within the perbekelan three definite spatial clusters of social loyalty to which the name village can be properly applied, while the perbekelan as a whole forms only the vaguest of social units. The three villages concerned are Pau, Penasan, and Tihingan proper (the seat of the Perbekel which, consequently, lends its name to the entire perbekelan). We shall be concerned here only with Tihingan proper.

Tihingan proper consists of a single hamlet of some 138 kitchens grouped into 85 house-compounds, and there is but one set of Kahyangan-Tiga temples to which all members of the hamlet belong, a rather untypically simple arrangement. There is a Brahmana priest living in the village, and there is a scattering of low-title Satria and Vesia families, but almost 90 per cent of the population is Sudra. From the structural point of view, however, the most striking characteristic of Tihingan is neither its territorial pattern nor its status system, but the rather unusual importance of kinship as an organizational force in social life. It is the four dadia, accounting for nearly 80 per cent of the village population, which form the axis around which Tihingan village life mainly revolves; and the implications of this simple fact can be traced through all the levels of its social organization. On the religious level, each major dadia owns a very large, handsomely carved temple (in the case of the two largest dadia, even larger and more handsomely carved than the theoretically superordinate Kahyangan-Tiga temples) near the center of the village. The upkeep of this temple and the carrying out of the requisite semi-annual ceremonies within it in suitable style are among the major functions of the dadia, and rivalries in those matters can become quite intense.

At the political level, the distribution of hamlet leadership roles is consciously and carefully designed to provide a realistic reflection of the balance of the dadia power. There are five klian or chiefs. Four of these are chosen, one from each of the major dadia; the fifth klian at the same time holds the office of Pengliman and is a member of the second largest dadia. Since the Perbekel himself, a man of some weight within Tihingan proper, is a member of the largest dadia, the kin group foundation for local leadership is clear and exact. Further, in supra-village political processes, institutionalized in the party system of the "New Indonesia," the two largest kin groups are allied as a faction against the next two plus all the families not belonging to a dadia. All of the first group belong to the Socialist party and all of the second to the Nationalist, so that party allegiance is absolutely predictable from kin group membership, and reflects the internal organization of the village rather than personal ideological conviction.

On the economic level, each dadia forms a cooperative work group for the manufacture of Balinese musical instruments — metallaphones, gongs, cymbals, etc. — a smithing craft in which this village is partially specialized; the personnel working in any given forge almost inevitably are members of the same dadia.[9] Further, most tenancy and exchange work patterns in rice field cultivation also follow kin group lines, introducing these alliances into the irrigation society context as well. More informal economic relationships — money lending, patronage, and so on — follow the same pattern.

Finally, even informal recreational interaction is shaped by extended kinship ties. It is only rarely that a man will enter the house-compound of a non-kinsman after nightfall when the most intensive gossiping takes place, though he will move freely among the yards of his dadia members. (A somewhat more consistent and literal adherence to the virilocal ideal in Tihingan than is common elsewhere means that house compounds of the same dadia tend to be fairly well clustered within the hamlet.) In cock fighting, a great part of the pattern of alliance and opposition — whose cock fights whose, who bets against whom — is only explicable in kinship terms. In religion, politics, economics, and informal social interaction, kin group membership therefore has a primacy in Tihingan which, though it is far from representing a universal pattern in Bali, is, like Njalian's lattice-work structure, a realized example of one possibility intrinsic in the intersecting plane type of village organization.

In this type of village organization the dangers of factionalism are obvious and the problem of containing kin group loyalties within the bounds of affiliation in hamlet, irrigation society, temple group, and so on becomes acute. Public activities are often marked by partially concealed kin group antagonisms. For example, when the hereditary priest of the origin and death temples died without an heir ten years ago, the kin groups could not agree on his successor so that responsibility for the ceremonies in these temples now rotates among the priests of the four dadia temples — a highly unsatisfactory and irregular pattern that the people themselves regard as "not quite right, but better than having an open war." At hamlet meetings in the balé the sort of universal agreement necessary to make decisions is difficult to accomplish, so that many proposals are blocked by the opposition of a minority kin group. For example, when the Perbekel tried to convince the hamlet to change funeral customs so as to bury people immediately, even on an unlucky day, rather than keep the corpse in the house for several days (a government-suggested health reform that the neighboring bandjar had adopted with little difficulty) the opposition of the dadia most hostile to the Perbekel's prevented the change from taking place, although the majority of vil-

[9] Economic specialization by village still persists to some degree in Bali, and is another factor to be considered in a full analysis of variation in Balinese village structure. It has been ignored here in favor of more formal considerations only for the sake of simplicity.

lagers were in favor of it. Antagonisms arising out of marriages and divorces across dadia lines, economic rivalries between the musical instrument manufacturing groups, and competitive prestige displays at dadia temple ceremonies also contributed to the heightening of this sort of intergroup tension.

Yet in general, the village is fairly well integrated and factionalization is usually kept within bounds.[10] In part this is accomplished by the concurrent application of two explicit rules of procedure. The first rule is that whenever a group formed on the basis of one principle of affiliation is allocated a given social function, no other principle of affiliation may receive any recognition whatsoever. Thus if the hamlet is cooperating in some task, the work is never suborganized in terms of kinship, caste, or any other bond. If subgroups are technically necessary, people are grouped in a random manner, each family being regarded as a hamlet member pure and simple, as having no qualitative difference from any other. ("The hamlet knows no kinship," runs a Balinese proverb.) Similarly, when a dadia is working at a temple festival, or whatever, the sub-dadia ties within the dadia are considered to have no reality and do not act as a basis for subgroup differentiation.

The second rule sets forth a hierarchy of precedence in which the needs of the hamlet outrank those of the dadia, those of the dadia outrank those of the sub-dadia, and those of the sub-dadia outrank those of voluntary groups. For example, if the hamlet as a whole wishes to harvest the fields of its members, then it has priority. The whole bandjar must harvest and does so as a group, with no internal differentiation. If the hamlet doesn't wish to harvest — per decision of the hamlet meeting — then the dadia have next rights, unaffiliated families either banding together or yielding their rights to one or another of the dadia. If the dadia also decides not to harvest, then the sub-dadia may; if the sub-dadia have no immediate needs then the task is surrendered to voluntary groups. The combination of these two rules of procedure — one prohibiting multiple bases of affiliation for a single task, one establishing an order of precedence — acts as a major integrative mechanism in this otherwise rather faction-prone village.

3. *Blaju.* Unlike Njalian, Blaju is not the name of a perbekelan, and unlike Tihingan, it is not the name of a fairly well defined villarge unit within a perbekelan. Rather, it is the name for a broadly defined region of about six square miles at the eastern edge of the Regency of Tabanan within which the influence of a particular ruling family was preponderant in the pre-Colonial period and to a great extent continues so today. As such, Blaju forms a minuscule state within a state, and its pattern of organization is characterized primarily by a stress on terri-

[10] The only time it has threatened to get completely out of bounds was at the time of the Indonesian general elections in 1955 when each of the two factions went armed in fear of massacre by the other, but no actual violence occurred.

toriality and caste (or title) as bases for social affiliation. Perhaps more than any other area of Bali, Blaju approaches the common stereotype of peasant social structure as being organized in terms of a pyramid of increasingly inclusive territorial units — barrios, villages, subdistricts, districts, and the like — each unit ruled by an attached political official of appropriate status. But, unfortunately for the sort of theory which would like to see in this system a survival of an "original" Balinese pattern from which all else could be adjudged a "deviation," this hierarchical territorialization is a quite recent phenomenon, occurring as a consciously motivated social innovation explicitly designed to intensify social integration.

The area commonly denominated as Blaju contains four perbekelan, three contiguous, one a kilometer or so to the north. The members of these four perbekelan — about 1,500 kitchens — support a common set of Kahyangan Tiga temples, a rather unusual circumstance, for commonly Kahyangan-Tiga congregations are usually smaller and are less extensive than a perbekelan. Within each of these perbekelan there are four hamlets, and each of these hamlets is further divided into from three to six territorial subunits called *kliran*. A kliran has arbitrarily fixed borders and each adult living within these borders is ipso facto a member of that kliran. It is the kliran, averaging eighteen to twenty kitchens, which performs most of the important day-to-day social functions, and it is the basic cooperative work unit in planting-harvesting, ritual, and the like, having its own independent treasury, rice shed, and meeting place. For larger and more important local tasks the klirans of one hamlet will fuse as a single unit; in the same way hamlets unite within perbekelan for affairs of government, and perbekelan unite within Blaju as a whole to support the Kahyangan-Tiga temples. As the irrigation societies in the Blaju area are small and land holdings are not so scattered, irrigation societies tend to be more or less informally identified with the perbekelan and hamlets closest to them, so that the whole system becomes territorialized through and through.

At the geographical center of this whole territorial complex, facing the market and the main crossroads, lies the "palace" (*puri*) of the ruling family, a walled-in, shabby-genteel complex of houseyards, temples, alleyways, and open courts about a city block square, tightly packed with more than five hundred people comprising a single Vesia-level dadia. The head of this dadia, Anak Agung Ngurah Njoman, is at the same time customary law chief for the whole area of Blaju — i.e., the four perbekelan within the Kahyangan-Tiga set. Though largely an honorary position concerned with giving advice in matters of custom, this apical role symbolizes the continuing dominance of the ruling family in the area. At the perbekelan level, two of the four perberkel are from this family (one of them again being the Anak Agung himself), the other two being ranking Sudra with traditional ties to the "castle."

The role of this elite group is strengthened in many ways. First, unlike many Balinese aristocrats, the Blaju ruling family is not impoverished. About one-fifth of all rice land in the area is still in their hands (though it is owned individually, not collectively, within the dadia), and as almost all this land is sharecropped by Sudra tenants who also have corvée obligations to their landlords, traditional patron-dependent ties remain of central integrative importance. Second, although the members of the ruling dadia live all in one place and so should be members of a single hamlet according to the territorial system, they are by traditional practice distributed among the sixteen bandjar in more or less equalized groups. They are assigned bandjar membership independent of their residence so as to insure a voice (and an ear) for the ruling house in each locality and to strengthen the unity of the whole region. Third, there is in Blaju a major temple, rivaling the Kahyangan-Tiga in importance, which is supported exclusively by all the people in the region who bear Triwangsa, upper-caste titles, thus symbolizing the importance of status and serving to ally all the local high prestige groups with the ruling dadia in its largely successful effort to maintain the traditional stratification system unimpaired.

As noted, this rather neat integration of territorialism and status is not altogether a traditional matter, but stems in part at least from rather recent reforms. The kliran subhamlet pattern, the distinctive element in the whole system, was only instituted in 1940. At this time the hamlet system was very weak, kinship unimportant, and most village functions had fallen into the hands of voluntary seka groups. "People" felt — evidently under prodding from the aristocracy, which began to reassert its leadership at this time — that there were too many such groups, that they made for conflict, for a decrease in valuable public activities, and led to a kind of individualism. "The seka got rich, but the bandjar got poor." Thus all the sixteen hamlets decided at once to institute the kliran system and to ban voluntary organizations for all important functions. And when the Dutch left in 1941 the ruling family further intensified its efforts to strengthen the status system which had also been weakened in the general move toward a less organic society, producing the present pattern of organization. Territorialism in Blaju is thus not a simple survival from the distant past, but the outcome of the interaction between traditional values and the quite untraditional events of the twentieth century.

In such a system integrative strains are likely to appear across caste lines, and despite all the bowing and scraping one sees in Blaju, Sudra resentment against Triwangsa domination is quite evident. When a small Sudra dadia of Sunguhu, which traditionally has the right to patronize priests appointed from among its own members rather than Brahmana ones, attempted to institute this system in Blaju a few years ago, they were expelled from their hamlet under intense Triwangsa pressure on the basis of "injuring local custom and denigrating the upper castes." Despite heavy pressures from the central bureaucracy and some local sympathy for the rebels, the Blaju upper castes held firm and the Sunguhu ultimately capitulated. But, irrespective of such strains, Blaju is rather more tightly knit than most Balinese villages: all the 1,500 families were members of a single national political party, and one of the few really effective consumer-producer cooperatives in Bali was located in Blaju, its effectiveness being mainly attributable to the fact that it, too, had 100 per cent membership.

SOME THEORETICAL IMPLICATIONS

Of the many theoretical issues growing out of the analysis of Balinese village organization, among the most interesting are those centering around questions of typology. Typologizing has always been a central concern of social anthropology because both descriptive simplicity and comparative generalization rest on the possibility of summarizing social organizations in terms of constructs at once ethnographically circumstantial and formally distinctive. Whatever their shortcomings from more sophisticated theoretical perspectives, such types as "The Indian Village," "The Chinese State," or "The Nuer Kinship System" (to say nothing of "Peasant Society," or "Segmentary Social Organization," which are perhaps best seen as second order types of types) seem essential to comparative analysis of even the most rudimentary sort. But the Balinese case, in which this methodologically fundamental task of discriminating wood from trees seems unusually difficult of accomplishment, suggests that some of the assumptions underlying our usual typologizing procedures may be in need of revision. Particularly, and perhaps paradoxically, they suggest that clues to the typologically essential may as often lie in rare or unique phenomena as they do in common or typical ones; that essential form may be seen more adequately in terms of a range of variation than in terms of a fixed pattern from which deviant cases depart.

In general, two main approaches to the problem of constructing first order typologies of social organization within a given culture area have been common in anthropology: the "lowest common denominator" approach, and the "representative unit" approach. In the first of these, the procedure is to create a synthetic picture of "Eskimo Life," or "Tale Society," or "Chinese Culture" by taking the various forms found throughout the greater part of the respective culture areas and integrating them so as to provide a generalized account of social structure in an overall sense. Here the anthropologist concentrates on sorting out what is typical from what is not within the entire social field, and the result is a picture which describes directly no actual, given social unit, but which rather summarizes the sort of social form characteristic of the society at whatever point one chooses to look at it. In such a view, variations are interpreted as circumscribed deviations from the general pattern caused by locally acting forces of an ecological, historical, or acculturative nature. This is the older and more popular approach of the two. It is the one usually taken by textbooks and simply descriptive monographs, by such summary volumes as Murdock's *Our Primitive Contemporaries* (1934), and for the most part by the British anthropologists in their African studies.

The "representative unit" approach might also be called the "Middletown" approach, because the procedure is to choose a concrete community — village, town, or tribal settlement — which is at least in a broad way "typical" of the sorts of community found within the culture area. Whether the choice is made on the basis of a systematic social and cultural survey of the whole area or in a more intuitive manner, the attempt is to find a community which forms a useful sample of the broader society, one in which idiosyncratic traits are few relative to those shared with other communities, and one in which most of the patterns deemed basic within the society generally are represented in a "normal" form. This procedure may be refined by choosing several such communities within subcultural areas, as in Steward's Puerto Rico study (Steward *et al.* 1956), but the methodological strategy is nevertheless the same: to choose a community which is to the greatest possible degree directly representative of more than itself.[11]

Both of these now established procedures yield rather strange results when applied to Bali. The lowest common denominator approach obviously depends on the possibility of finding some fairly simple fundamental patterns — a territorial village, a clan and lineage system, a developed caste structure — which appear over and over again in various parts of the culture area in a broadly similar fashion. But in Bali, though certain patterns are common throughout the whole area the form in which they actually appear differs so widely that any synthetic picture must be drawn in such a generalized fashion as to have little substantial reality of any kind. One could easily enough construct a "Balinese village" with a "typical" temple setup, hamlet organization, kinship system, irrigation society, title distribution, and so on; but such a composite construct would utterly fail to express the two most fundamental char-

[11] There is a third approach to typologizing, which is particularly prevalent in Dutch studies of Bali (Korn 1936), in which a community is chosen for study not so much on the basis of its representativeness in a statistical sense, but rather because it is held to show prototypical forms and patterns in a relatively uncomplicated, direct, and undistorted fashion. Highly traditionalized communities which have been relatively isolated from acculturative contacts are considered to have changed more slowly than other communities and so are favored as providing pictures of underlying social structures which are clouded over by adventitious elements in the more dynamic communities. This approach has tended to lose favor as it has become apparent that it is based on a dubious theory of social change and that the traditionalism of isolated communities is as often interpretable as an adaptation to peculiar environmental circumstances as it is a persistence of earlier and more fundamental patterns.

acteristics of Balinese village organization, namely, that these patterns take widely differing forms from village to village, and that their relative importance within any particular village integration varies greatly. For similar reasons, the representative unit approach is also almost certain to be misleading. Are we to take Njalian, Tihingan, or Blaju as typical of Bali? In a direct descriptive sense they are not typical of much beyond themselves; but neither, probably, is any other Balinese village. If we are to discriminate what is really essential and characteristic in Balinese village organization we need to take a somewhat different tack and conceptualize that organization not in terms of invariance in overt structure throughout the whole island, or from place to place within it, but rather in terms of the range of overt structure which it is possible to generate out of a fixed set of elemental components. Form, in this view, is not a fundamental constancy amid distracting and adventitious variation, but rather a set of limits within which variation is contained.

What is common to Njalian, Tihingan, and Blaju, and to Balinese villages generally, is the set of planes of social organization out of which they are built up; it is the fact that they are all constructed, although in different ways, of the same materials which accounts for the strong family resemblance they show despite their great structural diversity. In the actual investigation of Balinese village organization, one of course proceeds in a direction diametrically opposite to the logic of presentation followed in this paper: the planes are derived through an inspection of a series of villages rather than discovered in pure form and then combined to generate villages. As more and more villages are studied it soon becomes clear that a relatively small set of basic elements is involved; after one has discriminated temple units, hamlets, irrigation societies, the title hierarchy, the kinship system, voluntary organizations, and governmental units — he comes to feel that he is not likely to find a village in which one of these is wholly lacking nor one in which a completely new plane is present.[12] But though the number and type of elements are thus fairly quickly discovered the possible forms they can take and the ways in which they can unite with the other elements are not. Almost every village studied reveals some new organizational potentiality with respect to one or several of the planes, and a new mode of integration. The process of investigating Balinese village organization, in a typological sense, is therefore a process of progressive delimitation of the structural possibilities inherent in a set of fundamental social elements. What one derives is not a typical village in either the lowest common denominator

[12] There is a handful of the so-called *Bali Aga* ("original Balinese") villages whose organization differs markedly from those of the overwhelming majority, having age groups, a gerontocratic political structure, communal land tenure, etc. Though the significance of these villages from an ethnohistorical point of view is an interesting problem, their position within Balinese society generally is marginal in the extreme. For descriptions of such villages, see Bukian (1936), Korn (1933), and Bateson and Mead (1942).

or representative unit sense, but a differentiated and multidimensional social space within which actual Balinese village organizations are necessarily distributed. One discovers more and more what shapes a village can take and still be distinctively Balinese.

Among other things this means that the peculiar, the unique, and the odd take on a rather different significance than in the usual typologizing procedures, for they are seen not as exceptions to a general rule to be accounted for by ad hoc considerations which save the rule, but as providing valuable further clarification of the basic principles of social organization. From Njalian's crisscrossing structure we learn that the various component planes are to a very large degree independent of one another; from Tihingan we learn how the Balinese kinship system works when given full play and how the other planes then adapt to its dominance; from Blaju we learn what increased territorialism and a stress on caste imply for social integration. Each case we confront reveals something new about the implicit potentialities of the typological model we are constructing, sets new bounds on the range of variation possible within it; and it does so mainly not in terms of what is common but rather of what is unusual about it. In the same way that Cromwell has been adjudged the most typical Englishman of his time on the simple basis of his having been the oddest, so the general typological significance of any particular Balinese village lies primarily in its idiosyncracies.

REFERENCES CITED

Bateson, G., and M. Mead

1942 *Balinese Character: A Photographic Analysis*. New York: New York Academy of Sciences.

Belo, J.

1953 "Bali: Temple Festival." *Monographs of the American Ethnological Society*, XXII, Locust Valley, New York.

Bukian, I Dewa Putu

1936 "Kajoe Bihi, Een Oud-Balische Bergdesa," bewerkt dor C. J. Grader. Tijdschrift v.d. Bataavische Genootschaap, LXXVI.

Covarrubias, M.

1936 "*Island of Bali*." New York: Alfred A. Knopf.

Korn, V. E.

1933 *De Dorpsrepubliek Tnganan Pagringsingan, Kirtya Liefrinck van der Tuuk*. Singaradja, Bali.

1936 *Het Adatrecht van Bali* (Second revised edition). s'Gravenhage.

Murdock, G. P.

1934 *Our Primitive Contemporaries*. New York: Macmillan.

Raka, I Gusti Gde

1955 *Monographi Pulau Bali*. Djakarta: Indonesian Republic, Ministry of Agriculture.

Steward, J., *et al.*

1956 *The People of Puerto Rico*. Urbana: University of Illinois Press.

The Community-Nation Mediator in Traditional Central Italy

Sydel F. Silverman

One of the most strategic yet formidable problems in the anthropological study of complex societies is the relationship of the parts to the whole of such societies. Most attempts to tackle this problem have been concerned primarily with those parts which are localized social systems, or communities,[1] interdependent with though analytically separable from the whole, a national social system. The community and national levels of sociocultural integration of Steward (1955:43–63), the discussion of tensions between pueblo and state by Pitt Rivers (1954:202–210), the community-oriented groups and nation-oriented groups of Wolf (1956), and the local roles and national roles of Pitkin (1959) are only a few examples of this recurring contrast, the social analogue of the great-tradition/little-tradition approach to complex cultures. Such a model immediately sets the task of formulating the interaction between the two systems.

One of the more promising efforts to describe this interaction has been the concept of the "mediator," an individual or group that acts as a link between local and national social systems. Wolf introduced the idea of the cultural "broker" in a discussion of data from Mexico, defining as "brokers" the "groups of people who mediate between community-oriented groups in communities and nation-oriented groups which operate through national institutions" (Wolf 1956:1075). The mediating functions which Wolf emphasizes are economic and political, and he traces a succession of three phases in the post-Columbian history of Mexico during which these functions were carried out by different groups

This paper is an abridged version of "Patronage and Community-Nation Relationships in Central Italy," which appeared in *Ethnology*, Vol. IV, No. 2 (April 1965). Reprinted by permission of the author and the publisher. That article deals with changes in the community-nation linkage with passing time. Field work was carried out in a rural community of Central Italy from August, 1960 to September, 1961. The project was supported by a predoctoral fellowship (MF-11, 068) and grant (M-3720) from the National Institute of Mental Health, United States Public Health Service. A more detailed description of the community is given in my doctoral dissertation (Silverman 1963).

[1] The boundaries of the local system are not precisely coextensive with the community, since a local system may include regular relationships between members of different communities and since any community in a complex society has within it some representation of the national system. However, this paper will follow the common practice of using the term "community" interchangeably with "local system."

in the society. In his review of peasant-society research published the same year, Redfield (1956) observed that a recurrent phenomenon in many societies is the existence of a "hinge" group, administrative and cultural intermediaries who form a link between the local life of a peasant community and the state of which it is a part. The concept of the mediator is relevant to many studies of "part-societies" which exist within a larger encompassing whole. It describes the pivotal chiefs within colonial nations, whose positions derive from earlier periods of tribal autonomy, as well as the elites looked up to by peasants, deriving from a historical balance between two stable classes; the formal agents of national institutions, who penetrate into communities from distant capitals, as well as the upwardly mobile villagers who move into positions in national institutions.

In the analysis of material collected during field work in a Central Italian community, the concept of the mediator proved to be most pertinent for understanding the relationship of the community to the larger society during a particular period. However, it was found that if this relationship is followed over time, not only are there changes with regard to the groups which perform mediation functions, as Wolf (1956) showed for Mexico, and the roles through which mediation is effected, as Geertz (1960) showed for Java, but there are fundamental changes in the structuring of links between community and nation. These changes suggest that the concept of the mediator is most useful if defined narrowly and thus restricted to a particular form of part-whole relationship.

The concept refers to a status which functions as a link between a local system and a national system. In interactional terms, the mediator may be seen as one to whom action is originated from the national system and who in turn originates action to the local system; to some extent, the direction is reversible, the mediator still being the middle element. However, if the mediator were to be defined merely as anyone who acts as a means of contact between the systems, it would include such a wide range of phenomena as to become virtually meaningless. Moreover, such a definition would obscure the important differences between various kinds of contacts which may exist.

Wolf (1956:1075) referred to the "brokers" as persons who "stand guard over the critical junctures or synapses of relationships which connect the local system to the larger whole." By taking Wolf's terms in their full implications, it is possible to arrive at a more precise definition. First of all, the functions which those who are defined as mediators perform must be "critical," of direct importance to the basic structures of either or both systems. For example, a person who brings awareness of a new fashion in clothing from the national into the local system would not by virtue of this function alone be considered a mediator, even though he does act as a communicational intermediary. Second, the mediators "guard" these functions, i.e., they have near-exclusivity in performing them; exclusivity means that if the link is to be made at all between the two systems with respect to the particular function, it must be made through the mediators. As a result, the number of mediator statuses is always limited. To the extent that alternative links become available, so that the mediators lose their exclusive control of the junctures, they cease to be mediators. These two criteria, critical functions and exclusivity, limit the extension of the concept. Persons who provide contact between the two systems but who do not necessarily fulfill both criteria will be referred to here as "intermediaries." While the terminology is clumsy, it is felt that there is an important distinction which needs to be made between the broader category, "intermediary," and the special kind of intermediary, the "mediator."

It seems to be general that there is a rank difference between the mediator and the other persons in the local system who are involved in the mediated interaction. The mediators may take on their function because of previous possession of a higher rank, or they may achieve a higher rank as a result of assuming the mediator role. In either case, the relationship between the local and the national system assumes a "vertical" form.

The concept of the mediator emerged out of the study of particular kinds of societies, those to which anthropologists first turned when they began to move beyond the primitives, namely complex societies which still retain a strong "folk" element. That it is within such societies that the concept finds its widest applicability suggests that it may represent a form of part-whole relationship peculiar to the preindustrial state society. It is obvious that in a society at a pre-state level of integration there would be little necessity for mediators. On the other hand, the existence of mediators implies that the local units are separate from each other and from the larger society to the extent that a limited group can have exclusive control over the connections between part and whole — a situation associated with preindustrial societies.

This paper attempts to develop the "mediator" concept as an element of a particular kind of part-whole relationship, which is found at a particular level of development in complex societies. To this end, it examines the traditional mediators — in this instance a patron group — in the Central Italian community of Colleverde.

THE COMMUNITY

Colleverde (a pseudonym) is an Umbrian *comune* near the geographical center of Italy, about 50 kilometers from the provincial capital, Perugia, and approximately 150 kilometers north of Rome. The medieval castle-village which is the functional center of the community is situated on a hilltop overlooking the valley of the Tiber. The countryside of the comune covers a wide range of environmental variation, from a strip of level plain along the banks of the Tiber (about 150 meters above sea level), through a region of low and medium hills, to the woods, meadows, and wasteland of a high-hill zone (up to 650 meters). In 1960, Colleverde parish (one of two parishes in the comune, each of which may be considered a separate community) had a population of 1,885 in 465 households. About one-fifth of the inhabitants live in the village, the remainder on dispersed farms in the surrounding countryside.

About 80 per cent of the active population are agriculturalists. The majority work self-contained farmsteads, most of which comprise between two and fifteen hectares. Except for minor variations due to altitude, each farm produces the entire range of local crops and animals: wheat, olives, wine grapes, maize, a variety of minor crops grown for human and animal subsistence and for renewal of the land, meat calves (which since the advent of tractors after World War II have been rapidly eliminating the work oxen which were formerly raised), pigs, a few sheep, and barnyard fowl. In addition, industrial crops (tobacco, sugar beet, and tomato) have been introduced on a small scale in the irrigated tracts of the plain. Of these products, only the wheat, calves, and industrial crops are raised primarily or exclusively for sale. At least two-thirds of the land is cultivated under the *mezzadria* system of share-farming, while the remainder is worked by peasant proprietors, tenant farmers, and a few wage-laborers.

The mezzadria system is based on a contractual association between a landowner, who furnishes the farm (including cleared land, farmhouse, outbuildings, and livestock) and advances all working capital as needed, and a peasant family who provide labor and the minor equipment. All other expenses and the income of the enterprise are divided between them, theoretically half and half; in 1948 the peasant's share of the income was raised by law to 53 per cent. As compared with other sharecropping systems, the mezzadria is distinguished by three elements: the integrated farm, the family labor unit, and the active participation in investments and operation of the enterprise on the part of both owner and cultivators.

The integrity of the farm and the major dependence upon a family for its labor requirements imply a recurrent imbalance between the number of working hands and the size of the farm. Adjustment is made primarily by a movement of families among farms as major changes in family size occur. Partly because large households traditionally were advantageous to the mezzadri (enabling them to work a larger farm),[2] the ideal household consisted of a patrilocal extended family, in which all sons brought their brides to live in their father's household and in which authority and economic control were vested in the family head. Although during the

[2] The upper limit of household size was about twenty members. The average size, based on estimates from a population register covering the period 1881–1907, was seven or eight. Today, the average mezzadria household consists of about six members.

past few decades the largest households have been breaking up, more than half the mezzadria families still have at least one married son residing in the parental household. In the community as a whole, however, only a third of the households consist of extended families, and the predominant form is the nuclear family.

The community is economically and socially heterogeneous. The fundamental principle of settlement pattern, the segregation of village center and countryside, demarcates the most pervasive social division, the people of "inside" and those of "outside." This cleavage is occupational: those who do not work the land (landowners and administrators of agricultural properties, professionals, clerks, merchants, artisans, and laborers) as against those who do. It is the major correlate of social-class differentiation: the *signori* (the local upper class) and a middle group consisting of the working people of families resident in the village for generations, as against the great lower class. It describes, in general, political party alignments within the community: the Right and Center as against the Left. To some extent it parallels a difference in the spirit of religious participation: the "cynical" (in the view of the Colleverdesi) as against the devout. It is also a cultural division, for the village is regarded as the seat of civilization surrounded by rusticity, bringing *civiltà* (that which is "civilized," in the sense of "citified") to the countryside and bestowing the aura of civiltà on the whole community.

PATRONAGE IN COLLEVERDE

Until the recent postwar period, the mediation of relations between Colleverde and the larger society was the function of a patronage system. Before discussing this function, it will be helpful to describe the general features of traditional patronage in the community. Patronage patterns are familiar to all the older contemporary Colleverdesi, whose recollections (supplemented by local historical documents) were the basis for the following reconstruction. However, only vestiges of them remain today.

Patronage as a cross-cultural pattern may be defined as an informal contractual relationship between persons of unequal status and power, which imposes reciprocal obligations of a different kind on each of the parties. As a minimum, what is owed is protection and favor on the one side and loyalty on the other. The relationship is on a personal, face-to-face basis, and it is a continuing one.

As is the case in other cultures where a patron-client relationship receives explicit recognition, patronage in Central Italy is not coterminous with all the meanings of the term for "patron" (cf. Kenny 1960:14–15; Foster 1963:1282). In Colleverde, the term *padrone* is applied to: (1) the legal owner of something, for example a house or a dog; (2) one who controls something, such as the mistress of a household, or one who has self-control; (3) an employer, when reference is made to him by or to an employee; (4) the grantor of a mezzadria farm, whether or not he is actually the landowner and whether or not there is anything more than minimal contact with the cultivators; (5) a guardian deity; and (6) a patron in a patron-client relationship.[3] However, all of these usages which refer to one person as the padrone of another describe potential bases for the formation of a patron-client relationship.

The most important patron-client relationship in Colleverde was that between the parties to the mezzadria arrangement. The relationship developed informally, by extension of the formal terms of the contract. A peasant might approach the landlord to ask a favor, perhaps a loan of money or help in some trouble with the law, or the landlord might offer his aid knowing of a problem. If the favor were granted or accepted, further favors were likely to be asked or offered at some later time. The peasant would reciprocate — at a time and in a context different from that of the acceptance of the favor, in order to de-emphasize the material self-interest of the reciprocative action — by bringing the landlord especially choice offerings from the farm produce, by sending some member of the peasant family to perform services in the landlord's home, by refraining from cheating the landlord, or merely by speaking well of him in public and professing devotion to him.[4] Or the peasant might be the first to offer his "favors," in anticipation of those he would later have to ask of the landlord. Whether or not a true patronage relationship developed from the mezzadria association depended upon the landlord's inclination, his need of support, and his place of residence (or the length of an absentee owner's yearly sojourn in Colleverde).

The mezzadria association was particularly conducive to the development of a patronage relationship, for the institution had the effect of bringing landlord and peasant into long and personal contact with each other. The minimum duration of the contract is one year, but typically it persists for several years, and traditionally it was common for a farm to be occupied by the same family for many decades and even for generations. The landowner's role as director of the enterprise requires his continuing interest and his physical presence much of the time. Some proprietors employ managers (*fattori*), who range from unskilled foremen and commercial agents to highly trained agricultural technicians,

[3] In the third, fourth, and sixth instances, the term may also be used for address. Alternatively, the padrone may be addressed in the respectful form of using the given name preceded by *Sor* or *Signora* (rarely, *Sora*). In Colleverde, as in Foster's community, there is no specific term for "client."

[4] Until the reforms of recent years, the mezzadria contract required a number of "extra" obligations of the peasant to the landlord, including gifts of fowl and eggs in specific quantities at different times of the year and various forms of unreimbursed labor in the landlord's household. Thus it is not always apparent whether a peasant's offering was the fulfillment of the formal mezzadria contract or part of a voluntary patron-client relationship. However, the essence of the latter was that the quantity or value of the goods and services given exceeded the formal requirements.

but traditionally even when this was the case the landlords maintained close contact with their farms. In contrast to the typical situation in southern Italy, the landowning class throughout the mezzadria area has a strong tradition of active interest in agriculture; for example, many receive higher education in fields which equip them for the management of their property. There is, in fact, a marked tendency to glorify their attachment to their land and "their" peasants.

Until recent years, the owners of Colleverde's land were the nucleus of the village population, constituting a local upper class. In other communities of the area, those proprietors who did not reside in the rural centers lived in the nearby towns and small cities and often retained part-time residences near their land. Thus the landlords were accessible. Moreover, close and continuing contact between landlord and peasant was encouraged not only by the necessary interaction related to the operations of the farm but also by the cultural definition of the mezzadria relationship. The association was ideally a personal and affectionate tie ranging far beyond the formal contract covering the enterprise, a tie between two families, one the protector and benefactor and the other the loyal dependent. To the peasant, the landlord was the most immediately available person to turn to for economic aid or for knowledge about the world outside. To the landlord, a patronage relationship was at the least a great convenience. It provided a check against being taken advantage of, a check that was cheaper, more reliable, and in any case a useful supplement to supervision by fattori. It facilitated contacts with the peasant and contributed to the day-to-day efficiency of the enterprise. Finally, it was a means of controlling potentially disruptive influences from the outside. It is significant that the paternalism of the mezzadria landlords has often been pointed to as a factor in delaying the spread of labor agitation to the Central Italian hill region for several decades after its onset in many agricultural areas of the nation about 1870 (Bandini 1957:77–78).

A peasant whose own landlord was unavailable or who was unable or unwilling to dispense favors occasionally turned to other landowners. More common was the formation of a patron-client relationship between lower-class persons who were not mezzadri and a local landlord or other local person of high status and power. The potential client would approach one of the signori with a request, or he might attempt to establish the relationship first by presenting him with some small gift or by making himself available to run errands or help out in various ways. Such relationships, although they did not center about common participation in an agricultural enterprise, resembled and may be said to have been patterned after the landlord-peasant relationship.

The patron-client relationships in Colleverde differed from those which Foster observed in Mexico in one important respect. An essential aspect of such relationships in Tzintzuntzan is that they are dyadic; they can exist only between two individuals: "Ego conceptualizes his obligations and expectations as a two-way street, he at one end and a single partner at the other end" (Foster 1963:1281). In Colleverde, however, the dyad was not the only or even the most frequent form. When the relationship was formed between mezzadria landlord and peasant, the landlord became patron not to an individual but to an entire household. His obligations automatically extended to all members of the peasant family, unless some member specifically rejected his own obligations as client. On the other hand, the wife of the landlord became *la padrona,* and she was expected to adopt the role of patroness, especially toward the women of the peasant family. To a lesser extent, other members of the landlord's family were also treated as patrons and sometimes accepted the obligations of patronage. These extensions of the patron and client roles to whole households were not the result of independently established contracts; they were more or less automatic, although the other persons were not strictly bound to accept the role.

Furthermore, there was in Colleverde the concept of an individual (or a married couple or family) becoming patron to a group made up of unrelated persons. Traditionally, there were several community associations and organized projects (an important example was the 40-member band) which were initiated and/or maintained by local signori, who were considered their patrons. Such persons gave economic support and political protection to these groups (not to their members as individuals). Similarly, certain signori regarded themselves and were generally regarded by others as patrons of the community, with the responsibility to provide benefits for the community as a whole. One way in which this was done was by leaving a will providing that part of their patrimony be used in specific ways by the community. Such endowments were a major source of public funds and community charities.

THE PATRON AS MEDIATOR

The descriptions of patronage systems in various cultural settings suggest that one of the most important aspects of the patron's role is to relate the client to the world outside the local community. Pitt-Rivers (1954:141) emphasized this point in his analysis of an Andalusian village: "It is, above all, [the patron's] relationship to the powers outside the pueblo which gives him value." In Andalusia, a structure of patronage links the authority of the state to the network of neighborly relations and balances "the tension between the state and the community" (Pitt-Rivers 1954:154–55). Kenny (1960:17–18), writing about Castile, observed that the patrons are validly described as "gatekeepers," for "they largely dominate the paths linking the local infrastructure of the village to the superstructure of the outside urban world." In general, the patrons described from recent times in Spain and Latin America, and those of traditional Central Italy, are mediators in the full sense of the definition adopted here. Their functions are critical ones, for they have an essential part in the basic economic and political structures of the society. Moreover, persons become patrons precisely because their capacity to perform these functions is virtually exclusive.

It would appear, in fact, that patrons are particularly well adapted to performing the function of mediation between the local and the national system. The patron usually has a distinctly defined status in both systems and operates effectively in both. Furthermore, the relationship between patron and client is stable and durable. As Foster has pointed out, continuance of the relationship is assured by never permitting a balance to be achieved between the obligations of the parties; the account is never settled, but rather each constantly wins new credits which will be redeemed at a future time or incurs new debts which must later be paid. Stability of the patron-client tie is reinforced by its patterning after a kin relationship, the patron becoming "like a father" in obligations to and respect due from the client (as the close connection between "patronage" and "paternalism" suggests). Personalized terms of address are used, there generally are affective overtones to the relationship, and frequently there is a denial of utilitarian motives and an insistence instead upon the non-priced demands of "loyalty," "friendship," or being "almost like one of the family." (One Colleverde woman explained her economically advantageous relationship with her patroness with the statement, "We are old friends, so we always ask each other for favors.") In societies where social mobility is limited and where kinship therefore cannot function as a link between the local and the national system (cf. Friedl 1959), patronage provides a close, highly sanctioned, and self-perpetuating relationship between different social strata as a link between the systems.

Nevertheless, the data from Colleverde suggest that this aspect of patronage is a fairly recent acquisition. Until the unification of Italy in 1860, mediation of the client's dealings with the outside was only a minor aspect of the patron's role. The patronage system had its basis in the peasant's dependence upon the landlords, who historically were the peasants' sole recourse to physical protection and economic aid. However, under the domain of the States of the Church, the community had only tangential relations with the larger political unit, and for most Colleverdesi the sphere of social interaction extended no farther than the nearby market towns and a radius of neighboring communities within which there were cycles of fairs and religious festivals. Certainly for the lower classes extra-local contact was minimal, and there was little necessity for mediation.

After 1860, however, the new nation began the task of knitting together the separate regions and communities. The degree of contact between the national and the local system increased steadily, and more and more the nation encroached into the lives of Colleverdesi of all classes. The governmental bureaucracy entered the community, bringing to the peasants the bewildering demands of official papers and legal codes and occasionally offering equally bewildering economic benefits. New roads and railroads brought outsiders into the community and took Colleverdesi out. Obligatory military service and temporary labor opportunities in other areas took men to distant parts of the nation. To some the developing national institutions meant potential jobs, both within the community and outside it. In order to deal with their expanding world, the lower-class Colleverdesi needed help. The peasants turned to those who had always aided them. Persons who had no landlord, or whose landlord was unwilling or unable to help, sought other sources.

Of the functions performed by the patrons during the period from 1860 to 1945, some represent a continuity with the earlier role of the landlord: lending money or guaranteeing loans, giving employment, helping to provide dowries for the daughters of the client families, providing medicines and helping to obtain medical services. However, to these were added many new functions, involving the mediation of contacts with the world outside the community. The patron filled out the papers which were required at every significant step in the individual's life, and he spoke to bureaucrats on his client's behalf. As government benefits were introduced, the patron was needed to obtain them. For example, Sra. M., whose husband was killed during World War I, tried in vain for months to collect a government pension for war widows, and only after her patron spoke of her case to the appropriate officials did she succeed in getting it. The patron interpreted the law to his client and offered advice. If there were trouble with the authorities, the patron would intervene. Many cases could be cited of persons who were arrested by the *carabinieri* and released after intervention of the patron, and of others who were sentenced to prison and for whom the patron obtained pardons.

If a client had to go out of the community for any purpose, the patron would recommend him to some acquaintance at the destination. In fact, all dealings with institutions or persons outside the local system required personal recommendations from a mediator.[5] When M.'s grandfather tried to get the local tobacco concession, when R. applied to a military specialists' school, when F. took his deaf sister to a physician in Rome, when P. as a young man went periodically to the coastal plain to seek work, when T. took his bride to Perugia to choose a coral necklace — all would have considered it foolhardy to do so without a recommendation from a respected contact, and to get a recommendation a patron was

[5] The recommendation, the importance of which has diminished only slightly though the channels have changed, is a request for a personal favor to the recommender, and it is not at all concerned with the qualifications of the person on whose behalf it is made. The value of a recommendation depends first upon the status of the recommender, second upon the closeness of his connection to the addressee, and third upon the closeness of the connection between the recommender and the recommended.

needed. As jobs in the national institutions expanded, access to them was also a matter of recommendations, and this remained no less true even after adoption of the *concorso* system, an open competition for available jobs based on examinations.

In the patronage patterns of traditional Colleverde which were vividly recalled by older informants, the mediation functions were, in fact, the major importance of the patron. For example, the most valuable patron was neither the wealthiest nor the most generous, but the one with the best connections. Yet this aspect of the patron's role was elaborated only in the late nineteenth and early twentieth centuries. It was only after the community became incorporated into a complex nation, a nation which made demands upon and offered opportunities to individuals and which required extensive contact between the local and the national system, that the dominant features of "traditional" Colleverdesi patronage emerged.

In general, the patrons of Colleverde in the 1860–1945 years can be characterized as a small group of local signori, no more than a dozen heads of households at any given time. Most were mezzadria landlords, owning as little as two or three small farms or as much as several hundred hectares of land. Some of the landlords also occupied professional or administrative positions of authority in the community, as schoolteachers, pharmacists, physicians, tax collectors, priests, and elected administrators. In addition, some of these positions were held by non-landed members of local landowning families, who also formed part of the patron group. The non-landowning patrons also included a few bureaucrats and professionals (the comune secretaries, two of the pharmacists, a physician, and some of the priests), who came to Colleverde from other towns in Umbria.

The patrons were not an aristocratic group, although a few landowning families traced remote kinship ties to Umbrian nobility. New members were recruited from the commercial class of the towns and cities of the region, for it was this class that throughout Umbria was taking over the holdings of the traditional landowners and educating its sons for the burgeoning bureaucracy and the professions. There was little mobility into the patron group from the lower classes of Colleverde, for the sons of the prosperous peasants and artisans who were able to purchase land, even those who acquired substantial holdings, were not accepted as "true" signori, nor were they likely to possess the connections with signori in other communities which were an important foundation of patronage power. Despite their ties and sometimes their origins outside the community, the patrons were fully a local group. They lived in Colleverde, and their identification with it was strong.

Each patron performed a wide range of mediation functions, the same individual often being for his clients at once the economic, political, social, and ideological link to the larger society. As a group, the patrons controlled virtually all the critical junctures between the local and the national systems. Colleverde's economic relationships with the rest of the nation were for the most part the concern only of the major landlords. This follows from the duality of the traditional mezzadria economy: only the landowners sold produce on the market, while the peasants' share was consumed for their own subsistence. Direct participation in the political life of the nation was limited to the patrons. The mayor and the administrative council of the community were selected from this group; they were elected, but until well into the twentieth century few persons other than the signori were eligible to vote. Moreover, it was primarily members of this group who acted as local representatives of the state, for local jobs in the bureaucracy were passed from one member of the elite to another. Even the religious ties of the community to the Universal Church were to a large extent in the hands of the patrons. Not only were the priests of Colleverde themselves often part of the patron group (as major landlords holding the several Church-owned mezzadria farms and usually as members of landowning families), but the patrons constituted the lay leadership of the local Church, and many had kin connections with Church officials throughout Umbria and in the Vatican.

The patrons had numerous social relationships based on kinship and friendship extending beyond the community, and they practiced frequent inter-community visiting. The peasants, in contrast, maintained only rare ties of closest kinship outside the immediate area. Finally, because the patrons were long the only literate persons in Colleverde, they were the carriers of the national culture, and values and ideas filtered down through them to the rest of the community. In sum, this group were mediators precisely because they had, almost exclusively, direct access to the nation and because they occupied those formal positions which were the links between the local and national systems. In turn, this control of the mediation functions was the primary source of their power to exert patronage.

Looking outward from the community, the mediators' relationships with the national system were of two kinds. First, the local patrons had extensive ties with near and distant kinsmen, friends, and business associates — social and power equals to themselves — in other village centers, in towns, and in cities of the region. These were continuing relationships based on reciprocal, equivalent obligations. Second, the Colleverdesi patrons, as well as their equal numbers in other communities, were themselves clients to more powerful, higher-status patrons. These higher patrons did not function at the village level but belonged to the spheres of town and city. Thus, through a hierarchy of patronage (cf. Kenny 1960:22–23; Gillin 1962:37), Colleverde was linked to the higher units of organization within the nation.

The structure of the traditional relationship between Colleverde and the larger society may now be summarized. A small group of local upper-class families, the nucleus of which were the major landowners of the community, functioned as mediators. Although they considered themselves as Colleverdesi and were active in community life, they were also participants in the national society. Within the local context they acted out the national culture, creating — of a village of only 300 inhabitants — an urban-like, "civilized" center in the rustic countryside. Interaction between the mediators and those in the community for whom they mediated was based on a continuing and intimate patron-client relationship, which was an extension of the landlord-peasant relationship defined by the land-tenure system. Because of the nature of this relationship and the constant presence of the patrons, the clients were strongly aware of a wider social sphere without direct participation in it. Thus, the countryside was linked to the village (and the village lower class to its upper class) by the vertical bond of patronage, while the village was in turn linked to the outside through the patrons' participation in two kinds of networks: horizontal ties with equivalent members of other communities and vertical ties through hierarchies of patrons operating at progressively higher levels of national integration.

This description is an example of only one form that a part-whole relationship through mediators can take. Such a relationship varies significantly in at least five different ways. First, there is a tie between the mediators and those in the local system for whom they mediate, which need not be one of patronage. Not only are there other mechanisms by which the connection with a mediator may be established (such as kinship, ritual kinship, employment, or political appointment) and other cultural rationales for maintaining the connection, but the mutual rights and obligations and the kind of interaction involved may be different. The relationship may be limited to specific areas rather than as wide-ranging as the patron-client tie; the interaction may be sporadic rather than fairly continuous; and the quality of the relationship may be more or less emotionally intense than that between patron and client in Colleverde.

Second, the nature of the mediators themselves may vary greatly — their history, their traditions, and the manner in which they are recruited and replaced. For example, a mediating group recruited from economically successful peasants would be quite different from the patrons of Colleverde, a landowning class with quasi-aristocratic traditions.

Third, there is variation in the particular functions which the mediators perform and in the way in which these functions are combined. A political functionary whose main business is the collection of taxes is a mediator of a very different kind from the Colleverdesi patrons, whose functions touched every aspect of life. In the case of Colleverde, all mediating functions were combined and performed by the same group, but at the opposite extreme there might be a separate mediator for each function.

Fourth, the size of the mediating group may vary, determining a smaller or larger number of channels into the local system. In Colleverde there were multiple channels, intermediate between the extreme possibilities of a single individual as mediator and a situation in which each household has its own links to the national system.

A fifth dimension of variation is the kind of relationship of the mediators to the local system and the degree of their integration into it. The patrons of Colleverde were fully a part of the local system and locally resident. However, mediators may also be part of the local system yet not reside in the community, they may reside locally but remain detached from the local system, or they may be outsiders with only tangential relationships to the local system.

CONCLUSION: THE FATE OF THE MEDIATOR

Since World War II, a new kind of relationship between Colleverde and the larger society has developed. The patrons have been pushed out of the strategic link positions. Yet their control of the "critical junctures" has not passed to newly emerging groups in the society or to persons occupying different roles. New groups and new roles have appeared through which persons act as intermediaries, but the junctures can no longer be "guarded." Diverse, competing intermediaries, as well as an increase in direct participation by individuals in the national system, have replaced the mediators. It appears that the mediator represents a general form of community-nation relationship which characterizes an early phase in developing nation-states, and which regularly gives way as integration of the total society advances.

REFERENCES CITED

Bandini, M.

1957 *Cento Anni di Storia Agraria Italiana*. Roma.

Foster, G. M.

1963 "The Dyadic Contract in Tzintzuntzan, II: Patron-Client Relationship." *American Anthropologist* 65: 1280–1294.

Friedl, E.

1959 "The Role of Kinship in the Transmission of National Culture to Rural Villages in Mainland Greece." *American Anthropologist* 61: 30–38.

Geertz, C.

1960 "The Changing Role of Cultural Broker: The Javanese *Kijaji*." *Comparative Studies in Society and History* 2: 228–249.

Gillin, J. P.

1962 *Some Signposts for Policy. Social Change in Latin America Today*, pp. 14–62. New York.

Istituto Nazionale di Economia Agraria

1956 La Distribuzione della Proprietà Fondiaria in Italia, v. I: Relazione generale, a cura di Giuseppe Medici. Roma.

Kenny, M.
1960 "Patterns of Patronage in Spain." *Anthropological Quarterly* 33: 14–23.

Pitkin, D. S.
1959 "The Intermediate Society: A Study in Articulation." *Intermediate Societies, Social Mobility, and Communication*, ed. V. F. Ray, pp. 14–19. Proceedings of the 1959 Spring Meeting of the American Ethnological Society. Seattle.

Pitt-Rivers, J. A.
1954 *The People of the Sierra*. London.

Redfield, R.
1956 *Peasant Society and Culture*. Chicago.

Silverman, S. F.
1963 *Landlord and Peasant in an Umbrian Community*. Unpublished Ph.D. dissertation, Columbia University.

Steward, J. H.
1955 *Theory of Culture Change*. Urbana.

Wolf, E. R.
1956 "Aspects of Group Relations in a Complex Society: Mexico." *American Anthropologist* 58: 1065–1078.

PART FOUR

PEASANT PERSONALITIES

Introduction: Peasant Character and Personality

George M. Foster

City dwellers like to believe that rural life is marked by fundamental virtues and moral values which they themselves have lost in the impersonality and wickedness of the urban setting. This is an ancient and durable belief going back, as Caro Baroja recently pointed out, at least to the authors of classical antiquity. Citing such writers as Aristophanes, Varro, Caesar, and Tacitus, he summarizes the views they express: "In the city are found vice, corruption and artifice; in the country the ancient virtues, and still more than in the countryside of one's own land, in the countryside of distant regions which have a smaller number of cities" (1963:28).

Dreams die hard, and in all subsequent centuries writers and other intellectuals have extolled the traditional village and farm at the expense of the city. Not only are rural values described in glowing terms, but the golden view of this life has been a basic factor in determining many political, economic, and social policies. The United States national agricultural policy, for example, has long been based on the conviction that the single-family farm and the sturdy country people who operate it are essential to American democracy, whatever the financial cost may be to other sectors of society. Most community development programs in rural areas of newly developing countries reflect the belief that villagers are by nature friendly and cooperative people who look upon themselves as members of one big family which, with a modicum of outside encouragement and material help, will be able to solve many of its problems.

Anthropologists, too, have looked upon rural life in this way. When Robert Redfield described Tepoztlán in rather romantic and idyllic fashion, he was expressing a point of view accepted by most of his colleagues (1930). So, when twenty years later Oscar Lewis described these same Tepoztecos in a much less flattering way (1951) — as individualistic, suspicious, envious, and uncooperative — many anthropologists were shocked. Both the loyalty-to-people-studied code, unconsciously assumed in the ethics of the profession, and Western man's view of his good society, had been violated.

What, then, are the facts about the behavior, the personalities, of peasants? Are they Rousseauean as Redfield saw them, are they good sportsmen playing the game of life, as Pitt-Rivers saw them (1960–

1961), or do they display more than a touch of the characteristics that Lewis found in Tepoztlán? Obviously there is no simple answer. Peasants cannot be characterized as "nasty" or "nice" any more than can other people; they are both, and at the same time. Most anthropologists who have lived in peasant villages have found working there extremely pleasant, and after initial periods of distrust, they have formed deep attachments to and friendships with the local people, quite comparable to those in their home communities and with their peers. Peasants frequently — usually, we would say — display a profound sense of humor, an ability to enjoy life, a spirit of independence, and a compulsion to be loyal to friends. For an anthropologist, it is difficult to find a more pleasant or more satisfying type of community in which to work.

At the same time, few contemporary anthropologists or other scholars who have lived in peasant villages find the way of life to be idyllic. It is one thing to come to such a community, amply supplied with fellowship or other support, with none of the local worries of earning a living, and another thing to have to exist and care for a family on the meager resources available to most peasants. For poverty is a harsh fact of peasant life. Most peasants are poor, and they must struggle desperately for their small share of the economic and other good that is available in their villages. They are economically and socially and culturally deprived peoples, and to them, as to all deprived peoples, certain forms of nonidyllic behavior have real survival value. Most students of peasant life have found the people to be suspicious, distrustful, and envious of others, viewing the universe around them as essentially hostile. This cognitive orientation is accompanied by behavior forms that constitute defense mechanisms: the peasant criticizes and gossips about others, hoping thus to discourage them from taking undue advantage of him, and he cooperates not from a sense of village welfare, but rather in formally defined ways such as work-exchange institutions or through godparenthood ties. In brief, the "quality" of interpersonal relationships in most peasant villages is quite distinct from that which city people like to believe. A few years ago much evidence for this view was summarized by Foster, and an opposite point of view was offered by Pitt-Rivers (Foster 1960–61; Pitt-Rivers 1960–61).

Subsequent peasant studies generally substantiate a picture of much suspicion, criticism, and lack of cooperation. The Blums, for example, in their perceptive account of Greek village life, speak of the "vulnerability" felt by people. "For example, it was said that when good things happen to a villager, the other villagers express their envy in gossip, criticism, and calumny. The villagers described their life altogether as an uneasy one, with each family feeling competitive and jealous toward any other that might achieve success or happiness. The phrases they used over and over were 'We eat each other,' or 'They eat the bride,' 'They eat the newborn infant' "(1965:128). Among the peasants of Aritama, Colombia, the Reichel-Dolmatoffs found that cooperativeness is generally shunned, or at best is only nominal: "Most people are extremely wary of establishing such cycles of obligation. The motives of any favor done for a person are always analyzed with suspicion, the idea of disinterested help or friendship being quite incomprehensible. The smallest gift is interpreted as probably being but a bait used to establish a chain of mutual obligations, in which the one who did the first favor will invariably benefit most and put the other party in an unfavorable position" (1961:258).

Only in east and southeast Asia do we find marked exceptions to some of these behavior patterns. Anthropologists have noted cooperation and community responsibility in Japan, for example, that is quite lacking in Latin America, the Mediterranean, and perhaps India. Robert Smith, in the article reprinted in this book (pp. 246–255), describes the Japanese hamlet — the *buraku* — as a social unit showing "marked solidarity," where "the predominant tone is one of cooperative effort," in which in spite of tensions "to a remarkable degree the individual is ready to set aside personal interest in favor of the community." Potter, too, finds a strong cooperative tradition in traditional Chinese society that is lacking in non-Oriental peasant communities. Life may be bitter and tensions between families high, but means of enforcing cooperative efforts for communal welfare override these points of friction.

In Southeast Asia — the data are particularly good for Thailand — the picture is again different. Phillips notes an "absence among village residents of any strong sense of identification with the needs of their community as a whole. Except for religious activities and the reciprocal work groups organized for rice transplanting and harvesting — the rewards for which are directly personal — the villagers simply are not predisposed to participate in communal projects" (1965:17). At the same time, courtesy and a reluctance to offend others, is a marked character trait, and a desire to avoid conflict sometimes seems to Westerners to be reflected in a reluctance to become deeply involved emotionally *with anyone*. Certainly the suspicion, distrust, criticism, envy, and frequent physical violence found in peasant groups in India and westward are less common in Thailand.

In the selections that follow, several facets of the peasant personality question are dealt with. F. G. Friedmann describes the alienation and extreme suspicion that characterizes south Italian peasants as due, among other things, to the absolute poverty that characterizes their lives. Michael Maccoby, basing his conclusions in large measure on psychological tests, paints a picture of personality quite distinct from that described by Redfield, a fact all the more interesting because Las Cuevas and Tepoztlán are scarcely twenty miles apart. Foster's conclusions have much in common with those of Friedmann. Speaking generally of peasant behavior he sees lack of access to *all* the good things in life, not merely economic good — as promoting a particular type of behavior quite distinct from the urban stereotype of rural life — a behavior which is functional in traditional peasant communities, but which now severely handicaps peasants who must make major changes in their lives if they are to survive in the modern world.

Bernard Gallin directs himself to a topic that has interested anthropologists since Redfield first suggested it. Redfield saw a peasant as "a man who is in effective control of a piece of land to which he has long been attached by ties of tradition and sentiment. The land and he are parts of one thing, one old-established body of relationships" (1956:27–28). He also spoke of the "intimate and reverent attitude toward the land" (1956:112) held by some peasants, and he pointed out that agriculture is seen by villagers as a way of life and not a business for profit. In the face of evidence to the contrary in southern Europe, Redfield accepted the fact that mystical reverence for the land is not a universal characteristic of the peasant's view of the good life, although it was not easy for him to do so. Gallin's article points out that in an area far removed from the Mediterranean, love of the land also is not a generic characteristic of peasant attitudes, and he suggests that apparent attachment to the land is, in fact, an attachment to the only form of economic security that Chinese peasants have had. We suspect that this explanation has wide applicability.

REFERENCES CITED

Blum, Richard and Eva Blum
1965 *Health and Healing in Rural Greece*. Stanford, Cal.: Stanford University Press.

Caro Baroja, Julio
1963 "The City and the Country: Reflexions on Some Ancient Commonplaces," in *Mediterranean Countrymen* (Julian Pitt-Rivers, ed.), pp. 27–40. Paris — LaHaye: Mouton & Co.

Foster, George M.
1960–1961 "Interpersonal Relations in Peasant Society," *Human Organization* 19: 174–178.

Lewis, Oscar
1951 *Life in a Mexican Village: Tepoztlán Restudied*. Urbana, Ill.: University of Illinois Press.

Phillips, Herbert P.
1965 *Thai Peasant Personality: The Patterning of Interpersonal Behavior in the Village of Bang Chan*. Berkeley and Los Angeles: University of California Press.

Pitt-Rivers, Julian
1960–1961 " 'Interpersonal Relations in Peasant Society': A Comment," *Human Organization* 19:180–183.

Redfield, Robert
1930 *Tepoztlán: A Mexican Village. A Study of Folk Life*. Chicago: University of Chicago Press.

1956 *Peasant Society and Culture*. Chicago: University of Chicago Press.
Reichel-Dolmatoff, Gerardo and Alicia
1961 *The People of Aritama: The Cultural Personality of a Colombian Mestizo Village*. Chicago: University of Chicago Press.

PEASANT SOCIETY AND THE IMAGE OF LIMITED GOOD

George M. Foster

COGNITIVE ORIENTATION

The members of every society share a common cognitive orientation which is, in effect, an unverbalized, implicit expression of their understanding of the "rules of the games" of living imposed upon them by their social, natural, and supernatural universes. A cognitive orientation provides the members of the society it characterizes with basic premises and sets of assumptions normally neither recognized nor questioned which structure and guide behavior in much the same way grammatical rules unrecognized by most people structure and guide their linguistic forms. All normative behavior of the members of a group is a function of their particular way of looking at their total environment, their unconscious acceptance of the "rules of the game" implicit in their cognitive orientation.

A particular cognitive orientation cannot be thought of as world view in a Redfieldian sense, i.e., as something existing largely at a conscious level in the minds of the members of the group.[1] The average man of

From "Peasant Society and the Image of Limited Good" in *American Anthropologist*, Vol. 67, No. 2 (April 1965). Reprinted by permission of the American Anthropological Association. The Tzintzuntzan field work 1958–1963 which played an important part in the development of the ideas in this paper was supported in part by National Science Foundation Grant No. G7064, and by annual grants from the Research Committee of the University of California (Berkeley). In the preparation of this paper I am indebted for critical comments from Mary L. Foster and Richard Currier. This article appears under the title "El caracter del campesino" in *La Revista Mexicana de Psicoanálisis, Psiquiatría, y Psicologia*, Vol. 1, No. 1, 1965.

[1] Redfield describes world view as "that outlook upon the universe that is characteristic of a people" (1952:30). Redfield believes that "No man holds all he knows and feels about the world in his conscious mind at once" (1955:91), but at the same time he feels that a reasonably thoughtful informant can describe his world view so that an anthropologist can understand it, that if there is an "emphasized meaning" in the phrase it is "in the suggestion it carries of the structure of things *as man is aware of them*. It is the way *we see* ourselves in relation to all else" (1953:86. Emphasis added). Hallowell, on the other hand, tends to see world view in terms of a cognitive orientation of which the Ojibwa are not consciously aware and which they do not abstractly articulate (1960).

any society cannot describe the underlying premises of which his behavior is a logical function any more than he can outline a phonemic statement which expresses the patterned regularities in his speech. As Kluckhohn has pointed out, cognitive orientations (he speaks of "configurations") are recognized by most members of a society only in the sense that they make choices "with the configurations as unconscious but determinative backgrounds" (1943:218).

In speaking of a cognitive orientation — the terms "cognitive view," "world view," "world view perspective," "basic assumptions," "implicit premises," and perhaps "ethos" may be used as synonyms — I am as an anthropologist concerned with two levels of problems: (1) the nature of the cognitive orientation itself which I see as something "psychologically real," and the ways in which and the degree to which it can be known; and (2) the economical representation of this cognitive orientation by means of models or integrating principles which account for observed behavior, and which permit prediction of behavior yet unnoted or unperformed. Such a model or principle is, as Kluckhohn has often pointed out, an inferential construct or an analytic abstraction derived from observed behavior.

A model or integrating principle is not the cognitive orientation itself, but for purposes of analysis the two cannot be separated. A well-constructed model is, of course, not really descriptive of behavior at all (as is, for example, the term "ethos" as used by Gillin [1955] to describe contemporary Latin American culture). A good model is heuristic and explanatory, not descriptive, and it has predictive value. It encourages an analyst to search for behavior patterns, and relationships between patterns, which he may not yet have recognized, simply because logically — if the model is sound — it is reasonable to expect to find them. By the same token, a sound model should make it possible to predict how people are going to behave when faced with certain alternatives. A model therefore has at least two important functions: it is conducive to better field work, and it has practical utility as a guide to policy and action in developmental programs.

A perfect model or integrating principle of a particular world view should subsume *all* behavior of the members of a group. In practice it is unreasonable to expect this. But the best model is the one that subsumes the greatest amount of behavior in such fashion that there are no mutually incompatible parts in the model, i.e., forms of behavior cast together in what is obviously a logically inconsistent relationship. Kluckhohn speculated about the possibility of a single model, a dominant

---

Kenny recently defined "values" in much the same sense in which I understand "cognitive orientation": "In regard to values, I use the term to denote a series of conceptions from which a preferred type of conduct is evolved and imposed by the social system; which can be abstracted by analysis but which may not be consciously recognized or verbalized by every member of the society" (1962–1963:280).

"master configuration" characterizing an entire society, for which he suggested the terms "integration" (1941:128) and "ethos" (1943:221), but I believe he never attempted the task of describing a complete ethos. Opler, on the other hand, has described Lipan Apache culture in terms of twenty "themes" which are, however, to a considerable extent descriptive, and which in no way approximate a master model (1946).[2]

How does an anthropologist fathom the cognitive orientation of the group he studies, to find patterns that will permit building a model or stating an integrating principle? Componential analysis and other formal semantic methods have recently been much in vogue, and these techniques unquestionably can tell us a great deal. But the degree of dissension among anthropologists who use these methods suggests that they are not a single royal road to "God's truth" (cf. Burling 1964). I suspect there will always remain a considerable element of ethnological art in the processes whereby we come to have some understanding of a cognitive orientation. However we organize our thought processes, we are engaging in an exercise in structural analysis in which overt behavior (and the simpler patterns into which this behavior is readily seen to fall) is viewed somewhat as a reflection or representation of a wider reality which our sensory apparatus can never directly perceive. Or, we can view the search for a cognitive view as an exercise in triangulation. Of each trait and pattern the question is asked, "Of what implicit assumption might this behavior be a logical function?" When enough questions have been asked, the answers will be found to point in a common direction. The model emerges from the point where the lines of answers intersect. Obviously, an anthropologist well acquainted with a particular culture cannot merely apply simple rules of analysis and automatically produce a model for, or even a description of, a world view. In effect, we are dealing with a pyramidal structure: low-level regularities and coherences relating overt behavior forms are fitted into higher-level patterns which in turn may be found to fall into place at a still higher level of integration. Thus, a model of a social structure, sound in itself, will be found to be simply one expression of a structural regularity which will have analogues in religion and economic activities.

Since all normative behavior of the members of a group is a function of its particular cognitive orientation, both in an abstract philosophical sense and in the view of an individual himself, all behavior is "rational" and sense-making. "Irrational" behavior can be spoken of only in the context of a cognitive view which did not give rise to that behavior. Thus, in a rapidly changing world, in which peasant and primitive peoples are pulled into the social and economic context of whole nations, some of their behavior may appear irrational to others because the social, economic, and natural universe that in fact controls the conditions of their

[2] E.g., Theme 14: "The extended domestic family is the basic social and economic unit and the one to which first allegiance and duties of revenge are due" (1946:152).

life is other than that revealed to them — however subconsciously — by a traditional world view. That is, a peasant's cognitive view provides moral and other precepts that are guides to — in fact, may be said to produce — behavior that may not be appropriate to the changing conditions of life he has not yet grasped. For this reason when the cognitive orientation of large numbers of a nation's people is out of tune with reality, these people will behave in a way that will appear irrational to those who are more nearly attuned to reality. Such peoples will be seen as constituting a drag (as indeed they may be) on a nation's development, and they will be cutting themselves off from the opportunity to participate in the benefits that economic progress can bring.

In this paper I am concerned with the nature of the cognitive orientation of peasants, and with interpreting and relating peasant behavior as described by anthropologists to this orientation. I am also concerned with the implications of this orientation and related behavior to the problem of the peasant's participation in the economic growth of the country to which he may belong. Specifically, I will outline what I believe to be the dominant theme in the cognitive orientation of classic peasant societies,[3] show how characteristic peasant behavior seems to flow from this orientation, and attempt to show that this behavior — however incompatible with national economic growth — is not only highly rational in the context of the cognition that determines it, but that for the main-

[3] By the term "classic" peasant societies I follow Kroeber's statement: "They form a class segment of a larger population which usually contains also urban centers. . . . They constitute part-societies with part-cultures" (1948:284). My definition of peasant is structural and relational, only incidentally concerned with how people earn a living. Firth writes, "By a peasant economy one means a system of small-scale producers, with a simple technology and equipment, often relying primarily for their subsistence on what they themselves produce. The primary means of livelihood of the peasants is cultivation of the soil" (1956:87). This, and all other definitions stressing agriculture and purely subsistence economies, seem to me to be deficient. I find "classic" peasant societies rimming the Mediterranean, in the village communities of the Near East, of India, and of China. Emergent peasant communities probably existed in Middle America before the Conquest; today a large proportion of Indian and mestizo villages in Latin America must be thought of as peasant. Parts of Negro Africa, where there are indigenous cities and well-developed markets, are at least semi-peasant, although the lack of a Great Tradition perhaps excludes them from the "classic" label.

As I see it, classic peasant communities have grown up in a symbiotic spatial-temporal relationship to the more complex component of the society of which they are a part, i.e., the pre-industrial market and administrative city. Peasant communities "represent the rural expression of large, class-structured, economically complex, pre-industrial civilizations, in which trade and commerce, and craft specialization are well developed, in which money is commonly used, and in which market disposition is the goal for a part of the producer's efforts" (Foster 1960–1961:175).

The reader will realize, I am sure, that the model, drawn up on the basis of an ideal type of rural community in a pre-industrial world, does not in fact fit any contemporary peasant community with exactitude. All modern peasant communities have experienced to a greater or lesser degree inroads from the urban, industrial world, and to that degree they must depart from the model. I freely confess, too, that I tend to see peasant society in the image of Tzintzuntzan, Michoacán, Mexico, and that greater familiarity with other peasant communities might well lead me to different expressions of details in the model.

tenance of peasant society in its classic form, it is indispensable.[4] The kinds of behavior that have been suggested as adversely influencing economic growth are, among many, the "luck" syndrome, a "fatalistic" outlook, inter- and intra-familial quarrels, difficulties in cooperation, extraordinary ritual expenses by poor people and the problems these expenses pose for capital accumulation, and the apparent lack of what the psychologist McClelland (1961) has called "need for Achievement." I will suggest that peasant participation in national development can be hastened not by stimulating a psychological process, the need for achievement, but by creating economic and other opportunities that will encourage the peasant to abandon his traditional and increasingly unrealistic cognitive orientation for a new one that reflects the realities of the modern world.

THE IMAGE OF LIMITED GOOD

The model of cognitive orientation that seems to me best to account for peasant behavior is the "Image of Limited Good." By "Image of Limited Good" I mean that broad areas of peasant behavior are patterned in such fashion as to suggest that peasants view their social, economic, and natural universes — their total environment — as one in which all of the desired things in life such as land, wealth, health, friendship and love, manliness and honor, respect and status, power and influence, security and safety, *exist in finite quantity* and *are always in short supply*, as far as the peasant is concerned. Not only do these and all other "good things" exist in finite and limited quantities, but in addition *there is no way directly within peasant power to increase the available quantities*. It is as if the obvious fact of land shortage in a densely populated area applied to all other desired things: not enough to go around. "Good," like land, is seen as inherent in nature, there to be divided and redivided, if necessary, but not to be augmented.[5]

For purposes of analysis, and at this stage of the argument, I am considering a peasant community to be a closed system. Except in a special — but extremely important — way, a peasant sees his existence as de-

[4] I don't advocate maintenance of classic peasant society, nor do I think it has a permanent place in the world.

[5] I do not believe the Image of Limited Good is characteristic only of peasant societies. Quite the contrary, it is found, in one degree or another, in most or all socio-economic levels in newly developing countries, and it is, of course, equally characteristic of traditional socialist doctrine. I am not even sure that it is *more* characteristic of peasants than of other groups. I examine the hypothesis in the context of peasant societies simply because they are relatively less complex than many other groups, because good data are readily available, and because my arguments can easily be tested in the field by other anthropologists. I suspect, but will leave the ultimate decision to others, that the Image of Limited Good when applied to peasant society *goes further* in explaining behavior than when applied to any other type of society. That is, and by way of illustration, although the Image of Limited Good certainly is characteristic of many urban Mexicans, including those of the highest social and economic classes, the complexity of that society requires additional themes beyond those needed in peasant society to produce an equally coherent and satisfying explanation.

termined and limited by the natural and social resources of his village and his immediate area. Consequently, there is a primary corollary to the Image of Limited Good: if "Good" exists in limited amounts which cannot be expanded, and if the system is closed, it follows that *an individual or a family can improve a position only at the expense of others.* Hence an apparent relative improvement in someone's position with respect to any "Good" is viewed as a threat to the entire community. Someone is being despoiled, whether he sees it or not. And since there is often uncertainty as to who is losing — obviously it may be ego — *any* significant improvement is perceived, not as a threat to an individual or a family alone, but as a threat to *all* individuals and families.

This model was first worked out on the basis of a wide variety of field data from Tzintzuntzan, Michoacán, Mexico: family behavior, exchange patterns, cooperation, religious activities, court claims, disputes, material culture, folklore, language, and many other bits and pieces. At no point has an informant even remotely suggested that this is his vision of his universe. Yet each Tzintzuntzeño organizes his behavior in a fashion entirely rational when it is viewed as a function of this principle which he cannot enunciate.[6]

[6] I have long speculated that the economic world view of classic peasants, and particularly of people in Tzintzuntzan, the peasant community I know best (Foster 1948, 1960–1961, 1961a, 1961b, 1962, 1963, 1964a, 1964b, 1965) can be described by a principle I have called the Image of the Static Economy. Writing in 1948 I suggested that Tzintzuntzeños see their economic world as one in which "the wealth goal is difficult and almost impossible of achievement; hence, the stimulus of a reasonable chance of success is lacking" (1948:289). Much later I attempted to explain the frequent poor quality of interpersonal relations in peasant society in the same terms, suggesting that the "economic pie" is seen (quite realistically) as constant in size, and unexpandable. Consequently, "If someone is seen to get ahead, logically it can only be at the expense of others in the village" (1960 1961:177). Subsequently I spoke of the Image of the Static Economy as inhibiting village cooperation, particularly in community development programs (1961b). Several sentences by Honigmann about a West Pakistan village stimulated me to think about the wider applicability of the Image of the Static Economy, i.e., that this integrating principle is simply one expression of a total cognitive view with analogues in a great many other areas of life. Honigmann wrote, "One dominant element in the character structure (not only here but elsewhere in West Pakistan) is the implicit belief that good of all kinds is limited. There is only so much respect, influence, power, and love in the world. If another has some, then somebody is certainly deprived of that measure" (1960:287).

Other anthropologists also have recognized the Image of Limited Good, usually indirectly via the corollary that good fortune can be obtained only at the expense of others. Leslie, in describing world view in the Mexican Zapotec Indian peasant village of Mitla, comments that " . . . for the most part they [the Mitleños] assumed that one man's gains were another man's losses" (1960:71). Beals, speaking of a specific incident in an Indian village, writes, "There is only so much land in Gopalpur; what one man farms cannot be farmed by another. Although Danda [a farmer], by developing distant lands, has expanded the economy of Gopalpur, people do not think of his achievement in terms of the creation of wealth. They think rather that Danda's success contributes to their own failure" (1962:64). Mandelbaum, introducing the new edition of the Wisers' *Behind Mud Walls*, notes that the villagers fail to understand "that each may prosper best when all in a community prosper together. There is rather the idea that the good things of the village are forever fixed in amount, and each person must manipulate constantly to garner a large slice for his own" (1963:x).

The model of Limited Good, when "fed back" to behavior in Tzintzuntzan, proved remarkably productive in revealing hitherto unsuspected structural regularities linking economic behavior with social relations, friendship, love and jealousy patterns, health beliefs, concepts of honor and masculinity, *egoísmo* manifestations — even folklore (Foster 1964a). Not only were structural regularities revealed in Tzintzuntzan, but much peasant behavior known to me from other field work, and reported in the literature, seemed also to be a function of this cognitive orientation. This has led me to offer the kinds of data I have utilized in formulating this model, and to explain the interpretations that seem to me to follow from it, as characterizing in considerable degree classic peasant societies, in the hope that the model will be tested against other extensive bodies of data. I believe, obviously, that if the Image of Limited Good is examined as a high-level integrating principle characterizing peasant communities, we will find within our individual societies unsuspected structural regularities and, on a cross-cultural level, basic patterns that will be most helpful in constructing the typology of peasant society. The data I present in support of this thesis are illustrative, and are not based on an exhaustive survey of peasant literature.

In the following pages I will offer evidence under four headings that seems to me to conform to the model I have suggested. I will then discuss the implications of this evidence.

Economic Behavior. When the peasant views his economic world as one in which Limited Good prevails, and he can progress only at the expense of another, he is usually very near the truth. Peasant economies, as pointed out by many authors, are not productive. In the average village there *is* only a finite amount of wealth produced, and no amount of extra hard work will significantly change the figure. In most of the peasant world land has been limited for a long, long time, and only in a few places have young farmers in a growing community been able to hive off from the parent village to start on a level of equality with their parents and grandparents. Customarily land is not only limited but it has become increasingly limited, by population expansion and soil deterioration. Peasant productive techniques have remained largely unchanged for hundreds, and even thousands, of years; at best, in farming, this means the Mediterranean plow drawn by oxen, supplemented by human-powered hand tools. Handicraft techniques in weaving, pottery-making, woodworking and building likewise have changed little over the years.[7]

In fact, it seems accurate to say that the average peasant sees little or no relationship between work and production techniques on the one

[7] Cf. Wolf, "Marginal location and traditional technology together limit the production power of the community, and thus its ability to produce cash crops for the market. This in turn limits the number of goods brought in from the outside which the community can afford to consume. The community is *poor*" (1955:457).

hand, and the acquisition of wealth on the other. Rather, wealth is seen by villagers in the same light as land: present, circumscribed by absolute limits, and having no relationship to work. One works to eat, but not to create wealth. Wealth, like land, is something that is inherent in nature. It can be divided up and passed around in various ways, but, within the framework of the villagers' traditional world, it does not grow. Time and tradition have determined the shares each family and individual hold; these shares are not static, since obviously they do shift. But the reason for the relative position of each villager is known at any given time, and any significant change calls for explanation.

Friendship. The evidence that friendship, love, and affection are seen as strictly limited in peasant society is strong. Every anthropologist in a peasant village soon realizes the narrow path he must walk to avoid showing excessive favor or friendship toward some families, thereby alienating others who will feel deprived, and hence reluctant to help him in his work. Once I brought a close friend from Tzintzuntzan, working as a bracero in a nearby town, to my Berkeley home. When safely away from the camp he told me his brother was also there. Why did he not tell me, so I could have invited him? My friend replied, in effect, that he was experiencing a coveted "good" and he did not want to risk diluting the satisfaction by sharing it with another.

Adams reports how a social worker in a Guatemalan village unwittingly prejudiced her work by making more friends in one barrio than in the other, thereby progressively alienating herself from potential friends whose help she needed (1955:442). In much of Latin America the institutionalized best friend, particularly among post-adolescents, variously known as the *amigo carnal*, or the *cuello* or *camaradería* (the latter two described by Reina for Guatemala [1959]) constitutes both recognition of the fact that true friendship is a scarce commodity, and serves as insurance against being left without any of it. The jealousies and feelings of deprivation felt by one partner when the other leaves or threatens to leave sometimes lead to violence.

Widespread peasant definitions of sibling rivalry suggest that a mother's ability to love her children is viewed as limited by the amount of love she possesses. In Mexico when a mother again becomes pregnant and weans her nursing child, the child often becomes *chípil*. It fusses, cries, clings to her skirt, and is inconsolable. The child is said to be *celoso*, jealous of its unborn sibling whose presence it recognizes and whom it perceives as a threat, already depriving him of maternal love and affection. Chípil is known as *chip* or *chipe* in Guatemala, where it is described in a classic article by Paul (1950), as *sipe* in Honduras, and simply as *celos* ("jealousy") in Costa Rica. *Chucaque* in southern Colombia, described as the jealousy of a child weaned because of its mother's pregnancy, appears to be the same thing (communicated by Dr. Virginia Gutierrez de Pineda).

A similar folk etiology is used among the semi-peasant peoples of

Buganda to explain the onset of *kwashiorkor* in a child recently weaned. If the mother is again pregnant, the child is said to have *obwosi*, and shows symptoms of pale hair, sweating of hands and feet, fever, diarrhea, and vomiting. "The importance of pregnancy is such that if a woman takes a sick child to a native doctor the first question he asks is 'Are you pregnant?' " (Burgess and Dean 1962:24). The African logic is the reverse of, but complementary to, that of Latin America: it is the *unborn child* that is jealous of its older sibling, whom it tries to poison through the mother's milk, thereby forcing weaning (Burgess and Dean 1962:25). In both areas, insufficient quantities of love and affection are seen as precipitating the crisis. In Buganda, "In the local culture it is essential that the mother should devote herself to the unborn child or a child recently born, at the expense of any other children; *there does not seem to be an easy acceptance of the idea that there can be enough love for all*" (Burgess and Dean 1962:26. Emphasis added).

Similarly, in an Egyptian village, sibling rivalry is recognized at this period in a child's development. As in Latin America, jealousy is one way; it is always the older who is jealous of the younger. "It is also acknowledged that the youngest child becomes jealous immediately his mother's abdomen becomes enlarged on pregnancy and he is usually told of the forthcoming event." This jealousy, in excess, may have ill effects on the child, causing diarrhea, swellings, lack of appetite, temper tantrums, and sleeplessness (Ammar 1954:107–109).[8]

In parts of Guatemala chipe is a term used to express a husband's jealousy of his pregnant wife, for temporary loss of sexual services and for the attention to be given to the baby. Tepoztlán husbands also suffer from *chipilez*, becoming sleepy and not wanting to work. Oscar Lewis says a husband can be cured by wearing a strip of his wife's skirt around his neck (1951:378). In Tonalá, Jalisco, Mexico, husbands often are jealous of their adolescent sons and angry with their wives because of the affection the latter show their offspring. A wife's love and affection are seen as limited; to the extent the son receives what appears to be an excessive amount, the husband is deprived (communicated by Dr. May Diaz). In the Egyptian village described by Ammar a new mother-in-law is very affectionate toward her son-in-law, thereby making her own unmarried sons and daughters jealous. By showing affection to the outsider, the woman obviously is seen as depriving her own offspring of something they wish (Ammar 1954:51, 199).

Health. It is a truism to peasants that health is a "good" that

[8] In fact, the child who is chípil may have good reason to be fussy: withdrawn from the breast and put on an adult diet, he frequently experiences an acute protein-deficiency condition that stimulates his behavior. And, of course, sibling-rivalry exists, probably, in all societies. The significant thing is not the real physiological or psychological root of the condition, but rather that the condition is explained by a folk etiology which assumes a mother can give only so much love and affection to her children, so that the older ones are deprived in favor of the newest, even before the newest makes its appearance.

exists in limited quantities. Peasant folk medicine does not provide the protection that scientific medicine gives those who have access to it, and malnutrition frequently aggravates conditions stemming from lack of sanitation, hygiene, and immunization. In peasant societies preoccupation with health and illness is general, and constitutes a major topic of interest, speculation, and discussion. Perhaps the best objective evidence that health is viewed within the framework of Limited Good is the widespread attitude toward blood which is, to use Adams' expression, seen as "non-regenerative" (Adams 1955:446). For obvious reasons, blood is equated with life, and good blood, and lots of it, means health. Loss of blood — if it is seen as something that cannot be renewed — is thus seen as a threat to health, a permanent loss resulting in weakness for as long as an individual lives. Although best described for Guatemala, the belief that blood is non-regenerative is widespread in Latin America. This belief, frequently unverbalized, may be one of the reasons it is so difficult to persuade Latin Americans to give blood tranfusions: by giving blood so that someone can have more, the donor will have less.

Similar beliefs are found in Nigeria (communicated by Dr. Adeniyi-Adeniji Jones) and they are well known in Indian peasant villages. Here the psychological problem is further compounded by the equation of blood with semen: one drop of semen to seven (or forty, depending on area) drops of blood. The exercise of masculine vitality is thus seen as a permanently debilitating act. Only so much sexual pleasure is allotted man, and nothing he can do will increase his measure. Sexual moderation and the avoidance of bloodletting are the course of the prudent man.

In parts of Mexico (e.g., the Michoacán villages of Tzintzuntzan and Erongarícuaro) the limits on health are reflected in views about long hair. A woman's long hair is much admired, but the price is high: a woman with long hair is thought always to be thin and wan, and she cannot expect to have vigor and strength. Sources of vitality are insufficient to grow long hair and still leave an individual with energy and a well-fleshed body.

Manliness and Honor. Oft-noted peasant sensitiveness to real or imagined insults to personal honor, and violent reactions to challenges which cast doubt on a man's masculinity, appear to be a function of the belief that honor and manliness exist in limited quantities, and that consequently not everyone can enjoy a full measure. In rural Mexico, among braceros who have worked in the United States, American ethnologists have often been asked, "In the United States it's the wife who commands, no?" Masculinity and domestic control appear to be viewed much like other desirable things: there is only so much, and the person who has it deprives another. Mexican men find it difficult to believe that a husband and wife can share domestic responsibilities and decision making, without the husband being deprived of his *machismo*. Many believe a wife, however good, must be beaten from time to time, simply so she will not lose sight of a God-decreed familial hierarchy. They are astonished and shocked to learn that an American wife-beater can be jailed; this seems an incredibly unwarranted intrusion of the State into God's plans for the family.

The essence of machismo is valor, and *un hombre muy valiente*, i.e., a *macho*, is one who is strong and tough, generally fair, not a bully, but who never dodges a fight, and who always wins. Above all, a macho inspires *respeto* ("respect"). One achieves machismo, it is clear, by depriving others of access to it.

In Greece *philotimo*, a "love of honor," equates closely with Mexican machismo. A man who is physically sound, lithe, strong, and agile has philotimo. If he can converse well, show wit, and act in other ways that facilitate sociability and establish ascendency, he enhances his philotimo. One attacks another male through his philotimo, by shaming or ridiculing him, by showing how he lacks the necessary attributes for a man. Consequently, avoiding ridicule becomes a major concern, a primary defense mechanism among rural Greek males. In a culture shot through with envy and competitiveness, there is the ever-present danger of attack, so a man must be prepared to respond to a jeer or insult with a swift retort, an angry challenge, or a knife thrust. "Philotimo can be enhanced at the expense of another. It has a see-saw characteristic; one's own goes up as another's declines . . . the Greek, in order to maintain and increase his sense of worth, must be prepared each moment to assert his superiority over friend and foe alike. It is an interpersonal combat fraught with anxiety, uncertainty, and aggressive potentials. As one proverb describes it, 'When one Greek meets another, they immediately despise each other' " (R. Blum and E. Blum 1962:20–22).

PEASANT BEHAVIOR AS A FUNCTION OF THE "IMAGE OF LIMITED GOOD"

If, in fact, peasants see their universe as one in which the good things in life are in limited and unexpandable quantities, and hence personal gain must be at the expense of others, we must assume that social institutions, personal behavior, values, and personality will all display patterns that can be viewed as functions of this cognitive orientation. Preferred behavior, it may be argued, will be that which is seen by the peasant as maximizing his security, by preserving his relative position in the traditional order of things. People who see themselves in "threatened" circumstances, which the Image of Limited Good implies, react normally in one of two ways: maximum cooperation and sometimes communism, burying individual differences and placing sanctions against individualism; or extreme individualism.

Peasant societies seem always to choose the second alternative. The reasons are not clear, but two factors may bear on the problem. Cooperation requires leadership. This may be delegated democratically by the members of a group itself; it may be assumed by a strong man from within the group; or it may be imposed by forces lying outside the group. Peasant societies — for reasons that should be clear in the following analysis — are unable by their very nature to delegate authority, and assumption of authority by a strong man is, at best, temporary, and not a structural solution to a problem. The truncated political nature of peasant societies, with real power lying outside the community, seems effectively to discourage local assumption and exercise of power, except as an agent of these outside forces. By the very nature of peasant society, seen as a structural part of a larger society, local development of leadership which might make possible cooperation is effectively prevented by the rulers of the political unit of which a particular peasant community is an element, who see such action as a potential threat to themselves.

Again, economic activities in peasant societies require only limited cooperation. Peasant families typically can, as family units, produce most of their food, farm without extra help, build their houses, weave cloth for their clothes, carry their own produce to market and sell it — in short, take care of themselves with a degree of independence impossible in an industrial society, and difficult in hunting-fishing-gathering societies. Peasants, of course, usually do not live with the degree of independence here suggested, but it is more nearly possible than in any other type of society.

Whatever the reasons, peasants are individualistic, and it logically follows from the Image of Limited Good that each minimal social unit (often the nuclear family and, in many situations, a single individual) sees itself in perpetual, unrelenting struggle with its fellows for possession of or control over what it considers to be its share of scarce values. This is a position that calls for extreme caution and reserve, a reluctance to reveal true strength or position. It encourages suspicion and mutual distrust, since things will not necessarily be what they seem to be, and it also encourages a male self image as a valiant person, one who commands respect, since he will be less attractive as a target than a weakling. A great deal of peasant behavior, I believe, is exactly what we would predict from these circumstances. The works of Lewis (1951), Banfield (1958), Simmons (1959), Carstairs (1958), Dube (1958), the Wisers (1963), and Blackman (1927) (summarized by Foster 1960–1961) and many others testify to the "mentality of mutual distrust" (Friedmann 1953:24) that is widespread in peasant societies.

Since an individual or family that makes significant economic progress or acquires a disproportionate amount of some other "good" is seen to do so at the expense of others, such a change is viewed as a threat to the stability of the community. Peasant culture is provided with two principal mechanisms with which to maintain the essential stability: (a) an agreed-upon, socially acceptable, preferred norm of behavior for its people, and (b) a "club" and a "carrot," in the form of sanctions and rewards, to ensure that real behavior approximates this norm.

The agreed-upon norm that promotes maximum community stability is behavior that tends to maintain the status quo in relationships. The individual or family that acquires more than its share of a "good," and particularly an economic "good," is, as we have seen, viewed as a threat to the community at large. Individuals and families which are seen to or are thought to progress violate the preferred norm of behavior, thereby stimulating cultural mechanisms that redress the imbalance. Individuals or families that lose something, that fall behind, are seen as a threat in a different fashion; their envy, jealousy, or anger may result in overt or hidden aggression toward more fortunate people.

The self-correcting mechanisms that guard the community balance operate on three levels, viz: (1) Individual and family behavior. At this level I am concerned with the steps taken by *individuals* to maintain their positions in the system, and the ways in which they try to avoid both sanctions and exploitation by fellow villagers. (2) Informal and usually unorganized group behavior. At this level I am concerned with the steps taken by the *community*, the sanctions that are invoked when it is felt someone is violating the agreed-upon norm of behavior. Negative sanctions are the "club." (3) Institutionalized behavior. At this level I am concerned with the "carrot": major community expressions of cultural forms which neutralize achieved imbalances. Each of these forms will be examined in turn.

Individual and Family Action. On the individual-family level, two rules give guidance to preferred behavior. These can be stated as: (a) Do not reveal evidence of material or other improvement in your relative position, lest you invite sanctions; should you display improvement, take action necessary to neutralize the consequences. (b) Do not allow yourself to fall behind your rightful place, lest you and your family suffer.

A family deals with the problem of real or suspected improvement in its relative position by a combination of two devices. First, it attempts to conceal evidence that might lead to this conclusion, and it denies the veracity of suggestions to this effect. Second, it meets the charge head on, admits an improvement in relative position, but shows it has no intention of using this position to the detriment of the village by neutralizing it through ritual expenditures, thereby restoring the status quo.

Accounts of peasant communities stress that in traditional villages people do not compete for prestige with material symbols such as dress, housing, or food, nor do they compete for authority by seeking leadership roles. In peasant villages one notes a strong desire to look and act like everyone else, to be inconspicuous in position and behavior. This theme is well summed up in the Wisers' paragraph on the importance of dilapidated walls suggesting poverty as a part of a family's defense (1963:120).

Also much remarked is the peasant's reluctance to accept leadership roles. He feels — for good reason — that his motives will be suspect and that he will be subject to the criticism of neighbors. By seeking, or even accepting, an authority position, the ideal man ceases to be ideal. A "good" man therefore usually shuns community responsibilities (other than of a ritual nature); by so doing he protects his reputation. Needless to say, this aspect of socially-approved behavior heavily penalizes a peasant community in the modern world by depriving it of the leadership which is now essential to its development.

The mechanism invoked to minimize the danger of loss of relative position appears to center in the machismo-philotimo complex. A tough, strong man whose fearlessness in the face of danger and whose skill in protecting himself and his family are recognized does not invite exploitation. A "valiant" individual can command the "respect" so much sought after in many peasant societies, and he can strive toward security with the goal in mind (however illusory) of being able to live — as is said in Tzintzuntzan — *sin compromisos* ("without obligations" to, or dependency on, others). A picture of the ideal peasant begins to emerge: a man who works to feed and clothe his family, who fulfills his community and ceremonial obligations, who minds his own business, who does not seek to be outstanding, but who knows how to protect his rights. Since a macho, a strong man, discourages exploitation, it is clear that this personality characteristic has a basic function in peasant society. Not surprisingly, defense of this valuable self-image may, by the standards of other societies, assume pathological proportions, for it is seen as a basic weapon in the struggle for life.

The ideal man must avoid the appearance of presumption, lest this be interpreted as trying to take something that belongs to another. In tracing the diffusion of new pottery-making techniques in Tzintzuntzan I found that no one would admit he had learned the technique from a neighbor. The inevitable reply to my question was *Me puse a pensar* ("I dreamed it up all by myself"), accompanied by a knowing look and a tapping of the temple with the forefinger. Reluctance to give credit to others, common in Mexico, is often described as due to *egoísmo*, an egotistical conceited quality. Yet if egoísmo, as exemplified by unwillingness to admit profiting by a neighbor's new pottery knowledge, is seen as a function of an image of Limited Good, it is clear that a potter *must* deny that the idea is other than his own. To confess that he "borrowed" an idea is to confess that he has taken something not rightfully his, that he is consciously upsetting the community balance and the self-image he tries so hard to maintain. Similarly, in trying to determine how compadrazgo (godparenthood) ties are initiated, I found no informant who admitted he had asked a friend to serve; he always was asked by another. Informants appear to fear that admission of asking may be interpreted as presuming or imposing on another, trying to get something to which they may not be entitled.

A complementary pattern is manifest in the general absence of compliments in peasant communities; rarely is a person heard to admire the performance of another, and when admiration is expressed by, say, an anthropologist, the person admired probably will try to deny there is any reason to compliment him. Reluctance of villagers to compliment each other again looks, at first glance, like egoísmo. But in the context of the Limited Good model, it is seen that such behavior is proper. The person who compliments is, in fact, guilty of aggression; he is telling someone to his face that he is rising above the dead level that spells security for all, and he is suggesting that he may be confronted with sanctions.

Consider this interpretation as applied to an incident reported in southern Italy: "My attempt, in private, to praise a peasant friend for his large farm and able system of farming brought a prompt and vigorous denial that he did anything special. He said, 'There is no system, you just plant.' This attitude was expressed by others in forced discussions of farming" (Cancian 1961:8). Dr. Cancian offers this as illustrating the peasant's lack of confidence in his own ability to change his environment. Speaking specifically of agriculture, he writes that "All the examples indicate denial of the hope of progress in agriculture and alienation from the land" (Cancian 1961:8). I believe the peasant viewed Dr. Cancian's praise as threatening, since it reminded him of his vulnerability because of his superior farming methods. His denial is not of hope of progress, but of cause for anyone to envy him.

Informal, Unorganized Group Action. The ideal man strives for moderation and equality in his behavior. Should he attempt to better his comparative standing, thereby threatening village stability, the informal and usually unorganized sanctions appear. This is the "club," and it takes the form of gossip, slander, backbiting, character assassination, witchcraft or the threat of witchcraft, and sometimes actual physical aggression. These negative sanctions usually represent no formal community decision, but they are at least as effective as if authorized by law. Concern with public opinion is one of the most striking characteristics of peasant communities.

Negative sanctions, while usually informal, can be institutionalized. In peasant Spain, especially in the north, the charivari (*cencerrada*) represents such an instance. When an older man marries a much younger woman — usually a second marriage for the groom — marriageable youths serenade the couple with cowbells (*cencerros*) and other noisemakers, parade straw-stuffed manikins representing them through the streets, incense the manikins with foul-smelling substances, and shout obscenities. It seems clear that this symbolizes the resentment of youths, who have not yet had even one wife, against the inequalities represented by an older man who has already enjoyed marriage, who takes a young bride from the available pool, thereby further limiting the supply for the youths. By institutionalizing the sanctions the youths are permitted a degree of freedom and abuse not otherwise possible.

Institutionalized Action. Attempted changes in the balance of a peasant village are discouraged by the methods just described; *achieved* imbalance is neutralized, and the balance restored, on an institutional level. A person who improves his position is encouraged — by use of the carrot — to restore the balance through conspicuous consumption in the form of ritual extravagance. In Latin America he is pressured into sponsoring a costly fiesta by serving as *mayordomo*. His reward is prestige, which is viewed as harmless. Prestige cannot be dangerous since it is traded for dangerous wealth; the mayordomo has, in fact, been "disarmed," shorn of his weapons, and reduced to a state of impotence. There is good reason why peasant fiestas consume so much wealth in fireworks, candles, music, and food; and why, in peasant communities the rites of baptism, marriage, and death may involve relatively huge expenditures. These practices are a redistributive mechanism which permits a person or family that potentially threatens community stability gracefully to restore the status quo, thereby returning itself to a state of acceptability. Wolf, speaking specifically of the "closed" Indian peasant community of Mexico as it emerged after the Conquest, puts it this way: "the system takes from those who have, in order to make all men have-nots. By liquidating the surpluses, it makes all men rich in sacred experience but poor in earthly goods. Since it levels differences of wealth, it also inhibits the growth of class distinctions based on wealth. . . . In engineering parlance, it acts as a feedback, returning a system that is beginning to oscillate to its original course" (1959:216).

THE "OPEN" ASPECTS OF PEASANT SOCIETY

To aid in the development of the argument to this point, I have asked the reader momentarily to accept a contrary-to-fact assumption: that a peasant community is a closed system. By so doing he is better able to view the world through the eyes of traditional peasants. We can now abandon this fiction for, of course, by definition a peasant community is in fact *not* closed. And, although the typical peasant does not fully appreciate the implications for self-advancement of this "openness" of his society, he does recognize that for a lucky few success may be achieved by tapping wealth and resources that exist outside the village system. Such success, unlike that believed to be generated within the village, and hence at the expense of others, may be envied, but it is not seen as a direct threat to community stability, for no one within the community has lost anything. Still, such success must be explained. In today's transitional peasant communities, seasonal emigration for wage labor is the most available way in which one can tap outside wealth. Hundreds of thousands of Mexican peasants have come to the United States as braceros in recent years and many, through their earnings, have pumped significant amounts of capital into their communities. Braceros generally are not criticized or attacked for acquisition of this wealth; it is clear that their good fortune is not at the direct expense of others within the village. Fuller finds a similar realistic appraisal of the wealth situation in a Lebanese community: "they [the peasants] realize . . . that the only method of increasing their incomes on a large scale is to absent themselves from the village for an extended period of time and to find work in more lucrative areas" (1961:72).

These examples, however, are but modern variants of a much older pattern in which luck and fate — points of contact with an open system — are viewed as the only socially acceptable ways in which an individual can acquire more "good" than he previously has had. In traditional (not transitional) peasant communities an otherwise inexplicable increase in wealth is often seen as due to the discovery of treasure which may be the result of fate or of such positive action as making a pact with the Devil. Recently I have analyzed treasure tales in Tzintzuntzan and have found without exception they are attached to named individuals who, within living memory, have suddenly begun to live beyond their means. The usual evidence is that they suddenly opened stores, in spite of their known previous poverty (Foster 1964a). Erasmus has recorded this interpretation among Sonora villagers (1961:251), Wagley finds it in an Amazon small town (1964:128), and Friedmann reports it in southern Italy (1953:224). Clearly, the role of treasure tales in communities like these is to account for wealth that can be explained in no other manner.

The common peasant concern with finding wealthy and powerful patrons who can help them is also pertinent in this context. Since such patrons usually are outside the village, they are not part of the closed system. Their aid, and material help, like bracero earnings or buried treasure, are seen as coming from beyond the village. Hence, although the lucky villager with a helpful patron may be envied, the advantages he receives from his patron are not seen as depriving other villagers of something rightfully theirs. In Tzintzuntzan a villager who obtains a "good" in this fashion makes it a first order of business to advertise his luck and the source thereof, so there can be no doubt as to his basic morality; this behavior is just the opposite of usual behavior, which is to conceal good fortune.

Treasure tales and concern with patrons, in turn, are but one expression of a wider view: that any kind of success and progress is due to fate, the favor of deities, to luck, but not to hard work, energy, and thrift. Banfield notes in a south Italian community, "In the TAT stories, dramatic success came only as a gift of fortune: a rich gentleman gave a poor boy a violin, a rich gentlewoman adopted an abandoned child, and so on" (1958:66). Continuing, "Great success, then, is obtained by the favor of the saints or by luck, certainly not by thrift, work, and enterprise. These may be important if one is already lucky, but not otherwise, and few would invest large amounts of effort — any more than they would invest large amounts of fertilizer — on the rather remote possibility of good fortune" (Banfield 1958:114). Friedmann also finds that the south Italian peasant "firmly believes that the few who have succeeded in making a career were able to do so for some mysterious reason: one hit upon a hidden treasure; another was lucky enough to win in the lottery; another was called to America by a successful uncle" (1953:224).

All such illustrations underlie a fundamental truth not always recognized in comparing value systems: in the traditional peasant society hard work and thrift are moral qualities of only the slightest functional value. Given the limitations on land and technology, additional hard work in village productive enterprises simply does not produce a significant increment in income. It is pointless to talk of thrift in a subsistence economy in which most producers are at the economic margin; there is usually nothing to be thrifty about. As Fei and Chang point out, "In a village where the farms are small and wealth is accumulated slowly, there are very few ways for a landless man to become a landowner, or for a petty owner to become a large landowner. . . . It is not going too far to say that in agriculture there is no way really to get ahead. . . . To become rich one must leave agriculture" (1945:227). And again, "The basic truth is that enrichment through the exploitation of land, using the traditional technology, is not a practical method for accumulating wealth" (Fei and Chang: 1945:302). And, as Ammar says about Egypt, "It would be very difficult with the fellah's simple tools and the sweat involved in his work, to convince him that his lot could be improved by more work" (1954:36).

PEASANT COGNITIVE ORIENTATION AND ECONOMIC GROWTH

It is apparent that a peasant's cognitive orientation, and the forms of behavior that stem therefrom, are intimately related to the problems of economic growth in developing countries. Heavy ritual expenditures, for example, are essential to the maintenance of the equilibrium that spells safety in the minds of traditional villagers. Capital accumulation, which might be stimulated if costly ritual could be simplified, is just what the villager wants to prevent, since he sees it as a community threat rather than a precondition to economic improvement.

In national developmental programs much community-level action in agriculture, health and education is cast in the form of cooperative undertakings. Yet it is abundantly clear that traditional peasant societies are cooperative only in the sense of honoring reciprocal obligations, rather than in the sense of understanding total community welfare, and that mutual suspicion seriously limits cooperative approaches to village problems.[9] The Image of Limited Good model makes clear the peasant logic

[9] Cf. Geertz 1962:244, speaking of Javanese peasants and their need for periodic labor mobilization: "What has developed . . . is not so much a general spirit of cooperativeness — Javanese peasants tend, like many peasants, to

underlying reluctance to participate in joint ventures. If the "good" in life is seen as finite and nonexpandable, and if apart from luck an individual can progress only at the expense of others, what does one stand to gain from a cooperative project? At best an honorable man lays himself open to the charge — and well-known consequences — of utilizing the venture to exploit friends and neighbors; at worst he risks his own defenses, since someone more skillful or less ethical than he may take advantage of the situation.

The Anglo-Saxon virtues of hard work and thrift seen as leading to economic success are meaningless in peasant society. Horatio Alger not only is not praiseworthy, but he emerges as a positive fool, a clod who not knowing the score labors blindly against hopeless conditions. The gambler, instead, is more properly laudable, worthy of emulation and adulation. If fate is the only way in which success can be obtained, the prudent and thoughtful man is the one who seeks ways in which to maximize his luck-position. He looks for the places in which good fortune is most apt to strike, and tries to be there. This, I think, explains the interest in lotteries in underdeveloped countries. They offer the only way in which the average man can place himself in a luck-position. The man who goes without lunch, and fails to buy shoes for his children in order to buy a weekly ticket, is not a ne'er-do-well; he is the Horatio Alger of his society who is doing what he feels is most likely to advance his position. He is, in modern parlance, buying a "growth stock." The odds are against him, but it is the *only* way he knows in which to work toward success.

Modern lotteries are very much functional equivalents of buried treasure tales in peasant societies, and at least in Tzintzuntzan the correlation is clearly understood. One elderly informant, when asked why no one had found buried treasure in recent years, remarked that this was indeed true but that "Today we Mexicans have the lottery instead." Hence, the "luck" syndrome in underdeveloped countries is not primarily a deterrent to economic progress, as it is sometimes seen from the vantage point of a developed country, but rather it represents a realistic approach to the near-hopeless problem of making significant individual progress.

David C. McClelland has argued persuasively that the presence of a

---

be rather suspicious of groups larger than the immediate family — but a set of explicit and concrete practices of exchange of labor, of capital, and of consumption goods which operate in all aspects of life. . . . This sense for the need to support specific, carefully delineated social mechanisms which can mobilize labor, capital, and consumption resources scattered thinly among the very dense population, and concentrate them effectively at one point in space and time; is the central characteristic of the much-remarked, but poorly understood, 'cooperativeness' of the Javanese peasant. Cooperation is founded on a very lively sense of the mutual value to the participants of such cooperation, not on a general ethic of the unity of all men or on an organic view of society which takes the group as primary and the individual as secondary."

human motivation which he calls "the need for Achievement" (*n* Achievement) is a precursor to economic growth, and that it is probably a *causative* factor, that it is "a change in the minds of men which produces economic growth rather than being produced by it" (McClelland 1963:81; 1961). McClelland further finds that in experimental situations children with high *n* Achievement avoid gambling situations because should they win there would be no sense of personal achievement, while children with low *n* Achievement do not perform in a way suggesting they calculate relative risks and behave accordingly. "They [low *n* Achievement children] thus manifest behavior like that of many people in underdeveloped countries who, while they act very traditionally economically, at the same time love to indulge in lotteries — risking a little to make a great deal on a very long shot" (McClelland 1963:86). McClelland sees this as showing an absence of a sense of realistic risk calculation.

If the arguments advanced in this paper are sound, it is clear that *n* Achievement is rare in traditional peasant societies, not because of psychological factors, but because display of *n* Achievement is met by sanctions that a traditional villager does not wish to incur. The villager who feels the need for Achievement, and who does something about it, is violating the basic, unverbalized rules of the society of which he is a member. Parents (or government school programs) that attempt to instill *n* Achievement in children are, in effect, training children to be misfits in their society *as long as it remains a relatively static system.*

As indicated above, I would argue in opposition to McClelland that the villager who buys a lottery ticket *is not* behaving in an inconsistent fashion — that is, rationally in traditional economic matters, irrationally in his pursuit of luck — but in the most consistent fashion possible. He *has* calculated the chances and risks, and in a most realistic manner *in the context of the way in which he sees his traditional environment.* The man who buys a lottery ticket in a peasant society, far from displaying lack of *n* Achievement, is in fact showing a maximum degree of it. It simply happens that this is about the only display of initiative that is permitted him by his society, since it is the only form not viewed as a threat to the community by his colleagues.

Banfield, and Fei and Chang, appear to see the economic factors in the presence or absence of initiative in much the same light. The former writes about the Italian peasant, "The idea that one's welfare depends crucially upon conditions beyond one's control — upon luck or the caprice of a saint — and that one can at best only improve upon good fortune, not create it — this idea must certainly be a check on initiative" (Banfield 1958:114). The latter see, in the Chinese data, evidence that a particular economic attitude is a function of a particular view of life. The traditional economic attitude among Chinese peasants is that of "contentment . . . an acceptance of a low standard of material comfort" (Fei and Chang 1945:82), which is contrasted to "acquisitiveness" characteristic of "modern industry and commerce in an expanding universe" (Fei and Chang 1945:83). "Both attitudes — contentment and acquisitiveness — have their own social context. Contentment is adopted in a closed economy; acquisitiveness in an expanding economy. *Without economic opportunities the striving for material gain is a disturbance to the existing order, since it means plunder of wealth from others.* . . . Therefore, to accept and be satisfied with the social role and material rewards given by the society is essential. But when economic opportunity develops through the development of technology and when wealth can be acquired through the exploitation of nature instead of through the exploitation of man, the doctrine of contentment becomes reactionary because it restricts individual initiative" (Fei and Chang 1945:84. Emphasis added). In other words, change the economic rules of the game and change the cognitive orientation of a peasant society, and a fertile field for the propagation of *n* Achievement is created.

For the above reasons, I believe most strongly that the primary task in development is not to attempt to create *n* Achievement at the mother's knee but to try to change the peasants' view of his social and economic universe, away from an Image of Limited Good toward that of expanding opportunity in an open system, *so that he can feel safe* in displaying initiative. The brakes on change are less psychological than social. Show the peasant that initiative is profitable, and that it will not be met by negative sanctions, and he acquires it in short order.

This is, of course, what is happening in the world today. Those who have known peasant villages over a period of years have seen how the old sanctions begin to lose their power. Local entrepreneurs arise in response to the increasing opportunities of expanding national economies, and emulative urges, with the city as the model, appear among these people. The successful small entrepreneurs begin to see that the ideal of equality is inimical to their personal interests, and presently they neither seek to conceal their well being nor to distribute their wealth through traditional patterns of ritual extravagance. *N* Achievement bursts forth in full vitality in a few new leaders, and others see the rewards and try to follow suit. The problem of the new countries is to create economic and social conditions in which this latent energy and talent is not quickly brought up against absolute limits, so that it is nipped in the bud. This is, of course, the danger of new expectations — released latent *n* Achievement — outrunning the creation of opportunities.

Viewed in the light of Limited Good peasant societies are not conservative and backward, brakes on national economic progress, because of economic irrationality nor because of the absence of psychological characteristics in adequate quantities. They are conservative because individual progress is seen as — and in the context of the traditional society in fact is — the supreme threat to community stability, and all cultural forms *must* conspire to discourage changes in the status quo. Only by being conservative can peasant societies continue to exist as peasant societies. But change cognitive orientation through changing access to opportunity, and the peasant will do very well indeed; and his *n* Achievement will take care of itself.

REFERENCES CITED

Adams, Richard N.
1955 "A Nutritional Research Program in Guatemala," in *Health, Culture and Community*, Benjamin D. Paul, ed. New York: Russell Sage Foundation.

Ammar, Hamed
1954 *Growing up in an Egyptian Village: Silwa, Province of Aswan*. London: Routledge & Kegan Paul, Ltd.

Banfield, Edward C.
1958 *The Moral Basis of a Backward Society*. Glencoe: The Free Press.

Beals, Alan R.
1962 *Gopalpur: a South Indian Village*. Case Studies in Cultural Anthropology, G. and L. Spindler, eds. New York: Holt, Rinehart & Winston.

Blackman, Winifred S.
1927 *The Fellāhin of Upper Egypt*. London: George C. Harrap & Co., Ltd.

Blum, Richard and Eva
[1962?] "Temperate Achilles: Practices and Beliefs Associated with Alcohol Use. A Supplement to Health and Healing in Rural Greece." Pre-publication draft, Institute for the Study of Human Problems, Stanford University.

Burgess, Anne and R. F. A. Dean (eds.)
1962 *Malnutrition and Food Habits*. London: Tavistock Publications.

Burling, Robbins
1964 "Cognition and Componential Analysis: God's Truth or Hocus-pocus?" *American Anthropologist* 66:20–28.

Cancian, Frank
1961 "The Southern Italian Peasant: World View and Political Behavior." *Anthropological Quarterly* 34:1–18.

Carstairs, G. Morris
1958 *The Twice-Born: A Study of a Community of High-Caste Hindus*. Bloomington: University of Indiana Press.

Dube, S. C.
1958 *India's Changing Villages: Human Factors in Community Development*. London: Routledge and Kegan Paul, Ltd.

Erasmus, Charles J.
1961 *Man Takes Control: Cultural Development and American Aid*. Minneapolis: University of Minnesota Press.

Fei, Hsiao-Tung, and Chih-I Chang
1945 *Earthbound China: A Study of Rural Economy in Yunnan*. Chicago: University of Chicago Press.

Firth, Raymond

1956 *Elements of Social Organization*. London: Watts & Co.

Foster, George M.

1948 *Empire's Children: the People of Tzintzuntzan*. Mexico City: Smithsonian Institution, Institute of Social Anthropology, Publication no. 6.

1960–61 "Interpersonal Relations in Peasant Society." *Human Organization* 19:174–178.

1961a "The Dyadic Contract: A Model for the Social Structure of a Mexican Peasant Village." *American Anthropologist* 63:1173–1192.

1961b "Community Development and the Image of the Static Economy." *Community Development Bulletin* 12:124–128.

1962 *Traditional Cultures and the Impact of Technological Change*. New York: Harper & Brothers.

1963 "The Dyadic Contract in Tzintzuntzan, II: Patron-Client Relationship." *American Anthropologist* 65:1280–1294.

1964a "Treasure Tales, and the Image of the Static Economy in a Mexican Peasant Community." *Journal of American Folklore* 77:39–44.

1964b "Speech Forms and Perception of Social Distance in a Spanish-speaking Mexican Village." *Southwestern Journal of Anthropology* 20:107–122.

1965 "Cultural Responses to Expressions of Envy in Tzintzuntzan." *Southwestern Journal of Anthropology* 21:24–35.

Friedmann, F. G.

1953 "The World of 'La Miseria,' " *Partisan Review* 20:218–231.

Fuller, Anne H.

1961 *Buarij: Portrait of a Lebanese Muslim Village*. Cambridge, Mass.: Distributed for the Center for Middle Eastern Studies of Harvard University.

Geertz, Clifford

1962 "The Rotating Credit Association: A 'Middle Rung' in Development." *Economic Development and Cultural Change* 10:241–263.

Gillin, John

1955 "Ethos Components in Modern Latin America." *American Anthropologist* 57:488–500.

Hallowell, A. Irving

1960 "Ojibway Ontology, Behavior, and World View." In *Culture in History: Essays in Honor of Paul Radin*, S. Diamond, ed., New York: Columbia University Press.

Honigmann, John J.

1960 "A Case Study of Community Development in Pakistan." *Economic Development and Cultural Change* 8:288–303.

Kenny, Michael

1962–1963 "Social Values and Health in Spain: Some Preliminary Considerations." *Human Organization* 21:280–285.

Kluckhohn, Clyde

1941 "Patterning as Exemplified in Navaho Culture." In *Language, Culture, and Personality* (Leslie Spier, ed.). Menasha, Wis.: Sapir Memorial Publication Fund.

1943 "Covert Culture and Administrative Problems." *American Anthropologist* 45:213–227.

Kroeber, A. L.

1948 *Anthropology*. New York: Harcourt, Brace and Company.

Leslie, Charles M.

1960 *Now We Are Civilized: A Study of the World View of the Zapotec Indians of Mitla, Oaxaca*. Detroit: Wayne State University Press.

Lewis, Oscar

1951 *Life in a Mexican Village: Tepoztlán Restudied*. Urbana: University of Illinois Press.

McClelland, David C.

1961 *The Achieving Society*. Princeton, N.J.: D. Van Nostrand Co.

1963 "The Achievement Motive in Economic Growth." In *Industrialization and Society* (B. F. Hoselitz and Wilbert E. Moore, eds.) UNESCO, Mouton.

Mandelbaum, David G.

1963 Foreword to *Behind Mud Walls 1930–1960*, by William H. Wiser and Charlotte Viall Wiser. Berkeley and Los Angeles: University of California Press.

Opler, Morris Edward

1946 "An Application of the Theory of Themes in Culture." *Journal of the Washington Academy of Sciences* 36:137–166.

Paul, Benjamin D.

1950 "Symbolic Sibling Rivalry in a Guatemalan Indian Village." *American Anthropologist* 52:205–218.

Redfield, Robert

1952 "The Primitive World View." *Proceedings of the American Philosophical Society* 96:30–36.

1953 *The Primitive World and Its Transformations*. Ithaca: Cornell University Press.

1955 *The Little Community: Viewpoints for the Study of a Human Whole*. Chicago: University of Chicago Press.

Reina, Ruben E.

1959 "Two Patterns of Friendship in a Guatemalan Community." *American Anthropologist* 61:44–50.

Simmons, Ozzie G.

1959 "Drinking Patterns and Interpersonal Performance in a Peruvian Mestizo Community." *Quarterly Journal of Studies on Alcohol* 20:103–111.

Wagley, Charles

1964 *Amazon Town: A Study of Man in the Tropics*. New York: Alfred A. Knopf, Borzoi Book LA-4.

Wiser, William H. and Charlotte Viall Wiser

1963 *Behind Mud Walls 1930–1960*. Berkeley and Los Angeles: University of California Press.

Wolf, Eric R.

1955 "Types of Latin American Peasantry: A Preliminary Discussion." *American Anthropologist* 57:452–471.

1959 *Sons of the Shaking Earth*. Chicago: University of Chicago Press.

THE WORLD OF "LA MISERIA"

F. G. Friedmann

One of the chief characteristics of traditional peasant cultures is that for them "history," as well as the natural factors of the environment, belong to the realm of the given. That is to say, peasants see themselves as subject to the workings of history but scarcely as makers of it. In this respect the peasants of Calabria and Lucania differ in no way from the rural populations of other parts of the world. The difference lies, rather, in the special and intricate relationship between geography and history that prevails in southern Italy, for more history has passed over this region than over any comparable area.

Calabria and Lucania are above all isolated provinces. Most of the towns are situated at a distance from the main highways and railroads. Some are connected by dirt road or mule track with some larger center; others have only a footpath, impassable during the winter months, to link them with the outer world. Hence there is little trade between the various towns of the interior, and contact with the outside is still limited to such unusual events as emigration or conscription. Only here and there does a movie theater import the sights and sounds of the world at large.

The tillable soil is both scarce and of poor quality. Even in areas where a majority of the people own the land they farm, the average holding consists of no more than six to eight acres. To this factor must be added the deficiency of rainfall as well as the ancient and inefficient methods of cultivation. Also, nature has afflicted this region with two special handicaps — landslides and earthquakes. It is said that in Lucania the mountains walk. The same could be said of Calabria. Towns peel off, house by house, crashing down the mountainsides; roads sag and tracks disappear.

But historically these same regions, though poor in resources and plagued by natural catastrophes, have exerted an extraordinary power of attraction. In great part this has been due to their pointing toward the center of the Mediterranean world, their location on the trade routes leading from Hellas to the Middle East as well as to the trading capitals of Southern and Central Europe; and the very difficulty of internal communication has played a role in opening these regions to external conquest. For one thing, it has prevented the rise of cities and the develop-

From "The World of 'La Miseria'" in *Partisan Review*, Vol. 20, No. 2 (March–April 1953), pp. 218–231.

ment of a class capable of local leadership. For the same reasons the rulers of central and northern Italy have been unable to exert effective control over the provinces of the far south. Thus only the very big powers ever had the interest and the means to conquer and hold those provinces.

Through the centuries exploitation has been the motive of the conquerors, and the incursion of foreign armies could not but worsen the "natural" situation. One thinks of the sheer destruction wrought by the struggle between Greeks and natives and of the devastation caused by the second Punic War and the fight between Pompey and Caesar. The long-term effects of campaigns like those of Hannibal were to force the people to flee from the coastal plains, which, left uncultivated, soon turned into malarial swamps. And when after centuries of ruthless invasions a feudal order was established at long last, it came into existence under the sway of foreign barons at a time when the greater part of Europe (including the northern part of Italy) was fighting resolutely and with frequent success to rid itself of medieval economic forms. The belated imposition of feudalism on Calabria and Lucania, at a time when it had already lost its historical function, was again due in part to the geographical factors not permitting effective control of these provinces. (The period of Frederick II, who maintained his court in Calabria for a considerable length of time, is exceptional.) Southern Italy still suffers from certain after-effects of feudalism, such as the working of the land by sharecroppers or hired hands, without ever having benefited from the new forms that developed out of feudalism, namely the communes which in northern Italy and elsewhere led to the rise of an industrious middle class and the modern State. Nor did the unification of Italy under the House of Savoy affect the southern peasantry favorably. For when the laws and the system of taxation of highly advanced Piedmont were applied without substantial modification to the closed economy of the south, history added another cruel chapter to the old tale of exploitation.

As a result Calabria and Lucania still exhibit the most shocking poverty. More than a hundred years ago the poet-priest Vincenzo Padula wrote of the lowliest inhabitants of these regions that they are not human beings but appendages of the animals. "The peasant works in order to eat, he eats in order to have the strength to work; then he sleeps. This is his life." The impression of the visitor today is not very different. The peasant's home is still a hovel which he shares with his wife and a litter of children, and a mule is still his only possession.

However, the peasant's abysmal poverty is not nearly so touching as a certain attitude that colors every manifestation of his existence. Or, to put it another way, what moves the visitor in a confused upsurge of feelings (ranging from shame to pride) is the glaring contrast between the objective conditions of the life of these people and the nobility of their response. It teaches the visitor that "*la miseria*" is more than a set of material conditions, for he soon comes to see it as poverty turned into a philosophic outlook — an outlook not limited to the landless peasants but equally influential with the artisans, the professional men and even the landowners.

This nobility of response, this dignity peculiar to "la miseria," is based, no doubt, on a sense of acceptance that reminds us of the pre-Socratic thinkers who once inhabited these lands. Not only do the fire of mighty Etna, the rocks of Calabria, the rushing rivers, the transparent air represent the same ancient elements of which this world is composed; but as in the times of Magna Graecia, a sense of primitive speculative realism, of acceptance of the unavoidable, of recognition of an established order — both natural and moral — pervades the people's life.

The delicate sense of the hierarchy of things, natural and human, is well expressed in the remark of a landless peasant who, in attempting to describe his daily routine, had started by saying: "We hoe the earth" — then had interrupted himself with an apology to me (the gentleman) — "if you will forgive the expression, like beasts." Someone who wants to explain a difficult question to a visitor often starts by saying: "I am only a peasant" or "I am only a carpenter — but this is what I think about it." This matter-of-fact recognition of one's proper place in the general scheme of things has no taint of submissiveness of the poor to the rich. First of all, the criterion of the social order, in the minds of the peasants, is not primarily an economic one as it is for the baron or great proprietor, who for this reason does not participate in the dignity of the peasant and is not treated with the same kind of simple human regard that peasants are accustomed to show each other. It is as if each position, or function, had the same basic value within the general propriety of things.

From this results a broad understanding of every human phenomenon, a tendency to see something plausible in every human weakness. It also helps to explain a certain restraint in everyday behavior, particularly remarkable in a region where the passions are naturally fierce: people speak little and what they say is measured and precise; even when pointing to the hopelessness of their position, there is little tendency toward self-pity or playing upon the pity of the visitor.

We have mentioned a certain similarity between the pre-Socratic conception of life and the *Weltanschauung* of the present-day Lucanian or Calabrian peasant. In both cases we note a cosmic sanction of the various phases of life, including the social realm. In both cases we detect in the acceptance of the cosmic order the source of their dignity. With the Greeks, however, the cosmic sanction found its expression in social and political action: in the presence of the cosmic example they built their cities and ordered their social life. With the peasants of Calabria and Lucania the possibility of constructing and directing their own social, political and economic life does not exist. The cosmic order is not perceived as a stimulus to do but as an admonition to accept. The contrast between the awareness of the cosmic order, potentially the cosmic example, and of the inability to follow this example as a guiding light in social action creates, next to the real sense of dignity, and often overshadowing it, a pseudo-dignity, which is the result of pitiful attempts to hold the individual, the family and the society together. It may express itself in a disproportionate emphasis upon dress, in the raising of virginity to an absolute value, in the phenomenon of "*omertà*" (the conspiratorial silence of a whole community when a crime is committed). It is evident in the desire "not to be taken for dumb" (the worst thing that could happen to a member of a society in which education and intelligence are the only possible achievements); in fact, this desire, nourished by an almost pathological distrust of the "other world" (of government officials and landed nobility), may assume at times strange forms such as the gratuitous pretense of belonging to the Mafia.

The inordinately strong possessive attitude pervading every phase of the peasants' lives is a sure expression of the precariousness of their existence, of the need and the desire to create artificial supports for the human personality. This possessive attitude cannot be satisfactorily explained in terms of economic need alone even in the field of material goods.

Its full morbidity becomes evident in man's attitude toward woman. Though we may find deep in the heart of the peasant a feeling of respect toward woman, it is a feeling which seems to refer to the maternal function in general rather than to one's own wife in particular. As a rule, the wife is treated as a useful possession since she represents working power as well as the capacity to satisfy man's most elementary desire of possession.

It is difficult to exaggerate the importance of sex in a society as closed and limited in its expressions as is the peasant world of southern Italy. All factors seem to conspire to make sex the obsession of southern men. First there is the fact that in a society in which active participation in the political, social, economic, and even cultural life of the nation is impossible, sex is the only outlet for man's energies. Sex-life, furthermore, is limited to its most brutal, physiological aspects, since neither the male nor the female is permitted to develop his personality normally. Not only is the wife "protected" by custom from contact with the world, the man also lives in a world by himself: outside the home no contact between the sexes exists, and even within the home there are occasions when the wife is kept separate from the "world of man." During my visits to peasant homes no woman ever joined us in a meal. This, of course, was due not only to the conviction that a woman's place is in the kitchen but also to the desire of the man to protect her from possible dangers.

The unhealthy separation of the sexes, making friendships between men and women, and even participation of the wife in the friendships of the husband, almost impossible, creates in the man an attitude toward the woman not based on a precise knowledge of the partner's personality but on the emotional elaboration of her into a fantastic being upon whom his drives now concentrate. The woman — like the Family or the Nation — takes on a symbolic meaning. This becomes most strikingly evident in attitudes toward virginity — symbol of symbols — in which the elements of precariousness, of possession, and of dignity are clearly present. A peasant family regards a marriageable girl as an invaluable possession despite the fact that in the strictly material sense she represents a loss rather than an asset. The whole "honor" of the family, the whole psychological foundation of security, is based on her "virtue." In a society in which the essentials of freedom and security are lacking, to dispose of a daughter is the family's only expression of freedom.

On the other hand, the strong sense of modesty which the great majority of women in Lucania and Calabria exhibit is more than a defensive device in a society in which frequently all members of the family, male and female, are forced to live together in one room. Whatever the original motives, there can be no doubt that her modesty, the particular form of the woman's dignity, has become an autonomous human value. The precariousness of her social position, instead of leading to artificial forms of dignity, has been fully absorbed and sanctified by real dignity, at least so far as her modesty is concerned. Only when this modesty is compared with the demoralized condition of many a woman living in a city slum, where material conditions and crowding are equally bad, does one fully realize that it is the woman who has for centuries held the southern family and society together. This is the more remarkable if we keep in mind that the peasant society of southern Italy is considerably less "natural" than our "decadent," progressive society; as we have seen, of the "natural" drives of man only one has been developed in the peasant world, taking the place of all the others whose development has been inhibited. As a result we have a world full of complexes that explode in acts of exasperation, of which the violation of daughters and sisters is probably the most frequent.

A consequence of the effort of the woman to defend her dignity is a peculiar sense of solitude which pervades the whole of southern society. Never alone — not even when she has to satisfy a natural need — the woman of these regions is the loneliest being imaginable. This loneliness extends by reflection into the realm of the male. When reference is made to the philosophical sense of the Calabrian or Lucanian it is probably to this sense of loneliness which, in the man, expresses itself in contemplation. At times this sense may erupt in the grandiose philosophical constructions of a Campanella or in the prophecies of a Joachim of Fiore; more often, it will stay submerged in the hardly conscious play of ideas in the mind of a peasant walking toward the fields.

Even the contempt for manual labor conspicuous in all strata of southern society, with the exception perhaps of the lowest classes, seems to be as much an element satisfying certain needs of the social situation as a consequence of Spanish influence. In a society tortured for centuries by an unceasing tension between an almost pathological sense of insecurity and a commanding sense of dignity, we can expect, next to the acceptance of one's position in the cosmic scheme, a series of strong attempts to find a measure of dignity by self-distinction. In the world of "la miseria," possession in itself is an insufficient sign of distinction, particularly if we keep in mind that the use of wealth, the idea of investment by the individual, is largely unknown in southern Italy; exemption from labor then becomes the only true criterion of distinction: he who is at the lowest level of the economic and social scale has to work with his hands; he who belongs to the "better classes" gives proof of it by disdaining manual labor. The bitterest antagonism in southern society exists between two groups which do manual labor, the peasants and artisans; the artisans therefore welcome every occasion to show off their difference from the "serfs of the soil." For example, it is not difficult to find places where the artisans vote Communist *en bloc* if the peasants vote Demo-Christian, or Demo-Christian if the peasants vote Communist.

Phenomena like the peasant's solitude or his contempt for manual labor are, of course, closely related to his inability to use knowledge, and to use his acceptance of a cosmic order as stimulus toward the construction of a social and political order. No matter how great his sacrifice, governments and nature, landlords and drought, creditors and earthquakes will forever continue to conspire against him. He has lost confidence in himself (in his own ability to achieve) as well as trust in the government and in members of his own group. He firmly believes that the few who have succeeded in making a career were able to do so for some mysterious reason: one hit upon a hidden treasure; another was lucky enough to win in the lottery; another was called to America by a successful uncle.

This belief is also responsible for the peasant's attitude toward his neighbors. Since one's honest efforts are of no avail in making headway against the impossible odds of life, and, furthermore, since there is not enough to go around for everyone, one necessarily has to try to keep one's head above water by using means not entirely "fair." As far as collaboration for the common benefit is concerned, one must understand that working with others always involves an initial sacrifice which one has to be able to afford. If I want to join other members of my community in building a road for the common good I have to be able to donate a workday; if my margin of security is zero, I am unable to join. In a more general sense, the social contract ultimately is based upon my ability and willingness to give up something I possess in order to receive some other good. This refers not only to the material but to the more properly human realm as well: unless I possess a certain freedom of action (a measure of personal security) I am unable to surrender part of this freedom in order that what is left of it may be more solidly secured.

In the world of "la miseria," the individual is unable to give in the social-political realm. This is the more tragic as we know him to have preserved, outside that realm, a profound sense of human solidarity as witnessed, for example, by his hospitality. In fact, there are few things in this world more touching than the simple generosity of a peasant, than his joy at giving all to the stranger who, away from home, needs love and attention. Incapable of working together with his neighbor in the solution of the most insignificant problem of his daily life, he knows how to be a royal host to the guest who is not a neighbor but just a man.

This should explain why "*la omertà*" is practically the only form of social cooperation in Italy (aside, perhaps, from the recent occupations of land which seem to represent sporadic manifestations of a cosmic sense of justice rather than the expression of movements in which this sense has become a permanent and guiding force in the realization of lasting reforms). "La omertà" is a form of cooperation by which the individual surrenders nothing. He simply participates in a conspiracy of silence making it difficult if not impossible for the authorities to apprehend the delinquent. That the "conspiracy of silence," despite superficial indications to the contrary, is to be regarded as a positive value in the world of "la miseria" is attested, among other things, by the fact of its geographic distribution: in regions where the material conditions are such that the population is demoralized to the point of having lost its dignity, one finds little or nothing of the "conspiracy of silence."

The southern peasant's attitude toward the government is well expressed in the saying of Padula, according to which this peasant "has been educated to consider the government as his worst enemy while expecting that it do everything for him." Centuries of exploitation by various governments or by forces that acted under government protection have developed in him an absolute distrust of the intentions of all governments. At the same time, since he has no confidence in his own ability to solve the most elementary problems of his community, he feels he has no choice but to expect that the government act for him. Behind this contradiction lies the deeper hiatus of his own personality: the inability to create a continuum between the everyday reality and the objects of his aspirations. The government is real and ideal in its everyday reality; the State is incapable and unwilling to help the poor; in fact, they are the object of its exploitation. Ideally, however, the State is all-powerful and happy is he who can make use of some of its power.

The failure to achieve and the faith in transcendent ideals like the State are both present in the phenomenon of "*personalismo*," the institution of the influential person, which pervades southern Italy (and from there, great parts of central Italy). For it is believed that it is not the individual himself who achieves a certain result by his work and good judgment, but the "influential" person whose magic powers are due to his living close to still more influential persons who ultimately are in touch with the ideal power of the State. As far as the "influential" person is concerned, this system is rooted in the desire to *sell* influence (some feel that we have here the old Roman clientele system), so that, in effect, we have an extraordinary combination of a remarkable faith in the ideal nature of the State and, in the name of this same State, the most abysmal corruption.

Thus one does not so much "achieve" anything as "obtain" something. The rise of the parties and their activities in the south have scarcely changed this situation. Instead of the government and its agents or of local lords, it is now the parties and their representatives who "promise" and "obtain." The memorial plate on the promenade of a well-known Sicilian port is indicative of this attitude. Upon it is inscribed this line: "Citizens, this magnificent promenade has been obtained for you by the Honorable ———." At the same time, the ideality of the State has been taken over, in part at least, by the idealities or ideologies of the parties. As a friend said pointedly: "What people in the south are voting for is neither parties nor concrete programs but types of paradise (that is, of the American, Russian or heavenly variety)."

The lack of continuity between reality and ideality, the inability to "achieve" or to "realize," leads in the world of "la miseria" to the desire to flee the ugly reality of everyday life and to reach, by a magic leap, the "other," the ideal side of existence. This desire to escape expresses itself in a variety of ways. First there is the mind as an instrument of escape. For the member of the middle class in the world of "la miseria," this mental escape takes on the permanent forms of an abstract intellectualism and of a nauseating rhetoric. Freed by their privileged position from the responsibility of returning to concrete reality, they are satisfied to see the "ideal" world realized in the great examples of the past, the poems of the Greeks and the heroic deeds of the Romans with which they are more familiar than with the physical and social world in which they live.

Then there are the strenuous attempts to flee one's class — attempts grown more frequent since the contact with the outside world has increased. The classical way to escape is to use education: in many a peasant family sons were unable to marry until they were forty or even older in order to permit one of them "to get an education" and become a priest or a teacher. Another, and for the southern economy certainly unfavorable, means of flight, is the land itself. Also, between the peasant and his land there is often a lack of continuity: his attitude — where he has a choice — is that of wanting to exploit rather than to improve his land, so that in a sense the present hunger for land is, among other things, an indication of an increased desire to flee the land: one would like to have enough of it, and exploit it thoroughly and quickly enough, to be able to buy a ticket to America (or at least to northern Italy).

Of course, the most spectacular form of flight is emigration abroad. There were years in which the exodus from Lucania exceeded the birth-rate and in which two-thirds of the male population of some towns lived overseas. America, for a time, became identified with the ideal side of life and still today it is easy to find people who speak of it simply as "that country." Less spectacular perhaps, but of greater significance for the whole fate of Italy, is a form of internal emigration: the flight into government employment. Both in the national bureaucracy and in the police southerners constitute a solid majority. Instead of the normal growth of an individual, instead of the shifting continuity between actuality and possibility, we have a one-time jump out of "la miseria" into the immediate vicinity of the State, the ever-realized ideal, from which flows the magma of "influence" giving the lowliest bureaucrat his privileged position and separating him, as if by an insurmountable gulf, from the rest of the citizens. Another cause of the flight into the bureaucracy is the fact that the southern peasant economy, which exists virtually without the use of money, has no need of a middle class. Italian society finds it generally difficult to absorb academically trained personnel into creative jobs; and this difficulty is increased by the desire of the middle class to preserve its "standing" and therefore to send its children to the university, regardless of their inclination and ability, and by the intellectualistic type of education the universities offer.

The peasants or artisans who succeed in fleeing "la miseria" and enter government service, carry their mentality of mutual distrust and the petty curiosity of small communities into the police forces of the State. As for the bureaucracy, instead of being an instrument for the well-defined purposes of a government, it represents an end in itself and, therefore, is a dangerous parasite upon the body politic. And the police, far from being the objective custodians of the public order, represent an outmoded apparatus of petty spying with no other apparent purpose than that of satisfying their instincts of diffidence and curiosity. One may therefore say that the national bureaucracy represents the revenge of an often forgotten and otherwise exploited south upon the whole of Italian society. Themselves unable to "realize," the members of the bureaucracy consider as dangerous to their own position those modern spirits willing and able to "achieve."

This failure of self-fulfillment is perhaps best illustrated by the peasant's religious life. The fact is that in these regions the Church is no more than a superstructure upon an essentially pagan civilization. Norman Douglas had already observed that the adult Jesus was outside southern experience and that his teachings were repugnant. Indeed, theirs are not the Christian but the natural virtues of a realistic people living within the social and cosmic confines of "la miseria" — a world in which to love one's neighbor, to let down one's guard in the face of the relentless struggle for existence, would simply mean to commit suicide.

The Christian view of the abyss between sinful man and the Eternal Father and the mediating function of Christ the Savior has little meaning to the peasant, who is not afraid of death and hardly conscious of sin. Death and suffering are natural ingredients of "la miseria," while faults and shortcomings are no more than human. The abyss, to him, is rather between a perfect deity, a god who is the cosmic order personified, and the misery of daily life. In his religious existence this is evident in the contrast of two faiths held concurrently: the faith in a divine power, unsullied by earthly life, and in a magic conception, expressed in a myriad of saints and superstitions, in which the cosmic has been reduced to human proportions as it were, and made operative in the petty struggles of workaday existence.

The mediator, strange to say, is not Christ but the Madonna. In a sense, the Madonna is part and parcel of the magic life, and in fact, there is not one Madonna but a great variety of them. At one mountain sanctuary I was informed that the local Madonna was one of seven sisters, and when I asked which of the seven was the Mother of God, I was bluntly told that none of the seven had anything to do with the Madonna "down there in the village church." On the other hand, the Madonna is more than just a local saint: not only can help be magically obtained through her (as through any other saint) in our daily troubles, we can also orgiastically obtain union with her, the Cosmic Mother in whom all suffering has become meaningful.

This will explain why in the south of Italy feasts in honor of Christ are exceedingly few, why celebrations in honor of the Holy Trinity are vitiated by the earthiness of local pagan rites, why the Sacraments have often little more than a formal magic value, while religious passion seeks its satisfaction in the feasts of local saints and of the Madonna particularly. Characteristically enough, they are frequently held around sanctuaries on isolated mountainsides to which throngs of peasants come from faraway places. Often the feast starts in the evening and lasts a whole night and day. Then groups of peasants bivouac around open fires while a young goat is roasted and ancient songs in honor of the Madonna rise into the broad heavens. In other places the feast begins only in the morning when hundreds of small processions form, usually carrying images of the Madonna decorated with pagan symbols; and as they arrive, the whole procession, composed of animals and humans, walks around the sanctuary, church bells ring, a bagpiper plays his monotonous litany, and from a near-by hill fireworks burst in seemingly endless succession. The sanctuary is often too small for the crowd, and some women fight their way in to set a candle before the image of the Madonna. And often, when the police fail to intervene, they attempt to move toward the altar on their knees, licking the ground with their tongues.

No wonder that it is the women who set the tone of these celebrations. Among the followers of Dionysus, it was the maidens of Thrace who roamed the forests to catch and devour the sacred pig. So, in the realm of "la miseria" it is the women, the lowliest of a downtrodden society, who find in the orgiastic celebrations of the Madonna a momentary respite from their daily fate.

Our description so far has illustrated the initial statement that in the traditional peasant civilizations the historical element is a strictly objective factor. The peasant has no choice but to see in history something given in whose making he has no active part. We might ask now whether the experience of the last twenty or thirty years, and particularly of the period after World War II, has not made for a substantial change in the traditional position. War and emigration, the cinema and the rise of the political parties have no doubt created a new type of awareness. Until recently one's position had been interpreted in terms of a cosmic sense of justice, of the very laws of life which governed one's society. Now it is being compared, here and there — and more and more vividly and insistently — with the living standards of the people in Rome, in Moscow, in Hollywood. The organic conception of life in which each function was roughly equivalent to every other function, in which each aspect of life was intimately related to every other, makes way for an emphasis upon one plane of life, the economic-political one, and for an awareness of needs — a word practically unknown in the traditional society — demanding to be satisfied at any cost. The inability of the great majority to satisfy these needs increases social tension, while the belief in the cosmic sanction of the existing order and, with it, the sense of dignity and of understanding of everything human decreases.

More specifically, the historical element is gradually being removed from the realm of acceptance; the objective conditions of "la miseria" cease to be universally regarded as necessary. Some of these conditions are being recognized as having been caused by the will of men — men who once were thought to be qualitatively different, who lived forever outside of "la miseria" and therefore outside the consciousness of its citizens; of men who are now on a level with themselves, that is, a level of quantitative comparison. This new kind of awareness marks the passage from a static, hierarchic society to a dynamic one of social polarization, from an acceptance of the historical elements as necessary parts of the objective environment to a transfer of these elements into the subjective field: the peasant begins to see that among the causes of "la miseria" are the interests of men who are not essentially different from himself and certainly not outside of his own field of action. As he accepts, thus, the possibility of eventually overcoming the human causes of "la miseria" he begins to participate in the making of history.

But what is the nature of this new awareness? Must it take on the form of group consciousness, whether of the nation or of a class? In other words, will it find its final formulation in a new fascism, in the theory of a have-not nation in a world of mighty empires, or in Communism, the identification of the citizens of "la miseria" with the world-proletariat and its struggle against capitalist exploitation? Or is there a chance for an individual form of consciousness, for self-restraint (in the place of the weakened traditional cultural restraints), for cooperative effort on the part of free individuals to solve their own problem?

Despite the recent gains of the neo-Fascist party in southern Italy it is not likely that the new awareness will find its ultimate satisfaction in Fascist nationalism. Even in Mussolini's time the peasants showed little liking for the Fascist regime. Not only did their cold realism detect the fantastic character of its various enterprises; they also recognized in its leaders the allies of their local overlords. Communist gains, on the other hand, have to be taken much more seriously. In many situations, it is true, the people exhibit toward the parties — including the Communist party — the same attitude of skeptical expectancy which they have shown for centuries toward all who came to them bringing offers of friendship and assistance; it is also true that in most local elections what counts is still the feuds and alliances of families, the petty struggles of spite and influence.

But so far as larger issues are concerned, like land reform, the right to organize, the system of taxation, the Communist party has acquired considerable importance. To a great extent this is due to the inability (or unwillingness) of a government which, ultimately, is controlled by the industrialists of the north and the landowners of the south, to "realize" seriously much-advertised reforms. The peasant is no doubt aware of the increased investments in the south, but he is equally aware of waste and corruption and of an incredible confusion of competing or overlapping efforts. Furthermore, his new awareness excludes a solution of the problem exclusively from above. Investments on the part of a government, even if honestly made, would not be enough. "La miseria" always has been more than the sum of its objective conditions. Today, solving its problems according to the necessities of a dynamic age means more than the endeavor to raise the standard of living: it means giving the peasants a chance to participate in the determination of their destiny.

The policy of the Communist party consists in trying to show that only within the framework of dialectical materialism can the participation of the peasant in the making of history become real. Their successes are to be ascribed to their intimate knowledge of local conditions and also to their ability to translate their ideology into the mental language of the average peasant. In a society in which the newspaper is practically unknown, they have concentrated upon "explaining" the news orally in the local Union Halls. In a world in which a down-to-earth realism is closely related to a magico-religious conception of life, they have chosen St. Joseph, the protector of cattle, as their patron rather than the official party saints. As a consequence one can step today into some of the most miserable huts and find a map of the North Korean People's Republic as the only decoration on the fly-stained walls. "After all," you would be told, "is not theirs the same heroic fight against landlordism and exploitation?"

The democratic states must attempt to apply to the Communist problem the lessons learned in the struggle against fascism. We know now that the military defeat of fascism — itself the most disturbing symptom of the crisis of the middle classes — did not solve that crisis. But we still have to learn that the phenomenon of Communism in Italy, in India, and even in China or Russia, is but the symptom of a profound crisis in the peasant world. By limiting ourselves to the struggle against the symptom we are not reaching toward a basic solution of the problem.

Love and Authority: A Study of Mexican Villagers

Michael Maccoby

Over half the people in the world live in peasant villages. Social scientists who have observed rural life in many of the developing nations report that peasants from Latin America, India, and the Near East seem more like one another in many ways than like their urban compatriots. In Mexico, the city-trained technician or agricultural worker who enters the peasant village feels himself almost as much a stranger as does the North American, and has as little understanding of the peasant character. Mexicans experience the same frustration and puzzlement when their plans for agricultural improvement or community development meet the solid wall of peasant indifference and distrust. The Mexicans are not alone; peasants everywhere distrust townspeople.

In the peasant village we have studied, many problems stem from the same factors that have plagued peasants in other countries and in other eras. His small plot of land — all he can physically handle with slow, unprofitable methods of farming — and his loss of profit to city buyers have determined the peasant's life for centuries. He may switch from a wooden to a steel plow, but this makes no essential difference in the forces that control his existence. Only in the United States has industrialized agriculture all but wiped out the peasant population.

Erich Fromm, who has worked in Mexico for thirteen years, teaching and training Mexican psychoanalysts, first began the study six years ago, with financial support from the Foundations Fund for Research in Psychiatry. He had noted that almost all the anthropological studies in Mexico focused on Indian communities, which constitute no more than 10 per cent of the population and which reflect a history significantly

From "Love and Authority," *Atlantic*, Vol. 213, No. 3 (March 1964), pp. 121–126. Reprinted by permission of the author.

different from that of the Spanish-speaking mestizo, the descendant of mixed Spanish and Indian ancestry. Dr. Fromm was particularly interested in studying a mestizo village which had once been a hacienda (a large, semifeudal plantation) to discover how the character of the peasant, formed by generations of semifeudal peonage, has changed since the Revolution of 1910, which apportioned lands to the ex-peons and for the first time gave them the opportunity to direct their own destinies.

Las Cuevas, the village chosen, has a population of 850, small enough so that we can study each individual intensively. It is picturesque, dominated by a stone aqueduct built in the seventeenth century and by the ruins of the hacienda building, burnt early in the Revolution. Some of the older men served in Emiliano Zapata's army, which was formed from this district. Others fought against him. Many wished only to be left in peace, like Don Mardonio, who says that when Zapata's men entered the village, he would dress in the white manta shirt and trousers of the revolutionary, and when the government men came, he would hurriedly change his clothes. Others hid in the mountains and barely managed to survive.

While the village is reminiscent of the past, there are many signs of change. Although some people live in huts of sticks and sweep floors of packed dirt, others have houses of adobe, brick, or cement, with large patios shaded by banana and avocado trees, with purple bougainvillaea on the yellow walls and wild poinsettias blooming in the winter. The streets are unpaved, but within the last five years the village through its own efforts raised enough money to install running water and electricity. Over half the households have radios, and there is a television set in the town hall and in the houses of a few rich peasants.

Surrounding the village are some of the most fertile fields in Mexico, planted mainly with sugarcane, and in the summer rainy season, rice. In the distance, mountains separate the village from Taxco and Acapulco to the west and Mexico City to the east.

Just as striking as the setting of village life are the human problems that mar it. Many people lack work and barely manage to subsist. Others do not take advantage of what they have. They plant their fields with crops that pay little, or they neglect their work. Twenty per cent of the adult men are alcoholics, and another twenty per cent are heavy drinkers who waste at least two days of work a month and money desperately needed by their families. Alcohol leads them to magnify quarrels and insults, and a friendly exchange in a canteen may end in a machete or pistol fight; a misinterpreted look can be the cause of murder.

There is little deep friendship among the villagers. Few feel trust or fellowship outside their own families. Unless a common enemy threatens the group, the villagers seldom join together for community projects. Although they are ashamed of it and wish to be thought modern, most of the villagers are superstitious, suspicious that some women are witches, and will blame a child's illness on the evil eye. Although they respect modern medicine, they still turn to traditional curers to treat illnesses that resist the doctor's treatment, especially those of psychosomatic origin.

The villagers are not blind to these problems, for their ideals constantly clash with reality. They know that they gained from the Revolution. The land which was once part of the hacienda was parceled out to the villagers in *ejidos*, plots of rich land, averaging five acres in size, which belong to a man as long as he works them. Ejido land is meant to be inalienable and indivisible, to be passed on to a wife, son, or daughter. The ejido land symbolizes Zapata's ideals, which the villager willingly accepts. He is meant to be a free man and to work with his fellows cooperatively, in the spirit of the community. What keeps him from realizing this ideal? What are the roots of alcoholism, violence, and despair?

When Dr. Fromm and a group of his students, all Mexican psychiatrists, first entered the village, they told the leading men they wished to study just these problems, in the interest not only of this village but of other villages which suffered equally.

It is fair to ask why the villagers accepted the study and the many hours of answering personal questions, responding to inkblot and other projective tests. For most of them, such an abstract project made little sense, but they probably decided that the help promised — medical care and aid in working on the town plaza — were worth the bother; and in any event, they seemed to enjoy talking about themselves. The image of a new patron for the village fitted the dreams of many. But one leader, more intelligent and honest than most, had doubts. "I shall be frank," he told the group of investigators. "You say you are interested in helping us and in understanding us. I don't know what the others expect from you. But it has been my experience that when someone from the city comes to a peasant village, it is for one of two reasons. Either he wants to exploit us or he is interested in becoming senator or governor." The investigators told him there was some truth in what he said, but they asked him to give them a chance to prove that for once in his life, this reasoning could be wrong.

Our study has had three general aims: first, to describe the character of the villager, or the range of character types, in terms which, while not based on the value judgments of our own society, accurately portray his strengths and his weaknesses; second, to trace the major formative influences, the factors in his social and economic experience, in his beliefs, in his family background, which prove most pertinent to the molding of the villager's character; and finally, to determine whether violence, alcoholism, distrust of self, and lack of initiative are mainly his reactions to poverty and exploitation — expressions of anger and despair which would disappear if conditions changed — or whether they would persist even if the peasant saw before him the path to a better life.

The study is based on lengthy interviews, mainly given by Dr. Felipe

Sanchez, a Mexican physician who has also treated the villagers' illnesses and delivered their babies for more than five years. Two anthropologists, Dr. Theodore Schwartz and his wife, Lola, lived in the village for a year, observing the people at work and at leisure. Besides investigation by interview and observation, new stimuli have been introduced: readings in good literature (the villagers particularly liked the peasant stories of Tolstoy, and *Grimm's Fairy Tales*), weekly movies followed by discussions, a library, and an agricultural club for boys.

Except in those indigenous communities where land and religion are unified in mystical observances and where the society is self-contained, the conditions of peasant life in Mexico do not encourage love of land and agricultural work. A Mexican villager sees nature symbolized by the hot sun that drains his energy, or the land that gives him little for his effort: Five acres of sugarcane result in a year's profit of only forty dollars. Despite his industry and initiative, a planting of better paying crops can be ruined by bad weather, insects, or disease, and even if he has the luck to escape nature's displeasure, the market may be saturated. Under these circumstances, many peasants look with envy at the factory workers, sheltered from the elements, with less backbreaking work and more security.

Despite the hardships, a few peasants express love for their work. Perhaps in these peasants love for the land is part of appreciation for the experience of creation, of nurturing a plant, animal, or child, of seeing labor bear fruit. But a carpenter or skilled mechanic might feel the same way. Possibly this reaction is characteristically Mexican.

As a part of their intensive interview, all of the villagers were asked for their concept of love. Their answers tell a great deal about their attitudes toward life. The villager whom I shall quote first is one of 70 *ejidatarios* (55 men and 15 women). Doña Teresa, as I shall call her, is about fifty and has never attended school. She is unmarried but has a fifteen-year-old daughter, and she supports her younger sister who was left with two children by her husband. Doña Teresa's family is one of the oldest in the village; her ancestors worked in the hacienda. Although she does relatively little manual work on her own land, she runs a canteen and raises pigs and chickens profitably on her house site. She is passionate by nature, suspicious of outsiders, loyal and affectionate to her friends, violent and unforgiving to her enemies. She says:

> Love is very sacred, because without love there would not be the world we would have if we loved each other, because even though there is friendship, it is not enough. One must love. Beginning with love of parents, of sweethearts, love of a husband, love of children, love of a good friendship; even to raise an animal one must love. It is incomparable, because people even commit suicide if they do not know love. The love of a father is eternal. The love of friends one retains even when they are away. Love of God, one must have also, for God sends us love in the form of understanding.

Doña Teresa's answer is more detailed than those of many who share her attitude, but some 15 per cent of the villagers answer in a similar way. What these villagers express in their concept of love is the knowledge that love is not a bewitchment or a sexual attraction, but a deeply rooted trait of character, a respect for someone or an interest that is always different, depending on the person or object loved, but always essentially the same.

Don Nicolas, a peasant of fifty-eight years, states the same idea more briefly: "Love is a force that makes a person seek the well-being of those he esteems." Don Fortunato, a young farmer aged twenty-seven, says, "There are many kinds of love, for a plant, for the land. First, there is love of God. Second, for a father or mother. Love is to love a woman, the love that one's sons grow and develop. One has many loves."

Many villagers without an active, loving orientation express concepts of love that nevertheless move the listener by their authenticity. Their thoughts are deeply felt, but they react with passivity or resignation to the hardships which have eroded confidence in their own powers. Instead of creating love, they wait to be loved, and they receive little from the land or from others who also feel their inability to give.

The concept of love most often stated by villagers reflects the feeling that all good things of life lie outside oneself, beyond reach; one must await passively the experience of happiness or love, being grateful if it arrives but without power to keep it. For these receptive people, joy lasts only momentarily, if at all. It may remain no more than a dream, a promise that never materializes, but which soon sours into disillusion. Of course, these villagers are not so different from other people. Few in any society have developed an active loving orientation to others and to their work, or a sense of self not dependent on outside supports. But the villagers have more cause to lack hope than most people.

Some people with hoarding characters tend to apportion their love, like a limited supply of money, to those children who merit it by obedience and good behavior. Says Doña Soledad, "I cannot feel as much affection for a son who acts badly as I do for one who treats me well." In work as in love, the hoarding orientation implies storing one's forces, avoiding spending too much interest and energy. Such peasants make good storekeepers, and as farmers they are seldom lazy. They earn a better living than the poorest, but they stick to old methods and are suspicious of anything that demands a new burst of activity.

Why is it that some peasants are able to develop an active orientation to love and work, despite conditions that foster despair in others? Perhaps they were born with a stronger will to live, or they were fortunate to experience the loving care of parents who nurtured the force necessary for growth. A simple reason for the depth and beauty of the average Mexican peasant's concept of love, despite economic scarcity and lack of formal education, is that love is what interests him. What does he have to think about, other than his own feelings and those of his fellow villagers? The routinized work, unchanged for centuries, demands little thought or planning. It does not occur to him to start a new industry, partly because he lacks models and capital. In fact — and this is common to other peasant societies — he opposes projects initiated by any village entrepreneur. He believes the village's resources have been parceled out once and for all; a new use of them presages one person's gain at the cost of others.

Culturally, life is barren, without the traditions, legends, and rites of Indian communities. Television has arrived only recently. There are occasional movies or dances. Las Cuevas, which wishes to be progressive, has done away with *jaripeos*, local bullfights. After work, some young men, the most productive, play basketball. The others hang around the plaza or the bars. Nothing in the experience of most villagers leads to thoughts of life outside, except as alien and dangerous. In these circumstances most minds are dulled; some people leave, and the best of those who remain refine the experiences that do come to them, by directing their intellect into familiar channels.

As in all societies, the peasant develops the kind of intelligence that fits his needs. And it is noteworthy that our tests do not measure the kind of intelligence the peasant most values. The peasant may learn to detect fine differences in the state of a plant, an animal, or the weather. He studies people, trying to understand what lies behind their gestures and expressions. He does not respond to words alone, because he knows words often hide feelings or are meant to be polite. He may formally agree with another person, even though he does not mean it, in order not to insult him, and he is surprised when the man from the city who accepted his polite assent to some project then reproaches him for lack of responsibility. The productive peasant has developed his mind not as a machine, finely tooled to solve abstract problems, but in order to stimulate life and growth in all that he respects.

Don Guadalupe, aged seventy-five, who has never been to a school, tells us how a father should treat his sons. "If the Architect of the universe sends you a son, tremble. You cannot know if his soul will be good or evil. All you can do is to be a loving father, protecting him until he reaches the age of twelve. From twelve until he is twenty, be his teacher. And from twenty on, be his friend."

Why so few villagers develop productive characters is a complex problem, similar in peasant communities everywhere. Among other reasons are economic factors and social and psychological forces. The most important is based on scarcity — hunger, the vagaries of the market, lack of land and of the rational use of it. A few peasants by their industry have transcended these conditions, but many lack the hope or life force necessary to mature. As long as peasants are saddled with rudimentary methods of farming on small plots and remain subjugated to the cities, they will remain distrustful and fatalistic.

In the village today, despite the peasants' greatly improved conditions, the psychological attitudes of the peon persist. Peasants lacking faith in themselves still seek patrons with whom they act the part of humble supplicant. In fact, when the land was partitioned, some villagers refused to accept *ejidos*, because they feared that the old hacienda owner would return to punish them. The competitive and distrustful attitudes characteristic of all peasants were more deeply etched by the hacienda experience and persist even though they conflict with the revolutionary ideal of cooperation.

These social attitudes mirror family relationships in which bonds between brothers are weakened by the tie to parents. The parents, like the hacienda owners, demand strict obedience from children, although their treatment of infants who have not yet developed a strong sense of self is warm, giving, and undemanding, and mothers show a deep sense of responsibility for children combined with a willingness to sacrifice for their well-being. Their strictness is rooted in the idea, perhaps historically planted, that willfulness and independence are signs of *lo malo* ("badness") that must be eradicated. With this attitude parents probably saved their children from getting into trouble with the hacienda masters, but now it cripples the growth of self-reliance. It persists both because of its self-perpetuating effects and because peasant fathers and mothers imitate the child-rearing techniques of their parents.

After the age of six, when boys must work in the fields and girls in the household, the child is expected to obey without question. He is taught that what is right is what his parents consider right. He constantly feels guilt and seldom learns to distinguish between his own rational conscience and the fear that he will transgress a parental commandment. Since parents often punish but hardly ever reward, the child lacks a sense of doing anything worthwhile; it is enough to avoid trouble.

The chance that he might rebel against this irrational authority and band together with his peers, as children do in the United States and Western Europe, never materializes. Parents discourage play with other children. Furthermore, the society lacks models for fraternal cooperation. Even the games of children, unlike our games such as hide-and-seek and ring-a-levio, lack the symbolic acting-out of the group banding together to home-free-all their comrades from the central authority. Rather, in their hide-and-seek, called "burnt leather," the boys run from the central person, who has the right to whip each child he catches with a leather belt. Until the study entered the village, the young boys had never played such cooperative games as baseball or soccer, although a group of young men have been playing basketball, which was introduced twenty years ago by a schoolteacher.

The feudal heritage weakens the peasant's self-reliance and undermines the moral supports of reliability, cooperation, and fellow feeling. Those who assume authority tend to fall into the irrational, exploitative pattern of the hacienda system, and many of the most able villagers, to escape being a target for hostility and distrust, refuse to accept elected positions of command. One villager elected to office fell ill and remained ill until another person was chosen to replace him. Often the official positions fall to weak figureheads who excite no one's suspicions. The villagers distrust the community leaders, suspecting that those who institute communal projects siphon off the profits into their own pockets, whereas if a man openly assumes the role of patron for gain, they are more likely to admire his virtues and flatter him, seeking his favor.

Anyone who tries, as we did, to introduce new projects into the village runs up against the peasant's attempt to place him in the category of either a hypocritical do-gooder or an openly exploitative but manageable patron. It is deceptively easy to fall into the role of patron, cushioned by the flattery of the village and by the feeling that only in this way can anything get done. We had the idea of helping the boys of the village to start an agricultural club. The aim of this club, founded by Dr. Schwartz, has been to teach the boys new methods of farming and animal-raising, to give them the opportunity of earning some money by their work, and to stimulate a sense of responsibility and an experience of cooperation with their peers.

Perhaps we made our first error by giving them too much to start with, including hybrid seed, corn, chickens, milk-producing goats, pigs, and a cow. Instead of assuming responsibility, the boys treated us as patrons to whom they must remain submissive, awaiting orders. When because of bad luck and our inexperience, animals fell ill or the crops yielded little, the boys became apathetic and despairing instead of working harder. A volunteer from the American Friends Service Committee moved into the village to supervise the boys, but they worked well only so long as he was there. If he left for a few days, animals went thirsty and the fields stayed untended.

After two years of little progress, we decided to try to analyze with the boys the attitudes and feelings which caused their lack of initiative. Together with Señor Antonio de la Torre, the volunteer from the AFSC, I began to meet with the boys for two hours a week for a kind of group psychotherapy centered around the problems of work. At first the boys blamed their neglect of the animals on lack of time and lack of knowledge, but they soon saw this as a rationalization for deeper problems, since they had plenty of time to play and they avoided learning what we were eager to teach them.

What blocked their energy and self-development was the same feudal pattern of behavior that keeps the village from progressing as much as it might. Each boy felt his only bond within the club was his tie with us, the patrons. Cooperation meant only that if he worked more, others would work less and cut into his reward. Despite a new system of profits based on individual work, the boys still saw their fellows as rivals who were trying to get the most out of the club with the least work. Even in our meetings, when one boy spoke to another, it was to accuse him, never to support him. When the boys spoke to me, their words were tinged with guilt, as though they feared that whatever they did, I would be dissatisfied.

During the first meetings most of the time passed in painful silence. Finally I asked them to say what was on their minds. No one would speak, until Candido, the bravest and most responsible, admitted that he had been thinking about going to a dance that night. But he was afraid to tell me, sure that I would be angry. I said that I did not want to schedule meetings that conflicted with dances and that they were free to go, but I asked that we talk some more at the next meeting about their fear of saying what was on their minds.

In what followed we discussed the ever-present guilt that each boy felt before his parents and any other authority. He had been taught that to anger the authority for whatever reason meant punishment. Therefore, with parents, with employers, or with us, it was better to remain silent, to do only what one was told to do, to avoid any initiative. I pointed out to them how this attitude was rooted in centuries of hacienda life and how as long as they kept it, they would remain peons in their souls and never be free men. By accepting the idea that the right thing to do depends on another's judgment, they could never develop their own sense of right, they could never be the masters of their own activity, and they would always be more interested in escaping punishment than in their work.

After this meeting there was a surge of initiative and responsibility, but when I asked the boys what had happened when Antonio left for a few days, they all turned their eyes sheepishly to the ground. "I heard that you did a good job by yourselves," I said. Yes, it had been true, but they were unable to give themselves credit. The other side of guilt about disobeying authority was the conviction that nothing they did could be praiseworthy, for no one had ever stimulated the sense of satisfaction in a job well done. Their only rewards resulted from obedience.

We tried to interest the fathers of the boys in the club so that when we left, there would be a continuing direction. The club had by now grown to the stature of a small business with valuable animals and some 350 chickens which produce 220 eggs a day. But the parents either lacked interest or felt that like every other cooperative enterprise begun in the village, this would fail. Naturally, this attitude, well known by the boys, weakened their confidence.

In a last attempt to enlist the support of the fathers and mothers, we called a meeting. When the parents heard about the difficulties the boys had in cooperating, and the losses due to negligence, they were all for giving up the club. One father said, "You should move the club to a village that will appreciate it."

"Why do you waste your time?" asked another. "These boys are not worth it." We assured the fathers that the boys had done a great deal, and that we would not leave until the club was financially solid, but privately we wondered how the club would carry on without help from the older generation and how the boys who were present at the meeting would react to their fathers' fatalism and lack of hope.

At our next reunion, I asked them what they had thought of the meeting. By this time the group of boys who came to these discussions had shrunk from twenty to a hard core of six of the older boys, who always came. One said that the meeting seemed fine. He was immediately challenged by the others. "What do you mean fine?" asked Cheque. "They have no interest in helping us, they think we are no good, and they want the club to end." Cheque and others realized that they could expect no support from their parents, and they decided that they could do without it. "Already we know more about chickens than they do," said one boy, "and we have learned how to market the eggs. Even if they were to help, they would only order us around and take the profits."

After this discussion the boys began for the first time to cooperate in setting a day in which each one took the others' animals to pasture. Together they built a roof for the corral in which their goats were quartered. They demanded that others cooperate or leave the club. Those of the older boys who had before shunned any leadership in order not to seem to put themselves ahead of others accepted the fact that if they did not lead, nothing would be done. They organized a dance to raise money; and taking advantage of the Mexican love of lotteries, they sold chances on a pig, realizing a greater profit than they would have made in the market. They began to think of new projects, such as fixing up a village bathhouse, long run-down by disuse, and charging a few cents for showers. They petitioned and received village approval for the project.

It is still too early to conclude that these changes in attitudes will last. These boys who are now fifteen and sixteen years old will soon leave the club, marry, and work for their own families. Then the test will be whether they maintain the fraternal ties of the club, based neither on family nor on personal advantage but on shared work and play. As adults, will they have both the interest and ability to help another generation of boys? As fathers, will they encourage their sons' independence?

The aim of this project was not to change the village but to see whether the young people on their own could respond to opportunity. It is interesting to note, although statistically speculative, that just as 15 to 20 per cent of the adult population can be characterized as loving and productive, so five out of twenty of the boys have become responsible and cooperative. Perhaps our project has done little more than encourage the growth of those who with maturity might have developed anyway. But these boys are becoming different from the older peasants, who are still limited by the feeling that community progress is impossible and that love and interest are rooted only in the family and their own land.

Unlike their fathers, the boys are learning that leadership does not invariably mean exploitation, that a man can work with another who is neither his patron nor his peon.

Fatalism, distrust, and hopelessness were born in the experience of the hacienda and reinforced by the scarcity of land and living, common to peasants everywhere. Since the Revolution, some peasants have taken advantage of the greater opportunities. Others have fallen back into old ruts. Still others have left the village to work in the city or, under the bracero program, have traveled to the United States for a few months a year, where they earn more than they could make in the village. In the future, economic necessities will probably move more peasants from the villages into the cities. Industries will need more workers; good land is scarce, and the small holdings of the peasant are inefficient for a nation which must increase its food supply. Many of the young boys say they would go to the city if they could be assured of a good job, such as that of auto mechanic. A few aspire to be teachers, doctors, or engineers. But almost half of the others prefer to work in the fields, if they can make a living. To Aristeo's remark that when tilling the soil one is only burned by the sun, they answer that in an auto-repair shop one cannot breathe. "Besides," says Candido, "here in the country one can work with animals. And I like to be in the hen house, because the chickens sing to me."

SOCIAL CONTACT VS. SOCIAL PROMISE IN A SIAMESE VILLAGE

Herbert P. Phillips

Social life in a Siamese village is as paradoxical and inconsistent as it is among any group of human beings. This essay discusses one of the more important of these paradoxes, its cultural sources and behavioral expressions. The paradox is genuine in that it describes two fundamentally different ways in which Siamese villagers deal with other people. It is readily resolvable if we consider these ways as belonging to two fundamentally different categories of social behavior, requiring two entirely different methods of analysis.

The paradox is this: When adult Siamese peasants meet and interact with one another in a face-to-face situation they know almost precisely

This essay is a modification of selected sections of Chapter II, *Thai Peasant Personality*, University of California Press, 1965. Grateful acknowledgment is offered to the University of California Press for permission to quote from this study.

how to act; they can predict, within a relatively limited range of alternatives and with substantial certainty, the form, and often the content, of each other's questions, answers, comments, facial expressions, and postural effects. They have a clear idea of the alternative purposes, latent as well as manifest, of the meeting; and although they may occasionally suffer some anxiety about their own performance in the situation (a psychological consideration), they know that by conforming to the standard rules and rituals of interaction they can get by in a socially comfortable manner. In short, most face-to-face Siamese peasant situations approximate a sociologist's model of behavior: highly patterned, predictable, and conservative. Yet when these same people leave each other's presence they behave in a strikingly different manner. No longer occupants of a particular social role with its associated definitions and constraints, they do very much what they as individuals wish to do. They readily permit personal impulse, diversion, and unforeseen circumstance to take precedence over commitments they may have undertaken in the face-to-face encounter. They often pay little attention to the rights, obligations, and responsibilities which are supposed to form the substance of enduring relationships; the relationships themselves are uncertain, as are the underlying factors upon which they are based. The peasants even offer a Siamese maxim to sanction these tendencies: "To follow your own heart is to be a true Thai."

We shall discuss the dynamics of these two opposing tendencies — and two different modes of social behavior — as they appear in the life of the villagers of Bang Chan, a rice-growing community located 31 kilometers northeast of Bangkok.

THE VILLAGE OF BANG CHAN

The people of the community of Bang Chan are, like almost all ethnic Thai (82 per cent of the national population), peasants (84 per cent of the national labor force), in that they have a keen sense of membership in the nation-state with a deep loyalty to the Crown, speak the Thai language, are Therevada Buddhists (as is 94 per cent of the national population), are outwardly highly deferential to the authority of the central government, and have a conception of the good life that stresses fun, physical comfort and security, and a moral (as contrasted with a natural) ordering of the universe. Like the vast majority of their rural compatriots, 85 per cent of the population of the village are engaged in the production of rice, an activity which to them is not only an economic operation but almost a way of life, being bound up with their social structure, dietary habits, religious practices, and even their philosophical and aesthetic conceptions.

Unlike many Asian peasants, 64 per cent of the people of Bang Chan own the land which they cultivate and upon which they live. This relatively high rate of land ownership is a traditional Siamese peasant pattern — 82 per cent for the nation as a whole — although recent data indicate that with an increasing population (3.2 per cent per year), individual land holdings are becoming smaller and the tenancy rate higher as entrepreneurial villagers, rather than absentee landlords, are beginning to consolidate land holdings.

In terms of the 700 years of continuous and independent existence of the Thai nation-state, Bang Chan is a recently settled community, its founding tracing back to the 1870's when the entire Central Plain was opened up for commercial rice production. As with many villages in the central region, its founders *came from* Bangkok and areas immediately south of the capital city. Its current population of 1,771 people live in 296 households, either strung out along both sides of the village's canals or in isolated homesteads surrounded by rice fields. The latter settlement pattern is the more recent and commonplace and is not out of keeping with the independent propensities of the villagers. As one villager expressed it, "If people live far away from each other, there will not be any trouble."

There are essentially only five social units toward which Bang Chaners express continuing psychological commitment: the nuclear family; a loosely defined, laterally oriented kindred; the nation-state (mentioned not for formal reasons, but because it actually is psychologically important); the local Buddhist temple; and the village school. The last two institutions provide the villagers with a sense of belonging to "the community of Bang Chan" and also with a fundamental sense of being "civilized"; the lack of such institutions, they argue, is what marks "primitive people of the forest." Otherwise, there are within the community no castes, age-grade societies, occupational groups (other than the family), neighborhood groups, or groups expressive of village solidarity (such as councils, governing boards, etc.) which might impose a sense of obligation on the villagers or to whose norms or functions they might have to conform. Bang Chaners do not have to contribute their labor to their community, serve as village guards, contend with the dictates of village elders, or even actively cooperate with fellow villagers. All villagers have friends of varying degrees of intimacy both within and without the community, but these are dyadic, not group, relationships based on expectations of mutual benefit.

Although the monastery and school afford the villagers a sense of living in and belonging to a particular community, they are not sufficient to prompt identification with the needs of the village as a whole. Except for religious activities and the reciprocal work groups organized for rice transplanting and harvesting — the rewards for which are directly personal — villagers simply are not predisposed to participate in communal projects. Thus, activities which require large-scale cooperation or organization to be effective — clearing or deepening canals, repairing the road that leads from the main highway to the school — are either not carried out or are effected only with extreme difficulty. Most frequently it is the government, in the persons of the local district officers, that initiates and attempts to see such programs through, although even here lack of established cooperation patterns creates serious impediments to success. Although a few villagers recognize this as a defect of social organization, the majority clearly find it easier to live with the defect than to try to change the basic institutional framework that sustains it; maintaining their own freedom of action is simply more important, and more culturally "natural" to the villagers, than getting involved in public-service projects.

A few words should be said about the psychological environment of the villagers. In general, Bang Chaners are a people who do not live at, and rarely reach, a high emotional pitch. Their greatest pleasures are derived from experiences that are novel, diverting, comfortable, and frivolous. These are muted joys, completely lacking in Faustian intensity. In this kind of psychological environment people rarely permit themselves to become so committed to any person or activity that the frustration of that commitment will be overly disturbing to them. They proceed from a premise which says in effect: "Well, it is really not that important that I did not get the reward I had hoped for or that he did not do what I expected of him. I will simply have to make do." This fundamental orientation appears repeatedly in the social responses described below and serves to legitimize them cognitively and emotionally.

THE PLEASURES OF SOCIAL CONTACT

Of all the personality traits that come to the attention of the foreign observer, there is perhaps none more compelling than the affability, gentleness, and good humor of the villagers. It is difficult to think of a people more consistently ready, once contact has been made, to treat others amicably and convivially than the peasants of Bang Chan. However, this jovial cordiality is not an easy thing to conceptualize. In an earlier paper by Hanks and Phillips (1961) we spoke of these happy characteristics as "not so much the expressions of any basic light-heartedness as they are techniques for implementing the main precept of social interaction: 'Avoid face-to-face conflict!' " Although the villagers' good humor does serve this purpose, I would now suggest that it involves several additional dimensions and motives.

First, a whole complex of responses is represented here. The tendency to keep situations and conversations jocular, amusing, and at times gently ribald, is perhaps the most relaxed expression of this attitude. It is most obvious in the behavior of village gossip groups and in the relationships between individuals who consider themselves acquaintances but not quite close friends. The essential ingredient of this mode of affability is that interaction should be a great deal of fun but of little social consequence. Of a different order, and more common, is the villagers' ubiquitous politeness. This takes a host of forms: the genial hospitality that is expressed toward a newcomer, usually in the form of "personal" questions serving both to identify the person and to make him feel that others are interested in him ("How old are you? Any children? How much did you pay for your shirt or your land? Why don't you have any children?"); numerous linguistic and postural forms expressive of respect, such as lowering the body when passing near a social "superior" or supporting one's hand when offering something to somebody; the repeated hesitation to place others in embarrassing situations; the hesitation to tell others bad news so that "they will not feel sad" or will not have to dissemble (although more often the less delicate reason is the person's fear of embarrassing himself). Of a still different order is the uneasy affability that is expressed in the nervous giggling accompanying many face-to-face relationships and in the compulsive preoccupation with inconsequential or inoffensive topics while conversing with others. These responses appear to be either attempts to maintain minimal contact with others while jockeying to find out what they are really up to, or, in the negative sense, efforts to fulfill the minimum requirements of interaction while waiting (and hoping) for the contact to come to an end. And still different from all these is the affability associated with trying to make a good impression on others, expressed in the constant concern with displaying good manners, with using pleasing or flattering words, with being a good host, and the like. Although this category is in many respects behaviorally similar to the "politeness" referred to above, it seems to differ from the latter motivationally in that it is concerned not with the state and comfort of others, but with ego's effect on others.

It might help to think of these varying forms of politeness as a type of "social cosmetic." A cosmetic not only makes one appear more attractive and conceals one's blemishes, real or imagined, but permits one to deal with others more easily and comfortably. The cosmetic indicates that regardless of his basic intentions the person will conduct himself properly and agreeably; it defines the presence of and prompts conformity to certain behavioral rituals which simplify for the participants the kinds of behavior they may express. In a sense, the cosmetic of politeness represents one of the most "civilized" modes of social interaction: It is based on a fundamental concern with structuring one's behavior (again, irrespective of intentions) so as to disturb others least and thus permit them to act in socially easy, uncomplicated ways. Further, it stresses respect for the dignity and psychological integrity of others. The actual topic of conversation or nonverbal ritual that links the participating individuals may be either meaningful or inconsequential, but that is essentially irrelevant when compared with the fact that the respect the participants feel for each other is being communicated. In essence, much of the villagers' interaction is based on certain formal, rather than substantive, considerations,[1] the net effect of which is to minimize the effect that they might have upon each other but to maximize each person's sense of psychic independence and integrity.

That the villagers use social forms — stylized, often ritualized, modes of behaving — for expressing the degree and quality of contact that they feel toward others is crucial to understanding what is perhaps the major theme of Thai peasant interaction: that relations between people should be friendly, genial, and correct, but need have little personal commitment or involvement. As will be seen below, it is this readiness to phrase most face-to-face contact in terms of social rituals while at the same time feeling little commitment to others that lies at the root of what has been often called Thailand's "loosely structured social system."

CONTACTING OTHERS

The most relaxed, least contrived form of social contact is the cordiality that villagers extend to newcomers. Strangers to Bang Chan are hardly swept off their feet, but once contact has been established they are welcomed with a degree of attention far exceeding simple tolerance of their presence. People express a curious interest in them as individuals, as if somehow their presence were adding a new dimension to the lives of their hosts. For many Bang Chaners, this is probably true; the lives of these villagers are sufficiently routine and insular that the appearance of a new face is identified also with the advent of a significant and new experience. Still other villagers approach the newcomer with an attitude that says in effect: "One should try to meet and know as many persons as possible. Who knows what good may come of it?" The implied meaning here is that the cursory contact may in time develop into a firm relationship of reciprocal rights and obligations, whereby person A could turn to *B* to borrow money, ask his help in finding a job, help sponsor his son's ordination, and vice versa. There is in this attitude a gentle optimism combined with opportunism. And still other villagers, probably the majority, approach the newcomer with no self-reference at all, but with the simple intention of trying to make him feel comfortable. Whatever the intention, however, the dominant behavior exhibited to the newcomer is openness, amiability, and curiosity.

The actual expressions of conviviality are at all times simple and straightforward. They involve asking the person such questions as his age, place of birth, whether he is married, or whether he has yet served in the monkhood. (Notice the phrasing of this last question. The polite Thai form is never whether a person has been a monk or not, but rather whether he has already been a monk or not *yet* become one. The syntax

[1] All interaction is of course based on *both* formal and substantive considerations. The issue here is the relative emphasis given to one over the other, and how one may even be used as a substitute for the other when presenting the self.

of the interrogative form assumes the good intentions of the other person.) If the individual is identified as coming from a locale with special or distinguishing characteristics, the conversation will often involve humorous allusions to the place. For example, if he is from the North, there will most likely be joking references to the beautiful women of Chiengmai; if he is from the Northeast, to the funny accent of the people in that area. If the relative statuses of visitor and host can be quickly identified (based upon age, clothes, speech patterns, and occasionally surname), the conversation may turn to topics whose very purpose is to emphasize status considerations and thus make the participants more comfortable with one another. If they are social peers, the Bang Chaners would easily turn the conversation to a discussion of the technical aspects of rice farming or even gambling. The latter probably would be discussed with a social superior only after some acquaintance. On the other hand, if one were clearly the other's superior, the conversation would primarily express the superior's concern with the welfare of his new-found friend, which the latter would typically accept.

All this is usually accompanied by gentle laughter and careful attention to appropriate pronominal forms. The good host will also serve his guest rainwater, and if possible, scented rainwater. If opportunity and finances permit, he may even offer him a warm Coca-Cola. The youngster who will actually serve the refreshment will make sure that it is on a coaster and that his hands are in the proper ritual position when he offers the drink to the guest. Such are the ingredients from which potential friendships are made.

Although the particulars of the kind of politeness found among family and friends are different from the above, the forms are essentially the same. Villagers do not talk about the funny accents of the people who live next door to them, nor do they rush to serve scented water when a brother comes to call. But they do take pains to express respect for each other by using proper honorific and pronominal forms, by looking to the oldest competent family member for advice, by talking of subjects that are pleasant and amusing, but never threatening or embarrassing.

Avoiding embarrassing topics — even when the airing of such topics may be crucial or beneficial to one of the parties concerned — is one of the most pronounced facets of village social life. To a Westerner accustomed to outspokenness, the types of situations that villagers define as embarrassing and the lengths to which they will go to avoid them sometimes appear to border on the masochistic. Detailed interviews with two women whose husbands had taken second wives, for example, indicate that although at the time they were deeply disturbed by their husbands' actions (primarily for economic reasons; secondarily for emotional-sexual ones) they never once even brought the subject up with their husbands. They explained that they were too *ʔaaj* (embarrassed) to do so. In neither case did this embarrassment express any feeling of inadequacy on their parts. It was prompted rather by the desire to avoid an awkward and potentially rancorous confrontation. They did not want to put anybody on the spot.

Of somewhat different order from the above are the numerous instances in which "good friends" will avoid reporting to each other unhappy or distressing information although it is clearly to the other's advantage to have such information in order better to cope with the difficulty. In one case, a villager had been working for weeks on a land sale deal which would have netted him a brokerage fee of 2,000 baht (approximately $100, a considerable sum in a community where the average annual family income is, before expenses, only 8,500 baht). A friend had meanwhile learned that another villager, with whom he was not at all close, had sweet-talked the customer into permitting him to handle the sale, much to the detriment of his own friend, the original broker. However, rather than warn the friend of what was happening, he simply said nothing. When asked to explain why he kept his silence, he said that he was just too ʔaaj to speak up. Although the consequences of "ʔaaj-ness" were in this case more extreme than usual, the situation itself was not. In another, less dramatic instance, a villager mentioned that in coming across the rice fields that afternoon he had noticed that his neighbor's windmill had broken down. The belt connecting the wind mill to the irrigating machine used in raising water into the fields had slipped from the drive shaft. However, despite the obvious importance of this fact to his neighbor — the planting of his rice seedlings was completely dependent on the *noria* raising a sufficient amount of water into the field at the right time — the friend failed to tell his neighbor what had happened. When asked why, he said he was ʔaaj about making his friend unhappy.

What is important about the above illustrations is not so much their typicality — one can cite instances where friends are considerably more realistic and helpful — but rather the legitimacy of the rationalizations of the inactive friends. All Bang Chaners can understand and accept the reluctance of a villager to be the person who actually triggers another individual's discomfort. There is a genuine (albeit misplaced) sense of responsibility about not making another unhappy. What is important is the immediate, face-to-face situation. If a person must ultimately suffer, that is his own problem; but at least the friend can say, "I did not 'cause' it." Villagers also recognize the reluctance of an individual to become involved in another person's problems on the grounds of avoiding the accusation of actually having caused them. They say that frequently the person with good intentions is turned on by the very friend he is trying to help; for example, "Since you know so much about the broken windmill perhaps you were the one who broke it!" Both these attitudes result from a rather overinflated view of one's importance to the friend, as if the friend would be more concerned with the agent of information than with the information itself. This is not so much a confusion of means and ends as a reidentification of them. Finally, some of the villagers' reluctance is probably also due to simple indifference or laziness regarding the friend's plight.

Other expressions of the "ʔaaj-ness" complex are more clearly altruistic than the above. Villagers explain that the reason there is never any more than one candidate for the post of hamlet or commune headman, on the rare occasions when such elections are held, is to avoid embarrassing the individuals involved. The eventual headman would be embarrassed because the presence of a competitor would suggest doubt about his competence; the candidate who lost would be embarrassed by the very fact that he lost. To avoid hurt feelings, only one candidate is presented, voted on, and elected.

We have been talking above about politeness primarily in a negative sense, that is, about the lengths to which villagers will go to avoid discomforting others or upsetting peaceful relationships. This aspect was stressed because its expressions represent a somewhat unique form of patterned social interaction. However, the many positive forms of the villagers' politeness to friends and kin should not be minimized: their concern with choosing topics of conversation they think will interest or entertain others; their search for opportunities to flatter them, sometimes in pseudo-mocking fashion but more often to make them feel good; their attention to providing others with a pleasing audience — being silent, attentive, and eager when others are declaiming on a favorite subject. Of course, many times the villagers are not listening, but they try to behave as if they were. The aim here is to make others feel that what they are saying is worthwhile. An important part of this is that one almost never directly challenges the veracity or logic of the speaker's statements. If disbelief is the only appropriate response, it should be done silently. Nothing except personal pain and interpersonal tension would be gained from a direct challenge. If one feels strongly enough about the issue, which is very rare,[2] presenting an alternative view would not be inappropriate. But one must be extremely careful not to phrase it as a direct refutation. Again, there is present in this approach the Thai assumption that the most important aspect of a social relationship is the psychic comfort and welfare of the persons involved, not the truth or validity of the matter being discussed. The overriding ethic is that each person not only has a right to be heard, but should be made to feel comfortable as well.

Related to the above, but distinctive enough to require a category of its own, is the form of politeness expressed in the villagers' nervous laughter and in their preoccupation with inconsequential topics of conversa-

[2] Strong feelings are rare because, so often, the very purpose of such conversations is to convey politeness and nothing more. The actual topic of conversation is simply a medium of contact, not a matter to be seriously discussed.

tion. It is most obviously (and justifiably) expressed when a villager who wants to get something from another person — for example, a job, a loan, higher rent on land — is uncertain about the other's reaction and approaches him by hedging around the issue with giggles and light, irrelevant comments. This behavior usually occurs when there is no history of reciprocal benefits between the parties or when a middleman cannot be used. Although villagers themselves certainly do not consider such comments "irrelevant" (because from a ritualistic point of view they are not), it is hard to define a detailed discussion of a person's buttons or belt buckle as anything but a kind of phatic communion. Sometimes conversations of this type will go on for twenty and thirty minutes, often branching off to include more topical interests such as the size of eggs or the calls of birds before reaching the point. Frequently they do not reach the point at all, since somewhere along the line the individual recognizes from the tone of the conversation that the other person is not in the proper mood to entertain his request; in this case, the individual will explain that he came simply "to chat." Sometimes the friend will begin to giggle uneasily (particularly if the protagonist's references to him contain excessive flattery) as he becomes aware of the purpose of the conversation and wishes to evade facing the ultimate issue. Very often, even when the final request comes out, he can avoid it simply by giggling. Under such circumstances a giggle is crucially communicative. It is the person's polite substitute for "No," or "Let us bring this particular topic of conversation to an end." Giggling is a wonderfully effective way of carrying on a "conversation" (for those who can read its "vocabulary"), because one can so readily convey his refusal, wariness, and even hostility while at all times maintaining the illusion of friendliness. It is precisely because the villagers' giggling frequently rests on such devious attitudes that it appears to be somewhat nervous. Like the conversational topics mentioned above, its purpose is to maintain social contact, but at a minimal substantive level.

The third major form of the villagers' politeness — that associated with making a good impression on others — has to a certain extent been described by the materials already presented. Thus, in terms of the actual manifestations, there is really little difference between flattering another person, for example, because it will make him feel good, because it will make getting something out of him much easier, or because it will make one appear much more attractive in his eyes. However, it is clear that the motivations in these three cases are all quite different. It is for this reason that this last category has been introduced. When villagers meet a person whom they regard as significant (and this by no means includes all their contacts), they do put forth much effort to make a good impression on him. And being polite — courteous, helpful, flattering — is one of the most suitable means for achieving this effect.

Discussion of this interactive mode might not be necessary were villagers themselves not so keenly aware of it. Village children are continually and consciously taught, by word and deed, the necessity always to put their best foot forward. Bang Chaners assess themselves and others by their capacity to make themselves appealing. Both the "good" and the "competent" person is one who can make himself attractive by speaking softly, gently, and, if possible, beautifully and cleverly. Often villagers take offense at an individual who refuses to do this because his very refusal suggests that he does not feel respect for others.

What the ultimate psychological roots of this behavior are is unclear. It is apparent — largely because of the great attention given to considerations such as manners, proper speech, and the like — that this concern is not prompted primarily by the desire to be loved by others. Love would require a more substantial medium. Gaining the respect and approval of others is clearly an important component of the attitude, but one wonders why a people otherwise so self-loving and self-accepting should need to have their self-esteem repeatedly validated by others. Perhaps the villagers' concern with impressing others really has little to do with the others themselves, although obviously at the behavioral level it implicates them — that is, I suggest that the major factor behind the villagers' concern is essentially self-referring. It is both a manifestation and validation to the self that one is a fine, proper, and upstanding person; that to treat others well is to perform one's role as a civilized, meritorious person. This last word, "meritorious," is intentionally selected. It is meant to suggest that much of the villagers' politeness is consciously (although perhaps not explicitly) related to the notion of accumulating Buddhist merit, and that in being nice to others Bang Chaners are managing to fulfill, a little bit, what is to most of them the *raison d'être* of human experience.

THE DYNAMICS OF LOOSE STRUCTURE

The foregoing was concerned with the nature of some of the most frequently occurring forms of face-to-face contact in Bang Chan. We focused on manifestations of, and motives for, behavior when people actually meet and interact. However, human relationships involve considerably more than the forms and rituals of face-to-face interaction. They also include feelings, attitudes, and behavior toward others once the interactive situation has been left behind; a readiness to become involved with others in the first instance; and a sense of social linkage, functional or sentimental, that ties people to one another over time.

These latter considerations are perhaps the most difficult to talk about in Bang Chan because their most conspicuous expressions tend to be negative in nature; that is, empirically it often is considerably easier to point to cases wherein there are no enduring ties between individuals or wherein there is hesitation to become closely involved with others than it is to identify what links them together. There are a few relatively explicit means of linkage: the "dyadic contract" (to be discussed below); kinship ties, in many respects a special case of the dyadic contract; and, on some occasions, certain cosmological considerations ("I owe him this because we were friends in earlier lives," "We love each other because we were born on the same day"). However, even these modes of linkage require continuous behavioral validation and are recognized as ultimately unreliable. A Bang Chaner who fails to fulfill his "contract" by refusing to return a favor would at very worst be considered selfish. Most villagers would not even bother to assess his actions, assuming that he must have had a good reason for them.

To a large extent, the descriptive problem encountered here is the result of methodological conventions. An investigator concerned with how human beings relate to each other attempts initially to identify the bases of their contact. Having once identified these, he tends to assume that not only the bases but the relationships themselves are relatively constant and reliable. The relationship between Bang Chan employer and employee is an excellent example of the problem. An investigator concerned with specifying the bases of their relationship could readily point to two factors: contractual (in the strict meaning of the word) and sentimental. The former involves exchanging a sum of money for labor fulfilled. The latter involves an array of behaviors expressive of the employer's concern for his retainer: feeding him well, not making him work too hard, treating him like a younger sibling or "adopted" child, recognizing his birthday, or buying him small gifts. Interestingly, the subordinate's obligations to his superior are considerably less explicit and socially and psychologically less demanding: he must simply respect and obey him. However, accurate as these specifications are, they say nothing about the reliability of the relationship. It may be broken off over matters that have nothing to do with how well each is fulfilling his interactive responsibilities. The employee may become bored; he may have a sudden desire to take a trip or go to Bangkok; if he is from a distant village, he may suddenly become homesick and just as suddenly leave.

Again, there is nothing extraordinary or unique about personal desires and inclinations intruding on the stability of an interpersonal relationship. However, what is unique to Bang Chan and Thai culture in general is the frequency of such intrusions, the extent to which they take precedence over the responsibilities of the established relationship, and perhaps most important, their general expectability. No Bang Chaner is ever taken aback when another does not fulfill his assumptions about how that other will behave. These intrusions may have little effect on face-to-face contacts between people. A young man who leaves his job in the middle of harvest season will inform his boss of his departure in a most affable way, or there may not be any contact whatsoever between the parties. He may simply leave, trusting that his absence will indicate that the relationship is ended; weeks later a friend may come for his wages.

These modes of relationship received their first formal, and perhaps most elegant, formulation in a now-famous article entitled "Thailand — A Loosely Structured Social System," by the late John F. Embree (1950). Embree applied the notion of "loose structure" mainly in a descriptive rather than an analytic way. Thus (182): "The first characteristic of Thai culture to strike an observer from the West, or from Japan or Vietnam is the individualistic behavior of the people. The longer one resides in Thailand the more one is struck by the almost determined lack of regularity, discipline, and regimentation in Thai life. In contrast to Japan, Thailand lacks neatness and discipline; in contrast to Americans, the Thai lack respect for administrative regularity and have no industrial time sense." After providing many examples Embree concludes (184): "The point here once more is that . . . while obligations are recognized, they are not allowed to burden one unduly. Such as are sanctioned are observed freely by the individual — he acts of his own will, not as a result of social pressure."

While Embree's formulation is by definition phrased in social-structural terms, it inevitably directs our attention to an underlying motivational issue the nature of the villagers' disposition to conformity. Conformity to the expectations of others — whether such expectations are shared, complementary, or emergent — is of course a basic requisite of all effective [3] social action. It is perfectly clear, as demonstrated earlier, that Bang Chaners are highly motivated to conform while in the direct presence of others. Often there is overconformity when in such situations villagers become overly solicitous to what they think are the needs of others. However, the hallmark of Thai social relations is that there never is any certainty that such face-to-face contacts will take place, or if they do take place, that the conformity present during the direct encounter will be sustained once the contact has ended. The Bang Chaner's overriding inclination is to separate the encounter itself from that which precedes or follows it; psychologically, they are independent and unrelated experiences. The typical Bang Chaner excels at the art of indicating agreement with people — responsiveness, cooperativeness, and compliance with their verbal requests and orders — and then once the situation has been concluded, doing precisely what he wants, often exactly the opposite of that to which he had agreed.

Ordinarily, this is not intended as a form of duplicity. Villagers are quite sincere (and probably correct) when they say: "People are much happier when you agree with them and tell them what they want to hear." Too, the behavior is explained in part by the fact that most villag-

[3] The word "effective" is inserted here to acknowledge that social action is just as likely to be characterized by ambiguity, confusion, and misunderstanding — the absence of clear expectations — and that in some cases (as in greeting rituals) it is oriented mainly to *discovering* patterns of expectations. Further, insofar as such action occurs through time, it is never completely free of a minimum of both ambiguity and certainty: the ambiguity of not being able to anticipate what might next occur; the certainty of knowing that what does emerge has some relationship to what has gone before.

ers feel they can change their plans and intentions with impunity at the slightest provocation. Unfortunately, the other persons involved may not be informed of the change until it occurs. A Bang Chan employee who walks out on his superior because he does not like the food he is served or a villager who agrees to lend a person money and then is not at home when the person calls for the loan can easily account for his actions by saying that circumstances had changed.

It must be noted, and this is crucial, that there is generally no animosity felt toward the employer with the unpalatable food, the employee who left his job, nor toward the unreliable creditor. Villagers are thoroughly conditioned to the possibility of such events and accept them simply as part of the inauspicious nature of life. That they are in fact considered inauspicious rather than results of the willful or malevolent intentions of others is not accidental. Bang Chaners faced with a breakdown in the fulfillment of commitments can of course point to the individual who directly caused it. But no satisfaction is to be gained from this. The person who broke his obligation must have had his own good reason, and beyond this there probably were other factors, unknown to both parties, that caused the breakdown. For most Bang Chaners, all human intentions are forever set within a framework of cosmic, and particularly moral, unpredictability. If things do not work out the way one expects, it is most likely due to the inauspiciousness of the time, place, and persons involved. The proper time is particularly important. It is precisely for these reasons that the more important events in a person's life — marriage, trying to win a lottery or a maiden's heart, taking an important trip — are so often preceded by ceremonial attempts to decide the cosmologically auspicious conditions for the event. These involve consultations with monks, shamans, and other religious practitioners, and highly ritualized forms are followed to select the appropriate conditions. The kind of occurrences discussed above are not this significant, but they do partake of the same cognitive assumptions that lead to such highly institutionalized practices. Thus, whereas most Occidentals would point exclusively to the actions of the other person as being both the necessary and sufficient cause of the interactional breakdown, Bang Chaners, who have considerably less confidence in human capacities, would really not be sure. To them, human volition represents only one indeterminate and uncontrollable factor among the several that give rise to events. Who knows what accident, change of heart, sudden windfall — particularly one occasioned by something done by one of the parties several lives earlier — might intervene to alter what had originally been planned and agreed upon?

These assumptions about the indeterminacy of the universe and human actions are so integral to the villagers' cognitive orientation that Bang Chaners often hesitate to make even the most elementary predictions. Thus, in asking a village lad how he felt about his older brother's forthcoming ordination, I was told, "I don't know." The tone of his reply indicated that he was not evading the question, so I pursued the matter further. "Well, do you feel happy about it? Do you wish you were being ordained together with him?" He answered: "The ordination is not for another three days. I do not know how I will feel at that time. But when that time comes I will know." In another case, I was going up the canal with a villager to attend a *Kathin* being held at the monastery. (A Kathin is a fiestalike merit-making ceremony usually sponsored by a person or group of persons from outside the village at which new robes are presented to the monks.) Although not necessarily an annual event, Kathins are held often enough at Monastery Bang Chan so that this villager was thoroughly familiar with their every aspect. Simply to make conversation, I asked him: "What is the Kathin going to be like today?" to which he replied, "I do not know. I have not been to the monastery yet today." Assuming that his past experience with Kathins provided him with some knowledge of the goings-on, I went on: "Well, do you think there will be many people?" His answer: "I don't know. You never know what a situation is like until you meet it. I have not met this one yet today."

The point of these various illustrations is that they represent an uncertain and unpredictable psychological universe. And in this kind of universe — where one hesitates to build up sharply defined expectations and where one is forever aware of the mutability and frailty of the environment — it is not unusual that there should also be a high tolerance for interpersonal nonconformity. It is uncertain where the actual limits, theoretical or empirical, to this tendency to nonconformity, may lie. Much of the nonconformity is undoubtedly made possible, in the first instance, by the sociologically simple and relatively undifferentiated nature of Bang Chan society; that is, the actual number of functionally specific tasks and roles — those which require special competencies — are few, and any number of individuals can perform them. Thus, when a Bang Chan employee walks out on his boss or when a wife walks out on her husband, their actions do not, from a functional point of view, disable the system. Since the requirements of the role of house servant or farmhand are characteristically simple and understood by all, the departing employee can usually be replaced by another individual. Similarly, since any adult — aunt, grandparent, older sibling — can and often does rear another's children, and since there are always sufficient fish in the canal for an abandoned spouse to feed himself, the departure of a wife or husband need not, from a functional point of view and the point of view of most villagers, work any great hardship on the individuals involved.

It is recognized, of course, that the sociological simplicity of Bang Chan represents a necessary, but not sufficient, condition for the nonconformity found in the community. There undoubtedly are many cultures which are functionally and sociologically less complex than Bang Chan but where culturally defined requirements for interpersonal conformity are considerably greater. I would suggest that the loosely structured nature of relationships in Bang Chan is due primarily to psychological and philosophical ("world-view") factors and is permitted expression by the relatively undifferentiated social system. A more complex, highly differentiated social system, one whose functioning is completely dependent on the technical competencies of its members and on their meeting each other's expectations (a factory system, for example), obviously could not afford this luxury.

The ultimate psychological sources of the villagers' tendency toward loosely structured relationships are not easily determined. However, from the point of view of their etiology in the individual, it is clear that the villagers' tendencies toward loose relationships are related to early childhood experiences. A second source is their philosophical notions concerning the nature of the individual. These notions are largely cultural derivatives of Buddhist doctrine, although at the behavioral level they function simply as unstated premises which guide and tacitly define behavior.[4]

The basic assumptions governing the socialization of the Bang Chan child are most relevant here. When the child enters the world of human beings, he is already a partially formed and psychologically independent individual, with his own *ʔupanidsaj* (ingrained character) and *khwaan* (soul-stuff), not to mention his stock of accumulated merit and demerit from countless previous lives which predetermines his character. These definitions not only award to the child a psychic individuality that is partially independent of any social environment to which he is exposed, but assign to him a fundamental sense of psychological equality. We are not speaking here of *social* equality. The child is clearly a social inferior, and is due all the prerogatives of his position: he is to be dealt with gently, kindly, and benevolently, with sympathetic regard for his incompetence; correlatively, he must be taught to express deference and obedience to superiors. Rather, the equality awarded the child results from the recognition that in the workings of the cosmic scale it is impossible to ascertain what the child could once have been or eventually will become, and he, like any soul, is always potentially of the same value as any other person. It is precisely for this reason that most Bang Chaners, if they mention it at all, are only mildly pleased rather than particularly proud that one of their own grew up to become an admiral in the Thai

[4] From a strictly analytic point of view, it would probably be best to consider Buddhist doctrine as an abstract, codified representation of these premises rather than to consider the premises as explicit, logically coherent deductions from Buddhist doctrine. To be sure, many Bang Chaners explain and justify their actions by pointing directly to Buddhist doctrine, sometimes applying its tenets correctly and sometimes not. But for most, Buddhism is a diffuse, ubiquitous *Weltanschauung*, the precise effects and applications of which the villagers are tpyically unconscious. It would probably not be incorrect to think of most religious "traditions," particularly the "Great" codified ones, as functioning in this way.

Navy. It comes as no great surprise that such a thing can happen. To them, it is no more unusual than that the prime minister himself should be a person who was born and reared in a village. (By the same token, the peasant background of these two individuals creates no special sense of personal identification with them on the part of the villagers. They are perceived simply as two unique individuals, their peasant roots being only one of the literally countless factors that made them what they are today.) To a large extent, the child's equality derives from the premise that he is not so much a child as he is a human being who happens to be at a particular stage in his ontological career. From an epistemological point of view, there is of course nothing strange about such an approach. What is perhaps somewhat unique, however, is that the villagers actually use it as the point of departure in their treatment of the child.

The practical consequences of these equalitarian notions are manifold. For one thing, with the child defined as a separate and equal soul, the relationship between parent and child takes on a highly instrumental flavor. That is, rather than expressing love toward the child as an end in itself or otherwise treating him in ways that require no further justification (it is assumed that love is characteristically an absolute sentiment, not a means to any other satisfaction), villagers explicitly see the relationship between parent and child as contractual. Thus villagers say that they "are going to the trouble" of bringing up their children and "doing good things for them" (just as their own parents went to the trouble of bringing them up and doing good things for them) so that they will have someone to care for them in their old age and make merit for them when they die. Similarly, they say they love their parents because they are indebted to them for bringing them into the world. The language of the "contract" is poignantly explicit: "When I think of my mother, I think of the debt I owe her for bringing me into the world, and feeding me so I would survive"; "Parents who do not teach their children how to *waj* (exhibit respect to the parents) get nothing from them. I did many *bunkhuns* (good things requiring reciprocation) for my daughter, so now she gives me everything"; "When I was three my father gave me to my uncle who fed me and trained me, so I loved my uncle more."

Nothing is strange about these "contractual" criteria in themselves. However, they do reflect a fundamental recognition of the independence of parent and child and of the fact that parent and child have the *option* of fulfilling each other's needs. More specifically, they express the assumption that there is nothing intrinsic to the parent-child relationship that requires the two persons to be linked together. The relationship clearly is not fortuitous, but neither is it absolute. It functions primarily for the instrumental and symbiotic satisfactions that its participants can gain from it. Lacking the absolute elements of an ultimate relationship (*disinterested* appreciation or admiration of the other individual; loving the child or parent in his own right, rather than for his effect on the self), it has a strong undercurrent of unreliability. Since the maintenance of the relationship always depends on what the participants can gain from it — i.e., from the other person — and since the participants are essentially free to break the relationship once they feel that such rewards are not forthcoming, it is inevitable that there will be many instances when just that will happen. The important point is that there is nothing over and above the instrumental nature of the relationship to keep the individuals tied to one another. The only possible exception, an important one, is that which goes with the realization that by treating one's child or parent nicely, one is behaving in a moral way and is thus accumulating Buddhist merit; but even this purpose is avowedly self-referring. In this regard, it might be noted that other than the marriage ceremony, which is ignored by half of Bang Chan newlyweds, there are no institutionalized attempts to sanctify the solidarity of the family, or for that matter the solidarity of almost any social group. That is, unlike China and the West, there is nothing in traditional Thai folk belief and ritual or in the literature of the indigenous Great Tradition that alludes to the sacredness of the family as a social unit. All moral aphorisms concerning family relationships are phrased according to the dyadic relations between individuals, not affiliation with the family unit.

The second major source of the villagers' loose relationships lacks the developmental reference of the above. To a certain extent it is not even social-relational in nature, although our concern with it stems from its having crucial consequences to the social orientations of individuals. I am referring here to the Buddhist emphasis on the primacy of individual action and individual responsibility. Without discussing at length the subtleties of Buddhist doctrine, it is imperative to point out that the principal tenet of Hinayana Buddhism is the complete psychological freedom, isolation, and responsibility of every person. This is not the Occidental idea of "free will," but rather the notion that every person is a free agent, responsible only to and for himself, and that he inevitably reaps the fruits of his own conduct. Buddhist canonical literature is replete with references stressing the centrality of this doctrine. The last words of the Lord Buddha before he left this world to achieve the sublime state of *nibphaan* (nirvana) are said to have been: "Work out your own salvation with diligence." A frequently quoted passage of the *Dhamapada* reads: "By oneself is evil done; By oneself one suffers; By oneself evil is left undone; By oneself one is purified." The whole complex cosmology relating to the accumulation of merit and demerit is phrased in terms of the individual's lonely journey through cycles of interminable existences working out his own moral destiny. Who his progenitors were, what kind of environment he was born and reared in, what social advantages and disadvantages he was exposed to, all are considered secondary, and in some cases even insignificant, in influencing what he is and what he does. The life and career of Gautama himself testifies perfectly to the essential irrelevance of these factors. (On the other hand, the attention given to these considerations in Western ontology perfectly expresses our "sociological bias." In our system, even our original moral state is determined by what someone else — Adam and Eve — did.) In Therevada Buddhism, an individual's worldly and cosmological condition — the former essentially a temporary, special case of the latter — is for the most part self-generative, although because one never knows when the effects of one's karma may emerge, it is also unpredictable.

These formulations translate and function in workaday behavior in an extremely subtle manner. Every time a Bang Chaner is about to do something, he obviously does not ask himself whether it is in his own best moral interest. Similarly, every time he ignores another's expectations about how he will behave he does not justify his actions by the Buddhist doctrine of enlightened self-interest. However, these formulations do impart a fundamental legitimacy to the pursuit of individualistic self-concern. More important, they establish — in a diffuse, unreflective, but nonetheless highly meaningful way — a definition of social reality that assumes the ultimate reference of every person's act is himself. In this way, social relationships become defined as either artifacts of, or media for, attaining one's own ends. People need and use each other to satisfy their own purposes. (This is not to say that social relationships do not have many other functions. Our concern here is with the way villagers view the aims of their social relations.) What keeps the social system running relatively smoothly is the assumption that every person is acting on precisely the same bases, and the realization that one's own purposes are best served by acts of reciprocation. The basis of the system, however, is the continuous satisfaction of each participant's individual needs, for should such satisfactions not be forthcoming, there is always complete freedom and sanction to withdraw. Villagers typically define benefits gained from reciprocal acts to be materialistic (the food or gifts a parent gives to a child or an employer gives an employee); psychological (the respect a subordinate awards to a superordinate or the security the latter provides the former); and spiritual (the merit parents gain when their son enters the monkhood, the merit being repayment for their having gone to the trouble of rearing him).

In the above discussion some of the sources and supports of the loosely structured relationships that are found in Bang Chan were outlined. However, there remains the very important question of how villagers manage to develop the long-term relationships that they do have, for despite the inevitable unpredictability of all human contacts, most Bang Chaners do live together in family units for more or less long sustained periods of time; fathers do save for years in order to give their sons respectable ordinations into the monkhood; friends and relatives who have not seen each other since childhood do assemble for the cremation of a late kinsman or mutual friend; and mature adults do continue to feel profound respect for and obligation to those who were their teachers when they were youngsters. What are the bases and rewards for these enduring interpersonal commitments?

The immediate rewards are, on the one hand, quite apparent. They involve such things as the simple, unrationalized love found among any group of kin or close friends. In the case of the ordination and cremation, there is the reward of making merit, not only for the son and the departed soul, but for all those who sponsor and participate in the ceremonials. The satisfactions gained from increasing one's social prestige by putting on an ostentatious ceremonial are not to be overlooked, either. At a more subtle level, in the respectful student's case the reward is gained from knowing that one is behaving in a proper and courteous way toward one's *aacaan* (in its social-psychological connotations, similar to the Indian word *guru*) and is thus upholding established normative patterns. The rewards of maintaining the rituals of the moral order are not to be glossed over, for Bang Chaners, like most Siamese, are a deeply ethical people. This is not meant as an evaluation of their behavior or as a statement of their capacity to conform to their ethical prescriptions, but simply as a statement of their preoccupation with ethical concerns. The rewards of feeling (genuinely or self-deceptively) that one has behaved in an ethically and ritualistically prescribed way are among the most satisfying of sentiments, although, as indicated in the discussion of "social cosmetics," villagers often use the rituals of ethical behavior as substitutes for more demanding interpersonal involvements. Indeed, the great emphasis given to the performance of ethical rituals (speaking in soft and gentle words, honoring one's mentors) helps perpetuate the loosely structured relationships found in the community in that conformity to these rituals is perceived by many as comprising the fulfillment of their interpersonal obligations. Beyond this they are free to pursue their own interests. To a large extent the ritualistic forms serve as a comforting psychological justification for the pursuit of individualistic concerns e.g., "But I otherwise treat others so nicely." This is not the result of conscious psychological manipulation. The frequency with which villagers evaluate themselves and others according to the performance of these rituals and the high frequency of rituals in actual behavior attest to the seriousness which Bang Chaners attach to them. Their compensatory nature in no way detracts from their importance to the individual. In fact, precisely the opposite seems to be true. Bang Chaners are a highly ethical people regardless of the social-psychological functions such ethics may serve.

Less apparent than these immediate rewards for fulfilling interpersonal commitments, but perhaps the very factor that is common to most of them, is the sense of reciprocity that is the basis of all enduring relationships in Bang Chan. At several points the *quid pro quo* nature of Thai social relationships was referred to. However, the importance of this consideration cannot be fully appreciated without realizing that the functioning of the entire Thai social system is ultimately dependent on it. Individuals become involved with others and do things for them because they consciously expect others to respond in kind. This applies to the relationships between family members who live together *because* such an arrangement is most advantageous to each; to the father who gives his son an ordination *in order that* the latter will make merit for him and feel obligated to care for him when he becomes old; to the friends and relatives who make merit for the departed soul *because of* the good things he had done for them during his lifetime; to the adults who feel obligated to their childhood teacher *because of* the knowledge, and thus power, he imparted to them. It might well be, as Maus (1954. Originally 1923–1924, translated by Cunnison) and Homans (1961) have argued, that human relationships everywhere are based on just such considerations, usually concealed by ethically palatable amenities (such as in American culture, from which most of Homans' empirical materials come). What is so intriguing about the Thai, however, is that dyadic contracts are forever kept in mind to justify and explain why people relate to one another. Although villagers, because they are such polite people, rarely say to others: "I am helping you because I know the day will come when I need your help," or "Do this for me because you owe me a favor," they do use such arguments to explain the basis of their ties: "Of all my friends I love Lek the most because she has done me the most favors (bunkhuns)"; "The purpose of marriage is to have a companion who will take care of you when you get sick"; "Of all my daughters, the one who gives me the greatest pleasure is the one who sells things. . . . When she gets money she gives it to me"; "Friends are very useful because it means that you have people who will do you favors. And when they need help, you will take care of them. This is love."

In anthropological analysis it is customary first to seek and attempt to identify the factors which link human beings together rather than those which keep them apart. This is so much a part of our professional tradition that we tend to gloss over the question of the extent to which people *must* have enduring interpersonal commitments. This question has not been pursued in precise detail in our discussion. However, the realities of long-term relationships in Bang Chan are so weighted in the direction of atomistic and essentially conditional considerations that any coherent discussion of them should be organized in approximately equivalent fashion. It is hoped that this organization accurately reflects the tone and quality of Bang Chan social life as it is encountered and felt by an outside observer trying to understand its meaning to those who experience it.

REFERENCES CITED

Embree, John F.

1950 "Thailand — A Loosely Structured Social System." *American Anthropologist*, 52:181–193.

Hanks, Lucien M. Jr., and Herbert P. Phillips

1961 "A Young Thai from the Countryside: A Psychosocial Analysis," in *Studying Personality Cross-Culturally*, Bert Kaplan, ed. Evanston: Row, Peterson and Company.

Homans, George C.

1961 *Social Behavior: Its Elementary Forms*. New York: Harcourt, Brace & World.

Mauss, Marcel (Ian Cunnison, tr.)

1954 *The Gift: Forms and Functions of Exchange in Archaic Societies*. Glencoe, Ill.: The Free Press.

Chinese Peasant Values Toward the Land

Bernard Gallin

INTRODUCTION

Robert Redfield, in his last major essay on the nature of peasantry, devoted at least one chapter to "The Peasant View of the Good Life." In making generalizations based on comparative studies of peasantry, Redfield (1956:112) felt there existed "a cluster of three closely related attitudes or values: an intimate and reverent attitude toward the land; the idea that agricultural work is good and commerce not so good; and an emphasis on productive industry as a prime virtue." Later in the same essay, Redfield modified the form of these generalizations, but still held that peasant values included an "intense attachment to native soil; a reverent disposition toward habitat and ancestral ways. . . ." (1956: 140).

The views held by Redfield and shared widely by Western thinkers do not apply to China. Researchers on China have long assumed that such peasant attitudes towards the native soil did exist and, at least implicitly, seem to have accepted as fact the universality of these values.

From "Chinese Peasant Values Toward the Land" in *Proceedings of the 1963 Annual Spring Meeting of the American Ethnological Society*, pp. 64–71. Reprinted by permission of the University of Washington Press. Much of the data used in this paper I collected during almost two years (1956–1958) of field work in Taiwan; I wish to thank the Ford Foundation, which supported this work. I also owe thanks to the Office of International Programs, Michigan State University, for a grant providing partial support for the writing of this paper. Gratitude is also due to Herbert P. Phillips, of Michigan State University, for his helpful comments. To my wife Rita Schlesinger Gallin, goes my unending thanks for participation in the field work and for her constant aid and encouragement in my work.

A detailed ethnographic description and analysis of life in this changing Chinese village can be found in my book *Hsin Hsing, Taiwan: A Chinese Village in Change*, Berkeley: University of California Press, 1966.

They have frequently pointed out that the Chinese peasant has great feelings of reverence towards his land and closely associates it with his ancestors and with the continuation of his family through time.

The origins of this assumption are probably manifold. However, it seems clear that there is one major factor which contributes to its perpetuation: this conception has held a prominent place in the literature of the "great tradition" of China and in its articulation the "great tradition" has had a profound influence on both the observer and the observed in China.

The conscious role of the "great tradition" in China, by necessity, has been to stimulate social and political harmony. It has functioned in a society where agriculture has been the economic dominant and where an ever-growing population has depended on land with limited productive potential. To safeguard the traditional system of China it was essential that a set of values towards the land and agriculture be developed and stressed. It was fundamental first that the peasantry resign themselves to the laboriousness of physical survival, and second that a harmonious relationship between man and the land as well as the agricultural process be maintained. Fairbank (1959:207–208) has pointed out the necessity of perpetuating an "emphasis upon virtue of contentment and limitation of wants. . . . Only the firmest code of social conduct could have kept this old system operating and induced the peasant to make his rent, tax, or interest payments, or acquiesce in perpetual indebtedness and poverty. Plainly the sanctity of title to landed property, backed by the power of the landlord-official class, was one potent factor."

The "great tradition" was an important instrument in developing and fostering a firm set of values towards the land, agriculture, and the preservation of the social order of China. In the classical literature the primacy of agriculture and the tie to the land is constantly stressed and reinforced. For example, in an "Edict of Emperor Wen on the Primacy of Agriculture" (163 B.C. from Han shu, 4:15a-b; translated in de Bary, 1960:229), it is said that natural calamities exist because too many people are engaged in non-agricultural activities which are detrimental to agriculture. It does not take much to extend this idea down to the peasant level, so that events like family misfortunes, are also considered due to an imbalance in the family's relationship to its land.

In addition and perhaps more important, the classical literature is filled with allegories aimed at supporting the prescribed Confucian social and political order. The direct subject matter of the allegory is frequently the land and agriculture, as well as the symbolic care and proper processes necessary to enhance productivity. Although the allusion is clearly to proper social and political behavior, the land serves as a type of cognitive reference point even for the peasantry.

The notion of peasant reverence for the land has become so much a part of the "great tradition," that it has influenced the peasant mentally in such a way that he believes it, or at least is greatly concerned with it.

Further, as will be discussed later, this has been constantly reinforced by the nature of the qualifications for status and social mobility in the traditional socio-economic system. In fact, the values and attitudes projected into the peasant's consciousness through the "great tradition" have become so pervasive that the peasant's perception of his own life has been blurred, rendering him unable to distinguish clearly his values and attitudes from his actual behavior, or perhaps even from his conception of his own motivations. As a result, the researcher's problem of distinguishing between the ideal and the actual picture of social life has been greatly complicated.

It is the purpose of this paper, therefore, to discuss one possible instance of such distorted interpretation: some facets of the problem of Chinese peasant values toward the land. To do this, data drawn from traditional China as well as from a community study in contemporary Taiwan will be utilized.

PEASANT VALUES TOWARD THE LAND IN TRADITIONAL CHINA

Undoubtedly, the relationship of the Chinese peasant to his land did include an "attachment to the native soil" and a degree of "reverence for the land." It is unlikely, however, that such a feeling toward the land was an end in itself. There is evidence to suggest that the feeling existed because the land was considered the only means by which the family could be served, and its continuity secured.

This becomes clear when one considers the situation in traditional China. While the land may not have been overly productive of wealth and abundance, it did represent the only available and secure means of livelihood for the peasantry. Few other economic outlets were open to the average farmer in the Chinese preindustrial society and, the only alternative, work as a merchant or even an artisan, was considered to be of lower status. This was clearly communicated to and absorbed by the peasantry through the teachings of the "great tradition" which informed all levels of society that the peasant was a productive being who belonged on the land, while the merchant and the artisan belonged to, respectively, parasitic and less productive classes of society.

Such a situation was further complicated by the traditional Chinese social and political systems in which one's family, kinship group, and native place were the basis of identity for the individual. The only way to secure status for the individual and the family was through wealth from the land. A combination of increased landholding and education was the single road to increased status and eventual entry into the literati and bureaucracy of China.

This meant that the family and its members usually had little choice other than to remain on the land. For status purposes — at least for their children — even the merchants attempted to invest their wealth in land rather than increase their investment in business. While the merchant was often wealthy and even exerted much influence in the society, he belonged to a class of low esteem. His social and political aspirations in an open society were constantly thwarted by the bureaucracy whose members came from the landed gentry and shared their class's attitudes of disdain towards the merchants.

The classical literature of traditional times frequently points to the inferior status of the merchant in the society. The Legalist School of the 3rd and 4th centuries B.C., in order to promote the well-being of the state, proposed that, "Agriculture, as the basis of the economy, would be promoted intensively, while commerce and intellectual endeavor were to be severely restricted, as nonessential and diversionary." (de Bary 1960: 137).

On this basis, it is possible to understand how the native soil became identified as a symbol of the fate of a family so that an intimate and reverent relationship to the land was assumed to exist, perhaps more by the outsider than by the peasant himself. At the same time, the land did come to represent a way of life for the peasantry which could be understood, and from which psychic satisfaction as well as economic security could be attained. However, the sacred and symbolic value of the land as an end in itself was probably minimal, and the more basic peasant attitude regarded the land as an economic commodity which served as a means for securing the continuity and status of the family.

Events in the more modern period of China of the late 19th and early 20th centuries give additional substance to this interpretation. It was during this period that improved communication systems and new economic outlets provided greater freedom of movement for the individual family member so he no longer needed to feel completely bound to the land. Coupled with this new freedom was the problem of a growing land scarcity as the population grew so that the land was increasingly less able to provide satisfactory sustenance to its cultivators. Many took the opportunity to leave the land to seek other means of livelihood. Apparently this move was made by many peasants with little conscious thought or concern for "their overwhelming feeling of reverence and sacredness for the ancestral soil."

PEASANT VALUES TOWARD THE LAND IN A CHINESE VILLAGE COMMUNITY IN TAIWAN

The past few decades in Taiwan have witnessed a parallel situation. The Taiwanese agricultural village in which I did my field work is representative of a number in the area in which predominantly economic attitudes toward the land have become overt.

Hsin Hsing village, where I spent 16 months in 1957–1958, is on the west-central coastal plain of Taiwan. The ancestors of most of the present villages came from the coastal area of Fukien in Southeast China beginning in the latter part of the 18th century. At the time of the study the village had a population of about 650 people, clustered in approximately 115 family households, each an economic unit.

While there are 12 different surnames in the village, of these, four names comprise almost 80 percent of the village population. In most instances families bearing the same surname consider themselves to be part of the same *tsu*, or lineage (frequently referred to as a "clan" in the literature). However, those families sharing a common surname may not be members of the same larger kinship group if they do not share a common ancestor. There are also a number of related families which are not part of any lineage organization, and even several village families which have no relatives in the village at all. Of the lineages found in the village, two are most influential in village affairs. Although some village *tsu* are relatively large, their corporate landholdings both in quantity and symbolic value are insignificant. This seemingly is the prevailing condition in most of the villages of the local area: segmentary lineages whose corporate landholdings are of relatively little significance.

At the time of its founding, Hsin Hsing, like other villages in the area, was relatively isolated from the larger society. The land, the home village, and kinship ties were the main sources of security. Outlets were limited for work other than on the land.

However, beginning with the period of the efficient, centralized Japanese government in the early 1900's, and continuing in recent years with the Chinese Nationalist government, village contacts and associations with the larger society have increased. Effective administrative measures have helped to break down the insularity of village organization and the villagers' traditional identification with their village and the land. At the same time, improved systems of public health and sanitation have led to rapid population growth and, as a result, an acute problem of land scarcity has developed. This problem has not been greatly alleviated by the land reform of 1949–1953 since the land was still subjected to as much fractionalization as before and the amount of land tilled by any one family, for the most part, had not been increased. Under such economic pressures, the villagers were forced to seek means of support other than village agriculture. However, it was not until the post World War II period that the possibilities increased for earning a livelihood other than on the land. Sometimes these job opportunities were found in the local area; but more often the peasants had to go to a city, like Taipei, about 120 miles to the north. Although today the majority of the villages are still engaged in some form of agriculture, it has become necessary for increasing numbers of men and boys, and sometimes whole families, to go to the cities to supplement their income or even completely to change their economic mode of life.

Such mobility has heightened the villagers' urban contacts and relationships and loosened traditional ties to their home village and the land. Family members are separated, if only temporarily. But, as a result, the individual family unit has grown increasingly independent of its traditional wider kinship ties. At the same time, the land reform has tended to affect and change the means by which social status and leadership may be achieved in the future; the source of prestige is no longer limited exclusively to the land.

For many village families, whatever feeling of intimacy or reverence may have been held toward the native soil usually quickly becomes insignificant in the face of better economic opportunities off the land. Were it not for those villagers who still prefer the village and the agricultural way of life, it would be tempting completely to discount any real feeling of "reverence or intimacy" which the peasant may have held in the past along with his economic attitude toward the land.

At the time of their migration to the city to work, and eventually to live, most of the villagers still own or operate at least a small piece of land. This has been true of both the migrating landlords and peasants.

In the case of landlords, most of whose land had been accumulated over several generations, large percentages of their family holdings were expropriated with compensation through the land reform. They therefore had to find other outlets for capital investments. In doing so, many of them made investments in business or industry — often in the cities. Some of the landlords remained in the village even though they derived much of their income from non-village sources. Others have moved out of their villages since they no longer have much economic interest in the village of their ancestors. Many, primarily for purposes of income, still hold on to the land which the land reform permitted them to retain. Others, however, feel that today there is little opportunity to reaccumulate large landholdings. They have found other outlets for financial investment, and so have not only left the village but have also sold off their remaining landholdings. The land is sold usually to any person who is willing to pay the price. Little consideration is given to the landlord's lineal relatives who remain in the village and are interested in the land but unable or hesitant about paying the price. In these cases there is little evidence or concern by the sellers for maintaining land in the family line.

In the case of villagers who are small land cultivators (owners, or former and present tenant farmers) the need to supplement the income from the land is usually met by first sending an individual member of the family to work in the city. The women, the children and the old people are left to work the land. The men or older boys return to the village to help on the land usually at planting and harvest time, and to take part in festivals. They are important carriers of urban cultural elements to the village, and are one of several agents of change within the village social structure.

Most of the migrating villagers who go to work in the city, at least at first, usually find jobs as unskilled laborers and their income is often inadequate as well as insecure. As a result, their families may continue to live in the village for years since the men are unable to earn enough money or security to bring their entire families to live in the city. During this time they certainly cannot take the chance and give up the income from whatever land they own or rent in the village area. In addition, the decision to make the move to the city a permanent one for the entire family is usually rather slow in coming, even for those villagers who do earn good money in the city.

When individuals working in the city feel that their employment is economically secure or are perhaps able to establish a small business, they usually gradually bring the remaining family members from the village to live in the city with them. But even then, most — at least at first — retain their small village landholdings, whether as owners or tenants. They make an informal agreement with a village relative or even a close village friend to till their land for them, often allowing such people to keep most of the small income from the land for their work and trouble. In this way, a city-dwelling village family can for long periods of time retain some minimal form of economic security in the village in case things should go wrong in the city. Eventually, however, some families do feel secure enough to sell their land or their tenant rights. In such instances they usually also then sell their family's land to anyone who can afford it, rather than to a tsu (lineage) relative who would have wished to buy the land but who could not pay the price immediately. (It might be noted here that if, for economic reasons, the land is sold to a nonrelative, the family is likely to be critized by their relatives for not giving the family, and the tsu members, first choice and for not keeping the land in the family. But such criticism or censure is ineffectual and weak, at best.)

This failure of family or tsu pressure to keep the land in the hands of the family, or at least in the larger kinship group, can also be attributed to the generally small and weakened state of tsu organization in the Hsin Hsing village area. One must note that where the tsu is strong, the situation can be quite different. Fei and Chang (1948:126) note in their study in Yunnan province that,

> Because the land is mainly inherited from the ancestors and it is the duty of the descendants to keep it within the clan, custom decrees that the clan members shall have a preferential right to buy it. Only if the clan members are unable to buy the land or to lend him money to extricate him from his financial difficulty, may the individual sell to an outsider. In this case the buyer must secure the signatures of all the near members of the seller's clan; if the transaction takes place without their permission, the contract is both customarily and legally invalid.

But general knowledge of the nature of Chinese lineages makes it clear that the symbolic value attached to the land by the lineage derives primarily from the elite's desire to maintain the major source of the lineage's political and economic power rather than from a pervasive emotional attachment ("reverence") toward the land. For example, the necessity for the "clan" to rely on its rules and coercion in order to prevent its members from selling their land to outsiders (found by Fei and Chang, 1948:126) demonstrates the recognition of the need to control individual families from dissipating the land of the "clan." On the other hand, in the Hsin Hsing area, where the lineage is weak, there is virtually unobstructed sale of land to outsiders. For the individual family here the land is primarily significant as a form of economic security and, especially in the past, the means for potential social mobility. On this basis, it is retained or sold. The symbolic value of land, then, would seem to diminish in importance wherever the individual family is free to do with it what it will.

SUMMARY AND CONCLUSIONS

It would appear, then, that much of the farmer's traditional sentiment for his land and, to a lesser extent, his ancestral home, is frequently cast aside if there is an alternate way to earn a livelihood and accumulate status and wealth. While the work performed by many villagers in Taipei is often no more than coolie labor (usually referred to as "going to Taipei to be a water buffalo" or a "beast of burden"), for the man with too little land, there is just not enough to eat if he stays in the village. But now that there are new economic opportunities outside the village even the farmer who does manage to earn a living from the land may be heard to say, "the life of a farmer is hard and bitter." He does not want his son to be a farmer like himself and "suffer on the land." He wants him to become a businessman or teacher for, "although teachers and minor officials do not make much money their work is easy." He wants his daughters to marry businessmen because, "instead of having money only after the harvest the businessman always has money coming in." Similar remarks and attitudes expressed by rural peasants have been recorded by other field workers (e.g., Fei and Chang 1948:129) carrying on community studies on the China mainland.

We have seen that, in Taiwan, even those people who desire to remain in the village and on the land do not do so, as one might otherwise expect, for conservative reasons or as a reaction to change. In the Taiwanese villages examined, it is often this group of people who are the most active in the community. They bring about internal economic and social changes in the village through their attempt at improved agriculture methods which bring them into contact with government agriculture agents as well as with farmers in the surrounding rural area. This group stands in contrast to the larger group of villagers who have continued to cultivate their diminishing land base in the traditional manner.

The interpretation presented here of the attitude of the Chinese peasant to his land may have important significance. If, on the basis of this evidence, we revise our interpretation of this value, accept that even in pre-modern times the basis for the Chinese peasant's feeling for his land was primarily an economic and status-giving one and only secondarily a spiritual or emotional one, perhaps we can then project such findings and better understand the present situation on the Chinese mainland. We might then inquire into the effects of the Chinese Communist government's manipulations of the peasant and his land: To what degree has the peasant's emotional and spiritual tie to the land been an important factor on the mainland? What consequences has the loss of his individual landholdings produced in other aspects of the mainland peasant's life? With these questions in mind, one might then further inquire as to how the government's manipulation of the peasant and his land will affect the eventual position of the present regime in mainland China.

REFERENCES CITED

de Bary, William Theodore, (ed.)
1960 *Sources of Chinese Tradition.* New York: Columbia University Press.

Fairbank, John King
1959 *The United States and China.* Cambridge: Harvard University Press.

Fei Hsiao-tung and Chang Chih-i
1948 *Earthbound China: A Study of Rural Economy in Yunnan.* London: Routledge and Kegan Paul, Ltd.

Redfield, Robert
1956 *Peasant Society and Culture.* Chicago: University of Chicago Press.

PART FIVE

CONTEMPORARY PEASANT PROBLEMS

Introduction: Peasants in the Modern World

Jack M. Potter

In the rapidly developing field of comparative peasant studies there is, as Geertz (1962:5) has remarked, not only a proto-peasant problem but also a post-peasant problem. As anthropologists began to move away from the study of primitive societies to the serious study of peasants, peasants, like the primitives, were rapidly disappearing. The transformation of classical peasant societies into modern states is one of contemporary history's great themes, and the comparative study of this modernization process as it affects the world's peasantries has become one of the most important problem areas in anthropological research.

The major sources of change in peasant societies are the cultural, technological, scientific, and ideological influences which have come in part from the Western industrialized nations, and in part from the elites of the new countries themselves. This process of change began several centuries ago with the first expansion of the West, but it has accelerated to a breakneck pace in this century. Everywhere modern economic, cultural, and ideological influences are eroding traditional societies at national and village levels. Already peasant societies can no longer be found in what may be called their "classical" forms; change has carried them beyond this point. This transformation is one of the great social revolutions in history, comparable to the rise of civilizations, and it will have enormous effects on the human condition. Until recently, life in a peasant village was the most prevalent form of human existence, and probably more people have lived and died there than in any other social context.

In the modern world peasant societies are anachronisms, and it is inevitable that they disappear. Peasants themselves have demonstrated time and time again that they prefer a different, and what they believe to be a better life. Poverty, illiteracy, oppression, disease and early death, and a backbreaking life of sweating over a piece of land, have little nostalgic value to peasants, a great many of whom will take every reasonable opportunity to escape to the new life of the city. Modern technology as well as human desires have conspired to hasten the end of the traditional peasant.

Ever since its appearance in eighteenth-century England, industrialization has been the main force changing the traditional peasant order, and for most overcrowded and impoverished peasant societies in the world it represents the only alternative to a miserable and increasingly unsatisfactory existence. The phenomenal increase in population over the last century has created a problem that is, simply stated, one of too many people trying to live off too little land. With an ever-increasing population pressing against limited resources, many peasants are forced to seek a livelihood outside their traditional communities. Only with the expansion of industry and a sharp drop in the birth rate can remaining peasant societies escape their serious dilemma and achieve some measure of human dignity.

Urbanization inevitably accompanies industrialization. Classical peasant societies have always contained cities, but these preindustrial cities are changing from centers of commerce and handicrafts, and residences of traditional elites, to new centers of industry. It has been from the new urban centers that most modern influences have entered the countryside.

With the beginnings of industrialization, cities not only change in type; they also dramatically increase in size as peasants are attracted by jobs in the new industrial plants and by the novelties of modern urban life. The migration of peasants into urban centers is occurring on a dramatic scale all over the world and is often a traumatic experience for the peasant. The move from the small, personal world of the peasant community, where one is in the bosom of family, friends, and kinsmen, into the impersonal and confusing life of the city is an adaptation often difficult for the peasant to make. Made cautious by centuries on the land, the peasant often makes the move from village to city over several generations. At first young peasants leave the village to find temporary work in the city. Since this is at first a risky business, because of depressions and other imponderables to which modern economic systems are subject, the peasant may initially retain his village kinship ties and his rights to property as something he can fall back upon if he loses his job or in some other way fails to make it in the city. Often "making it" in the city is difficult because the peasant usually has to enter the urban job market at the lowest level as an unskilled laborer. Peasants rarely become members of the bourgeois middle class upon moving to the urban areas. In the mushrooming industrial cities the peasant finds that economic development does not proceed fast enough to absorb all migrants, and frequently he ends up unemployed, living in an urban slum where life is sometimes even worse than in the countryside. Only gradually, after he achieves some success and job security in the city, does the peasant finally break his ties with the countryside — which by that time have outlived their usefulness and become burdensome. It is largely through the influence of city migrants that modern political and social attitudes of the city, usually heavily influenced by Western culture, are introduced into the peasant village where they begin gradually to change traditional attitudes and customs.

The commercial network is another important avenue by which economic and technological innovations reach the countryside. New manufactured goods such as electric appliances, canned foods, and new clothing styles are made available to peasants in the market. The desire to acquire these new manufactured goods and all the other gadgets of modern industry gives rise to new expectations and furnishes the incentive for peasants to take advantage of new economic opportunities. As commerce and industry develop, the market nexus increasingly penetrates the subsistence sector of the peasant economy, and soon the peasant is caught up in market networks that extend to market towns, cities, and the outside world.

As the extension of the market network opens up wider trade channels to the world outside the village, agriculture frequently becomes commercialized. Participation in the market gradually changes traditional peasants, to whom agriculture was a way of life, into farmers, or agricultural businessmen, whose activities become a business for profit.

The impersonal forces of the city and the market, though inexorable, are not the only ways in which peasant life is being changed in the contemporary world. The elite groups which control the new nation-states, imbued with the idea of progress, deliberately attempt to transform their peasantries through programs of planned change. Rural-extension and community-development programs, in which efforts are made to introduce new farm technology, new crops, better sanitary and health facilities, birth-control methods, and so on, are common in most of the emerging nations. These attempts at social engineering meet with uneven success, sometimes because they are poorly planned and executed, and sometimes because the peasant's basic caution and conservatism do not permit him to change as rapidly as the more advanced sectors of his nation wish.

Peasants are crucial in the industrialization of new nations. In the initial stages of industrialization new nations have to raise capital to finance the building of factories, the importation of machinery, and the acquisition of necessary industrial skills. Since agriculture lies at the basis of traditional economies, some capital accumulation must come from this source. The peasants, therefore, must not only furnish the food requirements of an expanding urban labor force; they must also produce a surplus which can be sold abroad to obtain foreign exchange that will finance part of the industrialization program. At the same time, peasants must supply the manpower to create the urban labor force for the new factories and new service establishments.

Ultimately, modernization and industrialization so transform traditional peasant societies that almost all features which characterized the traditional peasant social, economic, and cultural order are significantly altered. The structural semi-isolation of the village community becomes less pronounced, and class groupings, occupational associations, and other horizontal social ties become more important in the peasant's life than his traditional village, as pointed out by Fallers in the article that appears in Part One. Traditional kinship groups, like the extended family and the lineage, where they exist, give way to the nuclear family, which is better suited to the social and geographical mobility required in modern industrial society. The old cultural separation between the Great and Little Traditions is blurred by modern communication facilities, which tend to create a common mass culture. The fatalistic attitude of traditional peasants, summarized in Professor Foster's "Image of Limited Good" model in Part Four of this volume, gives way — although slowly — to an achievement orientation as it becomes more and more possible to acquire newly created wealth and status in the wider society. Communal custom as a means of social control is replaced by the bureaucratic legal and political systems of the new states. The political and social independence of the local community is lessened as the modern state apparatus extends its power down to the local level. In all these ways the "part-society" characteristics of traditional peasants are significantly altered as the peasant becomes an organic part of a new social order.

At present there seem to be two main routes by which peasants enter the modern world, with many variations. The first peasant societies to be transformed into modern societies were those of Western Europe during the eighteenth and nineteenth centuries. In these, the transformation took place in laissez-faire fashion, because of industry and commerce. A similar though by no means identical process is taking place in those new nations which are trying to modernize within a democratic framework. India is perhaps the best example.

A second and contrasting alternative is the Communist route, pioneered by the Soviet Union and followed by the Communist countries of Eastern Europe, China, North Korea, and North Vietnam. These countries illustrate one of the great themes in contemporary history — the violent transformation of traditional peasant societies into modern nation-states by Communist-inspired and Communist-led revolutionary movements in which peasants take active part. This should dispel the widespread notion that peasants are inherently passive, meek, and nonviolent; a notion already proved false by the violent eruptions that have occurred throughout history in many peasant societies, including traditional Europe.

The great difference between modern and past peasant uprisings is that between rebellion and revolution (Cf. Gluckman 1963:8). Before the modern period, peasants often rose in desperation, in movements of the *Jacquerie* type, when their condition became hopeless under predatory states and ruling classes. In these violent outbursts they killed landlords, local officials, and any other members of the ruling class on whom they could get their hands. Rarely, however, did these uprisings fundamentally change the larger society's structure, though faces were changed, the bureaucratic and governmental channels were cleared, and pressures on the peasantry were often temporarily relieved. These were rebellions rather than revolutions.

In the modern period, however, peasant movements have received additional ideology and effective organization from Marx, Lenin, and Mao, which have transformed rebellions into revolutions and have completely destroyed the social structures of some traditional peasant societies and created new socialist states. The increased political awareness of peasants has not, of course, been manifested solely in Communist-led movements; the Mexican Revolution is a case in point.

Marx and the peasant are two of history's strangest and most unnatural bedfellows, whose marriage is at best one of convenience. As Mitrany (1951:205–206) has pointed out, the fact that some Communist governments such as China, Yugoslavia, and North Vietnam have ridden into power on the backs of peasant movements is one of the great paradoxes of modern history. To Marx, the peasant was anathema. The small-scale capitalistic mode of production to which the peasant was committed was ridiculously outmoded and had no place in a modern socialist society. To Marx, moreover, peasants as a group were grains of sand that were not only impossible to organize into a revolutionary movement, but often reactionary; the betrayal of the workers during the Paris Commune of 1871 particularly irritated Marx (1957). The peasant form of production was outmoded; the peasants were at best a force that had to be "neutralized" by the revolutionary urban proletariat; and, furthermore, as a social and economic type, peasants had no place in the new communist society that was to emerge from the revolution (1957:14). Marx went so far as to praise capitalism for forcing many of the European peasants out of their "rural idiocy" and into the urban factories. The new socialist society was to transform peasants into rural proletarians whose way of life was to be remolded to eliminate the differences between the country and the city. Individual peasant farming was to be replaced by large-scale cooperative farms worked by armies of rural workers using modern machinery. In other words, the ultimate Communist aim was to eliminate peasants as a social and economic class. As Mitrany has related so clearly (1951:22), European peasants were well aware of the Marxist program and were almost universally hostile to the European socialist movements.

With Lenin, however, political opportunism and the necessity of seizing power overrode any theoretical objections to bringing the peasants in as partners of the revolution. In the Eastern European and Asian countries where urban proletariats were not strong and where the peasants formed the great bulk of the population, there could be no revolution without peasant support. With his Theory of Imperialism, Lenin, by theoretical sleight of hand, spun a worldwide class warfare between the capitalistic countries and the non-Western world out of a theory of internal proletarian revolution (Lenin 1927–1942 20:280–281; Meyer 1957: 235–

292). Efforts were made to placate the peasants by adopting the essentially populist slogan of "Land to the Tillers," and by identifying the landed classes and traditional elites with feudal exploitation and with foreign imperialism. These efforts capitalized on the peasant's land hunger and also on his newly created nationalist feelings. All this served to blur effectively the basic conflicts of interest between Communists and peasants, and made possible their cooperation in revolution.

The peasants, however, are in one sense betrayed by their Communist organizers and allies, because once the revolution succeeds, the basic Marxist-Leninist program for eliminating peasants as a social and economic class is put into operation. Land reform is carried out in the initial stages of the postrevolutionary period and equalizes holdings and eliminates the landed classes in the countryside. This fulfills the Communist promise to redistribute the land. Soon after, however, the transformation of peasant social and economic organization begins in earnest by forming agricultural cooperatives on an ever-larger scale; and somewhere in this process the land is taken from the peasant. At the same time, the peasants have to shoulder much of the burden of producing the surpluses necessary to furnish capital for industrialization. The peasants find that their erstwhile allies use them as instruments to achieve power and to modernize the society, submerging their peasant identity so that they end up as a class of landless rural proletarians.

In the long run, however, peasants as a class (and not as individuals, of course) are no more betrayed by the Communist system than they are by capitalism, because both systems inevitably destroy the traditional peasant social and economic order — the former by rapid and traumatic reorganization under totalitarian state control, and the latter by the more gradual effects of industrialization and urbanization.

REFERENCES CITED

Geertz, Clifford
1962 "Studies in Peasant Life: Community and Society." In *Biennial Review of Anthropology*, 1961 (Bernard J. Siegel, ed.), 1–41. Stanford: Stanford University Press.

Gluckman, Max
1963 *Order and Rebellion in Tribal Africa*. London: Cohen and West.

Lenin, V. I.
1927–1942 *Collected Works*. New York: International Publishers.

Marx, Karl
1957 *The Eighteenth Brumaire of Louis Bonaparte*. New York: International Publishers.

Meyer, Alfred G.
1957 *Leninism*. Cambridge: Harvard University Press.

Mitrany, David
1951 *Marx against the Peasant*. Chapel Hill, N.C.: University of North Carolina Press.

MIGRANT ADJUSTMENT TO CITY LIFE: THE EGYPTIAN CASE

Janet Abu-Lughod

One of the most dramatic phenomena of recent decades has been the urbanization of large segments of the world's peasant folk, particularly in rapidly industrializing countries. In few places has this urban growth been as vigorous as in Egypt — at first spasmodically in the 1940's stimulated by a war economy, then more gradually in the 1950's in response to the indigenous demands of a developing economy [1] — until, at present, one out of every three Egyptians lives in an urban place having 20,000 or more persons.

Migration from rural areas has been chiefly responsible for Egypt's soaring rate of urbanization, even though natural increase, still as high in cities as in rural areas, accounts for half the annual rate of urban growth. This migration has favored the very largest cities of the country, bypassing those of moderate and small size. Therefore there has been a tendency for cities to conform to the principle of allometric growth, with high growth rates correlated positively with rank as to size.[2] Indeed, for the last three decades, cities of highest rank size have sustained average rates of growth which are more than twice the rate of natural increase, while smaller towns, of between 20,000 to 30,000, have failed to keep pace with rates of natural increase, i.e., have actually experienced net losses of population.

Migration, then, has had its prime impact on the largest cities, and the towering giant of Cairo, with a present population of close to three and one-half million, has been the most important recipient of the newly urbanizing population. This paper, therefore, concentrates on the adjust-

From "Migrant Adjustment to City Life: The Egyptian Case" in *The American Journal of Sociology*, Vol. 47, No. 1 (July 1961), pp. 22–32. Reprinted by permission of the author and The University of Chicago Press. This article is a revised summary version of a paper presented to a conference on "The Emerging Arab Metropolis" (Congress for Cultural Freedom and the Egyptian Society of Engineers, co-sponsors) in Cairo, December, 1960.

[1] Expulsion from supersaturated rural environment ranks as an equally important element in this growth.

[2] See Charles Stewart, Jr., "Migration as a Function of Population and Distance," *American Sociological Review*, XXV (June 1960), 347–56; George Zipf, *Human Behavior and the Principle of the Least Effort* (Cambridge, Mass.: Addison-Wesley Press, 1949). Application of hypothesis to Egyptian data prepared by present writer.

ment of Egyptian villagers to life in Cairo, inquiring into its nature and exploring the elements which mediate any dramatic transition between rural and urban life.

I. THE RURAL AND THE URBAN IN CAIRO

Sociologists studying the adjustment of rural migrants to city life have been trapped in a dilemma of their own making. Even after the replacement of the rural-urban dichotomy by the more reasonable continuum, the sequence and dynamics of adjustment have still been deduced as though the dichotomy were valid; the unconscious assumptions have led many students to an oversimplified image of a one-way adjustment of rural man to a "stable" urban culture, despite lip service paid to feedback and mutual assimilation.

This adjustment is assumed to be disorganizing in the extreme. Physically, it is envisioned as drastically altering the dwelling, changing the accouterments within the home as well as the neighborhood surrounding it, transforming the appearance and dress of the migrant himself. Economically, the migrant is seen as adjusting to changed occupations and rhythms of work, to a new division of labor within the family, and to different relationships between work associates. Socially, it is hypothesized that the migrant weans himself from the intimacy of the village to the harsh superficial relationships inherent in urban life, adapts himself from the homogeneous peer group to the diversified reference groups of the city, and suffers a reduction in proximity-centered social life and neighboring. Culturally, he is assumed to undergo a revolution in motivation, values, and ideology. In short, according to the rural-urban dichotomy, a hypothetical villager is to be dropped, unarmed, into the heart of urban Cairo to assimilate or perish. He is to be granted no cushions to soften his fall.

It is our contention here that the dichotomy is as invalid in Egypt and in many other newly awakening nations as it is in the Western nations, but for a somewhat different reason. In these cases the dichotomy has not yet sharpened due to the continual ruralization of the cities.[3]

Only one fact need be cited to support this allegation: More than one-third of the permanent residents of Cairo have been born outside the city, that is, one out of every three Cairenes is a migrant of one sort or another, and the overwhelming majority are from the rural hinterlands within Egypt.[4] To speak about one-way assimilation to a stable urban

[3] It probably *never* will sharpen to the same extent as it did in the West because simultaneously with this ruralization of the cities is occurring an urbanization of rural areas (extension of roads, education, and social services). These processes were temporarily distinct in Western development.

[4] The *1947 Census of the Governorate of Cairo* shows that, of a total population of little more than 2 million, only 1.3 million had been born within the city; 51,000 were born in other governorates (large cities); 59,000 were born outside Egypt. Thus more than 630,000 residents of Cairo came from more or less rural sections of Egypt.

culture when so large a minority comes equipped with needs and customs of rural origin is folly. Numbers alone should alert us to the probability that migrants are shaping the culture of the city as much as they are adjusting to it.

These rural migrants are drawn from two extreme types which face basically different problems of adjustment. One type, qualitatively the cream but numerically the less significant, consists of bright youths who migrate in search of education or wider opportunities. These have both the drive and the facility for rapid assimilation into the culture of the city. This paper ignores their real but different problems. The second type, referred to here as the "non-selective" migrants, are drawn primarily from the have-nots of the village. Numerically dominant, they are as much driven from the village by dearth of land and opportunity as they are attracted to the city.[5] With a lower capacity for assimilation, they tend to build for themselves within the city a replica of the culture they left behind. They are the subject of this article.

A second circumstance which has kept Cairo more rural than would be expected is the continual incorporation into the built-up metropolitan region of pre-existing villages. While some of these villages go back into history, such as Mataria, the pharaonic town of On (Greek, Heliopolis), some are of fairly recent origin. It would take a keen observer indeed to distinguish between a village within Cairo and one located miles beyond its fringes. In fact, the city of Cairo contains within its boundaries an extensive rural-urban fringe which stands juxtaposed against modern villas on the west, intervenes on the alluvial flats between urban Misr Qadima and suburban Maadi on the south, dips deep into the very heart of the city from the north, and, in somewhat different fashion, encircles Medieval Cairo on its eastern border. As can be seen from Figure 1, there are vast quarters within the mosaic of Cairo where, physically and socially, the way of life and the characteristics of residents resemble rural Egypt.

While full proof of this contention lies outside the scope of this paper,[6] a few figures may illustrate this point. High literacy is associated in Egypt with urbanism. In the largest urban centers, literacy rates in 1947 ranged between 40 and 45 per cent, while smaller towns and villages had literacy rates of under 25 per cent. Yet, in one out of eight census tracts in Cairo, the literacy rate was less than 25 per cent. As might be expected, the rural-urban fringe had the lowest literacy rates (5 and 7 per cent), but, surprisingly enough, even some of the more inlying zones contained populations no more literate than the rural. Similar comparisons made for

[5] See the unpublished findings of two American sociologists, Karen and Gene Petersen, who have made a sample study of 1,250 migrant families from five Delta villages.

[6] It is presented in full detail in a book on Cairo, prepared by the writer, to be published by the Social Research Center of the American University at Cairo.

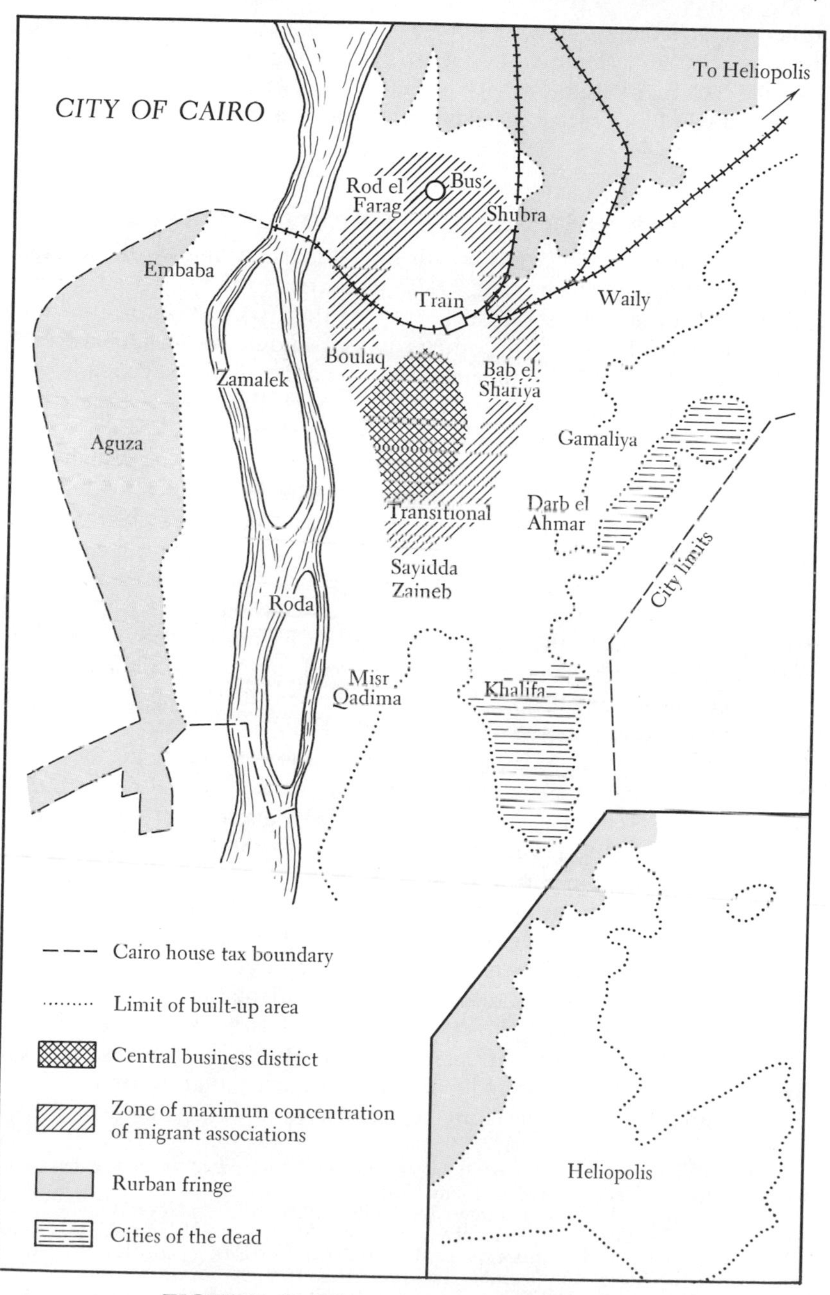

FIGURE 1. Map of Cairo showing major districts and location of migrant associations within the city.

other urban variables, such as refined fertility rates, religious and ethnic homogeneity, and condition and type of building, reveal the same inescapable fact that within the city of Cairo there exist numerous subareas whose physical and social characteristics closely approximate the villages of the countryside.

II. WHERE MIGRANTS SETTLE IN CAIRO

It is therefore possible for migrants to live in any of the large sections of the city which retain basic similarities to the village. To what extent do they actually select such areas as their ports of entry into the city's structure? Since our hypothesis is that one of the major cushions in the assimilation of rural migrants is the nature of the subcommunity to which they gravitate, our concern will be with the areas of first settlement of "non-selective" migrants.

Direct evidence of where migrants settle in the city is not available in the Cairo census.[7] In our attempt to approximate their ecological distribution, however, we are aided by several circumstances: First, small sample studies made in Egypt and other industrializing countries indicate that a fairly typical pattern of initial settlement is followed by many rural immigrants.[8] The typical migrant, here as elsewhere, is a young man whose first contact in the city is often with a friend or relative from his original village, with whom he may even spend the first few nights. Later, more permanent lodgings are found, usually within the same neighborhood. This process, in the aggregate, results in a concentration of migrants from particular villages within small subsections of the city, far beyond what would be expected by chance. Second, migration to Cairo has tended to occur in major spurts, the most important of recent times occurring in the early 1940's. Therefore, not only did the typical migrant gravitate to a small area of the city already containing persons from his home village, but he was not the only newcomer at the time of his arrival.

These two factors, operating together, resulted in the formation of small conclaves of ex-villagers sharing a common past in the village and a similar and often simultaneous history of adaptation to the city. A parallel between this and the ethnic ghettos of large American cities at the turn of the century readily suggests itself. While the congregations of villagers from Kafr Bagour and Garawan are smaller than were the Little Sicilys and although villagers are segregated (and segregate themselves)

[7] A table showing place of birth by census tract of current residence has, unfortunately, never been included in any Cairo census.

[8] See H. Saaty and G. Hirahayashi, *Industrialization in Alexandria* (Cairo: Social Research Center, 1959); "Demographic Aspects of Urbanization in the ECAFE Region," in *Urbanization in Asia and the Far East* (Calcutta: Research Center on the Social Implications of Industrialization in Southern Asia, 1957); a variety of papers in UNESCO, *Social Implications of Industrialization and Urbanization in Africa South of the Sahara* (Paris: United Nations, 1956), among others.

from the main stream of urban life by less powerful barriers than language and Old World customs, they also have developed the protective pattern of physical proximity and certain social institutions which help mitigate the difficulties of transition.

The formal associations founded for and developed by migrants are important, directly, in the dynamics of rural to urban adaptation, but are even more important indirectly, since their location and distribution in the city offer the *only* evidence as to where migrants settle in Cairo. Before analyzing the locational pattern of these institutions, however, some explanation of their nature is essential.

The *Directory of Social Agencies in Cairo* [9] lists more than 110 village benevolent associations. The Garawan Benevolent Society is typical. Garawan, a village of 8,000, is located in the heart of the Egyptian Delta some forty miles northwest of Cairo. Population pressure resulted first in the formation of several daughter villages, but eventually many of the men had to seek work in Cairo. (The village has a heavy excess of females.) The Garawan Benevolent Society was founded in 1944 to "extend aid to members" and to "provide burial facilities." Self-supporting, it sustains its activities through the dues contributed by "320 Egyptian Muslim adult males from Garawan," according to the directory's entry. Using a most conservative estimate of size of family (two dependents per adult male), one estimates that approximately 1,000 persons are to some extent involved in the core community of ex-Garawan residents.

One must make two basic assumptions if the locations of these societies are to be used as indirect evidence of migrant settlements. First, it must be assumed that migrants from specific villages are not distributed randomly throughout the city but that the processes described above result in aggregate settlements of persons from the same village.[10] Second, it must be assumed that the office of the migrant association is located in or near the subarea of the city which contains the maximum concentration of members. While this would not be true in every case, one might reasonably expect some relationship between office and clientele.

Even if these assumptions were absolutely beyond question (which they are not), an analysis of the locations of the associations would be irrelevant if they were scattered capriciously throughout the entire city. This, however, is fortunately not the case. When the addresses listed in the directory are located on a spot map, a definite, although not simple, pattern emerges which indicates in rough fashion the areas where rural migrants seem to be concentrated. Most associations fall within the ellip-

[9] Prepared by Isis Istiphan and published by the Social Research Center, American University at Cairo, 1956.

[10] Obviously, not all ex-residents would be found in the Cairo settlement of maximum concentration, since some, probably the most successful economically, may have already moved to other sections of the city, while others never did follow the typical pattern, for example, the selective migrants or those with intervening experiences, such as army service.

tical belt around but never within the central business district. The arc contracts both east and west to a bare quarter of a mile from central business district and expands north and south to more than a mile from city center, thus conforming to the general contours of the city.

Northern Settlement. One-third of the migrant associations cluster in the segment of the city which radiates northward from the central business district, circumscribed south and east by major rail lines, and bounded by the Nile to the west and an agricultural zone to the north. This section contains two subareas of densest concentration: the first in the vicinity of the Khazindar bus station; the other in Al Sharabiya, northeast of the main train terminal.

The Khazindar bus station has served since the 'twenties as the terminus of bus lines connecting Lower Egyptian provinces (the Delta) with Cairo. Within a radius of one-fourth of a mile of this station are eight village associations, all representing Delta villages; within half a mile are sixteen associations, ten actually concentrated in a four-by-six-block area just northeast of the station. This area has a strange mixture of urban and rural features. Behind the main street on which the station stands, narrow unpaved streets and alleys harbor prematurely aged, badly deteriorated, urban housing interspered with the rural type of structure. The two- and three-story buildings contrast markedly with the six- to eight-story structures which dominate the main street. A cluster of black-garbed women squat to gossip; old men sit in doorways; a sheep bleats; children swarm in packs. When this area received its major influx of migrants, it was an outpost of urban settlement. As recently as 1940 there were farms just to the north. By now, however, the city has swept beyond it.

The second concentration of migrant associations is located in the tiny quarter of Al Sharabiya, where seven associations almost all from Delta villages are located within four blocks. Occupationally, many residents are bound to the rail yards that virtually surround it. Despite its geographically central location, this section presents a distinctly rural aspect and retains a close functional tie to the rural fringe, since farms bound it where rail lines do not. Lower buildings, some of mud brick, predominate. Commercial establishments are those of the large village or small town. Al Sharabiya and Khazindar areas contain most of the migrant associations of the city's northern quadrant. (The remainder are scattered within the belt shown on Fig. 1.)

Most of the associations in this quadrant represent Lower Egyptian villages. Hence many migrants have presumably settled close not only to their point of origin but, even more specifically, to their point of entry into the city, i.e., the bus terminal. Moreover, the migrants settling in this part of the city selected areas which were, at the time of settlement at least, on the outer edge of the built-up city.

Southern Settlement. Another third or more of the migrant

associations are clustered directly south of the central business district, quite distant from the southern rural-urban fringe. The densest concentration is found in the transitional business district — a curved interstitial belt buffering the Western-style commercial zone north and west of it from the native market and residential quarters to its south and east. Twenty-five associations are located in this zone, while the remainder are scattered farther south toward Old Cairo.

Most striking is the fact that the majority of these associations represent villages of Upper Egypt. Thus the principle of least effort seems to determine migrant distribution. Villagers coming from north of the city favor the northern quadrant of the city, while those coming from the south prefer location in the southern quadrant. But, whereas the former have their associations in family residential zones near the city's fringe, the latter have theirs in a marginal commercial district characterized by a heavy excess of unmarried males.[11] Further examination reveals that the latter are primarily in rented offices, whereas the former are frequently in the home of the association's president.

What accounts for the remarkable difference? One hypothesis can be offered here. Migrants from Delta villages follow a different pattern of migration and hence make a different type of adjustment to the city than do migrants from Upper Egyptian villages. First, migrants from the Delta move primarily in family groups, while those from the south either remain single or leave their wives and children in their home villages. In Cairo in 1947, of the 400,000 migrants from Lower Egypt, half were males and half females, but 200,000 out of the 250,000 migrants from Upper Egypt were males. Thus the sex ratio of Delta migrants was remarkably well balanced, while there were four men for every woman among Upper Egyptian migrants in Cairo.

Second, significant occupational differences between the two migrant groups affect both adjustment patterns and spatial distribution. Upper Egyptian migrants go primarily into domestic and other personal services or work in unskilled labor gangs, while the occupations followed by Lower Egyptian migrants are both more varied and less likely to include housing as a part of wages.[12]

In the light of this the major differences between the location of migrant associations representing Upper and Lower Egyptian villages become more comprehensible. The associations of Upper Egyptians are located in an area which serves as a leisure-time focal point as well as a

[11] The sex ratio here is 129 in the ages most likely to be imbalanced by migration, 15 to 49; in the northern section it is only 104. Forty per cent of males of marriageable age are unmarried here, while only 25 per cent are unmarried in the northern section (computed from 1947 census).

[12] The *Directory of Social Agencies* lists the dominant occupations of members of each association. Government and manual workers are listed most frequently for Lower Egyptian associations, while servants, porters, and messengers are the most frequently mentioned occupations for Upper Egyptian associations.

residential area catering to single men. This is both cause and effect of the character of Upper Egyptian migrants. The associations play a more active role in their lives, in part because their members are denied access to the alternative social unit, the family.

Central Zone, East and West of the Central Business District. The remaining associations are divided between Boulaq, which forms the western quadrant of the ellipse, and Bab al-Shariya and Waily, the eastern portion of the belt. Ten associations are located within the former zone, while twenty have addresses in the latter. Just as the ecological position of these areas is midway between the northern concentration of Delta village associations and the southern concentration of Upper Egyptian associations, so, sociologically, they lie midway, containing associations from both regions of the country in roughly equal proportions. They share still other similarities. Both are close to the central business district; both rank low in socioeconomic status (below both shubra and the transitional business zone); both are primarily family areas; and both contain the densest slums of the city: densities of up to 900,000 persons per square mile are recorded for small subsections of Boulaq, and the over-all density of the community area of Bab al-Shariya is the highest in the city. Of the two, Boulaq is the older and hence the one retaining more rural qualities in its buildings and streets, but even Bab al-Shariya, despite its uniformly high apartment buildings looming above narrow access alleys, contains a population more rural than urban in its ways.

These, then, are the areas to which migrants have gravitated within the city. That they are relatively scarce in the highest rental zones of the city is attributable to their low socioeconomic status. Migrants are relatively absent, also, from the rural-urban fringe proper which would, as we have seen, provide them with the most familiar and protective environment. The lack of rental housing in these areas (privately owned farms with villages for laborers only), the dearth of public transportation, and their desire to live close to their new jobs are undoubtedly important reasons for their rejection of these areas. A second area surprisingly overlooked in the search for "near-the-fringe" living is Medieval Cairo, that rectangular belt of oldest structures toward the eastern edge of the city. The complete absence of new housing in these districts, coupled with a low turnover rate (the population works at traditional crafts and trades where production, selling, and living quarters are often in the same structure), have probably prevented mass invasions by new migrants.

III. HYPOTHESES CONCERNING MIGRANT ADJUSTMENT

Earlier, the hypotheses of migrant adjustment were broken down into four classes: physical, economic, social, and ideological. In light of the locational material presented above, plus observations of both rural and city life in Egypt,[13] these will be defined here in an attempt to describe the peculiarities of migrant adjustment in Egypt.

Physical. We have already suggested that many migrants gravitate to areas lying close to the rural-urban fringe, while others settle in areas which have at least a cultural resemblance to semirural areas. In these sections, interior streets and alleyways are seldom used for wheeled traffic, leaving undisturbed the rural functions of the street as pathway, meeting place, playground, and tethering area for animals.

Greater adjustments are required with respect to both the dwelling and the physical neighborhood. Housing occupied by the majority of migrants is more urban than rural in style. This results in functional overcrowding more severe than in the villages. The village home minimizes the number of inclosed rooms in order to maximize private open space (a ground-level interior courtyard or a protected roof courtyard in a more commodious two-story home). This cherished space is eliminated in the multifamily flats of the city. While many of the tasks assigned to the courtyard are no longer performed in the city (drying dung cakes, storing crops, tethering animals), other social uses such as cooking, eating, and just sitting are driven indoors or to the streets in the city.

Not only is the home more compressed due to the loss of outdoor "overspill" space, but the neighborhood is also more concentrated. While residential densities in Egyptian villages are surprisingly high, they nowhere approach the densities of Cairo's poorer districts. Many families using a common stairwell and public utilities means, paradoxically, more intensive contact with neighbors than in the village; and adjusting to the inadvertent intimacy may be extremely difficult for people new to the city, particularly for women.

Within the home itself are other changes, of which the loss of the overroom is perhaps the most important. In the rural home one full room is devoted to the massive flat-topped oven in which bread is baked daily and which, during the winter months, heats the adjacent areas and provides a snug bed for a blanketless family. That its loss is viewed with distress by at least some migrants is evidenced by the fact that some seek the top floor of an urban dwelling to construct a village oven and advise newcomers from their village to do the same.[14]

Other changes in the home are viewed more favorably, since they conform to the aspirations of villagers. Among the objects high in status found in the most prosperous rural homes are small kerosene burners instead of dung-cake fires for cooking, wardrobes and china closets to

[13] The author has spent more than three years in Egypt, one and a half at a UNESCO project in a village area and two years in Cairo studying the structure of that city. Many observations have been further authenticated by anthropologists and social workers with longer and more intimate experience in both areas, to whom the author expresses gratitude.

[14] Reported by Hind Abu el Seoud, an anthropologist studying a small Delta village and its ex-residents in Cairo.

store a growing stock of consumption items, and the high four-poster bed with its black wrought-iron frame embellished with gilt, which remains, in the city as in the village, the *most* important sign of status. These are items with which migrants tend to crowd their urban homes, as soon as they can afford them.

The dress of migrants changes little in the city. Only the selective migrants change completely from the *galabiya* (long loose robe) to pants and shirts; for non-selective migrants the change is rarely required to conform to the urban pattern, and it is occupation rather than status per se or place of birth which dictates appropriate attire. It is perhaps because of this that the change is more frequently attempted by Delta than by Upper Egyptian migrants.

Change in dress presents more difficult problems for the women. The universal dress of village women is a high-necked, long-sleeved printed gown which is then covered by a black one of similar cut. A kerchief and then a black mantilla completely cover the hair. While many village women retain this attire in the city (as do many old city residents), some of the younger of them first discard the black garment and later may adopt a modified urban version of the printed gown with cutout neckline and daring three-quarter-length sleeves.

The foregoing remarks apply best to Delta families making a relatively permanent adjustment to the city. They do not apply with equal force to Upper Egyptian migrants working as domestic servants or in other occupations where housing is provided or to those who remain unmarried or leave their families in the village. Paradoxically, this group, exposed most intensively to a completely new physical environment, is least assimilated to Cairo. A lifetime spent in sections of the city which contrast sharply with the village environment affects a superficial sophistication unmatched by the manual laborer from the Delta living in a quasi-rural district. It seems, however, that the very lack of gradual transition and of the mediating influences of family and neighborhood has the reverse effect of prolonging the period when one is a stranger. This type of migrant often completely rejects urban life, confining his periodic social contacts to co-villagers often in his own profession and his "real" life to infrequent sojourns to his village family.

Economic. In their villages of origin, migrants were engaged almost exclusively in agriculture. Men worked long and hard during the three sowing and harvesting periods in the Delta and the two crop-change periods in Upper Egypt, these periods of intense activity being followed by slower seasons of maintenance and community sociability. The basic rhythm of rural life thus dictated large finite jobs alternating with lighter routine work. The length of the work day varied with the stage of the cycle.

Women's work was more evenly distributed, with child care, the preparation of food and bread, the making of dung cakes, and the tending of livestock performed daily. Work in the fields was done during the early morning hours, except during the busy seasons, when it absorbed a greater portion of the day. Labor was communal within the extended family home and, when outdoors, was usually performed in company.

Laundry is a case in point. In the village, washing is done in the canal or now, increasingly, at the communal water taps. It is never a solitary activity. Contrast this with how laundry is done in Al Sharabiya, a migrant area described above.[15] Water is also secured from communal taps, but a man guards the tap, effectively discouraging women from washing at the site. Women carry their water home to wash in solitude within their dwellings. Other functions are similarly driven indoors or eliminated altogether. Thus the ex-village woman experiences a reduction in her work load (except where outside employment is taken), but, at the same time, she experiences an even greater reduction in the social life which formerly attended her labors.

The experience of migrant men, on the other hand, is often the reverse. The work of a city manual laborer is probably more taxing, certainly more evenly distributed over time, and usually *less* solitary than rural work. Exceptions must be made for migrants working as itinerant peddlers, shoe-shiners, tea-makers, etc., and, of course, for those working as domestic servants. These occupations are both more independently regulated and somewhat more isolating from contacts of a primary nature.

To what extent do migrants working at steady jobs in the company of others come into contact with associates from different backgrounds? Social heterogeneity is one of the distinguishing characteristics of urbanism, but for this to create the mental counterpart — cultural relativity — heterogeneous persons must come into intimate contact with each other. While in large-scale factories the mixing of diverse people undoubtedly occurs, the overwhelming majority of commercial and industrial firms in Cairo employ only a few persons, often within the same family. Furthermore, migrants often depend upon their compatriots to guide them to their first jobs. Sometimes, migrants seek out well-known "successes" from their village to give them employment. Thus migrants cluster together not only residentially but also on the job as well. In the smaller firms of Cairo, then, a far greater homogeneity of the work force exists than would have been expected by chance. Far from isolating the migrant from his fellow villagers, his job may actually consolidate his village ties.

Social. The hypotheses presented by Louis Wirth in his logical statement[16] of the differences between the rural and urban ways of

[15] Account provided by Abdel Monem Shawky, former social worker in the district for fourteen years.

[16] Louis Wirth, "Urbanism as a Way of Life," *American Journal of Sociology,* XLIV (July 1938), 1–24, which essentially reformulates the work of earlier German scholars, such as Max Weber, *The City,* ed. and trans. D. Martindale and G. Neuwirth (Glencoe, Ill.: Free Press, 1958); and George Simmel, "The Metropolis and Mental Life," in *The Sociology of Georg Simmel,* tr. Kurt Wolff (Glencoe, Ill.: Free Press, 1950), pp. 409–24.

life have been misused, as if they were facts, and many of the concepts almost self-evident to sociologists studying American cities have proved less valid when applied to the growing body of data about non-Western and preindustrial cities. While isolated refutations have appeared,[17] as yet there has been no major reformulation of the theory.

Wirth hypothesized that the ecological determinants of a city (large numbers of heterogeneous people in dense, permanent settlement) would have certain social consequences, notably anonymity, dependence upon impersonal relations and sanctions, sophistication, and tolerance of change. To what extent do the social relationships in Cairo conform to these predicated types, and, further, how much does the rural migrant really have to adjust his personality to become a functioning member of urban society?

While these questions are too ambitious to be answered here, two propositions are suggested. First, the culture of Cairo fails to be characterized chiefly by anonymity, secondary contacts, and the other attributes of urban life. Second, migrants to Cairo are active creators of a variety of social institutions whose major function is to protect migrants from the shock of anomie.

Middle Eastern culture places a high value on personal relationships, even at a sacrifice of privacy and internal development. This, combined with a system of relationships based on the extended kinship group, serves to increase the number of primary ties far beyond what Western sociologists, reasoning from their own experience, dare to assume possible.[18] This network of personal associations enmeshes not hundreds but thousands of individuals.

Were Cairo merely an amorphous mass of individuals, this network, large as it is, might account for but a small fraction of the individual's contacts. However, Cairo is not one community but, rather, many separate social communities. Functional sections of each community may be geographically separated — residence in one section, business in another, recreation in still another. A member of one community may pass daily through the physical site of communities other than his own, neither "seeing" them nor admitting their relevance to his own life. But, within his own community, there is little if any anonymity.

It is within this context of "urbanism" that the Egyptian migrant is called upon to adjust. His adjustment is further facilitated by the formal and informal institutions he develops within his small community, one of which has already been mentioned — the village benevolent society. Through it many migrants receive moral support from their compatriots

[17] See, e.g., Gideon Sjoberg, "The Preindustrial City," *American Journal of Sociology*, LX (March, 1955), 438–45; Horace Miner, *The Primitive City of Timbuctoo* (Princeton, N.J.: Princeton University Press, 1953).

[18] Weber himself rejected impersonal relations as a useful part of the city's definition, noting that "various cultural factors determine the size at which 'impersonality' tends to appear" (*op. cit.*, p. 65). See also Richard Dewey, "The Rural-Urban Continuum," *American Journal of Sociology*, LXVI (July 1960), 60–66.

as well as insurance against the insecurities of urban life, that is, isolation in poverty, sickness, and death.[19] It is unlikely, however, that more than 100,000 migrants are involved in these associations, while it will be recalled that their number exceeded 600,000 in 1947. Thus, even if these associations are important to the persons they serve, they fall short of absorbing most migrants.

Other formal institutions play a relatively minor role in providing social groups for migrant identification. Labor unions (except for craft guilds), civic associations, charitable organizations and political groups are all relatively undeveloped social institutions in Cairo. One must look, then, to the informal social institutions for a fuller understanding of patterns of adjustment. Unfortunately, documentation in this area is totally lacking. While a few may be singled out as playing important roles, no estimate of their magnitude can be offered.

First in importance is undoubtedly the coffee shop in which Middle Eastern males conduct their social and often their business lives. The comparable Western institution is probably the old style of British pub which, with its set of steady patrons and its intimate atmosphere, served as a social focus for the individual's life. Many an Egyptian coffee shop is run by a villager to serve men from that particular village. News of the village is exchanged, mutual assistance for employment is given, and the venture more resembles a closed club than a commercial enterprise.

For the women no such informal association is available. While within the village there are also no purely female informal associations, religious festivals, births, deaths, marriages, circumcisions, etc., are all village-wide events in which women have important roles to play. Within the city, however, these events become more private, and the role of women as full participants is probably reduced. Social life in the city is confined more and more to the immediate neighborhood.

It is this immediate neighborhood, however, which constitutes, after the family, the most important informal social institution for migrants in the city. The cohesiveness of the neighborhood is strengthened by the tendency of persons from the same village to settle together. Similar to the situation elsewhere, it is the women, children, and very old persons who are the most active participants in neighborhood-centered social life.

Motivations and Ideology. The Weltanschauung of the city man is presumed to differ from the peasant's in several significant ways. First, relaxation of the heavy hand of personal social control in the village is assumed to give greater latitude for individual differentiation. Second, cities are assumed to foster a more secular, rational, and mechanistic ordering of activities. Third, cities are gateways to a more sophisticated knowledge of the outside world. Finally, cities have traditionally been the centers of movements of social change, from new religions to new political ideologies and transfers of power.

[19] Burial services, offered by almost all associations, parallel the burial-insurance organizations of Negro rural migrants to northern cities.

While these statements are valid premises, data on Cairo are lacking which would permit us to place rural migrants along the continuum from the sacred, conformist, isolated, and relatively static state of the ideal folk society to the extreme of urbanism outlined above. For one thing, the Egyptian village hardly conforms to the ideal prototype of a folk society. Where farmers raise cash crops tied to international markets (cotton and sugar), listen to radios, travel often to market towns, have relatives or friends in the cities, and send their children to schools following a national curriculum, the magic ring of isolation has already been broken. On the other hand, as already demonstrated, it is possible within Cairo to lead a fairly circumscribed existence outside the main stream of urban life. Therefore, while there may be a wide gap between the least-sophisticated villager and the most-sophisticated urbanite, there is certainly no indication that migrants necessarily pass from one pole to the other.

CASTE AND COMMUNITY DEVELOPMENT

Gerald D. Berreman

The social scientist who studies a program of planned change as vast as India's Community Development Program is likely to be overwhelmed by its complexity. As a result, he may take refuge in minute local details or in gross generalizations, either of which may be of little interest to those responsible for carrying out the program. At the risk of the latter fault, I will attempt to generalize on the basis of local details in such a way as to point up a major problem inherent in the Community Development Program as it has functioned in India; one which seems not to have received adequate attention by planners. This is the problem of realizing a democratic program designed to improve standards of living in a rigidly stratified society.

THE PROBLEM

The research which led to this analysis was carried out in and around Sirkanda, a village of the lower Himalayas of Uttar Pradesh state in India. There, in 1957–58, I observed the first year of intensive com-

From "Caste and Community Development" in *Human Organization*, Vol. 22, No. 1 (Spring 1963), pp. 90–94. Reprinted by permission of the author and the Society for Applied Anthropology. This analysis was first presented in a lecture entitled "Community Development in India: II," given for the Committee for Arts and Lectures and the Department of Near Eastern Languages of the University of California, Berkeley, July 7, 1960, and broadcast over radio station KPFA, Berkeley, on October 20, 1960. The research upon which the analysis is based was financed by a Ford Foundation Foreign Area Training Fellowship.

munity development work in a village and area that had been touched only slightly by the program during two previous years when it was officially listed as part of an area of unintensive development (a National Extension Block). The year of my residence in Sirkanda coincided with that of the first Community Development Program employee to live and work in the village. This man was the multipurpose community development extension agent, known locally and throughout India as the Village Level Worker (VLW). His function was to work closely with the residents of Sirkanda and a number of surrounding villages, helping them to help themselves to a better way of life.

Up to the time of the VLW's final departure from the village, and my own departure shortly thereafter, the Community Development Program had been a failure in and around Sirkanda, albeit inspection of records filed by the VLW to higher authority would lead one to think it was entirely successful. It was a paper success and a practical failure. The reasons for this failure are several. They have been analyzed elsewhere as stemming in part from (1) inappropriateness of the content of the program as applied in this mountain area, (2) ineptness in its presentation to the people, (3) deficiencies in the selection, training and motivation of the personnel invested with the responsibility of introducing the program.[1] Any or all of these factors might be remedied, however, without significantly improving the success of the Community Development Program because it faces pervasive problems in the attitudes, beliefs and behavior of the people who are expected to benefit from and participate in it. That is, there are cultural and social impediments to the success of the program, ranging from the lack of a tradition of community-wide cooperation in the kinds of activities sponsored by the Community Development Program, and a traditionally hostile attitude toward anything associated with outside authority — in this case, the government — to resistance to particular items introduced by the program. Such factors have been described and analyzed in some detail elsewhere and by other authors.[2] In Sirkanda a fundamental problem which is manifest, directly or indirectly, in much of the resistance to community development, is that of social stratification, specifically caste organization, with the con-

[1] Gerald D. Berreman, *Hindus of the Himalayas,* University of California Press, Berkeley, 1963, pp. 326–330.

[2] *Ibid.,* pp. 321–326; S. C. Dube, *India's Changing Villages,* Routledge and Kegan Paul, London, 1958, pp. 132–146; David G. Mandelbaum, "Planning and Social Change in India," *Human Organization,* XII, 3 (Fall, 1953), 4–12; McKim Marriott, "Technological Change in Overdeveloped Rural Areas," *Economic Development and Cultural Change,* I (December, 1952), 261–273; Morris E. Opler, "Political Organization and Economic Growth, the Case of Village India," *International Review of Community Development,* No. 5 (1960), 187–197; Milton Singer, "Cultural Values in India's Economic Development," *The Annals of the American Academy of Political and Social Science,* CV (May, 1956), 81–91; J. Goheen, M. N. Srinivas, D. G. Karve, M. Singer, "India's Cultural Values and Economic Development: A Discussion," *Economic Development and Cultural Change,* VII (October, 1958), 1–12.

comitant traditional, rigid and marked differential access which various caste groups have to social, economic, and other advantages. This has become a problem with reference to the democratic, equalitarian stand of the government of India, the agency sponsoring the development program. This is the focus of the present paper.

RESPONSES TO COMMUNITY DEVELOPMENT IN SIRKANDA

Sirkanda and its region are populated predominantly by high-caste Hindu farmers (Khasiya Rajputs and Brahmins) who own and till their own lands. These people comprise about 90 per cent of the population. Beneath them, ritually, socially, and economically, are the untouchable artisan castes, most of whom (and until relatively recently all of whom) are dependent upon the farmers for their livelihood. There are real, readily cited and actively defended advantages which accrue to high-caste people as a result of their caste-based social and economic position. There are also real, readily cited and actively resented disadvantages which low-caste people bear as a result of their caste-based social and economic position.[3] Since people in the village are aware of this, stress is inherent in the system; stress which under most circumstances is covert. Overt expression of it is held in check partly by the threat of physical, economic, social, and religious sanctions, and partly by the fundamental necessity for continued social interaction which overt expression might impair or destroy.

Under these circumstances, community development, as it has been defined in India, is fraught with potential difficulty. Briefly the problem is this: the Community Development Program aims at economic development of rural villages, with emphasis on agriculture, and at the same time it aims at fundamental changes in the social life of villages, with emphasis on democratization. In practice, the program has functioned primarily to improve agricultural productivity. As a result, its effect has been, over much of India, to benefit primarily the farmers — those who own land — and these tend to be high-caste people who are already the most economically advantaged. Dube has remarked on this, noting that he found agricultural extension to be the significant and most effective aspect of development work in two villages of western Uttar Pradesh, and that

> . . . nearly 70 per cent of its benefits went to the *elite* group and to the more affluent and influential agriculturists.[4]

There has been little community development activity aimed at directly benefitting non-agriculturists or even non-landowners.

[3] Gerald D. Berreman, "Caste in India and the United States," *American Journal of Sociology*, LXVI (1960), 120–127.
[4] S. C. Dube, *op. cit.*, pp. 82–83.

In Sirkanda, community development has so far benefitted no one significantly. However, it is apparent to farmers and artisans alike (high and low castes, respectively) that the efforts which have been made are designed to benefit high-caste farmers and are of no immediate benefit to the artisan low castes. As a result, low-caste people are alienated from the program. When their cooperation is sought they ask why they should help the farmers increase the advantages which high-caste landowners already enjoy. In the eyes of the low-caste artisans, community development will only solidify the advantages of the dominant group to their own disadvantage.

Why then, one might ask, do the high castes not move ahead and increase their advantage through community development (assuming that they could be convinced that it would indeed help them), ignoring the low castes? The low castes in this area are too few in number to seriously impair the program by non-participation. The answer lies in large part in high-caste perception of the Community Development Program; their definition of the total situation. High-caste farmers are willing to admit the possibility of immediate advantage to themselves through an intelligently applied Community Development Program. However, community development is closely identified with the government of India and with the dominant Congress Party in India. These institutions are explicit advocates of an equalitarian society. They have outlawed untouchability and have attempted to discredit the caste system. To high-caste villagers who have a heavy stake in the social and economic status quo, these are dangerous — even subversive — doctrines. Their advocates are feared and resented. Ultimately, it is felt, the government will try to force high castes to associate with their inferiors and will aid the latter to independence, prosperity and arrogance, possibly at high-caste expense and certainly to their detriment. This leads high-caste people to be suspicious of any program sponsored by the government, and to fear that any cooperation on their part will contribute to the ultimate destruction of their cherished status and their advantageous economic position. Therefore, they oppose the Community Development Program; it is seen as a palliative to gain their confidence in order to undermine their social, ritual, and economic status. More immediately, they fear that the VLW, of whose caste status they cannot be sure since he is an alien, will give the low castes dangerous ideas or may insist on enforcing anti-untouchability legislation in the village.

Low-caste people, too, are aware of this phase of the government's activity. This knowledge tended to make them hopeful when they learned that a government officer (the VLW) was to come to live and work in the village. They thought he might give them advantages formerly denied them, or even grant them preferential treatment. They were quickly disillusioned, however, when he proved to advocate programs which could only reinforce the advantage of the high castes, and when he evinced no interest in the low castes and their problems. He thereby precluded the possibility of getting low-caste support for his program.

Therefore, all major groups in the village and area have been alienated from the Community Development Program. Low castes want their positions improved; high castes want their positions maintained by suppression of the low castes. The government has alienated the former by their actions and the latter by their words. To please either group would be to alienate the other. This is a real dilemma in Sirkanda. From the available literature it appears to be a dilemma over much of India; one that has been largely unrecognized and therefore unresolved.[5] The dilemma is aggravated by the rigidity of the caste system, but it is one which appears and functions in much the same way with regard to non-caste (class) groups where significant differences in economic well-being exist, for in such situations help to one group constitutes a threat to other groups. Generally caste status and economic advantage go together in India.[6] When there is marked disparity there is likely to be an effort to bring the two into conformity, e.g., via upward mobility in a well-off low-caste group. Rowe has documented this tendency and has analyzed it by reference to the concept of cognitive dissonance.[7]

RESPONSES TO GOVERNMENT PROGRAMS ELSEWHERE

While explicit discussion of this dilemma is largely missing in the literature on community development, there has been a good deal of discussion of aims and accomplishments of the program in which the dilemma is implicit. Dube is among those who has cited the predominance of benefits to the elite under the Community Development Program.[8] Mayer's book, *Pilot Project India,* has elicited critical comment

[5] John T. Hitchcock has made a very similar point in an article which appeared after this analysis was made: "Centrally Planned Rural Development in India: Some Problems," *Economic Weekly,* XIII (March 11, 1961), 435–441. It is significant that social scientists working in two quite different kinds of villages — villages with important differences in economic organization and caste structure — have independently found the same factors to be operative. Had Hitchcock's report not appeared, I would have been inclined to admit that the highly complex caste situation of the plains where there are found many castes intermediate between untouchables and twice-born high castes (in contrast to the Sirkanda situation), might result in a different type of reaction to community development. That it does not is significant. Rigid social stratification seems to have led to the same type of response to the Community Development Program in both areas, and for similar reasons.

[6] M. N. Srinivas, "The Dominant Caste in Rampura," *American Anthropologist,* LXI (1959), 1–6.

[7] William L. Rowe, *Social and Economic Mobility in a Low-Caste North Indian Community,* Ph. D. dissertation, Cornell University, 1960, p. 70ff. Cf. Leon Festinger, *A Theory of Cognitive Dissonance,* Row, Peterson, Evanston, 1957.

[8] Dube, *op. cit.,* pp. 82–83.

from Lewis [9] and from Thorner,[10] both raising the question of production versus "social justice" as goals of the Community Development Program. Lewis notes that ". . . the primary goals of [Mayer's] Etawah Project as well as of the Community Development Projects were increases in production rather than social justice," and he questions whether ". . . spiritual revitalization and democratization . . . [are] possible within the framework of the caste system.[11]

Thorner accuses Mayer of ". . . reluctance to come to grips with underlying problems," [12] and of assuming ". . . that structural obstacles to village progress are either non-existent or insignificant." [13]

This "reluctance to come to grips with underlying problems" is not, of course, unique to India. In fact, it is almost universal in action programs where strong vested interests are at stake. One is reminded, for example, of reactions to federal aid to education in the southern United States. There, many Negroes object to such aid on grounds that federal funds to which they have contributed will be used, as in the past, to perpetuate an untenable and unconstitutional educational system which discriminates against them. Many whites object on grounds that the government may use such funds to impose economic sanctions to achieve integration of the school system, thereby depriving the whites of advantages which they believe they derive from the status quo. This fear is based on the government's publicly stated equalitarian stand and specifically on decisions of the Supreme Court over the past eight years interpreting the United States Constitution as prohibiting segregation.

DEALING WITH THE PROBLEM

When a government or other agency deals with two groups whose interests are defined by one or both groups as being opposed, and when it intervenes in areas which their members consider to be central to that opposition, it is unlikely that the government will be able to succeed for long in pleasing both sides. This is obvious, yet it is rarely faced. The ideal solution to the problem is to get the groups to redefine their interests so that they are no longer in opposition. Needless to say, this is no easy task. Presumably it can be accomplished by education, which takes time, determination and skill, and by legislation effectively enforced, which takes both conviction and courage. The solution is

[9] Oscar Lewis, "Review of: *Pilot Project, India,* by Albert Mayer and Others," *American Anthropologist,* LXI (1959), 534–536. Cf. Albert Mayer *et al., Pilot Project, India,* University of California Press, Berkeley, 1959.

[10] Daniel Thorner, "Dropping the Pilot: A Review," *Economic Development and Cultural Change,* VII (1959), 377–380. Cf. Albert Mayer, "Comment on Thorner's Review of Pilot Project, India," *Economic Development and Cultural Change,* VII (1959), 477–478.

[11] Lewis, *op. cit.,* 536.

[12] Thorner, *op. cit.,* 380.

[13] *Ibid.,* 378. Cf. Mayer, "Comment on Thorner's Review," *op. cit.*

especially difficult when an attempt is made to go counter to the perceived self-interest of the dominant group in a society, as is the case in the examples cited here. In such cases very far-reaching choices must be made with regard to means and ends. In India and the United States, broad policies and goals with respect to the civil rights of individuals and groups are clearly spelled out in basic national documents, such as the Constitution; documents which receive a good deal of public respect. This makes relatively easy the problem of choosing and justifying a course of action when these matters come into question, but it by no means assures its success.

There is no simple, assured solution to the dilemma presented by the conflicting goals of production and democratic social justice in a rigidly stratified and economically underdeveloped society such as India, but the problem must at least be recognized and faced it it is not to continue to stand in the way of successful community development. Failure to recognize the problem can result in actions inappropriate to achieve its stated goals as has, indeed, happened.

DEMOCRATIC DECENTRALIZATION (PANCHAYATI RAJ)

This point can be illustrated with reference to recent events in the organization of the Community Development Program in India. In their report of 1957, the Mehta team which surveyed the program made a number of recommendations for its improvement.[14] An important problem area was found to be that the program tended to impinge on villagers from above and from afar and therefore failed in meeting their needs and in securing their participation. The report recommended that this be remedied by placing more responsibility for community development activities in the hands of local people.[15] Largely as a result of this recommendation, and a subsequent directive from the Ministry of Community Development, several states have acted to reorganize the administration of their programs. Rajasthan, the first state to undertake this reorganization, has granted wide powers and responsibilities for planning and implementing community development to village councils. At the next higher level, a committee of village council heads has replaced the former "block" administration of the program.[16]

Although it has not been made explicit, and may in fact be unrecognized, a choice has been made between production and social justice — a choice which an understanding of village social structure makes very

[14] Team for the Study of Community Projects and National Extension Service, *Report of the Team for the Study of Community Projects and National Extension Service*, Vol. I, The Manager of Publications, Delhi, 1957.

[15] *Ibid.*, pp. 5–23.

[16] Ralph Retzlaff, "Panchayati Raj in Rajasthan," *The Indian Journal of Public Administration*, VI (April–June, 1960), 141–158.

clear. The choice is, of course, for production. In fact, this is consistent with another recommendation of the Mehta team that more emphasis be placed on production as compared to welfare activities. However, there is no indication that the team or those who followed its recommendations were aware that in putting community development in the hands of local people they were likely to sacrifice democratic social justice. This sacrifice seems inevitable because local councils are dominated by local elites who are usually the high castes, and are nearly always the economically advantaged groups. Under current conditions they cannot be expected to do otherwise than enhance their advantages. They are extremely unlikely to move to achieve democratic, equalitarian goals, for to do so would be to undermine their own status and to increase the threat from their social, ritual, and economic inferiors — people about whose upward strivings they are already nervous. So far the democratic, equalitarian goals of national leaders as set forth in the basic national documents have influenced relatively few villagers. They have been incorporated into the world view of no high-caste villagers in Sirkanda.[17] To expect community development in a democratic idiom to succeed under these circumstances is even more unrealistic than to expect rapid, orderly integration of the schools in the southern United States to result from putting responsibility for school integration in the hands of local school boards. In the Indian case, the dominant groups have a more concrete and readily perceived economic stake in the status quo in addition to the important social status considerations which are found in both instances. There are also greater problems in communication of new and unfamiliar national ideals in India, and there are very complex religious and ritual factors which influence their reception.

The contemporary rural community in India is simply not structured for democratic, equalitarian self-administration. To put the administration of community development in local hands may well result in increased production on the part of the most productive segments of the community if it is properly handled, but in so doing a choice is made which will result in the subordination of social justice as democratically defined. Thus, one goal of the program has been sacrificed (at least for the time being) for another. One can paraphrase M. E. Opler and say that failure to recognize this is a failure to recognize the social organizational difficulty of expecting a social structure which is rigidly hierarchical and inequalitarian — where status, privilege, and power are jealously restricted to the dominant groups — to implement programs which are democratic, equalitarian and are perceived as being to the economic advantage of the dominant groups.[18]

[17] With time, education in the schools may alter this picture, especially if, as seems likely, newspapers and radios begin to make an impact on adults who have gone to school.

[18] Cf. Opler, *op. cit.*, 197.

Whether it has been planned that way or not, putting community development in the hands of local leaders will, in the nature of village social organization, aggravate the problem of inequality and privilege while possibly increasing productivity. This does not mean that through education and legislation villages cannot become democratic. In a few areas this has evidently happened. But it does mean that for the present they are not democratic, and to assume that they are or that they will suddenly become so is to seriously misunderstand their functioning.

CHOICES AND RESULTS

Confronted with a demand for a specific solution to the dilemma of introducing equalitarian reforms by democratic means in a traditionally non-equalitarian society, one is tempted to respond after the fashion of shamans in the Sirkanda area when faced with an insoluble case: to prescribe a cure guaranteed to be effective but impossible to perform and therefore never put to the test. That is, one might recommend impossibly vast amounts of funds for education and propaganda to be applied concurrently with enlightened social legislation unfailingly enforced. Incidentally, we in the United States are in an exceptionally weak position, by our example, to advocate this for others. Alternatively, one might advocate that a clear-cut choice be made and acted upon — that social justice or production be publicly declared primary and thenceforth the chosen goal be sought uncompromisingly. This, too, is evidently impossible in light of social and political realities in India. As I have indicated, a short-run choice for production seems, in fact, to have been made, although it has remained implicit. This may be the most realistic choice for the present.

Undoubtedly if democratic community development as conceived in the Community Development Program of India is to succeed in the long run, social justice must be achieved. For this, effective agrarian reform is crucial. Also crucial is serious attention to means to benefit non-agriculturists both in their village economic functions and in centralized and dispersed industry. Some such steps have been planned or taken already in India, but far more remains to be done. Effective action in these directions would increase production and reduce the diffierential access to livelihood which separates the high and the low and which is basic to the dilemma described here. That is, it would tend to reduce the economic correlates — the underpinnings — of differential social and ritual status. This would ultimately tend to reduce the differential in social and perhaps even ritual status.[19] More immediately, if these steps were combined with effective agricultural extension work of the kind which currently characterizes community development in some areas, tangible economic advantage might accrue to both high- and low-status groups

[19] Cf. Rowe, *op. cit.*

(to advantaged and disadvantaged segments of the society), thereby winning a degree of support for the Community Development Program in both groups. If the advantages were real and recognized this support could well come in spite of the fact that one group would realize that it might eventually have to pay the price of diminished social superiority, and that the other would realize that prosperous groups were in some respects being helped to become more prosperous. If this program were combined with education and enforced social legislation, making defiance of the social legislation costly in material terms through withholding the benefits of community development (or other benefits such as loans) from the defiant ones, then progress might be made toward the ultimate goals of community development. That is, if tangible material benefit (production) for all could be made the hallmark of the Community Development Program, it could then be used as an incentive to encourage compliance with social legislation and it would, by diminishing economic disparities, reduce the basis for the social structural impediments to acceptance of community development.

As in any such situation, the essence of the program would have to be the ability to produce results: an unequivocal statement of goals and of the policies through which the goals are to be achieved, followed by enforcement of the policies. The unanswered question remains whether this can be achieved in light of social, economic and political realities in India. Perhaps the Community Development Program, now that it covers all of India, has spread too widely and thinly to make possible the intensive application of human and material resources which would be necessary to achieve sufficiently rewarding benefits from the program to make it effective. If so, the prospects for achieving its ambitious goals are dim; the goals themselves may have to be redefined.

From Peasants to Rural Proletarians: Social and Economic Change in Rural Communist China

Jack M. Potter

In the mid-twentieth century peasant societies are ceasing to be peasant, or are significantly changing their traditional forms, in a number of different ways. In the non-Communist world the spontaneous and voluntary migration of peasants to urban centers, where they seek jobs and the material comforts of the city, is perhaps the most important mechanism of change. Temporary migration of males, who continue to maintain their families in home villages, is one significant way in which traditional communities receive infusions of outside capital and ideas. Mexican braceros in the United States and European Mediterranean peasants migrating northward to industrial Western European countries illustrate this phenomenon. Major national community-development programs, perhaps best exemplified by the Indian program, also are changing traditional villages and their inhabitants.

With totalitarian governments more dramatic, rapid, and sweeping changes can be brought about. In no country is such major change more clearly seen, or the reasons for it more easily understood, than in Communist China. When the Chinese Communist party achieved power in 1949, China was an overpopulated, poverty-stricken country with 80 per cent of her population living in more than a million peasant villages. In some parts of China peasants suffered from high rates of tenancy, usurious interest rates, and high rents. Farms controlled by peasants were extremely small, and individual farm units were divided into numerous small plots that were inefficient to work. Farm technology had changed little in two thousand years, and modern innovations such as chemical fertilizers and insecticides were lacking, except in some areas near coastal industrial centers. The rural Chinese economy, like most peasant economies, was not entirely based on subsistence agriculture, for both agricultural products and handicraft goods were sold in local and regional markets. Transportation facilities were so primitive and marketing arrangements so inefficient, however, that a great part of the peasant's potential income went to middlemen (Cf. Ong 1955a). Capital accumulation in the countryside was low because many villagers had barely enough income to meet their basic living expenses. The small savings accumulated by the peasants were spent on expensive marriage and funeral ceremonies to maintain family status in village society. Much of the surplus capital was siphoned off by the landlord-official class in the form of rents and usurious interest rates. Economic conditions in the countryside were made even worse by the interminable civil wars that swept over the countryside after the fall of the Imperial Government in 1911, and by the terrible destruction caused by the Japanese invasion prior to and during the Second World War.

The Chinese peasants for centuries had been accustomed to organizing their own affairs in the contexts of family, lineage, association, and village. Traditionally, the hand of the Imperial Government had rested lightly on the countryside, with a bureaucracy so small that for all practical purposes government did not interfere on the local level as long as order was maintained and taxes were paid. The leading group in Chinese society was the landlord-scholar-official class, whose power, wealth, and prestige enabled them to dominate the entire society. The peasants, always suspicious of the government, had as little to do with it as possible. The new concept of China as a nation-state embodying the interests and loyalty of all its people was created mostly by the Chinese reaction to foreign imperialism and the Japanese invasion. One major reason why the Chinese Communist party was able to achieve power in China and gain a mandate for change was that they championed the peasants' nationalist cause in the anti-Japanese War (Johnson 1962). The mandate that the Chinese people gave the new government called for modernizing and industrializing their society so that China could regain its national dignity and never again have to suffer the humiliations of the previous century.

To carry out this mandate the new Chinese government had to solve several basic problems. Transforming a traditional society into a modern industrial state requires capital. Since China was overwhelmingly peasant, most capital accumulation would have to come from this source. The Communists' assumptions as to the route to be followed in creating a new socialist society, and their ideas about the means that could legitimately be employed to acquire capital from the peasantry, would require that peasant social and economic organization be radically reorganized, preceded by the destruction of the old landlord-gentry class which held an ironclad political, economic, and cultural grip on the peasantry. Increased means of state control would have to be developed to regulate peasant consumption and to concentrate the small-scale capital accumulations into the state's hands. Moreover, the new social organization would have to effectively control the peasants and mobilize them to work in the state's interests.

The major program for reconstructing rural Chinese society and economy was formulated in the Basic Program on the Chinese Agrarian Law, issued in 1950 (Ong 1955b:15–19). The Communists had already had extensive experience in organizing the peasants and carrying out land reform before they achieved power, since changes had been effected in the Communist-controlled areas, sporadically, since 1927.

In describing the process of change in the rural areas since 1949, however, it is not essential to consider these early attempts because they were somewhat different from the later programs. The changes about to be described were carried out with much variation, and took place at different times and at different rates in different sections of China. Those areas which the Communists had previously controlled completed land reform and organizational change much earlier than the "newly liberated" areas. For convenience of presentation, however, the process of land reform and social and economic change will be described as if they had occurred all over China at the same time.

As is generally known by now, the first step in the change of peasant China was land reform. "Land to the Tillers" had been a popular slogan in China since Sun Yat-sen, and was recognized by most Chinese revolutionary parties, including the Kuomintang, as necessary to improve the Chinese peasants' livelihood. The objectives of the land reform were not simply economic, however, for the new government utilized land reform to achieve political as well as economic objectives.

The announced aim of the land-reform program was to eliminate the "feudalistic landlords" and redistribute their land, tools, houses, and excess wealth to the poor peasants and landless laborers (*Agrarian Reform Law* 1959:1–15). The government also wished to firmly establish its power at the village level. By emphasizing the reform's class-struggle aspect and using the poor peasants and landless laborers to overthrow the landlords, the government had an opportunity to organize the villagers and destroy the old organizations dominated by the landlord class. By redistributing land to the peasants, the government gave them a stake in the new order, since the peasants were well aware of what might happen if the landlords regained power. The aspect of "struggle" was heavily emphasized in land reform, and every effort was made to instill a sense of popular participation among the villagers. The government could easily have sent in troops to carry out the reform, but preferred to have the peasants become politically conscious of what the government defined as "feudal oppression" and destroy the very bastions of the old social order.

Land reform was carried out by means of a well-planned program. Once peace had been firmly established in an area, government cadres were sent into the villages to assess the local social structure and organize the poor and landless peasants into new associations which thereafter could control affairs in the village. Special care was taken to ensure that former landlord elements did not infiltrate the new peasant associations and use them to protect their interests by blunting the force of the revolution.

The peasant associations, with the aid of the cadres, divided the villagers into five major classes: (1) landlords, who lived on the rent from land which they did not work or manage themselves; (2) rich peasants, who worked part of their land themselves, worked another part by means of hired help, and rented out the balance to poor peasants; (3) middle peasants, who tilled their own holdings and owned most of their farms; (4) poor peasants, who usually had small plots of their own but managed to exist only by renting from the landlords and rich peasants; and (5) landless laborers, who owned no land and made a living by working for the landlords and rich peasants. The class status of every member of the village community was posted on slips and pasted on village walls so that everyone had a chance to challenge his status (Yang 1959:142). Class ranking was a life-and-death matter to villagers, because the higher one was placed the more difficult one's position would be in the new society.

After the classes in the village were analyzed, "struggle meetings" were held to consider cases of landlords against whom complaints were made by the poorer peasants, often under the urging of the cadres. In these meetings, held on stages erected outside the village much as traditional operas had been held in previous days, the people were encouraged to pour out their grievances against landlords and other local bullies who had been guilty of "oppression," "exploitation," or other criminal offenses. Landlords and other persons found guilty of especially heinous crimes were summarily executed or deprived of their property and sent to be "reformed through labor." Landlords who had not committed crimes were allotted enough land to support their families. Even today, persons with landlord backgrounds are still discriminated against in China, and their children have an especially difficult time obtaining higher education or responsible positions.

In the third stage of land reform, the excess land, cattle, equipment, and hoarded wealth of the landlords was distributed to the landless laborers and the poor peasants. Land belonging to ancestral shrines, temples, monasteries, churches, schools, and other such organizations was also confiscated and redistributed. When the reform was completed title deeds were issued by the government and the old deeds were destroyed. The land managed by rich peasants, who are among the most efficient producers in any peasant society, and the commercial property of merchants and landlords, was supposedly not taken because the government did not wish to disturb the economy any more than was necessary at this early stage of the revolution (*Agrarian Reform Law* 1959).

Land reform marked the end of the first period of change in rural Communist China and was substantially completed in all mainland areas, except the minority areas, by August of 1952. The effects of land reform on rural social structure can hardly be overemphasized. In many parts of China, especially the central and southeastern areas of the country, rural society was dominated by powerful landowning lineages (usually called "clans" in the literature on China), who exercised economic and political hegemony over the countryside. Since the ownership of land formed the economic basis of lineage power, the land reform wiped out at one stroke a major structural feature of pre-Communist rural society. Wealthy landowning families formerly admired as models of success by less fortunate villagers now had prestige, wealth, and power stripped from them and were paraded through village streets wearing tall paper hats, the most lowly and despised members of the new society. The revolutionary destruction of the landlord-gentry group, who had led the lower stratum of Chinese society beneath the imperial bureaucracy, and who had served as the buffer group that mediated between the villagers and outside centers of power, represented the destruction of one of the major structural features of traditional Chinese society. The disappearance of this group left no buffer between the peasant village and state power, which was now free to extend down into the villages in a way that was rare in traditional China. This power vacuum was filled by the new state-controlled organizations that enabled the state to carry out, unimpeded, its rural social and economic construction program.

During and immediately after land reform, several new kinds of associations were established in the villages. These included the women's associations, created to implement the new marriage law; the consumers' cooperatives, tied directly to state-owned trading corporations at the town, provincial, and national levels; new assemblies, which elected rural officials; and mutual aid teams.

Mutual aid teams were the first step in the economic reorganization that was to result, in 1958, in the communes. With middle peasants established as the typical productive organization in rural China after land reform, and landless agricultural wage labor largely eliminated, some new form of labor exchange in production was necessary. Mutual aid teams were frequently initiated by the peasant association or the consumers' cooperatives, or both acting together. Two types of mutual aid teams were established in rural China after land reform, one temporary and the other permanent. The temporary teams were modeled upon traditional forms of labor exchange that, in some parts of rural China (Fei 1939:172–183), furnished the labor required during peak periods in the agricultural cycle. Under the temporary system, peasants joined with a small group of fellow villagers to exchange labor and the use of draft animals during the planting and harvesting seasons. The second, more permanent type, was usually an aggregation of several temporary teams. Farm tools, draft animals, and labor were pooled with a year-round plan for their use.

At the mutual-aid-team stage, each peasant maintained absolute control over his property. The principle was to collectivize work without disturbing individual management of private property. Peasants theoretically were free to join or not join the teams, but in effect they were pressured by government cadres in the village, induced to join by a governmental propaganda campaign that extolled the new organization's economic benefits, and almost forced to join because the government provided loans, seeds, and marketing contracts mainly to members of the mutual aid teams.

After mutual aid teams were established, the Chinese government began to move the peasants to the second stage of agricultural collectivization, the semi-socialist cooperatives. In this more highly socialized unit, private ownership of land was still respected but the members placed their land in a collective pool along with their farm equipment, cattle, and labor. Another difference from the mutual aid team was that land was cultivated on a collective, and not an individual, field basis. Boundary stones between fields were removed so that the land could be worked in larger and supposedly more efficient tracts. The yearly cultivation of the land belonging to the cooperative was done according to an over-all plan which was to make maximum use of the group's resources. When the crops were harvested, some of the produce was set aside for the payment of taxes to the government; a second part was set aside for the collective purchase of fertilizer, machinery, draft animals, and other production instruments; the remainder was then divided among the members in proportion to their investment of labor, land, cattle, and equipment. As in the permanent mutual aid teams, a point evaluation was made of each member's contributions for accounting purposes. The average size of the semisocialist cooperatives was about 26 households, or 130 people, with most villages containing several of these new cooperatives.

This step in collectivization was carried out slowly and carefully in its early stages, with concentrated propaganda campaigns to lay the groundwork for the movement. As in all of these earthshaking revolutionary programs on the mainland, very little information about the peasant's reaction filters out. It is likely that this step in the reorganization of rural Chinese society ran into more difficulties than either land reform or the formation of mutual aid teams. Some reports indicate that many peasants were reluctant to place their newly acquired land in the cooperatives, and since the peasants were theoretically free to join or not, some stubborn individuals initially refrained from joining. It must be remembered, however, that Chinese peasants were accustomed to organizing associations in the traditional society, and the idea of subscribing shares in a corporate body was by no means foreign to them. Many also had experience in managing land owned in common by lineages and lineage subsegments. Still, the Chinese peasant's attachment to his land as the sole secure means of livelihood for his family and descendants, makes it easy to imagine what a wrenching and painful process this must have been for more than 500 million peasants.

It now became clear that the Chinese villagers were being moved by stages into the large-scale agricultural cooperatives that Communists had always held to be the ideal and most efficient means of production. No sooner had semisocialist cooperatives been formed throughout China, than the government began to organize more comprehensive cooperatives — the socialist cooperatives. These resembled the semisocialist cooperatives except that tools, animals, and land were made the permanent property of the cooperative, as a corporate body, and no longer belonged to individual peasants. The members of the unit received no compensation for their property and their only income was now derived from the labor points accumulated during the year. The higher-stage socialist cooperatives were also larger than the semisocialist type, averaging about 160 families, or about 800 persons — the size of one large village or several smaller villages.

This gigantic reorganization proceeded at a rate that staggers the imagination (see Tung 1959). In December, 1955, socialist cooperatives included about 40 per cent of the Chinese peasantry. By June, 1956, 90 per cent of China's peasants were in socialist cooperatives; and finally, by 1958, almost all Chinese peasants were organized into socialist cooperatives.

Still, this did not represent the end-stage of the socio-economic evolution that had begun immediately after land reform. In order to create a more efficient and more productive rural cooperative unit that could produce the agricultural surpluses necessary for their program of rapid industrialization, in 1958 with the Great Leap Forward the Chinese government began to organize people's communes throughout China.

In the spring and fall of 1958, almost all of China's peasant population was organized into about 26,000 commune units. The commune was to be the key rural organizational unit that would enable China to pass from the socialist to the communist stage of society, and was to be the rural configuration of the future utopia. The communes were formed by combining numerous fully socialist cooperatives of the most advanced type. They were based upon the *hsiang*, a rural administrative unit that was the lowest level of government in China, with the government of the hsiang being transformed into the government of the commune. The size of the communes varied greatly in different regions of China, from an average of 7,065 in Kweichow, a mountainous and sparsely populated province in the southwest, to 37,435 in Chekiang province on the Yangtsze River Delta, an agriculturally productive and densely populated region. For China as a whole, the average commune at the time of their initial formation was about 24,000, with most communes containing from 20,000 to 30,000 people.

The communes differed from the socialist cooperatives in three important ways. First, they were much larger and transcended the traditional village boundaries. The average commune contained more than twenty times as many people as the average socialist cooperative and usually included more than a score of villages. Second, the communes were multifunctional, in contrast to the socialist cooperatives, which were mainly agricultural production units. The communes not only carried out agricultural production; they also operated small factories, ran branch banks and commercial enterprises, and managed educational facilities. Since it was merged with the hsiang administration, the commune also took over political and police functions. In short, the commune organization was designed to control and organize the agricultural, commercial, educational, military, social, and welfare activities formerly carried out in a less centralized fashion on the rural level. Moreover, as Professor Schurmann has pointed out (1966:471), all these activities were to be performed within a more functionally specific and militaristic style of work that went far beyond the organization of labor in the socialist cooperatives. Production brigades, large labor units under the control of the commune, were to specialize in specific tasks. Among the agricultural brigades, some would grow basic grain crops; others would specialize in vegetable gardening or field crops such as cane or sweet potatoes. Other specialized brigades would operate the decentralized handicraft industries managed by the commune; still others ran mess halls, schools, and so on. All this was supposed to represent a more efficient and productive division of labor.

A third major difference between the commune and the socialist cooperatives was the degree of collectivization. At the socialist cooperative stage, though all land and major production instruments were collectivized, the peasants still retained ownership of their houses, fruit trees, domestic animals, and most important, their private garden plots on which they worked after their commitments to the cooperative were fulfilled. During the formation of communes almost all this private property was confiscated, leaving the peasant a true proletarian, dependent solely on his labor for a livelihood. With houses and even cooking utensils confiscated, and the women mobilized to carry out productive work alongside the men, new collective institutions such as common mess halls, kindergartens, and "happy homes for the aged" were to fulfill some of the old functions performed by the family.

An example of the quality of life in communes during late 1958 and early 1959 is given by Sripati Chandra-Sekhar (1961:47–55). The commune he visited, named the Commune of Sixteen Guarantees, was organized in July, 1958 by merging 68 villages. All the houses, implements, cottage industries, and even the kitchen utensils were the property of the commune. It also owned and operated iron smelters, repair plants, flour mills, tailoring establishments, tile and brick kilns, and fertilizer plants. All members ate in the canteens and dining halls operated by the commune. There were 35 nurseries and 130 kindergartens housing children from age 4 to 6; two middle schools (similar to American high schools) where 1,450 students received instruction; and 36 trade schools called "Red and Expert Schools," in which youngsters were taught practical trades. The commune also operated two hospitals with 14 outpatient departments.

The adult population of the commune was distributed over 146 production teams that specialized in growing rice, vegetables, and cotton, and operated small industries, canteens, public nurseries, schools, and hospitals. Since all adults, both women and men, worked in productive tasks, the children were cared for in nurseries and kindergartens and the old people were in the "happy homes for the aged." The workday started with the blare of loudspeakers in village streets. After participating in a half-hour of exercise, the people went to the dining halls for a communal breakfast. Then they broke up into their production teams to begin the day's work, with husbands and wives, parents and children not necessarily working on the same team. In military fashion, they marched off to perform their allotted tasks in the fields and factories. They reassembled at noon in the various canteens for lunch and then returned to work the balance of the day.

After the day's work was finished, all attended classes in which they learned to read and studied political ideology. They also listened to radio broadcasts which recited the latest editorial from the *People's Daily*, the latest production figures from agriculture and industry, the latest government measures to liquidate American imperialism and the Chiang Kai-shek clique, and figures on how China had surpassed Britain in producing various industrial goods. After this there was a movie, a play, or an acrobatic show; and finally the discussion meetings, led by a party cadre, which everyone attended. Here, according to Chandra-Sekhar's account, the art of self-criticism was practiced; people rose to confess their drawbacks and failings, criticize their colleagues, and swear to increase production. Thereafter, everyone retired.

The communes were heralded by the Chinese during this initial period as a kind of social organization within which most of rural China's social and economic problems could be solved, an efficient agricultural production unit that would produce enough to feed the people and also furnish the surpluses required for industrialization. Collectivization was supposed to solve the problems of small farms and scattered fields which, under the traditional agricultural system, had made for uneconomical use of labor. With boundary strips between the fields removed, not only could the land area be increased, but also the stage was set for future use of mechanized farm machinery when it became available. The more rational planning by the commune made better rotation of crops possible and also enabled managers to see that crops could be planted on the land best suited for their cultivation.

The commune was also supposed to be well suited for improving many other aspects of agricultural production. With the labor savings obtained from the more efficient specialized production teams, it was possible to expend labor on large-scale projects such as building better irrigation systems and flood-control facilities. Additional improvements could be achieved by large-scale reforestation projects. Moreover, agricultural-extension projects such as better seed selection, new varieties of crops, the control of pests and animal diseases, and so on, would supposedly be carried out much more easily under the highly centralized commune management.

Using labor efficiently, the commune could also become important in the manufacturing sector of the economy. The commune could be the basis for a large-scale, decentralized light industry, which could produce consumer products to satisfy the needs of the population and leave the urban factories free to concentrate on heavy industry (Schurmann 1959: 10). Many Chinese writers on the Chinese rural economy before the war had recommended that industry be established on such a decentralized basis because it would be more suitable to Chinese conditions and would furnish employment for the peasants during slack seasons in agricultural production (Fei and Chang 1945).

Another important feature of the commune was that it gave the state control over consumption and more opportunities for capital accumulation. With the commune's centralized management and accounting system it was possible for the state to regulate the consumption of the rural population by specifying the amount of income to be paid in taxes and the amount to be left for distribution to commune members. The surplus could be taken by the state and used for industrialization. In these ways, the commune offered a means by which the state could have much more control over the economy than was possible in the smaller and more decentralized cooperative system.

The commune organization was also supposed to be an ideal unit to improve social and cultural services for the rural population. Within this larger unit, enough surplus funds could be accumulated to maintain the services found in the urban areas. A larger unit could build and maintain schools, public utilities, hospitals, and entertainment facilities that would be difficult for separate villages to afford. For these reasons, the communes were enthusiastically organized during the Great Leap Forward movement that began in 1958. During this year news came from China of increases in agricultural and industrial production that astounded the world. Part of the increase was supposed to be due to this new utopian unit in the Chinese countryside (see Strong 1959; Cheng 1959; and *People's Communes* 1958).

As the world now knows, however, the Great Leap Forward movement fell flat on its face and China's over-all economic development suffered a serious setback. The statistics which purported to show astounding increases in agricultural production were enthusiastic overestimates sent up from the local levels rather than production accomplished. In spite of the great advantages of the communes on paper, they apparently failed. It is difficult to specify the exact reasons for this failure, but the following factors must have been important. First, the labor resources devoted to flood control, industry, and other nonagricultural tasks resulted in a shortage of agricultural labor; and the direction of agricultural production by cadres not familiar enough with local agricultural conditions led to agricultural disasters. Second, the commune seems to have brought about great confusion in accounting procedures. Third, the confiscation of the peasants' garden plots which, as in the Soviet Union, yielded astounding quantities of food, vegetables, and meat, must have substantially decreased production. Fourth, it appears that there was a serious lack of incentive on the part of the peasants, represented by the attitude, "If everything belongs to everyone, why should I break my back?" And finally, it is likely that the unsatisfactory mess halls, the disorganization of family activities as women participated in labor, the long hours of labor in flood-control and backyard-furnace schemes, and the unfamiliarity of militarized working procedures, must have seriously demoralized the rural population.

Whatever the reasons for the failure, the communes began to be modified almost as soon as they were formed, and a retreat was started to less radical forms of collective organization. From 1959 to 1961, the commune organization was broadly modified, and today it is a mere administrative shell of its former self.

T. A. Hsia, in his excellent analysis of *The Commune in Retreat* (1964), has pointed out the modifications in the commune organization that have occurred since 1958. Since the end of 1960, the peasant's private garden plots have been returned to him, along with his house, kitchen utensils, and domestic animals. The mess halls created so much trouble in 1959 and 1960 that in 1961 they were finally discontinued. Since 1961, economic policy has been liberalized with the creation of a relatively free sector of the economy in which the peasant can market the produce from his private garden plots. At present, industry gives greater attention to producing goods to fill the consumer needs of the peasantry (Cf. Schurmann 1966:492). Furthermore, there has been increased emphasis on capital investment in agriculture and a policy under which the peasants concentrate on agricultural production and largely ignore the tasks of light industry and other matters that interfered with agricultural production. Finally, as Hsia points out, beginning in late 1960 and 1961, a de-evolution has caused the control of production and management to retreat, first to the level of the production brigade (equivalent to the old socialist cooperatives, usually the natural village unit), and, finally, to the level of the production team, another term for the old semisocialist cooperatives that formed a small section of a village. Since 1962, the production team has been the effective organizational unit in rural China. In the last few years, the communist press has talked much more about production brigades and teams than communes, although the word is still retained as a matter of face.

The liberalization of organizational and economic policy by the government seems to have been effective. Since 1961, China has recovered from the economic debacle of the Great Leap Forward years (1958–1961) and economic conditions appear to have improved considerably. At present, no one knows whether the communes have been permanently discarded or will at some time in the future return to the Chinese scene. Theoretically, at least, the Chinese government still clings to the commune as the future form of rural society.

In spite of the great problem of transforming a traditional society and in spite of the setbacks here described, in less than two decades many inhabitants of rural China have been changed from traditional peasants to rural semiproletarians, and the old forms of social and economic organization have in many instances been changed beyond recognition. Perhaps in no other country has a peasant society been transformed so completely and so rapidly. The fate of the present revolutionary movement in China is uncertain, but whatever it may be, a knowledge of what has happened in China during recent years is essential if one wishes to understand one of the major processes of transformation of peasants and peasant society.

REFERENCES CITED

The Agrarian Reform Law of the People's Republic of China and Other Relevant
1959 *Documents*. Peking: Foreign Languages Press.

Chandra-Sekhar, Sripati
1961 *Red China: An Asian view*. New York: Frederick A. Praeger.

Cheng, Chu-yuan

1959 *The People's Communes.* Kowloon, Hong Kong: The Union Press.
Fei, Hsiao-tung
1939 *Peasant Life in China.* London: Kegan Paul.
1945 *Earthbound China.* Chicago: University of Chicago Press.
Hsia, T. A.
1964 *The Commune in Retreat as Evidenced in Terminology and Semantics.* Berkeley: Center for Chinese Studies, Institute of International Studies, University of California.
Johnson, Chalmers A.
1962 *Peasant Nationalism and Communist Power.* Stanford: Stanford University Press.
Ong, Shao-er
1955a *Chinese Farm Economy after Land Reform.* Technical Research Report No. 34. Texas: Lackland Air Force Base, Air Force Personnel and Training Research Center.
1955b *Agrarian Reform in Communist China to 1952.* Texas: Lackland Air Force Base, Air Force Personnel and Training Research Center.
People's Communes in China. Peking: Foreign Languages Press.
1958
Schurmann, H. Franz
1959 "The Communes: a One-Year Balance Sheet." *Problems of Communism* VIII (5).
1966 *Ideology and Organization in Communist China.* Berkeley and Los Angeles: University of California Press.
Strong, Anna Louise
1959 *The Rise of the Chinese People's Communes.* Peking: New World Press.
Tung, Ta-lin
1959 *Agricultural Cooperation in China.* Peking: Foreign Languages Press.
Yang, C. K.
1959 *A Chinese Village in Early Communist Transition.* Cambridge: Massachusetts Institute of Technology, The Technology Press.

How Would You Like to Be a Peasant?

Joseph Lopreato

Until a few years ago the insufficiency of tillable land was one of south Italy's most critical problems. Today the situation has so changed that in some places, given present work habits and technology, the land supply by far exceeds the demand. The evident cause of this

From "How Would You Like to Be a Peasant?" in *Human Organization,* Vol. 24, No. 4 (Winter 1965), pp. 298–307. Reprinted by permission of the Society for Applied Anthropology.

previously inconceivable turn of events lies in a flow from the farms which has gradually assumed the dimensions of a veritable exodus. Many towns of the south have been almost totally abandoned or at best reduced to waiting colonies of the aged, women, and children. In some places, the people depart as if a scourge were relentlessly pursuing them from the country. Thus, throughout south Italy there are numerous villages whose population has been more than halved by emigration since the end of World War II.

Although no precise statistics are available on the phenomenon, various unofficial estimates indicate that since 1951 the Italians who have migrated from southern regions amount to about 2,500,000 out of a total population of 17,433,530 present in the south in 1951. Most of these have gone to the industrial regions of the north or to various foreign countries in Europe and overseas. To a very large extent, they have been male agricultural workers. The massive nature of this male agricultural emigration is well attested by the fact that from November 4, 1951 to October 6, 1963 the number of employed male agricultural workers decreased from 2,688,756 to 1,661,000, while that of female agricultural workers increased slightly from 938,395 to 977,000.[1] What are the causes of this swelling wave away from the land?

NATIONAL WEALTH AND SOCIAL REORGANIZATION

The first cause of emigration that comes to mind, at least with respect to the internal migration, is the accelerating transformation of Italian society from a traditional, agricultural, quasi-feudal type of social organization to the more urban type that characterizes the industrial world. The factors underlying the social reorganization itself are of course numerous and complex. Roughly, however, they may be expressed by reference to the fact that at the end of World War II Italy threw her lot with a group of nations who had already gone far along in this transformation and were now organizing to pursue even more ambitious economic and social goals. As a result of external economic help, implication within a rapidly expanding European economic market, and a more rational utilization of natural resources, in the last few years Italy has been providing an additional 200,000 jobs per year. Most of these new jobs have opened up in the industrial triangle of the north, thus providing a formidable pull factor for the unemployed and underemployed workers of the south.

[1] See and compare: (a) Istituto Centrale di Statistica, IX Censimento Generale della Popolazione (4 novembre, 1951), IV, *Professioni*, pp. 603–605, Table 6; and (b) Istituto Centrale di Statistica, *Rilevazione Nazionale delle Forze di Lavoro, 20 ottobre, 1963*, p. 28, Table 11. It should be noted that the figures for 1963 include the southern part of the Latium region, so that the real difference between the two years is surely greater.

As Forte [2] rightly argues, the Italian internal migration can, therefore, be partly expressed in terms of the development of "an economy of well-being." That is to say that, given the dynamic economic conditions of the Italian nation in the past decade, the relatively idle and unproductive southern labor could not but be transferred to places where it could produce more and contribute more effectively to the expansion of the national economic system.

POVERTY OF LIFE CONDITIONS IN THE SOUTH

But Italian migrants, like migrants everywhere, do not merely respond to enticements from the outside; it must be specifically recognized also that in migrating they always reject at least some of the conditions existing in their own community. In what follows I shall examine, in part, this aspect of the south Italian emigration. The focus will be on the peasant, by which term I intend to indicate any worker directly engaged in manual agricultural activity as his major occupation. This definition will exclude from our interest such individuals as absentee land owners, managers, and the like whose occupational activity, though often fundamentally agricultural, is no more than supervisory in nature. Again, we shall exclude from our definition any agricultural worker who directly operates a total amount of land exceeding 30 acres, whether owned or rented, totally or partially. For, at this level of agricultural activity we are often faced by a level of economic power and a total style of life that are extraneous to the masses of agricultural workers in south Italy.

Poverty. The factors of rejection that operate in the south Italian peasant are numerous and very powerful. Very considerable among them is the combination of overpopulation and natural poverty of his region. In a 1952 report given in Venice, a representative of SVIMEZ (Association for the Industrial Development of the Italian South) divided the south into "economically homogenous zones" and estimated that more than seven million persons, that is, 42 per cent of the total southern population, which resided in 59 per cent of the total southern area, lived in zones without "consistent possibilities of development." Therefore, even without considering the highly unbalanced man-land ratio existing in other zones more capable of further economic development, there was a very large number of south Italians for whom, given the new needs and values that were being nationally developed and reinforced, there was little or no place in the economy of their region.

The fundamental characteristic of the Italian south is a terribly rugged country which only very rarely is interspersed with small strips of flat and tillable land. A tragic contradiction has dominated the economic history

[2] Francesco Forte, "Le Migrazioni Interne come Problema di Economia del Benessere," in Autori Vari (ed.), *Immigrazione e Industria,* Edizioni di Comunità, Milano, 1962, pp. 77–105.

of this region, which has had to shelter on its land a much denser population than nature would allow. As Professor Rossi-Doria, an expert on south Italy, has aptly stated, to eke out a living, the south Italian peasant has had to impose on a land largely fit for a pastoral economy the most absurd of all cultivations, namely wheat.[3]

Under such circumstances, the level of living of the southern population leaves much to be desired. According to a rough estimate by the DOXA public opinion research institute, in 1948, when the recent southern emigration was beginning to be noticeable, 59 per cent of the family units in the southern region of Calabria had a yearly income of less than $630. The percentages for such other classically southern regions as Sicily and the Abruzzi were 55 and 53 respectively. The picture was much more comfortable in the north. For instance, the corresponding figures for the industrial regions of Emilia, Piemonte, and Lombardia were, respectively, 39, 31, and 30 per cent.[4]

By 1957, when migration from the south had already become quite voluminous, per capita yearly income in south Italy as a whole was about $200, compared to around $500 in the north.[5] It is easy to guess, furthermore, that the income of the southern peasants themselves was considerably lower than the southern average.

The general life conditions of the southern peasant are truly penurious. After a decade of miraculous economic boom in his nation, many a peasant's home is still a one- or two-room hovel which he shares with his wife and three or four children, and very often with a donkey, a goat, or a pig. But the whims of history and terrain have also decreed that his hovel be often located in a village built high upon a hill. Not infrequently, therefore, the peasant spends several hours a day walking to and from his place of work loaded with his ancient hoe, a water receptacle, and a lunch bag consisting at best of bread, a piece of cheese, an onion, some olives, and dried fruit. When he arrives on the land, his body, already weakened by burden, disease, and starvation, is gravely fatigued by the interminable march in the mud or the dust. If by a supreme act of will and pride he succeeds in accomplishing a little work, too often it comes to nought.

After paying an exorbitant share to his landlord and losing much of his produce to thieves, birds, diseases, landslides, or drought, the peasant usually manages to store enough grain, fruit, or beans to keep him and his family barely alive until early spring, months before the new harvest. At such time, then, he is very frequently compelled to incur debts which

[3] Manlio Rossi-Doria, "La Struttura e i Problemi Fondamentali dell 'Agricoltura Meridionale,'" in Cassa per il Mezzogiorno, *Problemi dell'Agricoltura Meridiona*, Istituto Editoriale del Mezzogiorno, Napoli, 1953, pp. 145–148.

[4] Pierpaolo Luzzatto-Fegiz, *Il Volto Sconosciuto dell' Italia*, Giuffrè Editore, Milano, 1956, p. 1137, Table 3.

[5] Franco Angeli (ed.), *La Calabria*, Centro di Analisi di Opinione Pubblica e Mercato, Milano, 1958, p. 15.

keep him in continuous bondage. Writing about Butera, a Sicilian community of about 10,000 population, Sciortino Gugino has fittingly said:

Woe to those who find it necessary to be in debt, be it with private persons or with banks. From then on the family has lost its peace. With banks, when all is counted, the interest rate amounts to 13 per cent; very rarely, however, is a peasant judged a good risk by the director of the local bank. With usurers, interest rates are always higher than 20 per cent and often reach 50 per cent for a six-month loan or even for a two-month period in the spring.[6]

This state of chronic insolvency often induces the peasant to purchase a donkey, a goat, a pig, or sometimes even one or two calves. In his desperate estimate, the profit on the future sale of any of these may, and indeed sometimes does, permit him to make ends meet at the end of the year. But all too often the ends do not meet. Here is an actual case, admittedly extreme but in its basic elements not at all rare. In December 1962, a Calabrian sharecropper convinces his landlord to buy a calf at the cost of about $116. Four months later, in April 1963, the calf is sold for about $158. Total gross profit: $42. Sharecropper's share: $21. Daily gross profit: $.16. Major expenses: hay and straw for a total market value of $10. The labor factor: inestimable. Suffice it to say that in order to be kept fed and safe from thieves, the calf required constant attention, whether it was on a Sunday, on Christmas, or Easter. Total net profit? In the colorful words of the peasant himself: "the hen's udders." And this was that peasant's way of accepting a familiar economic loss.

But things are not always so bad. There are times when, after a few months' assiduous care, a peasant clears a net profit of $60–80, and there are years when nature is generous, and he brings in a fair harvest. Assuming now that he has no rapidly multiplying debts to be paid, there is always a daughter to marry off, a lawyer to counsel with, an illness to be cured, or a funeral to pay. It is no accident that the peasant is an inveterate pessimist. Ask him, in a good year, "how is the harvest?" and the answer is likely to be: "poor." Ask the healthiest one about his health, and the answer is almost surely, "not very good." To answer otherwise would amount to disturbing that precarious and mysterious equilibrium that sometimes yields a moment of peace, or even to inviting the *iettatura* (evil eye).

Rare is the peasant family in which there is not at least one member who does not suffer from illness. If it is not heart disease, it is a liver condition; if not anemia, it is kidney trouble; if not the eyes, then the teeth; if it is not arthritis, it is hernia. Despite a relative abundance of medical doctors in south Italy, these disorders have a peculiar way of being persistent. "Our ills are ours for the tomb," said an Abruzzese peasant recently.

[6] Carola Sciortino Gugino in U. Manfredi Editore, *Coscienza Collettiva e Giudizio Individuale nella Cultura Contadina*, Palermo, 1960, p. 44.

The peasant's sickness is understandably a source of constant worry for him — and for more reasons than one. Given as he is to occasional arduous labor, not infrequently he breaks a bone or suffers a heart attack. At such times as these he has urgent need of medical care. Each town has a medical doctor appointed by the High Commissioner for Health, but all too often the doctor is nowhere to be found. His residence may be in another town, several miles away, where he may also have a private practice. Or he may travel daily to his native town many miles away to visit his parents or to eat his mother's food. Thus it is that when he finally returns to his official place of work, sometimes late at night, he often finds someone who asks him to write a death certificate, and a large number of suffering patients who have been waiting many hours for him. As a Roman doctor who knows this situation said recently in a personal conversation, "then prescriptions for patent medicines start flying." By then it may happen, however, that the pharmacies nearby are closed — legally or otherwise — and there is nothing that the peasant can do short of cursing under his breath against his God, his ill fate, his fellowmen, and his *Miseria*. Or in the hours of resigned and meditative protest, he may merely create a stanza such as the following:

L'inferno è pieno
di notari e giudici,
uomini approbi (*sic*),
speziali e medici.

(Hell is full
of notaries and judges,
upright men,
druggists, and doctors.)

A 1952 DOXA survey of Italian *braccianti* (farm hands) found that 68 per cent of these workers were unhappy (*malcontenti*) of "their actual life conditions." No doubt, the percentage of unhappy southern *braccianti* was a great deal higher. The reasons given for their dissatisfaction were: "little work, irregular work, little money, high prices, hunger, and other economic reasons and various difficulties." [7] These are largely economic expressions, and they are crucial. Nevertheless, depth interviewing by this writer and other students of south Italian peasantry reveals additional important factors of another kind.[8]

[7] Luzzato-Fegiz, *op. cit.*, p. 1018, Table 2.

[8] See for instance, Joseph Lopreato, "Social Stratification and Mobility in a South Italian Town," *American Sociological Review*, XXVI (August, 1961), 585–596; "Interpersonal Relations in Peasant Society: The Peasant's View," *Human Organization*, XXI (Spring, 1962), 21–24; "Alienazione nella Società e nella Comunità," (forthcoming), Istituto di Statistica, Università di Roma. See also, Edward C. Banfield, *The Moral Basis of a Backward Society*, The Free Press, New York, 1958; Johan Galtung, "Componenti Psico-Sociali nella Decisione di Emigrare" in Autori Vari (ed.), *op. cit.*, pp. 429–435; Carola Sciortino Gugino, *op. cit.*; Guido Vincelli, *Una Comunità Meridionale*, Casa Editrice Taylor, Torino, 1958.

Interpersonal Relations. The precariousness of the peasant's economy gives rise to certain other conditions that keep him in a constant state of insecurity, fear, distrust, animosity, and conflict with his fellowmen. His life is in continual anguish. A Calabrian peasant, who returned from Canada to visit his parents and to satisfy his nostalgia for his birthplace, explained a few years ago:

> The village is too small a world to live in. It is impossible to breathe freely in it. It is dirty; you must always hide something or from some one; every one lies about everything: wealth, eating, friendship, love, God. You are always under the eyes of someone who scrutinizes you, judges you, envies you, spies on you, throws curses against you, but smiles his ugly, toothless mouth out whenever he sees you.

Suspicion of one's fellowmen is rampant in south Italian peasantry. In its purest state it reveals in the peasant an individual engaged in a one man's war against all others. The nuclear family itself is not free from intense internal conflict.[9] Basically this arises because an economy of dire scarcity encourages instrumental relations based on domination-submission terms within the family nucleus, and as a consequence, resentment and hostility. Children are needed to "pitch in." Each of them is an instrument of production and subsistence, and his energies are often utilized to the maximum. The suffering child is quick in attributing fault to his elders, and the positively affective aspect of family relations is weakened. Thus it is that by the age of ten, many a south Italian child has learned to bear a constant grudge against his father and his older brothers who command him and reflect their animus for their father on him. Communication is minimal, and then it is usually initiated by the older person in the form of a dry, abrupt command to do something. On those rare occasions in which the son addresses his father, he frequently does so in timid and formal language. When they return home from the fields, they often walk several yards apart. Their eyes hardly ever meet. They consume their evening meal in silence.

At home the father is considered a tyrant, frightful and ready to explode at the least provocation. It must be difficult to love such a person, to admire him, to feel friendly toward him. It is even difficult to talk with him. Is it then a surprise when we hear the lady of the home, who has just finished preparing the supper, call out curtly to her husband who has been waiting for it: "Don't you come to eat? What are you waiting for?" This statement comes at the end of an imagined but failed altercation in which she has vindicated her right to annul his arbitrary and afflicting authority. In her spiteful conclusion she seems to be saying: "It is ready, Mr. Belly. Come and choke on it!"

On this topic of interpersonal hostility, an elderly and wise peasant recently explained to me:

[9] In his study of Montegrano, Banfield, *op. cit.*, has vividly discussed conflict in interpersonal relations, but he has failed to observe such conflict within the context of the nuclear family itself.

Where there are hunger, grief, and uncertainty you can be sure that there is also carnage (*carneficina*) and not just among strangers, but also among friends and relatives. And mind you: things are getting worse. The young people are getting proud, demanding, and impatient. They get angry quickly and fall out with any one. In my youth I never heard of any one who killed his own father or brother with an axe. You would club a neighbor, alright. Today such cases happen frequently. We hear about them every day. . . . Nowadays everyone is every one else's enemy. In this village I could count on the fingers of one hand the young people who have not had a serious quarrel with their brothers or parents. It's frightful!

Whether in the family or in the community, interpersonal relations in peasant south Italy are stressful. It is not difficult to imagine why. In the last analysis stress and conflict in peasant society are rooted in the constant precariousness of its traditional economy.[10] In such economy, while the past evokes memories of painful hardships and the present is a tense and uncertain struggle for survival, the future constitutes a threat of hunger, sickness, humiliations, and futile toil. Under these circumstances, the peasant, like any other man, is *homo homini lupus*. He is constantly on guard against possible impingements on his meager share of the local "economic pie" and at the same time maneuvering against all but his own dependents to enlarge his own share so as to achieve a higher degree of comfort and security. It is such facts as these which explain such widely diffused maxims as: "Do not trust even your brother, Friends with all, loyal with no one, Even your best friend is a traitor."

It may be objected that stress and conflict do not arise only in economically insecure societies, and they do not always arise here. What distinguishes the peasant economy from other types of economy at the present time is its rapidly changing nature. Whether it be in south Italy or in South America, in Africa or in Asia, strong winds of transformation are blowing. But the ensuing economic improvement is not equally distributed. It follows that the traditional power and prestige structures are disturbed, resulting in an intensification of the pre-existing, economically-derived and possibly latent, conflict.[11]

Indeed, the peasant is so insecure about his economy, and so accustomed to the idea of an inalterable partition of the economic pie, that he may negate even personal improvement in absolute terms. And it is understandable. From the perspective of the observer, it is not difficult to envision a future state of affairs in peasant society in which the traditional pie has been vastly enlarged to provide for each person a much larger share than he ever had in the past. But the traditional peasant himself can see the future only from the perspective of the past, and from here, any changes, any differential improvements are likely to suggest to him a diminution of his own share of the pie, unless they be clearly

[10] George M. Foster, "Interpersonal Relations in Peasant Society," *Human Organization*, XIX (Winter 1960–1961), 174–178.

[11] Joseph Lopreato, "Interpersonal Relations in Peasant Society: The Peasant's View," *op. cit.*, 24.

advantageous to him. The struggle for survival is accentuated, and with it, of course, stress, animosity, conflict.

The peasant's life, already burdened by hunger, ill health, hard labor, and insecurity becomes unbearably tiring and equally menacing. It is like living at the foot of a volcano that has been threatening to erupt. At his first chance, the peasant packs up his rags and leaves — he emigrates.

The Prestige Structure. Still another powerful set of circumstances, closely related to the above, induces the peasant to abandon his land. "*Chi non ha non è*" (He who has not is not), states a Calabrian proverb. The peasant's economic poverty is translated into social insignificance, subordination, contemptibility. As sharecropper or farm hand, he is completely dependent on the capital of others for his minimal livelihood. Even as petty owner he disposes of little capital with which to exercise influence over any beyond his own family dependents. Lacking the support and the leadership to organize a protest, the traditional peasant seeks to insure his continued subsistence by practicing an abject servility. But such social response becomes the focus of general derision at his expense.

Again, his work conditions and habits are such that he is hardly ever present in the village, which is the center of social life and political affairs. It ironically happens, then, that in a village where peasants constitute as much as 90 per cent of the total population, they are in fact a vast minority excluded from public participation. Furthermore, the peasant has little or no schooling; consequently, in "a country of the thousand foreign languages," he lacks the speech refinements of the most foreign, but most prestigeful, of them all: the mother language. Finally, in a society which has recently raised fashion to a national institution he lacks the most manifest of all symbols of social importance, correct dress. All this and the cruel fate of centuries of suffering stamped clearly on his face and on his back, render him clearly identifiable from a distance, and reduce him nearly to the level of an untouchable. And so it may happen that a young high-school student, proud of his talcum powder and hair tonic, prefers to walk two or three miles to a nearby town rather than taking a bus "crowded with fetid *contadini*."

In her study of the prestige structure of Butera, Sciortino Gugino observes that peasants "continue to make up the lowest stratum." Nonfarming workers treat them with contempt; *pedi 'ncritati* (muddy feet) is their nickname. The peasant is credited with feeding everybody, and yet he is everybody's laughing-stock. "*Viddanu si e di viddanu ti trattu.*" (You are a rustic, and as such I treat you.)[12]

It is no surprise that already in 1948, according to a DOXA national survey, only 14 per cent of Italian parents wished their male children to become agricultural workers; yet the actual percentage of such workers was no less than 48.[13] And when in another such survey carried out in

[12] *Ibid.*, 51.
[13] Luzzato Fegiz, *op. cit.*, p. 1037.

1950 the respondents were divided by the four regional categories of North, Center, South, and Islands (Sardinia and Sicily), the percentages were respectively 25, 12, 8, and 19.[14] The people of the industrial north were more favorably disposed toward the agricultural way of life than the people of the agricultural south!

In a nation where it is generally recognized that "*ci vuole la raccomandazione per poter vivere* (you need pull to be able to live)," the poor and unpolished peasant's life chances are very low indeed. In the shops, at the market place, in the hospital, in the army, in court, in church, in the post office, everywhere but in his own smoky and malodorous hut, the peasant is either neglected or altogether ridiculed and humiliated.

In the spring of 1963, for instance, I was at the post office of a southern market town to buy some stamps. Among the thick crowd of waiting clients there was a visibly exhausted peasant woman who had most likely left her little village at sunrise that morning to come to sell her score of eggs at the market. One by one, many fellow customers passed her by, oftentimes by their own initiative, sometimes because invited to do so by the postal clerk. When she could tolerate it no longer, she whispered to the clerk in a meek tone that could have aroused general shame and compassion: "Be charitable. I have been waiting an hour." She must have wished she had never spoken! The clerk's immediate, violent reaction was to order her to hold her tongue until he would be ready to listen to her. Then he had a clever afterthought. "But what do you wish?" he jested. "An express stamp," she begged. "But why, my good woman? Can you write?" That question was indeed clever. It had the effect of a clown act in a children's circus; the spectators exploded in laughter. One of them, who until then had been merrily conversing with the clerk at the nearby window about the exploits of an Italian soccer team, appeared to be one of the local police authority. He could not help but volunteer a bit of his own wisdom for the occasion: "And what do *you* know about the difficulty of dealing with these blessed peasants?"

The tired and outraged lady retreated without the stamp and with the only form of protest open to her. In picking up her wicker basket from the floor, she exclaimed: "May you die with rabies, arrogant cowards!" Given her lowly social position, the whole thing ended there, for all but herself. When she returned home that day and heard her young son mention the possibility of going to seek work in Milan or Toronto, it is very likely that she did not discourage him.

AGENTS OF CHANGE

By now the thought must have emerged that emigration from south Italy is not merely or primarily a question of seeking one's fortune. To a very large extent it has become a question of escaping what a Basilicata peasant has recently referred to as "the inferno of the peasant's

[14] *Ibid.*, p. 1050, Table 1.6.

life."[15] There was a time, until a few decades ago, when, as Friedmann observes, south Italian peasants, like peasants elsewhere, saw themselves as subject to the working of history but scarcely as makers of it.[16] But the cultural evolution of recent years has altered this view in the south Italian peasant. He has now taken a step into the stream of history, and has started to manipulate the processes that go into making it. Channels of communication which link his society to the larger national society and to the world outside have opened up to an extent previously inconceivable, and have become objects of his awareness. The factors underlying their opening are numerous and quite complex, but the following appear to have been crucial in causing a new awareness in the peasant.

1. One of the most important factors has been the recent political struggle in his nation. The various political parties contending for the national power have better than ever recognized the conditions of the peasant's situation as an Italian problem and have vied for his vote, for his recognition of their efforts on his behalf, and for his own greater awareness of the problem. In so doing they have emphasized and publicized his pervasive poverty and displayed for him a future mode of life that excites his self-esteem, his achievement ideology, and his imagination. The government itself has now solemnly recognized a "southern problem" and instituted various concrete measures to solve it.

2. At least equally important has been emigration itself, particularly the first wave of it at the turn of the century. Emigration begets emigration. Whatever the original causes of departure, after some profitable years abroad, some of the old emigrants have returned to their old communities to enjoy at leisure the fruits of their labor. And here they have, by their improved style of life, displayed to the less fortunate previously unimagined possibilities of economic and social betterment. The impulse to throw away the hoe is thus strengthened.

[15] What happens to the peasant once he arrives in the new society would, of course, merit a fresh analytical look. There is reason to believe that many factors of acculturation and culture shock will cause the immigrant to lose the remembrance of original motives and values, or to modify them greatly. The immigrant often becomes demoralized and for some time may be expected to oscillate between nostalgia for the old society and thwarted hopes for the new in an uncomfortable succession of ambivalent feelings. In an interesting study carried out in Perth, Western Australia, Heiss found that 85 per cent of 107 Italian immigrants stated that they had gone to Australia solely for economic reasons. Again, most of them had originally left Italy with the alleged intention of returning to it permanently. (See Jerold Heiss, "The Italians of Perth," *Westerly* [March, 1964], 67–69.) In another paper dealing with the same body of data, Heiss interestingly found that migrants from south Italy displayed a significantly higher level of satisfaction with their life in Australia than migrants from northern Italy, where life conditions are initially more favorable than in the south. A more detailed analysis of the data then led Heiss to suggest that the level of satisfaction was directly related to the degree to which actual achievement was consonant with the expectations that immigrants had brought to the new country. (See Jerold Heiss, "Sources of Satisfaction and Assimilation among Italian Immigrants," *Human Relations*, forthcoming.)

[16] F. G. Friedmann, "The World of 'La Miseria,'" *Community Development Review*, VII (June, 1962), 91.

Away from his community, whether in New York, Milan, or Toronto, today's peasant then has experiences which reinforce his disaffection with his old society and his position in it. Or at home he hears about them. Particularly critical has been the migration to English-speaking countries, where the previous peasant has earned amounts of money which by his old standards are extraordinary, and has discovered forms of social relations which, despite the well-documented handicaps of the immigrant, he has found greatly more democratic and humane than those from which he escaped. Or so he says upon returning to Italy for one reason or another. The difference has been so impressive that the peasant very often idealizes the new well beyond recognizable proportions. In comparison, the old becomes altogether despicable. A few years ago a Calabrian peasant wrote to me from Canada:

> The beauty of it is that here, when five o'clock comes around, I clean my fingernails, dress like a king, and I *am* a king, like everyone else. I am not the son of So-and-So; I am not a hodman; I am just Mr. [name deleted], and I feel a hundred times better than those *vagabondi* [lazy do-nothings — persons of leisure in his old community].

Again, an Australian returnee told me in the anteroom of a radiologist in Messina, Sicily:

> In Australia you never have to wait very long in the office of a doctor. You have an appointment with him, and when it is time for you to go in, you go in. If you do not have an appointment, it is first-come-first-served. Here it is first-come-last-served, unless you come accompanied by a *commendatore* [honorific title].

He then proceeded to relate an experience he had had with a notary public in a town near his own village. It was the sort of story which in south Italy has been heard many, many times before. One day, shortly after temporarily returning from Australia, the poor fellow had left his village very early in the morning to arrange a transfer of property with the notary in the nearby town. He waited six or seven hours in the notary's waiting room while many other clients had gone in and out of the office. On those few occasions in which he had the courage to inquire about his own status in the obviously arbitrary procession of services, he was told by the notary's maid that when his turn came he would be informed of it. And he waited. Finally, late that afternoon the maid approached and lashed him with the information that there was no reason to wait any longer, for the *professore* had gone out two hours previously. "What are you waiting for? Can't you see he is not here? Return tomorrow." And so it was for several additional days.

The working of foreign bureaucracies has very favorably impressed many peasant emigrants. One of them expressed his admiration for the Canadian bureaucracy as follows:

In Canada you can often settle the most difficult official business with a single telephone call. In Italy you must take your hat off to hundreds of good-for-nothings throughout the country in order to solve the simplest problem. After many months or years, after having filled scores of officially stamped sheets of paper, and after having wasted large sums of money which end up in the pockets of thieves, you are told that you may not have the document because the law has changed.

Aside from the fact that migrants send remittances, or bring back sums of money, that by local standards are quite huge and permit the recipients to buy many cultural symbols of social importance and superiority, it is obvious that they are also important agents in the diffusion of customs and beliefs that feed the most cherished of the peasants' newly developing values. As it often happens, upon returning to his old village for a given period of time, after a few years abroad, the previously deprived magnifies the better reality of foreign cultures and titillates the imagination of those who have not yet left. Stories are told of the complete equality of the Americans, houses with incredible facilities in which one can go about in shirt sleeves when the streets outside are covered with snow, stores where one can buy most of his necessities in a few minutes and for little money, beefsteaks and milk that are fed to the pigs, public officials who serve with kindness and loyalty, notary publics who notarize a document for an insignificant fee from behind a drug counter, doctors who correct an old-standing disturbance with a single pill, gorgeous women who pursue "the passionate Italian." [17]

3. A third major factor in the new peasant awareness is the increasing operation of the modern media of communication. I shall briefly discuss only television, which is by far the most important of them. Those few times that the peasant watches television, whether it be at home, at the bar, or often in the form of peeking in the house of a neighbor while standing on the road, he is left with incipient new wants and a heightened discontent with his life situation. Television discloses a world which in comparison to his own is utterly fantastic: all light and color, wealth and comfort, beauty and joy. He learns to yearn for that world. In short, television generates and reinforces his discontent with the social world in which he has no respectable part.

Television creates a new awareness of still another sort. For a long time, the peasant submitted passively to the city and to the government — far away somewhere — from which came the orders that regulated

[17] This finding would suggest an affirmative answer to Merton's question whether there is "a tendency for outsiders to develop unrealistic images of nonmembership groups which, if they are positive reference groups, lead toward unqualified idealization (as the official norms are taken at face value). . . ." See Robert K. Merton, *Social Theory and Social Structure*, The Free Press, New York, 1957, p. 351. Again it would seem that one form of social organization which maximizes the probability of "distorted perception" of other individuals and groups (*Ibid.*, p. 336) is that represented by a peasant society in transformation.

many of his public activities. The orders were expressed and articulated by the local *intelligentsia*, namely the handful of administrative, religious, medical, and educational representatives of the upper and outer world. As Pitkin justly observes, the peasant had "very few opportunities for making decisions affecting his life in the community to say nothing of the nation." [18]

The "command center" in Rome and the decision-making processes that were emitted by it were formidable enigmas for the leisureless and uneducated peasant. As a result, he held his gentry in awe. Now television is revealing the very matrix of his social existence. By comparison, the old *intelligentsia* becomes puny and the expression of a cultural hoax too long tolerated. There is reason to believe that an individual's tendency in relation to the sources of power and decisions in his social milieu is generally centripetal in nature. For instance, the attempt to "get close to the leader" is a fairly well known phenomenon in small group research.[19] In larger social structures it does not seem unlikely that an individual will at least seek to learn about, and get close to, the proximate context of decision-making and public action. The possibility to do so is missing in the peasant's restrictive community, whereas television suggests that outside it is possible.

Three important clarifications are necessitated at this point of the discussion. First, the peasant's new social resoluteness must be viewed as a process that is at least a half century old. The considerations made so far would suggest only that the process has recently become more intensive.

Second, and relatedly, the recent wave of emigration from south Italy is *qualitatively* different from that which reached its peak around 1913. A very large number of the peasants who went to the United States a half century ago had to tolerate conditions which were not much better (if they were not worse) than those they had left at home. Many lived in unheated shanties, separate and lonely. Nor was their economic avail very high. The lucky ones were earning $1.50 for ten hours of work, while a pair of work shoes cost $1.75, and eggs sold for ten cents a dozen. These facts may explain the very large percentage of Italian migrants who returned home after only a year or two in the United States. Only those who persevered many years profited from the building of America. Of these, some never went back to their communities of origin; others returned and spread the word about the land of opportunities and equality.

The situation today is radically different. While until fifteen years ago the southern emigrant's community had changed but little in recent decades, the world they now see in Milan, in other parts of Europe, or

[18] Donald Pitkin, "A Consideration of Asymmetry in the Peasant-City Relationship," paper read at the annual meeting of the A.A.A., Chicago, December 27, 1957.

[19] See, for instance, Frederic M. Thrasher, *The Gang*, The University of Chicago Press, Chicago, 1927; and William F. Whyte, *Street Corner Society*, The University of Chicago Press, Chicago, 1943.

in any one of the English-speaking countries overseas often verges on the phantasmagoric. Needless to say, the migrant earns more money in real value; on the whole he finds a better reception by the native population; and of course he lives a fuller cultural life. As if all this were not enough, the modern media of communication encourage him to travel and to improve himself.

Third, no suggestion is here being made that current conditions are about to bring peasant life to an end in south Italy. The historical circumstances to which south Italian peasantry is anchored are very complex and deep-rooted. Furthermore, often human values change less than appearances lead us to believe. And, finally, much depends on the earnestness and the competence with which the Italian government's measures of economic and social development are carried out in south Italy. What is happening there at the present merely indicates that the peasant impatiently desires a change, that he wishes to help in bringing it about, and that in any case, barring a major setback, peasants will keep departing until the few remaining will have an opportunity to learn to farm rationally whatever land will prove itself tillable.

On the basis of "reference group theory,"[20] we may now hazard a general theoretical statement to help us better understand the recent massive movement of south Italian peasants from their land. It would seem that the peasant's abject and enduring poverty, the afflicting interpersonal relations that ensue therefrom, and the subservient, handicapped social status that also follows from his poverty and from his work conditions constitute the objective preconditions to his decision to escape his traditional situation. Once, however, for the various reasons mentioned, and no doubt for many others, the communication channels linking his peasant world to national and extra-national societies have opened up and become objects of his awareness, the peasant sees in the outside world a mode of life and standards of conduct that intensify the discomfort and discontent inherent in the objective preconditions. In his observation of this new world an intense feeling of relative deprivation has emerged.

What has happened is that the peasant has been put in a position to refer to the social values and opportunities of non-membership groups for an appraisal of the values and opportunities of his own peasant society. Within this comparative frame of reference, his society receives a negative judgment, and the need to escape it is heightened. We may, therefore, say that when an individual's self-image feeds on stimuli deriving from his own cultural milieu which tend to denigrate it, he is likely to search for non-membership groups who will provide stimuli to restore his self-respect. This is to say that he is likely to positively refer to non-membership groups for attitude-formation and for the rationale that bears on the pursuit of his future life chances. The evolution of personal goals follows

[20] See Merton, *op. cit.*, chapters VIII and IX.

an itinerary that frequently concludes itself with geographic mobility and usually also with an improvement in economic and social position as well as self-evaluation.

There was a time until recent decades when peasants turned aside from active comparison of themselves with others not of their own kind. In their forbidding contact with their local gentry in a static society, they pathologically learned to accept, through the centuries, the system of evaluation which publicly symbolized them as socially inferior by the basic tokens of social importance. In the near impossibility to transgress their own estate, they turned to creating various gradations of social worth within the stratum itself.

The evidence from south Italy contradicts Tumin and Feldman's proposition that "lower caste or class members [do not] accept the criteria of ranking by which they are deemed functionally and morally inferior." [21] Lacking in south Italy is any notion of the spirit of *dignidad* that Tumin and Feldman find in Puerto Rico in the form of

> . . . belief that all men are ultimately equal and equally worthy of respect, regardless of temporary or even enduring differences in their material standard of living, in the formal power they exercise or in the prestige which their occupations and educations evoke.[22]

The south Italian peasant, unlike the Puerto Rican *jibaro* is *not* romantically honored. May it suffice to say that in the Italian language all terms (*contadino, villano, terrone,* etc.) which designate the peasant are also synonyms of stupid, ill-bred, uncouth, and the like. When we turn to the local dialects themselves, we find a much vaster array of terms (like *zulu, tamarru, zammaru, picuni, pedi 'ncritati, viddanu,* etc.) which render even more obnoxious meanings.

How do the peasants themselves respond to such public denigration of them? Responses of course vary, but this writer has heard too many say of themselves:

> Well, what can one say? We peasants are poor earth worms. We live with the animals, eat with them, talk to them, smell like them. Therefore, we are a great deal like them. How would you like to be a peasant?

Under century-long debasement of his worth, the peasant has learned to consider valid the low evaluation of his status. He has learned to believe that as an occupational category he is indeed functionally and morally inferior. To be sure, Hesiodic attempts to glorify the peasant have not been lacking in Italian history. "*Scarpe grosse e cervello fino*" (Thick shoes and keen intellect), goes an old adage. But nobody believes it.

But could the peasant's approval of a low status for himself bring any

[21] M. M. Tumin and A. S. Feldman, *Social Class and Social Change in Puerto Rico*, Princeton University Press, Princeton, 1961, p. 480.

[22] *Ibid.*, p. 18.

comfort to his personal integrity? There is no reason to believe that he of all people is a stranger to the wish for recognition. In his case, this basic wish can only mean a cessation of agricultural activities. Emigration is patently suited to achieve this goal; barring few exceptions it involves also occupational mobility and social betterment.

In short, the peasants are leaving the land they have worked on for many reasons, but foremost among them seems to be a desire to regain, or to earn, their self-esteem, their dignity, and their personal integrity. To a large extent, the stimulus to do so has come from the outside, and particularly from various groups within the surrounding civilization whose economic and ideological forms have proved to be unusually benevolent.

In displaying before his eyes the conditions and possibilities of a more commodious, secure, and just life, the outside world has also intensified his sense of poverty, his *miseria*, and strengthened his wish to escape it. As Barnett might say, south Italian peasants are "resentful"; they are individuals who are not resigned have-nots; rather they are dissatisfied because they are denied the values that in their larger society are esteemed the most, and

> are markedly receptive to the suggestion of a change which will at least equalize opportunities or, perhaps even better, put them on top and their smug superiors on the bottom.[23]

CONCLUSIONS

1. Writing about peasant society and culture in 1956, Robert Redfield reiterated a thesis, in a somewhat modified form, that peasants are characterized by

> . . . an intense attachment to native soil; a reverent disposition toward habitat and ancestral ways; a restraint on individual self-seeking in favor of family and community; a certain suspiciousness, mixed with appreciation, of town life; a sober and earthy ethic.[24]

Redfield's case rested to a large extent on what he saw as supporting evidence from ancient Boeotia as presented by Hesiod, nineteenth-century England as discussed by George Bourne, and present-day Yucatan studied by himself. The evidence from the Mediterranean basin in general, and from south Italy in particular, was adverse to Redfield's thesis, but his commitment to it seemed to be much too strong to yield.

In his attempt to salvage whatever part of his scheme he could, Red-

[23] H. G. Barnett, *Innovation*, McGraw-Hill Book Co., New York, 1953, p. 401. Barnett's very keen proposition may also explain, in part, why a large number of south Italian emigrants eventually return, temporarily or permanently, to their old community. Enriched and proud of their recent cultural achievements, they now have an old question to settle.

[24] Robert Redfield, *Peasant Society and Culture*, The University of Chicago Press, Chicago, 1956, p. 140.

field raised the question as to whether differences reported about peasant values might be due, in part, to "choices made by observers and writers as to an aspect of a social situation to be stressed." [25] And this is a scientifically critical question, no doubt bearing with it an affirmative answer.

But true to his penetrating skill, he did not fail to make the equally important observation that any investigation of a people's values must answer such questions as: What do these people desire for themselves and for their children? To what kind of life do they attach highest esteem? The evidence presented in this paper bears precisely on these questions. As we have seen, large-scale public opinion surveys show that south Italian peasants do not wish their children to be like themselves. Depth interviews then reveal in the peasant an intense dislike of his life-situation and a strong desire to leave the inferno of his peasant community.

It may well be that, as Redfield suggests, the south Italian brings

> a distaste for rural life down from ancient times, while he also is influenced by the fact that he now lives in hardship in contrast to the life of the gentry and the rich.[26]

But it is unlikely that the south Italian peasant represents a special case, as Redfield proposes. Again, it is hard to understand his heavy dependence on Hesiod's poetic injunctions as to *ancient* agricultural industry. Finally, it is difficult to accept Redfield's observation that the south Italian peasant *now* lives in hardship in comparison to his gentry. Surely there is nothing in the economic history of south Italy that suggests less relative hardship in the past for the peasantry. Indeed, there is every indication that the opposite is true. The eighteenth and nineteenth centuries appear to have been particularly hard for the southern peasant whose control over his land was lost, regained, and then lost again in an endless chain of feudal vicissitudes, land reform measures, and seignorial seizing subterfuges.[27] In the meantime, the relative security provided by the early feudal system had disappeared.

Our own suggestion is that over and above whatever other differences may exist between south Italian peasants and many other peasants elsewhere, one is of utmost importance, and it concerns the rapid economic development and social transformations recently experienced by Italian society. The peasant's own share of the new benefits has lagged far behind the national average, but just the same he has been jerked out of his quasi-feudal state of acquiescence. He now has a *greater awareness* of his hardship and suffers from a deep sense of relative deprivation. This seems to me the *punctum* of the question. The south Italian peasant has

[25] *Ibid.*, p. 122.
[26] *Ibid.*, p. 118.
[27] For evidence on this question, see the numerous historical essays in Rosario Villari (ed.), *Il Sud nella Storia d'Italia*, Editori Laterza, Bari, 1963; and Rosario Villari, *Mezzogiorno e Contadini nell'Eta Moderna*, Editori Laterza, Bari, 1961.

learned to look around himself, then look at himself again, and in the words of Horatio complain: "*est modus in rebus.*" We suggest, therefore, that a direct approach to a study of peasants' values will reveal a similar reaction among them everywhere in peasant societies in transformation.

2. South Italian peasants have recently departed from farms in such great numbers that many study groups are busily seeking ways to solve what to them seems like a problem of great proportions impinging on the development of the entire Italian economy. The Italian government itself has recently instituted a law for the *ricomposizione fondiaria* whereby agricultural workers would be encouraged to continue working the land by helping, or forcing them, to *recompose* and reunite the infinitesimal pieces of land characterizing much of the Italian countryside, the south in particular. The rationale is that the agricultural worker would be happier to be such if he had one relatively large tract of good land to farm.

Such measure is no doubt a step in the right direction. The argument presented in this paper suggests, however, that much more is required to keep the peasant on the land. The peasant now demands that the wonders of urban civilization be transferred from the video screen to his village and farm. He requires competent and enlightened help to learn more comfortably to farm his land and to earn an equitable profit on it. Above all, a deliberate national effort will have to be made along all major channels, including the school and the modern media of communication, to develop a view of farming as a respectable occupation and to eradicate from the public mind the afflicting habit of heaping humiliation, derision, and all manner of wrongs on the peasant.

A Selected Bibliography

General Works

Anderson, Robert T.
1965 "Studies in Peasant Life." In *Biennial Review of Anthropology 1965* (Bernard J. Siegel, ed.), pp. 176–210. Stanford: Stanford University Press.

Caro Baroja, Julio
1963 "The City and the Country: Reflexions on Some Ancient Commonplaces." In *Mediterranean Countrymen* (Julian Pitt-Rivers, ed.), pp. 27–40. Paris, La Haye: Mouton & Co.

Chiva, I.
1959 "Rural Communities: Problems, Methods, and Types of Research." *Reports and Papers in the Social Sciences*, No. 10. Paris: UNESCO.

Firth, Raymond
1950 "The Peasantry of South East Asia." *International Affairs* 26:503–512.

Fitchen, Janet M.
1961 " 'Peasantry' as a Social Type." *Proceedings of the 1961 Annual Spring Meeting of the American Ethnological Society*, pp. 114–119. Seattle: University of Washington Press.

Foster, George M.
1953 "What Is Folk Culture?" *American Anthropologist* 55:159–173.

Franklin, S. H.
1962 "Reflections on the Peasantry." *Pacific Viewpoint* 3:1–26.

Friedl, Ernestine
1963 "Studies in Peasant Life." In *Biennial Review of Anthropology 1963* (Bernard J. Siegel, ed.), pp. 276–306. Stanford: Stanford University Press.

Gearing, Fred
1964 "Idioms of Human Interaction: Moral and Technical Orders." *Proceedings of the 1963 Annual Spring Meeting of the American Ethnological Society*, pp. 10–19. Seattle: University of Washington Press.

Geertz, Clifford
1962 "Studies in Peasant Life: Community and Society." In *Biennial Review of Anthropology 1961* (Bernard J. Siegel, ed.), pp. 1–41. Stanford: Stanford University Press.

Redfield, Robert
1939 "Introduction to *St. Denis: a French-Canadian Parish*, by Horace Miner, pp. xiii–xix. Chicago: University of Chicago Press.
1947 "The Folk Society." *The American Journal of Sociology* 52:293–308.
1953 *The Primitive World and Its Transformations*. Ithaca, N.Y.: Cornell University Press.
1956 *Peasant Society and Culture: An Anthropological Approach to Civilization*. Chicago: University of Chicago Press.

Sjoberg, Gideon
1952 "Folk and 'Feudal' Societies." *The American Journal of Sociology* 58:231–239.

Wolf, Eric R.
1966 *Peasants*. Englewood Cliffs, N.J.: Prentice-Hall.

Peasant Economics

Beidelman, Thomas
1959 A *Comparative Analysis of the Jajmani System*. Association of Asian Studies. Locust Valley, N.Y.: J. J. Augustin.

Berreman, Gerald
1962 "Caste and Economy in the Himalayas." *Economic Development and Cultural Change* 10:386–394.

Carrasco, Pedro
1957 "Some Aspects of Peasant Society in Middle America and India." Berkeley: *Kroeber Anthropological Society Papers* 16:17–27.

Dewey, Alice G.
1962 *Peasant Marketing in Java*. New York: The Free Press of Glencoe.
Erasmus, Charles J.
1956 "Culture Structure and Process: The Occurrence and Disappearance of Reciprocal Farm Labor." *Southwestern Journal of Anthropology* 12:444–469.
Firth, Raymond
1946 *Malay Fishermen: Their Peasant Economy*. London: Kegan Paul, Trench, Trubner & Co.
———, and B. S. Yamey (eds.)
1964 *Capital, Saving and Credit in Peasant Societies: Studies from Asia, Oceania, the Caribbean and Middle America*. Chicago: Aldine Publishing Co.
Firth, Rosemary
1943 *Housekeeping among Malay Peasants*. London School of Economics and Political Science Monographs on Social Anthropology, No. 7. London.
Foster, George M.
1948 "The Folk Economy of Rural Mexico with Special Reference to Marketing." *The Journal of Marketing* 13:153–162.
Gould, Harold A.
1964 "A Jajmani System of North India: Its Structure, Magnitude, and Meaning." *Ethnology* 3:12–41.
Halpern, Joel M.
1961 "The Economics of Lao and Serb Peasants: A Contrast in Culture Values." *Southwestern Journal of Anthropology* 17:165–177.
Harper, Edward B.
1959 "Two Systems of Economic Exchange in Village India." *American Anthropologist* 61:760–778.
Kolenda, Pauline Mahar
1963 "Toward a Model of the Hindu Jajmani System." *Human Organization* 22:11–31.
Levy, Harry L.
1956 "Property Distribution by Lot in Present-Day Greece." *Transactions of the American Philosophical Association* 87:42–46.
Mikesell, Marvin
1958 "The Role of Tribal Markets in Morocco: Examples from the 'Northern Zone.'" *The Geographical Review* 58:494–511.
Mintz, Sidney W.
1956 "The Role of the Middleman in the Internal Distribution System of a Caribbean Peasant Economy." *Human Organization* 15(2):18–23.
1959 "Internal Market Systems as Mechanisms of Social Articulation." *Proceedings of the 1959 Annual Spring Meeting of the American Ethnological Society*, pp. 20–30. Seattle: University of Washington Press.
1960a "A Tentative Typology of Eight Haitian Marketplaces." *Revista de Ciencias Sociales* 4:15–57. Rio Piedras: University of Puerto Rico.
1960b "Peasant Markets." *Scientific American* 203(2):112–118, 120, 122.
Nash, Manning
1966 *Primitive and Peasant Economic Systems*. San Francisco: Chandler Publishing Co.
Orenstein, Henry
1962 "Exploitation or Function in the Interpretation of Jajmani." *Southwestern Journal of Anthropology* 18:302–316.
Rowe, William L.
1963 "Changing Rural Class Structure and the Jajmani System." *Human Organization* 22:41–44.
Wiser, William H.
1936 *The Hindu Jajmani System: a Socio-economic System Interrelating Members of a Hindu Village Community in Services*. Lucknow, U.R.: Lucknow Publishing House.

Social Organization

General

Boissevain, Jeremy
1966 "Patronage in Sicily." *Man* 1:18–33.
Foster, George M.
1961 "The Dyadic Contract: A Model for the Social Structure of a Mexican

Peasant Village." *American Anthropologist* 63:1173–1192.
1963 "The Dyadic Contract in Tzintzuntzan, II; Patron-Client Relationship." *American Anthropologist* 65:-1280–1294.
1964 "Speech Forms and Perception of Social Distance in a Spanish-Speaking Mexican Village." *Southwestern Journal of Anthropology* 20:-107–122.
Geertz, Clifford
1960 "The Javanese Kijaji: The Changing Role of a Culture Broker." *Comparative Studies in Society and History* 2:228–249.
Gough, E. Kathleen
1955 "The Social Structure of a Tanjore Village." In *Village India: Studies in the Little Community* (McKim Marriott, ed.), pp. 36–52. Chicago: University of Chciago Press.
Kaut, Charles
1961 "*Utang Na Loob:* A System of Contractual Obligation among Tagalogs." *Southwestern Journal of Anthropology* 17:256–272.
Kenny, Michael
1960 "Patterns of Patronage in Spain." *Anthropological Quarterly* 33:14–23.
Lopreato, Joseph
1961 "Social Classes in an Italian Farm Village." *Rural Sociology* 26:266–281.
Moseley, P. E.
1943 "Adaptation for Survival: The Varžić Zadruga." *The Slavonic and East European Review* 21:147–173.
Moss, Leonard W., and
Stephan C. Cappannari
1962 "Estate and Class in a South Italian Hill Village." *American Anthropologist* 64:287–300.
Redfield, Robert, and Milton Singer
1954 "The Cultural Role of Cities." *Economic Development and Cultural Change* 3:53–73.
Silverman, Sydel F.
1966 "An Ethnographic Approach to Social Stratification: Prestige in a Central Italian Community." *American Anthropologist* 68:899–921.
Srinivas, M. N.
1955 "The Social System of a Mysore Village." In *Village India: Studies in the Little Community* (McKim Marriott, ed.), pp. 1–35. Chicago: Unviersity of Chicago Press.
Ullah, Inayat
1958 "Caste, Patti and Faction in the Life of a Punjab Village." *Sociologus* 8:170–186.

FICTIVE KINSHIP

Anderson, Gallatin
1956 "A Survey of Italian Godparenthood." Berkeley: *Kroeber Anthropological Society Papers* 15:1–110.
Deshon, Shirley K.
1963 "Compadrazgo on a Henequen Hacienda in Yucatan: A Structural Re-evaluation." *American Anthropologist* 65:574–583.
Eisenstadt, S. N.
1956 "Ritualized Personal Relations: Blood Brotherhood, Best Friends, Compadre, etc.: Some Comparative Hypotheses and Suggestions." *Man* 56:90–95.
Foster, George M.
1953 "Cofradía and Compadrazgo in Spain and Spanish America." *Southwestern Journal of Anthropology* 9:1–28.
Freed, Stanley A.
1963 "Fictive Kinship in a North Indian Village." *Ethnology* 2:86–103.
Ishino, Iwao
1953 "The Oyabun-Kobun: A Japanese Ritual Kinship Institution." *American Anthropologist* 55:695–707.
Miller, Beatrice D.
1956 "Ganye and Kidu: Two Formalized Systems of Mutual Aid among the Tibetans." *Southwestern Journal of Anthropology* 12:157–170.
Moss, Leonard W., and
Stephan C. Cappannari
1960 "Patterns of Kinship, Comparaggio and Community in a South Italian Village." *Anthropological Quarterly* 33:24–32.
Norbeck, Edward, and Harumi Befu
1958 "Informal Fictive Kinship in Japan." *American Anthropologist* 60:102–117.
Okada, Ferdinand E.
1957 "Ritual Brotherhood: A Co-

hesive Factor in Nepalese Society." *Southwestern Journal of Anthropology* 13:212–222.
Pitt-Rivers, Julian
1958 "Ritual Kinship in Spain." *Transactions of the New York Academy of Sciences*, Series II, 20:424–431.
Reina, Ruben E.
1959 "Two Patterns of Friendship in a Guatemalan Community." *American Anthropologist* 61:44–50.
Sayres, William C.
1956 "Ritual Kinship and Negative Affect." *American Sociological Review* 21:348–352.

Values, Personality, World View

Cancian, Frank
1961 "The Southern Italian Peasant: World View and Political Behavior." *Anthropological Quarterly* 34:1–18.
Cohen, Yehudi
1955 "Character Formation and Social Structure in a Jamaican Community." *Psychiatry: Journal for the Study of Interpersonal Processes* 18:275–296.
Foster, George M.
1960–61 "Interpersonal Relations in Peasant Society." *Human Organization* 19:174–178.
1964 "Treasure Tales, and the Image of the Static Economy in a Mexican Peasant Community." *Journal of American Folklore* 77:39–44.
1965 "Cultural Responses to Expressions of Envy in Tzintzuntzan." *Southwestern Journal of Anthropology* 21:24–35.
Hanks, L. M., Jr.
1962 "Merit and Power in the Thai Social Order." *American Anthropologist* 64:1247–1261.
Kenny, Michael
1962–63 "Social Values and Health in Spain: Some Preliminary Considerations." *Human Organization* 21:-280–285.
Lopreato, Joseph
1962 "Interpersonal Relations: The Peasant's View." *Human Organization* 21:21–24.
Lynch, Frank
1962 "Philippine Values II: Social Acceptance." *Philippine Studies* 10:-82–99.
McCormack, William C.
1957 "Mysore Villagers' View of Change." *Economic Development and Cultural Change* 5:257–262.
Nash, Manning
1963 "Burmese Buddhism in Everyday Life." *American Anthropologist* 65:285–295.
Peristiany, J. G. (ed.)
1966 *Honour and Shame: The Values of Mediterranean Society*. Chicago: University of Chicago Press.
Phillips, Herbert
1963 "Relationships Between Personality and Social Structure in a Siamese Peasant Community." *Human Organization* 22:105–108.
1965 *Thai Peasant Personality: The Patterning of Interpersonal Behavior in the Village of Bang Chan*. Berkeley: University of California Press.
Pitt-Rivers, Julian
1960–61 " 'Interpersonal Relations in Peasant Society': A Comment." *Human Organization* 19:180–183.
Quint, Malcolm N.
1958 "The Idea of Progress in an Iraqi Village." *The Middle East Journal* 12:369–384.

Europe

General Works

Arensberg, Conrad M.
1963 "The Old World Peoples: The Place of European Cultures in World Ethnography." *Anthropological Quarterly* 36:75–99.
Boissevain, Jeremy

1964 "Factions, Parties, and Politics in a Maltese Village." *American Anthropologist* 66:1275–1287.
Greenfield, Kent Roberts
1947 "The Mediterranean Way of Life." *The Yale Review* 36:435–446.
Kenny, Michael
1963 "Europe: The Atlantic Fringe." *Anthropological Quarterly* 36:100–119.
Pitkin, Donald S.
1963 "Mediterranean Europe." *Anthropological Quarterly* 36:120–129.
Pitt-Rivers, Julian (ed.)
1963 *Mediterranean Countrymen: Essays in the Social Anthropology of the Mediterranean.* Paris, La Haye: Mouton & Co.

SCANDINAVIA

Anderson, Robert T., and Barbara Gallatin
1964 *The Vanishing Village: A Danish Maritime Community.* Seattle: University of Washington Press.
Barnes, J. A.
1954 "Class and Committees in a Norwegian Island Parish." *Human Relations* 7:39–58.
1957 "Land Rights and Kinship in Two Bremnes Hamlets." *Journal of the Royal Anthropological Institute* 87:31–56.
Barth, Fredrik (ed.)
1963 *The Role of the Entrepreneur in Social Change in Northern Norway.* Bergen: Norwegian Universities Press. (Årbok for universitetet, Bergen, Humanistisk Ser. No. 3).

GREAT BRITAIN AND IRELAND

Arensberg, Conrad M.
1937 *The Irish Countryman: An Anthropological Study.* New York: Macmillan.
———, and Solon T. Kimball
1940 *Family and Community in Ireland.* Cambridge: Harvard University Press.
Frankenberg, Ronald
1957 *Village on the Border: A Social Study of Religion, Politics and Football in a North Wales Community.* London: Cohen and West.
Geddes, Arthur
1954 *Lewis and Harris: A Study in British Community.* Edinburgh: Edinburgh University Press.
Rees, A. D.
1950 *Life in a Welsh Countryside.* Cardiff: University of Wales Press.
Williams, W. M.
1956 *Gosforth: The Sociology of an English Village.* Glencoe, Ill.: The Free Press.
1963 *A West Country Village, Ashworthy: Family, Kinship and Land.* London: Routledge and Kegan Paul.

LOW COUNTRIES

Gadourek, I.
1956 *A Dutch Community. Social and Cultural Structure and Process in a Bulb-growing Region in the Netherlands.* Publications of the Netherlands' Institute of Preventive Medicine XXX. Leiden, N.V.: H. E. Stenfert Kroese.
Keur, John Y., and Dorothy L. Keur
1955 "The Deeply Rooted: A Study of a Drents Community in the Netherlands." American Ethnological Society, Monograph No. 25. Assen: Royal Van Gorcum.
Turney-High H. H.
1953 *Chateau-Gérard: The Life and Times of a Walloon Village.* Columbia, S.C.: University of South Carolina Press.

France

Bernot, L., and R. Blancard
1953 *Nouville: un village français*. Paris: Institut d'Ethnologie.

Burns, R. K.
1961 "The Ecological Basis of French Alpine Peasant Communities in the Dauphiné." *Anthropological Quarterly* 34:19–34.

Gallagher, O. R.
1953 "Looseness and Rigidity in Family Structure." *Social Forces* 31:332–339.

Pitt-Rivers, Julian
1960 "Social Class in a French Village." *Anthropological Quarterly* 33:1–13.

Porak, René
1943 *Un village de France: psychophysiologie du paysan*. Paris: G. Doin & Co.

Wylie, Lawrence
1957 *Village in the Vaucluse*. Cambridge: Harvard University Press.

Poland

Thomas, William I., and Florian Znaniecki
1958 *The Polish Peasant in Europe and America*. Second Edition. New York: Dover Publications. [First edition 1918.]

Iberian Peninsula

Dias, Jorge
1948 *Vilarinho da Furna, Uma Aldeia Cumunitaria*. Porto: Instituto para a Alta Cultura, Centro de Estudos de Etnología Peninsular.

Foster, George M.
1960 *Culture and Conquest: America's Spanish Heritage*. Viking Fund Publications in Anthropology, No. 27. New York.

Kenny, Michael
1961 *A Spanish Tapestry: Town and Country in Castille*. London: Cohen & West.

Pérez Díaz, Victor
1966 *Estructura Social del Campo y Éxodo Rural: Estudio de un Pueblo de Castilla*. Madrid: Editorial Tecnos, S.A.

Pitt-Rivers, J. A.
1954 *The People of the Sierra*. London: Weidenfeld & Nicolson.

Italy

Banfield, Edward C.
1958 *The Moral Basis of a Backward Society*. Glencoe, Ill.: The Free Press.

Friedmann, Fredrick G.
1960 *The Hoe and the Book: An Italian Experiment in Community Development*. Ithaca, N.Y.: Cornell University Press.

Lopreato, Joseph
1961 "Social Stratification and Mobility in a South Italian Town." *American Sociological Review* 26:585–596.

Moss, Leonard W., and W. H. Thompson
1959 "The South Italian Family: Literature and Observation." *Human Organization* 18(1):35–41.

Balkans

Balikci, Asen
1965 "Quarrels in a Balkan Village." *American Anthropologist* 67:1456–1469.

Durham, Mary Edith
1909 *High Albania*. London: Edward Arnold.
1928 *Some Tribal Origins, Laws and*

Customs of the Balkans. London: G. Allen & Unwin.
Erlich-Stein, Vera
1940 "The Southern Slav Patriarchal Family." *The Sociological Review* 32:224–241.
1945 "Phases in the Evolution of Family Life in Jugoslavia." *The Sociological Review* 37:50–64.
Halpern, Joel M.
1958 *A Serbian Village*. New York: Columbia University Press.
1963 "Yugoslav Peasant Society in Transition — Stability in Change." *Anthropological Quarterly* 36:156–182.
Hammel, Eugene A.
1957 "Serbo-Croatian Kinship Terminology." Berkeley. *Kroeber Anthropological Society Papers* 16:45–75.
Lodge, Olive
1941 *Peasant Life in Jugoslavia*. London: Seeley, Service & Co.
Moseley, Philip E.
1940 "The Peasant Family: The Zadruga, or Communal Joint-Family in the Balkans, and Its Recent Evolution." In *The Cultural Approach to History* (Caroline R. Ware, ed.), pp. 95–108. New York: Columbia University Press.
1953 "The Distribution of the Zadruga within Southeastern Europe." *The Joshua Starr Memorial Volume, Jewish Social Studies* 8:219–230. New York: Conference on Jewish Relations.
Sanders, Irwin T.
1949 *Balkan Village*. Lexington: University of Kentucky Press.

GREECE

Bent, James Theodore
1885 *The Cyclades; or Life among the Insular Greeks*. London: Longmans, Green and Co.
Blum, Richard, and Eva Blum
1965 *Health and Healing in Greece: A Study of Three Communities*. Stanford: Stanford University Press.
Campbell, J. K.
1964 *Honor, Family and Patronage: A Study of Institutions and Moral Values in a Greek Mountain Community*. Oxford: Clarendon Press.
Friedl, Ernestine
1959 "The Role of Kinship in the Transmission of National Culture to Rural Villages in Mainland Greece." *American Anthropologist* 61:30–38.
1962 *Vasilika, a Village in Modern Greece*. New York: Holt, Rinehart & Winston.
1964 "Lagging Emulation in Post-Peasant Society." *American Anthropologist* 66:569–586.
Rennell Rodd, James
1892 *The Customs and Lore of Modern Greece*. London: David Stott.
Sanders, Irwin T.
1962 *Rainbow in the Rock: The People of Rural Greece*. Cambridge: Harvard University Press.

Near and Middle East

GENERAL

Cohen, Abner
1965 *Arab Border-Villages in Israel: A Study of Continuity and Change in Social Organization*. Manchester: Manchester University Press.
Hamady, Sania
1960 *Temperament and Character of the Arabs*. New York: Twayne Publishers.
Tannous, Afif I.
1944 "The Arab Village Community of the Middle East." *Annual Report for 1943*, pp. 523–544. Washington, D.C.: Smithsonian Institution.

Egypt

Adams, John B.
1957 "Culture and Conflict in an Egyptian Village." *American Anthropologist* 59:225–235.

Ammar, Hamed
1954 *Growing up in an Egyptian Village: Silwa, Province of Aswan.* London: Routledge and Kegan Paul.

Aryout, Henry Habib
1963 *The Egyptian Peasant* (John A. Williams, tr.). Boston: Beacon Press.

Bergue, Jacques
1957 *Histoire sociale d'un village Égyptien au vingtième siècle.* Paris, La Haye: Mouton & Co.

Blackman, Winifred S.
1927 *The Fellāhīn of Upper Egypt.* London: George G. Harrap & Co.

St. John, Bayle
1852 *Village Life in Egypt; With Sketches of the Saïd.* London: Chapman & Hall.

Lebanon

Fuller, Anne H.
1961 *Buarij. Portrait of a Lebanese Muslim Village.* Cambridge: Harvard University Press.

Gulick, John
1955 *Social Structure and Culture Change in a Lebanese Village.* Viking Fund Publications in Anthropology, No. 21. New York.

Touma, Toufic
1958 *Un village de montagne au Liban, Hadeth El-Jobbé.* Paris, La Haye: Mouton & Co.

Jordan

Granqvist, Hilma Natalia
1931–35 *Marriage Conditions in a Palestinian Village* (2 vols.). Helsingfors: Societas Scientiarum Fennica. Commentationes Humanarum Litterarum, III. 8.

1965 *Muslim Death and Burial: Arab Customs and Traditions Studied in a Village in Jordan.* Helsinki: Societas Scientiarum Fennica. Commentationes Humanarum Litterarum, 34, 1.

Iraq

Salim, S. M.
1962 *Marsh Dwellers of the Euphrates Delta.* London School of Economics Monographs on Social Anthropology, No. 23. London: University of London.

Syria

Sweet, L. E.
1960 *Tell Toqaan: A Syrian Village.* Ann Arbor: University of Michigan Anthropology Papers, No. 14.

Turkey

Eberhard, Wolfram
1953 "Types of Settlement in South East Turkey." *Sociologus* 3:49–64.

Kolars, John F.
1963 *Tradition, Season, and Change in a Turkish Village.* Department of Geography, Research Paper No. 82. Chicago: University of Chicago Press.

Makal, Mahmut
1954 *A Village in Anatolia.* (Sir Wyndham Deedes, tr.) London: Vallentine, Mitchell & Co.

Pierce, Joe E.
1964 *Life in a Turkish Village*. New York: Holt, Rinehart & Winston.
Spencer, Robert F.
1960 "Aspects of Turkish Kinship and Social Structure." *Anthropological Quarterly* 33:40–50.
Stirling, Paul
1965 *Turkish Village*. London: Weidenfeld & Nicolson.

South and East Asia

PAKISTAN

Eglar, Zekiye
1960 *A Punjab Village in Pakistan*. New York: Columbia University Press.
Honigmann, John J.
1958 *Three Pakistan Villages*. Institute for Research in Social Science. Chapel Hill: University of North Carolina Press.

INDIA

Beals, Alan R.
1962 *Gopalpur: A South Indian Village*. New York: Holt, Rinehart & Winston.
Berreman, Gerald D.
1963 *Hindus of the Himalayas*. Berkeley: University of California Press.
Burling, Robbins
1963 *Rengsanggri: Family and Kinship in a Garo Village*. Philadelphia: University of Pennsylvania Press.
Carstairs, G. Morris
1958 *The Twice-Born: A Study of a Community of High-Caste Hindus*. Bloomington: University of Indiana Press.
Cohn, B., and McKim Marriott
1958 "Networks and Centres in the Integration of Indian Civilisation." *Journal of Social Research* (Bihar) 1:1–19.
Dube, S. C.
1955 *Indian Village*. London: Routledge and Kegan Paul.
1958 *India's Changing Villages: Human Factors in Community Development*. London: Routledge and Kegan Paul.
Lewis, Oscar
1958 *Village Life in Northern India: Studies in a Delhi Village*. Urbana: University of Illinois Press.
Mandelbaum, David G.
1953 "Planning and Social Change in India." *Human Organization* 12(3):-4–12.
Marriott, McKim (ed.)
1955 *Village India: Studies in the Little Community*. Chicago: University of Chicago Press.
Mayer, Adrian C.
1960 *Caste and Kinship in Central India: A Village and Its Region*. Berkeley: University of California Press.
Minturn, Leigh, and John T. Hitchcock
1966 *The Rajputs of Khalapur, India*. Six Culture Series, Vol. 3. New York, London, Sidney: John Wiley and Sons.
Opler, Morris E., William Rowe, and Mildred Stroop
1959 "Indian National and State Elections in a Village Context." *Human Organization* 18:30–34.
———, and Rudra Datt Singh
1952 "Economic, Political and Social Change in a Village of North Central India." *Human Organization* 11(2):5–12.
Orenstein, Henry
1965 *Gaon: Conflict and Cohesion in an Indian Village*. Princeton: Princeton University Press.
Rowe, William L. (ed.)
1963 "Contours of Culture Change in South Asia." Special issue of *Human Organization*, Vol. 22.
Singer, Milton
1955 "The Cultural Pattern of Indian

Civilization." *Far Eastern Quarterly* 15:23–36.
Singer, Milton (ed.)
1958 "Traditional India: Structure and Change." *Journal of American Folklore* 71:191–518.
Sinha, Surajit
1957 "Tribal Cultures of Peninsular India as a Dimension of Little Tradition in the Study of Indian Civilization: A Preliminary Statement." *Man in India* 37:93–118.
Srinivas, M. N.
1956 "A Note on Sanskritization and Westernization." *Far Eastern Quarterly* 15:481–496.
Wiser, William H., and Charlotte V. Wiser
1963 *Behind Mud Walls 1930–1960*. Berkeley: University of California Press. [First edition 1930.]

Ceylon

Leach, E. R.
1961 *Pul Eliya, a Village in Ceylon: A Study of Land Tenure and Kinship*. Cambridge: University Press.
Ryan, Bryce, L. D. Jayasena, and D. C. R. Wickremesinghe
1958 *Sinhalese Village*. Coral Gables, Fla.: University of Miami Press.

Burma

Leach, Edmund R.
1954 *Political Systems of Highland Burma: A Study of Kachin Social Structure*. Cambridge: Harvard University Press.
Nash, Manning
1965 *The Golden Road to Modernity: Village Life in Contemporary Burma*. New York: John Wiley & Sons.
Shway Yoe (Sir James George Scott)
1963 *The Burman: His Life and Notions*. New York: W. W. Norton & Co. [First edition 1882.]

Indonesia

Geertz, Clifford
1957 "Ritual and Social Change: A Javanese Example." *American Anthropologist* 59:32–54.
1960 *The Religion of Java*. Glencoe, Ill.: The Free Press.
1963a *Agricultural Involution: The Process of Ecological Change in Indonesia*. Association of Asian Studies. Berkeley and Los Angeles: University of California Press.
1963b *Peddlers and Princes: Social Change and Economic Modernization in Two Indonesian Towns*. Chicago: University of Chicago Press.
Geertz, Hildred
1961 *The Javanese Family: A Study of Kinship and Socialization*. New York: The Free Press of Glencoe.

Thailand

Embree, John F.
1950 "Thailand — A Loosely Structured Social System." *American Anthropologist* 52:181–193.
Hanks, L. M., Jr.
1958 "Indifference to Modern Education in a Thai Farming Community." *Human Organization* 17(2): 9–14.
———, and H. P. Phillips
1961 "A Young Thai from the Countryside." In *Studying Personality Cross-culturally* (Bert Kaplan, ed.), pp. 637–656. Evanston: Row, Peterson & Co.
Kaufman, Howard Keva
1960 *Bangkhuad: A Community Study in Thailand*. Association for Asian Studies Monographs, Vol. 10. Locust Valley, N.Y.: J. J. Augustin.

Kingshill, Konrad
1960 *Ku Daeng, the Red Tomb: A Village Study in Northern Thailand.* Chiangmai, Thailand: The Prince's Royal College.
Phillips, Herbert P.
1958 "The Election Ritual in a Thai Village." *Journal of Social Issues* 14(4):36–50.
Sharp, Lauriston
1950 "Peasants and Politics in Thailand." *Far Eastern Survey* 19:157–161.

PHILIPPINES

Leiben, Richard W.
1960 "Sorcery, Illness and Social Control in a Philippine Municipality." *Southwestern Journal of Anthropology* 16:127–143.
Nurge, Ethel
1965 *Life in a Leyte Village.* American Ethnological Society, Monograph No. 40. Seattle: University of Washington Press.
Nydegger, William F., and Corinne Nydegger
1966 *Tarong: An Ilocos Barrio in the Philippines.* Six Culture Series, Vol. 6. New York: John Wiley & Sons.

OKINAWA

Maretzki, Thomas W., and Hatsumi Maretzki
1966 *Taira: An Okinawan Village.* Six Culture Series, Vol. 7. New York: John Wiley & Sons.

CHINA

Chang, Chung-li
1955 *The Chinese Gentry: Studies on Their Role in Nineteenth-Century Society.* Seattle: University of Washington Press.
Cheng, Chu-yüan
1959 *The People's Communes.* Hong Kong: The Union Press.
Crook, David, and Isabel Crook
1959 *Revolution in a Chinese Village: Ten Mile Inn.* London: Routledge and Kegan Paul.
Fei, Hsiao-t'ung
1939 *Peasant Life in China: A Field Study of Country Life in the Yangtze Valley.* London: Kegan Paul.
1953 *China's Gentry: Essays in Rural-urban Relations.* Chicago: University of Chicago Press.
———, and Chih-i Chang
1949 *Earthbound China: A Study of Rural Economy in Yunnan.* London: Routledge and Kegan Paul.
Freedman, Maurice
1958 *Lineage Organization in Southeastern China.* London School of Economics Monographs on Social Anthropology, No. 18, University of London. London: The Athlone Press.
1966 *Chinese Lineage and Society: Fukien and Kwangtung.* London School of Economics Monographs on Social Anthropology, No. 33, University of London. London: The Athlone Press.
Fried, Morton
1953 *Fabric of Chinese Society: A Study of the Social Life of a Chinese Country Seat.* New York: Praeger.
Gallin, Bernard
1966 *Hsin Hsing, Taiwan: A Chinese Village in Change.* Berkeley: University of California Press.
Geddes, William R.
1963 *Peasant Life in Communist China.* Society for Applied Anthropology, Monograph No. 6. Ithaca, N.Y.
Hsiao, Kung-chüan
1960 *Rural China: Imperial Control in the Nineteenth Century.* Seattle: University of Washington Press.
Hsü, Francis L. K.
1948 *Under the Ancestors' Shadow: Chinese Culture and Personality.*

New York: Columbia University Press.
Hu, Ch'ang-tu
1960 *China: Its People, Its Society, Its Culture*. New Haven: HRAF Press.
Hu, Hsien-chin
1948 *The Common Descent Group in China and Its Functions*. Viking Fund Publications in Anthropology, No. 10. New York.
Johnson, Chalmers A.
1962 Peasant Nationalism and Communist Power. Stanford: Stanford University Press.
Kulp, Daniel
1925 *Country Life in South China: The Sociology of Familism*. New York: Teachers College, Columbia University.
Lin, Yüeh-hwa
1948 *The Golden Wing*. London: Kegan Paul.
Myrdal, Jan
1965 *Report from a Chinese Village*. New York: Pantheon Books.
Schurmann, H. Franz
1966 *Ideology and Organization in Communist China*. Berkeley: University of California Press.
Skinner, G. William
1964–65 *Marketing and Social Structure in Rural China*, Parts I, II, III. Reprinted from *The Journal of Asian Studies* 24:(1, 2, 3).
Strong, Anna Louise
1959 *The Rise of the People's Communes*. Peking: New World Press.
Yang, C. K.
1965 *Chinese Communist Society: The Family and the Village*. Cambridge: Massachusetts Institute of Technology Press.
Yang, Martin
1945 *A Chinese Village: Taitou, Shantung Province*. New York: Columbia University Press.

Korea

Osgood, Cornelius
1951 *The Koreans and Their Culture*. New York: Ronald Press.

Japan

Beardsley, Richard K., John W. Hall, and Robert Ward
1959 *Village Japan*. Chicago: University of Chicago Press.
Cornell, John B.
1956 "Matsunagi, a Japanese Mountain Community." *University of Michigan Center for Japanese Studies Occasional Papers*, No. 5, pp. 113–232. Ann Arbor: University of Michigan Press.
Embree, John F.
1939 *Suye Mura, a Japanese Village*. Chicago: University of Chicago Press.
Norbeck, Edward
1954 *Takashima, A Japanese Fishing Community*. Salt Lake City: University of Utah Press.
Smith, Robert J.
1956 "Kurusu, a Japanese Agricultural Community." *University of Michigan Center for Japanese Studies Occasional Papers*, No. 5, pp. 1–112. Ann Arbor: University of Michigan Press.
———, and Eudaldo P. Reyes
1957 "Community Interrelations with the Outside World: The Case of a Japanese Agricultural Community." *American Anthropologist* 59:463–472.
Smith, Thomas C.
1959 *The Agrarian Origins of Modern Japan*. Stanford: Stanford University Press.

Latin America

Mexico

Beals, Ralph L.
1946 *Cherán: A Sierra Tarascan Village*. Institute of Social Anthropology, Publication 2. Washington,

D.C.: Smithsonian Institution.
Cámara, Fernando
1952 *Chacaltianguis: Comunidad Rural en la Ribera del Papaloapan.* México: Gobierno del Estado de Veracruz.
Carrasco, Pedro
1952 *Tarascan Folk Religion: An Analysis of Economic, Social and Religious Interactions.* Middle American Research Institute, Publication 17: 1–64. New Orleans: Tulane University.
Diaz, May N.
1966 *Tonalá: Conservatism, Responsibility and Authority in a Mexican Town.* Berkeley and Los Angeles: University of California Press.
Foster, George M.
1948 *Empire's Children: The People of Tzintzuntzan.* Institute of Social Anthropology, Publication No. 6. Mexico, D.F.: Smithsonian Institution.
1967 *Tzintzuntzan: Mexican Peasants in a Changing World.* Boston: Little Brown.
de la Fuente, Julio
1949 *Yalalág: Una Villa Zapoteca Serrana.* México: Museo Nacional de Antropología, Serie Científica, No. 1.
Leslie, Charles M.
1960 *Now We Are Civilized: A Study of the World View of the Zapotec Indians of Mitla, Oaxaca.* Detroit: Wayne State University Press.
Lewis, Oscar
1951 *Life in a Mexican Village: Tepoztlán Restudied.* Urbana: University of Illinois Press.
1964 *Pedro Martínez: A Mexican Peasant and His Family.* New York: Random House.
Madsen, William
1960 *The Virgin's Children: Life in an Aztec Village Today.* Austin: University of Texas Press.
Parsons, Elsie Clews
1966 *Mitla, Town of the Souls, and Other Zapoteco-speaking Pueblos of Oaxaca, Mexico.* Chicago: University of Chicago Press.
Redfield, Robert
1930 *Tepoztlán: A Mexican Village. A Study of Folk Life.* Chicago: University of Chicago Press.
1941 *The Folk Culture of Yucatan.* Chicago: University of Chicago Press.
1955 *A Village That Chose Progress.* Chicago: University of Chicago Press.
———, and Alfonso Villa R.
1934 *Chan Kom, a Maya Village.* Carnegie Institution of Washington, Publication No. 448. Washington, D.C.
Romney, Kimball, and Romaine Romney
1966 *The Mixtecans of Juxtlahuaca, Mexico.* Six Culture Series, Vol. 4. New York: John Wiley and Sons.
Taylor, Paul
1933 *A Spanish-Mexican Peasant Community: Arandas in Jalisco, Mexico.* Ibero-Americana, No. 4. Berkeley: University of California Press.
Wolf, Eric R.
1955 "Types of Latin American Peasantry: A Preliminary Discussion." *American Anthropologist* 57:452–471.
1956 "Aspects of Group Relations in a Complex Society: Mexico." *American Anthropologist* 58:1065–1078.
1959 *Sons of the Shaking Earth.* Chicago: University of Chicago Press.

GUATEMALA

Gillin, John
1951 *The Culture of Security in San Carlos: A Study of a Guatemalan Community of Indians and Ladinos.* Middle American Research Institute, Publication No. 16. New Orleans: Tulane University.
Reina, Ruben E.
1960 *Chinautla, A Guatemalan Indian Community: A Study in the Relationship of Community Culture and National Change.* Middle American Research Institute, Publication 24:55–130. New Orleans: Tulane University.
Tax, Sol
1953 *Penny Capitalism: A Guatemalan Indian Economy.* Institute of Social Anthropology, Publication No. 16. Washington, D.C.: Smithsonian Institution.

Tumin, Melvin M.
1952 *Caste in a Peasant Society: A Case Study in the Dynamics of Caste*. Princeton: Princeton University Press.

Colombia

Fals-Borda, Orlando
1955 *Peasant Society in the Colombian Andes: A Sociological Study of Saucío*. Gainesville: University of Florida Press.
Gutierrez de Pineda, Virginia
1959 "El País Rural Colombiano, Ensayo de Interpretación." *Revista Colombiana de Antropología* 7:1–125.
Reichel-Dolmatoff, Gerardo, and Alicia Reichel-Dolmatoff
1961 *The People of Aritama: The Cultural Personality of a Colombian Mestizo Village*. Chicago: University of Chicago Press.

Ecuador

Leonard, Olen E.
1947 *Pichilingue: A Study of Rural Life in Coastal Ecuador*. Office of Foreign Agricultural Relations, Report No. 17. Washington, D.C.: Department of Agriculture.
Whitten, Norman E., Jr.
1965 *Class, Kinship and Power in an Ecuadorian Town: The Negroes of San Lorenzo*. Stanford: Stanford University Press.

Peru

Adams, Richard N.
1959 *A Community in the Andes: Problems and Progress in Muquiyauyo*. Seattle: University of Washington Press.
Gillin, John
1947 *Moche: A Peruvian Coastal Community*. Institute of Social Anthropology, Publication No. 3. Washington, D.C.: Smithsonian Institution.
Hammel, Eugene A.
1962 *Wealth, Authority and Prestige in the Ica Valley, Peru*. Albuquerque: University of New Mexico Press.
Simmons, Ozzie G.
1959 "Drinking Patterns and Interpersonal Performance in a Peruvian Mestizo Community." *Quarterly Journal of Studies in Alcohol* 20:103–111.
Stein, William W.
1961 *Hualcan: Life in the Highlands of Peru*. Ithaca, N.Y.: Cornell University Press.
Tschopik, Harry, Jr.
1947 *Highland Communities of Central Peru*. Institute of Social Anthropology, Publication No. 5. Washington, D.C.: Smithsonian Institution.

Paraguay

Service, Elman R., and Helen S. Service
1954 *Tobatí: Paraguayan Town*. Chicago: University of Chicago Press.

Brazil

Harris, Marvin
1956 *Town and Country in Brazil*. New York: Columbia University Press.
Hutchinson, Harry William
1957 *Village and Plantation Life in Northeastern Brazil*. Seattle: University of Washington Press.
Oberg, Kalervo
1965 "The Marginal Peasant in Rural Brazil." *American Anthropologist* 67: 1417–1427.

Pierson, Donald
1951 *Cruz das Almas, a Brazilian Village*. Institute of Social Anthropology, Publication No. 12. Washington, D.C.: Smithsonian Institution.
Wagley, Charles
1964 *Amazon Town: A Study of Man in the Tropics*. New York: Alfred A. Knopf.
Willems, Emílio
1961 *Uma Vila Brasileira: Tradição e Transição*. São Paulo: Difusão Européia do Livro.
———, and Gioconda Mussolini
1952 *Buzios Island: A Caiçara Community in Southern Brazil*. Monograph of the American Ethnological Society, No. 20. Locust Valley, N.Y.: J. J. Augustin.

WEST INDIES

Blake, Judith
1961 *Family Structure in Jamaica: The Social Context of Reproduction*. New York: The Free Press of Glencoe.
Cohen, Yehudi A.
1955 "Four Categories of Interpersonal Relationships in the Family and Community in a Jamaican Village." *Anthropological Quarterly* 3: 121–147.
Herskovits, Melville J.
1937 *Life in a Haitian Valley*. New York: Alfred A. Knopf.
———, and Frances S. Herskovits
1947 *Trinidad Village*. New York: A. A. Knopf.
Landy, David
1959 *Tropical Childhood: Cultural Transmission and Learning in a Rural Puerto Rican Village*. Chapel Hill: University of North Carolina Press.
Métraux, Alfred
1960 *Haiti: Black Peasants and Voodoo*. New York: Universe Books.
Smith, M. G.
1962a *Kinship and Community in Carriacou*. Yale Caribbean Series, No. 5. New Haven: Yale University Press.
1962b *West Indian Family Structure*. Seattle: University of Washington Press.
Steward, Julian, et al.
1956 *The People of Puerto Rico: A Study in Social Anthropology*. Urbana: University of Illinois Press.

Biographical Notes

Janet Abu-Lughod is Lecturer in Sociology at Smith College.

Victor Barnouw is Professor of Anthropology at the University of Wisconsin-Milwaukee.

Gerald D. Berreman is Professor of Anthropology at the University of California, Berkeley.

May N. Diaz is Associate Professor of Anthropology at the University of California, Berkeley.

L. A. Fallers is Professor of Anthropology at the University of Chicago.

George M. Foster is Professor of Anthropology at the University of California, Berkeley.

Ernestine Friedl is Professor of Anthropology at the City University of New York, Queens College.

F. G. Friedmann is Professor of Philosophy at the American Institute of the University of Munich.

Bernard Gallin is Associate Professor of Anthropology and Research Associate, Asian Studies Center at Michigan State University.

Clifford Geertz is Professor of Anthropology at the University of Chicago.

Mary R. Hollnsteiner is Research Associate at the Institute of Philippine Culture, Ateneo de Manila.

Oscar Lewis is Professor of Anthropology at the University of Illinois.

Joseph Lopreato is Associate Professor of Sociology at the University of Texas.

Michael Maccoby is a psychiatrist practicing in Mexico City, a research associate of Erich Fromm, and sometime professor at the University of California, Santa Cruz.

Sidney W. Mintz is Professor of Anthropology at Yale University.

Morris E. Opler is Professor of Anthropology at Cornell University.

Herbert P. Phillips is Associate Professor of Anthropology at the University of California, Berkeley.

Jack M. Potter is Assistant Professor of Anthropology at the University of California, Berkeley.

Robert Redfield was Robert Maynard Hutchins Distinguished Service Professor of the University of Chicago.

Sydel F. Silverman is Assistant Professor at the City University of New York, Queens College.

Gideon Sjoberg is Professor of Sociology at the University of Texas.

G. William Skinner is Professor of Anthropology at Stanford University.

Robert J. Smith is Professor of Anthropology at Cornell University.

Barbara E. Ward is Senior Lecturer in Anthropology at the School of Oriental and African Studies, University of London.

Eric R. Wolf is Professor of Anthropology at the University of Michigan.